P9-CMF-769

Records of Civilization

SOURCES AND STUDIES

EDITED BY

JAMES T. SHOTWELL, PH.D.
PROFESSOR OF HISTORY IN COLUMBIA UNIVERSITY

IN COLLABORATION WITH

FRANKLIN H. GIDDINGS, PH.D., LL.D.
PROFESSOR OF SOCIOLOGY AND THE HISTORY OF CIVILIZATION IN COLUMBIA UNIVERSITY

JULIUS A. BEWER, PH.D.
PROFESSOR OF OLD TESTAMENT EXEGESIS IN UNION THEOLOGICAL SEMINARY

MUNROE SMITH, J.U.D., LL.D.
PROFESSOR OF ROMAN LAW AND COMPARATIVE JURISPRUDENCE IN COLUMBIA UNIVERSITY

CARLTON H. HAYES, PH.D.
ASSOCIATE PROFESSOR OF HISTORY IN COLUMBIA UNIVERSITY

WILLIAM R. SHEPHERD, PH.D.
PROFESSOR OF HISTORY IN COLUMBIA UNIVERSITY

ELLERY C. STOWELL, PH.D.
ASSISTANT PROFESSOR OF INTERNATIONAL LAW IN COLUMBIA UNIVERSITY

GEORGE W. BOTSFORD, PH.D.
PROFESSOR OF HISTORY IN COLUMBIA UNIVERSITY

HAROLD H. TRYON, M.A., B.D.
INSTRUCTOR IN NEW TESTAMENT AND CHURCH HISTORY IN UNION THEOLOGICAL SEMINARY

New York
COLUMBIA UNIVERSITY PRESS
1920

RECORDS OF CIVILIZATION

SOURCES AND STUDIES

EDITED BY

JAMES T. SHOTWELL

A COMPREHENSIVE SERIES CONSISTING OF

DOCUMENTS IN TRANSLATION

COMMENTARIES AND INTERPRETATIONS

BIBLIOGRAPHICAL GUIDES

For titles of volumes, see list at end of this volume.

Records of Civilization: Sources and Studies

HELLENIC CIVILIZATION

EDITED BY

G. W. BOTSFORD

PROFESSOR OF HISTORY IN COLUMBIA UNIVERSITY

AND

E. G. SIHLER

PROFESSOR OF THE LATIN LANGUAGE AND LITERATURE
IN NEW YORK UNIVERSITY

WITH CONTRIBUTIONS FROM

Professor WILLIAM L. WESTERMANN (University of Wisconsin)
CHARLES J. OGDEN, Ph.D., and others

New York
COLUMBIA UNIVERSITY PRESS
1920

Set up and electrotyped. Published August, 1915.

Norwood Press
J. S. Cushing Co. — Berwick & Smith Co.
Norwood, Mass., U.S.A.

PREFACE

THE aim of the series of which this volume forms a part is twofold. In the first place, its intention is to make accessible those sources of the history of Europe and of the near East which are of prime importance for the understanding of Western civilization. In the second place, both by the treatment of these texts and by special studies it covers the work of modern scholars in these fields. It is, therefore, a guide both to the original documents and to recent criticism. The material, furthermore, is given in English translation, in order that it may be readily accessible to students and readers who do not have that knowledge of classical and other foreign languages which is essential for specialized research.

The present volume departs slightly from the general plan of the series owing to the peculiar editorial problems which it involves. While, in most other cases, documents are given *in extenso*, this is necessarily an anthology. The very wealth of the literary and monumental remains of Greek civilization renders any other treatment impossible. Even more important, however, is the fact that so much of the available material is of interest to the historian for other reasons than those which determined its original form. Casual references in literature, whether prose or poetry, frequently possess a distinctive value sufficient to make them by themselves, apart from their context, documents for the study of Hellenic civilization. Beside these must often be placed texts from obscure sources or fragments revealed by recent archæological research. In short, in this volume the intricacies of a very complex subject demanded an adjustment of text to topic in order to illustrate the general lines of Greek history.

In view of these difficulties, the volume as a whole was originally placed under the editorial control of Professor Botsford. As he found, however, that the labor of selecting and preparing excerpts illustrative of Hellenic civilization from the vast field of ancient Greek literature, inscriptions, and papyri exceeded the limits of time at his disposal, he was fortunate in securing the coöperation of his friend Professor Sihler in the editorial work, and contributions from other scholars. The parts severally taken by these associates are explained below, and the editors wish here to thank them for their aid and their interest in the work.

The selections have been made, not for specialists, but for those who are interested in general Hellenic culture. Nothing could be easier than to suggest the lengthening or shortening of passages and the addition or substitution of other selections. No two scholars could agree as to what is absolutely best for a volume of the kind; and those who have coöperated in its preparation can only hope that it may in some degree contribute to an understanding of the spirit of ancient Hellas and add to the interest in her culture.

For the selections from printed translations permission has been obtained from the translators or the publishers. Individual acknowledgments are made elsewhere. This permission has rendered it possible to give the volume a literary quality to which it could not otherwise have attained. The grouping of selections in chapters on society, religion, political conditions, etc., is necessarily more or less arbitrary, as the same passage often throws light on several of these aspects of life; yet this arrangement will probably be found as convenient as any that could be devised. The notes are for the general reader, and represent the minimum of information required for an understanding of the passages. Those who desire special knowledge are referred to the bibliographies, the compilation of which has extended through years. Throughout the book will be found occasional references to the closely interrelated "Hellenic History," by Professor Botsford, which will probably be ready for the printer within ten or twelve months after the appearance of the present work.

It is hoped that this volume may appeal to a wide range of users, that the student may find it an illuminating companion to his textbook or his course of lectures, and that men and women who are interested in the cultural history of mankind, even though classically educated, may obtain through it fresh and inspiring glimpses of the wonderfully endowed people from whom these messages have come.

JAMES T. SHOTWELL.

NEW YORK,
June 1, 1915.

DIVISION OF LABOR

PROFESSOR WESTERMANN has contributed Chapter XVI entire. Mr. Wallace E. Caldwell (fellow in history, Columbia University), Dr. Ogden, and Professor William C. Lawton (Hobart College) have translated the selections credited to them and have furnished the greater part of the material for the introductions and annotations of these excerpts. Professor Munroe Smith has aided in the interpretation of the Gortynian law. All have read the proofs of their respective contributions. Professor Sihler has made the translations credited to him, has revised, by a comparison with the original texts, the greater number of excerpts from published translations, and has furnished some of the material for the introductory chapter. He has also read the proofs of the whole work, with the aid of Mr. F. M. Barranco, and has prepared the index. Professor Shotwell has made suggestions at various points in the preparation of the volume and has read the proofs. Professor Botsford has chosen and arranged the selections, excepting those of Chapter XVI, has translated the passages credited to him, has prepared the introductory chapter and most of the special introductions and notes. He has compiled the bibliographies, read the proofs, and edited the selections contributed by others. The bibliographical work has been facilitated by the courteous aid of Miss Isadore G. Mudge of the Columbia University Library.

CONTENTS

ABBREVIATIONS MOST COMMONLY USED

Abbott = Abbott, E., History of Greece, 3 vols. (New York: Putnam, 1892–1900).
Acad. des Inscr. = Mémoires de l'académie des inscriptions et belles-lettres.
Acad. roy. de Belg. Bull. = Académie royale de Belgique: Bulletins de la classe des lettres et des sciences morales et politiques, etc.
Am. Journ. Arch. = American Journal of Archæology.
Am. Journ. Philol. = American Journal of Philology.
Archiv. soc. Bull. = Archives sociologiques, Bulletin (Brussels).
Ath. Mitt. = Mitteilungen des kaiserlich deutschen archäologischen Instituts: Athenische Abteilung.
B.S.A. = Annual of the British School at Athens.
Beloch, Griech. Gesch. = Beloch, J., Griechische Geschichte (I and II. 1, second ed.; the remainder, first ed.).
Berl. Philol. Woch. = Berliner philologische Wochenschrift.
Bury = Bury, J. B., History of Greece (revised ed., Macmillan, 1913).
Busolt, Griech. Gesch. = Busolt, G., Griechische Geschichte, 3 vols. (second ed., Gotha, 1893–1904).
Christ, Griech. Lit. = Christ, W. von, Geschichte der griechischen Litteratur, 2 vols. revised by Schmid, W. (fifth ed., Munich, 1908–1913).
CIA. = Corpus inscriptionum atticarum; *v.* Inscr. græc.
C.J.O. = Charles J. Ogden.
Class. Journ. = Classical Journal.
Class. Philol. = Classical Philology.
Class. Quart. = Classical Quarterly.
Class. Rev. = Classical Review.
Cl. Weekly = Classical Weekly.
Collitz, SGDI. = Sammlung der griechischen Dialektinschriften, 4 vols. (1884–1911).
Curtius = Curtius, E., History of Greece, 5 vols. (New York: Scribner, 1886).
Daremberg-Saglio, Dict. = Dictionnaire des antiquités grecques et romaines (beginning 1873).
Diss., Dissert. = Dissertation.
Ditt. Or. græc. inscrs. = Dittenberger, W., Orientis græci inscriptiones selectæ (Leipzig, 1903).
Ditt., Ditt. Syll. = Sylloge inscriptionum græcarum, 3 vols. (second ed., Leipzig, 1898–1901).
E.G.S. = Ernest G. Sihler.
Encycl. Brit. = Encyclopædia Britannica (eleventh ed.).
Eng. Hist. Rev. = English Historical Review.
Ergzb. = Ergänzungsband.

Gesch. u. Kult. des Alt. = Studien zur Geschichte und Kultur des Altertums.

Gilbert, Const. Antiq. = Gilbert, G., Constitutional Antiquities of Sparta and Athens (Macmillan, 1895).

Griech. = Griechisch.

Gött. gelehrt. Anz. = Göttingische gelehrte Anzeigen.

Gött. Gesellsch. = Nachrichten von der königlichen Gesellschaft der Wissenschaften zu Göttingen.

Greenidge, Gk. Const. Hist. = Handbook of Greek Constitutional History (Macmillan, 1896).

Grote = Grote, G., History of Greece, 12 vols. (reprint from original ed., New York: Harper).

G.W.B. = George W. Botsford.

Harv. St. in Cl. Philol. = Harvard Studies in Classical Philology.

Herm. = Hermes.

Hicks and Hill = Hicks, E. L., and Hill, G. F., Manual of Greek Historical Inscriptions (new ed., Oxford, 1901).

Hist. Zeitschr. = Historische Zeitschrift.

Holm = Holm, A., History of Greece, 4 vols. (Macmillan, 1895–1898).

Inscr. græc. = Inscriptiones græcæ, 14 vols. (Berlin, 1873–1890). The old edition is occasionally cited as CIA.

Jahresb. = Jahresberichte über die Fortschritte der klassischen Altertumswissenschaft.

J.H.S. = Journal of Hellenic Studies.

Jouguet, Pap. grecs = Papyrus grecs (Paris, 1907).

Journ. Philol. = (English) Journal of Philology.

Kock, Th., Com. att. frag. = Comicorum atticorum fragmenta.

Meyer, Ed., Forsch. = Forschungen zur alten Geschichte, 2 vols. (Halle, 1892, 1899).

—— Gesch. d. Alt. = Geschichte des Altertums, 5 vols. (I. 1, third ed.; I. 2, second ed.; II–V, first ed.).

Michel = Michel, Ch., Recueil d'inscriptions grecques (Brussels, 1900).

Mitt. Vorderas. Ges. = Mitteilungen der vorderasiatischen Gesellschaft.

Müller, Frag. hist. græc. = Fragmenta historicorum græcorum, 5 vols. (Paris: Didot, 1841).

Mus. belg. = Le Musée belge, revue de philologie classique.

N. Jahrb. = Neue Jahrbücher für das klassische Altertum, Geschichte, etc.

Pauly-Wissowa, Real-Encycl. = Pauly's Real-Encyclopädie der classischen Altertumswissenschaft, revised by Wissowa, G. (beginning 1894); the later vols. by Kroll, W., and Witte, K. References are all to the *erste Reihe*. A *zweite Reihe* began to appear in 1914.

Philol. = Philologus.

Pöhlmann Griech. Gesch. = Pöhlmann, R. von, Grundriss der griechischen Geschichte (fourth ed., Munich, 1909).

Pol. Sci. Quart. = Political Science Quarterly.

R. Acad. d. sci. atti = Atti della reale accademia delle scienze di Torino.

Rev. des ét. gr. = Revue des études grecques.

Rev. hist. = Revue historique.

Rhein. Mus. = Rheinisches Museum.

Roberts and Gardner = Roberts, E. S., and Gardner, E. A., Introduction to Greek Epigraphy, 2 vols. (Cambridge: University Press, 1887, 1905).

Sächs. Gesellsch. = Abhandlungen der königlich sächsischen Gesellschaft der Wissenschaften. Philologische-historische Klasse.

Sitz. Berl. Akad. = Sitzungsberichte der königlich preussischen Akademie der Wissenschaften zu Berlin.

Supplb. = Supplementband.

Supplem. = Supplementum (of the Inscr. græc.).

Trans. Am. Philol. Ass. = Transactions and Proceedings of the American Philological Association.

Versamml. d. Philolog. = Versammlung deutscher Philologen und Schulmänner. Verhandlungen.

W.C.L. = William C. Lawton.

W.E.C. = Wallace E. Caldwell.

W.L.W. = William L. Westermann.

Zeitsch. f. Ethnol. = Zeitschrift für Ethnologie.

HELLENIC CIVILIZATION

CHAPTER I

THE SOURCES OF HELLENIC HISTORY

I. Introduction

The sources for the history of Hellas include everything from which may be derived information of service to the historian. They comprise, accordingly, not only literature and written documents, but also products of workmanship found by exploration, and even the physical features and conditions of the country, the climate, soil, and products, the practicabilities of communication with other countries; in brief, everything that in any way throws light upon the factors that determined the historical development. The language itself is a highly important source for the origin of the Hellenes, their relations with other early peoples, their subdivision into the so-called races, which are in fact large dialect groups, and for the gradual development of their ideas on all subjects of which they thought. This volume, however, is limited to the written sources. It has to do, accordingly, with literature, with inscriptions on stone or bronze, and with documents committed to papyri, many of which have recently been discovered in Egypt.

To the scholar of a few decades ago, whose chief interest was in political and military narrative, the Greek historians were all-important sources. Recently, however, history has so expanded as to take into account all human conditions and activities, physical, mental, and emotional. In this wider view it embraces economy, society, philosophy and science, religion, poetry and art, as well as political institutions, party struggles, and warfare, and thus renders the lyric poet and the dramatist equal in importance to the historian. In all oscillations of judgment regarding the relative importance of things there is danger of going to extremes. The culture of a people without their economy and politics is like the decorations of a dwelling without its foundation and framework. It is for the purpose of illustrating all these aspects of Greek civilization that the material of the present volume has been selected and organized.

II. The Minoan Age

Our sources for the Minoan period, approximately 3000–1200 B.C., are nearly all archæological. Various Hellenic authors, however, have written of that time and have referred to it the origin of certain conditions and institutions existing in historical Greece. Some of this material has been included in this present volume, and the reasons for so doing have been given in the introduction to Chapter II. Whereas scholars have thus far taken great interest in pointing to artistic and religious survivals from the Minoan age, the present study breaks ground in calling attention also to survivals of social and political conditions.

III. Homer

The ancients are at variance regarding the place and time of Homer. The weight of their evidence, however, connects him with Smyrna, Chios, or their neighborhood, where with an original Æolic population Ionians were afterward mingled. They are at one in placing him after the Trojan war, although they differ by centuries as to the length of time that intervened between that event and his birth (*cf.* Christ, *Griech. Lit.* I. 34 *sq.*). Their idea of his personality, that of a blind old minstrel who wandered about chanting his sweet lays, is best expressed in the Homeric *Hymn to the Delian Apollo* (165 *sqq.*): —

> "But come now, be gracious, Apollo, be gracious, Artemis, and ye maidens all, farewell; but remember me even in time to come, when any of earthly men, yea, any stranger that much hath seen and much endured, comes hither and asks: —
>
> "'Maidens, who is the sweetest to you of singers here conversant, and in whose song are ye most glad?'
>
> "Then do you all with one voice make answer: —
>
> "'A blind man is he, and he dwells in rocky Chios; his song will ever hav the mastery, ay, in all time to come.'" (Lang.)

The picture is that of the typical rhapsodist, the professional chanter of epic verse, rather than of a historical person. For a time all existing epics were indiscriminately assigned to Homer; but as early as Herodotus the work of sifting was under way. On the ground of internal contradictions he separated in authorship the poem entitled *Cypria* from the *Iliad* and the *Odyssey* (ii. 117). The work of criticism thus begun resulted in the definite segregation, apart from Homer, of the group of epics known as cyclic. In this use, as in the word cyclopedia, cycle has reference merely to a definite scope or range of material. In the Alexandrian age the so-called separatists, Xenon and Hellanicus, advanced a step farther in Homeric criticism when they assumed distinct authors for the two poems. Here the work of sifting rested till near the close of the eighteenth century, when Wolf in his *Prolegomena ad Homerum*, on the basis of inconsistencies and other alleged defects, pronounced both poems the work of a number of poets. From his time throughout the nineteenth century scholars of all countries have devoted their lives to laborious analysis of the poems to discover earlier and later parts and to establish theories as to their process of growth.

During all this time there were conservatives who protested against such dissection; and since the beginning of the present century a strong reaction has set in in favor of unity, although there remain doughty champions of plural authorship. Meanwhile, the minute studies in Homer mentioned above have not been in vain, as they have given us a knowledge of the poet which could not otherwise have accumulated.

To the student of history the chief interest is not whether these poems were the product of one mind, but rather what historical value they have. As it is evident that they are not history pure and simple, the chief problem is, by sifting out the fiction, to discover the residuum of truth. If we are in search of light on political and social conditions and on material civilization, we may begin by rejecting the gods, their relations with men, and everything supernatural. Here it is possible to discard more than is necessary, for the Homeric Olympus is evidently a glorified reflection from a royal court; so that by a study of the gods we may gain knowledge of Homeric men and society. The individual human beings,

Agamemnon, Helen, Aretê, and the rest, are also fictions. Should any Homeric person have had a real being, there are no criteria by which we may discover the fact, or having discovered it, separate the fiction in his character from the reality. The same principle holds for the activities of persons individually and in combination. We cannot be certain even of the main event — the siege and sack of Troy by an army that had come from the Greek mainland. Some scholars are ready to affirm the truth of this event, while others as strenuously deny it. We know that the "sixth" city, the most splendid of the successive settlements at Troy, was destroyed by fire, and was followed by a poor village; we know that at about this time the Æolians colonized Asia Minor; but whether they attacked and destroyed Troy cannot as yet be proved. The migration of the Æolians, their conflict with the natives, the hardships of life in the new world, and the sight of the ruined city, burned by whatever hands, would be enough to inspire the poet to his great achievement.

The elimination of the elements thus far mentioned leaves but a small residuum. The question arises, why should we not continue the process of elimination still farther? Why could not Homer have invented his palaces, the armor of men, the dress of women, and all the products of handicraft which he mentions? Perhaps he could; but the fact is that many of these objects actually existed in the Minoan age and can now be seen in the museums by readers of Homer. The poet describes them so accurately as to force us to the conclusion that he must either have seen them or learned of them through trustworthy sources; either he lived in the splendor of the Minoan age or a literature, oral or written, descriptive of Minoan material civilization must have been preserved to his time.

Many reasons compel us to place him in a later period. On this point scholars are agreed. There is, however, the widest difference of opinion as to when, within the approximate limits, 1200–700 B.C., lived and wrought this transcendent genius. On this subject, which is still under controversy, the writer can do no more than express his own view. The weight of ancient authority, as has been said, places Homer in Chios, Smyrna, or their neighborhood — that is, after the Hellenic colonization of Asia Mi[illegible]

His dialect was an Æolizing Ionic, such as must have been spoken in those places, and so far as we are aware, nowhere else in Hellas. It has often been assumed that the culture of Homer was that of Ionia, about 1000–700 B.C. To that view, however, Andrew Lang (*World of Homer*) has offered insuperable objections. It is in fact well established that the Ionian civilization of this period was essentially decadent Minoan, whereas many Homeric ideas and usages were distinctly Indo-European. Thus far Lang's conclusions are acceptable. But instead of placing Homer back to 1100 or 1200, as he does, it is well to note the fact that the Æolians of Thessaly, and hence of their colonies, were thoroughly Indo-European, scarcely touched by Minoan culture (Wace and Thompson, *Prehistoric Thessaly*, 1912). This fact completes the evidence that Homer's habitat was the borderland between Æolis and Ionia.

We may suppose, then, that songs and perhaps other literature descriptive of the splendors of Minoan life passed down into the Middle Age, which followed the Minoan period, and into the language of the Hellenes, and that Hellenic bards on the Greek mainland and in the colonies continued to sing the glories of gods and heroes, intermingling their own customs and ideas with traditions. The greatest of these bards was Homer, who lived in Asia Minor, perhaps in the ninth or in the eighth century. He incorporated nothing, but created his great poems afresh, making use, however, of much traditional subject matter. The *Odyssey* was composed after the *Iliad;* yet both may have been the product of one genius. After their completion by Homer the poems were to some extent interpolated.

No analysis of the subject matter for historical purposes will satisfy every scholar. Much of the material civilization is clearly Minoan, and may be distinguished by archæological study, although important elements are later than that period. In the political sphere the vast pretensions of king and nobles and their contempt for the commons seem Minoan, whereas the actualities of political life are largely those of Homer's time and place. The same principle holds for society. The religion, too, is composite; earlier and contemporary elements are mingled. In a word, each detail of Homeric life requires individual consideration, and on many points, because of a lack of determinative facts, it will be impossible for scholars to agree.

BIBLIOGRAPHY

I. The Homeric Question; Artistic Aspect. — Under this heading are included questions of time and place, origin, historical relations, unity, personality, and literary character. All histories of Greek literature deal with the subject, and do not require individual mention. The books and articles here enumerated treat mainly of the subjects above mentioned, while those which have to do chiefly with life are placed under (2). The amount of literature on Homer produced during the present century is enormous. A few only of the vast number of titles are given here. Indispensable guides to this literature are Mülder, D., "Bericht über die Literatur zu Homer," in *Jahresb.* CLVII (1912). 170–325; CLXI (1913). 73–171; Rothe, C., *Der augenblickliche Stand der homerischen Frage* (Berlin, 1912); Shewan, A., in *Class. Rev.* XXVII (1914). 128–32.

Burrows, R. M., *Discoveries in Crete*, ch. xii; Browne, H., *Handbook of Homeric Study* (Longmans, 1905); Stawell, F. M., *Homer and the Iliad: an Essay to determine the Scope and Character of the Original Poem* (London: Dent, 1909); Shewan, A., "Does the Odyssey imitate the Iliad?" in *Class. Quart.* VII (1913). 234–42; "Continuation of the Odyssey," in *Class. Philol.* VIII (1913). 284–300; IX. 35 *sqq.*; Perrin, B., "The Odyssey under Source-Criticism," in *Am. Journ. Philol.* VIII (1887). 415–32; Lang, A., *Homer and the Epic* (1893); Allen, T. W., "Canonicity of Homer," in *Class. Quart.* VII (1913). 221–33; "Lives of Homer," in *J. H. S.* XXXII (1912). 250–60; XXXIII. 19–26; "Homeridæ," in *Class. Quart.* I (1907). 135–43; "Peisistratus and Homer," *ib.* VII (1913). 33 *sqq.*; "Homeric Catalogue," in *J. H. S.* XXX (1910). 292–322; Scott, J. A., various articles in *Class. Philol.* V (1910). 41 *sqq.*; VI. 156 *sqq.*, 419 *sqq.*; VII. 293 *sqq.*; *Class. Rev.* XXIV (1910). 8 *sqq.*

Bonitz, H., *Ueber den Ursprung der homerischen Gedichte* (5th ed. Vienna, 1881); Cauer, *Grundfragen der Homerkritik* (Leipzig, 1909); "Erfundenes und Ueberliefertes bei Homer," in *N. Jahrb.* VIII (1905). 1–18; "Soll die Homerkritik abdanken?" *ib.* XV (1912). 98–111; Croiset, M., "La question homérique au debut du XXe siècle," in *Rev. des deux mondes*, 1907, p. 600 *sqq.*; Laurand, L., *Progrès et recul de la critique* (Paris, 1912); Rothe, C., *Ilias als Dichtung* (Paderborn, 1910); *Die Odyssee als Dichtung und ihr Verhältnis zur Ilias* (*ib.* 1914), by one of the greatest upholders of unity; Belzner, E., *Homerische Probleme*, I: *Die Kulturellen Verhältnisse der Odyssee als kritische Instanz* (Teubner, 1911); Bethe, E., "Die trojanischen Ausgrabungen und die Homerkritik," in *N. Jahrb.* XIII (1904). 1–11; "Die Einheit unserer Ilias," *ib.* XXXIII (1914). 362–71; Maas, E., "Die Person Homers," *ib.* XIV (1911). 539–50; Kammer, E., *Ein aesthetischer Kommentar zu Homer's Ilias* (3d ed. Paderborn, 1906); Lawton, W. C., *Art and Humanity in Homer* (Macmillan, 1896).

II. Life. — Lang, A., *Homer and his Age* (Longmans, 1906); Leaf, W., *Troy: A Study of Homeric Geography* (Macmillan, 1912); Keller, A. C., *Homeric Society* (London, 1902); Isham, N. M., *Homeric Palace* (Providence, 1898); Dickins, G., "Some Points with regard to the Homeric House," in *J. H. S.*

XXIII (1903). 325 *sqq.*; Sihler, E. G., *Testimonium Animæ*, ch. iii; Harrison, J. E., *Myths of the Odyssey in Art and Literature* (London, 1882); Seymour, D., *Life in the Homeric Age* (Macmillan, 1907); "Slavery and Servitude in Homer," in *Am. Journ. Arch.* V (1902). 23 *sqq.*; Symonds, J. A., *Studies in the Greek Poets*, II. ch. iii (women); Bonner, "Justice in the Age of Homer," in *Class. Philol.* VI (1911). 12–36; Sidgwick, H., "Trial Scene in Iliad xviii. 497–508," in *Class. Rev.* VIII (1894). 1–3.

Buchholz, E., *Homerische Realien*, 3 vols. (Leipzig, 1871–84); Finsler, G., *Homer* (Teubner, 1908), a new ed. is appearing in pts.; Drerup, E., *Anfänge der hellenischen Kultur: Homer* (Munich, 1903); *Omero* (Bergamo, 1910), revision of preceding German work; Reichel, W., *Homerische Waffen* (2d ed. Vienna, 1891); Helbig, W., *Das homerische Epos aus den Denkmälern erläutert* (2d ed. Teubner, 1887).

IV. The Cyclic Epics, the Homeric Hymns, and Hesiod

The cyclic epics (p. 3), which have all disappeared with the exception of a few scant fragments, once constituted a large body of literature. Among them were the *Theogonia*, *Œdipodeia*, *Thebais*, *Epigoni*, *Cypria*, *Æthiopis*, *Little Iliad*, and *Nosti*. Younger than Homer, they belong, some to the eighth and more to the seventh century. Even the ancients did not know the authors by name; and we can only say that the bulk of this literature seems to have been Ionic. The value of the poems lies in the fact that they were the chief sources for the Attic dramatists. They were the creations of talent rather than of genius; but the customs they pictured, their ideas and general tone were better adapted to the Attic stage than were those of the true Homeric poems. Particularly the priestly lore, the oracles, the belief in ghosts, in the guilt wrought by homicide and its purification by swine's blood, in the hereditary curse that brought the family to ruin, finally the gloomy aspects of religion characteristic of Minoan civilization but foreign to Homer, were all far more appropriate to Attic tragedy than was the sunny life of the *Iliad* and *Odyssey*. To the student of history the important fact is that the characteristics of the cyclic epos above mentioned belong to Ionia along with other regions formerly under Minoan dominance, as distinguished from Indo-European Thessaly and Æolis. It was in fact from the conditions represented by these inferior poems, far more than from Homeric life, that the Athenian civilization developed.

As a prelude to his epic recitation at a festive gathering it was customary for the rhapsodist to chant a song in honor of the god to whose glory the festival was held. A group of songs ostensibly composed for this purpose was collected in ancient times, and is still preserved, under the name of Homeric Hymns. The earliest among these poems is the *Hymn to the Delian Apollo*, which belongs most probably to the seventh century. Composed at widely different times and places, they throw light on the thought and feeling of poet and audience, and reveal in occasional passages charming pictures of life.

Hundreds of rhapsodists assumed and transmitted in epics a poetry of gods and heroes which mirrored the aristocratic form of Greek life. It was a world of song and noble feats which certainly — apart from the broader sketches of the *Shield* — was somewhat one-sided though lofty. Thersites and Eumæus, men of the lower class, appear too, but they are foils for an essentially aristocratic society.

In Hesiod we come down to an actuality which moves no longer among gods and men of might; but in his work the common and the commonplace are mirrored, we may say, with photographic fidelity. The father of Hesiod (*Works*, 633 *sqq.*) came from Cymê in the Æolic littoral of Asia Minor to Æolic Bœotia, fleeing from poverty at home. He acquired a farmstead at Ascra at the foot of Mount Helicon, near Thespiæ. The poet, a shepherd and farmer, suffered from scoundrelly litigation at the hands of his brother Perses. Out of such experiences the *Works and Days* came forth. The seasons of the year, and all the tasks and toil which they bring in their train, are here set forth. The poet's time has been computed for about 700 B.C. or perhaps somewhat later. In his personality there are reflected thoughtfulness and meditation rather than imagination and enthusiasm. His *Theogony* was the first effort of the Hellenic world to construct through a system of genealogies and pedigrees a unity of Heaven and Earth and their history. The epic of the *Heroines* (ἢ οἵα) continued this constructive process and dovetailed it into the ancestral legends of the chief families associated with the principal communities or states of Greece. The fact that but one elaborate simile occurs in Hesiod is significant of his prosaic character, while the deliberate and didactic trend of his manner and mind is equally manifest in both epics. There are two sides in him: he is gifted in presenting actual, even minor and petty things, with remarkable precision. On the other hand, he is indeed a man of deep reflection. From this vein, particularly in the *Theogony*, a world of abstractions arises, which the poet of Ascra knows how to clothe with dazzling nomenclature. "Common to both epics, specifically speaking, is the conception of Woman, a gift of Zeus which he bestowed on mankind in his wrath. The Pandora-myth in both poems is episodical; but favorite themes and favorite plaints are apt to crop out and to steal in — as episodes — particularly in didactic poetry. If anything, the Pandora episode of the *Works* (94 *sqq.*) is more malicious, because there woman is made responsible for the diffusion of evils through the world, evils tempered only by the retention of Hope. Hesiod's ethics are those of Cato the Censor and Franklin's *Poor Richard:* they are largely based on the virtues clustering around *Frugalitas*." (Sihler, in *Am. Philol. Assoc.* 1902, p. xvii.)

If we take the art of Homer, of Pindar, of Æschylus, there is a trend toward large and lofty themes, there is a certain affinity for a splendid elevation of being and feeling which many readers are tempted to use as the atmosphere and perspective for their general outlook upon the Hellenic world. It is the privilege, nay the proper function of such art to eliminate or ignore the common and the commonplace. For this one-sided estheticism of vision and of judgment the *Works and Days* of Hesiod furnishes an admirable corrective. We are brought into a world of the workday and of the toil requisite for the support of life. The hero and the man of splendid feats have entirely disappeared. In Hesiod the word *Basileus* ("king") evidently means nothing very great. The judges are called "kings": the poet describes them as "*swallowers of bribes*" (δωροφάγοι, *Works*, 264).

So far as we know, it was Hesiod who made the first attempt to divide the past into periods; and far from conceiving a development, he assumed a succession of declines. He calls his own time the Iron age, before which have come and passed the Golden, the Silver, and the Bronze. Curiously enough, this process of recession and decline was for an epoch stopped or inhibited, — that is, the Fourth age was an heroic age, the period of the Seven against

Thebes and of the Trojan war, but now there is no intimation of any survival of that heroic spirit. Socially the horizon of the Ascran farmer is narrow, morally it is large and wide. If we look at the abundant data of material living, there is here a detail of the year and of the husbandman's changing task, of house and home, of summer and winter, of wife and children and fireside, of servants and slaves, of crops and harvests and vintage, of seafaring and of a form of trade, which, in part, may still have been barter. No other piece of ancient literature brings us into so close and realistic touch with country people and rural conditions.

It is obvious that the proverbs and general truths in which the *Works and Days* abound were not all composed by Hesiod himself, but constitute a gradual aggregation. The whole, however, had a large place in Greek schools and schooling to the latest times.

BIBLIOGRAPHY

I. The Cyclic Epos. — The fragments of the cyclic epics have been collected by Kinkel, G., *Epicorum Græcorum fragmenta*, I (Teubner, 1877). Most of them are too brief to be serviceable to the historian. All in which the student of history could take an interest are translated by Lawton, W. C., *Successors of Homer* (London: Innes, 1898), ch. i. From this work a few selections have been taken for this volume. The most complete discussion of the subject is by Welcker, F. G., *Der epische Cyclus*, 2 vols. (Bonn, 1835, 1849; vol. I, 2d ed. 1865). See also Wilamowitz-Moellendorff, in *Homerische Untersuchungen*, VII. 328–80. On the illustration of cyclic subjects in Greek art, see Luckenbach, O., "Das Verhältniss der griech. Vasenbilder zu den Gedichten des epischen Kyklos," in *Jahrb. f. Philol.* Supplb. XI (1880), 491–637; Jahn, O., *Griech. Bilderchroniken*, ed. by A. Michaelis (Bonn, 1873); Robert, K., *Winckelmannsprogram* (Halle, 1891); Bendorff, O., and Niemann, G., *Das Heroon von Gjölbaschi-Trysa* (Vienna, 1889).

A briefer treatment of the cyclic epos will be found in any history of Greek literature. Especially new and valuable is Allen, T. W., "The Epical Cycle," in *Class. Quart.* II (1908). 81–8.

II. The Homeric Hymns. — Edition by Baumeister, A. (Teubner, 1910). See also the English edition by A. Goodwin and T. W. Allen (Oxford, 1893), and by Allen and Sikes (1904). Lang, A., *Homeric Hymns: A New Prose Translation* (Longmans, 1899), is a charming translation. From it the material in the present volume has been drawn. The best treatment in English is by Lawton, W. C., *Successors of Homer*, chs. iv–vi. See in general the histories of Greek literature.

III. Hesiod. — An excellent guide to the recent literature on Hesiod is

Rzach, A., "Bericht über die Publikationen zu Hesiodos 1899–1908," in *Jahresb.* CLII (1911). 1–75. The most recent critical edition is that by Rzach (Leipzig, 1902). The explanatory notes in Flach's revision of Göttling's edition have also proved useful to the editors. The best English translation is Mair, A. W., *Hesiod: The Poems and Fragments done into English Prose* (Oxford: Clarendon Press, 1908), from which the selections of the present volume have been taken, verified on the basis of the text by E. G. S. There is also a translation by C. A. Elton (London, 1894). Newly discovered fragments may be found in Grenfell, B., and Hunt, A., *Oxyrhynchus Papyri*, various volumes; *cf.* especially Wilamowitz-Moellendorff, V., "Neue Bruckstücke der hes. Kataloge," in *Sitzb. Berl. Akad.* 1900, pp. 839–51; *Berliner Klassiker Texte*, V. 1. On Hesiod's life and writings, in addition to the histories of Greek literature, see Schwartz, E., *Charakterköpfe aus der antiken Literatur* (3d ed. Teubner, 1911), ch. i; Symonds, J. A., *Studies of the Greek Poets*, II, ch. iv; Sihler, E. G., *Testimonium Animæ*, ch. iii; Aly, W., "Hesiod von Ascra und die Verfasser der Theogonie," in *Rhein. Mus.* LXVIII (1913). 22–67; Waltz, P., *Hésiode et son poème moral* (Bordeaux, 1906); Meyer, E., "Hesiods Erga und das Gedicht von den fünf Menschengeschlechtern," in *Carl Robert zum 8. März, 1910 Genethliakon;* Steitz, A., *Die Werke des Landbaus in den Werken und Tagen des Hesiodos* (Frankfurt am Main, 1866); Scott, J. A., *Comparative Study of Hesiod and Pindar* (Chicago, 1898); Bonner, R. J., "Administration of Justice in the Age of Hesiod," in *Class. Philol.* VII (1912). 17–23; Rzach, A., in Pauly-Wissowa, *Real-Encycl.* VIII. 1167–1240.

V. The Elegiac, Iambic, and Lyric Poets

700–479 B.C.

For the period extending from the seventh century to the close of the great war between Hellas and Persia almost our only contemporary sources are the poets of that time. Of elegiac, iambic, and lyric poetry we have in general nothing but fragments; but from this material, however scanty, may be derived precious information on a great diversity of subjects, including personal traits, society, economy, warfare, religion, and intelligence. Below are presented brief sketches of the lives and literary works of the poets represented in the present volume. They give expression to a period of stormy life and of brilliant varied emotion. "The change from rural to industrial economy in this time, the growth of cities and of a leisurely class, as well as contact with the entire Mediterranean world through commerce and colonization, afforded the means and the impetus to a magnificent literature. The abolition of kingship and the rise of aristocracies and tyrannies, involving fierce factional struggles, added to the intensity of life. To express these complex conditions the old epic verse of calm stately meter — the dactylic hexameter — proved wholly inadequate. It gave way, accordingly, to new and varied measures, which would better exhibit the play of individual or communal thought and emotion characteristic of the new era. The first variation from the epic verse is found in the elegiac pentameter, whose spirit may be either meditative or emotional. Accompanied by the pipe, it lent itself equally to the expression of political and social thought, religious devotion, and martial fire." (Botsford, *Hellenic History*, ch. viii.)

Among the earlier elegiac poets was Tyrtæus, who composed martial elegies at Sparta in the second half of the seventh century. The story that he was an Athenian schoolmaster, sent on request to lead the Lacedæmonians in war with the Messenians, is an insipid fiction. It would harmonize far better with the conditions of the time to connect his origin with Ionia, the home of the elegy, as Suidas actually does (Λάκων ἢ Μιλήσιος, "Laconian or Milesian"). It is perfectly possible, however, that he was a Laconian by birth; at all events he addresses the Spartans as a native, and enters into their spirit like one of their number. Philochorus, the Attic chronicler (Frag. 56), who is no mean authority, states that through his generalship the Spartans overcame the Messenians. If this assertion is true, he was a commander in war, and therefore a native. In addition to martial songs, he composed a poem entitled *Eunomia* (Good Order), in which he counsels the Spartans to cease from political dissensions. It would not be difficult to think of him as a general and statesman, like Solon, who used the elegy, in lack of prose, to inspire his troops with courage and to make known his political views.

Alcman, a contemporary of Tyrtæus, is likewise reputed to have been of foreign birth. An allusion in one of his poems led the ancients to believe that he was a native of Sardis. It was even said that he was brought as a slave to Sparta and there emancipated. Some modern scholars regard him as an Ionian, invited, like other foreign poets, to Sparta, to devote his genius to the good of that community. Another tradition represents him as a native Spartan of the deme Messoa, where he was buried (Suidas *s.* Ἀλκμάν;

Pausanias iii. 15. 2). The fact is that this century saw the culmination of Laconian civilization, and that after the decline had far advanced, no Greek critic or antiquarian could believe that Sparta had ever been capable of producing a poet of the rank of Alcman or Tyrtæus. Whatever his origin, he identifies himself heart and soul with Spartan life. He writes not of war and politics, however, but of sleeping nature, dancing, ceryl birds, and fair athletic girls. Here is an expression of the gentle refinement of early Sparta, which centuries of cramping military discipline gradually crushed. The form of poetry in which he excelled is the choral lyric, to be sung by a group of persons appropriately dressed and trained to dance in accompaniment. The Doric state set the example of using this form of song and dance as a means of civic education.

In our review of the seventh-century poets we now pass from the mainland on either side of the Ægean to the islands of that sea. A native of Paros, land of marble, was Archilochus, the reputed inventor of the iambic. This form of verse is adapted to the expression of the passions from love to hate, scorn, and invective. It is the measure used by the Greek dramatists in their dialogues and by modern poets in the so-called heroic verse. The iambic is appropriate to satire, and its inventor was the first to write that kind of poetry. He was the author, too, of certain grotesque combinations in which the stately hexameter is fused with scolding iambics, a truly mongrel verse. This poet, the son of an aristocratic father and slave mother, pours into his verse the storm and strife that filled the age. In early life he joined a colony, a pack of scoundrels as he describes it, on the island of Thasos. It was rich in gold, of which little fell to his lot, while he had to fight along with his fellow-colonists against the native barbarians. On one of these occasions he threw away his shield, a most disgraceful act, and afterward boasted of it in verse. Unable to remain in Thasos, because, as he says, he was too insolent, abusing friend and foe alike, and perhaps fearing to return to Paros, he became a wanderer over land and sea, a soldier of fortune, and seemingly a pirate. This life is reflected in the fragments of his verse. Admiring his bold inventiveness, the courage that always rallied from every overthrow, the versatility of his poetic genius, and his intense personality, the ancients placed him, as the unrivaled master of personal song, next to Homer.

Regarding Semonides of Amorgos little was known even to the ancients. As he used the iambic measure, he must be placed after Archilochus, seemingly as a younger contemporary. It is said that he was born in Samos and himself conducted a colony to Amorgos. This author is interesting to us chiefly for his satire on women, in which he compares their various types to animals. In homeliness of thought and style he is akin to Hesiod, while his treatment of animals makes him a forerunner of Æsop. The tone of contempt for women, his denunciation of them as the main or only source of human ills, he shares with Hesiod; in fact this spirit, in contrast with Homer's chivalry, extended far beyond the limitations of these two authors.

In our study of Solon, about 639–559, we pass from the seventh to the sixth century. While reaching firmer historical ground, we come to deal with a far more conspicuous personality than any mentioned above, made known to us through Aristotle's *Constitution of the Athenians*, 5–13, Plutarch's genial biography, and the mediocre life by Diogenes Laertius. In the spirit of Tyrtæus, Solon composed at least one martial elegy, all of which, with the exception of eight lines, has perished. Like Tyrtæus, he used the elegy for the propagation of his statesmanly views, for informing and persuading the people. In fact, from the fragments of his political verses, scant as they are, we may gather the aims and the results of his social and constitutional reforms. Not limiting himself to one kind of verse or to the topics above mentioned, he employed the iambic and expressed his views on various social and moral subjects. With Solon Athens entered upon a new era. Through him she acquired a body of liberal statutes and such an extension of the civic franchise as to interest the masses in her well-being, an open door to desirable alien immigrants, a commercial and cultural touch with Ionia, Egypt, and other countries, and lastly a worthy beginning of the most beautiful literature known to the world. It is not strange, then, that after ages looked back to Solon as the father of free government, the greatest of beneficent legislators, and the wisest of men.

Mimnermus of Colophon, a contemporary of Solon and perhaps his elder in years, lived in the shadow of Lydian imperialism which hung over the Asiatic Greeks. In one of his poems, a martial lay worthy of Tyrtæus, he glorifies a Smyrnæan hero, who battled with the Lydians, probably against King Gyges, and "scattered the dense phalanxes of Lydian cavalry throughout the plain of Hermus stream." This elegy was perhaps to encourage his fellow-citizens to defense against King Sadyattes (Christ, *Griech. Lit.* I. 163 *sq.*), who died about 604. His poems in general offer us the lively and impressionable strain of Ionic character. To the ancients, who knew his verse more fully than we do, his poetry was the typical note of sadness for the brief and passing springtime of human life and human joys, soft and mournful but too devoid of the elements of firmness, virility, and endurance, an embodiment of the "voluptuous and melancholy worldweariness of Ionia." Most of the larger remnants have been preserved to us by Stobæus.

The poets thus far mentioned have been Dorian and Ionian. With Alcæus we return to the home of the Æolians, who were a factor in the creation of the Homeric poems, and who in Lesbos kept equal pace with their Ionic kinsmen. This island lay in the highest cultural area of the age; it shared with the Ionians the advantages of trade with Orient, and while equally refined and intellectual, it showed less tendency than Ionia to physical and moral enfeeblement. Its people had their political troubles. The aristocracy, to which Alcæus belonged, had weakened itself through factions, till the government fell a prey to demagogues and tyrants. In the midst of such turmoil Alcæus passed his troubled life, an active participator in events, now the inspiring genius of his party, now wandering in lonely exile. Some of the details of his life are given in connection with his poems (ch. v). He was the first great master of the lyric monody, the song of individual experience sung to oneself or to friends. The lyric was so named because it was accompanied by the lyre, in contrast with the pipe, which was used with the elegy. His songs covered a wide range of subjects, including war, politics, drinking, love, and the beauties of nature. We have one or two entire poems remaining and many small fragments — enough for a high appreciation of his genius and for affording a glimpse of his island home within his lifetime.

In all human history, down nearly to our own time, the sixth century, B.C., with a part of the early fifth, formed the great age of women, the age in which their gifted representatives reached the utmost height of art and intelligence. It is true that in Ionia the tendency was to her segregation, and in Athens her liberty, once large, was being restricted by legislation. The high place of women in Laconia is well known; there they shared in the education of men, an education which was athletic rather than intellectual, and often appeared as the moral advisers of sons, husbands, or fathers. Throughout the greater part of Hellas they enjoyed large freedom and influence, while the reach of their intelligence is proved by the great number of poetesses who flourished in this period. They include Myrtis and Corinna of Bœotia, Praxilla of Sicyon, Telesilla of Argos, and especially Sappho of Lesbos.

Sappho was a contemporary and a friend of Alcæus; their lives belong to the early part of the sixth century. Little is known of the poetess. It is said that she was banished for political reasons, and afterward recalled. In Mytilene, appreciation of her genius grew till the state stamped her image on its coins. There was perhaps no place in Hellas where women were so free to develop their taste for music and poetry as Lesbos; and Sappho took advantage of this liberty to gather about her a school of brilliant, beautiful girls, her pupils in the composition of verse and melody. Many of her poems refer to these companions, their social relations, partings, marriages, and the telepathic sympathy of widely separated friends. She gives attention also to other subjects, to her spendthrift brother in Egypt, to a chorus of Cretan women about an altar, to the stars and moon, to orchards where cool streams call through the branches of apple-trees and slumber streams from quivering leaves. In all themes her inspiration is love and loveliness.

Anacreon of Teos, an Ionic city, is distinctly later than Sappho and belongs to the latter half of the century, yet the erotic tone of his verse connects him in a way with the Lesbic group of poets. When in 545 Harpagus, the lieutenant of Cyrus, assailed Anacreon's native city, he fled, with his fellow-citizens, to the Teian colony Abdera on the Thracian coast. This event found an echo in his song. During the reign of Polycrates, the magnificent tyrant of Samos (533–522), he served at his court as a sort of minister of pleasure. Afterward invited by Hipparchus to Athens, he made the acquaintance of Athenians who were then prominent or destined to prominence in the impending war with Persia. Still later it is said that he visited the mighty family of the Aleuadæ in Thessaly. The Alexandrian scholars had at hand his elegies, epigrams, iambics, and lyrics in five books, of which we have but two poems and many diminutive fragments. In his generation Ionia was full of intellectual energy; it was the age in which Hellenic philosophy, science, geography, and history were born. But as in every highly developed civilization luxury, dissipation, and vice also abounded; and it was the ambition of Anacreon to represent the decadent tendencies of his period.

Theognis, a contemporary of Anacreon, was an aristocrat of Megara, that little Doric commonwealth which lay between Attica and Corinth. His time was the second half of the sixth century and beyond, for in some of his verse (764 *sqq.*) the eastern horizon is darkened by the impending danger of Persian invasion. Much of his life he lived in exile, as at Thebes and in Sicily, where Megara Hyblæa was a colony of his native commonwealth. It would seem to be an elusive task to reconstruct his life and movements in detail from the verses traditionally ascribed to him, as the English scholar John Hookham Frere attempted to do (*Works*, 2 vols. 1842). This work was brilliant for its time, but the critical labors of Bergk have rendered many of its assumptions untenable.

In his wanderings the Megarian exile visited Sparta, too, and Eubœa, and received much kindly hospitality (784 *sqq.*), but nothing, he declared, could assuage the yearning for home and country. Much of his elegiac verse was composed to embellish a social occasion. The pipe (241) still accompanied the recitation. The general truths relating to the wise conduct of life gave to much of his verse a lasting currency among the Hellenes. In fact the remnants are an anthology in which social moralizing predominates. For the general purposes of this volume have been chosen some passages which exhibit the proud and stubborn consciousness of the aristocrat who considers the political and social domination of his own class as a self-evident principle, nay as a very postulate of nature. The aristocrats are the good and the excellent; the common folk are the mean and the bad.

As the life of Theognis connects the old aristocratic régime with the great war of Hellenic independence, that of Simonides of Ceos (556–469) spans the period between the age of the Peisistratidæ and the age of Themistocles. It is a curious fact that the same poet enjoyed the patronage of the last Athenian tyrant and of the founder of the Athenian naval supremacy. Like Anacreon he wandered about from place to place at the call of tyrant, aristocrat, or imperial democrat, ever ready to compose for the one who offered a sufficient fee. We hear of him at the court of Hippias, at the aristocratic courts of the tyrant's friends in Thessaly; then after the battle of Marathon we find him again at Athens, where in poetical competition he won a victory over Æschylus. Still later, Hieron called him to Sicily, where he entered into rivalry with Pindar. There he ended his days, and his tomb stood long before the gates of Syracuse.

The conspicuous success of his art in a characteristic way illustrates an aspect of the Greek spirit — a craving for immortality by means of a literary monument. The faculty of inscriptional composition which Simonides possessed in a high degree was sought for by aristocrats, tyrants, wealthy individuals of every party, and even by commonwealths such as Athens in the age of Themistocles. The most lasting of his verses are of the character mentioned above, which we may call commemorative, to give enduring distinction to historical monuments erected for great achievements and eminent persons of his time. He was one of the famous figures and voices of his own age; his muse, ready at the tinkle of silver, possessed a certain adroitness and versatility of worldly wisdom noted in his own generation. The Alexandrian critics studied and perpetuated his commemorative verse, called *Epigramma* by the Greeks. In addition to this kind of poetry, however, he wrote choral songs for religious and secular purposes, pæans, hymns, odes for the victors in the games, skolia, dithyrambs, lamentations, in brief every kind of verse of which his age had knowledge.

BIBLIOGRAPHY

I. General. — Sitzler, J., "Bericht über die griech. Lyriker, 1898–1905," in *Jahresb.* CXXXIII (1907). 104–322, for editions and literature appearing in the years indicated. Standard texts are those of Bergk, Th., *Anthologia Lyrica* (Teubner); Hiller, E., *Anthologia Lyrica* (Teubner); Smyth, H. M., *Greek Melic Poets* (Macmillan, 1900), the best English edition; Hartung, J. A., *Die griech. Lyriker*, 2 vols. (Engelmann, 1856), with German translations; Appleton, W. H., *Greek Poets in English Verse* (Houghton Mifflin, 1893), selected translations by various authors.

II. SEVENTH-CENTURY POETS. — Hauvette, A., *Un poète ionien du VIIe siècle, Archiloque; sa vie et ses poesies* (Paris, 1905); Crusius, in Pauly-Wissowa, *Real-Encycl.* II. 487–507.

Schwartz, E., "Tyrtæos," in *Hermes*, XXXIV (1899). 428–68; Verrall, A. W., "Tyrtæus, a Græco-Roman Tradition," in *Class. Rev.* X (1896); Schulhof, J. M., "Callinus and Tyrtæus," in *Class. Rev.* XIV (1900). 103 *sqq.*; Opitz, R., "Ueber den Weiberspiegel des Semonides von Amorgos," in *Philol.* L (1891). 13–30.

III. ALCÆUS, SAPPHO, CORINNA, AND TELESILLA. — Easby-Smith, J. S., *Songs of Alcæus, Memoir and Text with Literal and Verse Translations* (Washington: Lowdermilk, 1901), from which some of the selections of this volume have been taken; Edmonds, J. M., *The New Fragments of Alcæus, Sappho, and Corinna* (London: Bell, 1909), text of new fragments discovered before that date; "Newly discovered Fragments of Alcæus," in *Class. Rev.* XXIII (1910). 72–4, 241–3; "New Lyric Fragments," *ib.* XXVIII (1914). 73–8, from these three articles selections have been taken for the present volume. A criticism on the last-named article is made by Hunt, A. S., *ib.* 126 *sq.* See also Schubart, W., "Neue Bruchstücke der Sappho und des Alkaios," in *Sitzb. Berl. Akad.* 1902, pp. 195–214; Wilamowitz-Moellendorff, V., "Neue lesbische Lyrik," in *N. Jahrb.* XXXIII (1914). 225–47.

Wharton, H. T., *Sappho: Memoir, Text, and Selected Renderings* (Chicago: McClurg, 1887), from which selections have been made for this volume; Easby-Smith, J. S., *Songs of Sappho* (Washington: Stormont and Jackson, 1891), English translation; Brandt, P., *Sappho: Ein Lebensbild aus den Frühlingstagen altgriechischer Dichtung* (Leipzig, 1905), biography and literary appreciation; Steiner, B., *Sappho* (Jena, 1907), selections and appreciation; Bascoul, J. M. F., Ἡ ἁγνὰ Σαπφώ: *La chaste Sappho de Lesbos et le movement fémeniste à Athènes au IVe siècle avant J.-C.* (Paris, 1911); Paulides, I. I., Σαπφὼ ἡ Μυτιληναία (Leipzig, 1885), doctorate dissertation in modern Greek; Reinach, Th., "Nouveaux fragments de Sappho," in *Rev. des ét. gr.* XV (1902). 60–70; Wilamowitz-Moellendorff, V., *Sappho und Simonides: Untersuchungen über griechische Lyriker* (Weidmann, 1913).

Crönert, G., "Corinnæ quae supersunt," in *Rhein. Mus.* LXIII (1908). 161–89, contains text; Herzog, R., "Auf den Spuren der Telesilla," in *Philol.* LXXI (1912). 1–23, a few short fragments.

IV. SOLON, MIMNERMUS, THEOGNIS, ANACREON, AND SIMONIDES OF CEOS. — Wilamowitz-Moellendorff, V., *Aristoteles und Athen*, I. 39–75; II. 304–15; Keil, B., *Die Solonische Verfassung in Aristoteles' Verfassungsgeschichte Athens* (Gaertner, 1892); Mitchell, J. M., "Solon," in *Encycl. Brit.* 11th ed.; Platt, A., notes on Solon, in *Journ. of Philol.* XXIV (1896). 248–62; XXVI. 64–8; Jebb, R. C., "On a Fragment of Solon," *ib.* XXV (1897). 98–105.

Wilamowitz-Moellendorff, V, "Mimnermos und Properz," in *Sitzb. Berl.*

Akad. 1912, pp. 100–22; Frere, J. H., *Works*, 2 vols. (London: Pickering, 1872), containing translations and interpretations of Theognis; Hudson-Williams, T., *Elegies of Theognis and other Elegies included in the Theognidean Sylloge* (London: Bell, 1910), best edition; "Theognis and his Poems," in *J. H. S.* XXIII (1903). 1–23; Unger, G. F., "Die Heimat des Theognis," in *Philol.* XLV (1886). 18–33; Bullen, A. H., *Anacreon*, with Th. Stanley's translation (London, 1893); Crusius, "Anakreon," in Pauly-Wissowa, *Real-Encycl.* I. 2035–50; Wilamowitz-Moellendorff, V., *Sappho und Simonides*, mentioned under III.

VI. The Logographi and Herodotus

In the sixth century B.C., the age that saw the birth of Hellenic science, the epics current under the name of Homer and Hesiod's genealogical poems formed in the mind of the Greeks the background of their history. Thus far they had taken no literary interest in recent or contemporary happenings, and for that reason had produced no chronicles, as had the Oriental kings from immemorial time. The awakening of the scientific spirit, however, which led the Hellenes in search of the origin of the physical world, interested them equally in the beginnings of mankind, of their own race, of the various states, and of the leading families in each. Hence arose a class of writers, who, in a manner parallel with that of the contemporary "philosophers," busied themselves with such matters. They have been called logographi, "writers of prose" (*logos*), as distinguished from the composers of poetry (*epos*). If Cadmus of Miletus, reputed the earliest writer of this class, and author of the *Settlement of Ionia* (Pliny, *Natural History*, v. 112; *cf.* vii. 205), was a real person, at least nothing has been preserved from his book. Acusilaüs of Argos, about 500 B.C., is the earliest of whose work we have fragments. He composed *Genealogies*, a treatise which converted into prose and perhaps further expanded the Hesiodic genealogies. The fragments are but meager quotations by later writers. So far as we may infer from these scant remains, Acusilaüs limited himself to the beginnings of the gods, of the great things of nature, and of the human race. Nowhere does he approach historical times. Such was doubtless the nature of all early logography. In no respect, therefore, could it be termed history. The change, however, from verse to prose clipped the wings of imagination and accentuated correspondingly system and reason.

A notable advance was made by Hecatæus of Miletus, a younger contemporary of Acusilaüs. He was the author of a geography entitled *Circuit of the Earth.* The voyages of the Ionians to all parts of the Mediterranean and its tributary waters for commerce and colonization supplied him with the knowledge necessary for such a work. If the fragments collected by Müller, *Frag. Hist. Græc.* I. p. 1 *sqq.*, actually belong to this treatise, it must have been a great achievement for that age. The genuineness has been questioned, seemingly on insufficient ground (see Jacoby, F., "Hekataios," in Pauly-Wissowa, *Real-Encycl.* VII. 2667 *sqq.*). His *Genealogies* differs from those of his predecessors in dealing extensively with the historical period. The extant fragments prove, too, that he was gifted with a nascent critical spirit. There can be no doubt that Herodotus drew extensively from him, and that though he is set down among the logographi, he deserves to be called the earliest of historians.

From Hecatæus to Herodotus the advance is not so much in critical ability and accuracy of statement as in literary genius, in largeness of mind, and amiability of character. It is clear, however, that Herodotus doubted some things which Hecatæus accepted, that in the later writer there was an appreciable growth of the historical spirit.

Herodotus was born in Halicarnassus, a Dorian city which had become so Ionized as to use the Ionic dialect for official purposes (see Hicks and Hill, no. 27 with comment). Thus it was that this dialect, which Herodotus adopted for his *History*, was his native speech. He was born in 484 or thereabout and lived through the early years of the Peloponnesian war, to about 425. In early life he was involved in a civil war with Lygdamis, the Carian tyrant of his city. In this struggle his uncle Panyasis, an epical poet of some note, was killed, and Herodotus had to flee into exile, about 452. Thence arose his journeyings, which resulted in the creation of his great work. It is not easy or even necessary to determine whether the historian developed from the traveler, or the traveler from the historian. Doubtless the two parallel interests stimulated each other; and certainly the delight in geographical and ethnographical knowledge, gained by direct experience and vision, was a leading motive in his literary planning. He went to Egypt and ascended the Nile as far as Elephantine; he visited Cyrene and Phœnicia; he traversed the Persian empire as far as Susa. He came into personal acquaintance with the Black Sea region, including the Hellenic communities along its northern shore. For a time he was a citizen of the Periclean colony of Thurii in southern Italy. Attempts have been made, with partial success, to establish the chronology of his journeys and of the composition of his history. For a study of this subject the reader is referred to the bibliography given below.

The object of his literary labor is expressed in his preface: "This is a presentation of the Inquiry — *Historia* — of Herodotus of Halicarnassus to the end that time may not obliterate the great and marvellous deeds of the Hellenes and the Barbarians, and especially that the causes for which they waged war with one another may not be forgotten." So far as we know, he is the first to apply the word *Historia* to the department of literature of which he was laying the foundation. In his mind the term cause (*αἰτίη*), far from signifying historical causation in the modern sense, meant in particular the grievances of the parties to the war, which expressed themselves in the series of events leading to that struggle. In tracing these events he narrates from the earliest known times the notable achievements of all the peoples engaged in the great struggle. His production may be described therefore as a universal history, the unifying element of which is the ultimate conflict.

The word history in the sense of inquiry aptly describes his method of collecting information. It is true that he gathered some material from books, but the greater part of his knowledge came through personal inquiry of those who were supposed to know the facts. Not content with what he learned from one class of informants or from one locality, he visited different places to make inquiry of different persons (*cf.* ii. 3, 44); thus he introduced the method of comparative inquiry with a view to the sifting of his material. The object of his *History*, as he conceived it, required him to tell all he had thus heard, but not necessarily to accept it as fact: "I am under obligation to tell what is reported, though I am not bound altogether to believe it; and let this saying hold good for every narrative in the *History*." We find him accordingly comparing the less with the more credible account and expressing doubt as to this or that story.

One of the greatest of his qualities is his breadth of mind which enabled him to sympathize with foreigners, and to see that among them there could be good customs, able men, and admirable characters (*cf.* especially iii. 38). Ordinarily this quality lifts him above the prejudices of nationality, of states, and parties to the high level of the universal historian. On the other hand, the very lack of a well-developed critical method placed him at the mercy of his sources. It was but natural that he should gravitate to Athens, already becoming the intellectual metropolis of the world, and should write from the Athenian point of view, with the prejudices roused in Athens by the opening of the Peloponnesian war (see especially ix. 54). This prejudice colors many of the details of his chapters on Athenian and Peloponnesian history. It was but natural, too, that his chief informants on the internal affairs of Athens during the past were in the Periclean circle; and thus it happens that the enemies of the Alcmeonidæ suffer at his hands. He has, for instance, no just appreciation of Themistocles, the founder of Athenian greatness, the ablest statesman who had thus far appeared in history. The fault is not one of character; and in fact no historian has ever been readier to do justice to men than Herodotus.

In the religious sphere Herodotus is by no means credulous, but accepts the enlightened orthodoxy of his age. Although a generation younger than Æschylus, he looks upon human life and human pride essentially with the same eyes. Under the sunny gleam of his rippling narrative there is a substratum of deep melancholy and of the awe concerned with the anger and envy of the gods. King Crœsus, whom the auriferous Pactolus made the richest of men, Polycrates, tyrant of Samos, or Periander, despot of opulent Corinth — their pride and their end are merely iterations and reverberations of the stern melody of human success and divine retribution and the humiliation of man, exemplified most signally in Xerxes himself. An exponent of this doctrine is the Great King's adviser Artabanus, from whose lips issues the wisdom of Æschylus: "Thou seest how the Deity strikes with thunderbolt those beasts that tower above their fellows, but the little ones worry him not; and thou seest also how his missiles always smite the largest buildings and trees of such kind; for God loves to truncate all those things that rise too high. Thus, too, a large army may be ruined by a small one, when God in his jealousy hurls a panic or a thunderbolt, through which they are shockingly destroyed; for God permits none but himself to entertain grand ideas" (vii. 10. 5).

BIBLIOGRAPHY

I. Logographi. — Christ, *Griech. Lit.* I (1909). 424–34; Bury, *Ancient Greek Historians*, lect. i; Busolt, *Griech. Gesch*, I. 146–50; Gercke and Norden, *Einleitung in die Altertumswissenschaft*, III (1912). 76–8. Schwartz, "Akusilaus," in Pauly-Wissowa, *Real-Encycl.* I. 1222 *sq.* Fragments in Müller, *Frag. hist. græc.* I. 100–103. Jacoby, F., "Hekataios," in *Pauly-Wissowa, op. cit.* VII. 2666–769; Bunbury, E. H., *History of Ancient Geography* (London, 1883), I. ch. v; Berger, H., *Geschichte der wiss. Erdkunde bei den Griechen* (Leipzig, 1903), see Index. Pirro, "Studi erodotei, Ecateo e Xanto," in *Studi Storici*, I (Pisa, 1893). 424 *sqq.* Fragments in Müller, *op. cit.* I. 1–31.

II. Herodotus. — Report on recent literature, in *Jahresb.* 1910. Standard critical edition by Stein, H., 2 vols., Berlin, 1869–71. The same editor's annotated edition, 5 vols. (Berlin, 1883–93), Bks. iv–vi (1895), vii–ix (1908), ed. with excellent commentary by Macan, R. W. (London). How, W. W., and Wells, J., *Commentary on Herodotus*, 2 vols. (Oxford: Clarendon Press, 1912). English translations by Rawlinson, G., 4 vols. with abundant notes (3d ed., London, 1874); Macaulay, G. C., 2 vols. (Macmillan, 1890). Selections taken from the latter for this volume have been revised on the basis of the Greek text by E. G. S.

Hauvette, A., *Hérodote historien des guerres médiques* (Paris, 1894); "Hérodote et les Ioniens," in *Revue des études grecques*, I. 257 *sqq.*; Höck, A., *Herodot und sein Geschichtswerk* (Gütersloh, 1904); Kirchhoff, A., *Ueber die Entstehungszeit des herodoteischen Geschichtswerkes* (2d ed., Berlin, 1878); Diels, H., "Herodot und Hekataios," in *Hermes*, XXII (1887). 411–444; Lipsius, J. H., "Der Schluss des herod. Werks," in *Leipziger Studien*, XX (1902). 195–202; Grassl, A., *Herodot als Ethnologe; ein Beitrag zur Geschichte der Völkerkunde* (Munich, 1904); Myres, J. L., "Herodotus and Anthropology," in Marett, R. R., *Anthropology and the Classics* (1908), 121–68; Croiset, A., "La véracité d'Hérodote," in *Revue des études grecques*, I. 154 *sqq.*; Sihler, E. G., *Testimonium Animæ*, 159–68; Bury, *Ancient Greek Historians*, lect. ii.

VII. Hellanicus and Thucydides; Inscriptions

Hellanicus of Mytilene lived to see the close of the Peloponnesian war, and occupied accordingly a place next after that of Herodotus. In spirit and method, however, he connected closely with the logographi; his chief interest was in myth and genealogy. It was his task to carry much farther than his predecessors the extension and systematizing of pedigrees. As a basis he seems to have taken the list of priestesses in the Argive Heræum (see his *Priestesses of Hera*, in Müller, *Frag. hist. græc.* I. p. 51 *sq.*). In the form in which he employed it, this list, beginning in the thirteenth century B.C., continued unbroken to his own time, and included the number of years that each priestess officiated (Frag. 53, Müller). It is evident that the first five centuries or thereabout were fictitious, but we cannot say through whose hands the reconstruction took place. A part of the work of Hellanicus was to bring the early chronology of other states into harmony with that of Argos. In his *Atthis* — Attic chronicle — for example, he inserted new names in the existing list of kings in order to synchronize Athenian with Argive history; and we may assume that in the case of other states his method was similar. His works, *Bœotica*, *Argolica*, *Lesbica*, *Thettalica*, *Founding of Chios*, etc., included all or nearly all Hellenic countries, while accounts of prominent foreign nations were given in his *Concerning Lydia*, *Phœnicica*, *Ægyptiaca*, *Persica*, etc. (*cf.* Müller, *op. cit.* I. pp. 45–69). It seems clear that the chronological outline of early Hellas accepted by later authors was largely his work. The portion dealing with the period anterior to about 750 is almost wholly fictitious, an arbitrary system of myth and actual invention joined with an extremely scant and uncertain tradition. While his chief interest was in remote antiquity, he treated meagerly of recent times. His *Atthis* extended to the close of the Peloponnesian war.

While we possess mere shreds of the vast works of Hellanicus, we are fortunate in having the entire production of Thucydides, universally reputed the greatest of ancient historians. We do not know when he was born. He says (v. 26) that at the beginning of the Peloponnesian war he was at the height of his power, a statement which would make him perhaps about thirty years old at the time, and he must have died soon after the close of the Peloponnesian war, as he left his *History* of that conflict unfinished. He was related to Cimon, the Athenian general and statesman, and was probably with him a descendant of the Thracian chief Olorus.

Evidently these connections gave him an interest in the gold mines at Scapte-Hyle, Thrace. A man of wealth and of distinguished family, he was elected to the board of generals for the year 424. His failure to protect Amphipolis from the Lacedæmonians under Brasidas, whatever may have been its cause, resulted in his exile for twenty years, 424–404. We do not know whether he was actually banished or withdrew in fear of trial and condemnation. However that may have been, his exile presented to the wealthy man of affairs a leisure which he resolutely and consistently used in the collection of information for his history of the war. From its very beginning, 431, nay even before the outbreak of hostilities, he had conceived the purpose of writing this history. It was a well-matured resolution. Probably no man in the Hellenic world, not even Herodotus, had at the time so good a knowledge and so clear a grasp of Hellenic affairs. This preparation he enlarged by the persistent industry of his long exile in gathering all possible facts relating to the conflict.

The period anterior to the war he surveys by way of introduction to his theme; and yet this portion, brief as it is, is of the highest value not only for the facts it contains, but also as an illustration of the author's method: "The character of the events which preceded (the war), whether immediately or in more remote antiquity, owing to the lapse of time cannot be made out with certainty" (i. 1). This utterance is likely to weaken our faith in the logographic accounts of early Hellas. If the events of the Persian war and of the pentecontaëtia which followed, 480–431, could not be made out with certainty by Thucydides, it would be absurd for us to accept the Greek stories of so remote happenings, as for instance the Dorian migration. The difficulty of knowing the past, he continues, lies partly in the nature of our sources. For the Trojan war, which he regards as a fact, he has the authority of Homer: "He was a poet, and may therefore be expected to exaggerate" (i. 10). The difficulty lies partly, too, in our dependence on oral tradition: "Men do not discriminate, and too readily receive ancient traditions about their own as well as about other countries" (i. 20). Even regarding events of a hundred years before his time, events of profound interest to his countrymen, they entertained the grossest misconceptions. Notwithstanding these uncertainties the historian sketches the political development and the progress of civilization from the earliest time to the beginning of the war (i. 2–23): "Yet anyone who upon the grounds I have given arrives at some such conclusion as my own about those ancient times, would not be far wrong. He must not be misled by the exaggerated fancies of the poets or by the tales of logographi, who seek to please the ear rather than to speak the truth. He cannot test their accounts; and most of the facts in the lapse of ages have passed into the regions of romance. At such a distance he must make up his mind to be satisfied with conclusions resting upon the clearest evidence which can be had" (i. 21).

He attempts to reconstruct the primitive condition of Hellas (1) from survivals of customs and conditions. Certain tribes remained primitive down to his own day, and he infers that all the Hellenes once lived as did these tribes in his time. These conclusions, he adds, are confirmed by the ancient poets (i. 5, 6). (2) He makes use of archæology. The primitive islanders he studied by means of their tombs. When the Athenians purified Delos in the Peloponnesian war and opened the tombs in that island, it appeared that more than half of the occupants were Carian, as was proved by their arms and their mode of burial (i. 8). He is wrong, however, in supposing that he here has evidence of race; he has proved only that the occupants had a civilization like that of the present Carians. His method of drawing deductions from the survival of customs and conditions and from archæological remains and of making allowances for the mistakes and exaggerations of earlier authors has been adopted by modern historians.

Historians before Thucydides limited themselves to the time before the Persian war or to that war itself. The period intervening between the Persian and the Peloponnesian war was omitted by all with the exception of Hellanicus; and he, where he touched upon it in his Attic chronicle (*Syngraphê*), was very brief, and in his chronology inaccurate (i. 97). Thucydides adopts what he considers a better chronological system: "I would have a person reckon the actual periods of time and not rely upon catalogues of the archons or other official personages whose names may be used in different cities to mark the dates of past events. For whether an event occurred in the beginning or in the middle, or whatever might be the exact point of a magistrate's term of office, is left uncertain by such a mode of reckoning. But if he measures by summers and winters as they are here set down, and counts each summer and each winter as a half year, he will find that ten summers and ten winters have passed in the first part of the war" (v. 20). The advantage of reckoning time by the natural year, rather than by the conflicting civil years of the various states, Thucydides fully appreciates, although he seems to have no conception of the importance of an era of chronology for fixing the period of his history in its appropriate universal relation.

This shortcoming is probably due in the main to the concentration of his attention upon the present, which he regards as all-important: "Former ages were not great either in their wars or in anything else" (i. 1); "The greatest achievement of former times was the Persian war; yet even this conflict was decided in two battles by sea and two by land. The Peloponnesian war, on the other hand, was a protracted struggle, and attended by calamities such as Hellas had never known within a like period of time. Never were so many cities captured and depopulated — some by barbarians, others by Hellenes themselves fighting against one another. . . . Never were exile and slaughter more frequent, whether in the war or in civil strife. . . . There were earthquakes unparalleled in their extent and fury, and eclipses of the sun more numerous than are recorded to have happened in any former age; there were also in some places great droughts causing famines, and lastly the plague, which did immense harm and destroyed numbers of people" (i. 23). This high valuation of the present as compared with the past he shares with the sophists. He is at one with them also in his desire to impart useful information. The chief object of Herodotus had been to entertain the public, that of Thucydides was to furnish information useful to the general and statesman: "Very likely the strict historical character of my narrative may be disappointing to the ear. But if he who desires to have before his eyes a true picture of the events which have happened, and of the like events which may be expected to happen hereafter in the order of human affairs, shall pronounce what I have written to be useful, then I shall be satisfied. My history is a possession forever, not a prize composition to be heard and forgotten" (i. 23).

Although it is now recognized that history does not repeat itself, there can be no doubt that a knowledge of the past greatly aids the statesman in maturing his judgment and in enlarging his experience of human affairs. Such knowledge must above all things be accurate; and this quality Thucydides claims for himself: "As to the events of the war I have not ventured to speak from any chance information, nor according to any notion of my own; I have described nothing but what I either saw myself or learned from others, of whom I made the most careful and particular inquiry. The task was laborious because eye-witnesses of the same occurrences give different accounts of them according as they remember or are interested in the actions of one side or the other" (i. 22). It is universally granted that Thucydides, though by no means infallible, possesses the quality of accuracy in an extraordinarily high degree.

His theme is extremely narrow — a war rather than a period of national development; yet within this limited field he is deep and thorough. With marvelous analytical power he lays bare the spirit of government and the soul of political factions. When he has to do with persons, he tells us nothing of their outward appearance, their habits, or mannerisms, but reveals the mind only. His philosophy has taught him that as a rule the individual counts for little in history. The life of a nation is the surging of mighty currents, in which ordinary statesmen are mere straws whose movements indicate the ebb and flow and conflict of forces. A few master spirits combine reason and force in a sufficient degree to control the destinies of their people. They have their creative plan, which they are able to realize by bending the masses to their will. Such were preëminently Themistocles and Pericles. They have a universal and eternal interest, whereas a Cleon or Hyperbolus is the type of a politician ofttimes repeated.

A large place in his history is occupied by the speeches, which must not be taken as verbatim reports: "As to the speeches which were made either before or during the war, it was hard for me and for others to recollect the exact words. I have therefore put into the mouth of each speaker the sentiments appropriate to the occasion, expressed as I thought he would be likely to express them, while at the same time I endeavored as nearly as I could to give the general purport of what was actually said" (i. 22). They are usually grouped in pairs expressing the opposing sides of a crisis, and may be regarded as largely the author's interpretation of the situation or the events to which they apply.

In the year 411 his narrative comes abruptly to an end. At that point he seems to have ceased writing, to devote his attention to the revision of the part already written — a work which he did not complete before his death; for the fifth and eighth books lack his stylistic finish.

A means of verifying and correcting our literary sources and of greatly enlarging our knowledge of Hellenic life is afforded by the inscriptions. Reference is made to Minoan writing in the introduction to Chapter II. With the decline of the Minoan civilization the art of writing seems to have been lost to Hellas, and the Greek alphabet was not invented before the tenth, or possibly the ninth, century. In the seventh century, with the first importation of papyrus from Egypt, writing began to be extensively used. From that century, too, come the earliest extant inscriptions. They appear in increasing numbers during the sixth century and in the fifth they become abundant. From that time to the end of ancient civilization they are among the most important of our sources.

BIBLIOGRAPHY

I. Hellanicus. — Fragments in Müller, *Frag. hist. græc.* I. 45–69; IV. 629 *sqq.* Kullmer, H., "Die historiai des Hellanikos von Lesbos," in *Jahrb. f. kl. Phil.* Supplb. XXVII (1901). 455–698, an attempt at reconstruction; Von Wilamowitz-Moellendorff, *Arist. u. Ath.* II. 19 *sq.*; Bury, *Anc. Greek Historians*, 27 *sqq.*; Perrin, in *Am. Journ. Philol.* XXII (1901). 38 *sqq.* The most recent and thorough treatment is by Gudeman, "Hellanikos," in Pauly-Wissowa, *Real-Encycl.* VIII (1912). 104–55.

II. Thucydides. — Critical edition by Bekker (2d ed., Berlin, 1892); by Poppo, E. F., rev. by Stahl, J. M., 4 vols. (Leipzig, 1875–89); by Sitzler, J. (Gotha, 1891–1901); by Hude, C., 2 vols. (Leipzig, 1898, 1901); by Jones, H. S. (Oxford: Clarendon Press, 1902); with detailed explanatory notes by Classen, J., 8 vols. (4th ed., Berlin, 1897). The best English translation is by Jowett, B. (see review by Freeman, E. A., in *Fortnightly Review*, 1882, pp. 273–92). Selections from this translation for the present volume have been revised and improved by comparison with the Greek text by E. G. S.

Reports of recent literature on Thucydides in *Jahresb.* 1905, 1908; and by Lange, E., "Die Arbeiten zu Thukydides seit 1890," in *Philol.* LVI (1897).

658–711; LVII (1898). 436–500, 658. See also Cornford, F. M., *Thucydides Mythhistoricus* (London: Arnold, 1907); Grundy, G. B., *Thucydides and the History of his Age* (London: Murray, 1911); Bury, J. B., *Ancient Greek Historians*, lect. iii; Meyer, Ed., "Thukydides und die Entstehung der wissenschaftlichen Geschichte," in *Mitt. des Wiener Vereins der Freunde des hum. Gymn.* XIV; *Forsch.* II (1899). 269–436; Kirchhoff, A., "Ueber die von Thukydides benutzten Urkunden," in *Berl. Akad.*, 1881–1884; Büdinger, M., *Poesie und Urkunde bei Thukydides* (Vienna, 1891); Jebb, R. C., "Speeches of Thucydides," in *Essays and Addresses* (Cambridge, 1907), 359–445; Lange, E., *Thukydides und sein Geschichtswerk* (Gütersloh, 1893); Von Wilamowitz-Moellendorff, "Die Thukydides-Legende," in *Herm.* XII (1877). 326–67; *Aristoteles und Athen*, I. 99–120; Milchhöfer, A., "Athen und Thukydides ii. 15," in *Philol.* LV (1896). 170–9; Petersen, E., "Zu Thukydides. Urathen und Tettix," in *Rhein. Mus.* LXII (1907). 536–49; Morris, C., "Chronology of the πεντηκονταετία," in *Am. Journ. Philol.* VII (1886). 323–43; Busolt, *Griech. Gesch.* III. 616–93; Kornemann, E., "Thukydides und die römische Historiographie," in *Philol.* LXIII (1904). 148–53.

VIII. The Fifth-century Poets

For the spirit of the great age of Hellas, 480–404 B.C., its social customs and thought, religious rites and aspirations, moral and intellectual attainments and ideals, we have to depend upon the poets even more than upon the historians. The study of Pindar leads us to the very heart of the national games, which were among the most characteristic of Hellenic activities. The devotion of the Greeks to competitions was in a high degree stimulating and fruitful. The fact that their communities were small and isolated, either surrounded by water or narrowly limited by mountain ranges, added importance to their periodic reunions, "all-gatherings" (*panegyreis*). In time as they spread in colonies to the mouth of the Nile, to Cyprus, to the Black Sea, to Sicily and southern Italy, and to the coasts of Gaul and Spain, these gatherings, with the contests which gradually grew more diversified, came to be almost the only form of union known to their national life. The competitions (*agones*) were connected with their legends and religion, with their literature and art. They furnished, too, a sphere in which music was almost equal to the other forms of art in dignity, importance, and technical development. The games were many and were frequently held. In addition to the annual festivals of every city, there were four great national games: those at Olympia and Delphi came once in four years, the Isthmia and Nemea once in two years.

Through his *Odes of Victory* (Epinikia) Pindar of Bœotia (about 520–441) is one of the most important exponents of the Greek spirit. His relations were mainly with the rich and great. They alone were able not only to contend at the national games, but also to remunerate the poet, whose Muse wrought for money. He was the composer not only of the verses but also of the accompanying music and the instructor who trained the chorus chosen to chant the Odes. As the singers had to be taken from the locality where the prize-winner resided, or at the place of the actual contest, it is clear that Pindar had the opportunity through visit and sojourn to make himself acquainted with many parts of Hellas. His rivalry with his eminent contemporary Simonides was noted by their own generation. Hieron of Syracuse was patron of both. To the modern reader Pindar's most striking feature is the heavy proportion of myth and legend in these choral odes. The reason is not only that the several communities, but specifically the more eminent families therein, so cherished legendary traditions that their very pedigree and pride of race were inextricably bound up with such myths. Thus the tone of the *Odes* is essentially noble and lofty, and the spirit intensely aristocratic. Pindar was a contemporary of Æschylus. There are many points of resemblance between them, and their handling of legends is not essentially different. In the nature of the case the lyre of the Bœotian devoted itself to the happy and brilliant side of myth and of human life, whereas the tragic poet necessarily presented their somber aspects. In style Pindar, like Æschylus, is bold, original, and elevated. Many obscurities of allusion may never be cleared up; and the texts, without the music, without the choral chanting, without the well-ordered movements of the original production in strophe, antistrophe, and epode, in its present effects must fall far short of the poet's actual achievement.

In addition to choral lyric Pindar composed many forms of poetry. His writings were collected in seventeen books, probably by the Alexandrine scholar Aristophanes of Byzantium. Dionysius of Halicarnassus makes the same scholar responsible, too, for the editing of the lines and the metrical schemes.

Valuable to the student of Greek history are Pindar's ideas on religion, morals, and other features of society. From what has already been said it will be understood that these ideas are decidedly conservative, aristocratic. This side of Hellenic life and thought is especially recommended for examination in view of the fact that most modern histories of the fifth century treat almost exclusively of democratic ideas and movements.

A contemporary of Pindar was Æschylus of Athens, who was born in 525. When the Persians were driven back to their fleet at Marathon, 490, he was in the prime of manhood and fought on that field. In the time of Xerxes' invasion he witnessed the abandonment of town and country, and Persian torches in the sanctuaries and homes of Athens, a requital for the burning of Sardis. These experiences were the inspiration of his life's work. In his earlier career he was a composer of what we may roughly compare with modern cantatas and oratorios. His choruses sang; and only gradually, as two actors were introduced, his productions became more distinctly dramatic. He composed about seventy plays, not counting the so-called satyr dramas; the function of the latter was to lighten the gloom and the severe strain superinduced by the presentation of the three tragedies which each of the authors produced in competition for the first prize. Æschylus distinctly excelled the competitors of his earlier manhood and middle life, such as Phrynichus and Pratinas. He came forward for the first time in 500 B.C., and, according to the *Marmor Parium*, gained his first victory, *i.e.* the First Prize, in 485. In all, he won this distinction thirteen times, each time with three pieces: thus thirty-nine of his tragedies were crowned. Twice he visited Sicily: the first time, it seems, in consequence of an invitation by Hieron, tyrant of Syracuse, whose splendid generosity to men of letters, such as Pindar and Simonides, was well known to that generation. In 468, at the first competition in which Sophocles appeared on the Attic stage, the latter triumphed over the veteran. It was not for this reason, however, as some have imagined, that Æschylus retired from Athens to Sicily. The brilliant court of Hieron, the great demand in Syracuse for dramatic productions, were sufficient attractions. His last days were spent in Gela, where he died in 456.

The austere loftiness of Æschylus was coupled with a genuine religious spirit, deepened by the stirring experiences of the struggle with Persia. He was bold, original, and creative — in a large sense the intellectual and moral parent of the succeeding Attic dramatists and of the philosophers.

Sophocles, mentioned above as a younger rival of Æschylus, lived through the greater part of the fifth century, 496–406. Though he learned much from his elder contemporary, he belongs distinctly to a new age. Whereas Æschylus gives expression to the notable achievements and gigantic aspirations of the war heroes, Sophocles represents the calmer and more reasoned spirit of the Periclean age. The father of Sophocles was a manufacturer, probably of knives and swords; so that the Peloponnesian war, while impoverishing the majority of Athenians, by no means diminished his income or detracted from the serenity of his life. His easy circumstances, joined with a naturally balanced character, found reflection in his dramas. For the problems of religion and of human life and character he was inclined to accept gentle solutions. In opposition to the sophistic movement he was strongly conservative, and in religion he represents, with Herodotus, an enlightened orthodoxy. We appreciate him as a man of wonderful intellectual and moral strength, as well as a perfect master of dramatic art, in brief, as the highest expression of Hellenism both in the age of Pericles and in the subsequent conflict between conservatism and the more modern thought of Euripides and the sophists.

Euripides was about fifteen years younger than Sophocles, though both died in 406. Throughout his life, therefore, he was a rival of the older poet. In the conflict, however, between Hellenism and modernism which arose within this century Euripides was wholly for the new movement. Thus it happens, that though Æschylus and Sophocles, when compared with one another, stand an age apart, they should be placed together in contrast with Euripides. We know little of his life. His father seems to have been a landowner of moderate circumstances but of no distinction; and certainly the gifted son was free from all aristocratic connections with the past. As a youth he had an athletic training, and it is said that he afterward studied as a painter; at all events he had a keen eye for art and landscape. Of science and philosophy he learned what he could from books. While attaching himself to no system, he shows a lively interest in all manner of philosophic problems. With the sophists he rejects traditional religion; and in his own field he casts away the art of his predecessors, to build the drama anew on principles which we recognize as relatively modern. He shows a deep and varied knowledge of human nature, and especially sympathizes with the weak and unfortunate, with women, slaves, beggars, and cripples. While as an exponent of Hellenism Sophocles has a voice for the Greeks only and their admirers, the humanism of Euripides appeals to the world.

In the use of dramatic literature as a historical source we have to consider (1) what elements are traditional, (2) what are the ideas of the poet, (3) what is contemporary thought or custom. In considering the personal element of the author we have further to distinguish between settled conviction and the passing thought or feeling assigned to a character. The persons and the essentials of the plot are an inheritance from the remote past, from the epics and especially from those of the cycle; the rest of the drama is the poet's creation from his own imagination, character, and environment. Beyond this point the problem of analysis is complex and difficult, and incapable of solution by any ready-made process. Each drama requires individual study; and although there is much that defies analysis, it cannot be doubted that the plays of the three great tragic poets constitute an invaluable store of information relating to the customs, thought, feeling, and character of the Hellenes in the most splendid period of their history.

Much later than was the case with tragedy did the Attic government recognize comedy and provide choruses for it. This occurred probably between 465 and 460. In a certain sense the Old Comedy of Athens is but a single symptom, but certainly the most significant symptom, of that absolute freedom of speech (*παρρησία*) which attained its most unbridled development in the Periclean democracy. Aristophanes, born about 450, was a mere lad when Pericles died. A few years later the young genius, incomparably endowed for political satire — beyond all Dean Swifts or Punches of a later time — secured from the archon choruses for the children of his rollicking muse. His first three plays, *Daitalês* (Banqueters),

427 B.C., *The Babylonians*, 426, and *The Acharnians*, 425, were presented under the imaginary authorship of an actor, Callistratus.

It was long the custom, as in the heavy and ultra-serious essay by Ferdinand Ranke, to assign to the author of the *Knights*, *Clouds*, *Wasps*, *Peace*, *Birds*, and *Frogs* a niche among the thoughtful patriots, deep political thinkers, and even moral reformers who gave lasting distinction to Athens. On this subject, however, there is room for difference of opinion. It is always a question how far our poet should be taken seriously. Thucydides and his great work afford a curious foil to the political comedy of the Peloponnesian war: they illumine one another in the most admirable manner. The faculty of symbolical caricature and a drastic felicity of allegory and invective, intermingled with lofty lyrics and harlequinade, language sometimes running on the even keel of current Attic dialogue, but often interlarded with sudden and incalculable spurts of slang and vulgarity, an abandon of obscenity and semi-intoxication of demeanor — all in close harmony with the essential character of the vintage festivals — sudden attacks on some familiar minor figures, with sustained persecution of some greater personage in public life — these, and many other ingredients may be found in the plays of Aristophanes. Besides the eleven plays preserved he wrote about twenty-nine others. Was the political influence of an Aristophanes comparable to that of the orators who addressed the Ecclesia directly, when all were sober and in a deliberative frame of mind? Plato has borne witness that the caricature of Socrates in the *Clouds* had a lasting and an evil effect on the reputation of that philosopher. The typical humanist who would duly revere both the philosopher and his reckless traducer finds himself in a somewhat difficult plight. That Aristophanes pleaded for peace, and that, with his brilliant and piercing intellect, he discerned the evils of the developed Attic democracy cannot be denied; but it seems to be equally true that sheer love of fun interfered with the earnest pursuit of any serious object.

BIBLIOGRAPHY

I. PINDAR. — Edition by Christ, W. (2d ed., Teubner, 1896); by Schröder, O., in Bergk, Th., *Poetæ lyrici græci*, I (Teubner, 1900). *Olympian and Pythian Odes*, by Gildersleeve, B. L. (2d ed., N. Y., 1890). The best translation is by

Myers, E. (Macmillan, 1892), from which selections have been taken for this volume.

Wilamowitz-Moellendorff, V., "Hieron und Pindaros," in *Sitzb. Berl. Akad.* 1901, pp. 1273–1318; Christ, *Griech. Lit.* I. 216–35.

II. BACCHYLIDES. — Editio princeps of the newly discovered poems by Kenyon, F. G. (London, 1897); also by Blass, F. (3d ed., Teubner, 1904); by Jebb, R. C., with introduction, notes, and prose translation (Cambridge, 1905). There is also an English translation by Poste, E. (Macmillan, 1898). See further the article by Jebb on Bacchylides in *Encycl. Brit.* 11th ed.; Meiser, O., *Mythographische Untersuchungen zu Bacchyl.* (Munich, 1904), dissertation. Although no selections have been made from Bacchylides for this volume, he may be recommended for study along with Pindar.

III. ÆSCHYLUS. — Edition by Weil, H. (2d ed., Teubner, 1907); by Campbell, L. (Macmillan, 1898); by Sidgwick, A. (Clarendon Press, 1902). English translation by Blackie, J. W. (London: Parker, 1850), verse; by Headlam, W., 5 vols. (London: Bell, 1900–08), from revised text; by Plumptre, E. H., 2 vols. (Boston: Heath, 1901); text with verse translation by Way, A. S., 3 pts. (Macmillan, 1906–08), from which selections, revised by E. G. S., have been made for this volume; *Persians, Seven against Thebes, Prometheus*, and *Suppliants*, by Morsehead (Macmillan, 1908).

Myers, E., "Æschylus," in Abbott, E., *Hellenica* (London: Rivingtons, 1880), 1–32; Cauer, F., "Aischylos und der Areopag," in *Rhein. Mus.* L (1895). 348–56; Sihler, E. G., *Testimonium Animæ*, 148–59; V. Wilamowitz-Moellendorff, "Die Bühne des Æschylus," in *Hermes*, XXI (1886). 597–622; Dieterich, "Aischylos," in Pauly-Wissowa, *Real-Encycl.* I. 1065–84.

IV. SOPHOCLES. — Edition by Schneidewin, F. W., and Nauck, A. (Berlin, 1897–1909); by Tyrrell, R. V. (London, 1897); by Campbell, L., and Abbott, E., 2 vols. (Oxford, 1899, 1900); with explanatory notes by Wecklein, N., 2 vols. (Munich, 1897); by Jebb, R. C., plays in separate vols. with copious notes and Eng. trans. (Cambridge: University Press). Translations by Whitelaw, R. (Longmans, 1904); by Storr, F. (Loeb Cl. Libr. 1912, 1913); by Campbell, L. (London: Frowde, 1906); by Way, A. S., 2 vols. (Macmillan, 1909, 1914); by Coleridge, E. P. (Bohn); by Jebb, R. C. (Cambridge: University Press, 1912), from which the selections for this volume have been taken.

For studies in the author, see Campbell, L., *Sophocles* (Macmillan, 1880); Abbott, E., "Theology and Ethics of Sophocles," in *Hellenica* (London, 1880). 33–66; Tyrrell, R. Y., *Essays on Greek Literature* (London, 1909); Post, C. R., "Dramatic Art of Sophocles," in *Harv. St. in Cl. Philol.* XXIII (1912). 71–129; Müller, A., *Æsthetischer Kommentar zu den Tragödien des Sophokles* (Paderborn, 1904); Patin, A., *Æsthetisch-kritische Studien zu Sophokles* (Paderborn, 1911); Sihler, E. G., *Testimonium Animæ*, ch. ix.; Botsford, *Hellenic History*, ch. xvii. § 2.

V. EURIPIDES. — Edition by Prinz, R., and Wecklein, N., 3 vols. (Leipzig, 1883–1902); by Nauck, A., 3 vols. (3d ed., Teubner, 1892–1895); by Murray, G., 2 vols. (Oxford, 1902, 1905). Among the editions of individual plays especially valuable for interpretative matter are Wilamowitz-Moellendorff, U. v., *Herakles*, 2 vols. (2d ed., Berlin, 1895); *Hippolytos* (Berlin, 1895). The scholia are edited by Schwartz, E., 2 vols. (Berlin, 1887, 1895). Translations by Way, A. S., with text, Loeb Cl. Libr., 4 vols. (Macmillan, 1912); Coleridge, E. P., 2 vols. (Bohn); *Medea, Trojan Women and Electra* by Murray, G. (Oxford, 1907). The selections for this volume are from Coleridge and Way.

For studies in Euripides, see Macurdy, G. H., *Chronology of the Extant Plays of Euripides*. Diss. (Lancaster, Pa., 1905); Decharme, P., *Euripides and the Spirit of his Dramas*, trans. by Loeb, J. (Macmillan, 1905); Murray, G., *Euripides and his Age* (Holt, 1913); Verrall, A. W., *Euripides the Rationalist; a Study of Art and Religion* (Cambridge: University Press, 1913); Steiger, H., *Euripides, seine Dichtung und seine Persönlichkeit* (Leipzig: Dieterich, 1912); Haussleiter, F., *Ueber die Frage der Sittlichkeit bei Sophokles und Euripides* (Erlangen, 1907); Bartels, R., *Beziehung zu Athen und seiner Geschichte in den Dramen des Euripides*, Progr. (Berlin, 1889); Huddilston, J. H., *Greek Art in Euripides, Aischylos and Sophokles*, Diss. (Munich, 1898); Sihler, *Testimonium Animæ*, ch. x.; Kirchhoff, C., *Dramatische Orchestik der Hellenen* (Leipzig, 1899); Verrall, A. W., *The Bacchants of Euripides and other Essays* (Cambridge: University Press, 1910); Nestle, W., "Die Bacchen des Euripides," in *Philol.* LVIII (1899). 362–400.

Fragments of all the tragic poets: Nauck, A., *Tragicorum græcorum fragmenta* (2d ed., Teubner, 1889).

VI. Aristophanes. — Edition by Leeuwen, J. van (Leiden, 1893–1906); by Hall, F. W., and others (Clarendon Press, 1902); facsimile of the Codex Venetus Marcianus 474 by White, J. W. (Boston, 1902); text with translation and explanatory notes by Rogers, B. B., each play in a separate vol. (Macmillan, 1902–), from which selections for the present volume have been taken. Scholia by Rutherford, W. G., 3 vols. (London, 1896–1905). Translations, in addition to Rogers, by Walsh, B. D., 3 vols. (London, 1837); by Hickie, W. J., 2 vols. (Bohn); select plays by Frere, J. H. (London: Routledge, 1887).

Dunbar, H., *Complete Concordance to the Comedies and Fragments of Aristophanes* (Oxford, 1883); Müller-Strübing, H., *Aristophanes und die historische Kritik*, etc. (Leipzig, 1873); Mazon, P., *Essai sur la composition des comédies d'Aristophanes* (Paris, 1904); Leeuwen, J. van, *Prolegomena ad Aristophanem* (Leiden, 1908); Sihler, E. G., *De parodiis comicorum græcorum*, etc. (Leipzig, 1875); White, J. W., "The 'Stage' in Aristophanes," in *Harv. St. in Cl. Philol.* II (1891). 159–205; Richards, H., *Aristophanes and Others* (London: G. Richards, 1909); Süss, W., *Aristophanes und die Nachwelt*, 2 vols. (Leipzig, 1911); Emerson, A., "On the Conception of Low Comedy in Aristophanes," in *Am. Journ. Philol.* X (1889). 265–79; Droysen, J. G., "Des Aristophanes Vögel und die Hermokopiden," in *Kleine Schriften* (2d ed., 1894). 1–51; Kock, Th., "Aristophanes als Dichter und Politiker," in *Rhein. Mus.* XXXIX (1884). 118–40; Croiset, M., *Aristophanes and the Political Parties at Athens*, trans. by Loeb, J. (Macmillan, 1909); Willems, A., "Aristophane et la démocratie

Athénienne," in *Acad. roy. de Belg. Bull.* 1907, pp. 338–73; Sheppard, J. T., "Politics in the Frogs of Aristophanes," in *J. H. S.* XXX (1910). 249–59; Jebb, R. C., "Aristophanes," in *Encycl. Brit. s. v.* (11th ed.); Kaibel, G., "Aristophanes," in Pauly-Wissowa, *Real-Encycl. s. v.*

IX. The Fourth-century Historians and Chroniclers

Whereas in general the fourth century is the great age of prose, of oratory and philosophy, in history we find a notable decline. Xenophon, whose works are preserved to us mainly by the interest of after ages in Socrates, is far inferior to Thucydides. Xenophon was born about the beginning of the Peloponnesian war and lived to 354 or thereabout. As a member of a well-to-do family of pronounced conservative sentiments he grew up in the narrow laconizing circle of aristocrats at Athens, whose most commendable interests lay in athletics, hunting, and the exercise of conventional virtue and religion. It was his good fortune to become a pupil of Socrates, whose character and teachings were henceforth the inspiration of his life. The pupil's *Memorabilia of Socrates* not only gives the author's impressions of the great teacher, but forms an invaluable source for the social condition of Athens during the Peloponnesian war and the early years of the fourth century. His *Anabasis* describes the expedition of Cyrus the Younger against his brother Artaxerxes the Persian king, and more particularly the retreat of the Ten Thousand Greeks who had accompanied Cyrus as mercenaries. Among the Greeks was Xenophon, who after the death of Cyrus in battle was elected to their board of generals, and who according to his own account was the inspiring genius of the retreat. His narrative affords us a rare insight into this mercenary force, its organization and spirit, and the characters of prominent officers. At the same time it gives interesting information concerning the countries and peoples along the route. The publication of the work must have had an important influence on the Hellenic attitude toward Persia.

The chief historical product of this author is the *Hellenica*, a continuation of the history of Thucydides. It is a narrative of Hellenic affairs during the period extending from 411 to the battle of Mantineia, 362. The greater part of the work (bks. iii–vii) was composed while the author was an exile from Athens and a protégé of Sparta. It represents, accordingly, the Lacedæmonian point of view. Although in comparison with the history of Thucydides it is shallow and partisan, we value it as our only continuous narrative of the period which it covers. The author has the qualities of a biographer rather than of a historian; and for that reason the *Hellenica* shows an interest in personal traits and incidents, which are totally wanting in Thucydides but which appeal strongly to the student of Hellenic life and culture. Xenophon had a wide experience with the world; and in his breadth of mind, his liberal education, and his ethical and religious principles he represents the best features of the cultured class of his generation. Other works of the author, such as his *Constitution of the Lacedæmonians*, *Economicus*, and *Ways and Means*, of great value as sources, are introduced in their appropriate places.

We are made to feel keenly the loss of the great historians of the fourth century by the recent discovery of a fragment of what was evidently a far more detailed and more valuable *Hellenica* than that of Xenophon. It is published by Grenfell and Hunt, *Oxyrhynchus Papyri*, V (1908). 147 *sqq.* The fragment gives an account of the events of 396, and includes a surprisingly interesting digression on the Bœotian federal constitution. Scholars assign the treatise variously to Theopompus, Ephorus, and Cratippus. On the whole the weight of evidence seems to incline in favor of the last-named historian.

Both Thucydides and Xenophon are philosophic, akin to the sophists and Socrates. After Xenophon and Cratippus the greater part of the historical field is usurped by rhetoric, which acquires an excessively powerful influence over literature. It was largely through Isocrates that this development took place; and accordingly the first rhetorical historians were his pupils, Ephorus of Cymê, Asia Minor, and Theopompus of Chios. The principal work of Ephorus was a *History of Universal Affairs*, which treated of Hellas from the Return of the Heracleidæ to his own time. Our interest in this last history is due to the fact that it was the chief source of Diodorus for the period which it covered, and that Strabo and Plutarch drew extensively from it. Although Ephorus possessed some degree of critical ability, his work fell lamentably below the standard of accuracy set by Thucydides.

Theopompus wrote a *Hellenica* in twelve books, which was a continuation of Thucydides, and, more important, a *Philippica* in fifty-eight books, which treated in great detail of recent and contemporary affairs, with Philip of Macedon as a unifying center. The extant fragments, preserved especially in Athenæus, show a noteworthy interest in culture and character, with a disproportionate love of exhibiting the luxuries and vices of mankind. In spite of the shortcomings of Ephorus and Theopompus, the discovery of the works of either author would doubtless vastly enlarge our knowledge of Greek history and civilization.

A portion of the historical field scarcely touched by rhetoric was occupied by the chroniclers of Athens, whose interest, like that of the scientists, lay in the collection and the systematizing of facts. Such chronicles of Athens were termed *Atthides* (plural of *Atthis*). They began with the earliest mythical kings; and for the regal period they seem to have grouped events and institutions according to reigns. For the historical period the material was arranged annalistically under the appropriate archons. Far from limiting himself to political and military happenings, the atthid-writer included all kinds of institutional, personal, and cultural matter. The earliest of the class after Hellanicus (see p. 25) was Cleidemus, whose *Atthis* evidently appeared after 378, but of whose work we have little information. To us the chronicler of greatest interest was Androtion, a pupil of Isocrates and for thirty years a prominent statesman of Athens. While he was in exile at Megara he completed and published his *Atthis* in 330. His attraction for us lies in the circumstance that his chronicle was the chief source for Aristotle, *Constitution of the Athenians*, published a few years afterward. An introduction to the latter work will be found in no. 27 *infra*. With the help of his pupils Aristotle composed the constitutional histories of a hundred and fifty-eight states, most of them Hellenic. Each work consisted of (1) the narrative of constitutional growth to the philosopher's own time, (2) a contemporary survey of the constitution. The treatise on the Athenian constitution, the greater part of which was recovered in Egypt about the close of the year 1890, is the only one we have of the vast collection. To the early Hellenistic age belongs Philochorus, who was murdered about 260 at the instigation of the Macedonian ruler, and whose *Atthis* seems to have been the ablest and most extensive of the series. In addition to his chronicles he composed a variety of works on religion and other subjects.

BIBLIOGRAPHY

I. Xenophon. — Review of recent literature on Xenophon in *Jahresb.* 1903, 1909. Edition by Sauppe, G. A., 5 vols. (Leipzig, 1867–70); by Marchant, E. C., 3 vols. (Clarendon Press, 1900); *Hellenica* by Keller, O. (Leipzig, 1890); by Breitenbach, L., with explanatory notes (Weidmann); *Economicus* by Holden, H. A., 5th ed. (London, 1895). Translation by Dakyns, H. G., 3 vols. (Macmillan, 1890–97). Selections from this work for the present volume have been compared with the Greek text and revised by E. G. S.

Bury, *Ancient Greek Historians*, lect. v; Wachsmuth, C., *Einleitung in das Studium der alten Geschichte*, 529–36; Richter, E., *Xenophon-Studien* (Teubner, 1892); Lincke, K., "Xenophon's persische Politie," in *Philol.* LX (1901). 541–71; Taine, H., "Xenophon: L'Anabase," in *Essais de critique et de l'histoire* (11th ed., Paris, 1908), 49–95; Guernsey, R., "Elements of Interest in the Anabasis," in *Cl. Weekly*, III. 66; Morris, C. D., "Xenophon's Economicus," in *Am. Journ. Philol.* I (1880). 169–86; Thalheim, Th., "Zu Xenophons Oikonomikos," in *Hermes*, XLII (1907). 630–42; Köhler, U., "Ueber die Πολιτεία Λακεδαιμονίων," in *Berl. Akad.* 1896, pp. 361–77; Schanz, M., "Beiträge zur Kritik der Schrift Περὶ Πόρων," in *Rhein. Mus.* XXXVI (1881). 215–36; Dümmler, F., "Zu Xenophons Agesilaos," in *Philol.* LIV (1895). 577–86.

II. The Lost Historians. — Fragments of Ephorus in Müller, *Frag. hist. græc.* I. 234–77; IV. 641 *sq.* For studies in Ephorus, see Mess, A. v., "Untersuchungen über Ephoros," in *Rhein. Mus.* LXI (1906). 360–407; Niese, B., "Wann hat Ephoros seine Geschichtswerk geschrieben?" in *Hermes*, XLIV (1909). 170–8; Schwartz, E., "Die Zeit des Ephoros," *ib.* XLIV (1909). 481–502; "Ephoros," in Pauly-Wissowa, *Real-Encycl.* VI. 1–16; Laqueur, R., "Ephorus," *ib.* XLVI (1911). 161–206, 321–54; Ciaceri, E., "Sulla reintegrazione della antichissima storia greca in Eforo," etc., in *Rivista di Storia antica*, N. S. VI. 2. 17–24.

The fragments of Theopompus are in Müller, *Frag. hist. græc.* I. 278–333; IV. 643–5; for additions, see Crönert, W., in *Rhein. Mus.* LXII (1907). 382 *sqq.* For studies in this author and in the newly discovered *Oxyrhynchus Hellenica*, see Meyer, Ed., *Theopomps Hellenika* (Halle, 1909); Busolt, G., "Zur Glaubwürdigkeit Theopomps," in *Hermes*, XLV (1910). 220–49; "Der neue Historiker und Xenophon," *ib.* XLIII (1908). 255–85; Mess, A. von, "Die Hellenika von Oxyrhynchos," in *Rhein. Mus.* LXIII (1908). 370–91, favors Cratippus as author; "Die Hellenika von Oxyrhynchos und die Berichte Xenophons und Diodors," *ib.* LXIV (1909). 235–43; Bonner, R. J., "The New Greek Historian," in *Class. Journ.* V (1910). 353–9; Roberts, W. R., "Theopompus in the Greek Literary Critics," in *Class. Rev.* XXII (1908).

118–22; Goligher, W. A., "The New Greek Historical Fragment attributed to Theopompus or Cratippus," in (Eng.) *Hist. Rev.* XXIII (1908). 277–83; Judeich, W., "Theopomps Hellenika," in *Rhein. Mus.* LXVI (1911). 94–139; Walker, E. M., *The Hellenica Oxyrhynchia: Its Authorship and Authority* (Clarendon Press, 1913), contends for Ephorus.

The fragments of Cratippus are in Müller, *Frag. hist. græc.* II. 75 *sqq.* On the question as to whether he was the author of the newly discovered *Hellenica*, see the works cited above; also Grenfell and Hunt, *Oxyrhynchus Papyri*, V (1908). 110 *sqq.* For other studies in the historian, see Susemihl, F., "Die Zeit des Historikers Kratippos," in *Philol.* LIX (1900). 537 *sqq.*; Schmidt, W., "Kratippos zum dritten Mal," *ib.* LX. 155–7.

III. The Atthid-Writers and Aristotle's Constitution of the Athenians. — On the Atthis in general, see Schwartz, "Atthis," in Pauly-Wissowa, *Real-Encycl.* II. 2180–3; Wilamowitz-Moellendorff, V., *Aristoteles u. Ath.* I. 260–90; Busolt, *Griech. Gesch.* II. 7 *sqq.*

On Androtion, see Keil, B., *Die solonische Verfassung*, etc. (Berlin, 1892), 190 *sqq.*; Schwartz, "Androtion," in Pauly-Wissowa, *Real-Encycl.* I. 2173–5; De Sanctis, G., "L'Attide di Androzione e un papirio di Oxyrhynchos," in *R. Acad. d. sci. atti.* XLIII (1908). 331–56. On Philochorus, see Wright, J. H., "Did Philochorus quote the Ἀθηναίων Πολιτεία as Aristotle's?" in *Am. Journ. Philol.* XII (1891). 310–18.

The editio princeps of Aristotle, *Constitution of the Athenians*, is that of Kenyon, F. G. (London, 1891: 3d ed., 1892); the most thoroughly annotated edition is by Sandys, J. E. (2d ed., Macmillan, 1912); see also ed. by Herwerden, H. van, and Leeuwen, J. van (Leyden, 1891); by Blass-Thalheim (Teubner, 1909). The best complete translation is by Kenyon (London: Bell, 1912). There is one also by Poste, E. (Macmillan, 1891). For studies in the subject, see Adcock, F. E., "Source of the Solonian Chapters," *Klio*, XII (1912). 1–16; Bauer, A., *Literarische und historische Forschungen zu Aristoteles* Ἀθηναίων Πολιτεία (Munich, 1891); Berard, J., "Aristote, la constitution d'Athènes," in *Rev. hist.* 1892, pp. 285–305; Blass, F., "Die sogenannte drakontische Verfassung," in *N. Jahrb.* CLI (1895). 476–9; Botsford, G. W., *Development of the Athenian Constitution* (Ginn, 1893); "Beginnings of the Athenian Hegemony," in *Class. Rev.* VIII. 195 *sq.*; "Trial of the Alcmeonidæ and the Cleisthenean Constitutional Reform," in *Harv. St. in Class. Philol.* VIII (1897). 1–22; Bruck, S., "Heliastengerichte im 4 Jahrh." in *Philol.* LII (1893). 295–317, 395–421; "Heliastentäfelchen," *ib.* LIV. 64–79; Busolt, G., "Aristoteles oder Xenophon," in *Hermes*, XXXIII (1898). 71–86; Cauer, F., *Hat Aristoteles die Schrift vom Staate der Athener geschrieben?* (Stuttgart, 1891); Cauer, P., "Aristoteles Urteil über die Demokratie," in *N. Jahrb.* CXLV (1892). 581–93; Corssen, P., "Das Verhältniss der aristotelischen zu der thukidideischen Darstellung des Tyrannenmordes," in *Rhein. Mus.* LI (1896). 226–39; Droysen, H., *Vorläufige Bemerkungen zu Aristoteles* Ἀθηναίων Πολιτεία (Berlin, 1891); Dufour, M., *La constitution d'Athènes et l'œuvre d'Aristote* (Paris, 1896); Fowler, H. N., "Dates of the Exiles of Peisistratus," in *Harv. St. in Class. Philol.* VII (1896). 167–75; Francotte, A., *L'Organisation de la cité athénienne et la réforme de Clisthène* (Paris, 1893); Fredericks, J., "La valeur de la Ἀθηναίων Πολιτεία," in *Rev. de l'instr. publ. en Belgique*, XXXVII (1894). 26–43; Gilliard, *Quelques réformes de Solon* (Lausanne, 1907); De Sanctis, G., Ἀτθίς, *Storia della repubblica ateniese* (2d ed., Torino, 1912); Hofmann, J., *Studien zur drakontischen Verfassung* (Straubing, 1899); Keil, B., *Die solonische Verfassung*, etc. (Berlin, 1892); *Anonymus Argentinensis*, etc. (Strassburg, 1902); Lecoutere, C., *L'Archontat . . . d'après la* Ἀθηναίων Πολιτεία (Louvain, 1893); Lehmann-Haupt, C. F., *Solon of Athens, the Poet, the Merchant, and the Statesman* (Liverpool, 1912); Lipsius, J. H., "Ueber das neugefundene Buch des Aristoteles," etc., in *Sächs. Gesellsch.* XLIII (1891). 41–69; Mess, A. v., "Aristoteles Ἀθηναίων Πολιτεία und die politische Schriftstellerei Athens," in *Rhein. Mus.* LXVI (1911). 356–92; Meyer, P., *Des Aristoteles Politik und die* Ἀθηναίων Πολιτεία (Bonn, 1891); Milchhöfer, A., *Untersuchungen über die Demenordnung des Kleisthenes* (Berlin, 1892); "Attische Localverfassung," in *Ath. Mitt.* 1893, pp. 277–304; Newman, W. L., "Aristotle on the Constitution of Athens," in *Class. Rev.* V. 155–64; Nordin, R., *Themistoklesfrage* (Upsala, 1893); Seeck, O., "Quellenstudien," in *Klio*, IV. 164–326; Stern, E. v., "Solon und Peisistratos," in *Hermes*, XLVIII (1913). 426–41; Thalheim, Th., "Die drakontische Verfassung," in *Hermes*, XXIX (1894). 458–63; Viedebantt, O., "Metrologische Beiträge, I, II," in *Hermes*, XLVII (1912). 422 *sqq.*, 562; Wright, J. H., "The Date of Cylon," in *Harv. St. in Class. Philol.* III (1892). 1–74; Ziehen, L., "Die drakontische Gesetzgebung," in *Rhein. Mus.* LIV (1899). 321–44.

X. The Attic Orators

From Homeric times the Greeks had paid great attention to oratory; but it was not till the period of the Peloponnesian war, in the mature growth of rhetoric, that men began to write their speeches. Oratory was of three kinds; (1) epideictic for the display of literary skill at funerals, great public gatherings, or similar occasions; (2) symbouleutic, deliberative, for council or assembly, (3) judicial, for prosecution or defense in the law courts. In the democratic tribunals every man had to plead his own case, and the party to the trial who was not himself a rhetorician had his pleading composed for him by a professional speech writer, a rhetorician equipped with at least a smattering of the law. These professional composers preserved their speeches chiefly that they might serve as models for similar work in the future. Literary critics of the Alexandrian age made up a list, termed the canon, of ten Attic orators to represent the various excellences of style. It is mainly to the interest of these critics that we owe the preservation of a large body of Attic oratory. Those orators only whose works are represented in the present volume are mentioned below.

Lysias belonged to a wealthy resident-alien family, whose estate was destroyed by the tyranny of the Thirty, 404–403. This misfortune converted him into a teacher of rhetoric and a professional writer of speeches for others to deliver. He died in 380 or shortly afterward, and could not therefore have followed this profession more than a quarter of a century; and yet we are informed by a credible authority that he composed at least two hundred and thirty-three speeches. His productive power was in fact astounding. Of the whole number we have but thirty-four, of which one or two are fragmentary. Most of them are judicial. They are composed in a simple graceful style, resembling in appearance the language of every-day life though in fact artistic. They are dramatic in their adaptation to the characters of the individual pleaders and possess the quality known to the Greeks as *ethos* — the gentle current of feeling which wins the sympathy of the hearers. The orations deal fully with the parties to the trial, their characters, history, financial and social circumstances; thus they bring us into contact with actual persons and social-economic conditions. While the other orators differ in style and mentality, it may be said once for all that their productions, equally with those of Lysias, lead us into direct touch with public and private life.

Regarding the personal affairs of Isæus we have little information. His activity as a speech writer extended from the close of the Peloponnesian war to about the middle of the fourth century, while his extant speeches lie within the years 389–353. Though he is reputed a pupil of Isocrates, he betrays no sign of that master's influence, and should be regarded rather as the successor, and younger contemporary, of Lysias, and a connecting link between that writer and Demosthenes. All the twelve extant speeches are concerned with the law cases in which the writer excelled— inheritances and adoptions. His best recent editor, Wyse, has added no glory to the orator's moral reputation. Isæus was an extremely clever family lawyer who knew how to twist legal points most skilfully in order to win his case. The same thing, in a varying degree, may be said of all Greek writers of judicial speeches; and with careful criticism the speeches of Isæus may be made as profitable for history as those of Lysias.

The general tendencies of life and thought during the fourth century were toward the breaking down of the city-state with all its traditional associations and the corresponding enlargement of ideas and sympathies, of social and political relations. These tendencies, recognizable in Xenophon, found more complete expression in Isocrates of Athens, 436–338, whose life was contemporary with the whole development of prose literature, and with the culmination and incipient decay of the city-state system. He was a schoolmaster, who for a fee of 1000 drachmas gave a course of three or four years in statesmanship. Along with a training in oratory he supplied the pupil with such ethical and political knowledge as he deemed essential to public leadership. The sons of princes and other notables throughout Hellas, particularly in the East, gathered at his feet, and received from him most helpful instruction. From his school issued generals, statesmen, orators, and historians. Undoubtedly through his pupils he exercised a wide influence on Hellenic opinion. While teaching, Isocrates engaged in the composition of *Orations*, which, not being intended for delivery, may more properly be termed essays. With a delicate taste for literary form he gave the most minute and prolonged attention to the elaboration of a nicely adjusted periodology, and to the exquisite choice and arrangement of words. At least in appearance the stylist in him dominates over the thinker. His writings treat of political conditions; he was the first and most eminent of ancient publicists. In home politics he was a conservative who preferred the constitution of Solonian and Cleisthenean times when the Council of the Areopagus kept parental watch over citizens and magistrates. These views he sets forth in his *Areopagiticus*. In the larger field of inter-state politics he long favored the union of all the Hellenes, under the joint leadership of Athens and Sparta, for a war of conquest against Persia. The *Panegyricus*, his greatest masterpiece, 380 B.C., embodies this doctrine. Finally recognizing the futility of this hope, he appealed to various eminent men to take the leadership. Among them were Dionysius of Syracuse, Archidamus of Sparta, and lastly Philip of Macedon. The study of Isocrates has been given a new importance and a new impetus by the contention of certain German scholars, among whom is Eduard Meyer, that he is the truest interpreter of his time, that the study of fourth-century conditions should proceed from his outlook (*Cf. Gesch. d. Alt.* V. p. 280). Although space does not permit a discussion of this view, it is to be presumed that no thinker, however useful as sources his writings may be, possesses a monopoly of the political wisdom of his age. See further on this subject the introduction and notes to the *Philippus*, no. 127 *infra*.

With Isocrates, his fellow-citizen Demosthenes, 384–322, presents a striking contrast, that of the practical against the theoretical, energy against lassitude, the dense massing of facts in irresistible phalanxes of persuasion as opposed to a high dilution of ideas in multitudes of perfumed, sweet-sounding words. The circumstances of his early life, his mistreatment at the hands of unfaithful guardians, and his prosecution of the latter are touched upon in connection with the excerpt from his *Oration against Aphobus*, no. 156 *infra*. From this prosecution he emerged with a reputation as a writer of judicial speeches — the foundation of his worldly fortune. These orations have equal value with those of Lysias as sources for social, economic, judicial, and general cultural conditions. In his early life appear two forces which admirably support and supplement each other: the first is a certain sternness and severity, the second a clear and direct manner of going to his point and of making it. The bald truth and its intrinsic force, rather than any technical skill in rousing emotion, form the vital quality of his oratory. In the general sweep of history the private orations are lost sight of in the struggle of this rare man against the power, the policy, and the personality of Philip, who, succeeding to the throne of Macedon in 359, made of his country, formerly insignificant, the most formidable monarchy of Europe. It was Philip's achievement to establish in his country a world power organized and fitted for the purpose which his son Alexander with dazzling promptitude accomplished — the destruction of the Persian realm and the erection on its ruins of a vast Hellenistic empire.

Against the growth of this power, which overshadowed the freedom of the Greek republics, Demosthenes almost alone struggled like a hero but in vain. In the past century the pendulum of judgment on his character and principles has swung to violent extremes.

At the time when Napoleon I was crushing Prussia beneath his iron heel, B. G. Niebuhr, the patriot scholar, saw a close resemblance between Philip of Macedon and the tyrant emperor, while he looked to Demosthenes as the champion of human freedom. But times have changed; and the grasping imperialism of Europe cannot afford to tolerate the memory of a man who contended according to his power for the liberty of the weak commonwealth. It is true that the empire of Alexander was the means of diffusing Hellenic civilization among mankind; it is equally true that in the end, even if not so soon as Demosthenes expected, imperialism, beginning with Alexander and continuing with Rome, crushed local freedom and brought to ruin the civilization of the world. From these considerations it appears clear that while the success of the Macedonian cause brought great though not unalloyed benefits to the world, there was right also on the side of the local patriot; and though he failed, his inspired eloquence and heroic struggle are a priceless and eternal treasure.

Æschines, about 389–314, remembered chiefly as the political adversary of Demosthenes, was the son of a schoolmaster of humble circumstances. In earlier life Æschines became a public scribe, then for a time an actor, and finally, under the patronage of Eubulus, he entered the political arena. At first he favored the formation of a Hellenic league against Philip; but in 346 he was a member of a peace embassy to the Macedonian king. After this first contact with Philip he remained a steadfast leader of the pro-Macedonian party at Athens. Whether this somersault was due to a change of conviction or a bribe is under controversy. Demosthenes, a member of the same embassy, prosecuted him on the charge that he had sold himself to Philip to betray his country; and he narrowly escaped condemnation (343). The opposing speeches of Demosthenes and Æschines *On the Faithless Embassage* (Parapresbeia) are extant; they are a hopeless tangle of contradictions. Afterward, Æschines prosecuted Ctesiphon for proposing high honors to Demosthenes. This great case, begun in 336, was decided in 330. The aim of Æschines to destroy Demosthenes in public life called forth the noblest pleading of antiquity, the oration of Demosthenes *On the Crown*, a defense of the speaker's career and character. The failure of Æschines was so complete that he was forced to retire into exile. Besides the orations of Æschines on these two occasions we have his speech *Against Timarchus*, from which an excerpt is given in this volume. It hardly need be said that modern scholars who condemn Demosthenes are equally strenuous in attempting to rehabilitate Æschines as a far-sighted statesman and a man of honor. Something can be done in this direction.

Lycurgus, a distinguished contemporary and collaborator of Demosthenes, was like the latter firm in support of measures hostile to the aggression of Macedon. In the difficult times which followed the catastrophe of Chæroneia he was preëminent through the firmness and the purity of his Attic patriotism. For twelve years he directed the finances, the first period of four years under his own name, the next two periods, eight years in all, under the formal control of others. During this time of twelve years, 14,000 talents, or according to some, 18,650 talents, passed through his hands. Modern scholars highly extol his financial administration. The extant discourse *Against Leocrates* exhibits a public character of great sternness. Of the published discourses mentioned in Suidas as genuine, eight were prosecutions. A vulnerable politician as a rule eschews this form of public service. Uncompromising, vigorous no less than rigorous, he appears in the preserved speech as a man who appropriated the literature of the past in a practical and patriotic manner, to illustrate the underlying principles of right conduct and civic duty.

Hypereides, 389–322, long an associate of Demosthenes in opposition to Macedon, was a man fond of the pleasures of life. In oratory he possessed in a notable degree the quality of grace (χάρις) in contrast with the Demosthenic power, and an all-round ability rather than preëminence in any one oratorical feature. The ancients had fifty-two undoubted speeches; but all were lost, and the world of scholarship could judge of him through the medium of ancient critics only, till about the middle of the nineteenth century, when individual orations began to come to light. We now have in whole or in large part six orations. Among them is the *Epitaphios*, delivered at the public funeral of those who had fallen in the Lamian war in defense of their country. The fact that Hypereides was chosen for this function is evidence of his repute both as a patriot and as an eloquent orator.

BIBLIOGRAPHY

I. Attic Orators. — Recent literature reviewed in *Jahresb.* 1907, 1912. Jebb, R. C., *Attic Orators from Antiphon to Isæus,* 2 vols. (2d ed., Macmillan, 1893); Blass, Fr., *Geschichte der attischen Beredsamkeit,* 4 vols. (2d ed., Teubner).

II. Lysias, Isæus, and Isocrates. — Edition of Lysias by Cobet, C. G. (2d ed. 1882); by Scheibe (2d ed., Teubner, 1885); by Thalheim, Th. (Leipzig, 1901); by Hude, C. (Clarendon Press, 1913). German translation by Falk, A. (Breslau, 1843). For studies in Lysias, see Jebb, *Attic Orators,* I. 142–316; II. 1–368; Devries, W. L., *Ethopoiïa. A Rhetorical Study of the Types of Character in the Orations of Lysias.* Diss. Johns Hopkins University (Baltimore, 1892); Wolff, *Ueber Lysias Epitaphios und Isokrates Panegyrikos* (Berlin, 1896).

The best edition of Isæus is by Wyse, W., with detailed notes on matters of Attic law (Cambridge: University Press, 1904); see also the ed. of Thalheim (Leipzig, 1903). For studies in Isæus, see Jebb, *Attic Orators;* Blass, *Attische Beredsamkeit,* II. 452–541; Goligher, W. A., "Isæus and Attic Law," in *Hermathena,* XIV (1907). 183–204, 481–515.

Edition of Isocrates by Blass, F., 2 vols. (Teubner, 1885); by Drerup, E., vol. I ready (Leipzig, 1906). English translation by Freese, J. H., vol. I (Bohn), from which selections have been taken for this volume. The entire work is translated by Dinsdale, J., rev. by Young (London, 1752). A useful work is the *Index Isocrateus* by Preuss, S. (Teubner, 1904). For studies in this author, see Adams, C. D., "Recent Views of the Political Influence of Isocrates," in *Class. Philol.* VII (1912), 343–50; Gercke, A., "Isokrates und Alkidamas," in *Rhein. Mus.* LIV (1899). 404–13; "Die Replik Isokrates gegen Alkidamas," *ib.* (1907). 170–202; Hagen, B. v., "Isokrates und Alexander," in *Philol.* LXVII (1908). 113–33; Hubbell, H. M., *Influence of Isocrates on Cicero, Dionysius, and Aristeides,* Diss. (Yale University Press, 1913); Kessler, J., "Isokrates und die panhellenische Idee," in *St. z. Gesch. u. Kult. des Alt.* IV. 3 (1911); Köpp, F., "Isokrates als Politiker," in *Preuss. Jahrb.* LXX (1892). 472–87; Meyer, Ed., "Isokrates' zweite Philippika," in *Sitzb. Berl. Akad.* 1909, pp. 758–79; Münscher, K., "Die Isokratesüberlieferung," in *Philol.* LVIII (1899). 88–110; Pöhlmann, R. v., "Isokrates und das Problem der Demokratie," in *Münch. Akad.* (Munich, 1913); Raeder, H., "Alkidamas und Platon als Gegner des Isokrates," in *Rhein. Mus.* LXIII (1908). 495–511; Scala, R. v., "Isokrates und die Geschichtschreibung," in *Versamml. d. Philolog.* (Leipzig, 1892), 102–21; Wilamowitz-Moellendorff, U. v., *Aristoteles u. Ath.* II. 380–99.

III. Demosthenes. — Edition by Dindorff, rev. by Blass, F., 3 vols. (Leipzig, 1891–1907). In 1805 there was published at Leipzig a translation of his public orations, "in order that, by an example from ancient times, the German people might be warned against the tyranny of Napoleon which threatened them." An English translation by Kennedy, C. R., 4 vols. (Bohn) from which one or two of the selections from Demosthenes for this volume have been taken, after a revision, on the basis of the Greek text, by E. G. S. An *Index Demosthenius* by Preuss, S. (Teubner, 1892), will be found useful.

For studies in this orator, in addition to Jebb and Blass, see Brodribb, W. J., *Demosthenes* (new ed., London, 1898); Butcher, G. H., *Demosthenes* (Macmillan, 1881); Droysen, J. G., "Ueber die Echtheit der Urkunden in der Rede vom Kranz," in *Kleine Schr.* I (Leipzig, 1893). 95–297; Hug, A., "Demosthenes als politischer Denker," in *Stud. aus dem cl. Alt.* I (1881). 51–103; Kahrstedt, *Forschungen zur. Gesch. d. ausgehenden 5. u. des 4. Jahrh.* (Berlin, 1910). 1–154 (rev. *Berl. Philol. Woch.* XXX, 1913, p. 498 *sqq.*; *Gött. gelehrt. Anz.* 1912, p. 17 *sqq.*, unfavorably); Francotte, H., "Études sur Démosthène," in *Mus. Belg.* XVII (1913). 69–91, 237–88; Pickard-Cambridge, A. W., *Demosthenes and the last Days of Greek Freedom* (Putnam, 1914); Schäfer, A., *Demosthenes und seine Zeit*, 3 vols. (Teubner, 1885–87); Thalheim, "Demosthenes," in Pauly-Wissowa, *Real-Encycl.* V. 169–88, with references to modern literature.

IV. Æschines, Lycurgus, and Hypereides. — Edition of Æschines by Schultz, F. (Leipzig, 1865); by Weidner, A. (Leipzig, 1872); by Blass, F. (2d ed., Leipzig, 1908). Recent literature on Æschines reviewed in *Jahresb.* 1913, pp. 214–40. German translation by Benseler, G. E., 3 vols. (Leipzig, 1855–60; *Two Orations on the Crown* by Biddle, G. W. (Phila. 1881). See also Preuss, S., *Index Æschineus* (Teubner, 1896). For other studies, in addition to Blass, see Bougot, A., *Rivalité d'Æschine et de Démosthène* (Paris, 1891); Bruns, I., *Das literarische Porträt der Griechen*, etc. (Stuttgart, 1896), ch. iv. § 5; Thalheim, "Aischines," in Pauly-Wissowa, *Real-Encycl.* I. 1050–62.

Edition of Lycurgus by Blass, F. (Leipzig, 1899); a new fragment by Rabe, H., in *Rhein. Mus.* LXIII (1908). 143 *sqq.*; Index to Andocides, Lycurgus, and Dinarchus by Forman, L. L. (Oxford, 1897). German translation by Bender, H. (3d ed., 1909). See also Dürrbach, F., "L'Orateur Lycurge. Étude hist. et lit.," in *Bibl. des écoles franc. d'Athènes*, etc. LVII (Paris, 1887); Dröge, C., *De Lycurgo atheniensi pecuniarum publicarum administratore*, Diss. (Bonn, 1880).

Edition of Hypereides by Blass. F. (3d ed., Leipzig, 1894); by Kenyon F. G. (Oxford, 1907); *Orations against Athenagoras and Philippides*, with a translation, by Kenyon (London, 1893); Grenfell and Hunt, *Oxyrhynchus Papyri*, IV (1904). Recent literature on Hypereides in *Jahresb.* 1913, pp. 186–213; Sandys, J. E., "Recent Editions of Hypereides," in *Class. Rev.* IX (1895). 71–4. See also Bruner, L., *Studien zur Gesch. u. Sprache des Hypereides*, Progr. (Bamberg, 1906).

IX. Plato and Aristotle

Plato, 427–347, belonged to the oldest nobility of Athens, and enjoyed the literary, musical, and athletic education of his class. Through such accomplishments and more through his long pupilage under Socrates he unfolded a brilliant literary genius paralleled in the fourth century by that of Demosthenes alone. His nature was essentially poetic: his *Dialogues* are, in poetic prose, the creation of a wonderfully versatile imagination. His philosophy, which need not concern us here, is not, as expressed in the *Dialogues*, an orderly consistent system of reason; it is rather an ever changing revelation of mingled thought and emotion. The only permanent element is idealism. In politics he was by birth and education a pronounced oligarch, whose hatred of the democracy was intensified by the condemnation of Socrates. For the attitude of men of his class the democracy was only in small part responsible. The oligarchs had long preferred conspiracy and sedition to open political conflict or to conciliation and compromise. When opportunity offered, as in the time of Critias, a relative of Plato, they seized despotic power, throttled free speech, robbed and murdered their fellow-citizens, and tried to reduce the masses to serfdom. In times of quiet their aloofness from public life was due largely to a narrowness of political vision and class egoism and to a selfish love of sensual, social, or intellectual pleasure. If their abnegation of civic duty made the democracy worse, they and not the masses of voters should bear the weight of blame.

Plato was the most refined and gifted of his class. In him antipathy to free institutions, the ambition of the few for class despotism, is glorified by aspirations for perfect knowledge, justice, and righteousness. But the standard of judgment which permits him to condemn Themistocles, Pericles, and the greatest statesmen of his country is one which would equally force the condemnation of every government in the world's history to the present day.

Only three or four of his masterpieces will here be mentioned. His *Protagoras*, a work of great dramatic interest, assails the fundamental principles and the thought methods of the more eminent sophists. His *Gorgias* is a protest against democracy as well as against rhetoric. His *Republic* sets forth the ideal state, in which the masses, practically serfs, are absolutely ruled by a military-aristocratic-philosophic class. It is his greatest masterpiece, the most splendid of Utopias. As the expression of a brilliant intellect on educational, social, moral, and political questions, it commands our attention; but the state here pictured, if realized, would have crushed the genius of the author, a state that no man, not even a member of the ruling class, could endure. The *Laws*, composed in later life, is a more sober and practicable construction of the ideal state, and hence more serviceable to the student of actual conditions. To one interested in social history, however, the ideas of Plato are less valuable than his many and diverse pictures of life, which, if not true of the individual persons portrayed, are at least representative of existing social phases.

In passing from Plato to Aristotle, 384–322, we come to a new type of mind. Whereas the authors of prose and verse thus far mentioned are essentially creative, Aristotle is a scholar, in fact the greatest as well as the first scholar in history. It was his achievement to systematize and reduce to writing the knowledge which the Hellenes had thus far accumulated, and to add to this store by his own researches. His writings include metaphysics, psychology, the natural and physical sciences, logic, rhetoric, ethics, and politics. His authorship of a hundred and fifty-eight constitutional histories has already been noticed (p. 41). On the basis of accumulated facts relating to the institutions of individual states Aristotle constructed his *Politics*, the most notable treatise on the state thus far produced in the history of the world. The circumstance that this work, published within the years 336–332, appeared somewhat earlier than the collection of individual constitutions (p. 41) presents no serious problem; the gathering of material for the vast collection was undoubtedly far advanced before the composition of the *Politics*. For an introduction to the treatise we must look to his *Nicomachean Ethics*, which in discussing the principles of virtuous living conducts the reader logically to the state, as to an organism, not merely for the protection, but for the perfection of human life (*Ethics*, x. 10).

The *Politics* treats exclusively of the city-state untrammeled by connection with any higher political organization. Its appearance at the time when Alexander was founding his world monarchy has puzzled modern scholars. In justification it may be said that although under Alexander and his successors Greek communities enjoyed a high degree of local freedom, this condition existed on sufferance only. The imperial statesmen of the ancient world failed to guarantee to the municipalities local freedom and self-government. It is only in modern times, notably in the case of Great Britain, that monarchy has been reconciled with democracy. As against the world monarchy, therefore, Aristotle was right in his exclusive devotion to the city-state. The same thing, however, cannot be said of his neglect of the federation; but it was long after his death that Greece saw the maturity of the federal union — the most highly developed and perfected political creation of the Hellenes, and in fact of the world before the founding of the United States of America. Regarding Aristotle's views of the several forms of government the selected passages, with their introductions and notes, will afford the necessary information.

BIBLIOGRAPHY

I. Plato.—Edition by Burnet, J., 5 vols. (Oxford, 1900–1907); *Protagoras* by Sihler, E. G. (Harper); *Gorgias* and *Protagoras* by Sauppe, H., and Gercke, A. (Weidmann); *Republic* by Jowett, B., and Campbell, L., 3 vols. (Oxford, 1894); by Adams, J., 2 vols. (Cambridge, 1902). Translation of works by Jowett, 5 vols. (3d ed., Macmillan, 1892); of *Republic* by Vaughan, D. J., and Davies, J. L. (Macmillan, 1912). The selections in this volume are from Jowett. Recent literature on Plato is reviewed in *Jahresb.* 1912, 1913.

For studies in Plato, see the various histories of Greek philosophy by Zeller, Gomperz, etc.; also Adams, J., *The Vitality of Platonism*, etc. (Cambridge: University Press, 1911); Adamson, J. E., *Theory of Education in Plato's Republic* (London, 1903); Barker, E., *Political Thought of Plato and Aristotle* (London: Methuen, 1906); Boyd, W., *Introduction to the Republic* (London: Sonnenschein, 1904); Dittenberger, W., "Sprachliche Criterien für die Chronologie der platonischen Dialoge," in *Hermes*, XVI (1881). 321–45; Grote, G., *Plato and the Other Companions of Socrates*, 4 vols. (new ed., London, 1888); Huit, C., *Études sur la politique attribuê à Platon* (Paris, 1888); *La vie et l'œuvre de Platon*, 2 vols. (Paris, 1893); Müller, J., *Platons Staatslehre und der moderne Socialismus*, etc. (Sondershausen, 1886); Nettleship, R. L., "Theory of Education in the Republic of Plato," in Abbott, E., *Hellenica*, 67–180; Pater, W. H., *Plato and Platonism* (Macmillan, 1908); "Genius of Plato," in *Contemp. Rev.* 1892, pp. 249–61; Ritchie, D. G., *Plato* (Scribner, 1902); Ritter, C., *Platon: sein Leben, seine Schriften* (1909); *Platons Gesetze; Kommentar* (Teubner, 1896); Sihler, E. G., "Vergil and Plato," in *Trans. Am. Philol. Assoc.* 1880; Taylor, A. E., *Plato* (New York: Dodge, 1908); Usener, H., "Platon und Aristoteles," in *Vorträge und Aufsätze* (Teubner, 1907). 67–102.

II. Aristotle. — Edition of complete works, Acad. reg. boruss. 5 vols. (Berlin, 1831–70), the pages of which are generally cited; the fragments by Rose, V. (Teubner, 1886); *Politics*, by Susemihl, F. (Teubner, 1909); ed. with essays and notes, by Newman, W. L., 2 vols. (Clarendon Press, 1887). Translation of works under editorship of Smith, J. A., and Ross, W. D. (under way,

Oxford: Clarendon Press). *Politics*, translated by Welldon, J. E. C. (Macmillan, 1905); by Jowett, B., 2 vols. (Clarendon Press, 1885), from which the selections in this volume have been taken. For literature on Aristotle prior to 1896, see Schwab, M., *Bibliographie d'Aristote* (Paris, 1896). See also Barker, E., *Political Thought of Plato and Aristotle* (Putnam, 1906); Bradley, "Aristotle's Conception of the State," in Abbott, E., *Hellenica*, 181–243; Eucken, R., *Lebensanschauungen der grossen Denker* (7th ed., Leipzig, 1907), I. 3; Giesen, K., "Quæstiones græcæ und Aristoteles Politien," in *Philol.* LX (1901). 446–71; Loos, I. A., *Studies in the Politics of Aristotle and the Republic of Plato* (Iowa City: University Press, 1899); Oncken, W., *Staatslehre des Aristoteles*, 2 vols. (Leipzig, 1870, 1875); Shute, R., *History of the Process by which the Aristotelian Writings arrived at their Present Form* (Clarendon Press, 1888). Further studies in the political theories of Aristotle will be found in the various histories of Greek philosophy by Zeller, Gomperz, and others, and in works on the political theories of the ancients, such as Dunning, W. A., *History of Political Theories, Ancient and Mediæval* (Macmillan, 1902), and Willoughby, W. W., *Political Theories of the Ancient World* (Longmans, 1903).

XII. Writers of the Hellenistic and Roman Periods

As to minor authors and those but briefly excerpted for this volume, the necessary facts are given in the introductions to the selections from their writings. This arrangement applies also to the scientific and medical works quoted in the volume. Polybius, who ranks among the greatest historians of antiquity, is given especial attention in connection with the selections from his history which illustrate the condition of historical science in the Hellenistic age (ch. xviii).

A characteristic form of literature of this period is the New Comedy, which has been given fresh interest by the discovery of a considerable part of four plays of Menander, 342–290, its chief representative. Other productions in the field are the comedies of Plautus and Terence, which are translations of contemporary Greek plays modified more or less in adaptation to their Roman audience. The change in the character of comedy, beginning in the last activities of Aristophanes, was now complete; particularly it had forsaken politics, to devote itself wholly to social life. It had also shaken off many of the coarser indecencies and immoralities of the Aristophanic period. As has been pointed out by Ferguson (*Hellenistic Athens*, 75 *sqq.*), however, respectable women still kept themselves for the most part modestly within doors, so that the female characters on the stage were as a rule those of ill repute. Restricting itself to street scenes, the New Comedy had to avoid the inner life of the family and the more respectable activities of society, to picture the exposure of infants, the intrigues of young men and hetæræ, and other such immoral or indecent aspects of life. But however one-sided and imperfect may be the information contained in this branch of literature, it throws a welcome light on its limited field of thought, feeling, character, and social customs of an age but scantily known.

Another equally characteristic form of literature is the Idyll, represented in this volume by Theocritus. He was born about 305, probably in Syracuse (Christ, *Griech. Lit.* II. 141 *sq.*), and passed some years at the courts of Syracuse and Alexandria. His pictures of common life are marked by delicacy and grace. "Theocritus gives us nature, not behind the footlights, but beneath the truthful blaze of Sicily's sunlit sky" (Kynaston); and certainly nothing can bring us into so close and pleasing touch with life in the home and on the streets of Alexandria as the fifteenth *Idyll* reproduced in this volume. A few epigrams, too, of the age, whose authors are uncertain, will be found in their appropriate chapter (xix).

As we pass from the Hellenistic to the Roman age, we may notice but briefly the Roman biographer Cornelius Nepos, about 99–24 B.C., a part of whose work *On Famous Men* (*De viris illustribus*) has been preserved. The greater number of biographies in this fragment are of Greek generals. We see in his *Epaminondas*, for example, a love of artificial characterizations. His work is universally pronounced unreliable, and must be used for historical purposes with great caution.

His Greek contemporary, Diodorus of Sicily, affords us no better proof of the historiographic capabilities of the age. The work of the latter was a *Library* so named — in fact a general history of the world from the earliest times at least to 60 B.C., in forty books. In his Preface (i. 4) he makes great pretensions that he has labored thirty years on his work, and has experienced extreme sufferings and dangers in visiting the scenes of his narrative in Europe and Asia that he might write with the knowledge of an eye-witness. The truth is that he was merely a compiler. Much of his work he vitiated by the use of inferior sources; in general he shows a lack of knowledge of military and political affairs, and still worse, a want of judgment. Some parts of his historical library, however, are better than others; and for some subjects and periods, as for Sicily during the fifth and fourth centuries and for the earlier Hellenistic age, he is our only continuous source. We feel the loss, therefore, of the second half of his compilation, books xxi–xl, covering 301–60 B.C., now represented only by fragments. Books vi–x likewise exist only in fragments, arranged in order with great intelligence in Vogel's edition.

In Strabo we come into touch with an authority immeasurably superior to Diodorus. He was born in Pontus about 64 B.C. and lived to 19 A.D. His principal work was a history, *Historical Memoirs*, in forty-three books, mainly a continuation of Polybius. This treatise has been lost and we know little of it. As a supplement to his history he wrote a *Geography* in seventeen books, which is still preserved. Composed in the main under Augustus, it was revised and slightly extended under Tiberius (Pais, *Ancient Italy*, ch. xxvi). In his own words it was a "colossal work," requiring many years, including travel and personal inspection, for the collection of details relating to thousands of localities distributed over the known world. The treatise is not a geography pure and simple, but includes much mythical and historical information associated with the various localities. In the earlier part he gives the general views of the earth held by himself and his predecessors of the Alexandrian age. While he cannot compare in originality with Eratosthenes (no. 210), he is a credit to his generation, and his treatise is worthy of respectful consideration as a geographical and historical source of the first rank.

Pliny the Elder, 23–79 A.D., was a native of the Roman municipality of Como (Novum Comum) and an officer of the empire. His leisure he devoted with amazing diligence and economy to study and authorship in many fields (Pliny the Younger, *Letters*, iii. 5). The only work preserved is his *Natural History* in thirty-seven books, an encyclopedia of arts, sciences, and antiquities by a gentleman with a keen interest in every kind of knowledge, yet lacking in scientific method and precision. In his treatment of the arts and sciences he necessarily has to do chiefly with the Greeks.

Three late Hellenic writers will be briefly grouped together.

Pausanias, who lived in the latter part of the second century A.D., wrote a *Description of Greece* in ten books, which is still extant. The author was an amateur in his subject and an archaist in style. His work, however, though compiled with mediocre talent, is a treasury of information on topography, archæology, religion, and mythology, including much historical and biographical matter. It is the foundation of modern studies in the topography and archæology of Greece. Diogenes Laertius, probably belonging to the early third century, composed the *Lives of the Philosophers*, a work of perhaps even less ability than that of Pausanias, yet valuable for the information contained in it. Athenæus, seemingly a contemporary, composed a work named *Symposium of the Sophists*, a great part of which has come down to us. The dinner he assigns to a time shortly after the death of Commodus (Christ, *Griech. Lit.* II. 626 *sq.*). During the symposium the learned guests (sophists) hold discourse, centering in the food and the customs of banquets, but extending to a multiplicity of subjects. The aim of the writer seems to be to display his erudition by quoting as many authors — the majority of whom we know only through him — and on as wide a variety of subjects as possible. Through this work, accordingly, we come to appreciate how vast a treasure of ancient literature has been lost to the world.

It is a pleasure to close this introduction with a notice of one of the most admirable and lovable spirits of classical antiquity, Plutarch of Chæroneia, Bœotia, about 46–125 A.D. He belonged to an old and respectable family, and received a many-sided education in rhetoric, history, biography, physics, mathematics, and philosophy. While broadening his experiences by travel, he retained to the end his attachment to his native city. His writings on social, political, moral, and philosophic subjects are grouped together under the title *Moralia*. They show a surprising versatility and productive power operating in the Platonic spirit, which at that time and through him was entering a new religious-mystic path. Much of this material can be utilized in historical study. Our chief interest here, however, is in his *Parallel Lives*, the most popular work created by classical antiquity. Forty-six biographies are in pairs, notable Greeks and Romans compared and contrasted, with only four — Artaxerxes, Aratus, Galba, and Otho — standing as individuals.

Several important biographies, including the *Epaminondas*, have been lost. The parallelism is artificial; far better would be a historical order. It is to be noted, too, that Plutarch has no conception of historical development. Men of primitive times, like Lycurgus, Romulus, and Theseus, are furnished with the same mental equipment as the author himself. He is equally devoid of the faculty of historical criticism. With him all sources enjoy equal credibility. The truth of any statement therefore can be determined only by an inquiry into its source. We must admit further that in dealing with conflicting statements regarding a person or event under consideration he rarely seems conscious of the necessity of eliminating the contradiction. Generally such critical discussions as appear in his *Lives* have been introduced from his authorities. By way of summary it may be stated that his biographies, only critically sifted, constitute one of the most important sources for the customs, institutions, and personal characters of Greece and Rome.

The author himself regarded the *Lives* as a means of philosophic instruction, closely akin to his *Moralia*. The object of his philosophy was to preserve the great, the good, and the ennobling from the classic past, and to use this material as a guide and an encouragement to virtuous living and to the upbuilding of a broad, humane, moral character. He never descends to mere preaching, and therefore never grows wearisome; but through every page shines in sunny happiness the liberal kindly human soul, warming the reader's heart to the author and awakening in it aspirations for the Beautiful and Good.

BIBLIOGRAPHY

I. Menander and Theocritus. — Edition of the newly found plays together with the earlier fragments, by Kock, Th., *Com. att. frag.* III. Ed. of the newly found *Four Plays of Menander* by Capps, E. (Ginn, 1910); by Lefebvre and Croiset, M. (Cairo, 1907); ed. with translation by Unus Multorum (2d ed., Oxford: Parker, 1909), the basis for the selection in the present volume. See also Arnim, H. v., "Kunst und Weisheit in den Komödien Menanders," in *N. Jahrb.* XIII (1910). 241–53; Capps, E., "Plot of Menander's Epitrepontes," in *Am. Journ. Philol.* XXIX (1908). 410–31; Gerhard, G. A., "Zu Menanders Perikeiromene," in *Philol.* LXIX (1910). 10–34; Leo, F., "Der neue Menander," in *Hermes*, XLIII (1908). 120–67; Lübke, H., *Menander und seine Kunst.*

Progr. (Berlin, 1892); Post, C. R., "Dramatic Art of Menander," in *Class. Philol.* XXIV (1913). 111–45; Richards, H., "The New Menander," in *Class. Quart.* II (1908). 132–6, on the finding and the character of the plays.

Edition of Theocritus with English notes by Kynaston, H. (5th ed., Clarendon Press, 1892); by Edmonds, J., *Greek Bucolic Poets*, with Eng. trans. (Macmillan, 1912). Translation also by Way, A. S. (Cambridge: University Press, 1913); by Lang, A. (Macmillan, 1892), from which the selection in this volume has been taken; *Theocritus and Vergil's Eclogues*, trans. by Calverley (London: Bell, 1908).

II. Nepos and Diodorus Siculus. — Edition of Nepos by Fleckeisen, A. (Teubner, 1898); English translation by Watson, J. S. (Bohn), the basis of the selections for this volume.

Edition of Diodorus by Müller, C. (Paris: Didot, 1842–4); by Vogel, F., continued by Fischer, C. T., 5 vols. (Teubner, 1888–1906). There is an old and poor English translation by Booth, G., 2 vols. (London, 1814), out of print; German translation by Wurm, J. F., 19 vols. (Stuttgart, 1827–40). See also Mess, A. v., "Untersuchungen über die Arbeitsweise Diodors," in *Rhein. Mus.* LXI (1906). 244–66; Schwartz, E., "Diodorus," in Pauly-Wissowa, *Real-Encycl.* V. 663–704, an especially valuable study.

III. Strabo, Pliny, and Pausanias. — Edition of Strabo by Casaubon, J., (Paris, 1587), to which page citations refer; by Müller, C., with maps (Paris, 1858); by Meineke, A., 3 vols. (Teubner, 1866–77). Fragments of his *History* in Müller, *Frag. hist. græc.* III. 490–4; Otto, P., "Strabonis Ἱστορικῶν ὑπομνημάτων frag.," in *Leipziger Stud.* XI (1889). 1–224. English translation by Hamilton and Falconer, 3 vols. (Bohn), from which selections, compared with the Greek text and revised by E. G. S., have been taken for this volume. For studies in Strabo, see Bunbury, E. H., *History of Ancient Geography*, II. chs. xxi, xxii; Tozer, H. F., *History of Ancient Geography* (Cambridge: University Press, 1897), ch. xii; Berger, H., *Geschichte der wissenschaftlichen Erdkunde der Griechen* (2d ed., Leipzig, 1903), see Index; Pais, E., *Ancient Italy*, ch. xxvi; "Straboniana," in *Rivista di filologia*, 1887, pp. 97–246; Otto, P., "Quæstiones strabonianæ," in *Leipzig. Stud.* XI (1889). 225–350; Niese, B., "Beiträge zur Biographie Strabos," in *Hermes*, XIII (1878). 33–45.

Edition of Pliny's *Natural History* by Jahn and Mayhoff, 6 vols. (Teubner, 1892–1906). English translation by Bostock, J., and Riley, H. T., 6 vols. (Bohn). *Chapters on the History of Art*, trans. by Jex-Blake, K., with commentary by Sellers, E. (Macmillan, 1896), from which selections have been made for the present volume. See further Furtwängler, A., *Plinius in seinen Quellen über die bildenden Künste* (Teubner, 1877); Kalkmann, A. D., *Quellen der Kunstgeschichte des Plinius* (Berlin, 1898); Jahn, O., "Uber die Kunsturtheile bei Plinius," in *Sächs. Gesellsch.* 1850. 2. pp. 105–42.

Edition of Pausanias by Hitzig, H., and Blümner, H., 3 vols. (Leipzig, 1896–1910). English translation with extensive commentary and thirty maps by Frazer, J. G., 6 vols. (2d ed., London, 1913); also by Shilleto, A. R., 2 vols. (Bohn), from which have been taken the selections for this volume. See also

Robert, C., *Pausanias als Schriftsteller. Studien und Beobachtungen* (Berlin, 1909). Works on Greek topography generally serve as commentaries on Pausanias.

Works for General Reference

I. Works on Greek Literature and Kindred Studies. — Bergk, Th., *Griechische Literaturgeschichte*, 4 vols. (Berlin, 1872–1887); Bruns, I., *Das literarische Porträt der Griechen*, etc. (Berlin, 1896); Capps, E., *From Homer to Theocritus* (Scribner, 1901); Christ, W., *Geschichte der griechischen Litteratur*, 2 vols. rev. by Schmid, W. (Munich, 1908–1913); Croiset, A. and M., *Histoire de la litterature grecque*, 5 vols. (Paris, 1887); *Abridged History of Greek Literature* (Macmillan, 1904); Hall, F. W., *Companion to Classical Texts* (London, 1913); Keble, A. J., *Lectures on Greek Poetry* 1832–1841, translated from the Latin by Francis, 2 vols. (Oxford: Clarendon Press, 1912); Kirchner, J., *Prosopographia Attica*, 2 vols. (Berlin, 1901, 1902); Lawton, W. C., *Introduction to Classical Greek Literature* (Scribner, 1903); Jebb, R. C., *Growth and Influence of Classical Greek Poetry* (London, 1893); *The Attic Orators from Antiphon to Isæus*, 2 vols. (Macmillan, 1876); Mackail, J. W., *Lectures on Greek Poetry* (Longmans, 1910); Mahaffy, J. P., *History of Classical Greek Literature*, 2 vols. (new ed., Macmillan, 1908); Murray, G., *History of Ancient Greek Literature* (Appleton, 1897); Misch, G., *Geschichte der Autobiographie*, I: Das Altertum (Leipzig, 1907); Putnam, G. H., *Authors and their Public in Ancient Times* (Putnam, 1894); Peck, H. T., *History of Classical Philology from the Seventh Century* B.C., etc. (Macmillan, 1911); Sandys, J. E., *History of Classical Scholarship*, 3 vols. (1906–1908); Schwartz, E., *Charakterköpfe aus der antiken Litteratur* (Leipzig, 1906); Symonds, J. A., *Studies in the Greek Poets*, 2 ser. (London, 1873, 1876); Thompson, E. M., *An Introduction to Greek and Latin Palæography* (Oxford: Clarendon Press, 1912); Whibley, L., *Companion to Greek Studies* (Cambridge: University Press, 1905); Wilamowitz-Moellendorf, U. von, Krumbacher and others, *Griechische und lateinische Literatur und Sprache* (Teubner, 1905); *Greek Literature: A Series of Lectures delivered at Columbia University* (Columbia University Press, 1912).

II. General Histories of Greece. — Grote, G., *History of Greece*, 12 vols. (Harper, reprint from the edition of 1849–1853); Curtius, E., *History of Greece*, 5 vols. (Scribner, 1886); Abbott, E., *History of Greece*, 3 pts. (Putnam, 1895–1900); Holm, A., *History of Greece*, 4 vols. (Macmillan, 1895–1898); Bury, J. B., *History of Greece* (2d ed. Macmillan, 1913); Hall, H. R., *Ancient History of the Near East* (Methuen, 1913); Busolt, G., *Griechische Geschichte*, 3 vols. (2d ed. Gotha, 1893–1904); Beloch, J., *Griechische Geschichte*, 3 vols. (I and II. 1, 2d ed.; the remainder, 1st ed. Strassburg, 1912–1914; 1897–1904); Meyer, *Geschichte des Altertums*, 5 vols. (I, 3d ed. 1910; II–V, 1st ed. 1893–1902); Freeman, E. A., *History of Sicily*, 4 vols. (Oxford: Clarendon Press, 1891–1894).

III. Inscriptions. — *Inscriptiones Græcæ*, 14 vols., ed. Kirchhoff, A., Kaibel, G., and others (Berl. Akad. 1873–1890); this is the new edition abbreviated in this volume as *Inscr. græc.*, whereas the earlier edition of the *Corpus Inscriptionum Atticarum*, occasionally cited, is abbreviated as *CIA.*; Dittenberger, W., *Sylloge Inscriptionum Græcarum*, 2d ed., 3 vols. (Leipzig, 1898–1901); Hicks, E. L., and Hill, G. F., *Manual of Greek Historical Inscriptions*, (new ed., Oxford: Clarendon Press, 1901); Roberts, E. S., and Gardner, E. A., *Introduction to Greek Epigraphy*, 2 vols. (Cambridge: University Press, 1887, 1905); Michel, Ch., *Recueil d'inscriptions grecques* (Brussels, 1900); Dareste, R., Haussoullier, B., and Reinach, Th., *Recueil des inscriptions juridiques grecques*, 2d ser. fasc. i–iii (Paris: Leroux, 1898, 1904); Collitz, H., *Sammlung der griechische Dialektinschriften*, 4 vols. (1884–1911); Larfeld, W., *Griechische Epigraphik* (3d ed., Munich: Beck, 1914); Wilhelm, A., *Beiträge zur Inschriftskunde* (Vienna, 1909); "Attische Psephismen," in *Hermes*, XXIV (1889). 108–152, 326–36; Böckh, A., *Urkunden über das Seewesen des attischen Staates* (Berlin, 1840); Köhler, U., "Attische Inschriften des V[ten] Jahrhunderts," in *Hermes*, XXXI (1896). 137–54; Bleckmann, F., *Griechische Inschriften zur griechischen Staatenkunde* (Kleine Texte, no. 115, Bonn, 1913); Gardthausen, V., "Wiedergefundene Originale historischer Inschriften des Altertums," in *N. Jahrb.* XXXIII (1914). 248–54, inscriptions quoted in ancient works; Kern, O., *Tabulæ in usum scholarum editæ*, etc. (Bonn: Marcus and Weber, 1913).

IV. Atlases, Dictionaries, and Kindred Helps. — Shepherd, W. R., *Atlas of Ancient History* (Holt, 1913), the best historical atlas; Sieglin, W., *Schulatlas zur Geschichte des Altertums* (imported by Lemcke and Büchner, N. Y.); Kiepert, H., *Atlas Antiquus* (Boston: Sanborn). Harper's *Dictionary of Classical Literature and Antiquities*, by H. T. Peck (Harper, 1887), most convenient; Smith, W., *Dictionary of Greek and Roman Biography and Mythology*, 3 vols. (Boston, 1849), useful though old; *Dictionary of Greek and Roman Geography*, 2 vols. (Boston, 1854, 1857); *Dictionary of Greek and Roman Antiquities*, 2 vols. (3d ed., London: Murray, 1890, 1891); Daremberg et Saglio, *Dictionnaire des antiquités grecques et romaines* (Paris, beginning 1873), in many volumes, still under way; Pauly, *Real-Encyclopädie der classischen Altertumswissenschaft*, revised and greatly enlarged edition under the supervision of Wissowa, G., and (the later volumes) of Kroll, W. (Stuttgart, beginning 1894), in many volumes, still under way; Hermann, K. F., *Lehrbuch der griechischen Antiquitäten* (Freiburg i. B.: Mohr), new editions of the several volumes are constantly appearing; Müller, I. von, *Handbuch der klassischen Altertumswissenschaft* (Munich: Beck), new editions of the several volumes are constantly appearing; Gercke, A., and Norden, E., *Einleitung in die Altertumswissenschaft* (Teubner), in several volumes, still incomplete.

Works devoted to special periods or to special subjects will be mentioned in the several chapter bibliographies.

CHAPTER II

THE MINOAN AND HOMERIC CIVILIZATIONS

Approximately 3000–750 B.C.

THE Minoan period begins with the Bronze age, in which it is probable that copper was used for a time before the introduction of bronze; see Mosso, A., *Dawn of the Mediterranean Civilization.* The entire period is divided by Evans (*Nine Minoan Periods*, 1915), into three large epochs, which he terms Early, Middle, and Late Minoan, respectively. In the Middle Minoan period Crete reached the height of her brilliant civilization; in the Late Minoan age, called also the Mycenæan age, she stagnated and declined, while Troy ("sixth city"), Mycenæ, and other cities on the Greek mainland rose to a brilliant height of culture and power. The Minoans had systems of writing, first pictographs, out of which developed linear scripts; and a great store of inscribed tablets has been found in a room of the palace at Cnossus, Crete. No one as yet has been able to read the script, but there can be no doubt that the accumulated tablets just mentioned were the archives of accounts, of dues, receipts, etc., belonging to the king. That the Minoans, endowed as they were with splendid mentality, possessed a literature of songs, epics, and perhaps chronicles, as did the less gifted Orientals of the same period, seems certain. Such literature, however, must have been consigned to less durable material, doubtless papyrus from Egypt, and for that reason perished. One of the most important questions bearing upon the relation of the Minoan civilization to that of historical Hellas is whether any of this literature survived, in any form, the downfall of the culture, so as to be used by the Greeks. The accuracy with which Homer pictures the material civilization, not of the decadent period but of the splendid Middle Minoan age, suggests the possibility of a survival to his time. If his sources were unwritten, at least the oral traditions were remarkably definite and concrete. It is noteworthy, too, that Aristotle and Ephorus speak with such confidence of the conditions and institutions of the age of Minos, and at the same time in such harmony with the facts revealed by the spade, as to tempt us to believe it possible that they or their sources made use of written material directly or indirectly transmitted from the Minoan age to their time.

Notwithstanding this possibility we are forced to deal with the fact that our sources are almost wholly archæological, and that references in Greek literature to the Minoan age can be accepted as facts or as probabilities only in so far as they are supported by archæological discoveries. With this understanding a few selections from literature are presented below. Preceding those which relate to the Minoan age is an excerpt from Æschylus which treats of the beginnings of civilized life.

1. The Primitive Condition of Man and the Origin of Civilization

(Æschylus, *Prometheus*, 442–506. Paley's translation, revised on the basis of Weil's text by G. W. B.)

It is a remarkable fact that twenty-five hundred years before the dawn of anthropology a Greek dramatist should come so near the truth regarding the origin of civilization. It is interesting, too, to notice what Æschylus considered the most vital elements of civilization, and especially the great prominence given to its religious features.

Hear of the evils that existed among mortals, — how I[1] made them, hitherto without reasoning powers, to have mind and to be possessed of intelligence. I shall tell you this, without any wish to disparage mankind, but by way of explaining the good feeling implied in my gifts. They in the first place, though seeing saw to no purpose, hearing they did not understand; but like the forms of dreams, during all that long time they did everything in a confused and random way, and knew not brick-built houses turned to the sun, nor the craft of carpentry. But they used to dwell in holes made in the earth, like the tiny ants in the sunless recesses of caves. Further, they had no sign either of winter or of flowery spring, or of fruitful summer, to rely upon; but they used to do everything without judgment, till at length I showed them the risings of the stars and their laboriously determined settings. Moreover, numbers, the best of inventions, I devised for them, and the combining of letters, at once the origin of literature, and the means of remembering every event. I was the first, too, to join together under the yoke the animals that served them for drawing and for riding, that they might be used by mortals to relieve them in their severest toils. I brought also under the car horses, taught to love the rein,

[1] The speaker is Prometheus, the friend of mankind, ancestor of the Hellenic race through Deucalion and his sons.

the ornament of luxurious wealth.[1] Besides, no other than myself found out for them the sea-traversing canvas-winged cars to convey mariners. Such were the contrivances I devised for man. . . .

If any one had fallen into an illness there were no remedies to avert it, either to be swallowed as food, or to be used as ointments, or to be taken as draughts; but for want of drugs they used to pine and waste away, till I showed them how to compose these assuaging remedies, by which they now repel from themselves every kind of malady.[2] Many ways, too, of divination I arranged for them: first I taught them what sort of dreams were destined to prove realities: the obscure import of ominous sounds I made clear to them, and the meaning of objects met on the way. The flight too of crooked taloned birds of prey I clearly defined, both those which are lucky in their nature and the unlucky ones. . . . I showed them also what the smoothness of the liver meant, and what particular color it should have to be pleasing to the gods.[3] Such then were my services in these matters; but those great benefits to man which lie hidden under the earth, — copper, iron, silver, and gold, — who can assert that he found them out before I did? . . . In fine, hear the whole matter: all arts came to mortals from Prometheus.

2. The Carians

(Herodotus i. 171)

It is now generally accepted that the Minoans were not Indo-Europeans, but belonged to the "Mediterranean" race (*cf.* Sergi, *Mediterranean Race*). Of the same race were the Carians who inhabited a part of Asia Minor, and in earlier time, as Herodotus states, the islands of the Ægean Sea. Connections between the religion of Caria, Asia Minor, and Minoan Crete have been pointed out by scholars. It is to be noted, however, that the Caria here referred to had no part in the brilliant Minoan civilization.

The Carians came to the mainland from the islands; for being of old time subjects of Minos and being called Leleges, they used

[1] Horses were not used by the Greeks as ordinary work animals, but for riding, driving in carriages, and war. They were so expensive that only the relatively wealthy could afford to have them.

[2] In the time of Æschylus, early fifth century, medical science was rapidly developing. Hippocrates flourished in the latter part of the same century; see nos. 79–81.

[3] This system of divination is now supposed to have been derived from Babylonia.

to dwell in the islands, paying no tribute, so far back as I am able to arrive by hearsay; but whenever Minos required it, they used to supply his ships with seamen: and as Minos subdued much land and was fortunate in his fighting, the Carian nation was of all nations much the most famous at that time together with him. And they produced three inventions of which the Hellenes adopted the use: that is to say, the Carians were those who first set the fashion of fastening crests on helmets, and of making the devices which are put upon shields, and these also were the first who made handles for their shields, whereas up to that time all who were wont to use shields carried them without handles and with leathern straps to guide them, having them hung about their necks and their left shoulders.[1] Then after the lapse of a long time the Dorians and Ionians drove the Carians out of the islands, and so they came to the mainland.[2]

(Thucydides i. 8)

The islanders were even more addicted to piracy than the mainlanders. They were mostly Carian or Phœnician settlers. This is proved by the fact that when the Athenians purified Delos during the Peloponnesian war and the tombs of the dead were opened, more than half of them were found to be Carians. They were known by the fashion of their arms which were buried with them, and by their mode of burial, the same which is still practised among them.[3]

[1] The Minoans used a man-covering shield suspended from the neck as here described. The question as to the origin of the round shield is uncertain. In the opinion of Ridgeway, *Early Age of Greece*, ch. vi, the round shield was introduced from central Europe by invading Hellenes.

[2] In the colonization described by no. 11.

[3] From this passage it is clear that Thucydides, the writer, used a method of research followed by the archæologists of to-day. By this means he proves that the people buried in past ages in the island of Delos had the same civilization as the Carians of his own time. That they were of the same race is an inference which he and most archæologists have considered legitimate. Modern historians, on the contrary, are convinced that widely diverse races, as the Japanese, the negroes of North America, and the western Europeans, may enjoy the same civilization.

3. Minos

(Homer, *Odyssey* xix. 178 *sq.*)

In this excerpt "them" refers to the hundred cities of Crete. The "nine-year" period of the Cretan king was the same as in Laconia; the Cretan king and the Lacedæmonian kings were compelled, on the renewal of a nine-year period, to seek divine sanction. The close connection of the Cretan king with his deity is also paralleled in Lacedæmon. In brief, the royal office in both countries seems to have been a Minoan heritage.

Among them was Cnossus, a mighty city, wherein Minos ruled in nine-year periods, he who had converse with great Zeus.

(Diodorus v. 78)

This excerpt from Diodorus is evidently derived from early Greek sources and well represents the conventional Greek idea of Minos and his legislation and naval power. The colonization of western Hellas (Sicily and southern Italy), too, is repeated by many writers. There can be no doubt whatever that the later Minoans colonized this region; *cf.* no. 6.

They say that many generations after the birth of the gods many heroes arose in Crete, the most illustrious of whom were Minos and Rhadamanthys and Sarpedon, who they say were the sons of Zeus and Agenor's sister Europa. She, the story goes, had by a device of the gods been carried off on a bull's back to Crete. Minos as the eldest was king of the island, in which he planted no few cities, the most famous among them being Cnossus in the part which inclines toward Asia, Phæstus on the southern coast, and Cydonia in the western regions opposite Peloponnesus. He enacted for the Cretans many laws, professing to receive them from his father Zeus and to hold converse with him in a certain cave. It is said, too, that he acquired a great naval power, conquered most of the islands and was the first Greek to establish an empire at sea. After winning great repute for bravery and justice, he ended his life in Sicily in an expedition against Cocalus.

(Thucydides i. 8)

In the opinion of Thucydides settled life and civilization made progress till the time of the Trojan war, after which came a period of confusion due to the Dorian and other migrations. Archæological discoveries, on the contrary, seem to have proved that Troy, the "sixth" and most splendid city, was destroyed in a period, probably toward the end of the period, of confusion and turmoil of migration. The chronology of these early times could not be so well known to the historical Greeks as the spade has revealed it to us. On the other hand, the connection of economy with political history is stated with remarkable clearness and accuracy: the willingness of many to submit to empire for the protection of their property, and the use of wealth as a means of conquest.

After Minos had established a navy, communication by sea became more general. For after he had expelled the pirates, when he colonized the greater part of the islands, the dwellers on the sea-coast began to grow richer and to live in a more settled manner; and some of them, finding their wealth increase beyond their expectations, surrounded their towns with walls. The love of gain made the weaker willing to serve the stronger, and the command of wealth enabled the more powerful to subjugate the lesser cities. This was the state of society which was beginning to prevail at the time of the Trojan war.

4. Theseus and the Minotaur

(Hellanicus, *Atthis*, quoted by Plutarch, *Theseus*, 15–17, who cites also Philochorus and Aristotle)

There seems to be a kernel of truth in the myth related below. The favorite sport of the king and grandees of Cnossus came in the festival in which trained youths and girls grappled with bulls, turned somersaults over their backs, etc.; Botsford, *Hellenic History*, ch. ii. The subject states, including some of the towns of Attica, had to furnish the girls and youths as tribute. The labyrinth was the palace at Crete. The word is Carian and has reference to the double-ax, which was an attribute of Zeus. The Cnossian palace, in which this Zeus was worshiped, was named accordingly "the house of the double-ax." In time, however, the word labyrinth lost its original meaning, and came to refer to the intricate system of corridors and halls included in that palace. A further historical truth contained in the story is doubtless the liberation of Attica from the tribute by the hero.

They (the Athenians) sent an embassy to Minos and prevailed on him to make peace on condition that every nine years they should send him a tribute of seven youths and seven girls. The most tragic of the legends states that these poor children, when they reached Crete, were thrown into the Labyrinth, and there were devoured by the Minotaur [1] or else perished with hunger, being unable to find their way out. The Minotaur, as Euripides tells us, was

> A form commingled, and a monstrous birth,
> Half man, half bull, in twofold shape combined.

Philochorus states that the Cretans do not recognize this story, but say that the Labyrinth was merely a prison, like any other, from which escape was impossible, and that Minos instituted gymnastic games in honor of Androgeus, a son who had been treacherously slain, in which the prizes for the victors were these children, who till then were kept in the Labyrinth. . . . Aristotle himself, in his treatise on *The Constitution of the Bottiæans*,[2] evidently does not believe that the children were put to death by Minos, but that they lived in Crete as slaves to extreme old age, and that once the Cretans, in performance of an ancient vow, sent first-fruits of their population to Delphi. Among those who were thus sent were the descendants of the Athenians; and as they could not maintain themselves there, they first passed over to Italy, and settled near Iapygia.[3] Thence they removed to Thrace, and took the name of Bottiæans. For this reason the Bottiæan maidens, when performing a certain sacrifice, sing, "Let us go to Athens."

Plutarch next narrates the sailing of Theseus to kill the Minotaur, after which (§ 17) he quotes from Hellanicus the excerpt given below.

Hellanicus says that the City did not select the youths and girls by lot, but that Minos himself came thither and chose them, and that he picked out Theseus first of all upon the usual conditions, that the Athenians should furnish a ship, and that the youths should embark in it and sail with him, not carrying with them any weapon of war; and that when the Minotaur was slain, the tribute should cease. Formerly no one had any hope of safety; hence they used to send out the ship with a black sail, as if it were going to a certain

[1] The idea and the name of the Minotaur ("Minos-bull") easily arose from stories of the great king Minos, his labyrinthine palace, and the festival of bull grappling, which circulated through Hellas.

[2] Bottia, Bottiæa, was a Macedonian, not a Thracian, town; *cf.* Oberhummer, in Pauly-Wissowa, *Real-Encycl.* III. 794 *sq.* The basis of Aristotle's connection of the inhabitants with Delphi, Italy, and Crete is unknown.

[3] Here again is a reference to the Minoan colonization of Italy; *cf.* nos. 3, 6.

doom; but now Theseus so encouraged his father, and boasted that he would overcome the Minotaur, that he gave a second sail, a white one, to the pilot, and charged him on his return, if Theseus were safe, to hoist the white one, if not, the black one as a sign of mourning.

5. Crete and the Relation of her Institutions with those of Lacedæmon

(Aristotle, *Politics*, ii. 10. 1–5, 1271 b. Jowett's translation, revised on the basis of Susemihl's text, by G. W. B.)

The opinion of the writer is that the Lacedæmonians adopted many of their institutions from Crete, and the Hellenic Cretans from the earlier inhabitants. We know, however, that the Minoan civilization flourished in Laconia, and it seems to us, therefore, at least equally probable that the Lacedæmonians derived these institutions directly from the Minoans of their own country. If what Aristotle says regarding the Minoan origin is true, it follows that the institutions which we have looked upon as peculiarly Dorian belong to this earlier civilization. The view is reasonable, especially as the complex social organization of Laconia and historical Crete seems to be the product of a highly developed civilization, like the Oriental, rather than of a relatively crude race of invaders, such as were the Dorians.

The Cretan constitution nearly resembles the Lacedæmonian, and in some few points is quite as good, but for the most part less perfect in form. The Lacedæmonian is said to be, and probably is, in most respects a copy of the Cretan. In fact older constitutions are generally less elaborate than later. According to tradition, Lycurgus, when he ceased to be guardian of King Charilaüs, went abroad and spent most of the time of his absence in Crete. For the two countries are nearly connected; the Lyctians are a colony of the Lacedæmonians, and the colonists, when they came to Crete, adopted the system of laws which they found existing among the inhabitants. [Even to this day the periœci are governed by the original laws which Minos enacted. The island seems to be intended by nature for dominion in Hellas and to be well situated; it extends right across the sea, around which nearly all the Hellenes are settled; and while one end is not far from Peloponnesus, the other almost reaches to the region of Asia about Triopium and

Rhodes. Hence Minos acquired the empire of the sea, subduing some of the islands and colonizing others; at last he invaded Sicily, where he died near Camicus.][1]

The Cretan institutions resemble the Lacedæmonian. The helots were the husbandmen of the one, the periœci of the other; and both Cretans and Lacedæmonians have common meals, which were anciently called by the Lacedæmonians, not phiditia but andreia; and the Cretans have the same word, the use of which proves that the common meals (syssitia) originally came from Crete.

6. Occupation Classes; the Public Tables and the Colonization of Italy

(Aristotle, *Politics*, vii. 10. 1–6, 1329 b. Revision by G. W. B., as in no. 5)

It is no new or recent discovery that the state ought to be divided into classes, and that the warriors ought to be separated from the husbandmen. The system has continued in Egypt and in Crete to the present day, and was established, as is said, by Sesostris in Egypt and by Minos in Crete. The institution of common tables (syssitia) also appears to be of ancient date, being in Crete as old as the reign of Minos, and in Italy far older. The native historians there say that a certain Italus was king of Œnotria, from whom the inhabitants were called Italians instead of Œnotrians, and who gave the name Italy to the promontory of Europe which lies between the Scylletic and Lametic gulfs, which are distant from one another only a half-day's journey. They say that this Italus converted the Œnotrians from shepherds into husbandmen, and besides giving them other laws, he was the founder of their common meals. Even in our day some who are derived from him retain this institution and certain other laws of his. On the side of Italy toward Tyrrhenia (Etruria) dwelt the Opici, who are now, as of old, called Ausones; and on the side toward Iapygia and the Ionian Gulf, in the district called Siritis, the Chones, who are likewise of Œnotrian race. From this part of the world originally came the institution of the common tables; the separation into classes, which was much older, from Egypt; for the reign of Sesostris is of far greater antiquity than that of Minos.

[1] Bracketed by Susemihl. On the naval power of Minos, see no. 3.

(Athenæus xii. 24, probably quoting from Clearchus, *Lives*, iv)

As indicated by their language, the Iapygians were related to the Illyrians, and must have migrated to Italy far later than the Minoan age. There can be no doubt, however, that toward the end of the Minoan age the Cretans or other Ægean people colonized southern Italy and Sicily; hence there may have been a Cretan element in the Iapygian population. This passage, however, refers mainly to later time.

Now the race of the Iapygians came originally from Crete, being descended from those Cretans who came to seek for Glaucus, and settled in that part of Italy. Afterward forgetting the orderly life of the Cretans, they came to such a pitch of luxury and thence to such a degree of insolence that they were the first people who painted their faces, and who wore headbands and false hair, and who clothed themselves in robes embroidered with flowers, and who considered it disgraceful to cultivate the land or to do any kind of labor. Most of them made their houses more beautiful than the temples of the Gods. Thus, they say, the leaders of the Iapygians, treating the Deity with insult, destroyed the images of the Gods in the temples, ordering them to yield place to their superiors. For this reason, stricken with fire and thunderbolts, they gave rise to this report; for in fact the thunderbolts with which they were stricken down were visible a long time afterward. To this very day all their descendants live with shaven heads and in mourning apparel, in want of the luxuries which previously belonged to them.

7. Cretan Education and the Public Tables

(Ephorus, *Histories*, quoted by Strabo x. 4. 20)

The most illustrious and powerful of the youths form troops (ἀγέλαι), each individual assembling together as many youths of his age as possible. Generally the governor of the troop is the father of the youth who has gathered it, the former has the function of taking them to hunt, of exercising them in running, and of punishing the disobedient. They are maintained at the public expense. On certain set days troop encounters troop, marching in time to the sound of the pipe and lyre, as is their custom in actual war. They inflict blows, some with the hand and some even with iron weapons.

A certain number are selected from time to time from the troop and compelled forthwith to marry. They do not, however, take the young women whom they have married immediately to their homes, but wait until they are qualified to administer household affairs.

(Dosiades, *Cretica*, iv, quoted by Athenæus iv. 22, 143)

Dosiades was a native of Crete of the Hellenistic age, who composed the work named above, dealing evidently with the history and antiquities of his island. Little else is known of him (*cf.* Schwartz, in Pauly-Wissowa, *Real-Encycl.* V. 1596 *sq.*); but he must have had access to abundant sources of information lost to us.

The people of Lycti conduct their public tables as follows. Each brings in a tenth of the produce, and also the revenues of the state, which the authorities of the state distribute among the several houses. And each slave contributed an Æginetan stater as poll tax.

On reaching manhood the youth then passed from the troop to the club (*hetæria*). All the citizens are grouped in clubs. These institutions they call andreia. The management of a syssition (common table of an andreion) is in charge of a woman, who calls to her assistance three or four common men (*δημοτικοί*). Each of these men is accompanied by two slaves as wood-carriers, called *καλοφόροι*. In every Cretan city are two houses for syssitia. One they call the andreion: the other, in which they entertain strangers, the inn (*κοιμητήριον*). In the andreion stand in the first place two tables assigned to guests, at which aliens who are present sit, then the other tables in their order.

An equal portion is served to each one present, whereas a half portion is assigned to the younger men, who touch nothing of the other dishes. Then wine mixed with water is served, and all who sit at a common table drink together. When they have finished eating, a further supply of wine is furnished. For the boys, too, a common bowl is mixed, while to the elders, if they wish, the privilege is given of drinking more. The best of everything the woman in charge of the syssition takes from the table in the sight of all and gives to those who have distinguished themselves in war or by their wisdom. After dinner it is customary first to deliberate on public affairs, then to converse about the deeds of war and to praise those who have shown themselves good men, the object being to encourage the young to manliness.

(Pyrgion, *Cretan Customs*, quoted by Athenæus iv. 22, 143. Translated by G. W. B.)

In their syssitia the Cretans eat sitting. The youngest (the children) stand and serve the rest. After pouring an offering to the gods for good fortune, they divide among all the food brought to the table. They assign to the sons who stand behind their fathers' chairs portions one half of those placed before men. The orphans, however, have equal portions. Whatever is served them is prepared without seasoning according to the specifications of their customary law.

8. The Pyrrhic Dance and the Hymn of the Curetes

(Ephorus, *Histories*, quoted by Strabo x. 4. 16)

That courage and not fear might predominate, they were accustomed from childhood to the use of arms and to endure fatigue. Hence they disregarded heat and cold, rugged and steep roads, blows received in gymnastic exercises and in set battles.

They practised archery and the dance in armor, which the curetes first invented, and which was afterward perfected by Pyrrhichus and called after him Pyrrhic. Hence even their sports were not without their use in training for war. With the same intention they used the Cretan measures in their songs. The tones of these measures are extremely loud; they were invented by Thales (Thaletas), to whom are ascribed the pæans and other native songs and many customs. They adopted a military dress and shoes, and considered armor the most valuable of all presents.

THE HYMN

The curetes, mentioned above, were young, unmarried men, initiated into the mystic rites of the society, and worshipers of Zeus *Kouros*, the Divine Youth, with emotional rites and ecstatic dances in armor. See Harrison, J. E., "The Kouretes and Zeus Kouros," in the *Annual of the British School at Athens*, XV (1908–9). 308–338. A hymn of the curetes, recently discovered and published in *op. cit.* XV. 357 *sqq.*, is translated as follows by Gilbert Murray.

Io, Kouros most Great, I give thee hail, Kronion, Lord of all that is wet and gleaming, thou art come at the head of thy Daimones (spirits). To Dicte for the year, Oh, march, and rejoice in the dance and song,

That we make to thee with harps and pipes mingled together, and sing as we come to a stand at thy well-fenced altar.

Io, etc.

For here the shielded Nurturers took thee, a babe immortal, from Rhea, and with noise of beating feet hid thee away.

Io, etc.

(The next stanza is unintelligible.)

And the seasons began to be fruitful year by year (?) and Justice to possess mankind, and all wild living things were held about by wealth-loving Peace.

Io, etc.

To us also leap for full jars, and leap for fleecy flocks, and leap for fields of fruit, and for hives to bring increase.

Io, etc.

Leap for our cities and leap for our sea-borne ships and leap for young citizens and for goodly law.[1]

9. The Condition of Greece during and after the Hellenic Migration

(Thucydides i. 2–12. Jowett, verified on the basis of the Greek text by E. G. S.)

This passage best applies to the period of Indo-European immigration into Greece and of the gradual emergence of Hellenic civilization from the blending of the invaders with the decadent Minoans. At the same time the selection illustrates the method of Thucydides in dealing with early times.

2. The country which is now called Hellas was not regularly settled in ancient times. The people were migratory, and readily left their homes whenever they were overpowered by numbers.

[1] The curetes were themselves the daimones, spirits, attendant on the god. He was a year god, who brought fertility, increase, and prosperity. The curetes are called nurturers because they received the child Zeus from his mother Rhea and hid him from the father Cronos. Though the exhortation "leap" is addressed to Zeus, the curetes themselves performed the act while singing. From Crete the institution of the curetes extended to many parts of Greece.

There was no commerce, and they could not safely hold intercourse with one another either by land or sea. The several tribes cultivated their own soil just enough to obtain a maintenance from it. But they had no accumulations of wealth, and did not plant the ground; for, being without walls, they were never sure that an invader might not come and despoil them. Living in this manner and knowing that they could anywhere obtain a bare subsistence, they were always ready to migrate; so that they had neither great cities nor any considerable resources. The richest districts were most constantly changing their inhabitants; for example, the countries which are now called Thessaly and Bœotia, the greater part of the Peloponnesus with the exception of Arcadia,[1] and all the best parts of Hellas. For the productiveness of the land increased the power of individuals; this in turn was a source of quarrels by which communities were ruined, while at the same time they were more exposed to attacks from without. Certainly Attica, of which the soil was poor and thin, enjoyed a long freedom from civil strife, and therefore retained its original inhabitants. And a striking confirmation of my argument is afforded by the fact that Attica through immigration increased in population more than any other region. For the leading men of Hellas, when driven out of their own country by war or revolution, sought an asylum at Athens; and from the very earliest times, being admitted to rights of citizenship, so greatly increased the number of inhabitants that Attica became incapable of containing them, and was at last obliged to send out colonies to Ionia.[2]

3. The feebleness of antiquity is further proved to me by the circumstance that there appears to have been no common action in Hellas before the Trojan War. And I am inclined to think that the very name was not as yet given to the whole country, and in fact did not exist at all before the time of Hellen, the son of Deucalion; the different tribes, of which the Pelasgian[3] was the most

[1] It was the common belief of his time that Arcadia alone of all Peloponnesian states had never changed inhabitants; it is certain that they were among the oldest of Hellenic races.

[2] Thucydides has in mind especially the tradition that the inhabitants of northern Peloponnese, expelled by the invading Dorians, took refuge in Attica and afterward joined in the colonization of Ionia.

[3] In the time of Thucydides it was commonly believed that the Pelasgians had

widely spread, gave their own names to different districts. But when Hellen and his sons became powerful in Phthiotis, their aid was invoked by other cities, and those who associated with them gradually began to be called Hellenes, though a long time elapsed before the name prevailed over the whole country. Of this Homer affords the best evidence; for he, although he lived long after the Trojan War, nowhere uses this name collectively, but confines it to the followers of Achilles from Phthiotis, who were the original Hellenes; when speaking of the entire host he called them Danaäns, or Argives, or Achæans. Neither is there any mention of Barbarians in his poems, clearly because there were as yet no Hellenes opposed to them by a common distinctive name. Thus the several Hellenic tribes (and I mean by the term Hellenes those who, while forming separate communities, had a common language, and were afterward called by a common name), owing to their weakness and isolation, were never united in any great enterprise before the Trojan War. And they only made the expedition against Troy after they had gained considerable experience of the sea.

4. Minos is the first to whom tradition ascribes the possession of a navy. He made himself master of a great part of what is now termed the Hellenic sea; he conquered the Cyclades, and was the first colonizer of most of them, expelling the Carians and appointing his own sons to govern in them. Lastly, it was he who, from a natural desire to protect his growing revenues, sought, as far as he was able, to clear the sea of pirates.

5. For in ancient times both Hellenes and Barbarians, as well the inhabitants of the coast as of the islands, when they began to find their way to one another by sea had recourse to piracy. They were commanded by powerful chiefs, who took this means of increasing their wealth and providing for their poorer followers. They would fall upon the unwalled and straggling towns, or rather villages, which they plundered, and maintained themselves by the plunder of them; for, as yet, such an occupation was held to be

once occupied a great part of Hellas. This opinion, however, seems to have been due to an erroneous method of reconstructing the past. Homer knew only of a Pelasgic Argos and Pelasgians in Crete; from such small beginnings the antiquarians developed their great theory; *cf.* Meyer, E., *Forsch. zur alten Geschichte*, I. 1–124.

honorable and not disgraceful. This is proved by the practice of certain tribes on the mainland who, to the present day, glory in piratical exploits, and by the witness of the ancient poets, in whose verses the question is invariably asked of newly-arrived voyagers, whether they are pirates; which implies that neither those who are questioned disclaim, nor those who are interested in knowing censure, the occupation. The land too was infested by robbers; and there are parts of Hellas in which the old practices still continue, as for example among the Ozolian Locrians, Ætolians, Acarnanians, and the adjacent regions of the continent. The fashion of wearing arms among these continental tribes is a relic of their old predatory habits.[1]

6. For in ancient times all Hellenes carried weapons because their homes were undefended and intercourse was unsafe; like the Barbarians they went armed in their every-day life. And the continuance of the custom in certain parts of the country proves that it once prevailed everywhere.

The Athenians were the first who laid aside arms and adopted an easier and more luxurious way of life. Quite recently the old-fashioned refinement of dress still lingered among the elder men of their richer class, who wore undergarments of linen, and bound back their hair in a knot with golden clasps in the form of grass-hoppers; and the same customs long survived among the elders of Ionia, having been derived from their Athenian ancestors. On the other hand, the simple dress which is now common was first worn at Sparta; and there, more than anywhere else, the life of the rich was assimilated to that of the people. The Lacedæmonians too were the first who in their athletic exercises stripped naked and rubbed themselves over with oil. But this was not the ancient custom; athletes formerly, even when they were contending at Olympia, wore girdles about their loins, a practice which lasted until quite lately, and still prevails among Barbarians, especially those of Asia, where the combatants at boxing and wrestling matches wear girdles. And many other customs which are now confined

[1] The method of the historian is to study the undeveloped peoples of Hellas for information on the early condition of those peoples who had made progress. The same method is employed at present in the study of religion, social conditions, and other elements of civilization.

to the Barbarians might be shown to have existed formerly in Hellas.[1]

7. In later times, when navigation had become general and wealth was beginning to accumulate, cities were built upon the seashore and fortified; peninsulas too were occupied and walled-off with a view to commerce and defence against the neighboring tribes. But the older towns both in the islands and on the continent, in order to protect themselves against the piracy which so long prevailed, were built inland; and there they remain to this day. For the piratical tribes plundered, not only one another, but all those who, without being sailors, lived on the sea-coast. . . .

9. I am inclined to think that Agamemnon succeeded in collecting the expedition,[2] not because the suitors of Helen had bound themselves by oath to Tyndareus, but because he was the most powerful king of his time. Those Peloponnesians who possess the most accurate traditions say that originally Pelops gained his power by the great wealth which he brought with him from Asia into a poor country, whereby he was enabled, although a stranger, to give his name to the Peloponnesus; and that still greater fortune attended his descendants after the death of Eurystheus, king of Mycenæ, who was slain in Attica by the Heraclidæ. For Atreus the son of Pelops was the maternal uncle of Eurystheus, who, when he went on the expedition, naturally committed to his charge the kingdom of Mycenæ. Now Atreus had been banished by his father on account of the murder of Chrysippus. But Eurystheus never returned; and the Mycenæans, dreading the Heraclidæ, were ready to welcome Atreus, who was considered a powerful man and had ingratiated himself with the multitude. Thus he succeeded to the throne of Mycenæ and the other dominions of Eurystheus. The house of Pelops accordingly prevailed over that of Perseus.

[1] In their admiration for the human form, their recognition of its nobility, and their pleasure in viewing it unclad, especially in action, the Hellenes contrasted with the Orientals, who thought it shameful to expose the body to view. It was this attitude of the Greeks which made possible the creation of their art and the elevation of the human being to a dignity and nobility of which the Orientals appear never even to have dreamed.

[2] Ch. 8 has not been omitted, but merely transferred; see nos. 2, 3. At the close of the chapter Thucydides speaks of the Trojan war. The expedition here mentioned, therefore, is that of the Hellenes against Troy.

And it was, as I believe, because Agamemnon inherited this power and also because he was the greatest naval potentate of his time that he was able to assemble the expedition; and the other princes followed him, not from good-will, but from fear. Of the chiefs who came to Troy, he, if the witness of Homer be accepted, brought the greatest number of ships himself, besides supplying the Arcadians with them. In the 'Handing down of the Sceptre' he is described as 'The king of many islands, and of all Argos.' But, living on the mainland, he could not have ruled over any except the adjacent islands (which would not be 'many') unless he had possessed a considerable navy. From this expedition we must form our conjectures about the character of still earlier times.

10. When it is said that Mycenæ was but a small place, or that any other city which existed in those days is inconsiderable in our own, this argument will hardly prove that the expedition was not as great as the poets relate and as is commonly imagined. Suppose the city of Sparta to be deserted, and nothing left but the temples and the ground-plan, distant ages would be very unwilling to believe that the power of the Lacedæmonians was at all equal to their fame. And yet they own two-fifths of the Peloponnesus, and are acknowledged leaders of the whole, as well as of numerous allies in the rest of Hellas. But their city is not regularly built, and has no splendid temples or other edifices; it rather resembles a straggling village like the ancient towns of Hellas, and would therefore make a poor show. Whereas if the same fate befell the Athenians, the ruins of Athens would strike the eye, and we should infer their power to have been twice as great as it really is. We ought not then to be unduly sceptical. The greatness of cities should be estimated by their real power and not by appearances. And we may fairly suppose the Trojan expedition to have been greater than any which preceded it, although according to Homer, if we may once more appeal to his testimony, not equal to those of our own day. He was a poet, and may therefore be expected to exaggerate; yet, even upon his showing, the expedition was comparatively small. For it numbered, as he tells us, twelve hundred ships, those of the Bœotians carrying one hundred and twenty men each, those of Philoctetes fifty; and by these numbers he may be presumed to indicate the largest and the smallest ships; else why in

the catalogue is nothing said about the size of any others? That the crews were all fighting men as well as rowers he clearly implies when speaking of the ships of Philoctetes; for he tells us that all the oarsmen were likewise archers. And it is not to be supposed that many who were not sailors would accompany the expedition, except the kings and principal officers; for the troops had to cross the sea, bringing with them the materials of war, in vessels without decks, built after the old piratical fashion. Now if we take a mean between the crews, the invading forces will appear not to have been very numerous when we remember that they were drawn from the whole of Hellas.[1]

11. The cause of the inferiority was not so much the want of men as the want of money; the invading army was limited by the difficulty of obtaining supplies to such a number as might be expected to live on the country in which they were to fight. After their arrival at Troy, when they had won a battle (as they clearly did, for otherwise they could not have fortified their camp), even they appear not to have used the whole of their force, but to have been driven by want of provisions to the cultivation of the Chersonese and to pillage. And in consequence of this dispersion of their forces, the Trojans were enabled to hold out against them during the whole ten years, being always a match for those who remained on the spot. Whereas if the besieging army had brought abundant supplies, and, instead of betaking themselves to agriculture or pillage, had carried on the war persistently with all their forces, they would easily have been masters of the field and have taken the city; since, even divided as they were, and with only a part of their army available at any one time, they held their ground. Or, again, they might have regularly invested Troy, and the place would have been captured in less time and with less trouble. Poverty was the real reason why the achievements of former ages were insignificant, and why the Trojan War, the most celebrated of them all, when brought to the test of facts, falls short of its fame and of the prevailing traditions to which the poets have given authority.

[1] From this passage it is evident that Thucydides regarded the *Iliad* as history, modified somewhat by poetic exaggeration. Historians of to-day do not take this view; they regard the persons and events of the poem as mainly fictitious, while admitting that the story may contain a nucleus of fact.

12. Even in the age which followed the Trojan War, Hellas was still in process of ferment and settlement, and had not time for peaceful growth. The return of the Hellenes from Troy after their long absence led to many changes; quarrels too arose in nearly every city, and those who were expelled by them went forth and founded other cities. Thus in the sixtieth year after the fall of Troy, the Bœotian people, having been expelled from Arnê by the Thessalians, settled in the country formerly called Cadmeis, but now Bœotia: a portion of the tribe already dwelt there, and some of them had joined in the Trojan expedition. In the eightieth year after the war, the Dorians led by the Heraclidæ conquered the Peloponnesus. A considerable time elapsed before Hellas became finally settled; after a while, however, she recovered tranquillity and began to send out colonies. The Athenians colonized Ionia and most of the islands; the Peloponnesians the greater part of Italy and Sicily, and various places in Hellas. These colonies were all founded after the Trojan War.

10. Crete after the Hellenic Colonization

(Homer, *Odyssey*, 170–9)

This excerpt describes the ethnic composition of Crete as it was in the time of Homer. The "Cretans of Crete" (Eteo-Cretans, "genuine Cretans") and the Cydonians were the pre-Hellenic inhabitants, the Minoans. The Pelasgians had possibly migrated from Thessaly, where, according to Homer, was a "Pelasgic Argos"; *cf.* no. 9, n. 3. The Achæans and Dorians were Greeks. Although the idea arose in ancient times, and has found modern supporters, that the Dorians here mentioned came directly from Thessaly, it is far more probable that they were from Peloponnese.

The selection is especially interesting as a description of a part of Hellas after the immigration of the Indo-Europeans but before assimilation had perceptibly advanced.

Yet even so I will tell thee what thou askest and inquirest. There is a land called Crete in the midst of the wine-dark sea, a fair land and a rich, begirt with water, and therein are many men innumerable, and ninety cities. And all have not the same speech, but there is confusion of tongues; there dwell Achæans and there too Cretans of Crete, high of heart,[1] and Cydonians there and

[1] Naturally the natives prided themselves on their descent.

Dorians of waving plumes[1] and goodly Pelasgians. And among these cities is the mighty city Cnossus, wherein Minos ruled in nine-year periods,[2] he who held converse with great Zeus, and was the father of my father, even of Deucalion, high of heart.

11. Ionian, Dorian, and Æolian Colonization

(Herodotus i. 142–50. Macaulay, revised by E. G. S.)

The material contained in this selection Herodotus drew from a study of the situation, climate, soil, customs, and traditions of the Greek cities of Asia Minor. It is highly probable that he found considerable of this work already done by the logographers and especially by Hecatæus, his most distinguished predecessor (see p. 21). While he correctly described the customs, his explanation of their origin, for instance the separation of women and men at tables, does not always seem probable.

142. These Ionians to whom belongs the Panionion[3] had the fortune to build their cities in the most favorable position for climate and seasons of any men whom we know: for neither the regions above Ionia nor those below, neither those toward the East nor those toward the West, produce the same results as Ionia itself, the regions in the one direction being oppressed by cold and moisture, and those in the other by heat and drought. These people do not use all the same speech, but have four different variations of language. First of their cities on the side of the South lies Miletus, and next to it Myus and Prienê. These are settlements made in Caria, and speak the same language with one another; and the following are in Lydia, — Ephesus, Colophon, Lebedus, Teos, Clazomenæ, Phocæa: these cities resemble not at all those mentioned before in the speech which they use, but they agree one with another. There remain besides three Ionian cities, of which two

[1] Of all the inhabitants the Dorians were most conspicuously warriors.

[2] See no. 3 (introd.).

[3] The Panionion was a shrine of all the Ionians for the worship of Poseidon. It was situated on the promontory of Mycale in the territory of Priene, one of the twelve Ionic cities; see ch. 148 of this selection. The league of twelve cities was for protection from foreign enemies, especially from the Lydians and Persians; but the union was loose and the component states often fought among themselves or failed to support one another in foreign wars; see Wilamowitz-Moellendorff, U. v., "Panionion," in *Sitzb. Berl. Akad.* 1906. pp. 38–57.

are established in the islands of Samos and Chios, and one is built upon the mainland, namely Erythræ. Now the men of Chios and of Erythræ use the same form of language, but the Samians have one for themselves alone. Thus there result four separate forms of language.

143. Of these Ionians those of Miletus were sheltered from the danger, since they had sworn an agreement; and those of them who lived in islands had no cause of fear,[1] for the Phœnicians were not yet subjects of the Persians and the Persians themselves were not seamen. Now these were parted off from the other Ionians for no other reason than this: the whole Hellenic nation was at that time weak, but of all its races the Ionian was much the weakest and of least account. With the exception of Athens, indeed, it had no considerable city. The other Ionians, and among them the Athenians, avoided the name, not wishing to be called Ionians, nay even now I perceive that the greater number of them are ashamed of the name;[2] but these twelve cities not only prided themselves on the name but established a temple of their own, to which they gave the name of Panionion, and they made resolution not to grant a share in it to any other Ionians; nor indeed did any ask to share it except those of Smyrna.[3]

144. Likewise the Dorians of that district which is now called the Five Cities, but was formerly called the Six Cities, take care not to admit any of the neighboring Dorians to the temple of Triopion, and even exclude from sharing in it those of their own body who commit any offence as regards the temple. For example,

[1] Herodotus has in mind the situation in 546, after Cyrus had conquered Lydia and was on the point of proceeding against the Greek cities along the coast; see Botsford, *Hellenic History*, ch. x.

[2] At the time when the *History* of Herodotus was being composed, third quarter of the fifth century, the Ionians had greatly declined in creative power and personal worth, and were subject allies of the Athenians. There was reason then that the Athenians should be ashamed of kinship with them; but in the time of which he writes no such reason existed; in fact the Athenians claimed the Ionians as their colonists. The true reason why the Athenians did not call themselves Ionians seems to be, (1) the Ionians were only in part of the same race, having come from other places besides Attica and having mixed extensively with the natives of Asia Minor, (2) the name "Ionian" seems to have originated in Asia Minor and to have extended but faintly as far west as Attica.

[3] The people of Smyrna were originally Æolian, but their city had afterward been taken by the Ionians; see ch. 150.

in the games of the Triopian Apollo they used formerly to set bronze tripods as prizes for the victors, and the rule was that those who received them should not carry them out of the temple but dedicate them then and there to the god. There was a man then of Halicarnassus, whose name was Agasicles, who being a victor paid no regard to this rule, but carried away the tripod to his own house and hung it up there upon a nail. On this ground the other five cities, Lindus, Ialysus and Cameirus, Cos and Cnidus, excluded the sixth city Halicarnassus from sharing in the temple.[1]

145. Upon these people they laid this penalty: but as for the Ionians, I think that the reason why they made of themselves twelve cities and would not receive any more into their body, was because when they dwelt in Peloponnesus there were of them twelve divisions, just as now there are twelve divisions of the Achæans who drove the Ionians out:[2] for first, (beginning from the side of Sicyon) comes Pellenê, then Ægeira and Aigæ, in which last is the river Crathis with a perpetual flow (whence the river of the same name in Italy received its name), and Bura and Helicê, to which the Ionians fled for refuge when they were worsted by the Achæans in fight, and Ægion and Rhypes and Patreis and Phareis and Olenus, where is the great river Peirus, and Dymê and Tritæeis, of which the last alone has an inland position. These now form twelve divisions of the Achæans, and in former times they were divisions of the Ionians.

146. For this reason then the Ionians also made for themselves twelve cities; for at any rate to say that these are any more Ionians than the other Ionians, or have at all a nobler descent, is mere folly, considering that a large part of them are Abantians from Euboea, who have no share even in the name of Ionia, and Minyæ of Or-

[1] Originally a Dorian city, Halicarnassus became so Ionized before the fifth century as to use the Ionic language for official purposes; see the inscription in Ionic of about 460–455 B.C. in Hicks and Hill, no. 27. Herodotus, who was a native of this city, and who wrote in the Ionic dialect, undoubtedly learned it at home.

[2] The supposition of Herodotus is that the northern coast land of Peloponnese, in his time called Achæa, was formerly inhabited by Ionians, who at the time of the Dorian invasion were expelled by the Achæans. These Ionians passed ultimately to Ionia in Asia Minor. The notion that the Ionians of Asia Minor in any way imitated those of northern Peloponnese is baseless. It was usual for early peoples to adopt an arithmetical scheme of organization, in which the numbers three and four play an important part.

chomenus have been mingled with them, and Cadmeians and Dryopians and Phocians who seceded from their native State, and Molossians and Pelasgians of Arcadia, and Dorians of Epidaurus, and many other races have been mingled with them. Those of them who set forth to their settlements from the Prytaneum [1] of Athens and who esteem themselves the most noble by descent of the Ionians, these, I say, brought no women with them to their settlement, but took Carian women, whose parents they slew: and on account of this slaughter these women laid down for themselves a rule, imposing oaths on one another, and handed it on to their daughters, that they should never eat with their husbands, nor should a wife call her own husband by name, for this reason, because the Ionians had slain their fathers and husbands and children and then having done this had them to wife. This happened at Miletus.[2]

147. Moreover some of them set Lycian kings over them, descendants of Glaucus and Hippolochus, while others were ruled by Cauconians of Pylos, descendants of Codrus the son of Melanthus, and others again by princes of these two races combined. Since however these hold on to the name more than the other Ionians, let them be called, if they will, the Ionians of truly pure descent; but in fact all are Ionians who have their descent from Athens and who keep the feast of Apaturia; [3] and this they all keep except the men of Ephesus and Colophon: for these alone of all the Ionians do not keep the Apaturia, and that on the ground of some murder committed.

148. Now the Panionion is a sacred place on the north side of Mycalê, set apart by common agreement of the Ionians for Poseidon of Helicê; and this Mycalê is a promontory of the mainland running out westward towards Samos, where the Ionians gathering together from their cities used to hold a festival which they called the Panionia. [And not only the feasts of the Ionians but also those of all the Hellenes equally are subject to this rule, that their

[1] The City Hall, containing a sacred hearth of the community.

[2] For a time after the colonization the social condition of Ionia closely resembled that of Crete and Laconia; there were lords, serfs, public tables for the men, and military training; *cf.* Botsford, *Hellenic History*, ch. iii. These facts help explain the separation of women and men at table, a custom afterward accentuated by the Orientalizing tendency to seclude women.

[3] The phratric festival of the Ionians; see no. 144.

names all end in the same letter, just like the names of the Persians.][1]

149. These then are the Ionian cities; and those of Æolis are as follows: Kymê, which is called Phriconis, Larisæ, Neonteichus, Temnus, Cilla, Notion, Ægiroessa, Pitanê, Ægaiæ, Myrina, Gryneia; these are the ancient cities of the Æolians, eleven in number, since one, Smyrna, was severed from them by the Ionians; for these cities, that is those on the mainland, used also formerly to be twelve in number. The Æolians had the fortune to settle in a land which is more fertile than that of the Ionians but in respect of climate less favored. 150. Now the Æolians lost Smyrna in the following manner: certain men of Colophon, who had been worsted in party strife and had been driven from their native city, were received there for refuge: and after this the Colophonian exiles watched for a time when the men of Smyrna were celebrating a festival to Dionysus outside the walls, and then they closed the gates against them and got possession of the city. After this, when the whole body of Æolians came to the rescue, they made an agreement that the Ionians should give up the movable goods, and that on this condition the Æolians should abandon Smyrna. When the men of Smyrna had done this, the remaining eleven cities divided them amongst themselves and made them their own citizens. 151. These then are the Æolian cities upon the mainland, with the exception of those situated on Mount Ida, for they are separate from the rest. Of those which are in the islands, there are five in Lesbos, for the sixth which was situated in Lesbos, namely Arisba, was enslaved by the men of Methymna, though its citizens were of the same race as they; and in Tenedos there is one city, and another in what are called the "Hundred Isles." Now the Lesbians and the men of Tenedos, like those Ionians who dwelt in the islands, had no cause for fear; but the remaining cities came to a common agreement to follow the Ionians whithersoever they should lead.[2]

[1] Evidently an interpolation by a Greek grammarian.

[2] Before narrating the conquest of the Asiatic Greeks by the Persians, Herodotus pauses to describe, in the selection here given, the condition of the Greek colonies of Asia Minor. The "common agreement to follow the Ionians" refers to measures of defence against Persia.

12. Homeric Council and Assembly; Preparation for Battle

(Homer, *Iliad*, ii. 1–483. The following selections from Homer, translated by Lang, have been verified on the bases of the Greek text by E. G. S.)

The selection here given presents an interesting view of public life as pictured by Homer. At the same time it affords information on social classes and social feeling as Homer conceives them. Noteworthy are the vast pretensions of the king, and only in a less degree, of the councilors, and their utter contempt for the commons. We may learn from it, too, the essentials of Homeric religion.

Now all other gods and chariot-driving men slept all night long, only Zeus was not holden of sweet sleep; rather was he pondering in his heart how he should do honor to Achilles and destroy many beside the Achæans'[1] ships. And this design seemed to his mind the best, to wit, to send a baneful dream upon Agamemnon son of Atreus. So he spake, and uttered to him winged words: "Come now, thou baneful Dream, go to the Achæans' fleet ships, enter into the hut of Agamemnon son of Atreus, and tell him every word plainly as I charge thee. Bid him call to arms the flowing-haired Achæans with all speed, for that now he may take the wide-wayed city of the Trojans. For the immortals that dwell in the halls of Olympus are no longer divided in counsel, since Hera hath turned the minds of all by her beseeching, and over the Trojans sorrows hang."[2]

So spake he, and the Dream went his way when he had heard the charge. With speed he came to the Achæans' fleet ships, and went to Agamemnon son of Atreus, and found him sleeping in his hut, and ambrosial slumber poured over him. So he stood over his head in seeming like unto the son of Neleus, even Nestor, whom most of all the elders[3] Agamemnon honored; in his likeness spake to him the heavenly Dream:

[1] The host besieging Troy are called Achæans, Argives, and Danaäns, apparently without discrimination. It is not likely that all who are represented as taking part in the expedition against Troy had a common name (Thuc. i. 3; no. 9); but a common name was necessary for Homer's literary purpose, and we may accordingly suppose that the use of the terms Achæan in his poems is essentially literary.

[2] Zeus seems to have harbored no scruple about practising deception, and in general the Homeric gods were far from being patterns of virtue.

[3] The "elders" were the members of his council. Throughout the *Iliad* we find Nestor initiating most of the plans of the council.

"Sleepest thou, son of wise Atreus tamer of horses? To sleep all night through beseemeth not one that is a counsellor, to whom peoples are entrusted [1] and so many cares belong. But now hearken straightway to me, for I am a messenger to thee from Zeus, who though he be afar yet hath great care for thee and pity. He biddeth thee call to arms the flowing-haired Achæans with all speed, for that now thou mayest take the wide-wayed city of the Trojans. For the immortals that dwell in the halls of Olympus are no longer divided in counsel, since Hera hath turned the minds of all by her beseeching, and over the Trojans sorrows hang by the will of Zeus. But do thou keep this in thy heart, nor let forgetfulness come upon thee when honeyed sleep shall leave thee."

So spake the Dream, and departed and left him there, deeming in his mind things that were not to be fulfilled. For indeed he thought to take Priam's city that very day; fond man, in that he knew not the plans that Zeus had in mind, who was willed to bring yet more grief and wailing on Trojans alike and Danaäns throughout the course of stubborn fights. Then woke he from sleep, and the heavenly voice was in his ears. So he rose up sitting, and donned his soft chiton, fair and bright, and cast around him his great cloak, and beneath his glistening feet he bound his fair sandals, and over his shoulder cast his silver-studded sword, and grasped his sire's sceptre, imperishable for ever, wherewith he took his way amid the mail-clad Achæans' ships.

Now went the goddess Dawn to high Olympus, foretelling daylight to Zeus and all the immortals; and the king bade the clear-voiced heralds summon to the assembly the flowing-haired Achæans. So did those summon, and these gathered with speed.[2]

But first the council [3] of the great-hearted elders met beside the ship of king Nestor the Pylos-born. And he that had assembled

[1] Here is a hint of the divine basis of the king's office. Immediately below is an indication that the king was the special object of Zeus' care.

[2] The usual Homeric manner of calling the assembly of the people is here indicated. Ordinarily the warriors formed the assembly, but sometimes the working-people on the ships attended; in fact it was not in this age in any way exclusive.

[3] Here are pictured the summoning of the council of elders and with great brevity the procedure of its meeting. From other meetings we learn that it was customary to continue the discussion till opposition to the proposal ceased. There was no idea of a majority vote.

them framed his cunning counsel: "Hearken, my friends. A dream from heaven came to me in my sleep through the ambrosial night, and chiefly to goodly Nestor was very like in shape and bulk and stature. And it stood over my head and charged me saying: 'Sleepest thou, son of wise Atreus tamer of horses? To sleep all night through beseemeth not one that is a counsellor, to whom peoples are entrusted and so many cares belong. But now hearken straightway to me, for I am a messenger to thee from Zeus, who though he be afar yet hath great care for thee and pity. He biddeth thee call to arms the flowing-haired Achæans with all speed, for that now thou mayest take the wide-wayed city of the Trojans. For the immortais that dwell in the palaces of Olympus are no longer divided in counsel, since Hera hath turned the minds of all by her beseeching, and over the Trojans sorrows hang by the will of Zeus. But keep thou this in thy heart.' So spake the dream and was flown away, and sweet sleep left me. So come, let us now call to arms as we may the sons of the Achæans. But first I will speak to make trial of them as is fitting, and will bid them flee with their benched ships; only do ye from this side and from that speak to hold them back."

So spake he and sat him down; and there stood up among them Nestor, who was king of sandy Pylos. He of good intent made harangue to them and said: "My friends, captains and rulers of the Argives, had any other of the Achæans told us this dream we might deem it a false thing, and rather turn away therefrom; but now he hath seen it who of all Achæans avoweth himself far greatest. So come, let us call to arms as we may the sons of the Achæans."

So spake he, and led the way forth from the council, and all the other sceptred chiefs rose with him and obeyed the shepherd of the host; and the people hastened to them.[1] Even as when the tribes of thronging bees issue from some hollow rock, ever in fresh procession, and fly clustering among the flowers of spring, and some on this hand and some on that fly thick; even so from ships and huts before the low beach marched forth their many tribes by companies to the place of assembly. And in their midst blazed forth Rumor, messenger of Zeus, urging them to go; and so they gathered. And

[1] Here begins the gathering of the people in the assembly. There can be no doubt that the popular assemblies of the Hellenic states originally had this informal character.

the place of assemblage was in an uproar, and the earth echoed again as the hosts sat them down, and there was turmoil. Nine heralds restrained them with shouting, if perchance they might refrain from clamor, and hearken to their kings, the fosterlings of Zeus.[1] And hardly at the last would the people sit, and keep them to their benches and cease from noise. Then stood up lord Agamemnon bearing his sceptre, that Hephæstus had wrought curiously. Hephæstus gave it to king Zeus son of Cronos, and then Zeus gave it to the messenger-god the slayer of Argus;[2] and king Hermes gave it to Pelops the charioteer, and Pelops again gave it to Atreus shepherd of the host. And Atreus dying left it to Thyestes rich in flocks, and Thyestes in his turn left it to Agamemnon to bear, that over many islands and all Argos he should be lord. Thereon he leaned and spake his saying to the Argives[3]:—

"My friends, Danaän warriors, men of Ares' company, Zeus Cronos' son hath bound me with might in grievous blindness of soul; hard of heart is he, for that erewhile he promised me and pledged his nod that not till I had wasted well-walled Ilios should I return; but now see I that he planned a cruel wile and biddeth me return to Argos dishonored, with the loss of many of my folk. So meseems it pleaseth most mighty Zeus, who hath laid low the head of many a city, yea, and shall lay low; for his is highest power. Shame is this even for them that come after to hear; how so goodly and great a folk of the Achæans thus vainly warred a bootless war, and fought scantier enemies, and no end thereof is yet seen. For if perchance we were minded, both Achæans and Trojans, to swear a solemn truce, and to number ourselves, and if the Trojans should gather together all that have their dwellings in the city, and we Achæans should marshal ourselves by tens, and every company choose a Trojan to pour their wine, then would many tens lack a cup-bearer: so much, I say, do the sons of the Achæans outnumber the Trojans that dwell within the city. But allies from many cities, even warriors that wield the spear, are therein, and they

[1] These were Agamemnon, the over-lord, and the members of his council, all of them "kings" (basileës) and all under divine protection.

[2] The meaning of the word Ἀργειφόντης, Argeiphontes, is uncertain; possibly it signifies, not "slayer of Argus," but "appearing in brightness."

[3] The history of the scepter is further evidence of the divine origin of Agamemnon's royalty.

hinder me perforce, and for all my will suffer me not to waste the populous citadel of Ilios. Already have nine years of great Zeus passed away, and our ships' timbers have rotted and the tackling is loosed; while there our wives and little children sit in our halls awaiting us; yet is our task utterly unaccomplished wherefor we came hither. So come, even as I shall bid let us all obey. Let us flee with our ships to our dear native land; for now shall we never take wide-wayed Troy."

So spake he, and stirred the spirit in the breasts of all throughout the multitude, as many as had not heard the council. And the assembly swayed like high sea-waves of the Icarian Main that east wind and south wind raise, rushing upon them from the clouds of father Zeus; and even as when the west wind cometh to stir a deep cornfield with violent blast, and the ears bow down, so was all the assembly stirred, and they with shouting hasted toward the ships; and the dust from beneath their feet rose and stood on high. And they bade each man his neighbor to seize the ships and drag them into the bright salt sea, and cleared out the launching-ways, and the noise went up to heaven of their hurrying homeward; and they began to take the props from beneath the ships.

Then would the Argives have accomplished their return against the will of fate, but that Hera spake a word to Athene: "Out on it, daughter of ægis-bearing Zeus, unwearied maiden! Shall the Argives thus indeed flee homeward to their dear native land over the sea's broad back? But they would leave to Priam and the Trojans their boast, even Helen of Argos, for whose sake many an Achæan hath perished in Troy, far away from his dear native land. But go thou now amid the host of the mail-clad Achæans; with thy gentle words restrain thou every man, neither suffer them to draw their curved ships down to the salt sea."

So spake she, and the bright-eyed goddess Athene disregarded not; but went darting down from the peaks of Olympus, and came with speed to the fleet ships of the Achæans. There found she Odysseus standing, peer of Zeus in counsel, neither laid he any hand upon his decked black ship, because grief had entered into his heart and soul. And bright-eyed Athene stood by him and said "Heaven-sprung son of Laertes, Odysseus of many devices, will ye indeed fling yourselves upon your benched ships to flee homeward to your dear native land? But ye would leave to Priam and the Trojans their boast, even Helen of Argos, for whose sake many an Achæan hath perished in Troy, far from his dear native land. But go thou now amid the host of the Achæans, and tarry not; and with thy gentle words refrain every man, neither suffer them to draw their curved ships down to the salt sea."

So said she, and he knew the voice of the goddess speaking to him, and set him to run, and cast away his mantle, the which his herald gathered up, even Eurybates of Ithaca, that waited on him. And himself he went to meet Agamemnon son of Atreus, and at his hand received the sceptre of his sires, imperishable for ever, wherewith he took his way amid the ships of the mail-clad Achæans.

Whenever he found one that was a captain and a man of mark, he stood by his side, and refrained him with gentle words:[1] "Good sir, it is not seemly to affright thee like a coward, but do thou sit thyself and make all thy folk sit down. For thou knowest not yet clearly what is the purpose of Atreus' son; now is he but making trial, and soon he will afflict the sons of the Achæans. And heard we not all of us what he spake in the council? Beware lest in his anger he evilly entreat the sons of the Achæans. For proud is the soul of heaven-fostered kings; because their honor is of Zeus, and the god of counsel loveth them."

But whatever man of the people he saw and found him shouting, him he drave with his sceptre and chode him with loud words: "Good sir, sit still and hearken to the words of others that are thy betters; but thou art no warrior, and a weakling, never reckoned whether in battle or in council. In no wise can we Achæans all be kings here. A multitude of masters is no good thing; let there be one master, one king, to whom the son of crooked-counselling Cronos hath granted it, [even the sceptre and judgments, that he may rule among you"].[2]

So masterfully ranged he the host; and they hasted back to the assembly from ships and huts, with noise as when a wave of the loud-sounding sea roareth on the long beach and the main resoundeth.

[1] Contrast the bearing of Odysseus toward the captains and the people respectively.

[2] This line seems to have been interpolated.

Now all the rest sat down and kept their place upon the benches, only Thersites [1] still chattered on, the uncontrolled of speech, whose mind was full of words many and disorderly, wherewith to strive against the chiefs idly and in no good order, but even as he deemed that he should make the Argives laugh. And he was ill-favored beyond all men that came to Ilios. Bandy-legged was he, and lame of one foot, and his two shoulders rounded, arched down upon his chest; and over them his head was warped, and a scanty stubble sprouted on it. Hateful was he to Achilles above all and to Odysseus, for them he was wont to revile. But now with shrill shout he poured forth his upbraidings upon goodly Agamemnon. With him the Achæans were sore vexed and had indignation in their souls. But he with loud shout spake and reviled Agamemnon: "Atreides, for what art thou now ill content and lacking? Surely thy huts are full of bronze and many women are in thy huts, the chosen spoils that we Achæans give thee first of all, whene'er we take a town. Can it be that thou yet wantest gold as well, such as some one of the horse-taming Trojans may bring from Ilios to ransom his son, whom I perchance or some other Achæan have led captive; or else some young girl, to know in love, whom thou mayest keep apart to thyself? [2] But it is not seemly for one that is their captain to bring the sons of the Achæans to ill. Soft fools, base things of shame, ye women of Achæa and men no more, let us depart home with our ships, and leave this fellow here in Troy-land to gorge him with meeds of honor, that he may see whether our aid avail him aught or no; even he that hath now done dishonor to Achilles, a far better man than he; for he hath taken away his meed of honor and keepeth it by his own violent deed. Of a very surety is there no wrath at all in Achilles' mind, but he is slack; else this despite, thou son of Atreus, were thy last."

So spake Thersites, reviling Agamemnon shepherd of the host. But goodly Odysseus came straight to his side, and looking sternly at him with hard words rebuked him: "Thersites, reckless in words,

[1] Thersites was a man of the people. It was not forbidden such people to speak in the assembly, but they were under obligations to show respect to the nobles. Thersites failed in the requirement and was punished.

[2] A right of the assembly of warriors after a victory was to divide the spoil and assign shares even to the leaders.

shrill orator though thou art, refrain thyself, nor aim to strive singly against kings. For I deem that no mortal is baser than thou of all that with the sons of Atreus came before Ilios. Therefore were it well that thou shouldest not have kings in thy mouth as thou talkest, and utter revilings against them and be on the watch for departure. We know not yet clearly how these things shall be, whether we sons of the Achæans shall return for good or for ill. Therefore now dost thou revile continually Agamemnon son of Atreus, shepherd of the host, because the Danaän warriors give him many gifts, and so thou talkest tauntingly. But I will tell thee plain, and that I say shall even be brought to pass: if I find thee again raving as now thou art, then may Odysseus' head no longer abide upon his shoulders, nor may I any more be called father of Telemachus, if I take thee not and strip from thee thy garments, thy mantle and chiton that cover thy nakedness, and for thyself send thee weeping to the fleet ships, and beat thee out of the assembly with shameful blows."

So spake he, and with his staff smote his back and shoulders: and he bowed down and a big tear fell from him, and a bloody weal stood up from his back beneath the golden sceptre. Then he sat down and was amazed, and in pain with helpless look wiped away the tear. But the rest, though they were sorry, laughed lightly at him, and thus would one speak looking at another standing by: "Go to, of a truth Odysseus hath wrought good deeds without number ere now, standing foremost in wise counsels and setting battle in array, but now is this thing the best by far that he hath wrought among the Argives, to wit, that he hath stayed this prating railer from his harangues. Never again, forsooth, will his proud soul henceforth bid him revile the kings with slanderous words."

So said the common sort; but up rose Odysseus waster of cities, with the sceptre in his hand. And by his side bright-eyed Athene in the likeness of a herald bade the multitude keep silence, that the sons of the Achæans, both the nearest and the farthest, might hear his words together and give heed to his counsel. He of good intent made harangue to them and said: "Atreides, now surely are the Achæans for making thee, O king, most despised among all mortal men, nor will they fulfil the promise that they pledged thee when they still were marching hither from horse-pasturing Argos; that thou shouldest not return till thou hadst laid well-walled Ilios waste.

For like young children or widow women do they wail each to the other of returning home. Yea, here is toil to make a man depart disheartened. For he that stayeth away but one single month far from his wife in his benched ship fretteth himself when winter storms and the furious sea imprison him; but for us, the ninth year of our stay here is upon us in its course. Therefore do I not marvel that the Achæans should fret beside their beaked ships; yet nevertheless is it shameful to wait long and to depart empty. Be of good heart, my friends, and wait a while, until we learn whether Calchas [1] be a true prophet or no. For this thing verily we know well in our hearts, and ye all are witnesses thereof, even as many as the fates of death have not borne away. It was as it were but yesterday or the day before that the Achæans' ships were gathering in Aulis, freighted with trouble for Priam and the Trojans; and we round about a spring were offering on the holy altars unblemished hecatombs to the immortals, beneath a fair plane-tree whence flowed bright water, when there was seen a great portent: a snake blood-red on the back, terrible, whom the god of Olympus himself had sent forth to the light of day, sprang from beneath the altar and darted to the plane-tree. Now there were there the brood of a sparrow, tender little ones, upon the topmost branch, nestling beneath the leaves; eight were they and the mother of the little ones was the ninth, and the snake swallowed these cheeping pitifully. And the mother fluttered around wailing for her dear little ones; but he coiled himself and caught her by the wing as she screamed about him. Now when he had swallowed the sparrow's little ones and the mother with them, the god who revealed him made of him a sign; for the son of crooked-counselling Cronos turned him to stone, and we stood by and marvelled to see what was done. So when the dread portent brake in upon the hecatombs of the gods, then did Calchas forthwith prophesy, and said: 'Why hold ye your peace, ye flowing-haired Achæans? To us hath Zeus the counsellor shown this great sign, late come, of late fulfilment, the fame whereof shall never perish. Even as he swallowed the sparrow's little ones and herself, the eight wherewith the mother that bare the little ones was the ninth, so shall we war there so many years, but in the tenth year shall we

[1] Calchas the seer (*Il.* i. 68 *sqq.*).

take the wide-wayed city.' So spake the seer; and now are all these things being fulfilled. So come, abide ye all, ye well-greaved Achæans, even where ye are, until we have taken the great city of Priam."

So spake he, and the Argives shouted aloud, and all round the ships echoed terribly to the voice of the Achæans as they praised the saying of god-like Odysseus. And then spake among them knightly Nestor of Gerenia: "Out on it; in very truth ye hold assembly like silly boys that have no care for deeds of war. What shall come of our covenants and our oaths? Let all counsels be cast into the fire and all devices of warriors and the pure drink-offerings and the right hands of fellowship wherein we trusted. For we are vainly striving with words nor can we find any device at all, for all our long tarrying here. Son of Atreus, do thou still, as erst, keep steadfast purpose and lead the Argives amid the violent fray; and for these, let them perish, the one or two Achæans that take secret counsel — though fulfilment shall not come thereof — to depart to Argos first, before they know whether the promise of ægis-bearing Zeus be a lie or no. Yea, for I say that most mighty Cronion pledged us his word that day when the Argives embarked upon their fleet ships, bearing unto the Trojans death and fate; for by his lightning upon our right he manifested signs of good. Therefore let no man hasten to depart home till each have lain by some Trojan's wife and paid back his strivings and groans for Helen's sake. But if any man is overmuch desirous to depart homeward, let him lay his hand upon his decked black ship, that before all men he may encounter death and fate. But do thou, my king, take good counsel thyself, and hearken to another that shall give it; the word that I speak, whate'er it be, shall not be cast away. Separate thy warriors by tribes and by phratries, Agamemnon, that phratry may give aid to phratry and tribe to tribe.[1] If thou do thus and the Achæans hearken to thee, then wilt thou know who among thy captains and who of the common sort is a coward, and who too is brave; for they will fight each after their sort. So wilt thou know whether it is even by divine com-

[1] The division of the host into tribes and phratries was doubtless the military organization of the primitive Greeks. In time the phratries disappeared from the army, but in many states, as in Athens, the tribes continued in it to the end.

mand that thou shalt not take the city, or by the baseness of thy warriors and their ill skill in battle."

And lord Agamemnon answered and said to him: "Verily hast thou again outdone the sons of the Achæans in speech, old man. Ah, father Zeus and Athene and Apollo, would that among the Achæans I had ten such councillors; then would the city of king Priam soon bow beneath our hands, captive and wasted. But ægis-bearing Zeus, the son of Cronos, hath brought sorrows upon me, in that he casteth my lot amid fruitless wranglings and strifes. For in truth I and Achilles fought about a damsel with violent words, and I was first to be angry; but if we can only be at one in council, then will there no more be any putting off the day of evil for the Trojans, no not for an instant. But now go ye to your meal that we may join battle. Let each man sharpen well his spear and bestow well his shield, and let him well give his fleet-footed steeds their meal, and look well to his chariot on every side and take thought for battle, that all day long we may contend in hateful war. For of respite shall there intervene no, not a whit, only that the coming of night shall part the fury of warriors. On each man's breast shall the baldrick of his covering shield be wet with sweat, and his hand shall grow faint about the spear, and each man's horse shall sweat as he draweth the polished chariot. And whomsoever I perceive minded to tarry far from the fight beside the beaked ships, for him shall there be no hope hereafter to escape the dogs and birds of prey."

So spake he, and the Argives shouted aloud,[1] like to a wave on a steep shore, when the south wind cometh and stirreth it; even on a jutting rock, that is never left at peace by the waves of all winds that rise from this side and from that. And they stood up and scattered in haste throughout the ships,[2] and made fires in the huts and took their meal. And they did sacrifice each man to one of the everlasting gods, praying for escape from death and the tumult of battle. But Agamemnon king of men slew a fat bull of five years to most mighty Cronion, and called the elders, the princes of the Achæan host, Nestor first and king Idomeneus, and then the two Aiantes and Tydeus' son, and sixthly Odysseus peer of Zeus

[1] This was an emphatic affirmative, dissent being indicated by silence.

[2] This closes the fullest account of the popular assembly given in Homer's poems.

in counsel. And Menelaüs of the loud war-cry came to him unbidden, for he knew in his heart how his brother toiled. Then stood they around the bull and took the barley-meal. And Agamemnon made his prayer in their midst and said: "Zeus, most glorious, most great, god of the storm-cloud, that dwellest in the heaven, vouchsafe that the sun set not upon us nor the darkness come near, till I have laid low upon the earth Priam's palace smirched with smoke, and burnt the doorways thereof with consuming fire, and rent on Hector's breast his doublet cleft with the blade; and about him may full many of his comrades prone in the dust bite the earth."

So spake he, but not as yet would Cronion grant him fulfilment; he accepted the sacrifice, but made toil to wax unceasingly.

Now when they had prayed and sprinkled the barley-meal they first drew back the bull's head and cut his throat and flayed him, and cut slices from the thighs and wrapped them in fat, making a double fold, and laid raw collops thereon. And these they burnt on cleft wood stript of leaves, and spitted the vitals and held them over Hephæstus' flame. Now when the thighs were burnt and they had tasted the vitals, then sliced they all the rest and pierced it through with spits, and roasted it carefully and drew all off again. So when they had rest from the task and had made ready the banquet, they feasted, nor was their heart aught stinted of the fair banquet. But when they had put away from them the desire of meat and drink, then did knightly Nestor of Gerenia open his saying to them: "Most noble son of Atreus, Agamemnon king of men, let us not any more hold long converse here, nor for long delay the work that god putteth in our hands; but come, let the heralds of the mail-clad Achæans make proclamation to the folk and gather them throughout the ships; and let us go thus in concert through the wide host of the Achæans, that the speedier we may arouse keen war."

So spake he and Agamemnon king of men disregarded not. Straightway he bade the clear-voiced heralds summon to battle the flowing-haired Achæans. So those summoned and these gathered with all speed. And the kings, the fosterlings of Zeus that were about Atreus' son, eagerly marshalled them, and bright-eyed Athene in the midst, bearing the holy ægis that knoweth neither age nor death, whereon wave an hundred tassels of pure gold, all deftly woven and each one an hundred oxen worth. Therewith she passed dazzling through the Achæan folk, urging them forth; and in every man's heart she roused strength to battle without ceasing and to fight. So was war made sweeter to them than to depart in their hollow ships to their dear native land. Even as ravaging fire kindleth a boundless forest on a mountain's peaks, and the blaze is seen from afar, even so as they marched went the dazzling gleam from the innumerable bronze through the sky even unto the heavens.

And as the many tribes of feathered birds, wild geese or cranes or long-necked swans, on the Asian mead by Cayster's stream, fly hither and thither joying in their plumage, and with loud cries settle ever onwards, and the mead resounds; even so poured forth the many tribes of warriors from ships and huts into the Scamandrian plain. And the earth echoed terribly beneath the tread of men and horses. So stood they in the flowery Scamandrian plain, unnumbered as are leaves and flowers in their season. Even as the many tribes of thick flies that hover about a herdsman's steading in the spring season, when milk drencheth the pails, even in like number stood the flowing-haired Achæans upon the plain in face of the Trojans, eager to rend them asunder. And even as the goatherds easily divide the ranging flocks of goats when they mingle in the pasture, so did their captains marshal them on this side and on that, to enter into the fray, and in their midst lord Agamemnon, his head and eyes like unto Zeus whose joy is in the thunder, and his waist like unto Ares and his breast unto Poseidon. Even as a bull standeth out far foremost amid the herd, for he is pre-eminent amid the pasturing kine, even such did Zeus make Atreides on that day, pre-eminent among many and chief amid heroes.

13. The Shield of Achilles and the Scenes from Life that were wrought upon it

(Homer, *Iliad*, xviii. 467–608)

At the request of the goddess Thetis, Hephæstus the divine artisan fashions for her son Achilles a great shield and adorns it with scenes from life.

It was formerly supposed that such Homeric creations were purely imaginary; but since the explorations at Mycenæ, Troy, Cnossus, and other Minoan sites have revealed a pre-Homeric skill in the fashioning and decoration of metals that fills us with astonishment, we can no longer doubt that his pictures of art objects have a basis of reality. We are by no means to suppose that he had knowledge, for example, of a shield precisely like the one here described, but rather that many of the elements of his pictures are real.

In like manner the scenes from life wrought on the shield were probably taken from the world about him but idealized after the manner of a great creative poet.

Thus saying he left her there and went unto his bellows and turned them upon the fire and bade them work. And the bellows, twenty in all, blew on the crucibles, sending deft blasts on every side, now to aid his labor and now anon howsoever Hephæstus willed, and the work went on. And he threw bronze that weareth not into the fire, and tin and precious gold and silver, and next he set on an anvil-stand a great anvil, and took in his hand a sturdy hammer, and in the other he took the tongs.

First fashioned he a shield great and strong, adorning it all over, and set thereto a shining rim, triple, bright-glancing, and therefrom a silver baldrick. Five were the folds of the shield itself; and therein fashioned he much cunning work from his wise heart.

There wrought he the earth, and the heavens, and the sea, and the unwearying sun, and the moon waxing to the full, and the signs every one wherewith the heavens are crowned, Pleiads and Hyads and Orion's might, and the Bear that men call also the Wain, her that turneth in her place and watcheth Orion, and alone hath no part in the baths of Ocean.

Also he fashioned therein two fair cities of mortal men. In the one were espousals and marriage feasts, and beneath the blaze of torches they were leading the brides from their chambers through the city, and loud arose the bridal song. And young men were whirling in the dance, and among them flutes and viols sounded high; and the women standing each at her door were marvelling. But the folk were gathered in the assembly place; for there a strife was arisen, two men striving about the blood-price of a man slain; the one claimed to pay full atonement, expounding to the people, but the other denied him and would take naught; and both were fain to receive arbitrament at the hand of a daysman. And the folk were cheering both, as they took part on either side. And heralds kept order among the folk, while the elders on polished stones were sitting in the sacred circle, and holding in their hands staves from the loud-voiced heralds. Then before the people they rose up and gave judgment each in turn. And in the midst lay two talents of gold, to be given unto him who should plead among them most righteously.[1]

But around the other city were two armies in siege with glittering arms. And two counsels found favor among them, either to sack the town or to share all with the townsfolk even whatsoever substance the fair city held within. But the besieged were not yet yielding, but arming for an ambushment. On the wall there stood to guard it their dear wives and infant children, and with these the old men; but the rest went forth, and their leaders were Ares and Pallas Athene, both wrought in gold, and golden was the vesture they had on. Goodly and great were they in their armor, even as gods, far seen around, and the folk at their feet were smaller. And when they came where it seemed good to them to lay ambush, in a river bed where there was a common watering-place of herds, there they set them, clad in glittering bronze. And two scouts were posted by them afar off to spy the coming of flocks and of oxen with crooked horns. And presently came the cattle, and with them two herdsmen playing on pipes, that took no thought of the guile. Then the others when they beheld these ran upon them and quickly cut off the herds of oxen and fair flocks of white sheep, and slew the shepherds withal. But the besiegers, as they sat before the speech-places [2] and heard much din among the oxen, mounted forthwith behind their high-stepping horses, and came up with speed. Then they arrayed their battle and fought beside the river banks, and smote one another with bronze-shod spears. And among them mingled Strife and Tumult, and fell Death, grasping one man alive fresh-wounded, another without wound, and dragging another dead through the mellay by the feet; and the raiment

[1] We notice that the court was made up of "elders" without the king. The case was not criminal; it was a question of property, brought before the elders for arbitration. The elders gave their opinion in succession while the people cheered. Probably that elder was thought to have spoken most wisely whom the people most vigorously cheered. Here, then, was the germ of popular jurisdiction. The talent here mentioned must have been a small weight, far less than the later Attic talent.

[2] From which the orators spoke; Aristarchus, cited by Lang, Leaf, and Myres.

on her shoulders was red with the blood of men. Like living mortals they hurled together and fought, and haled the corpses each of the other's slain.

Furthermore he set in the shield a soft fresh-ploughed field, rich tilth and wide, the third time ploughed; and many ploughers therein drave their yokes to and fro as they wheeled about. Whensoever they came to the boundary of the field and turned, then would a man come to each and give into his hands a goblet of sweet wine, while others would be turning back along the furrows, fain to reach the boundary of the deep tilth. And the field grew black behind and seemed as it were a-ploughing, albeit of gold, for this was the great marvel of the work.

Furthermore he set therein the demesne-land of a king, where hinds were reaping with sharp sickles in their hands. Some armfuls along the swathe were falling in rows to the earth, whilst others the sheaf-binders were binding in twisted bands of straw. Three sheaf-binders stood over them, while behind boys gathering corn and bearing it in their arms gave it constantly to the binders; and among them the king in silence was standing at the swathe with his staff, rejoicing in his heart. And henchmen apart beneath an oak were making ready a feast, and preparing a great ox they had sacrificed; while the women were strewing much white barley to be a supper for the hinds.

Also he set therein a vineyard teeming plenteously with clusters, wrought fair in gold; black were the grapes, but the vines hung throughout on silver poles. And around it he ran a ditch of cyanus, and round that a fence of tin; and one single pathway led to it, whereby the vintagers might go when they should gather the vintage. And maidens and striplings in childish glee bare the sweet fruit in plaited baskets. And in the midst of them a boy made pleasant music on a clear-toned viol, and sang thereto a sweet Linos-song[1] with delicate voice; while the rest with feet falling together kept time with the music and song.

Also he wrought therein a herd of kine with upright horns, and the kine were fashioned of gold and tin, and with lowing they hurried from the byre to pasture beside a murmuring river, beside the

[1] "Probably a lament for departing summer;" Lang, Leaf, and Myres.

waving reed. And herdsmen of gold were following with the kine, four of them, and nine dogs fleet of foot came after them. But two terrible lions among the foremost kine had seized a loud-roaring bull that bellowed mightily as they haled him, and the dogs and the young men sped after him. The lions rending the great bull's hide were devouring his vitals and his black blood; while the herdsmen in vain tarred on their fleet dogs to set on, for they shrank from biting the lions but stood hard by and barked and swerved away.

Also the glorious lame god wrought therein a pasture in a fair glen, a great pasture of white sheep, and a steading, and roofed huts, and folds.

[Also did the glorious lame god devise a dancing-place like unto that which once in wide Cnossus Dædalus[1] wrought for Ariadne of the lovely tresses. There were youths dancing and maidens of costly wooing, their hands upon one another's wrists. Fine linen the maidens had on, and the youths well-woven doublets faintly glistening with oil. Fair wreaths had the maidens, and the youths daggers of gold hanging from silver baldrics. And now would they run round with deft feet exceeding light, as when a potter sitting by his wheel that fitteth between his hands maketh trial of it whether it run: and now anon they would run in lines to meet each other. And a great company stood round the lovely dance in joy; and among them a divine minstrel was making music on his lyre, and through the midst of them, leading the measure, two tumblers whirled.] [2]

Also he set therein the great might of the River of Ocean around the uttermost rim of the cunningly-fashioned shield.

14 (a). A Visit to the Homeric Palace at Sparta

(Homer, *Odyssey*, iv. 1–46)

Telemachus, son of Odysseus, king of Ithaca, resolves to go to Sparta to make inquiry of King Menelaüs concerning his father, who in returning from Troy has been wandering far and wide, driven by angry Poseidon. Telemachus

[1] Such a dancing-place, orchestra, actually exists in the ruins of the palace at Cnossus; Botsford, *Hellenic History*, ch. ii.

[2] This entire passage is bracketed by Dindorf-Hentze, ed. of 1909.

is accompanied by Peisistratus, son of Nestor, king of Pylos. They make their journey in a two-horse car.

The account of the palace, given in this selection and in the number following, corresponds so closely with the palaces unearthed at Tiryns, Mycenæ, and elsewhere as to force us to the conclusion that Homer either actually saw palaces of the kind or learned of them through a perfectly reliable source.

Excavations on the site of Sparta have shown that no Minoan city had existed there, and that the settlement was made about 1000 B.C. There were, however, Minoan cities in the vicinity and in various parts of Laconia. We should keep in mind the fact that whereas the ancients supposed Homer to have lived before the "Dorian migration," evidence now exists that he lived afterward: he knew, for instance, that there were Dorians in Crete (no. 10) and that at Sparta were Castor and Pollux, deities of the two royal families.

And they came to Lacedæmon lying low among the caverned hills, and drave to the dwelling of renowned Menelaüs. Him they found giving a feast in his house to many friends of his kin, a feast for the wedding of his noble son and daughter. His daughter he was sending to the son of Achilles cleaver of the ranks of men, for in Troy he first had promised and covenanted to give her, and now the gods were bringing about their marriage. So now he was speeding her on her way with chariot and horses, to the famous city of the Myrmidons [1] among whom her lord bare rule. And for his son he was bringing to his home the daughter of Alector out of Sparta, for his well-beloved son, strong Megapenthes, born of a slave woman, for the gods no more showed promise of seed to Helen, from the day that she bare a lovely child, Hermione, as fair as golden Aphrodite. So they were feasting through the great vaulted hall, the neighbors and the kinsmen of renowned Menelaüs, making merry; and among them a divine minstrel was singing to the lyre, and as he began the song two tumblers in the company whirled through the midst of them.

Meanwhile those twain, the hero Telemachus and the splendid son of Nestor, made halt at the entry of the gate, they and their horses. And the lord Eteoneus came forth and saw them, the ready squire of renowned Menelaüs; and he went through the palace to

[1] A tribe in Thessaly non-existent in historical times. The intermarriage between families of different states continued down to the early fifth century, when Athens and doubtless other states became too exclusive to permit the continuance of the custom; Botsford, *Hellenic History*, ch. xiii.

bear the tidings to the shepherd of the people,[1] and standing near spake to him winged words:

'Menelaüs, fosterling of Zeus, here are two strangers, whosoever they be, two men like to the lineage of great Zeus. Say, shall we loose their swift horses from under the yoke, or send them onward to some other host who shall receive them kindly?'

Then in sore displeasure spake to him Menelaüs of the fair hair: 'Eteoneus son of Boëthous, truly thou wert not a fool aforetime, but now for this once like a child thou talkest folly. Surely ourselves ate much hospitable cheer of other men, ere we twain came hither, even if in time to come Zeus haply give us rest from affliction. Nay go, unyoke the horses of the strangers, and as for the men, lead them forward to the house to feast with us.'

So spake he, and Eteoneus hasted from the hall, and called the other ready squires to follow him. So they loosed the sweating horses from beneath the yoke, and fastened them at the stalls of the horses, and threw beside them spelt, and therewith mixed white barley, and tilted the chariot against the shining faces of the gateway, and led the men into the hall divine. And they beheld and marvelled as they gazed throughout the palace of the king, the fosterling of Zeus; for there was a gleam as it were of sun or moon through the lofty palace of renowned Menelaüs. But after they had gazed their fill they went to the polished baths and bathed them.[2] Now when the maidens had bathed them and anointed them with olive oil, and cast about them thick cloaks and doublets, they sat on chairs by Menelaüs, son of Atreus. And a handmaid bare water for the hands in a goodly golden ewer, and poured it forth over a silver basin to wash withal; and to their side she drew a polished table, and a grave dame bare food and set it by them, and laid upon the board many dainties, giving freely of such things as she had by her, and a carver lifted and placed by them platters of divers kinds of flesh, and nigh them he set golden bowls. So Menelaüs of the fair hair greeted the twain and spake:

'Taste ye food and be glad and thereafter when ye have supped, we will ask what men you are; for the blood of your parents is not

[1] A common designation of the Homeric king.

[2] A bathroom with drains has been found in the palace at Tiryns.

lost in you, but ye are of the line of men that are sceptered kings the fosterlings of Zeus; for no churls could beget sons like you.'

So spake he, and took and set before them the fat ox-chine roasted, which they had given him as his own mess by way of honor. And they stretched forth their hands upon the good cheer set before them. Now when they had put from them the desire of meat and drink Telemachus spake to the son of Nestor, holding his head close to him, that those others might not hear:

"Son of Nestor, delight of my heart, mark the flashing of bronze through the echoing halls, and the flashing of gold and of amber and of silver and of ivory. Such like, methinks, is the court of Olympian Zeus within, for the world of things that are here; wonder comes over me as I look thereon." [1]

14 (b). The Visit of Odysseus to the Palace of Alcinoüs, the Phæacian King

(Homer, *Odyssey*, vii. 78–132)

Odysseus in his wanderings has been wrecked on Scheria, the Phæacian island, and rescued by the princess Nausicaa, who sends him to the palace of her father Alcinoüs. The goddess Athena has met and conversed with him on the way, after which she takes her flight to Athens, and Odysseus enters the palace. This selection gives some features of the palace not mentioned in no. 14(a), and presents a charming picture of the garden attached to the palace.

Therewith grey-eyed Athene departed over the unharvested seas, and left pleasant Scheria, and came to Marathon and wide-wayed Athens, and entered the good house of Erechtheus.[2] Meanwhile Odysseus went to the famous palace of Alcinoüs, and his heart was full of many thoughts as he stood there or ever he had reached the threshold of bronze. For there was a gleam as it were of sun or moon through the high-roofed hall of great-hearted Alcinoüs. Brazen were the walls which ran this way and that from the threshold to the inmost chamber, and round them was a frieze of

[1] Excavations of palaces and tombs show that this passage is no great exaggeration of their interior decorations.

[2] These lines have been included in this selection in order to call attention to the existence of a temple to Athena and Erechtheus at Athens at the time of the composition of this poem. It is curious that the poet thought of Marathon as the proper way of approach to Athens.

blue,[1] and golden were the doors that closed in the good house. Silver were the door posts that were set on the brazen threshold, and silver the lintel thereupon, and the hook of the door was of gold. And on either side stood golden hounds and silver, which Hephæstus wrought by his cunning, to guard the palace of great-hearted Alcinoüs being free from death and age all their days. And within were seats arrayed against the wall this way and that, from the threshold even to the inmost chamber [2] and thereon were spread light coverings finely woven, the handiwork of women. There the Phæacian chieftains were wont to sit eating and drinking, for they had continual store. Yea, and there were youths fashioned in gold, standing on firm-set bases, with flaming torches in their hands, giving light through the night to the feasters in the palace. And he had fifty handmaids in the house, and some grind the yellow grain on the millstone, and others weave webs and turn the yarn as they sit, restless as the leaves of the tall poplar tree: [3] and the soft olive oil drops off that linen, so closely is it woven. For as the Phæacian men are skilled beyond all others in driving a swift ship upon the deep, even so are the women the most cunning at the loom, for Athene hath given them notable wisdom in all fair handiwork and cunning wit. And without the courtyard hard by the door is a great garden, of four ploughgates,[4] and a hedge runs round on either side. And there grow tall trees blossoming, pear-trees and pomegranates, and apple-trees with bright fruit, and sweet figs, and olives in their bloom. The fruit of these trees never perisheth neither faileth, winter nor summer, enduring through all the year. Evermore the West Wind blowing brings some fruits to birth and ripens others. Pear upon pear waxes old, and apple

[1] This blue-glass paste has been found in considerable quantities at Tiryns, a fact which proves that Homer in speaking of the frieze is dealing with something real. For patterns of friezes and other interior decorations, see any illustrated work on Minoan civilization.

[2] Such seats, arrayed along the wall, have been found in the palace at Cnossus. For an illustration, see Botsford, *Ancient World*, 71.

[3] In the palace at Cnossus an "industrial quarter" has been found, in which were manufactured by hundreds of hands the objects of use and luxury of the royal family and their attendants. The palace of Alcinoüs was far more modest, and the industrial equipment was on a correspondingly smaller scale. In Homeric life most of the working people of the palace were women.

[4] This measure is unknown.

upon apple, yea and cluster ripens upon cluster of the grape, and fig upon fig. There too hath he a fruitful vineyard planted, whereof the one part is being dried by the heat, a sunny plot on level ground, while other grapes men are gathering, and yet others they are treading in the wine-press. In the foremost row are unripe grapes that cast the blossom, and others there be that are growing black to vintaging.[1] There too, skirting the furthest line, are all manner of garden beds, planted trimly, that are perpetually fresh, and therein are two fountains of water, whereof one scatters his streams all about the garden, and the other runs over against it beneath the threshold of the courtyard, and issues by the lofty house, and thence did the townsfolk draw water. These were the splendid gifts of the gods in the palace of Alcinoüs.

15. The Creation of Earth, Heaven, and the Gods

(Hesiod, *Theogony*, 116–138)

When the Greeks first began to think of the origin of things, their lively imagination hit upon birth as the process of creation. In the following passage Hesiod expresses no idea of the manner in which Chaos, Earth, Tartarus, and Love were formed, but of them were born the remaining elements of the world.

First verily was created Chaos, and then broad-bosomed Earth, the habitation unshaken forever of all the deathless gods who keep the top of snowy Olympus, and misty Tartarus within the wide-wayed Earth, and Love (Eros) which is the fairest among the deathless gods; which looseth the limbs and overcometh within the breasts of all gods and all men their mind and counsel wise.

From Chaos sprang Erebus and black Night; and from Night in turn sprang Bright Sky (Ether) and Day, whom Night conceived and bare after loving union with Erebus. Earth first bare the starry Heaven, of equal stature to herself, that he might cover her utterly about, to the end that there might be for the blessed gods a habitation steadfast forever; and she bare the lofty Hills, the pleasant haunts of the goddess Nymphs who dwell among the gladed Hills. Also she bare the unharvested deep with raging flood,

[1] It is evident that Homer was acquainted with all these fruits, although the garden, particularly with reference to the seasons, is idealized.

even the Sea (Pontus), without the sweet rites of love. And then in the couch of Heaven (Ouranos) she bare the deep-eddying Oceanus, and Cœus and Crius, and Hyperion and Iapetus and Theia and Rhea and Themis and Mnemosyne and Thebe of the golden crown and lovely Tethys. After these was born her youngest son, even Cronos of crooked counsels, of all her children most terrible, and he hated his lusty sire.

16. Earliest Attempts at History in Prose

(Acusilaüs, *Genealogies*)

The numbers of the excerpts are those of Müller, *Frag. Hist. Græc.* I. p. 100 *sqq.* Translated by G. W. B.

7. Deucalion, in whose time was the Deluge, was the son of Prometheus and, as most writers say, of Clymenê, according to Hesiod however, of Pandora; but the authority of Acusilaüs is that he was born of Hesionê, daughter of Oceanus, and of Prometheus.

Well known is the story of Deucalion and Pyrrha, and Acusilaüs testifies that the stones thrown behind their backs were made men.

11 *a*. Throughout his first book Acusilaüs has made it clear that Acheloüs is the eldest of all rivers, for he says: Oceanus married Tethys, his own sister; and of them were born three thousand rivers, and Acheloüs is the eldest and most highly honored.

12. Of Niobe and Zeus was born a son Argos, as Acusilaüs says, and Pelasgus, after whom were named the Pelasgians who inhabited Peloponnese.

13. Before Ogyges nothing was done among the Hellenes worth mentioning, apart from (the deeds of) Phoroneus, his contemporary, and Phoroneus' father Inachus, who, as Acusilaüs narrates, was the first king of the Argives.

15. Hellanicus and Acusilaüs and, in addition to them, Ephorus and Nicolaüs narrate that the ancients lived a thousand years.

16. The account ascribed to Acusilaüs which makes Myceneus son of Sparto, and Sparto of Phoroneus, I could not for my part accept, as the Lacedæmonians themselves would not accept it.

31. The Homeridæ: a genos of Chios, as Acusilaüs states in his third book.

(Hecatæus, *Circuit of the Earth* and *Genealogies*. Translated by G. W. B.) The numbers are those of Müller.

1. I laugh when I see that many have drawn the circuit of the earth with no show of sense, who mark out the Ocean flowing around it, and assume that the earth is a circle, as though drawn by a pair of compasses, and that Asia is equal to Europe (from Herodotus iv. 36).

276. Formerly when Hecatæus the logopoios was in Thebes and had traced his descent and connected his family with a god in the sixteenth generation before his time, the priests of Zeus did for him about the same as they did for me, although I had not traced my lineage. They took me into the sanctuary of the temple, which is of great size, and showing colossal wooden statues in number as they stated, they counted them up to that number; for each chief priest in his lifetime sets up an image of himself. The priests, accordingly, counting and showing me these statues, declared that each one of them was a son succeeding his father, and they went up through the series of images from the image of the one who had died last, until they had declared this of the whole number. When Hecatæus had traced his descent and connected his family with a god in the sixteenth generation, they traced a descent opposed to his, in addition to their numbering, not accepting his idea that a man had been born of a god. In the following manner they traced their counter-descent, saying that each one of the statues had been 'piromis' son of 'piromis,' until they had declared this of the whole three hundred and forty-five statues, each surnamed 'piromis,' and neither with a god nor with a hero did they connect their descent. Now 'piromis' means in Greek 'honorable and good man' (from Herodotus ii. 143).

355. Hecatæus of Miletus in the third book of his *Genealogies*, in describing an Arcadian dinner, says it consisted of barley-bread and pork.

362. After the Pelasgians had been expelled from Attica by the Athenians, whether justly or unjustly I am unable to say except what is reported, that Hecatæus son of Hegesander says in his narratives that it happened unjustly; for when the Athenians saw the land at the foot of Hymettus which they had given them to

inhabit as pay for building the wall around the Acropolis, — when they saw this land well cultivated which was formerly barren and worthless, they entertained a grudge, and a desire for the land, and for that reason expelled them, not alleging any other pretext (from Herodotus vi. 137).

17. Certain Kings of Attica

(Philochorus, *Atthis*, ii, quoted by Eusebius, *Chronica*, i; Müller, *Frag. Hist. Græc.* I. 385. 10. Translated by G. W. B.)

In their attempts to reconstruct the regal period of their country the chroniclers adopted the habit of assigning existing customs and institutions to the various kings — a process illustrated by the following selections.

Cecrops the diphyes (double-natured) reigned as king over Akte, now Attica, fifty years, so called because of the height of his person, as Philochorus says, or because, being an Egyptian, he understood two languages.[1]

(Philochorus, *op. cit.* in Strabo ix. 20; Müller, *op. cit.* I. 386. 11)

Philochorus says that as the country was harried from the sea by Carians and on the land by the Bœotians, whom they called Aones, Cecrops first gathered the multitude into twelve cities, whose names are Cecropia,[2] Tetrapolis, Epacria, Deceleia, Eleusis, Aphidna, which many call also by the plural number Aphidnæ, Thoricus, Brauron, Cytherus, Sphettus, Cephisia, Phalerus. Later, too, Theseus is said to have concentrated the twelve into the one city which now exists.

(Philochorus, *op. cit.* in Athenæus ii. 7)

Philochorus relates that Amphictyon,[3] king of the Athenians, having learned of Dionysus the art of mixing wine, was the first man who ever did mix it, and that it is owing to him that men who have been drinking on his system can afterward walk straight, when before they used to stagger about after drinking clear wine. On

[1] In myth he was half-man, half-serpent, and in this respect "double-natured"; but the chronicler has rationalized the myth, as was the habit of such writers.

[2] Traditionally the earlier name of Athens.

[3] The historical truth at the basis of this mythical king is the fact that Athens in early time became a member of the Delphic amphictyony.

this account he erected an altar to the straight Dionysus in the temple of the Seasons; for they are the Nymphs who cherish the fruit of the vine. Near it he built also an altar to the Nymphs as a memorial to all who used diluted drinks; for the Nymphs are said to have been the nurses of Dionysus. Further he made a law to bring unmixed wine after meals, only just enough to taste, as a token of the power of the Good Deity. But the rest of the wine was put on the table ready diluted in whatever quantity any one chose. Then he enjoined the guests to invoke in addition the name of Zeus Saviour, for the sake of instructing and reminding the drinkers that by using wine in that way they would be preserved from injury.

18. The Fully Developed List of Kings of Argos and of Athens

Homer, Hesiod, and the logographers reckoned time by generations and by reigns. Gradually greater precision was acquired, and attempts were made to reconstruct the lists of kings with the length of their respective reigns. In earlier time the list of kings of a country contained few names, but new names were gradually inserted. In the Alexandrian period scholars busied themselves with such chronologies, and their work has come down to us mainly through Eusebius, who lived in the fourth century A.D. The two lists given below will sufficiently illustrate the nature of their work. It is to be noted that perhaps not a single name in either list (or at most one or two) is that of a real person.

ARGIVE AND ATHENIAN KINGS

(Eusebius, *Chronicle*, ed. Karst, p. 148 *sq.*)

ARGIVE KINGS		ATHENIAN KINGS	
Inachus	50 yrs.		
Phoroneus	60		
Apis	35		
Argus	70	In the thirty-second year of the reign of Phorbas, the first (king) reigned over the Athenians	
Criasus	54	1. Cecrops Diphyes	50 yrs.
Phorbas	35	2. Cranaus	9
Triopas	47	3. Amphiction	10
Crotopus	21	4. Erichthonius	50
Sthenelus	11	5. Pantion	40
Danaüs	50	6. Erechtheus	50
Linceus	41	7. Cecrops II	40

ARGIVE KINGS		ATHENIAN KINGS	
Abas	23	8. Pantion	25
Proïtus	17	9. Egeus (son) of Pantion	48
Acrisius	31	10. Theseus (son) of Egeus	30
		11. Menestheus (son) of Peteus	23
		12. Demophon (son) of Theseus	33
		13. Oxintes	12
		14. Aphidas	1
		15. Thimoitus	8
		16. Melanthus	37
		17. Codrus	21

19. Dates of Certain Great Events

(Porphyry, *Philosophic History*, i, quoted by Eusebius, *Chronicle*, i. 31. Migne, *Patrologiæ Græcæ*, XIX. 220.)

From the capture of Ilium to the descent of the Heracleids upon Peloponnese, according to Apollodorus, 80 years elapsed; then from the descent to the colonization of Ionia, 60 years; thence to Lycurgus, 159 years; from Lycurgus to the first Olympiad, 108 years; the sum total of years from the capture of Ilium to the first Olympiad was 407 years.

For bibliography on the Homeric age, see p. 6.

BIBLIOGRAPHY FOR THE MINOAN CIVILIZATION

I. Sources. — Substantially the only sources are the objects discovered in explorations. They may be studied directly or by means of illustrations and descriptions. In addition to the illustrations in the works mentioned below, see especially Evans, A., *Atlas of Cnossian Antiquities* (Macmillan, 1915); Maraghiannis, G., *Antiquités crétoises*, 2 vols. (Vienna, 1906, 1911). Traditions from that period have been so contaminated by later conditions as to retain little or no independent value.

II. General. — Botsford, *Hellenic History*, ch. ii.; Bury, *History of Greece* (new ed. 1913), ch. i; Hall, *Ancient History of the Near East*, 31–72; Meyer, E., *Gesch. d. Alt.* I. pp. 677–803.

Schuchhardt, C., *Schliemann's Excavations*, trans. by E. Sellers (Macmillan, 1891), contains the results of his labors, and the substance of his writings; Hawes, C. H. and H., *Crete the Forerunner of Greece* (Harper, 1909), excellent scholarly summary, without illustrations; Evans, E., *Nine Minoan Periods* (Macmillan, 1915), by the excavator of Cnossus; Baikie, J., *Sea-Kings of Crete* (London: Adam and Ch. Black, 1910), popular but generally accurate; Mosso, A., *Palaces of Crete* (Putnam, 1907), useful for special topics; *Dawn of Mediterranean Civilization* (N. Y.: Baker and Taylor, 1911), asserts the existence of a copper age of considerable length; Dessaud, R., *Les civilizations prêhellênique dans le bassin de la mer Egée* (2d ed., Paris, 1914), the most thoroughly illustrated treatment of the general subject; Lichtenberg, R. F. v., *Aegäische Kultur* (Leipzig, 1911); Fimmen, D., *Die Zeit und Dauer der kretisch-mykenischen Kultur* (Freiburg, 1909), most valuable for chronology; Myres, J. L., *Dawn of History* (Holt, 1911), general study of beginnings in the ancient world; Tsountas, C., and Manatt, J. I., *Mycenæan Age* (Houghton Mifflin, 1897), a brilliant work, in need of revision; Ridgeway, W., *Early Age of Greece*, I (Cambridge: University Press, 1901); Hall, H. R., *Ægean Archæology* (London: Warner, 1915).

III. Special. — (*a*) Of primary importance are the reports of excavators, as those of Evans and others, *Annual of British School at Athens*, beginning with vol. VII (1900–1901); *Journal of Hellenic Studies*, beginning 1899; Boyd, H., in *Transactions of the Department of Archæology*, University of Pennsylvania, I (1904), for her excavations at Gournia; *Monumenti Antichi*, beginning XII (1900–1901), for excavations at Phæstus, etc.; Dörpfeld, W., and others, *Troja und Ilion*, 2 vols. (Athens, 1902); Seager, R. B., *Exploration in the Island of Mochlos:* American School of Classical Studies at Athens, 1912; *Excavations on the Island of Pseira* (University Museum, Phila. 1910); Atkinson, T. D., and others, *Excavations at Philakopi in Melos* (Macmillan, 1904); Wace, A. J. B., and Thompson, M. S., *Prehistoric Thessaly* (Cambridge: University Press, 1912); Ashmolean Museum *Report*, 1907; Frickenhaus, A., and others, *Tiryns. Die Ergebnisse der Ausgrabungen des K. deutsch. arch. Inst. in Athen* (Athens, 1912); Hall, E. H., *Excavations in Eastern Crete*, Anthropological Publications, University of Pennsylvania, 1913.

(*b*) *Palaces and Tombs.* — Dörpfeld, W., "Die kretischen, mykenischen und homerischen Paläste," in *Ath. Mitt.* XXX (1905). 257–97; Mackenzie, D., "Cretan Palaces and the Ægean Civilization," in *Annual of the British School at Athens*, XI (1904–1905). 181–223; XII. 216–57; XIII. 423–45; XIV. 343–422 (aims to derive civilization from north Africa); Noack, F., *Homerische Paläste* (Leipzig, 1903); *Ovalhaus und Palast in Kreta* (Teubner, 1908), important; Evans, A., "Prehistoric Tombs of Knossos," in *Archæologia*, LIX (1905). 391–562; Lichtenberg, R. F. v., *Haus, Dorf, Stadt* (Leipzig, 1909).

(*c*) *Pottery and Painting.* — Hall, E. H., *Decorative Art of Crete in the Bronze Age* (Phila.: Winston, 1907); Mackenzie, D., "Pottery of Knossus," in *J. H. S.* XXIII (1903). 157–206; "Middle Minoan Pottery," *ib.* XXVI. 243–67; Forsdyke, E. J., "Minoan Pottery from Cyprus and the Origin of the Mycenæan Style," *ib.* XXXI. 110–18; Furtwängler and Loeschke, *Mykenische Vasen*

(Berlin, 1886); Pfuhl, E., "Die griechische Malerei," in *N. Jahrb.* XIV (1911). 161–85.

(*d*) *Religion.* — Harrison, J. E., *Themis: A Study of the Social Origins of Greek Religion* (Cambridge University Press, 1912), speculative; Prinz, H., "Bemerkungen zur altkretischen Religion," *Ath. Mitt.* XXXV (1910), 149–76; Reichel, A., "Die Stierspiele in der kretisch-mykenischen Kultur," *Ath. Mitt.* XXIV (1909). 85-99, has religious connections.

Aly, W., "Ursprung und Entwickelung der kretischen Zeusreligion," in *Philologus*, LXXI (1912). 457–78; Bethe, "Minos," in *Rhein. Mus.* LXV (1910). 200–32; Frothingham, A. L., "Medusa, Apollo, and the Great Mother," in *Am. Journ. Arch.* XV (1911). 349–77, connections with Crete; Pernier, L., "Culto di Rhea a Phaestos," in *Saggi di Storia antica*, etc. (Rome, 1910), 241–53; Schaefer, J., *De Jove apud Cretas culto.* Diss. (Halle, 1912).

(*e*) *Writing.* — Evans, A., *Scripta Minoa*, I (Oxford: Clarendon Press, 1909); Sundwall, J., *Ueber die vorgriechische linearische Schrift auf Kreta* (brief study, 1914); Meyer, E., "Der Diskus von Phaestos und die Philister auf Kreta," in *Sitzb. Berl. Akad.* 1909, pp. 1022–9; Hall, H. R., "Note on the Phæstus Disk," in *J. H. S.* XXXI (1911). 119–23; Hempl, G., in *Harper's Monthly*, Jan. 1911, pp. 187–98, vain attempt at solution.

(*f*) *Problems and Connections.* — Burrows, R. M., *Discoveries in Crete and their Bearing on the History of Ancient Civilization* (London: Murray, 1907); Lichtenberg, R. F. v., in *Mitt. Vorderas. Ges.* XVI (1912), for influence on Egypt and Palestine; Müller, W. Max, *Asien und Europa nach altägyptischen Denkmälern* (Leipzig, 1893); Baur, P., "Pre-Roman Antiquities in Spain," in *Am. Journ. Arch.* XI (1907). 182–93.

(*g*) *The Ethnic Question.* — Sergi, G., *Mediterranean Race* (Scribner, 1901); Conway, R. S., "Pre-Hellenic Inscriptions of Præsos," in *B. S. A.* VIII (1901–1902). 125–56; "A Third Eteo-Cretan Fragment," *ib.* X. 115–26; Kiessling, M., "Das ethnische Problem des alten Griechenland," in *Zeitschr. f. Ethnol.* XXXVII (1905). 1009–24; Luschan, F. v., "Beiträge zur Anthropologie von Kreta," *ib.* XLV. 307–93, includes ancient period; Hirt, H., *Die Indogermanen*, 2 vols. (Strassburg, 1905, 1907); Schmidt, L., "Die Ursachen der Völkerwanderung," in *N. Jahrb.* VI (1903). 340–50; Meltzer, H., "Griechen und Germanen," *ib.* XXIX (1912). 385–405; Forrer, R., *Reallexikon der prähistorischen, klassischen und frühchristlichen Altertümer* (Berlin, 1907); Schrader, O., *Reallexikon der indogermanischen Altertumskunde* (Strassburg, 1901); *Sprachvergleichung und Urgeschichte*, 2 vols. (3d ed., Jena, 1906, 1907).

Kretschmer, P., *Einleitung in die Geschichte der griech. Sprache* (Göttingen, 1896), epoch-making; Fick, A., *Vorgriechische Ortsnamen als Quelle für die Vorgeschichte Griechenlands verwertet* (Göttingen, 1905); Hoffmann, O., *Geschichte der griech. Sprache*, I (Leipzig, 1911); Buck, C. D., *Introduction to the Study of the Greek Dialects* (Ginn, 1910); "Interrelations of the Greek Dialects," in *Class. Philol.* II (1907). 241 ff.

Meyer, E., "Die Pelasger," in *Forsch. zur alt. Gesch.* I (1892). 1–124;

Myres, J. L., "History of the Pelasgian Theory," in *J. H. S.* XXVII (1907). 170 *sqq.*; Aly, W., *Karer und Leleger*, in *Philol.* LXVIII (1909). 428–44.

(*h*) *Miscellaneous.* — Müller, S., *L'Europe préhistorique* (Paris, 1907); Kropp, P., *Die minoisch-mykenische Kultur im Lichte der Ueberlieferung bei Herodot* (Leipzig, 1905); Assmann, E., "Zur Vorgeschichte von Kreta," in *Philol.* LXVII (1908). 161–201; Fimmen, D., "Die Besiedlung Böotiens bis in frühgriech. Zeit," in *N. Jahrb.* XV (1912). 521–41; Frost, K. T., "The Critias and Minoan Crete," in *J. H. S.* XXXIII (1913). 189–206.

CHAPTER III

COLONIZATION

During the Period 750–479 B.C.

THE period extending from about 750 to the close of the great war with Persia, 479, is one of colonial expansion, of economic development from pastoral and agricultural conditions to commerce and industry, and of such progress in literature, art, and intelligence, including the beginnings of science and philosophy, that it may well be named the era of "intellectual awakening." The colonial movement did not continue to the end of the period, but came substantially to an end about the middle of the sixth century.

20. THE PHYSICAL CONDITION OF EUROPE AND ITS EFFECT ON THE INHABITANTS

(Strabo ii. 5. 26)

Now the whole of Europe is habitable with the exception of a small part which cannot be dwelt in, on account of the severity of the cold, and which borders on the Hamaxœci,[1] who dwell by the Don, Mæotis, and Dnieper. The wintry and mountainous parts of the habitable earth would seem to afford by nature but a miserable means of existence; nevertheless, by good management, places scarcely inhabited by any but robbers may be got into condition. Thus the Greeks, though dwelling amidst rocks and mountains, live in comfort, owing to their economy in government and the arts and all the other appliances of life. Thus, too, the Romans, after subduing numerous nations who were leading a savage life, either induced by the rockiness of their countries or want of ports or severity of the cold, or for other reasons scarcely habitable, have taught the arts of commerce to many who were formerly in total ignorance, and spread civilization among the most savage. Where the climate is equable and mild, nature herself does much toward

[1] "Dwellers in wagons," a nomadic people.

the production of these advantages. As in such favored regions everything inclines to peace, so those which are sterile generate bravery and a disposition to war. These two races receive mutual advantages from each other, the one aiding by their arms, the other by their husbandry, arts, and institutions. Harm must result to both when failing to act in concert, but the advantage will lie on the side of those accustomed to arms, except in instances where they are overpowered by multitudes. This continent is very much favored in this respect, being interspersed with plains and mountains, so that everywhere the foundations of husbandry, civilization, and hardihood lie side by side. The number of those who cultivate the arts of peace, is, however, the most numerous, which preponderance over the whole is mainly due to the influence of the government, first of the Greeks, and afterward of the Macedonians and Romans.[1]

Europe has thus within itself resources both for war [and peace]. It is amply supplied with warriors, and also with men fitted for the labors of agriculture, and the life of the towns. It is likewise distinguished for producing in perfection those fruits of the earth necessary to life, and all the useful metals. Perfumes and precious stones must be imported from abroad, but as far as the comfort of life is concerned, the want or the possession of these can make no difference. The country likewise abounds in cattle, while of wild beasts the number is but small. Such is the general nature of this continent.

21. The Fertility of Sicily; the Worship of Demeter

(Diodorus v. 2 *sq.*)

Diodorus, who was a Sicilian, writes with great enthusiasm, as well as with truth, of the beauty and fertility of his native island.

Having designed this book as a description of the islands, we will first speak of Sicily, as it is the most important of the islands and stands first in the antiquity of its stories.

In ancient times it was called Trinacria from its form. After-

[1] The alliances and federations of the Greeks contributed to peace, but far greater progress was made in this direction by the Macedonian and Roman empires, particularly the latter.

ward it was named Sicania by the Sicanians, its first inhabitants, and at last called Sicily, from the Sicilians,[1] who, with all their people, transported themselves thither from Italy.

In circuit it is four thousand three hundred and sixty stadia;[2] for one of the three sides, from the promontory Pelorus to Lilybæum, is a thousand and seven hundred stadia; the other from Lilybæum to Pachinum, a promontory of Syracuse, runs out in length a thousand and five hundred stadia. The rest contains a thousand one hundred and forty stadia.

The Sicilian inhabitants (from old tradition continued down to them from their forefathers) say that this island is dedicated to Demeter and Persephonê. Some of the poets feign that at the marriage of Pluto and Persephonê this island was given to the new bride by Zeus for a present. The most approved authors say that the Sicanians, who were the ancient possessors, were the indigenous inhabitants of this isle, and that the goddesses whom we have before mentioned appeared first in their country; and that the fertility of the soil was such, that grain first grew here of itself, which the most eminent of all the poets confirms in these words: —

> Within this island all things grow,
> Without the help of seed or plow,
> As wheat and barley, with the vine
> From whence proceed both grapes and wine,
> Which with sweet showers from above
> Are brought to ripeness by great Jove.

For in the territory of Leontini and in many other parts of Sicily there grows up wild wheat at this very day. If it be asked in what part of the world these grains were first known, before the use of corn was found out, it is most probable that they were first brought to the best and richest country, and therefore upon that account we see that the Sicilians most especially worship those goddesses who were the first discoverers of these fruits. That the rape of Persephonê was in this country (they say) is most clear and evident from hence, that neither of these goddesses ever resided in

[1] By the "Sicilians" is here meant the Siculi, whose origin ancient writers assign to Italy.

[2] A stadium is 600 Greek feet.

any other place but in this island, wherein they delighted above all others.[1] The rape, they say, was in the meadows of Enna, not far from the city, a place decked with violets and all sorts of other flowers, affording a most beautiful and pleasant prospect. It is said that the fragrance of the flowers is such, that the dogs sent out to hunt the game thereby lose the benefit of their sense, and are made incapable by their scent to find out the prey. This meadow-ground, in the middle and highest part of it, is level and well watered, but all the borders round are craggy, guarded with high and steep precipices, and it is supposed to lie in the very heart of Sicily, whence it is called by some the navel of Sicily. Near at hand are groves, meadows, and gardens, surrounded with morasses, and a deep cave with a passage underground opening toward the north, through which, they say, Pluto passed in his chariot when he forced away Persephonê. In this place the violets and other sweet flowers flourish continually all the year long, and present a pleasant and delightsome prospect to the beholders over all the flourishing plain.

22. The Colonization of Sicily

(Thucydides vi. 2–5. Jowett, verified by E. G. S.)

Thucydides probably drew this information from Antiochus of Syracuse, a slightly older contemporary, who wrote a treatise on *Sicilian and Italian Affairs*, now lost. We may contrast the serious tone of this selection with the uncritical, semi-poetic passage from Diodorus given under the preceding number.

2. I will now describe the original settlement of Sicily, and enumerate the nations which it contained. Oldest of all were (1) the Cyclopes and Læstrygones,[2] who are said to have dwelt in a district of the island; but who they were, whence they came, or whither they went, I cannot tell. We must be content with the legends of the poets, and every one must be left to form his own opinion. (2) The Sicanians appear to have succeeded these early races,

[1] These claims to the exclusive possession of the Goddesses Twain and to the earliest use of grain are merely evidence of an exaggerated insular pride. In like manner the Athenians claimed that Demeter gave them grain originally and that through them the knowledge of its cultivation extended to the rest of Hellas. There is no more truth in the one claim than in the other.

[2] It hardly need be said that these two races are mythical.

although according to their own account they were still older; for they profess to have been children of the soil. But the fact is that they were Iberians, and were driven from the river Sicanus in Iberia by the Ligurians.[1] Sicily, which was originally called Trinacria, received from them the name Sicania. To this day the Sicanians inhabit the western parts of the island. (3) After the capture of Troy, some Trojans who had escaped from the Achæans came in ships to Sicily; they settled near the Sicanians, and both took the name of Elymi. The Elymi had two cities, Eryx and Egesta. (4) These were joined by certain Phocians, who had also fought at Troy, and were driven by a storm first to Libya and thence to Sicily. (5) The Sicels were originally inhabitants of Italy, whence they were driven by the Opici, and passed over in Sicily; according to a probable tradition they crossed upon rafts, taking advantage of the wind blowing from the land, but they may have found other ways of effecting a passage; there are Sicels still in Italy, and that country itself was so called from Italus, a Sicel king.[2] They entered Sicily with a large army, and defeating the Sicanians in battle, drove them back to the southern and western parts of the country; from them the island, formerly Sicania, took the name of Sicily. For nearly three hundred years after their arrival until the time when the Hellenes came to Sicily they occupied the most fertile districts, and they still inhabit the central and southern regions. (6) The Phœnicians at one time had settlements all round the island.[3] They fortified headlands on the sea-coast, and settled in the small islands adjacent, for the sake of trading with the Sicels; but when the Hellenes began to find their way by sea to Sicily in greater numbers, they withdrew from the larger part of the island, and forming a union established themselves in Motya, Soloeis, and Panormus, in

[1] Most modern scholars, accordingly, connect the Sicanians in stock with the Iberians of Spain and the Ligurians of northern Italy. Others (*cf.* De Sanctis, *Storia dei Romani*, I. 98 *sq.*) consider the Sicani and Siculi branches of the same stock, which they pronounce Italic.

[2] The hypothesis that the Sicels, Siculi, were immigrants from Italy, and of Italic stock, receives support from the fact that certain names, common and proper, in their language seem related to Latin.

[3] The absence of archæological remains throws doubt upon this statement. Yet it is certain that the Phœnicians receded to some extent in the face of the Hellenic colonization.

the neighborhood of the Elymi, partly trusting to their alliance with them, and partly because this is the point at which the passage from Carthage to Sicily is shortest. Such were the barbarian nations who inhabited Sicily, and these were their settlements.

3. (7) The first Hellenic colonists sailed from Chalcis in Eubœa under the leadership of Thucles, and founded Naxos;[1] there they erected an altar in honor of Apollo the Founder, which is still standing without the city, and on this altar religious embassies sacrifice before they sail from Sicily. (8) In the following year Archias, one of the Heraclidæ, came from Corinth and founded Syracuse, first driving the Sicels out of the island of Ortygia; and there the inner city, no longer surrounded by the sea, now stands; in process of time the outer city was included within the walls and became populous. (9) In the fifth year after the foundation of Syracuse Thucles and the Chalcidians went forth from Naxos, and driving out the Sicels by force of arms, founded first Leontini, then Catana. The Catanæans however chose a founder of their own, named Evarchus.

4. (10) About the same time Lamis came from Megara bringing a colony to Sicily, where he occupied a place called Trotilus, upon the river Pantacyas; but he soon afterwards joined the settlement of the Chalcidians at Leontini; with them he dwelt a short time, until he was driven out; he then founded Thapsus, where he died. His followers quitted Thapsus and founded the city which is called the Hyblæan Megara; Hyblon, a Sicel king, had betrayed the place to them and guided them thither. There they remained two hundred and forty-five years, and were then driven out of their town and land by Gelon[2] the tyrant of Syracuse; but before they were driven out, and a hundred years after their own foundation, they sent out Pamillus and founded Selinus; he had come from Megara, their own mother state, to take part in the new colony. (11) In the forty-fifth year after the foundation of Syracuse, Antiphemus of Rhodes and Entimus of Crete came with their followers and together built Gela. The city was named from the river Gela, but the spot which is now the Acropolis and was first fortified is called

[1] The Greek colonization began about 750 B.C. The dates of the various foundings are unreliable.

[2] Gelon became tyrant of Syracuse in 485; Busolt, *Griech. Gesch.* II. 785.

Lindii. The institutions of the new settlement were Dorian. Exactly a hundred and eight years after their own foundation the inhabitants of Gela founded Acragas (Agrigentum), which they named from the river Acragas;[1] they appointed Aristonoüs and Pystilus founders of the place, and gave to it their own institutions. (12) Zanclê was originally colonized by pirates who came from Cymê the Chalcidian city in Opicia; these were followed by a large body of colonists from Chalcis and the rest of Eubœa, who shared in the allotment of the soil. The first settlement was led by Perieres of Cymê, the second by Cratæmenes of Chalcis. Zanclê was the original name of the place, a name given by the Sicels because the site was in shape like a sickle, for which the Sicel word is Zanclon. These earlier settlers were afterward driven out by the Samians and other Ionians, who when they fled from the Persians found their way to Sicily. Not long afterward Anaxilas, tyrant of Rhegium, drove out these Samians. He then repeopled their city with a mixed multitude, and called the place Messenê after his native country.

5. Himera was colonized from Zanclê by Eucleides, Simus, and Sacon. Most of the settlers were Chalcidian, but the Myletidæ, Syracusan exiles who had been defeated in a civil war, took part in the colony. Their language was a mixture of the Chalcidian and Doric dialects, but their institutions were mainly Chalcidian. (13) Acræ and Casmenæ were founded by the Syracusans, Acræ seventy years after Syracuse, and Casmenæ nearly twenty years after Acræ. Camarina was originally founded by the Syracusans exactly a hundred and thirty-five years after the foundation of Syracuse; the founders were Dascon and Menecolus. But the Camarinæans revolted, and as a punishment for their revolt were violently expelled by the Syracusans. After a time Hippocrates, tyrant of Gela, receiving the territory of Camarina as the ransom of certain Syracusan prisoners, became the second founder of the place, which he colonized anew. The inhabitants were once more driven out by Gelon, who himself colonized the city for the third time.

[1] See no. 23.

23. Acragas

(Polybius ix. 27)

The city of Acragas is not only superior to most cities in the particulars I have mentioned, but above all in beauty and elaborate ornamentation. It stands within eighteen stadia of the sea, so that it participates in every advantage from that quarter; while its circuit of fortifications is particularly strong both by nature and by art. For its wall is placed on a rock, steep and precipitous, on one side naturally, on the other side artificially. And it is inclosed by rivers: for along the south side flows the river of the same name as the town, and along the west and southwest, the river called Hypsas. The citadel overlooks the city exactly at the southeast, girt on the outside by an impassable ravine, and on the inside with only one approach from the town. On the top of it is a temple of Athena and of Zeus Atabyrius as at Rhodes: for as Acragas was founded by the Rhodians, it is natural that this deity should have the same appellation as at Rhodes. The city is sumptuously adorned in other respects also with temples and colonnades. The temple of Zeus Olympius is still unfinished, but in its plan and dimensions it seems to be inferior to no temple in Greece.

24. Cumæ, Dicæarchia, and Naples

(Strabo v. 4. 4–7. Hamilton and Falconer, revised by E. G. S.)

It is to be noted that in the time of Strabo the country described in this selection was far less populous and wealthy than it had been before the Roman conquest.

After these [cities] comes Cumæ, the most ancient settlement of the Chalcidenses and Cumæans, for it is the oldest of all [the Greek cities] in Sicily or Italy. The leaders of the expedition, Hippocles the Cumæan and Megasthenes of Chalcis, mutually agreed that one of the nations should have the management of the colony, and the other the honor of conferring upon it its own name. Hence at the present day it is named Cumæ, while at the same time it is said to have been founded by the Chalcidenses. Formerly this city was prosperous, as well as the Phlegræan plain, which mythology has made the scene of the adventures of the giants, for no other reason, as it appears, than because the fertility of the country had given rise to battles for its possession.[1] Afterwards, however, the Campanians becoming masters of the city, inflicted many outrages on the inhabitants, and even took their wives. Still, however, there remain numerous traces of the Grecian taste, both in their temples and in their laws. Some are of opinion that Cumæ was so called from τὰ κύματα, the waves, the sea-coast near having a heavy and incessant surf. These people have excellent fisheries. On the shores of this gulf there is a scrubby forest, extending over numerous stadia of parched and sandy land. This they call the Gallinarian wood. It was there that the admirals of Sextus Pompeius assembled their gangs of pirates, at the time when he drew Sicily into revolt.[2]

Beyond is the strand and city of Dicæarchia. Formerly it was nothing but a naval station of the Cumæans. It was built on an eminence. But at the time of the war with Hannibal, the Romans established a colony there, and changed its name into Puteoli, [an appellation derived] from its wells; or, according to others, from the stench of its waters, the whole district from hence to Baïæ and Cumæ being full of sulphur, fire, and hot-springs. Some too are of opinion that it was on this account [that the country about] Cumæ was named Phlegra, and that the fables of the giants struck down by thunderbolts owe their origin to these eruptions of fire and water. This city has become a place of extensive commerce,[3] having artificially constructed harbors, which were much facilitated by the nature of the sand, which contains much gypsum, and will cement and consolidate thoroughly. Therefore, mixing this sand with chalk-stones, they construct moles in the sea, thus forming bays along the open coast, in which the largest transport ships may safely ride. Immediately above the city lies the Forum-Vulcani,[4] a plain surrounded with hills which seem to be on fire, having in many parts

[1] This explanation shows the bookish side of Strabo. Actually these legends arose from the abundant traces of former volcanic activity.

[2] 43–42 B.C.; *cf.* Livy, epitome, 123.

[3] The largest on the west coast of Italy in the time of Seneca and St. Paul, a generation after Strabo.

[4] The modern Solfatara.

mouths emitting smoke, frequently accompanied by a terrible rumbling noise; the plain itself is full of drifted sulphur.

7. After Dicæarchia is Neapolis, [founded originally] by the Cumæans; but afterwards being peopled in addition by Chalcidians, and certain Pithecussæans and Athenians, it was on this account denominated Naples.[1] Here is pointed out the tomb of Parthenope, one of the sirens, and a gymnastic sport is celebrated by command of an oracle. In course of time the inhabitants, having disagreed amongst themselves, admitted certain Campanians, thus being forced to regard in the light of friends those most inimical to them, since their friends were estranged. This is proved by the names of their demarchi, the earlier of which are Grecian, but the latter a mixture of Campanian with Grecian names. Many traces of Grecian civilization are still preserved, the gymnasia, the ephebeia,[2] the phratries,[3] and the Grecian names of people who are Roman citizens. At the present time they celebrate, every fifth year,[4] public games for music and gymnastic exercises during many days, which rival the most famous games of Greece. There is here a subterranean passage, similar to that at Cumæ, extending for many stadia along the mountain, between Dicæarchia and Neapolis: it is sufficiently broad to let carriages pass each other, and light is admitted from the surface of the mountain, by means of numerous apertures cut through a great depth. Naples also has hot springs and baths not at all inferior in quality to those at Baïæ, but much less frequented, for another city has arisen there, not less than Dicæarchia, one palace after another having been built. Naples still preserves the Grecian mode of life, owing to those who retire hither from Rome for the sake of repose, after a life of labor from childhood, and to those whose age or weakness demands relaxation. Besides these, Romans who find a charm in this style of life, and observe the numbers of persons of the same tastes dwelling there, are attracted by the place, and make it their abode.

[1] Nea-polis, "Newtown."

[2] Places of exercise for youths.

[3] "Brotherhoods," associations of families assumed to be related in blood; no. 144.

[4] Actually once in four years.

25. THE VOYAGES OF THE PHOCÆANS AND THEIR COLONIZATION OF CORSICA

(Herodotus i. 163–6. Macaulay, revised by E. G. S.)

About the middle of the seventh century B.C. a Samian explorer, Colæus, reached Tarshish, Tartessus, in Spain, the first of the Hellenes to visit that city. Shortly afterward the Phocæans began making voyages to that place in the way described in the subjoined excerpt. The "round boats" had been in use for mercantile shipping along the coasts, but the fifty-oared galleys of the Phocæans were relatively narrow and straight, and were provided with bronze beaks for battering; *cf.* Busolt, *Griech. Gesch.* I. 432 *sqq.* About 560 they founded Alalia in the island of Corsica (Greek Cyrnos). The new settlement was exposed to danger from the Etruscans (Tyrsenians, Tyrrenians) and Carthaginians, who were actively trading with each other on the basis of commerical treaties. The decisive naval battle off Alalia was fought about 535. Harpagus, mentioned in the selection, was a lieutenant of Cyrus the Persian king, who after the conquest of Lydia, was aiming to subdue the Greek cities along the coast.

163. Now these Phocæans were the first of the Hellenes who made long voyages, and these are they who discovered the Adriatic and Tyrsenia [1] and Iberia and Tartessus: and they made voyages not in round ships, but in vessels of fifty oars. These came to Tartessus and became friends with the king of the Tartessians whose name was Arganthonius: he was ruler of the Tartessians for eighty years and lived in all one hundred and twenty. With this man, I say, the Phocæans became so exceedingly friendly, that first he bade them leave Ionia and dwell wherever they desired in his own land; and as he did not prevail upon the Phocæans to do this, afterward, hearing from them of the Mede how his power was increasing, he gave them money to build a wall around their city: and he did this without sparing, for the circuit of the wall is many stadia in extent, and it is built all of large stones closely fitted together.

164. The wall of the Phocæans was made in this manner: and Harpagus having marched his army against them began to besiege them, at the same time holding forth to them proposals and saying that it was enough to satisfy him if the Phocæans were willing to throw down one battlement of their wall and dedicate one single

[1] Tyrsenia (Tyrrenia), the Greek for Etruria.

house. But the Phocæans, being very greatly grieved at the thought of subjection, said that they wished to deliberate about the matter for one day, and after that they would give their answer; and they asked him to withdraw his army from the wall while they were deliberating. Harpagus said that he knew very well what they were meaning to do, nevertheless he was willing to allow them to deliberate. In the time that followed, accordingly, when Harpagus had withdrawn his army from the wall, the Phocæans drew down their fifty-oared galleys to the sea, put into them their children and women and all their movable goods, and besides them the images from the temples and the other votive offerings except such as were made of bronze or stone or consisted of paintings; all the rest, I say, they put into the ships, and having embarked themselves, they sailed toward Chios; and the Persians obtained possession of Phocæa, the city being deserted by the inhabitants.

165. But as for the Phocæans, since the men of Chios would not sell them at their request the islands called Œnussæ, from the fear lest these islands might be made a seat of trade and their island might be shut out,[1] therefore they departed for Cyrnos:[2] for in Cyrnos twenty years before this they had established a city named Alalia, in accordance with an oracle (now Arganthonius by that time was dead). And when they were setting out for Cyrnos they first sailed in to Phocæa and slaughtered the Persian garrison, to whose charge Harpagus had delivered the city; then after they had achieved this they made solemn imprecations on any one of them who should be left behind from their voyage, and moreover they sunk a mass of iron in the sea and swore that not until that mass should appear again on the surface would they return to Phocæa. However as they were setting forth to Cyrnos, more than half of the citizens were seized with yearning and regret for their city and for their native land, and they proved false to their oath and sailed back to Phocæa. But those of them who still kept the oath weighed anchor from the islands of Œnussæ and sailed.

166. When these came to Cyrnos, for five years they dwelt together with those who had come thither before, and they founded temples there. Then, since they plundered the prop-

[1] Here is one of many evidences of keen commercial rivalry among the Hellenes.

[2] Corsica.

erty of all their neighbors, the Tyrsenians and Carthaginians made expedition against them by agreement with one another, each with sixty ships. And the Phocæans also manned their vessels, sixty in number, and came to meet the enemy in that which is called the Sardinian sea: and when they encountered one another in the sea-fight the Phocæans won a kind of Cadmean victory,[1] for forty of their ships were destroyed and the remaining twenty were disabled, having had their prows bent aside. So they sailed in to Alalia and took up their children and their women and their other possessions as much as their ships proved capable of carrying, and then they left Cyrnos behind them and sailed to Rhegium.

BIBLIOGRAPHY

I. Sources for Colonization. — We have no knowledge of any contemporary source which treated of this period of colonization. Among the earliest sources known to us who touched upon the founding of cities were Hellanicus of Lesbos (Müller, *Frag. Hist. Græc.* I. p. 45 *sqq.*) and Antiochus of Syracuse (*ib.* I. p. 12 *sqq.*), both belonging to the fifth century B.C. For the colonization of Sicily, see Thuc. vi. 1–5. Ephorus, Timæus, and other later writers treated of the subject. The authors thus far mentioned collected the material from which were drawn the late accounts that have survived to our time; *e.g.*, Diodorus v–viii, Strabo, and Pausanias. See also Scymnos of Chios (Müller, *Geogr. gr. min.* I. p. 196 *sqq.*). The chronology, as we have it at present, was gradually elaborated, and reached its final form in Eusebius, who lived in the fourth century A.D.

II. Modern Works. — Botsford, *Hellenic History*, ch. iv; Bury, ch. ii; Holm, I. ch. xxi; Abbott, I. ch. xi; Curtius, bk. II. ch. iii; Grote, III. chs. xxii, xxiii; IV. chs. xxvi, xxvii; Freeman, E. A., *Story of Sicily*, chs. ii. iv; *History of Sicily*, I (entire); Greenidge, A. H. J., *Gk. Const. Hist.* ch. iii; Phillipson, C., *International Law and Custom of Ancient Greece and Rome*, II. ch. xix; Cunningham, *Western Civilization in its Economic Aspects*, bk. II. ch. i; Morris, H. C., *History of Colonization*, I. 85–125.

Beloch, *Griech. Gesch.* I. 1. 229–64 (colonization); 264–308 (economy); Holm, A., *Geschichte Siziliens*, I. 108–44; Giuliano, L., *Storia di Siracusa antica*, 1–15; Pais, E., *Storia della Sicilia e della Magna Grecia* (Torino, 1894); *Ancient Italy* (Chicago: University Press, 1908), especially for the relations between the Greeks and Rome; Raoul-Rochette, D., *Histoire critique de l'établissement des colonies grecques*, 4 vols. (Paris, 1815); Hertzberg, G. F., *Kurze Geschichte der altgriechischen Kolonisation* (Gütersloh, 1892).

[1] The idea of a Cadmean victory is perhaps derived from the story of the Sparti at Thebes (their mutual annihilation) or from that of Polyneices and Eteocles. The nature of that kind of victory may be inferred from the text; see Stein's note *ad loc.*

CHAPTER IV

GOVERNMENT AND POLITICAL CONDITIONS

During the period 750–479 B.C.

26. Spartan Discipline

(Xenophon, *Constitution of the Lacedæmonians*. Dakyns, revised on the basis of the Greek text by E. G. S.)

The chief interest in the Lacedæmonian system lies not so much in the political institutions as in the severe discipline exercised by the government over the citizens from birth to the grave. For that reason the following passage has been selected; unfortunately space does not permit the inclusion of the entire treatise. The picture drawn by Xenophon is idealized; it may be supplemented by Plutarch, *Lycurgus*, and offset by the criticisms of Aristotle, *Politics*, ii. 9. For other selections, see Botsford, *Source-Book of Ancient History*, ch. xii. No legislator could have been the author of all the institutions ascribed to Lycurgus; in fact his historical personality has been seriously questioned.

1. I recall the astonishment with which I first noted the unique position of Sparta amongst the states of Hellas, the relatively sparse population, and at the same time the extraordinary power and prestige of the community. I was puzzled to account for the fact. It was only when I came to consider the peculiar institutions of the Spartans that my wonderment ceased. Or rather, it is transferred to the legislator who gave them those laws, obedience to which has been the secret of their prosperity. This legislator, Lycurgus, I must needs admire, and hold him to have been one of the wisest of mankind. Certainly he was no imitator of other states. It was by a stroke of invention rather, and on a pattern much in opposition to the commonly accepted one, that he brought his fatherland to this pinnacle of prosperity.

Take for example — and it is well to begin at the beginning — the whole topic of the birth and rearing of children. Throughout the rest of the world the young girl, who will one day become a mother (and I speak of those who may be held to be well brought up), is nurtured on the plainest food attainable, with the scantiest addition of meat or other condiments; whilst as to wine they train them either to total abstinence or to take it highly diluted with water. And in imitation, as it were, of the handicraft type, since the majority of artificers are sedentary, we, the rest of the Hellenes, are content that our girls should sit quietly and work wools. That is all we demand of them. But how are we to expect that women nurtured in this fashion should produce a splendid offspring?

Lycurgus pursued a different path. Clothes were things, he held, the furnishing of which might well enough be left to female slaves. And believing that the highest function of a free woman was the bearing of children, in the first place he insisted on the training of the body as incumbent no less on the female than the male; and in pursuit of the same idea instituted rival contests in running and tests of strength for women as for men. His belief was that where both parents were strong their progeny would be found to be more vigorous. . . .

So opposed to those of the rest of the world are the principles which Lycurgus devised in reference to the birth of children. Whether they enabled him to provide Sparta with a race of men superior to all in size and strength any one who desires may examine.

II. After this exposition of the customs in connection with the birth of children, I wish now to explain the systems of education in fashion there and elsewhere. Throughout the rest of Hellas the custom on the part of those who claim to educate their sons in the best way is as follows. As soon as the children are of an age to understand what is said to them they are immediately placed under the charge of Paidagogoi (boy-escorts), who are also attendants, and sent off to the school of some teacher to be taught "letters," "music," and the concerns of the palæstra. Besides this they are given shoes to wear which tend to make their feet tender, and their bodies are made soft by various changes of clothing. As for food, the only measure recognized is that which is fixed by appetite.

But when we turn to Lycurgus, instead of leaving it to each member of the state privately to appoint a slave to be his son's escort, he set over the young Spartans a public guardian, the paidonómos or "manager of boys" to give him his proper title, with complete authority over them. This guardian was selected from those who fill the highest magistracies. He had authority to hold musters of the boys, and as their overseer, in case of any misbehavior, to chastise severely. The legislator further provided him with a body of youths in the prime of young manhood and bearing whips, to inflict punishment when necessary, with this happy result that in Sparta reverence and obedience ever go hand in hand, nor is there lack of either.

Instead of softening their feet with shoes, his rule was to make them hardy through going barefoot. This habit, if practised, would, as he believed, enable them to go up steep ascents more easily and to go down descending slopes with less danger. In fact, with his feet so trained the young Spartan would leap and jump high and run faster unshod than another shod in the ordinary way.

Instead of pampering them with a variety of clothes, his rule was to habituate them to a single garment the whole year through, thinking that so they would be better prepared to withstand the variations of heat and cold.

Again, as regards food, according to his regulation the Eirên, or head of the flock, must see that his messmates gathered to the club meal, with such moderate food as to avoid that heaviness which is engendered by repletion, and yet not to remain altogether unacquainted with inadequate sustenance. His belief was that by such training they would be better able when it proved necessary to undergo hardships without food. They would be all the fitter, if the word of command were given, to remain on the stretch for a long time without extra dieting. The craving for a finer dish would be less, the readiness to take any victual set before them greater, and, in general, the régime would be found more healthy. Under it he thought the lads would increase in stature and shape into finer men, since, as he maintained, a dietary which gave suppleness to the limbs must be more conducive to both ends than one which added thickness to the bodily parts by feeding.

On the other hand, in order to guard against a too great pinch of starvation, though he did not actually allow the boys to help themselves without trouble to what they needed more, he did give them permission to steal this thing or that in the effort to alleviate their hunger. It was not of course from any real difficulty how else to supply them with nutriment that he left it to them to provide themselves by this crafty method. Nor can I conceive that any one will so misinterpret the custom. Clearly its explanation lies in the fact that he who would live the life of a robber must forego sleep by night, and in the daytime he must enjoy shifts and lie in ambuscade; he must prepare and make ready his scouts, and so forth, if he is to succeed in capturing the quarry.

It is obvious, I say, that the whole of this education tended, and was intended, to make the boys craftier and more inventive in getting in supplies, whilst at the same time it cultivated their warlike instincts. An objector may retort: "But if he thought it so fine a feat to steal, why did he inflict many blows on the unfortunate who was caught?" My answer is: for the self-same reason which induces people, in other matters which are taught, to punish the mal-performance of a service. So they, the Lacedæmonians, visit penalties on the boy who is caught thieving as being but poor thieves. So to steal as many cheeses as possible off the shrine of Orthia was a feat to be encouraged; but, at the same moment, others were enjoined to scourge the thief, which would point a moral not obscurely, that by pain endured for a brief season a man may earn the joyous reward of lasting glory. Herein, too, it is plainly shown that where speed is requisite the sluggard will win for himself much trouble and scant good.

Furthermore, and in order that the boys should not want a ruler, even in case the overseer himself was absent, he gave to any citizen who chanced to be present authority to lay upon them injunctions for their good, and to chastise them if they failed in anything. By so doing he brought it about that boys of Sparta were more respectful. Indeed there is nothing which, whether as boys or men, they respect more highly than the ruler. Lastly, and with the same intention, that the boys must never be bereft of a ruler, even if by chance there were no grown man present, he laid down the rule that in such a case the most seasoned of the Leaders or Prefects was to become ruler for the nonce, each of his own division. The conclusion is that under no circumstances whatever are the boys of Sparta destitute of one to rule them. . . .

III. Coming to the critical period at which a boy ceases to be a boy and becomes a youth, we find that it is just then that the rest of the world proceed to emancipate their children from the boy-escorts and from the teachers, and without substituting any further ruler, are content to launch them into absolute independence.

Here, again, Lycurgus took an entirely opposite view of the matter. This, if observation might be trusted, was the season when the greatest conceit is developed in them, and insolence most luxuriates, when, too, the strongest desires for pleasures arise. At this point he imposed very many hardships upon them and devised the largest occupation. By a crowning enactment, which said that he who shrank from the duties imposed on him would forfeit henceforth all claim to the glorious honors of the state, he caused, not only the public authorities, but those personally interested in each of them to take serious pains so that no single individual of them should by an act of craven cowardice find himself dishonored within the body politic.

Furthermore, in his desire firmly to implant in their youthful souls a root of modesty he imposed upon these bigger boys a special rule. In the very streets they were to keep their two hands within the folds of the cloak; they were to walk in silence and without turning their heads to gaze, now here, now there, but rather to keep their eyes fixed upon the ground before them. There also it has become manifest that, even in the matter of self-control, the males are stronger than the nature of females. At any rate, you might sooner expect a stone image to utter a sound than one of those Spartan youths; to divert the eyes of some bronze statue were less difficult. As to quiet bearing, no bride ever stepped in bridal bower with more natural modesty. Note them when they have reached the public table. The plainest answer to the question asked, — that is all you need expect to hear from their lips.

IV. But if he was thus careful in the education of the stripling, the Spartan lawgiver showed a still greater anxiety in dealing with those who had reached the prime of opening manhood; considering their immense importance to the city in the scale of good, if only they proved themselves the men they should be. He had only to look around to see that wherever the spirit of emulation was most deeply seated, there, too, their choruses and gymnastic contests would present alike the highest charm to eye and ear. On the same principle he persuaded himself that he needed only to match his youthful warriors in the rivalry of excellence, and with like result. They also, in their degree, might be expected to attain to the fullest measure of manly virtue.

What method he adopted to engage these combatants I will now explain. Their ephors select three men out of the whole body of the citizens in the prime of life. These three are named hippagretæ, or masters of the horse. Each selects one hundred others, being bound to explain for what reason he prefers some and rejects others. The result is that those who fail to obtain the distinction are now at open war, not only with those who rejected them, but with those who were chosen in their stead; and they keep ever a jealous eye on one another to detect some slip of conduct contrary to the high code of honor there held customary. Thus is set on foot that strife, in truest sense acceptable to heaven, and for the purposes of state most politic. It is a strife in which not only is the pattern of a brave man's conduct fully set forth, but where each of them separately train themselves for the highest efficiency, and if there be any need, they will individually come to the aid of the commonwealth with all their strength.

Necessity, moreover, is laid upon them to study a good habit of the body, coming as they do to blows with their fists on account of their feud wherever they meet. Albeit any one present has a right to separate the combatants, and, if obedience is not shown to the peacemaker, the manager of boys hales the delinquent before the ephors, and the ephors inflict heavy damages, since they will have it plainly understood that rage must never override obedience to law.

With regard to those who have already passed the vigor of early manhood, and on whom the highest magistracies henceforth devolve, there is a like contrast. In Hellas generally we find that at this age the need of further attention to physical strength is removed, although the imposition of military service continues. But Lycurgus made it customary for men of that age to regard hunting as the highest honor suited to their time of life; albeit not to the exclusion of any public duty. His aim was that they might be equally able to undergo the fatigues of campaigning with those in the prime of early manhood.

27. The Constitution of Athens before Solon

(Aristotle, *Constitution of the Athenians*, i–iv. All the following selections from this treatise have been translated by G. W. B.)

The greater part of Aristotle's treatise on the Athenian Constitution, written on a papyrus, was discovered in Egypt near the end of 1890, and the *editio princeps*, by F. G. Kenyon, appeared in the following January. The author's name is not given in the papyrus, but from quotations by ancient writers the authorship is established beyond a reasonable doubt. On internal evidence it is clear that the work was composed between 328 and 325, some years after the publication of the *Politics* and shortly after the appearance of Androtion's *Atthis*, which Aristotle seems to have used as his main source. The discovery is especially helpful in clarifying our conceptions as to the nature of such treatises, and has helped solve many problems. For details, see introductions to the editions of Kenyon and Sandys, and bibliography, p. 43.

In the earlier part of the treatise, now lost, Aristotle evidently arranged his material according to reigns, as was the custom of ancient chroniclers (*cf.* no. 16 *sq.*), narrating in each the institutions and events traditionally assigned to it. The first period, that of the monarchy, extended to the accession of Theseus. Then began the first period of constitutional government, being originally a slight deviation from kingship.. During this period the government was aristocratic. At a time, not precisely dated, before Draco, began a new period of government (timocracy of the heavy infantry) in which the right to vote was enjoyed by all who could at their own expense furnish a panoply. This form of government continued to the archonship of Solon, 594.

The extant fragment opens with the trial of the Alcmeonidæ for sacrilege committed some years earlier in the slaughter of the followers of Cylon who had placed themselves under the protection of Athena. In giving an account of this event Plutarch (*Solon* 12) states that Solon persuaded the Alcmeonidæ "to be tried before a court of three hundred chosen on the ground of nobility. With Myron as accuser the men were convicted, and the living were banished," etc. By a comparison with this statement it is easy to reconstruct in substance the opening sentence of Aristotle's treatise.

1. With Myron as accuser (they were tried) by a court taken from the noble families and sworn on the sacrifices. Convicted of impiety, they themselves [1] were cast forth from the tombs and their gens (genos) was condemned to eternal exile. Thereupon Epimenides of Crete purified the city.[2]

[1] As years had elapsed between the sacrilege and the trial, all or nearly all the actual perpetrators were dead. The procedure admirably illustrates the belief in hereditary guilt.

[2] The date of the visit of Epimenides is exceedingly uncertain, as is everything connected with him; see Sandys' note.

2. Afterward it came about that for a long time the nobles and commons disturbed the state by their sedition. For the government was oligarchic in all respects; and particularly the poor, with their children and wives, were in slavery to the rich. They were called pelatæ (clients) and hectemori (sixth-part men), for they tilled the fields of the wealthy for that amount of rent. All the land was in the hands of the few; and if they (the tenants) failed to render the rents due, they and their children were liable to enslavement. There were loans on the security of every one's person down to the time of Solon; and he was in fact the first to stand forth as a patron of the commons. Now it was a most hard and grievous feature of the constitution that the masses should be in slavery; not but that they had other grounds of complaint, for they were, so to speak, excluded from everything.

3. The organization of the original government (of the republic) as it existed before Draco, was as follows. Their appointments to office were based on the qualifications of birth and wealth. Originally the offices were life-long and afterward decennial. The first and most important magistrates were the king, polemarch, and archon. The earliest of these three was the kingship, for it existed from the beginning. Secondly was instituted in addition the polemarchy because of the fact that some of the kings had proved incapable in war; hence they had sent for Ion on an occasion of especial need.[1] The last was the archonship:[2] the majority say it was instituted in the time of Medon, others in the time of Acastus. The latter urge as proof the circumstance that the nine archons swear that they will fulfil their oaths as in the time of Acastus, with the idea that in his magistracy the Codridæ sur-

[1] The institution of the polemarchy is connected in tradition with the war waged by Athens against Eleusis (*cf.* Hdt. viii. 44; Paus. i. 131. 3), and it seems probable that on the annexation of Eleusis all Attica was organized, or reorganized, in the four Ionic tribes. This connection helps explain why Ion was regarded as a polemarch. It seems probable further that the office was instituted before the kingship was thrown open to all the eupatrids (conventional date 713–712). The chroniclers before Aristotle pushed the institution of this office and of the archonship some three centuries back into the past.

[2] The archonship was instituted about 700, a decade or two after the polemarchy. The reason for the pushing back of these institutions (see preceding note) was the desire to make the republic begin as early as possible — with Acastus or Medon or even with Theseus.

rendered some of their royal power, corresponding prerogatives being transferred to the archons. Whichever way it was it matters little, for the change took place in that period. That is was the last of these offices, however, is proved by the circumstance that the archon administers none of the ancestral functions, as do the king and polemarch, but only those which were afterward added.[1] It is therefore only recently that the office has become great, increased by gradual accretions.

The thesmothetæ were for the first time chosen many years later — when the magistrates had already come to be elected annually — in order that they might record the customary laws and keep them for the trial of offenders. Therefore this alone of the offices has never been longer than a year in duration. Thus much do they precede one another in the time (of their institution). All nine archons did not occupy the same office; but the king used the building now called the boucoleum, near the prytaneum; and a proof of it is that even now the marriage and union of the king's wife with Dionysus takes place there. The archon had the prytaneum, the polemarch the epilyceum; formerly it was called the polemarcheum, but after Epilycus had rebuilt and furnished it in his polemarchy, it was named the epilyceum.[2] The thesmothetæ occupy the thesmotheteum. In the time of Solon all (nine archons first) met together in the thesmotheteum.[3]

They had absolute power to settle cases without appeal, and not as now merely to hold a preliminary trial. These, then, were the regulations regarding the offices. The council of the Areopagus had the function of watching over the laws; but in fact it managed the most numerous and important public affairs with full power to chastise and fine all who acted disorderly. Birth and wealth were required of those who were elected archons; and from them the Areopagites were constituted. Hence the office of the latter has alone remained lifelong to the present day.

[1] Such reasoning, found in many parts of the treatise, proves that Aristotle or his source had no contemporary record of the matters under consideration, but followed the method of inferring the past from present conditions.

[2] Epilyceum (ἐπὶ Λυκείῳ) doubtless means "Near the Lyceum." The author's explanation is characterisitic of the naïve reasoning of the ancients in such matters.

[3] In other words, it was not till the time of Solon that these nine magistrates came to constitute a board — that of the nine archons.

4. Such is an outline of the original constitution. No long time afterward, in the archonship of Aristæchmus, Draco drew up his laws. But the constitution itself (as it then existed) had the following character.[1] The franchise had (already) been granted to those who could furnish a panoply. They elected the nine archons and the treasurers from such as possessed an estate worth not less than ten minas [2] free from encumbrance, and the other, less important offices from those who had the franchise. The generals and hipparchs must show an estate free from encumbrance, worth no less than a hundred minas, and must be the fathers of children above ten years of age, born of a lawful wife. It was necessary for these persons, namely the prytaneis,[3] generals and hipparchs, to give security for the year to the time of their audit, furnishing four securities of the same census class as the generals and the hipparchs. There was to be a Council of Four Hundred and One, appointed by lot from those who had a right to vote. This and other offices were filled by lot from the citizens above thirty years of age, and it was not permitted to hold the same office a second time till all had their turn, then the lot was drawn anew from the beginning. When there was a session of the council or assembly, if any councillor was absent, he was fined if a pentacosiomedimnus three drachmas,[4] if a knight two, if a zeugite one. The council of the Areopagus was guardian of the laws, and supervised the offices to see that they were legally administered. It was permitted to anyone who was injured, to bring an impeachment before the Areopagites, citing the law in violation of which he was suffering harm. However, there were

[1] Most modern scholars have declared this chapter, or the greater part of it, an interpolation. There is no space here for the discussion of the extremely complicated subject. The writer of these notes has preferred to assume, at least tentatively, the genuineness of the chapter and to attempt a translation in accordance with that view. It is to be noted that Aristotle does not say here or elsewhere that Draco was the author of a constitution; and the abruptness of the change in this passage from "laws" to "constitution" may be due to the omission of material found in his source relating in detail to the laws and courts of homicide.

[2] This and the following property qualifications for office are suspicious; but mistakes are easily made in copying numbers.

[3] They were either prytaneis of the naucraries or of the council of four hundred and one mentioned below.

[4] There was little currency in Attica at this time, and that was of the Æginetan standard. A drachma of this standard was about twenty-five cents; a mina was a hundred drachmas.

loans on the security of the person, as has been said, and the land was in the hands of the few.[1]

28. The Athenian Constitution from Solon to Peisistratus

594–560 B.C.

(Aristotle, *Constitution of the Athenians*, 5–13. Of the poem in § 5 the first sentence only is from Aristotle, the rest is from another source (*Anthologia Lyrica*, ed. Bergk, 4, also translated by G. W. B.)

With this selection compare Plutarch, *Solon*.

5. Such being the organization of the government, while the many were in slavery to the few, the commons rose in revolt against the nobles. After the sedition had grown strong and the two parties had long been arrayed against each other, they in common elected Solon as arbitrator and archon,[2] and intrusted to him the constitution. The occasion was his composition of the elegy beginning thus: —

"I perceive, and within my heart lie griefs, as I see the oldest country of Iaonia in distress. Never is it the will of Zeus and the thought of the blessed immortal gods that our city perish; for in such wise the high-souled guardian of the city, Pallas Athena, daughter of a mighty sire spreads over it her hands. The nobles, persuaded by their love of money, desire recklessly to destroy the great city. And as to the people, the mind of their magistrates is dishonest — magistrates who are destined to suffer many ills because of their monstrous violence. For they know not how to be satisfied or to enjoy the present feast in quiet. . . . They grow wealthy in obedience to unjust deeds.[3] . . . They spare neither sacred nor public property and they rob and steal, one here and one there. They guard not the revered foundations of Justice, who though silent, knows what is going on, what went on before, and has come to demand full settlement in time. This wound inevitable hath come upon all the city, namely evil slavery into which the state hath quickly fallen, and which stirs up civil strife and war, — war that destroys our lovely youth in numbers.[4] For our well-beloved city is consumed by the evil-minded in their meetings, in which unjust plans are held dear. These are the ills prevailing in the commons;

[1] Draco's legislation in no way relieved the economic distress of the poor.

[2] Solon was elected archon, 594, and at the same time thesmothete ("legislator") with absolute power. Although one object of this extraordinary authority was for the arbitration of the civil strife, there was in Athens no political officer called "arbitrator."

[3] These two lacunæ are in the text.

[4] Evidently civil war had broken out, and blood was shed.

but many of the poor are going into a foreign land, sold and bound in unseemly chains and suffer hateful woes by force of slavery. Hall doors no longer will to hold the evil, it leapeth over the lofty hedge, and you find it everywhere, even if you hide in a chamber corner. This my soul bids me teach the Athenians, that misrule brings most ills to a city; but good rule makes all things harmonious and at one. Good order puts bonds upon the wicked, smooths the rough, stays satiety, weakens violence, withers flowers that grow of Ate (reckless guilt), straightens crooked judgments, softens acts of cruelty, ends disputation, ends the wrath of hateful strife."

Thus he marched to the attack and contended with each side against the other, reasoning with them, and finally exhorted them in common to put a stop to the existing strife. By birth and reputation Solon was among the first men in the state, whereas in property and circumstances he belonged to the middle class,[1] as all admit, and as he himself testifies in his poems in which he urges the wealthy to refrain from avarice: —

"Still your lordly heart within your breasts, you who have come into surfeit of abundant blessings; nourish your proud soul in moderation; for we shall not yield, nor shall you in everything have your way."

From first to last he lays the blame of the sedition upon the wealthy; hence in the beginning of the elegy he says he fears "their greed of gain and their overweening mind," with the idea that this spirit was the cause of the existing strife.

6. When he had become master of the state, Solon freed the commons both for the present and for the future by forbidding loans on the security of the person; and he enacted laws and made an abolition of debts both private and public, which they term seisachtheia ('disburdening'), with the idea that thus they shook off their burden.[2] In these matters some attempt to slander him;

[1] In Greek literature the "middle class" is the social class of moderate wealth, not necessarily the industrial or commercial class.

[2] Aristotle does not say here that he abolished *all* debts. The only reliable information on the subject which he had was derived from Solon's poems quoted by him. From these poems we have a right to infer that Solon canceled those debts only which were based on the security (1) of land, (2) of the person. It is a pertinent fact, too, that Androtion (*Atthis*, quoted below, § 10) understood that Solon left some debts uncanceled. Grote (*History of Greece*, III. 102 *sqq.*), a man of robust common-sense, maintains substantially the view presented in this note. Associated with the festival of the seisachtheia, however, was a popular but ill-founded tradition that Solon abolished all debts.

for it happened that when Solon was about to make the seisachtheia, he told his plan in advance to some of the nobles; and then, as the popular party say, he was outgeneraled by his friends; but as they say who wish to calumniate him, he shared in the gain. Now these nobles, borrowing money, bought up a large tract of land, and no long time afterward, when the abolition of debts took place, they became wealthy; thus they say arose the families reputed to be of ancient wealth.[1] In point of fact, however, the account given by the popular party is more credible; for it is not reasonable that a man who in other matters proved himself so moderate and so patriotic that, when it was permitted him by conspiring with either party to make himself tyrant of the state, he incurred the enmity of both factions and placed a higher value on honor and on the safety of the state than on his own advantage — it is not reasonable, I say, that such a man should debase himself in transactions so mean and unworthy. That he had this opportunity the disordered condition of affairs testifies, and he himself often mentions it in his poems, while all acknowledge it to be so. It is necessary, therefore, to consider the charge false.

7. He established a constitution and made laws besides, and the ordinances of Draco they ceased using with the exception of those concerning homicide. Engraving the laws on tablets, he set them up in the King's Porch, and all swore to obey them. The nine archons, taking oath on a stone, swore that they would dedicate a golden statue in case they transgressed any of the laws, hence to the present day they continue to take this oath. He made the laws binding for a hundred years, and organized the constitution in the following manner.

He divided (the population) into four census classes, just as it had been divided before, into pentacosiomedimni, knights (hippeis), zeugitæ, and thetes. He assigned the offices to be filled from the pentacosiomedimni, knights and zeugitæ, namely the nine archons, the treasurers, the commissioners of contracts, the eleven, and the

[1] This passage illustrates the extent to which the politics of the Athenians molded their conceptions of the past. Democrats and oligarchs had their opposing views of Solon, which found their way into literature. The statement regarding the dishonorable origin of families of ancient wealth (eupatrids) must have come from one who was an oligarch but not a noble.

colacretæ, distributing them among the several classes according to their property ratings. To the thetic class he granted a share in the assembly and the popular courts only. A pentacosiomedimnus was one who produced from his own estate five hundred measures [1] wet and dry together, a knight three hundred measures, but as some say, one who could support a horse; and they adduce as proof the name of the class, with the idea that it was derived from this circumstance, and they cite the dedicatory offerings of the ancients, for there stands on the Acropolis a statue with the following inscription: —

> "Anthemion, son of Diphilus, dedicated this statue to the gods when he exchanged the thetic for the knightly census."

The horse stands there in evidence that the word knightly ('hippic,' ἱππάς, ἱππικός, from ἵππος, 'horse') has this meaning. But in fact it seems more reasonable that the class, like that of the pentacosiomedimni, was defined in terms of measures.[2]

The zeugitæ were those who produced two hundred measures of both kinds, and the rest were thetes, who had no right to any magistracy. Hence even now when the question is asked of one who is to be taken by lot for any office, what census class he belongs to, no one answers, the thetic.

8. The archonship he caused to be filled by lot from nominees whom the tribes severally selected. Each tribe chose ten nominees for the archonships and lots were drawn from them; hence even now remains the custom for the tribes to draw severally by lot ten candidates, from whom the archons are then appointed by lot.[3] A proof that he caused them to be taken by lot from the census classes is the law which they continue even now to use concerning the treasurers; it prescribes that they be appointed by lot from the pentacosiomedimni. Thus Solon legislated regarding the nine

[1] The standard dry measure of Athens from the time of Solon was the medimnus, about 1½ bu. The wet measure was the metretes, 8½ gal.

[2] There is no contradiction in Aristotle's sources on this subject: the class was doubtless defined in terms of measures, and members were required to furnish each a horse for military service.

[3] It is clear that Aristotle had no Solonian document for his statement regarding the mode of appointment of archons, but merely inferred the Solonian method from that of his own time. There can be no doubt, however, that he has here made a mistake, that election to the office continued to the year 487–486; *cf.* § 22 *infra*.

archons, whereas in the original form of constitution the council of the Areopagus had called up men and of its own judgment had assigned them according to their qualifications to the several offices for the year. There were four tribes as before and four tribe-kings. From the several tribes were formed three trittyes, with twelve naucraries to each. Over the naucraries were established, as a magistracy, the naucrars, having charge of the current receipts and expenditures. In the laws of Solon, therefore, which they no longer use, it is often written that the naucrars shall pay into and expend from the naucraric fund.[1] He constituted further a council of four hundred, a hundred from each tribe; and he assigned the council of the Areopagus to the duty of protecting the laws, just as formerly it was guardian of the constitution. In fact it continued to supervise in addition the most numerous and most important administrative matters, while it corrected wrong-doers with full power to fine and punish, and it brought up the fines to the Acropolis without the obligation of stating the ground for their exaction. Furthermore it tried conspirators against the state under a law of impeachment which Solon enacted concerning such offenders. Seeing the state often disturbed by sedition and many of the citizens through sheer inertness allowing such affairs to take their own course, he enacted with reference to them a peculiar law, that whoever, when the country is disturbed by sedition, shall not take up arms with either faction, shall be disfranchised and deprived of all part in the state.

9. Such were Solon's regulations regarding the offices. Three features of his constitution seem to have been especially favorable to the people: the first and most important was his prohibition of lending money on the security of the person; the second his permission to anyone who wished to go to law in behalf of injured persons;[2] the third (by which they say the populace has chiefly gained

[1] Noteworthy is the circumstance that Aristotle, or his source, had access to obsolete laws preserved in the archives. Most of the institutional history of early Attica had been drawn by the chroniclers (atthid-writers) from such documents.

[2] This regulation is here mentioned by Aristotle for the first time. The injuries here referred to were not homicide, assault with intent to kill, or the like, for in such cases prosecution could be begun by kinsmen only. The author has in mind injury to parents by children; to orphans, heiresses, etc., by their guardians. In such cases any citizen could bring an accusation.

power) the right of appeal to a popular court; for being master of the vote, the commons have become master of the constitution. Still further because of the fact that the laws have not been composed simply and clearly, but like the statute concerning heiresses and wards of state,[1] necessarily many disputes arise and the popular court comes to be arbiter of all things public and private. Some accordingly suppose that he made the laws obscure on purpose, that the commons might have power to determine their meaning. It is not reasonable: (their obscurity is owing rather) to his inability to reach perfection in the general terms of a statute; for it is right to judge him, not by the present consequences, but by the intention he has shown in the rest of his constitutional legislation.

10. These features of his laws, accordingly, seem to be favorable to the people; but before his legislation he abolished debts, and afterward he made the increase in the measures and weights and in the money standard, for in his time the measures became greater than the Pheidonian;[2] and the mina, which formerly contained nearly seventy drachmas, was filled up to a hundred.[3] The ancient type of coin was the double drachma.[4] He established also standard weights corresponding to the coinage, sixty-three minas making a talent, and divided the mina into staters and other denominations.

For the sake of comparison a passage from Androtion, *Atthis*, quoted by Plutarch, *Solon*, 15, is here inserted.

Some authorities, among whom is Androtion, have written that he relieved the poor, not by an abolition of debts, but by lowering

[1] Statutes relating to inheritance, adoption, and kindred subjects of family law were indeed complicated. This condition, however, is not due to any legislator but to the very complexity of family relations. The legislator did little more than embody in enactments traditional customs in such matters.

[2] Pheidon and his weights and measures are exceedingly obscure; for references to the essential sources, see Sandys' note *ad loc.* It should be noticed that Aristotle speaks of him here only in connection with *metra*, measures of capacity.

[3] This statement has reference to the coinage. The usual explanation has been that Solon introduced the Euboic standard of coinage in place of the Æginetan, and that the proportion between the two was about as Aristotle has here stated it — that 70 drachmas of the Æginetan standard equaled 100 drachmas of the Euboic. In that case Aristotle is wrong in assuming an increase instead of a diminution. Head, *Historia Numorum* (2d ed., 1911), 367 *sq.*, presents in vindication of Aristotle a new interpretation, which however is not wholly convincing.

[4] *I.e.*, the Æginetan double drachma.

the rate of interest,[1] and that this benevolent act was called seisachtheia, and together with it the increase of the measures and the value of the coinage; for the mina, which formerly contained seventy-three drachmas, he made to contain a hundred, so that they (the drachmas) yielded an equal amount in number but less in value,[2] and those who had great debts to pay were benefited, while the creditors remained uninjured.

Aristotle's account is now resumed.

11. When he had arranged the government in the manner described, many people kept coming to him and annoying him in regard to the laws, finding fault with some points and asking questions concerning others; and as he wished neither to disturb these arrangements nor to remain and incur enmities, he went on a journey for trade and sight-seeing to Egypt, saying he would not return for ten years; for he thought it was not right that he should remain and interpret the laws but that everyone should obey them to the letter. It was at the same time his misfortune that many of the nobles were at variance with him because of the abolition of debts and that both factions had shifted their attitude because his reform had turned out contrary to their expectation. For the commons supposed he would redistribute everything, whereas the nobles hoped he would restore to them the same constitution or make but little change in it. He, however, opposed both parties, and though it was permitted him by conspiring with either to make himself tyrant, he preferred to incur the enmity of both parties by saving his country and legislating for the best.

12. All others agree that such was the case, and he in a poem mentions it in the following terms: —

"I gave the commons as much power as sufficed, neither detracting from their honor nor adding thereto. Those who possessed might and were illustrious in wealth, for them I planned that they should suffer naught unseemly. I stood, too, with my strong shield about both parties, suffering neither to gain an unjust victory."

[1] There was a law of Solon which permitted any interest agreed upon by the contracting parties; Lysias x. 18. As Androtion, an Athenian statesman, must have known this fact, we may only suppose that Plutarch has misquoted him.

[2] Here we have the authority of Androtion, against that of Aristotle, that the value of the coins was diminished; and on the whole this seems to be the reasonable view. We have also his authority that some debts remained uncanceled.

Again, revealing his mind regarding the populace, as to the way it ought to be treated: —

"Thus the commons would best follow their leaders,[1] neither given too much rein nor yet oppressed. For satiety breeds insolence when abundant wealth comes upon men whose minds are not right."

Again somewhere else he says concerning those who sought a redistribution of land: —

"They came for plunder, cherishing a hope of riches, each one imagining he would get abundant bliss, and that I, now smoothly flattering, would reveal a harsh intent. Then they idly prated; now in wrath they all look at me askance as at an enemy. It is not fitting; for what I promised, with the gods' help I performed. I wrought not in vain, nor did it please me to accomplish aught with a tyrant's force, nor that the good should share equally with the base in the rich soil of the fatherland."

Again in speaking of the abolition of debts and of those who had formerly been in slavery and had been set free by the seisachtheia, he says: —

"As to the purpose for which I organized the populace, why should I have desisted before reaching this end. In the just fulness of time the most mighty mother of the Olympian gods will bear me witness, even black Earth, most excellent, that I removed the mortgage pillars which stood in many places, — she was formerly in slavery but now set free. To Athens our country divinely founded, I restored many men who had been sold, some illegally, others under the law, others whom hard necessity forced into exile, who in their many wanderings had forgot the Attic tongue. Others held here in unseemly slavery and trembling under their masters' caprices I set free. These things I did by the power of law, uniting force with justice, and I fulfilled my promise. Ordinances, too, alike for the bad and the good I enacted, adapting straightforward justice to every case. Had another than I, some evil-minded, avaricious man, seized the goad, he would not have restrained the commons; for had I willed what would then have pleased this opposing party, or again what their foes devised for them, this state would now be bereft of many men. Therefore gathering courage from every source, I stood at bay like a wolf amid a pack of dogs."

Further, while rebuking both parties for their later grumblings:

"If I ought openly to reprove the commons — what they now have they would never have set eyes on even in dreams, while those who are greater, and superior in might, should commend me and hold me as their friend."

[1] Magistrates. This quotation proves that Solon had no intention of creating a democracy.

For if anyone else, he says, had obtained this office —

"He would not have restrained the commons or held them back till by their disturbance they had robbed the milk of its richness. Therefore I took my stand as a landmark between two armies."

13. For these reasons, accordingly, he went on a journey abroad. During Solon's absence, while the state was still in confusion, they kept the peace for four years; but in the fifth year after Solon's archonship they failed to elect an archon because of the sedition, and again in the fifth year they left the office vacant for the same reason. Then after an equal interval[1] Damasias, elected archon, ruled two years and two months, till he was forcibly expelled from his office. Thereupon they resolved because of the sedition to elect ten archons,[2] five from the eupatridæ, three from the farmers (ἄγροικοι), and two from the artisans (δημιουργοί),[3] and these persons held office in the year after Damasias. From this circumstance it is evident that the archon possessed the chief power, for they seem always to have been striving with one another for his office. Altogether they continued in a state of disorder among themselves, some taking as a cause and pretext the abolition of debts; for it had resulted in their impoverishment. Others were discontented

[1] In the interpretation of these chronological data editors are widely at variance; see Sandys' note *ad loc.* The subject is too complicated for treatment here.

[2] In the opinion of Meyer, *Forsch.* II. 537 *sqq.*, this measure transferred the functions of the office of Archon (eponymus), chief archon, to a commission of ten. Logically this was Aristotle's idea, for he considered that the dissensions concerned the chief archonship only. In truth, however, he or his source found the fact of the "ten archons" in a document, and interpreted it as in the text. While the view of Meyer is in any event perfectly possible, it is equally possible that the lower classes were content to leave the chief archonship in the hands of the eupatrids, provided they were fairly represented on the board. Furthermore Aristotle does not state whether the ten archons and the peculiar representation of the three classes were a temporary expedient or a lasting arrangement; but as there were no more dissensions over the office we may infer that the arrangement continued to the usurpation of Peisistratus. In the Cleisthenean system the secretary of the board counted, in the representation of the tribes, as a tenth archon.

[3] This measure is generally set down as reactionary, a return to conditions existing before the introduction of property qualifications for office. We may believe, however, that in spite of the broadening of eligibility the eupatrids still monopolized the offices, and that the measure here mentioned, like the Lex Licinia-Sextia at Rome, required actual usage to conform with law. This explanation was proposed by Botsford, *Development of the Athenian Constitution* (1893), 182 *sq.* See also De Sanctis, *Atthis* (2d ed., 1912), 264–8.

with the constitution because of the great change that had taken place, while others were actuated by mutual hatred. There were (accordingly) three factions: one of the Paralians (Shore Men), led by Megacles the Alcmeonid, who seemed particularly to favor a moderate form of government; another of the Pediæans (Plain Men), who favored an oligarchy, and who were under the leadership of Lycurgus; the third of the Diacrians (Hill Men) led by Peisistratus, who seemed most devoted to the people's interest. To the last-named faction were joined, because of their poverty, those whose securities had been cancelled, and, through fear, those who were not of pure descent. A proof is that after the overthrow of the tyranny they made a revision of the lists of citizens, with the idea that many were enjoying the franchise who had no right to it.[1] The several names of these factions were derived from the districts where they held their lands.

29. The Tyranny

(Aristotle, *Constitution of the Athenians*, 14–19)

14. Peisistratus appeared to be most devoted to the popular cause, and had won a brilliant reputation in the war with Megara. Having wounded himself, he persuaded the people, on the supposition that his injuries were inflicted by political enemies, to grant him a guard for his person. Taking the club-bearers, as they were called, he conspired with them against the state, and seized the Acropolis in the archonship of Comeas,[2] in the thirty-second year after (Solon's legislation). The story is told that when Peisistratus was asking for a guard, Solon opposed him, saying that he was wiser than some and braver than others — wiser than those who failed to see that Peisistratus was aiming at the tyranny, and braver than those who knew it but kept silent. As he accomplished nothing with words, he brought out his armor and placed it before his door, saying he had aided his country to the best of his ability

[1] This revision was probably made by the party of Cleisthenes after its return from exile but before Cleisthenes took up the cause of the people; § 20; Hdt. v. 69; *cf.* Botsford, in *Harvard Studies in Classical Philology*, VIII (1897). 9–11.

[2] 560 B.C. "Thirty-second" is probably a copyist's error for "thirty-fourth" (δευτέρῳ for τετάρτῳ).

(for he was at this time a very old man) and asking the rest now to perform this service. But Solon accomplished nothing by his exhortations at that crisis. Peisistratus, however, assuming the government, managed affairs constitutionally rather than despotically. Before his supremacy was firmly rooted, the party of Megacles, joining in friendship with that of Lycurgus, expelled him in the sixth year after his first establishment, in the archonship of Hegesias. But in the twelfth year afterward Megacles, harassed by sedition, again made overtures of peace to Peisistratus on condition that the latter should take the daughter of the former in marriage.[1] Megacles brought him back in an exceedingly old-fashioned and simple way. Spreading a report that Athena was restoring Peisistratus, he found a tall, handsome woman — of the Pæanian deme as Herodotus says, whereas others describe her as a Thracian flower-girl, named Phyê, of Collytus [2] — and dressing her up in imitation of the goddess, he brought her in along with Peisistratus, the latter seated in the chariot with the woman at his side, while the people of the city on their knees received them with adoration.

15. Thus was brought about the first restoration. He went again into exile about the seventh year after his return; for he did not maintain himself long, but because he was unwilling to treat the daughter of Megacles as his wife, and consequently feared a combination of the two factions, he secretly withdrew from the country. First he colonized a place called Rhæcelus about the Thermaic Gulf; then he crossed over to the neighborhood of Mount Pangæus. Making money in that locality and hiring soldiers, he came to Eretria in the eleventh year. Then for the first time he attempted to recover his supremacy by force, with the coöperation of the Thebans, of Lygdamis of Naxos, and of the knights who had the government at Eretria. Gaining a victory at Pallene and thus recovering his authority, he deprived the people of their arms and

[1] These chronological data are unreliable; *cf.* also § 17 and Aristotle, *Politics*, v. 9. 23, 1315 b. There is an utter lack of harmony among the various statements. On the whole it would seem reasonable that his first tyranny and first exile were relatively brief, amounting together to perhaps ten years, that his second exile was ten years in duration and his final tyranny ten or eleven years.

[2] Many demes (townships) must have existed under the tyranny, though they had no legal being before Cleisthenes; no. 30.

firmly established his despotism. Then taking possession of Naxos, he appointed Lygdamis governor. The people he deprived of their arms in the following manner. Holding a review of the citizens under arms at the Theseum, he attempted to address them, but spoke in a low voice; and when they declared they could not hear him, he bade them come up near the gateway of the Acropolis in order that his voice might sound louder. While he was passing the time making his speech, persons appointed to the task took the arms and locking them in a building near the Theseum, came and made a sign to Peisistratus. He finished his speech and then told them about the arms, bidding them not wonder or be dejected but go and attend to their private affairs, as he would himself manage all public matters.

16. Such was the origin of the tyranny of Peisistratus and such were its vicissitudes. He, as has been said, conducted the government moderately and more in the character of a statesman than of a tyrant. In general he was humane and unusually mild and forgiving to wrong-doers, and especially he lent money to the needy for use in their labors, in order that they might gain a livelihood by agriculture. This he did for two reasons, that they might not pass their time in the city but be scattered throughout the country, and that, being moderately well off and occupied with their private concerns, they might have neither the desire nor the leisure to attend to public affairs. At the same time the cultivation of the land resulted in the increase of his revenues, for he collected a tenth of the produce. For this reason, too, he established judges to go throughout the demes, and he himself often journeyed into the country to inspect it and to settle disputes. While Peisistratus was on one of these expeditions, it is said that he had the adventure with the man on Hymettus who was cultivating the so-called tax-free farm. Seeing a certain man digging and working among the rocks with a stake, he bade his servant ask what was produced in the place. The other replied, "Only aches and pains, and of these aches and pains Peisistratus must have his tenth." The man answered without knowing him; but Peisistratus, pleased with his candor and his love of work, made him exempt from all taxes.

In all other respects he absolutely refrained from disturbing the masses by his government, and he always preserved peace and maintained quiet; so that the tyranny of Peisistratus was often spoken of proverbially as the age of Cronos (golden age); for afterward when his sons had succeeded to the throne, the result was that the government became much harsher. Most praiseworthy of all his qualities was his popular and kindly character; for in general he chose to manage all affairs in accordance with the laws, giving himself no advantage, and once when cited for murder before the council of the Areopagus, he presented himself with a view to making his defence, but the accuser failed through fear to come forward. Hence he remained in power for a long time, and whenever he was banished, he easily recovered his position; for many of the nobles and commons were pleased with his rule. The former he attached to himself by his associations with them, the latter by aid in their private affairs. Throughout these times the laws of the Athenians concerning tyrants were mild, and particularly the one referring to the establishment of tyranny. The law runs thus: "These are the ancestral usages of the Athenians. If anyone attempts to make himself tyrant, or if anyone has a hand in establishing a tyranny, let him and his gens be disfranchised."

17. Peisistratus accordingly grew old in office and died of illness in the archonship of Philoneos,[1] having lived thirty-three years after the time when he first became tyrant, but having actually remained in power nineteen years; for during the rest of the time he was in exile. Evidently therefore they speak foolishly who assert that Peisistratus was a youthful favorite of Solon and a general in the war with Megara for the possession of Salamis. Their ages do not agree, if one reckons the length of their respective lives and the dates of their deaths. After the decease of Peisistratus his sons secured the power and conducted the administration in the same way. Of his lawful wife he had two sons, Hippias and Hipparchus, and two of his Argive wife,[2] Iophon and Hegesistratus, surnamed Thettalus. Peisistratus had married from Argos the daughter of an Argive named Gorgilus. This lady, Timonassa, had formerly

[1] 527 B.C.

[2] In 451 a statute of Pericles ordered that those only should be citizens whose parents were both Athenians. Aristotle and other ancient writers wrongly assumed that this regulation was in force from the earliest times. Naturally they regarded the foreign marriage of Peisistratus as illegal.

been the wife of the Cypselid Archinus of Ambracia. Thence arose his alliance with the Argives, a thousand of whom fought on his side in the battle of Pallene, having been brought by Hegesistratus. Some say he married the Argive woman after his first banishment, others while he was in possession of his authority.

18. Because of their greater reputation and age Hipparchus and Hippias were rulers of the state, while Hippias the elder, who was naturally statesmanlike and intelligent, was at the head of the government. Hipparchus, however, was youthful and amorous, and fond of literature. He it was who invited to Athens Anacreon and Simonides and the rest of the poets. [But Thettalus was much younger, and was bold and insolent in manner.] [1] He was the source of all their misfortunes. In love with Harmodius but failing to win his affection, he could not restrain his anger. On all occasions he showed himself bitter; and finally when the sister of Harmodius was about to act as basket-carrier at the Panathenæa, he forbade it, at the same time accusing Harmodius of being effeminate.

Hence it resulted that in their rage Harmodius and Aristogeiton did the deed with the help of many others. At the Panathenæa they were watching Hippias on the Acropolis (as he chanced to be sacrificing while Hipparchus was arranging the procession), and seeing one of the participants in the plot talking in a friendly manner with Hippias, they believed he was informing against them. Wishing accordingly to accomplish something before their arrest, they descended, and beginning action before the others, they killed Hipparchus while he was arranging the procession near the Leocorium. Thus they ruined the whole plot.[2] Harmodius was immediately killed by the guards, and Aristogeiton, arrested afterward, died by prolonged torture. Under constraint he accused many who belonged by birth to the nobility and were friends of the tyrants. For they were unable forthwith to find a clue to the plot. The current opinion, however, that Hippias disarmed those who were in the procession and searched them for concealed daggers is untrue, for they did not march armed in the procession; this custom was afterward introduced by the democracy.

[1] This sentence seems to be an interpolation.

[2] With this account of the conspiracy compare Thucydides i. 20; vi. 53–59.

He accused the tyrants' friends, purposely as the democratic writers say, in order that the tyrants might commit impiety and at the same time be weakened by the destruction of innocent persons and their own friends, though as some say, he did not deceive but actually informed against his accomplices. Lastly as he was unable, whatever he did, to find death, he proposed to denounce many others, and after persuading Hippias to give him his right hand as a pledge, he grasped it, at the same time reproaching Hippias with having offered his hand to the murderer of his brother. In this way he so exasperated Hippias that the latter could not restrain his wrath but drew his dagger and killed him.

19. From these events it resulted that the tyranny became far harsher; for in taking vengeance for his brother and in slaying and banishing many citizens, Hippias became distrustful and embittered toward all. About the fourth year after the death of Hipparchus, as his affairs in the city were in a bad condition, he undertook the fortification of Munichia with the idea of changing his residence to that place.

While engaged in this work he was expelled by Cleomenes, king of the Lacedæmonians, inasmuch as oracles were continually given to the Laconians to the effect that they should abolish the tyranny. The reason for the oracles is as follows. The exiles, led by the Alcmeonidæ, were unable by their own means to effect their return. In all their other undertakings they failed and particularly when they fortified Leipsydrium on Mount Parnes within the country of Attica. Here, joined by certain men from the city, they were besieged by the tyrants, wherefore after their disaster people used to sing in skolia[1]: —

"Alas, Leipsydrium, traitor to your friends, how good the men you slew, how brave in fight, how nobly born! They showed in that fray their illustrious parentage."

Having failed in everything else, they contracted to build the temple at Delphi. This transaction provided them well with the means of gaining the aid of the Laconians. Whenever, accordingly, the Lacedæmonians consulted the oracle, the Pythia always replied that they must set Athens free, till she succeeded in persuading the

[1] On the meaning of the term, see no. 52.

Spartans, notwithstanding that they were guest-friends of the Peisistratidæ. There was added a no small cause of the undertaking on the part of the Laconians in the alliance existing between the Argives and the Peisistratidæ. In the first place they despatched Anchimolus with an army by sea. He was beaten and slain with the aid of Cineas the Thessalian, who came with a thousand cavalry. Enraged at the event, they sent by land with a larger force Cleomenes the king, who after defeating the Thessalian horsemen in their endeavor to prevent his invasion of Attica, drove Hippias into the so-called Pelargic wall, and besieged him there with the aid of the Athenians. This event took place in the archonship of Harpactides,[1] after they had held the tyranny about seventeen years since the death of their father, and including his reign, forty-nine years in all.

30. Cleisthenes and the Democracy

508–480 B.C.

(Aristotle, *Constitution of the Athenians*, 20–22)

20. When the tyranny had fallen, a sedition arose between Isagoras, son of Teisander, a friend of the tyrants, and Cleisthenes of the gens of the Alcmeonidæ. Beaten by means of the clubs, Cleisthenes attached the commons to himself by promising the franchise to the masses. Isagoras, now proving inferior in strength, called to his aid Cleomenes, his guest-friend, and persuaded him to expel the pollution; for it was the common opinion that the Alcmeonidæ were under a curse.[2] Thereupon Cleisthenes with a few persons secretly withdrew from the country, while Cleomenes proceeded to expel as polluted seven hundred Athenian families. Having accomplished this object, he attempted to dissolve the council[3] and to make Isagoras and three hundred of his partisans masters of the state. But as the council opposed and the multitude

[1] 510 B.C. On the tyranny and its downfall, *cf.* Hdt. i. 59–64; v. 57–65.

[2] The curse was brought upon them by the guilt incurred in slaughtering the followers of Cylon; no. 27.

[3] This was the council of Four Hundred; that of the Five Hundred had not yet been instituted.

gathered, Cleomenes and Isagoras with their party took refuge in the Acropolis. The commons thereupon encamped and besieged them two days; on the third day they permitted Cleomenes and all with him to depart under a truce, but recalled Cleisthenes and the rest of the exiles. Now that the commons had become masters of the state, Cleisthenes was their leader and champion: for the Alcmeonidæ were perhaps the chief cause of the tyrants' expulsion and were almost always at sedition with them. Still earlier Cedon the Alcmeonid had made an attempt on them, hence the people used to sing to him in skolia [1]: —

"Pour out to Cedon, boy, and forget it not, if ever our duty is to pour an offering of wine to the memory of brave men."

21. For these reasons the people trusted Cleisthenes. On that occasion, as he was leader of the people in the fourth year after the overthrow of the tyrants, in the archonship of Isagoras,[2] in the first place he distributed all the people among ten tribes in place of four, with the object of intermixing them in order that more might have a share in the franchise. Hence arose the saying, "Do not discriminate between the tribes" with reference to those who wished to scrutinize the gentes.[3] Then he constituted the council of five hundred in place of four hundred, fifty from each tribe instead of a hundred as formerly. The reason for his not distributing the people among twelve tribes was his desire to avoid the division into the existing trittyes as the four tribes contained twelve trittyes; so that, had he made twelve tribes, he would not have succeeded in redistributing the population.[4]

The country he divided by demes into thirty parts, ten about the city, ten in the paralia, ten in the midland; and calling these parts trittyes, he assigned three by lot to each tribe in such a way that every tribe might have a trittys in each of the three local

[1] For an explanation of the term, see no. 52.

[2] 508 B.C.

[3] The meaning seems to be that whereas in the old tribe lists of citizens account was taken of the gentes, under the new system that was not the case. The proverb, however, may or may not have arisen from such a circumstance.

[4] Aristotle feels called upon to make this explanation in view of the fact that twelve tribes, one for each month, would have been a far more convenient arrangement. The number was increased to twelve in 307; Ferguson, *Hellenistic Athens*, 64.

sections. The inhabitants of the respective demes he made demesmen of one another in order that they might not expose the new citizens by calling them after the names of their fathers, but that they might be named after their demes. Hence the Athenians continue to call themselves by the names of their demes. He instituted demarchs with the same function as the earlier naucrars, for he made the demes to take the place of the naucraries. Some of the demes he named after localities, others after their founders; for all the localities did not preserve the names of their founders. Their gentes and phratries and priesthoods he permitted them severally to keep according to ancestral usage.[1] As eponyms of the tribes he appointed the ten whom the Pythia had selected from the hundred founders nominated to her.[2]

22. Through these changes the constitution became far more democratic than that of Solon. The fact is that the tyranny had abolished some of the laws of Solon through failure to observe them, and Cleisthenes in his effort to win the populace enacted new regulations, among which was the law of ostracism. It was not however till the fifth year after his legislation that, in the archonship of Hermocreon,[3] they drew up for the council of Five Hundred the oath which the members continue even now to swear. Then they began to elect the generals by tribes, one from each tribe,[4] whereas the commander of the entire army was the polemarch. In the twelfth year afterward, in the archonship of Phænippus,[5] they won the battle of Marathon. Two years after the victory, while the people were elated, they for the first time made use of the law of ostracism through suspicion of persons in power, because it was as

[1] It is sufficiently known that Cleisthenes did not disturb the composition of the gentes. From Aristotle, *Politics*, vi. 4. 18, 1319 b, we infer that he increased the number of phratries. It would be easy to reconcile the two passages by assuming that the old citizens remained in their several phratries, while new phratries were created for the multitude of new citizens. Many sacerdotal offices, too, remained hereditary in the noble families which had originally held them.

[2] *I.e.*, he sent to the prophetess of Apollo at Delphi the names of a hundred local heroes (founders), from which she selected the ten tribal eponyms.

[3] The Attic year 501–500.

[4] From the fact that the council of Five Hundred and the army of ten tribal regiments were not definitely organized before the date here given, we may assume that some years had been required for organizing the demes and fixing their boundaries.

[5] 490–489.

popular leader and general that Peisistratus had made himself tyrant. The first to be ostracized was one of his kinsmen, Hipparchus, son of Charmus of Collytus, on account of whom in particular Cleisthenes had enacted the law, as he wished to expel him.[1] But the Athenians with the accustomed leniency of the democracy permitted to remain in the city such friends of the tyrants as refrained from joining in their evil deeds in times of civil disturbance. The leader and patron of these friends was Hipparchus. In the next year following, in the archonship of Telesinus,[2] they appointed by lot the nine archons, according to tribes, from five hundred nominees presented by the demesmen.[3] This was the first time after the tyranny, for hitherto all had been elected. Megacles, son of Hippocrates[4] of Alopece, was ostracized. For three years in fact they continued to ostracize the friends of the tyrants, on account of whom the law had been enacted; and in the fourth year they began to ostracize any others who had the reputation of possessing excessive power. The first to be ostracized who had no connection with the tyranny was Xanthippus,[5] son of Ariphron. Three years later, in the archonship of Nicodemus,[6] as mines had been opened in Maroneia and a hundred talents had accrued to the state from the works, while others were advising the division of the silver among the people, Themistocles prevented it. He did not say what use he would make of the money but bade them lend it to the hundred wealthiest Athenians, a talent to each; then if the use of it should prove satisfactory, the expense should be the state's; otherwise the state should recover the money from the borrowers.[7] Receiving the money on these terms, he built a hundred triremes, each of the hundred men constructing one; and with these ships they fought at Salamis against the barbarians. In

[1] This statement seems most unlikely.

[2] 487–486.

[3] Through this change in the method of appointment the archons lost their importance; they ceased to be the chief magistrates, that position passing to the ten generals.

[4] Hippocrates was a brother of Cleisthenes. From the fact that Megacles was considered a friend of the tyrants, we may perhaps infer that he had made a political "deal" with them.

[5] 485–484. As the vote of ostracism took place in the winter, Xanthippus was exiled early in 484.

[6] 483–482.

[7] The anecdote certainly does not belong here.

these times Aristeides, son of Lysimachus, was ostracized. Four years afterward, in the archonship of Hypsichides,[1] they recalled all the ostracized because of the invasion of Xerxes; and for the future they laid down for the ostracized the rule that they must not dwell within Geræstus and Scyllæum on penalty of being forever disfranchised.[2]

31. The Procedure in Votes of Ostracism

In view of the fact that the question as to the number of votes required for the ostracism of an individual has been reopened by Carcopino, J., *Histoire de l'ostracisme athênien*, in Mélanges d'histoire ancienne (Paris, 1909), the two principal passages bearing upon the question are given below.

(Plutarch, *Aristides*, 7. Translated by G. W. B.)

The general character of the procedure was as follows. Each man took an ostrakon,[3] and having written on it the name of the citizen whom he wished to exile, brought it to a part of the market-place which had been fenced in with palings. Then in the first place the archons counted the whole number of ostraka; for if the number of voters was less than 6000, the vote of ostracism was ineffectual.[4] Next they counted by itself the number of times each name occurred, and proclaimed the banishment for ten years of the one whose name had been written by the greatest number, permitting the banished the enjoyment of his own property.[5]

[1] 481–480.

[2] The object was to prevent the ostracized from living so near at home as to interfere in politics.

[3] The ostrakon was a potsherd, specimens of which, with the names of famous Greeks, may be seen in the British Museum.

[4] The object was to determine whether a quorum of 6000, required for the vote of a privilegium, had actually voted. If the number fell below 6000, the individual names remained uncounted in order that no one might be prejudiced. After the introduction of pay for attendance at the assembly, early in the fourth century, there were officials who kept a record of every citizen's attendance; but it is unlikely that Cleisthenes made any such arrangement. It was only through the preliminary counting described in the text, therefore, that the number present could be ascertained.

[5] Plutarch's statement of the procedure is remarkably clear, and seems to have come from a reliable source. According to this statement 6000 constituted a quorum, and a plurality (not majority) of votes decided. His interpretation is confirmed by the well-known fact that privilegia (ψηφίσματα ἐπ' ἀνδρί) required a quorum of 6000; *cf.* Gilbert, *Const. Antiq.* 307 *sqq.*

(Philochorus, *Atthis*, iii, Müller, *Frag. hist. græc.* I. p. 396, frag. 79 b. Translated by G. W. B.)

Philochorus, writing in the third book, explains ostracism thus.[1] Before the eighth prytany the people in assembly, by a preliminary vote, determine whether they will have recourse to ostracism. Whenever the decision was affirmative, the market-place was fenced in with palings, and there were left open ten approaches through which (the citizens), entering by tribes, carried their ostraka, keeping the inscriptions concealed. The nine archons and the council presided. The votes were counted; the one against whom the greatest number was cast, and not less that 6000,[2] having settled his cases at law regarding his private business transactions, had to leave the country within ten days, for a period of ten years. The term was afterward changed to five. He could enjoy the use of his own property but was not permitted to enter within a line drawn through the promontory of Eubœa. Hyperbolus alone of men of no repute was ostracized through [3] . . . because of the baseness of his character, not through suspicion of his attempting the tyranny. After his exile they abolished the custom which originated through the legislation of Cleisthenes, after he had overthrown the tyranny, in order that he might also banish the friends (of the tyrant).[4]

[1] It is to be noted that Philochorus himself is not speaking; this passage is a quotation, made directly or indirectly from him by Photius. The passage is exceedingly condensed and obscure, and contains at least one primary error — the statement that the period of ten years was afterward cut down to five. The statement, too, regarding the limitation of the exile's movements is imperfect; *cf.* Aristotle, *Const. Ath.* 22, in no. 30 *supra*. These imperfections detract from the reliability of the passage.

[2] It is possible that this phrase, too (see preceding note), has suffered through excessive condensation. The statement of Philochorus may have read substantially, "and the total number of votes being not less that 6000," which would put it into agreement with the source of Plutarch's account.

[3] The person or persons (Alcibiades, Nicias) instrumental in his ostracism were probably named by Philochorus, but in Photius only the word "through" (διά) remains.

[4] On the whole this imperfect quotation from Philochorus cannot be taken in disproof of the clear, consistent account given by Plutarch.

32. Persian Tolerance of Greek Religion

(Letter of Darius to the Persian official Gadatas, about 500 B.C.; Hicks and Hill, no. 20; Ditt. I. no. 2; Cousin and Deschamps, in *Bulletin de Correspondance hellénique*, XIII (1889). 529–42, text with French translation and commentary. Translated by C. J. O.)

From this number to the end of the chapter the selections illustrate the relations between the Hellenes and their enemies, the Persians.

Though dating from Roman time, the inscription is proved to be a copy of the original rescript of the Persian king Darius I (reigned 522–486 B.C.) by the resemblance between its style and that of the Old Persian inscriptions. We have no further information about the Gadatas to whom the letter is addressed; but he must have been an official of the Ionian province, perhaps the governor (satrap), more probably the overseer of a royal park. The document shows both the careful administration and the religious tolerance of Darius, who, though himself a worshiper of Auramazda, maintains here the immunities of a sanctuary of Apollo.

The king of kings, Darius, the son of Hystaspes, to his slave Gadatas says thus: — I learn that thou dost not obey my commands in all respects. In that thou cultivatest my land by transplanting the fruits (of the country) beyond the Euphrates [1] to the lower parts of Asia, I commend thy purpose, and by reason of this there shall be laid up for thee great favor in the king's house.[2] But, in that thou settest at naught my policy towards the gods, I will give thee, if thou dost not change, a proof of my wronged feelings; for thou didst exact a payment from the sacred gardeners of Apollo and didst command them to dig unhallowed ground, not knowing the mind of my forefathers towards the god, who hath told the Persians the whole truth.[3] . . .

[1] Syria, which was "beyond the Euphrates" to the Persians.

[2] *I.e.*, Gadatas is enrolled in the official list of the king's benefactors, concerning which see Herodotus, viii. 85; *Esther*, chap. 6. A similar expression occurs in a letter of Xerxes quoted by Thucydides, i. 129.

[3] The reference seems to be to oracles of Apollo received by Cyrus or Cambyses, the predecessors of Darius.

On the selection in general, see E. Meyer, *Entstehung des Judentums* (Halle, 1896), 19–21.

33. The Attempt of the Persians to Conquer Naxos, 500 B.C.

(Herodotus v. 30–34)

In his policy of aggression Darius was gradually pushing the western boundary of his empire into Europe. He had conquered Thrace, had received the nominal subjection of Macedon, and had thus extended the empire to the northern border of Thessaly. The Ægean Islands lying near the coast of Asia Minor had submitted. The subjoined excerpt describes an attempt to extend the empire across the Ægean to the island of Naxos. The selection especially illustrates the fact that the greatest enemies of Hellas were her own people.

30. . . . At the time of which I speak evils began to come to Ionia from these states (Paros and Miletus, mentioned in the preceding paragraph) in the following manner: — From Naxos certain men of the wealthier class were driven into exile by the people, and having gone into exile they arrived at Miletus. Now of Miletus it happened that Aristagoras son of Molpagoras was ruler in charge, being both a son-in-law and also a cousin of Histiæus son of Lysagoras, whom Darius was keeping at Susa:[1] for Histiæus was despot of Miletus, and it happened that he was at Susa at this time when the Naxians came, who had been in former times guest-friends of Histiæus. When accordingly the Naxians arrived, they made request of Aristagoras, to see if perchance he would supply them with a force, that so they might return from exile to their own land: and he, thinking that if by his means they should return to their own state, he would be ruler of Naxos, but at the same time making a pretext of the guest-friendship of Histiæus, made proposal to them thus: "I am not able to engage that I can supply you with sufficient force to bring you back from exile against the will of those Naxians who have control of the state; for I hear that the Naxians have an army which is eight thousand shields strong and many ships of war; but I will use every endeavor to devise a means; and my plan is this: it chances that Artaphrenes[2] is my friend. Now Artaphrenes, ye must know, is a son of Hystaspes and brother of

[1] Why Darius summoned Histiæus to Susa and kept him there in honorable captivity is told by Herodotus v. 23 *sq.*

[2] Artaphrenes, the correct spelling; Cauer, in Pauly-Wissowa, *Real-Encycl.* II. 1306. On this person, *ib.* 1037. 2.

Darius the king; and he is ruler of all the people of the sea-coasts in Asia, with a great army and many ships. This man, then, I think will do whatsoever we shall request of him." Hearing this, the Naxians gave over the matter to Aristagoras to manage as best he could, and they bade him promise gifts and the expenses of the expedition, saying that they would pay them; for they had full expectation that when they should appear at Naxos, the Naxians would do all their bidding, and likewise all the other islanders. For of these islands — the Cyclades — not one was as yet subject to Darius.

31. Aristagoras, accordingly, having arrived at Sardis, said to Artaphrenes that Naxos was an island not indeed large in size, but fair nevertheless and of fertile soil, as well as near to Ionia, and that there were in it much wealth and many slaves: "Do thou therefore send an expedition against this land, and restore to it those who are now exiles from it; and if thou shalt do this, first I have ready for thee large sums of money apart from the expenses incurred for the expedition (which it is fair that we who conduct it should supply), and next thou wilt gain for the king not only Naxos itself but also the islands which are dependent upon it, Paros and Andros and the others which are called Cyclades; and setting out from these thou wilt easily attack Eubœa, an island which is large and wealthy, as large indeed as Cyprus, and very easy to conquer. To subdue all these a hundred ships are sufficient." He made answer in these words: "Thou makest thyself a reporter of good things to the house of the king; and in all these things thou advisest well, except as to the number of the ships; for instead of one hundred there shall be prepared for thee two hundred by the beginning of spring. And it is right that the king himself also should join in approving this matter."

32. So Aristagoras hearing this went back to Miletus greatly rejoiced; and Artaphrenes meanwhile, when he had sent to Susa and communicated that which was said by Aristagoras, and Darius himself also had joined in approving it, made ready two hundred triremes and a very great multitude both of Persians and of their allies, and appointed to be commander of these Megabates a Persian, one of the Achæmenidæ [1] and a cousin to himself and to Darius,

[1] The royal family of Persia, to whom Darius belonged. For the principal members of this dynasty, see Pauly-Wissowa, *Real-Encycl.* I. 200 *sqq.*

to whose daughter afterward Pausanias the son of Cleombrotus the Lacedæmonian (at least if the story be true) betrothed himself, having formed a desire to become despot of Hellas. Having appointed Megabates, I say, to be commander, Artaphrenes sent away the armament to Aristagoras.

33. So when Megabates had taken up from Miletus Aristagoras and the Ionian force together with the Naxians, he sailed with the pretence of going to the Hellespont; but when he came to Chios, he directed his ships to Caucasa, in order that he might from thence pass them over to Naxos with a North Wind. Then, since it was not fated that the Naxians should be destroyed by this expedition, there happened an event which I shall narrate. As Megabates was going round to visit the guards set in the several ships, it chanced that in a ship of Myndos there was no one on guard; and he being very angry bade his spearsmen find out the commander of the ship, whose name was Scylax, and bind him in an oar-hole of his ship in such a manner that his head should be outside and his body within. When Scylax was thus bound, some one reported to Aristagoras that Megabates had bound his guest-friend of Myndos and was doing to him shameful outrage. He accordingly came and asked the Persian for his release, and as he did not obtain anything of that which he requested, he went himself and let him loose. Being informed of this, Megabates was exceedingly angry and broke out in rage against Aristagoras; and he replied: "What hast thou to do with these matters? Did not Artaphrenes send thee to obey me, and to sail whithersoever I should order? Why dost thou meddle with things which concern thee not?" Thus said Aristagoras; and the other being enraged at this, when night came on sent men in a ship to Naxos to declare to the Naxians all the danger that threatened them.

34. For the Naxians were not at all expecting that this expedition would be against them; but when they were informed of it, forthwith they brought within the wall the property which was in the fields, and provided for themselves food and drink as for a siege, and strengthened their wall. These then were making preparations as for war to come upon them; and the others meanwhile having passed their ships over from Chios to Naxos, found them well defended when they made their attack, and besieged them for four

months. Then when the money which the Persians had brought with them had all been consumed by them, and not only that, but Aristagoras himself had spent much more in addition, and the siege demanded ever more and more, they built forts for the Naxian exiles and departed to the mainland again with ill success.

34. Proceedings of the Hellenic Congress of 481 B.C.

(Herodotus vii. 145–162. Macaulay, revised by E. G. S.)

This congress was called at the suggestion of Athens, but on the formal invitation of Lacedæmon, to meet at the shrine of Poseidon on the Isthmus of Corinth. It was composed of deputies from the loyal states of Hellas, and its object was to concert measures of defense against Xerxes, who was on the point of invading Greece.

The nucleus of the Hellenic union thus forming was the Peloponnesian league, which had grown up in the preceding century. For sources illustrative of the latter institution, see Botsford, *Source-Book of Ancient History*, 119–21. The preceding selection and the one given below throw light upon the internal condition of the Greek states and their relation to one another at a time when they were facing the greatest crisis in their history.

For a selection from Æschylus, *Persians*, describing the battle of Salamis, see Botsford, *op. cit.* 169–74.

145. When those Hellenes who had the better mind about Hellas came together to one place, and considered their affairs and interchanged assurances with one another, then deliberating together they thought it well first of all things to reconcile the enmities and bring to an end the wars which they had with one another. Now there were wars engaged between others also, and especially between the Athenians and the Æginetans. After this, being informed that Xerxes was with his army at Sardis, they determined to send spies to Asia to make observation of the power of the king; and moreover they resolved to send envoys to Argos to form an alliance against the Persian, and to send others to Sicily to Gelon[1] the son of Deinomenes and also to Corcyra, to urge them to come to the assistance of Hellas, and others again to Crete; for they made it their aim that if possible the Hellenic race might unite in one, and that they might join all together and act toward the same end,

[1] Tyrant of Syracuse.

since dangers were threatening all the Hellenes equally. Now the power of Gelon was said to be great, far greater than any other Hellenic power.

146. When they had thus resolved, they reconciled their enmities and then sent first three men as spies to Asia. These men, having come to Sardis and having got knowledge about the king's army, were discovered, and after having been examined by the generals of the land army were being led off to die. For these men, I say, death had been determined; but Xerxes, being informed of this, found fault with the decision of the generals and sent some of the spearmen of his guard, enjoining them, if they should find the spies yet alive, to bring them to his presence. Therefore having found them yet surviving, they brought them into the presence of the king; and upon that Xerxes, being informed for what purpose they had come, commanded the spearmen to lead them round and to show them the whole army both foot and horse, and when they should have had their fill of looking at these things, to let them go unhurt to whatsoever land they desired. 147. Such was the command which he gave, adding at the same time this saying, namely that if the spies had been put to death, the Hellenes would not have been informed beforehand of his power, how far beyond description it was; while on the other hand by putting to death three men they would not very greatly have damaged the enemy; but when these returned back to Hellas, he thought it likely that the Hellenes, hearing of his power, would deliver up their freedom to him themselves, before the expedition took place which was being set in motion; and thus there would be no need for them to have the labor of marching an army against them. This opinion of his is like his manner of thinking at other times; for when Xerxes was in Abydos, he saw vessels which carried corn from the Pontus sailing out through the Hellespont on their way to Ægina and the Peloponnese. Those then who sat by his side, being informed that the ships belonged to the enemy, were prepared to capture them, and were looking to the king to see when he would give the word; but Xerxes asked about them whither the men were sailing, and they replied: "Master, to thy foes, conveying to them corn:" he then made answer and said: "Are we not also sailing to the same place as these men, furnished with corn as well as with other things nec-

essary? How then do these wrong us, since they are conveying provisions for our use?"

148. The spies then, having thus looked at everything and after that having been dismissed, returned back to Europe; and meanwhile those of the Hellenes who had sworn alliance against the Persian, after the sending forth of the spies proceeded to send envoys next to Argos. Now the Argives report that the matters concerning themselves took place as follows: They were informed, they say, at the very first of the movement which was being set on foot by the Barbarian against Hellas: and having been informed of this and perceiving that the Hellenes would endeavor to get their alliance against the Persian, they had sent messengers to inquire of the god at Delphi, and to ask how they should act in order that it might be best for themselves; because lately there had been slain of them six thousand men by the Lacedæmonians and by Cleomenes[1] the son of Anaxandrides, and this in fact was the reason that they were sending to inquire: and when they inquired, the Pythian prophetess made answer to them as follows: —

"Thou to thy neighbors a foe, by the gods immortal belovèd,
Keep thou thy spear within bounds, and sit well-guarded behind it:
Guard well the head, and the head shall preserve the limbs and the body."

Thus, they say, the Pythian prophetess had replied to them before this; and afterwards when the messengers of the Hellenes came, as I said, to Argos, they entered the council-chamber and spoke that which had been enjoined to them; and to that which was said the council replied that the Argives were ready to do as they were requested, on condition that they got peace made with the Lacedæmonians for thirty years and that they had half the leadership of the whole confederacy: and yet by strict right (they said) the whole leadership fell to their share, but nevertheless it was sufficient for them to have half. 149. Thus they report that the council made answer, although the oracle forbade them to make the alliance with the Hellenes; and they were anxious, they say, that a truce from hostilities for thirty years should be made, although they feared the oracle, in order, as they allege, that their sons might grow to manhood in these years; whereas if a truce did not exist,

[1] King of the Lacedæmonians.

they had fear that, supposing another disaster should come upon them in fighting against the Persian in addition to that which had befallen them already, they might be for all future time subject to the Lacedæmonians. To that which was spoken by the council those of the envoys who were of Sparta replied, that as to the truce they would refer the matter to their public assembly, but as to the leadership they had themselves been commissioned to make reply, and did in fact say this, namely that they had two kings, while the Argives had one; and it was not possible to remove either of the two who were of Sparta from the leadership, but there was nothing to prevent the Argive king from having an equal vote with each of their two. Then, say the Argives, they could not endure the grasping selfishness of the Spartans, but chose to be ruled by the Barbarians rather than to yield at all to the Lacedæmonians; and they gave notice to the envoys to depart out of the territory of the Argives before sunset, or, if not, they would be dealt with as enemies. . . .

153. That which concerns the Argives has now been said. Meanwhile envoys had come to Sicily from the allies, to confer with Gelon, among whom also was Syagrus from the Lacedæmonians. . . . 157. . . . They came to speech with him and said as follows: "The Lacedæmonians and their allies sent us to get thee to be on our side against the Barbarian; for we suppose that thou art certainly informed of him who is about to invade Hellas, namely that a Persian is designing to bridge over the Hellespont, and to make an expedition against Hellas, leading against us out of Asia all the armies of the East, under color of marching upon Athens, but in fact meaning to bring all Hellas to subjection under him. Do thou therefore, seeing that thou hast attained to a great power and hast no small portion of Hellas for thy share, being the ruler of Sicily, come to the assistance of those who are endeavoring to free Hellas, and join in making her free; for if all Hellas be gathered together in one, it forms a great body, and we are made a match in fight for those who are coming against us; but if some of us go over to the enemy, and others are not willing to help, and the sound portion of Hellas is consequently small, there is at once in this a danger that all Hellas may fall to ruin. For do not thou hope that if the Persian shall overcome us in battle he will not come to thee, but guard thyself

against this beforehand; for in coming to our assistance thou art helping thyself; and the matter which is wisely planned has for the most part a good issue afterwards." 158. The envoys spoke thus; but Gelon was very vehement with them, speaking to them as follows: "Hellenes, a selfish speech is this, with which ye have ventured to come and invite me to be your ally against the Barbarian; whereas ye yourselves, when I in former time requested of you to join me in fighting against an army of Barbarians,[1] contention having arisen between me and the Carthaginians, and when I charged you to exact vengeance of the men of Egesta for the death of Dorieus the son of Anaxandrides, while at the same time I offered to help in setting free the trading-places, from which great advantages and gains have been reaped by you, — ye, I say, then neither for my own sake came to my assistance, nor in order to exact vengeance for the death of Dorieus; and so far as ye are concerned, all these parts are even now under the rule of the Barbarians. But since it turned out well for us and came to a better issue, now that the war has come round and reached you, there has at last arisen in your minds a recollection of Gelon. However, though I have met with contempt at your hands, I will not act like you; but I am prepared to come to your assistance, supplying two hundred triremes and twenty thousand hoplites, with two thousand horsemen, two thousand bowmen, two thousand slingers and two thousand light-armed men to run beside the horsemen; and moreover I will undertake to supply corn for the whole army of the Hellenes, until we shall have finished the war. These things I engage to supply on this condition, namely that I shall be commander and leader of the Hellenes against the Barbarians; but on any other condition I will neither come myself nor will I send others." 159. Hearing this Syagrus could not contain himself but spoke these words: "Deeply, I trow, would Agamemnon son of Pelops lament, if he heard that the Spartans had had the leadership taken away from them by Gelon and by the Syracusans. Nay, but make thou no further mention of this condition, namely that we should deliver the leadership to thee; but if thou art desirous to come to the assistance of Hellas, know that thou wilt be under the command of the Lacedæmonians; and if thou dost

[1] The historian, who composed this speech, has confused the chronology: the Carthaginian invasion occurred in the following year, 480.

indeed claim not to be under command, come not thou to our help at all."

160. To this Gelon, seeing that the speech of Syagrus was adverse, set forth to them his last proposal thus: "Stranger from Sparta, reproaches sinking into the heart of a man are wont to rouse his spirit in anger against them; thou, however, though thou hast uttered insults against me in thy speech, wilt not bring me to show myself unseemly in my reply. But whereas ye so strongly lay claim to the leadership, it were fitting that I should lay claim to it more than ye, seeing that I am the leader of an army many times as large and of ships many more. Since however this condition is so distasteful to you, we will recede somewhat from our former proposal. Suppose that ye should be leaders of the land army and I of the fleet; or if it pleases you to lead the sea forces, I am willing to be leader of those on land; and either ye must be contented with these terms, or go away without the alliance which I have to give." 161. Gelon, I say, made these offers, and the envoy of the Athenians, answering before that of the Lacedæmonians, replied to him as follows: "O king of the Syracusans, it was not of a leader that Hellas was in want when it sent us to thee, but of an army. Thou however dost not set before us the hope that thou wilt send an army, except thou have the leadership of Hellas; and thou art striving how thou mayest become commander of the armies of Hellas. So long then as it was thy demand to be leader of the whole army of the Hellenes, it was sufficient for us Athenians to keep silence, knowing that the Lacedæmonian would be able to make defense even for us both; but now since being repulsed from the demand for the whole thou art requesting to be commander of the naval force, we tell thee that thus it is:—not even if the Lacedæmonian shall permit thee to be commander of it, will we permit thee; for this at least is our own, if the Lacedæmonians themselves do not desire to have it. With these, if they desire to be the leaders, we do not contend; but none others beside ourselves shall we permit to be in command of the ships; for then to no purpose should we be possessors of a sea force larger than any other which belongs to the Hellenes, if, being Athenians, we should yield the leadership to Syracusans, we who boast of a race which is the most ancient of all and who are of all the Hellenes the only people who have not

changed from one land to another; to whom also belonged a man who Homer the Epic poet said was the best of all who came to Ilion in drawing up an army and setting it in array. Thus we are not justly to be reproached if we say these things." 162. To this Gelon made answer thus: "Stranger of Athens, it would seem that ye have the commanders, but that ye will not have the men to be commanded. Since then ye will not at all give way, but desire to have the whole, it were well that ye should depart home as quickly as possible and report to the Hellenes that the spring has been taken out of their year." [1] Now this is the meaning of the saying: — evidently the spring is the noblest part of the year; and so he meant to say that his army was the noblest part of the army of the Hellenes: for Hellas therefore, deprived of his alliance, it was, he said, as if the spring had been taken out of the year.

BIBLIOGRAPHY

I. Lacedæmon. (1) *Sources.* — The sources for early Lacedæmon are relatively abundant. New light has been thrown on her civilization by the excavations of the English, see *B. S. A.*, beginning with XI (1904–05). The seventh century is represented by Alcman and Tyrtæus. A large part of Herodotus (see Index) is given to Lacedæmonian affairs. Xenophon, *Constitution of the Lacedæmonians,* treats mainly of early conditions, as does also Plutarch, *Lycurgus.*

(2) *Modern Writers.* — Botsford, *Hellenic History,* ch. vi; Bury, ch. iii; Greenidge, *Gk. Const. Hist.* ch. v; Gilbert, *Const. Antiq.* 1–81; Abbott, I. chs. vi, viii; Curtius, bk. II. ch. i; Grote, II. chs. vi, vii; Busolt, *Griech. Gesch.* I. 510–611, 700–11.

The following studies are more special: Niese, B., "Herodotstudien besonders zur spartanischen Geschichte," in *Hermes,* XLII (1907). 419–68; Decker, De, "La genèse de l'organisation civique des Spartiates," in *Archiv soc. bull.* no. 25 (Brussels, 1913). 306–13; Nilsson, M. P., "Die Grundlagen des spartanischen Lebens," in *Klio,* XII (1912). 308–40; Bölte, F., "Beiträge zur Topographie Lakoniens," in *Ath. Mitt.* XXXIV (1909). 376–92; Sihler, E. G., "Aristotle's Criticisms on the Spartan Constitution," in *Class. Rev.* VII (1893), 439–43; Niese, "Neue Beiträge zur Geschichte und Landeskunde Lakedämons," in *Gött. Gesellsch.* (1906). pp. 101–42, very valuable; Heidemann, L., *Die territoriale Entwickelung Lakedaimons bis auf Alexander* (Berlin, Diss.); Toynbee, A. J., "The Growth of Sparta," in *J. H. S.* XXXIII (1913). 246–75; Kuchtner, K., *Entstehung und Ursprüngliche Bedeutung des spartanischen Ephorats* (Munich,

[1] The foregoing conversation, though a fiction, truly represents the Greek spirit.

1897); Jeanmaire, H., in *Rev. des ét. gr.* XXVII. no. 117, on the crypteia; Girard, P., "Crypteia," in Daremberg-Saglio, *Dict.* III. 871–3; Caillemer, E.; *γερουσία*, *ib.* II. 1549; "Hypomeiones," *ib.* III. 350–2; "Homoioi," *ib.* III. 233–4; Lecrivain, C., "Helotæ," *ib.* III. 67–71; Miller, J., "Gerontes, Gerusia," in Pauly-Wissowa, *Real-Encycl.* VII. 1264–7; Szanto, "Ephoroi," *ib.* V. 2860–4; Oehler, J., "Heloten," *ib.* 203–6; Schulthess, "Homoioi," *ib.* VIII. 2252–9;. Solari, A., *Ricerche spartane* (Livorno, 1907), reprints of studies; Wide, S., *Lakonische Kulte* (Leipzig, 1893); Droop, J. P., "Dates of the Vases called 'Cyrenaic,'" in *J. H. S.* XXX (1910). 1–34; Bethe, E., "Die dorische Knabenliebe," in *Rhein. Mus.* LXII (1907). 438–75; Semenov, A., same subject, in *Philol.* LXX (1911). 146–50.

II. Athens. (1) *Sources.* — For Attica before the middle of the seventh century, no contemporary written material, excepting perhaps a list of annual officials, is know to have existed. The earliest known source is the Draconian *code*, a part of which has survived. On the conditions immediately following Draco the *Poems* of Solon throw a clear light. His *Laws*, too, including some which soon became obsolete, are known to us through later writers. From about 600, inscriptions begin to appear, though during the sixth century they remain scant. A considerable part of the *History* of Herodotus (*cf.* i. 59–64; v. 62–96, and see Index) is given to Athens; then Thucydides i. 20; iii. 104; vi. 53–9. In the fourth century special histories of Attica, termed *Atthides*, began to appear; the most important were those of Androtion and Philochorus. The former was the main source of Aristotle, *Constitution of the Athenians*, which traces the development of the constitution from the earliest times to 404–03, and describes in detail the government and administration during the writer's own time. From the *History* of Ephorus, also fourth century, Diodorus drew the greater part of his material on Athenian history. Later sources, though of great value, are Plutarch, *Theseus; Solon; Aristeides; Themistocles;* Pausanias, bk. i. See also references to the scattered literature in the modern authorities on the subject.

(2) *Modern Writers.* — Botsford, *Hellenic History*, ch. vii; Bury, chs. iv, v; Holm, I. chs. xxvi, xxviii; Curtius, bk. II. ch. ii (tyranny); Greenidge, *Gk. Const. Hist.* 124–62.

More special are Gilbert, *Const. Antiq.* 95–153; Busolt, *Griech. Gesch.* II. 1–449, most thorough treatment; Grote, III. chs. x, xi; IV. xxx, xxxi; Botsford, *Ath. Const.* chs. vii–xi; Glotz, G., *Études sociales et juridiques sur l'antiquité grecque* (Paris, 1906); De Sanctis, G., *Storia della repubblica ateniese* (2d ed. Torino, 1912); Reinach, A., "Atthis, les origines de l'état athénien," in *Revue Synthèse historique*, XXIV (1912). 297–318; XXV. 1–25, 143–80; Ledl, A., *Studien zur älteren athenischen Verfassungsgeschichte* (Heidelberg: Winters, 1914); Wellmann, M., "Beiträge zur Geschichte der attischen Königsliste," in *Hermes*, XLV (1910). 554–63; Wilbrandt, M., "Politische und sociale Bedeutung der attischen Geschlechter vor Solon," in *Philol.* supplb. VII (1899). 133–228; Szanto, E., "Die griechischen Phylen," in *Ausgewählte Schriften* (Tübingen, 1906). 216–88; Lezius, "Gentilizische und lokale Phylen in Attika," in *Philol.* LXI (1907). 321–35; Bolkstein, H., "Zur Entstehung der 'ionischen' Phylen," in *Klio*, XIII (1913). 424–50; Solmsen, F., Ναύκραρος, Ναύκλαρος, Ναύκληρος, in *Rhein. Mus.* LIII (1898). 151–8; Helbig, W., "Les vases du Dipylon et les naucraries," *Acad. des inscr.* XXXVI. 1 (1898). 387–421: "Les ἱππεῖς atheniens," *ib.* XXXVII. 1 (1904). 157–264; Hofmann, J., *Studien zur drakontischen Verfassung* (Straubing, 1899); Ziehen, L., "Die drakontische Gesetzgebung," in *Rhein. Mus.* LIV (1899). 321–44; Hirzel, R., *Themis, Dike und Verwandtes* (Leipzig, 1907); Adcock, F. E., "Source of the Solonian Chapters of the Athenaion Politeia," in *Klio*, XII (1912). 1–16; "Source of Plutarch, Solon, 20–24," in *Class. Rev.* XXVIII (1914). 38–40; Gilliard, *Quelques reformes de Solon* (Lausanne, 1907); Viedebantt, O., "Metrologische Beiträge, I, II," in *Hermes*, XLVII (1912). 422 *sq.*, 562 *sq.*, includes Solon's coinage; Stern, E. v., "Solon und Peisistratos," in *Hermes*, LXVIII (1913). 426–41; Ure, "Origin of the Tyrannies," in *J. H. S.* XXVI (1906). 131–42; Milchhöfer, A., "Untersuchungen über die Demenordnung des Kleisthenes," *Abhdl. Berl. Acad.* (1892); "Zur attischen Lokalverfassung," in *Ath. Mitt.* XVIII (1893), 277 *sqq.*; Schoeffer, v., "Δῆμοι," in Pauly-Wissowa, *Real-Encycl.* V. 1–131; Martin, A., *Notes sur l'Ostracisme dans Athènes* (Paris, 1907); Carcopino, J., "Histoire de l'ostracisme athénien," in *Mélanges histoire ancienne* (Paris, 1909). 85–266.

Dörpfeld, W., "Alt-Athen zur Königszeit," in *Philol.* LXV (1906). 129–41; Drerup, E., "Beiträge zur Topographie von Alt-Athen," *ib.* LXIV (1905). 66–94; Milchhöfer, A., "Athen und Thukydides II. 15," *ib.* 170–9; Gräber, F., "Die Enneakrunos," in *Ath. Mitt.* XXX (1905). 1–64, the water-system; Schrader, H., *Auswahl archaischer Marmorskulpturen im Akropolis Museum;* Frickenhaus, A., "Das Athenabild des alten Tempels in Athen," in *Ath. Mitt.* XXXIII (1908). 17–32; "Erechtheus," *ib.* 171–6.

III. The Ionic Revolt and the Great War with Persia and Carthage. (1) *Sources.*—Besides memorial inscriptions the only contemporary literary source is Æschylus, *Persians.* With book iv Herodotus, in narrating the "Scythian expedition" of Darius, begins his account of the great conflict between the Orient and Hellas, which continues through the remainder of his history. Scattered through all subsequent literature of the ancients are passages of varying length and reliability relating to the same period.

(2) *Modern Writers.*—Botsford, *Hellenic History*, chs. x, xi; Bury, *History of Greece*, vi, vii; Holm, I. ch. xxiii; II. chs. i–vi; Abbott, II. i–v, xii; Grote, IV. chs. xxxii–xxxv, xxxviii–xliii; Freeman, *History of Sicily*, II. chs. v, vi; Grundy, G. B., *Great Persian War* (Scribner, 1901); Hall, H. R., *Ancient History of the Near East* (Methuen, 1913), ch. xii.

Beloch, *Griech. Gesch.* II. 1–74; Busolt, *Griech. Gesch.* II. 450–806; Meyer, *Gesch. d. Alt.* III. 3–484.

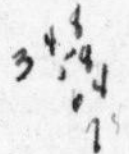

CHAPTER V

ECONOMY AND SOCIETY

During the period 750–479 B.C.

THE only contemporary sources for this subject are the poets (see p. 7 *sqq.*). The character of the extant fragments of their poems is such as to make a topical arrangement impracticable. In most cases, therefore, the poet's name is given as the heading. A few passages from prose writers of a later date are also included.

35. A PROTOTYPE OF THE MALTHUSIAN THEORY

(*Cypria*, opening lines; from Lawton, *Successors of Homer*, 16 *sq.*)

Once on a time was Earth by the races of men made weary,
Who were wandering numberless over the breadth of her bosom.
Zeus with pity beheld it, and took in his wise heart counsel
How to relieve of her burden the Earth, life-giver to all things,
Fanning to flame that terrible struggle, the war upon Troia.
So should the burden by death be removed: and they in the Troad
Perished — the heroes; the counsel of Zeus was brought to fulfilment.

36. THE CAPTIVE WIDOW AND HER YOUNG SON

(*Little Iliad;* from Lawton, *op. cit.* 32)

Then the illustrious son [1] of the noble-hearted Achilles
Down to the hollowed vessels the widow of Hector conducted.
As for the child, from the breast of the fair-tressed servant he tore him,
Grasped by the feet, and hurled him down from the tower; and upon him
Crimson death as he fell laid hold — and a destiny ruthless.

[1] Neoptolemus. The widow of Hector is Andromache, and her son is Astyanax.

37. The Festival to Apollo at Delos

(Homeric *Hymn to the Delian Apollo*, 140–64)

But thyself, O Prince of the Silver Bow, far-darting Apollo, didst now pass over rocky Cynthus, now wandering among temples and men. Many are thy fanes and groves, and dear are all the headlands, and high peaks of lofty hills, and rivers flowing onward to the sea; but with Delos, Phœbus, art thou most delighted at heart, where the long-robed Ionians gather in thine honor, with children and chaste dames. Mindful of thee, they delight thee with boxing and dances and minstrelsy in their games. Whoso then encountered them at the gathering of the Ionians, would say that they are exempt from eld and death, beholding them so gracious, and would be glad at heart, looking on the men and fair-girdled women and their much wealth and their swift galleys. Moreover, there is this great marvel of renown imperishable, the Delian damsels, handmaidens of the far-darter. They, when first they have hymned Apollo and next Leto and Artemis the Archer, then sing in memory of the men and women of old time, enchanting the tribes of mortals. They are skilled, too, to mimic the notes and dance music of all men, so that each would say himself were singing, so well woven is their fair chant.

38. The Five Races

(Hesiod, *Works and Days*, 109–201. All the selections from Hesiod are from Mair's translation, revised on the basis of the Greek text by E. G. S.)

First of all, a golden race of mortal men did the Immortal Dwellers in Olympus fashion. These lived in the time of Cronos when he was king in Heaven. Like gods they lived, having a soul unknowing sorrow, apart from toil and travail. Neither were they subject to miserable eld, but ever the same in hand and foot, they took their pleasure in festival apart from all evil. And they died as overcome of sleep. All good things were theirs. The bounteous earth bare fruit for them of their own will, in plenty and without stint. And they in peace and quiet lived on their lands with many good things, rich in flocks and dear to the blessed gods. But since this race was hidden in the earth, Spirits they are by the will of mighty Zeus: good Spirits, on earth, keepers of mortal men: who watch over dooms and the sinful works of men, faring everywhere over the earth, cloaked in mist: givers of wealth. Even this kingly privilege they received.

Then next the Dwellers in Olympus created a far inferior race, a race of silver, nowise like to the golden race in body or in mind. For a hundred years the child grew up by his good mother's side, playing, in utter childishness within his home. But when he grew to manhood and came to the full measure of age, for but a little space they lived and in sorrow by reason of their foolishness. For they could not keep heinous insolence from the other, neither would they worship the deathless gods, nor do sacrifice on the holy altars of the Blessed Ones, as is the manner of men wheresoever they dwell. Wherefore Zeus in anger put them away, because they gave not honor to the blessed gods who dwell in Olympus. Now since this race too was hidden in earth, they are called the blessed mortals under ground: of lower rank, yet they too have their honor.

Then Zeus the Father created a third race of mortal men, a race of bronze, not resembling the silver race, terrible and strong from their ashen spears: whose delight was in the dolorous works of Ares and in insolence. Bread they ate not; but souls they had stubborn of adamant, unapproachable: great was their might and invincible the arms and hands that grew from their shoulders on stout frames. Of bronze was their armor, of bronze their dwellings, with bronze they wrought. Black iron was not yet. These by their own hands slain went down to the dank house of chill Hades, nameless. And black Death slew them, for all that they were mighty, and they left the bright light of the sun.

Now when this race also was hidden in earth, yet a fourth race did Zeus the Son of Cronos create upon the bounteous earth, a juster race and better, a godlike race of hero men who are called demigods, the earlier race upon the boundless earth. And them did evil war and dread battle slay, some at seven-gated Thebes, the land of Cadmus, fighting for the flocks of Oidipodês: some when war had brought them in ships across the great gulf of the sea to Troy for the sake of fair-tressed Helen. There did the issue of death cover them about. But Zeus the Father, the Son of Cronos, gave them a life and an abode apart from men, and established them at the ends of the earth afar from the deathless gods: among them is Cronos king. And they with soul untouched of sorrow dwell in the Islands of the Blest by deep eddying Oceanos: happy heroes, for whom the bounteous earth beareth honey-sweet fruit fresh thrice a year.

I would then that I lived not among the fifth race of men, but either had died before or had been born afterward. For now verily is a race of iron. Neither by day shall they ever cease from toil and woe, neither in the night from wasting, and sore cares shall the gods give them. Howbeit even for them shall good be mingled with evil. But this race also of mortal men shall Zeus destroy when they shall have hoary temples at their birth. Father shall not be like to his children, neither the children like unto the father: neither shall guest to host, nor friend to friend, nor brother to brother be dear as aforetime: and they shall give no honor to their swiftly ageing parents, and shall chide them with words of bitter speech, sinful men, knowing not the fear of the gods. These will not return to their aged parents the price of their nurture: but might shall be right, and one shall sack the other's city. Neither shall there be any respect of the oath abiding or of the just or of the good: rather shall they honor the doer of evil and the man of insolence. Right shall lie in might of hand, and Reverence shall be no more: the bad shall wrong the better man, accosting him with crooked words and abetting them with an oath. Envy, brawling, rejoicing in evil, of hateful countenance, shall follow all men to their sorrow. Then verily shall Reverence and Retribution veil their fair bodies in white robes and depart from the wide-wayed earth unto Olympus to join the company of the Immortals, forsaking men: but for men that die shall remain but miserable woes: and against evil there shall be no avail.

39. Righteousness and Justice

(Hesiod, *Works and Days*, 202–69)

Now will I tell a tale to princes though they themselves are wise. Thus spake the hawk to the nightingale of speckled neck, as he bore her far aloft to the clouds in the clutch of his talons, while she, on his crooked talons impaled, made pitiful lament: unto her he spake masterfully: 'Wretch! wherefore dost thou shriek? Lo! thou art held in the grasp of a stronger. There shalt thou go, even where I carry thee, for all thy minstrelsy. And as I will, I shall make my meal of thee, or let thee go. A fool is he who would contend with the stronger. He loseth the victory and suffereth anguish with his shame.' So spake the swift-flying hawk, the long-winged bird. . . .

Whoso to stranger and to townsman deal straight judgments, and no whit depart from justice, their city flourisheth and the people prosper therein. And there is in their land peace, that reareth the young, and Zeus doth never decree troublous war for them. Neither doth Famine ever consort with men who deal straight judgments, nor Doom: but with mirth they tend the works that are their care. For them earth beareth much livelihood, and on the hills the oak's top beareth acorns, the oak's midst bees: their fleecy sheep are heavy with wool: their wives bear children like unto their fathers: they flourish with good things continually, neither go they on ships, but bounteous earth beareth fruit for them. But whoso pursue evil insolence, and froward works, for them doth Zeus of the far-seeing eyes, the Son of Cronos, decree justice. Yea, oftentimes a whole city reapeth the recompense of the evil man who sinneth and worketh the works of foolishness. On them doth the Son of Cronos bring from Heaven a grievous visitation, even famine and plague together, and the people perish. Their women bear not children: their houses decay by devising of Olympian Zeus: or anon He destroyeth a great host of them within a wall it may be, or the Son of Cronos taketh vengeance on their ships in the sea.

O Princes, do ye too consider this vengeance. For the Immortals are nigh among men and remark them that with crooked judgments oppress one another, taking no heed of the anger of the gods. Yea, thrice ten thousand Immortals are there on the bounteous earth, who keep watch over mortal men: who watch over judgments and froward works, clad in mist, faring everywhere over the earth. Also there is the maiden Justice, the daughter of Zeus, glorious and worshipful among the gods who hold Olympus. And whenever one injureth her with crooked reviling, straightway she sitteth by Zeus the Father the Son of Cronos, and telleth of the unrighteous mind of men, till the people pay for the folly of their kings, who with ill thoughts wrest aside judgments, declaring falsely.

Beware of these things, O Kings, and set straight your speech, bribe-devourers, and utterly forget crooked judgments. He deviseth evil for himself who deviseth evil for another, and the evil counsel is worst for him that counselleth. The eye of Zeus, that seeth all things and remarketh all, beholdeth these things too, and He will, and He faileth not to notice what manner of justice this is that our city holdeth. . . .

40. Rural Economy

(Hesiod, *Works and Days*, 405–705)

Get a house first and a woman and a plowing ox [1] — a slave woman — not a wife — who might also follow the oxen: and get all gear arrayed within the house, lest thou beg of another and he deny thee and thou go lacking, and the season pass by, and thy work be minished. Neither put off till the morrow nor the day after. The idle man filleth not his barn, neither he that putteth off. Diligence prospereth work, but the man who putteth off ever wrestleth with ruin.

What time the might of the keen sun abateth sweltering heat, when Zeus Almighty raineth in the autumn and the flesh of men turneth lighter far — for then the star Sirius goeth over the heads of men born to death but for a brief space in the daytime, and taketh a greater space of the night — then is wood cut with iron axe less liable to be wormeaten, but sheddeth its leaves to earth and ceaseth to sprout. Then be thou mindful to cut wood: a seasonable work. Three foot cut thy mortar, a pestle of three cubits an axle of seven feet: so will it be right meet. Howbeit if thou cut it of eight feet, thou canst cut therefrom a mallet. Three spans cut thou the felloe for a wagon of ten palms. Cut therewithal many bent planks. And bring thou home a plowbeam, when thou findest it by search on hill or field — of holm oak: For this is the strongest to plow with, when Athene's servant fasteneth it in the share beam and fixeth it with dowels to the pole. Get thee two plows, fashioning them at home, one of the natural wood, the other jointed, since it is far better to do so. So if thou break the one,

[1] These directions evidently are for the farmer of small means. Soon, however, and without notice, he takes in mind the lord of a considerable estate.

thou canst yoke the oxen to the other. Freest of worms are poles of bay or elm. Get thee then sharebeam of oak, plowbeam of holm, and two oxen, bulls of nine years. For the strength of such is not weak, in the fulness of their age: they are best for work. They will not quarrel in the furrow and break the plow, and leave their work undone. And with them let a man of forty follow, his dinner a loaf of four quarters, eight pieces, who will mind his work and drive a straight furrow, no more gaping after his fellows, but having his heart in his work. Than he no younger man is better at sowing. For the mind of a younger man is fluttered after his age-fellows.

Take heed what time thou hearest the voice of the crane from the high clouds uttering her yearly cry, which bringeth the sign for plowing and showeth forth the season of rainy winter, and biteth the heart of him that hath no oxen. Then feed thou the oxen of crooked horn in their stalls. For an easy thing it is to say, Give me a team of oxen, and a wagon; but easy also is it to refuse: Mine oxen have work to do. The man whose wealth is in his imagining saith he will build a wagon. Fool! who knoweth not that a wagon hath a hundred pieces of wood? Whereof take thou thought beforehand to lay them up at home. And when first plowing appeareth for men, then haste thyself and thy thralls in wet and dry to plow in the season of sowing, hasting in the early morn that so thy fields may be full. Plow in spring, but the field that is fallowed in summer will not belie thee. Sow the fallow field while yet the soil is light. Fallow land is a defender of doom, a comforter of children.

And pray thou unto Zeus the Lord of Earth and unto pure Demeter that the holy grain of Demeter may be full and heavy: thus pray thou when first thou dost begin thy plowing, when grasping in thy hand the end of the stilt-handle thou comest down on the backs of the oxen as they draw the pole by the yoke collar. And let a young slave follow behind with a mattock and cause trouble to the birds by covering up the seed. For good husbandry is best for mortal men and bad husbandry is worst. So will the grain ears nod with ripeness to the ground, if the Lord of Olympus himself vouchsafe a good issue. So shalt thou drive the spider's web from thy vessels and I have hope that thou wilt rejoice as thou takest of thy store of livelihood. And in good case thou shalt come to grey spring and shalt not look to others, but another shall have need of thee.

But if at the turning of the sun thou dost plow the goodly earth, sitting shalt thou reap, grasping a little in thy hand, binding it contrariwise, covered with dust, no way rejoicing. And in a basket shalt thou bring it home, and few there be that shall admire thee. Otherwise at other times is the will of Zeus the Lord of the Ægis and hard for mortal men to know. But if thou plowest late, this shall be a charm for thee. When first the cuckoo uttereth his note amid the leaves of the oak and rejoiceth men over the limitless earth, then may Zeus rain on the third day and cease not, neither overpassing the hoof[1] of an ox nor falling short thereof: so shall the late plower vie with the early. Keep thou all things well in mind nor fail to mark either the coming of grey spring or seasonable rain.

But pass by the smith's forge and crowded assembly place[2] in the winter season when cold constraineth men from work, wherein a diligent man would greatly prosper his house, lest the helplessness of evil winter overtake thee with poverty and thou press a swollen foot with lean hand. But the idle man who waiteth on empty hope, for lack of livelihood garnereth many sorrows for his soul. Hope is a poor companion for a man in need, who sitteth in an assembly place of men when he hath no livelihood secured. Nay, declare thou to thy thralls while it is still midsummer: It will not be summer always; build ye barns.

But the month Lenaion,[3] evil days, cattle-flaying every one, do thou shun, and the frosts that appear for men's sorrow over the earth at the breath of Boreas, which over Thrace the nurse of horses bloweth on the wide sea and stirreth it up: and earth and wood bellow aloud. Many an oak of lofty foliage and many a stout pine in the mountain glens doth his onset bring low to the bounteous earth, and all the unnumbered forest crieth aloud, and wild beasts shudder and set their tails between their legs, even they whose hide is covered with fur. Yea, even through these, shaggy-breasted though they be, he bloweth with chill breath. Through the hide of the ox he bloweth, and it stayeth him not, and through the thin-

[1] *I.e.*, filling the cavity in the soil made by the imprint of a hoof.

[2] Meeting place of a club.

[3] December–January.

haired goat: but nowise through the sheep doth the might of the wind Boreas blow, because of their year's growth of wool. But it maketh the old man trip along. Through the delicate maiden it bloweth not, who within the house abideth by her dear mother's side, not yet knowing the works of golden Aphrodite: when she hath bathed her tender body and anointed her with olive oil and lieth down at night within the house, on a winter day, when the Boneless One [1] gnaweth his own foot within his fireless house and cheerless home.

In the flower of thine age lead thou home thy bride, when thou art not far short of thirty years nor far over. This is the timely marriage. Four years past maturity be the woman: let her marry in the fifth. Marry a maiden that thou mayest teach her good ways. Marry a neighbor best of all, with care and circumspection, lest thy marriage be a joy to thy neighbors. For no better spoil doth a man win than a good wife, even as than a bad wife he winneth no worse — a gluttonous woman, that roasteth her husband without a brand, and giveth him over to untimely age.

41. Items from a Farmer's Calendar

(Hesiod, *Works and Days*, 793–828)

On the great twentieth [2] at full day [3] should a wise man be born. Verily such a one shall be of discreet mind.

The tenth day is a good day for the birth of males, the middle fourth for the birth of a girl. On that day tame thou by touch of hand sheep and horned trailing kine and sharp-toothed dog and sturdy mules. But beware in thy heart that griefs assail thee not on the fourth, whether of the waning or the waxing month. It is a very fateful day.

On the fourth of the month lead home thy bride, distinguishing the birds that are best for this business.

The fifth days avoid since they are hard and dread. On the fifth day they say the Erinyes attended the birth of Horcos, whom Eris bare to be the bane of men that swear falsely.

[1] A mollusk.

[2] The twentieth of that month in which is the longest day of the year; Flach's note.

[3] The Romans, too, considered a birth in the daytime as of better omen, hence the frequency of their prænomen Lucius.

On the middle seventh circumspectly cast the grain of Demeter on the rounded threshing-floor. And let the woodman cut wood for the house, and much timber for ship-building, even such timber as is meet for ships.

On the fourth day begin the building of slender ships.

The middle ninth is a better day toward afternoon. The first ninth is utterly harmless for men. A good day is this to beget or to be born, whether for man or woman: and it is never a day of evil.

Few men, however, know that the twenty-seventh is best to broach the jar and to set the yoke on necks of oxen and of mules and swift-footed horses, and to draw down to the wine-dark sea the swift ship many-benched. Few men call it truly. On the fourth day open the jar. The middle fourth is above all a holy day. Few again know that the fourth which followeth the twentieth of the month is the best at dawn, but it is worse toward afternoon. These days are a great boon to men on earth. But the others are shifty and fateless, and bring naught. Another praiseth another day but few men know. Anon a day is a stepmother, anon a mother. Therein happy and blessed is he who, knowing all these things, worketh his work blameless before the deathless gods.

42. Tyrtæus

For a translation of the only extant poem, substantially complete, of Callinus, see Botsford, *Source-Book of Ancient History*, 141. For a translation of a fragment of Tyrtæus not given here, *op. cit.* 141–3.

(The fragments given below are from the *Eunomia*, "Good Government." The numbers are those of Bergk, *Anthologia Lyrica*. Translated by E. G. S.)

Aristotle, Politics, v. *6. 2:* "In the aristocratic governments risings occur . . . further, whenever one class is excessively resourceless, and the others are well off, and especially does this happen in wars. And this came to pass also in Lacedæmon at the time of the Messenian war. It is also evident from the verse of Tyrtæus, the so-called Eunomia; for some, being hard-pressed on account of the war, demanded that the land be divided afresh."

Pausanias iv. *18. 1:* "The Lacedæmonians made a decree, since they were tilling the soil more for those in Eira (a fortress held by the Messenians) than for themselves, that Messenia and the contiguous strip of Laconia, while they were engaged in war, should be left unseeded. And from this resulted a scarcity of grain in Sparta, and with the scarcity of grain a civil disturbance: for those who had their possessions there would not endure it that their own should be untilled: and for these Tyrtæus solved their differences."

2. For Cronion himself, the spouse of fair-wreathed Hera,
Zeus, gave this commonwealth to the scions of Heracles,
With whom, forsaking windy Erineos, we arrived in the Broad Isle of Pelops.[1]

3. Greed for money will undo Sparta and nothing else;[2]
For thus he with the silver bow, the far-working lord Apollo,
He of the Golden locks, gave oracle from his rich shrine.

4. Having listened to Phœbus, they bore from Delphi home
The oracles of the god and consummating words:
That god-honored kings should be rulers of counsel
Whose concern is the winsome commonwealth of Sparta,
And aged elders; and then men of the people
In full harmony with straightforward sentences
Should utter what is fair and nought but justice do,
Nor counsel for this town [unseemly things] . . .
And for the commons' multitude should victory and power ensue:
For thus did Phœbus reveal for the commonwealth about these things[3]

5. To our king Theopompus, beloved of the gods,
On whose account we captured broad Messenê,
Messenê good to plow and good to plant;
For it they fought full nineteen years,
Ceaselessly ever, possessing enduring spirit,
Men of the lance, the sires of our sires;
And in the twentieth year the one party did leave their fertile fields,
And fled from the great mountains of Ithomê.[4]

[1] This is the earliest reference to the "Dorian migration." Erineos is a town in Doris, from which according to the view here presented the "scions of Heracles" with their followers migrated to Peloponnese.

[2] From this statement and from other evidence it is clear that the social conditions at Sparta in the seventh century were quite different from those of the fifth and fourth centuries; *cf.* Botsford, *Hellenic History*, chs. vi, xxi.

[3] In this stanza the poet declares that the organization of the Lacedæmonian government into kings, elders, and assembly of citizens, with their several functions, is a divine dispensation, the revelation of Apollo. On this ground it is the religious duty of every one to attend to his appointed function.

[4] The first Messenian war, here briefly described, was waged about 700 B.C.; Busolt, *Griech. Gesch.* I. 589 *sq.* According to the text the object of the Spartans was conquest. The two remaining stanzas, 6 and 7, describe the condition of the subject Messenians.

6. Like asses ground by heavy burdens,
Bringing to their masters from grievous necessity
One half of all the product that the soil doth bear,

7. Lamenting their masters, both wives and themselves,
Whenever the pernicious lot of death overtakes one.

43. Alcman

(*Parthenion,* "Girls' Choral Song," 4. 36 *sqq.* Translated by E. G. S.) On Alcman and the importance of his poetry, see p. 12.

4. From the gods is vengeance; but he is happy who cheerily weaves the web of his days unweeping. I sing the light of Agido; I see her like the sun, which Agido attests is shining for us. As for myself, may the illustrious maiden-leader of the choir not let me be either praised or blamed at all.[1] For she seems to be distinguished for her comeliness in such a manner, as though one were to place among the grazing cattle a steed compactly made, that won the prizes with ringing hoof, (a creature) of winged dreams.

5. Indeed, seest thou not? The swift steed is an Enetan;[2] and the streaming tresses of my maiden-cousin grace her like gold unalloyed; silver-like her countenance: frankly what shall I tell you? Agesichora is she. But she who is second after Agido in form, will run as a steed from Scythia to the Eibeni.[3] For the stars of the Pleiades struggle with us as we are bearing a mantle to Artemis, rising during the ambrosial night like Sirius.

6. For neither is there so great a satiety of purple as to ward off (our competitors), nor serpent-shaped variegated (bracelet), nor Lydian head-band, adornment of maidens with long eyelashes,[4] nor the tresses of Nanno, but not even divine Areta, nor Sylacis and Cleësisera; nor will you come into the chorus of Ænesimbrota and say: "Would that Astaphis were mine! and would that Philylla

[1] Evidently Alcman is the trainer of the chorus for whom he is writing this ode.

[2] The Eneti were a people of Paphlagonia; Pauly-Wissowa, *Real-Encycl.* V. 2562. Hence the horse is supposed to have come from that country.

[3] The word Kolaxaios signifies "Scythian" (Hdt. iv. 5). The Eibeni were a race in Lydia that bred horses, Greek forerunners perhaps of the Ionians — the Ionitæ; *cf.* Stephanus of Byzantium, *s.v.*

[4] If the text is correct, it means eyelashes like a garment, veiling the eye.

direct her glance toward me!" But Agesichora keeps me safe.[1] . . .

44. Archilochus

(Translated by E. G. S.)

3. In my lance is kneaded bread; in my lance is wine of Ismarus; and I drink while leaning on my lance.[2]

5. But come, with earthen drinking-vessel through the rowers' seats of the swift ship[3] wend thou thy way, and pull the lids from hollow jars, and gather red wine from the must: for not even we will be able to be sober on this watch.

6. My shield is now the boast of some Saïan, (my shield) which by a thicket unscathed I forsook against my will; but I myself escaped death's consummation. As for that shield, good riddance! another time I shall acquire one that will not be worse.[4]

9. Groanful troubles lamenting, O Pericles,[5] neither will any one of the citizens nor the city itself rejoice in feasts; such men the wave of the loud-roaring sea washes away, and our hearts are swollen with grief. But for incurable ills, the gods, my friend, have set endurance as the mighty remedy: sometimes this one, sometimes that one has the affliction; but now it has turned to us, and we lament a bleeding wound. Another time to others it will turn; but forthwith bear up, thrusting from you womanish sorrowing sore.

20. This (island)[6] like a donkey's spine doth stand; covered

[1] Agido and Agesichora, daughters of the king, are leaders of the chorus for whom Alcman writes. Stanzas 4 and 5 sing their praises. Stanza 6 describes the competing chorus: Agesichora alone saves us from defeat at its hands! On the poem in general, see Diels, H., "Alkmans Partheneion," in *Hermes*, XXXI (1896) 339–74.

[2] This verse is a drastic expression of his mercenary life.

[3] He is serving on shipboard; perhaps he is now a pirate, as when he says: "There were seven dead men trampled under foot and we were a thousand murderers;" Murray.

[4] Here he boasts of having thrown away his shield — a soldier's most disgraceful act.

[5] This stanza is addressed to Pericles on the death of friends by shipwreck; it illustrates the character of a man subject indeed to great griefs, but whose courageous spirit forthwith rallies from despondency.

[6] The island is Thasos, to which he had gone as a colonist in quest of gold. He contrasts the island with charming Italy in the neighborhood of Sybaris.

with savage forests; for there is no fair spot nor a lovely one, nor charming such as is about the currents of the Siris stream.

24. For Gyges [1] care I not, the one so rich in gold, nor ever did envy possess me, nor do I look with jealousy upon the works of gods; of mighty princely power I shall not speak: for it is far away from mine eyes.

56. Glaucus, look! for now the deep is troubled by the waves, and about the heights of Gyros stands a towering cloud, a sign of storm: from lack of hope doth fear come over me.

58. Leave all things to the gods: ofttimes from evils they lift men up that lie upon the black soil, and ofttimes do they overturn them, even when they stand firmly, and lay them on their backs; then many troubles come; and in quest of life he wanders, and his mind is overturned.

45. Semonides (Simonides) of Amorgos

(Translated by E. G. S.)

In way diverse did God fashion woman's mind
At first; one out of the long-bristled swine,
In whose abode all is upside down in mire,
And lies in foul disorder, rolls along the ground,
Herself unwashed, her garments unlaundered
She sits mid filth and groweth fat.

Another woman God created from the wicked fox,
Of all aknowing; of evil nothing
Nor of better things doth aught escape her mind;
And some of this she often calleth bad,
Another, excellent: her wrath is ever so or so.

Another from the dog, of speedy gait, her mother's other self.
Set all to hear and all to know
Agazing everywhere and roving so,
She screams, though she sees no mortal soul.
Not even though he threatened could her husband make her stop,

[1] Gyges was king of Lydia about this time. The poem is the expression of moderation in desires.

Not even if in angry fit he'd break her teeth with a stone
Nor even if to gentle speech resorteth he
Nor either if 'mid guest-friends she should chance to sit,
But firmly does she hold her ineffectual scream.

Another the Olympians shaped of earth
And then bestowed on man — half-witted she
Nor evil nor the good such woman knows;
Of works she only knows how to eat;
Not even when God an evil tempest makes,
Though shivering will she draw her chair closer to the fire.

Another from the sea, which has but two-fold thought;
One day she laughs and blithesome is;
The guest within the house who sees her will commend:
No other woman better than this one
In all mankind nor fairer is to see.
Another day she is insufferable, to see her with one's eyes
Or to approach her, but she rages then
Without measure, like bitch for pups concerned,
Ungentle she to all, repelling them.
To foes and friends alike demeans herself
Just as the sea without a quiver often
Stands propitious, a great joy to seafaring men
In Summer's season, but oftentimes does rage,
With heavy beating billows moving on;
To such, a woman of such kind resembles.

Another from the ashen-colored and much beaten ass,
Which whether by constraint or by the urging call
Is satisfied to do all her toilsome task,
With full complacence: meanwhile she munches in a corner
All night, all day, she eateth by the hearth. . . .

Another one a dainty steed with flowing mane produced,
Who turns aside from servile work and toil.
A gristmill she'd not touch nor sieve
Would lift, nor dirt throw from the house,
Nor sit by the fire, keeping from the soot:

It is by sheer constraint she wins her husband's friendship.
On every day she washes off each spot
Twice, sometimes thrice; with ointments fragrant is:
And always wears her manelike tresses combed
Deep; with blossoms shades she them.
A comely thing to see is such a wife
For others, but to him who weds her proves an ill,
Unless he be a prince or sceptered sovereign,
Who with such things his fancy doth adorn.

Another from the ape: this decidedly Zeus
Did bestow on husbands as the greatest evil.
Most ugly is her face; a woman such as she
Goes through the town, all mankind laughs at her.
Thickest in neck, she barely plies her limbs,
No curving hips, of withered limbs: O wretched goodman he
Who does embrace such evil thing;
All counsels and the ways of people does she know,
Just like a monkey, ridicule concerns her not,
Nor would she do a goodly turn to anyone, but this she sees
And this all day long doth she plot and plan,
To work the greatest evil in her might.

The other from the bee; fortunate he who gets her:
For she alone to censure furnishes no occasion,
But by her life doth bloom and doth increase;
Dear to her loving spouse she groweth old.
Often hath she given birth to children fair and famed.
Distinguished is she among the women all —
A grace divine doth play about her form.
Nor does she pleasure take to sit among the women,
Where they do hold converse of scandals bold.
Such are the wives which Zeus doth grant to men
A boon of grace, the best there are, the wisest of the sex.

For Zeus did make this greatest evil,
The woman; for even if they seem to furnish usefulness,
To him who weds them most they prove a bane.

For never he with cheerful spirit passes through a day
Complete, who with a woman is. . . .
And when the husband most does seem to please his mood
At home abiding, be it fate divine or kindliness of man,
She finds some word of censure, helms herself to fight.
For where a woman is, not even into the home
With willing mind (the husband) would receive a stranger
Who arrives. . . .

46. Mimnermus

(Translated by E. G. S.)

1. What living is there and what charm without golden Aphrodite?
I would be dead, when no more these things were my concern. . . .
If youth's blossoms may be plucked
For men and for women; but when there comes on
Lamentable age, which renders ugly even the comely man,
Ever his mind is ground by evil cares about,
Nor does he rejoice in gazing at beams of the sun,
But he is hateful to boys, unhonored by women,
So grievous has God rendered old age.

2. Our growth is like the leaves in the season of much-blossoming
Spring; when swiftly they do increase in the beams of the sun,
Like unto these, for a mere ell of time youth's blossoms
Do we enjoy, from gods knowing nor evil
Nor good. The murky Fates stand by our side,
This one holding goal of troublesome old age,
And the other, of death; slender the measure of the
Harvest of youth; as far as the sun sheds his light on the earth.
But when this consummation of bloom has passed,
Straightway to die is better than living;
For many evils ensue in the spirit; one time one's house
Is ruined, lamentable are the works of poverty;
Another again lacks children, yearning chiefly for whom
He passes under the earth to Hades' realm;
Another has a disease that consumes his spirit, nor is there
Any of men to whom Zeus gives not evils abundant.

14. Not *his* courage[1] and spirit heroic, such as I learn from my fathers, who saw him driving before him the lines of the Lydians fighting on steeds, all through the Hermian plain, wight with ashen spear, — by no means his spirit did censure Pallas Athene; piercing was his hearty courage, when he among the fore-fighters would sally, in the onset of bloody war, bitterly beset by the missiles of foemen; for not any wight 'mong the enemies was better then he, to advance into the performance of the mighty din of battle, when it was borne along in the beams of the swift sun-god.

47. Alcæus

There was fierce strife between the nobles and the democracy. The people were led by demagogues, who, Alcæus protested, were aiming to make themselves tyrants. Chief among them was Myrsilus. Alcæus, the inspiring genius of the aristocratic faction, inveighed against Myrsilus in the following well known lines: —

This man, this raving idiot here,
With rank supreme and power great,
Will quickly overthrow the state;
Already is the crisis near.

The conspiracy of the poet and his adherents against Myrsilus is vouched for in a scholium attached to a new fragment: "In the first banishment, when after conspiring against Myrsilus, Alcæus and Phan . . . and their adherents failed in their plot and fled to Pyrrha [Lesbos] before they could be brought to trial." While in exile Alcæus thus addressed his country: —

A. Apostrophe to his Country

(Newly discovered fragment; translated by J. M. Edmonds, *Classical Review*, XXIII, 1910, pp. 241–3)

What purpose or intent is in thee, my country, that thou hast been so long time afraid? Be of good cheer; for thus saith the great son of Cronos himself, whensoever fear of dread war hath seized upon thee, never shall neighbor foeman, nay nor one that

[1] The object of this poem, which portrays an Ionian hero battling for his country against the Lydians, is evidently to hold up to his fellow-citizens a pattern of martial virtue at a time when the Ionians were too devoted to peace to defend their fatherland against hostile neighbors.

with far-flung misery hither on shipboard passeth the sea, compass thee about with tearful combat, unless thou of thyself send afar all the best of thy people to sunder them from thee. For 'tis men that are a city's tower in war. But if one do other than Zeus did will it, him, strive as he may, fate ever overwhelmeth. . . . For what did Tenages, son of Æolus prove, whom in woeful war the spear of his brother Macar slew of old. Touching such matters, this is now my prayer: may I no longer behold the sunlight, if the son of Cleanax, or yonder Split-Foot, or the son of Archeanax, be suffered yet to live by one whom, casting him forth from his dear, sweet home, Myrsilus hath done to death.

While in exile Alcæus addressed the following poem to Melanippus, who besought him to come back. To return home, the poet says, would be as difficult as to recross the Acheron from Hades' realm. Sisyphus hoped to escape death but met with a worse fate.

B. TO MELANIPPUS

(Newly discovered fragment; translated by J. M. Edmonds, *Classical Review*, XXVIII, 1914, p. 76)

There are extensive lacunæ, which the translator has filled by conjecture.

O why, Melanippus, do you pray you might be with me? or why, when once fate has sent me to eddying Acheron, shall I hope to recross it and see again the pure light of the sun? Nay, set not your desire on things too great. King Sisyphus son of Æolus thought with a craft unsurpassed to have escaped death, but for all his cunning he crossed the eddying Acheron in fate the second time; and the son of Cronos ordained that he should have below a toil the woefullest in all the world. So I pray you bewail not these things [*or* lament not so]. If ever cries were unavailing, our cries are unavailing now. Assuredly some of these things were to be suffered with an enduring heart. When the wind rises in the north, no skilful pilot puts out into the wide sea.

We do not know how long after these events the death of Myrsilus, perhaps by violence, gave Alcæus occasion for the following outburst of joy: —

Now for wine and joy divine,
Myrsilus is dead!

Now 'tis meet the earth to beat
With quick and happy tread;
For Myrsilus is dead,
Myrsilus is dead!

This version is the rendering of an amended text. The manuscript reading (Bergk, 20) is simpler; "Now 'tis meet to drink perforce and get thoroughly drunk, for Myrsilus is dead." It was on a similar occasion of civil strife, when his fortunes were at a low ebb, that he composed the following poem.

C. THE SHIP OF STATE

(Newly discovered fragment; translated by J. M. Edmonds, *Classical Review*, XXVIII. 78)

The sailors have cast all their cargo overboard and are saving themselves as best they can. Meanwhile beaten with the roaring wave, she (the ship) bethinks her that she no longer desires to fight with storm and tempest, but would willingly strike a reef and go to the bottom. That is her plight; but for me, dear companions, I would forget these things and make merry here with you and with Bacchus. And yet why do we take our love off our country, even though fools have thrown all she hath into confusion?

D. THE ARMORY

This is one of his "Songs of Party Strife," in which he tried to inspire his comrades with new courage and new hope of success.

The spacious hall in brazen splendor gleams,
And all the house in Ares's honor beams.
The helmets glitter; high upon the wall
The nodding plumes of snowy horse's hair,
Man's noblest ornaments, wave over all;
And brightly gleaming brazen greaves are there,
Each hanging safe upon its hidden nail,
A sure defence against the arrowy hail.
And many coats of mail, and doublets stout,
Breast-plates of new-spun linen, hollow shields,
Well-worn and brought from foe-abandoned fields,
And broad Chalcidian swords are stacked about.
Bear well in mind these tools of war, they make
Easy and sure the work we undertake.

E. Spring

I feel the coming of the flowery Spring,
Wakening tree and vine;
A bowl capacious quickly bring
And mix the honeyed wine.

Weave for my throat a garland of fresh dill,
And crown my head with flowers,
And o'er my breast sweet perfumes spill
In aromatic showers.

48. Sappho

A. CONCERNING THE PUPIL ATTHIS WHO HAS GONE TO ANOTHER TEACHER

A newly discovered fragment, translated with commentary by J. M. Edmonds, *Classical Review*, XXIII (1910) 103 *sq.* Atthis, a pupil, left Sappho for another teacher named Andromeda. This fact comes from frag. 41 (Bergk): "Atthis, it has become hateful for thee to think of me, and now thou flutterest after Andromeda." In frag. 33 she says, "I loved thee once, Atthis, long ago." The new fragment is from a different poem, as the meter is different and the third person is used, though the subject is the same. Contrary to our own notion of propriety, Sappho felt no repugnance to regarding the details of toilet and the eating of dainties as subjects for lyrical treatment. The chief interest, however, is the relation between teacher and pupil.

So my Atthis has not come back, and in sooth I would I were dead. And yet she wept full sore to leave me behind, and said, 'Alas! how sad our lot, Sappho; I swear 'tis all against my will I leave thee.' To her I answered, 'Go thy way rejoicing and remember me; for thou knowest how fond I was of thee. And if thou rememberest not, Oh then I am fain to remind thee of what thou forgettest, how dear and beautiful was the life we led together. For with many a garland of violets and sweet roses mingled thou hast decked thy flowing locks by my side, and with many a woven necklet made of a hundred blossoms thy dainty throat; and with many a jar of myrrh both of the precious and of the royal hast thou anointed thy fair young skin before me, and lying upon the couch, hast thou satisfied thyself with dainty meats and with sweet drinks.'

B. MNASIDICA, SOMETIME PUPIL OF SAPPHO

A newly discovered fragment, translated with commentary by J. M. Edmonds, *Classical Review*, XXIII (1910) 99–104. The poem is addressed to a pupil who is still with Sappho, but the subject is another pupil, who has gone to live at Sardis, probably having married some Lydian grandee. The poem throws further light on Sappho's school, and affords an interesting glimpse of the social relations between Lesbos and Lydia.

Atthis, our beloved Mnasidica dwells in far-off Sardis, but she often sends her thoughts hither, recalling how once we used to live in the days when she thought thee like a glorious goddess, and loved thy song the best. Now she shines among the dames of Lydia, as after sunset the stars that are about her, when she spreads her light o'er briny sea and eke o'er flowery field, while the good dew lies on the ground and the roses revive and the dainty anthrysc and the honey lotus with all its blooms. And oftentimes when our beloved, wandering abroad, calls to mind her gentle Atthis, the heart devours her tender breast with the pain of longing; and she cries aloud for us to come thither; and what she says we know full well, thou and I, for Night, the many-eared, calls it to us across the dividing sea.

C. TO A LADY UNLEARNED

(Translated by J. A. Symonds)

Yea, thou shalt die,
And lie
  Dumb in the silent tomb;
Nor of thy name
Shall there be any fame
  In ages yet to be or years to come:
For of the flowering Rose,
Which on Pieria blows,
  Thou hast no share:
But in sad Hades' house,
Unknown, inglorious.
  'Mid the dim shades that wander there
Shalt thou flit forth and haunt the filmy air.

D. FAIREST IS THE HEART'S BELOVED

(Newly found fragment translated by J. M. Edmonds, *Classical Review*, XXVIII, 1914, p. 75)

Mr. Edmonds supposes that Sappho is in exile and that Anactoria and another woman are in Mytilene. Anactoria has fallen in love with a soldier and therefore neglects her girl friend. Sappho writes to Anactoria lamenting that she (Sappho) has not the joy of close contact with the girl neglected by Anactoria. It is possible, however, that Sappho personates a young man.

All these newly discovered fragments abound in lacunæ and the conjectures offered for filling them are only tentative.

The fairest thing in all the world some say is a troop of horsemen, and some a host of foot, and some again a navy of ships; but to me 'tis the heart's beloved. And 'tis easy to make this understood by any. When Helen surveyed much mortal beauty, she chose for best the destroyer of all the honor of Troy, and thought not so much either of child or of parent dear, but was led astray by Love to bestow her heart afar; for woman is ever easy to be bent when she thinks lightly of what is near and dear. Even so you to-day, my Anactoria, remember not, it seems, when she is with you one of whom I would rather the sweet sound of her footfall and the sight of the brightness of her beaming face than all the chariots and armored footmen of Lydia. I know that in this world man cannot have the best; yet to pray for a share in what was once shared is better than to forget it.

E. A LOVE SONG

(Translated by J. A. Symonds)

Peer of gods he seemeth to me, the blissful
Man who sits and gazes at thee before him,
Close beside thee sits, and in silence hears thee
    Silverly speaking,

Laughing love's low laughter. Oh this, this only
Stirs the troubled heart in my breast to tremble!
For should I but see thee a little moment,
    Straight is my voice hushed;

Yea, my tongue is broken, and through and through me
'Neath the flesh impalpable fire runs tingling;
Nothing see mine eyes, and a noise of roaring
    Waves in my ear sounds;
Sweat runs down in rivers, a tremor seizes
All my limbs, and paler than grass in autumn,
Caught by pains of menacing death, I falter,
    Lost in the love-trance.

For other selections from Alcæus and Sappho, see Botsford, *Source-Book of Ancient History*, 143–6.

49. Anacreon

THE UPSTART ARTEMON

(Preserved in Athenæus xii. 533 e. Translated by E. G. S.)

Blond Eurypytê is interested in Artemon, who moves in a litter, who formerly had a shabby garment, coverings tied about him, and wooden dice in his ears, and a worn oxskin about his flanks, the unwashed cover of a worthless shield, the comrade of bread-selling women and voluntary prostitutes, the scoundrelly Artemon, devising the life of a cheat; oft putting his neck in the stocks, and oft in the wheel, and often scourged on back with leather whip, his hair and beard pulled out. But now he bravely moves along in chariot, wearing golden ear-rings, the son of Cycê, and carries an umbrella with ivory frame, quite like the women.

50. Theognis

(Translated by E. G. S.)

Know this thus: but have no fellowship with the bad, yet always hold to the good,[1] and with them do drink, and eat and with them do sit, and them do please: for from the noble thou wilt learn noble lessons but if thou minglest with the bad, thou wilt destroy even what sense thou hast. Hast thou learned this, then have fellowship with the good and some day thou wilt say that well I counselled my friends. . . .

[1] Generally with Theognis "the good" are the blooded nobility, "the bad," the commons whether rich or poor.

No *good men*, O Cyrnus, ever did ruin any town: but whenever it pleases *the bad* to be overweening, and they ruin the land, and give their verdicts in favor of the unrighteous for their own lucre's sake, and power, — then do not hope that long that commonwealth will be still, not even if now it lies in perfect rest, whenever these things prove pleasing to the bad men, namely gains that come about attended with evil to the land. For from them come risings and civil slaughter of men: never may autocrat[1] be pleasing to this state. . . .

Cyrnus, the city is still the same, but the people are other, who before knew neither rightful verdicts nor laws, but about their flanks wore out the skins of goats, and 'yond the town like stags did feed from soil. And now they are the *Good*, O son of Polypais, and those erst noble now are *mean*. Who could endure to behold this? One another they cheat while laughing at each other, knowing neither the minds of the *bad* nor minds of the *good*.[2] . . .

Rams we seek and asses, O Cyrnus, and stallions of noble breed, and men desire to have the acquisition of the good, yet a nobleman does not care to marry a mean woman daughter of a mean man, (even) if she bring him much money. But a maid does not decline to be the spouse of a mean man; she wills a rich man instead of a good. For it is money they honor, and mean man's offspring marries the noble, and the mean man mates with the child of the good:[3] riches blended the stocks. Thus marvel thou not, O son of Polypais, that the race of the citizens loses its lustre, for the noble is mixed with the mean.

He himself though he knows this maid to be of mean sire, leads her to his home, induced by money, he of fine repute, her of mean repute: since forceful necessity urges him on, (necessity) which rendered patient the mind of the groom.

[1] Monarch (μούναρχος).

[2] *I.e.*, the country people, once clad in skins, have come to power, and the blooded nobles are beneath them.

[3] Theognis, the noble, is horrified at such mésalliances.

51. Simonides

(Translated by E. G. S.)

A. ON THE BATTLE OF PLATÆA

Centre held these who dwell in Ephyra [1] blessed by fountains,
Experts in every form of valor in war;
And they who reside in the city of Glaucus, Corinthian town,
Who set up fairest witness of their toils,
Of precious gold in open sky; and for them it extols
Their own wide fame and their fathers:
For of witnesses best is gold resplendent in ether.

B. VARIOUS EPITAPHS

Battling for Greece the Athenians at Marathon level'd the power of Persians, wearers of gold.

With myriads three hundred here once fought from Peloponnesus thousands four.[2]

Stranger, report to the Spartans, that here we lie, obedient to their laws.

Stranger, once we dwelled in well-watered Corinth;
But now Salamis, isle of Ajax, possesses us;
[Capturing with ease Phœnician ships and Persians and
Medians, holy Hellas we saved.] [3]

[1] An earlier name of Corinth.

[2] This epitaph on the Peloponnesians who fought at Thermopylæ is taken from Herodotus vii. 228. From the same source is the following epitaph on the three hundred Spartans who fell in the same battle.

[3] This epitaph is quoted by Dio Chrysostom, *Or.* XXXVII. 109 (R) under the name of the poet Simonides. It is quoted likewise but without the name by Plutarch, *De malignitate Herodoti*, to show the unfairness of Herodotus in even repeating the story that the Corinthians tried to run away from the battle of Salamis (Hdt. viii. 94). Herodotus adds that the story is told and believed only by the Athenians, while the Corinthians maintain that they were among the bravest in the battle — a contention in which they are borne out by the rest of the Greeks.

In 1895 M. Dragoumis found in Salamis a stone which had long served as a doorstep to a peasant's cottage, and which was inscribed with the first two lines of the epitaph. The remainder, — the part inclosed in brackets, — did not belong to the genuine epitaph. Before this discovery it had been suspected by certain scholars on philological grounds. The information contained in this note has been kindly supplied by Professor E. D. Perry, Columbia University.

Sons of Athenians having destroyed the host of the Persians,
Warded away from their fatherland grievous slavery.[1]

This is the tomb of that Adimantus, on account of whose plans
Hellas placed on her head the wreath of freedom.[2]

C. TO ARCHEDICE, DAUGHTER OF HIPPIAS, TYRANT OF ATHENS

Of a man who once in Hellas in his own generation held foremost rank,
Of Hippias, the daughter Archedice this dust doth conceal;
Who, with father and husband and brothers as princes,
And children, was not elated in mind to sinful presumption.

52. SKOLION TO HARMODIUS AND ARISTOGEITON

(Translated by E. G. S.)

Skolia the Greeks called brief poems declaimed by individual guests at banquets, in turn, or when some one of them was called upon, to the accompaniment of a lyre played by the contributor himself. They were called *Skolia* (crooked) on account probably of a permissible freedom or irregularity of metre. The subjoined specimen was ascribed to an Athenian, Callistratus. — E. G. S.

In a branch of myrtle will I bear my sword
Just like Harmodius and Aristogeiton,
When they slew the tyrant,
And made Athens a place of equal rights.[3]

Dearest Harmodius, you are not dead, I ween,
But in the islands of the Blessed they say thou art,
Where are swift footed Achilles
And Tydeus' son, they say, the worthy Diomede.

In a branch of myrtle will I bear my sword,
Just like Harmodius and Aristogeiton,

[1] This epitaph probably refers to the achievements of the Athenians at Platæa.

[2] Adimantus was admiral of the Corinthians in the battle of Salamis.

[3] For the story of the assassination of Hipparchus by Harmodius and Aristogeiton, see no. 29, § 18. As a reward for this deed the democratic government of Athens decreed to the descendants of the two tyrannicides exemption from public burdens and various public honors forever.

When at the sacrifices of Athena,
They slew the autocrat Hipparchus.

Ever the renown of you two will be upon the earth,
Dearest Harmodius and Aristogeiton,
Because you slew the tyrant
And made Athens a place of equal rights.

53. A Sedition in Miletus

(Heracleides of Pontus, *Concerning Justice*, ii, quoted by Athenæus xii. 26)

Heracleides of Heracleia on the Pontus was a pupil of Plato. He wrote many works on a great variety of subjects, literary, musical, scientific, and philosophical. His treatise on Justice, from which the following excerpt was taken by Athenæus, contained three books; Diogenes Laertius v. 86. The fragments are collected in Müller, C., *Frag. hist. græc.* II. p. 254 *sqq.* See also Christ, *Griech. Lit.* II. 52–4.

Heracleides of Pontus, in the second book of his treatise on Justice, says, — "The city of the Milesians fell into misfortunes, on account of the luxurious lives of the citizens, and on account of the political factions; for the citizens, not loving equity, destroyed their enemies root and branch. For all the rich men and the populace formed opposite factions (and they call the populace Gergithæ). At first the people got the better, and drove out the rich men, and, gathering the children of those who fled into some threshing-floors, collected a lot of oxen, and so trampled them to death, destroying them in a most impious manner. Therefore, when in their turn the rich men got the upper hand, they smeared over all those whom they got into their power with pitch, and so burnt them alive. And when they were being burnt, they say that many other prodigies were seen, and also that a sacred olive took fire of its own accord; on which account the God drove them for a long time from his oracle; and when they asked the oracle on what account they were driven away, he said —

My heart is grieved for the defenceless Gergithæ,
So helplessly destroy'd; and for the fate
Of the poor pitch-clad bands, and for the tree
Which never more shall flourish or bear fruit.

54. Luxury of Athenian Grandees in Early Time

(Heracleides of Pontus, *Concerning Pleasure*, in Athenæus xii. 5)

The city of the Athenians, while it indulged in luxury, was a very great city, and bred very magnanimous men. For they wore purple garments and were clad in embroidered chitons. They bound their hair in knots, and wore golden grasshoppers over their foreheads and in their hair. Their slaves followed them, carrying folding chairs for them, in order that if they wished to sit down, they might not be without some proper seat, and be forced to put up with any chance seat. These men were such heroes that they conquered in the battle of Marathon, and alone worsted the power of combined Asia.

55. Luxury of the Ionians

(Democritus, *Concerning the Temple of Diana at Ephesus*, quoted by Athenæus xii. 19)

Democritus of Ephesus, who wrote the work with the title given above, lived in the Hellenistic age. See Susemihl, *Griech. Lit.* II. 387. The subjoined excerpt is the only known fragment of the work; *cf.* Müller, *Frag. hist. græc.* IV. 383 *sq.*

The Magnesians also, who lived on the banks of the Mæander, were undone because they indulged in too much luxury, as Callinus relates in his Elegies; and Archilochus confirms this: for the city of Magnesia was taken by the Ephesians. And concerning these same Ephesians, Democritus, who was himself an Ephesian, speaks in the first book of his treatise on the Temple of Diana at Ephesus; where, relating their excessive effeminacy, and the dyed garments which they used to wear, he uses these expressions: — "And as for the violet and purple robes of the Ionians, and their saffron garments, embroidered with round figures, those are known to every one; and the caps which they wear on their heads are in like manner embroidered with figures of animals. They wear also garments called sarapes, of yellow, or scarlet, or white, and some even of purple: and they wear also long robes called calasires, of Corinthian workmanship; and some of these are purple, and some violet-colored and some hyacinth-colored; and one may also see some which are of a fiery red, and others which are of a sea-green color. There are also Persian calasires, which are the most beautiful of all. And one may see also," continues Democritus, "the garments which they call actææ; and the actæa is the most costly of all the Persian articles of dress: and this actæa is woven for the sake of fineness and of strength, and it is ornamented all over with golden millet-grains; and all the millet-grains have knots of purple thread passing through the middle, to fasten them inside the garment." And he says that the Ephesians use all these things.

(Duris of Samos, *Annals of the Samians*, quoted by Athenæus xii. 30)

Duris was a pupil of Theophrastus, and for a time ruler of his native island. He wrote in twenty-nine books a work entitled *Histories*, beginning with the battle of Leuctra, 371, and some minor works. Among the latter was his *Annals of the Samians* in at least two books. For his fragments, see Müller, *Frag. hist. græc.* II. pp. 466–88. See also Christ, *Griech. Lit.* II. 160 *sq.*; Schwartz, "Duris," in Pauly-Wissowa, *Real-Encycl.* V. 1853–6.

Duris, speaking concerning the luxury of the Samians, quotes the poems of Asius, to prove that they used to wear armlets on their arms: and that, when celebrating the festival of the Heræa, they used to go about with their hair carefully combed down over the back of their head and over their shoulders; and he says that this is proved to have been their regular practice by this proverb — "To go, like a worshipper of Hera, with his hair braided."

Now the verses of Asius run as follows: —

And they march'd, with carefully comb'd hair
To the most holy spot of Hera's temple,
Clad in magnificent robes, whose snow-white folds
Reach'd the ground of the extensive earth,
And golden knobs on them like grasshoppers,
And golden chaplets loosely held their hair;
Gracefully waving in the genial breeze;
And on their arms were armlets, highly wrought,
* * * * * and sung
The praises of the mighty warrior.

But Heracleides of Pontus, in his treatise on Pleasure, says that the Samians, being most extravagantly luxurious, destroyed the city, out of their meanness to one another, as effectually as the Sybarites destroyed theirs.

56. The Sybarites

(Clearchus, *Lives*, v, quoted by Athenæus xii. 15)

Clearchus of Soli, Cyprus, was a pupil of Aristotle. His *Lives*, in at least eight books, were not biographies but descriptions of various classes of people. They were an important source for Athenæus. For the fragments, see Müller, *Fragmenta historicorum græcorum*, II. pp. 302–27. See also Christ, *Griech. Lit.* II. 60.

Why need we mention the Sybarites, among whom bathing attendants and pourers of water were first introduced in fetters, in order to prevent their going too fast, and to prevent their scalding the bathers in their haste? The Sybarites were the first people, too, who forbade those who practise the noisy arts from dwelling in their city, such as braziers, smiths, carpenters, and similar mechanics, thus providing that their slumbers should always be undisturbed. It used to be unlawful also to rear a cock in the city.

(Timæus, *Sicelica et Italica*, vii, quoted by Athenæus xii. 15–18)

On Timæus, see ch. xviii, D. introduction.

Timæus relates concerning them that a citizen of Sybaris, once going into the country and seeing the farmers digging, said that he himself felt that he had broken his bones by the sight; and some one who heard him replied: "And I, when I heard you say this, felt as if I had a pain in my side." Once at Croton some Sybarites were standing near one of the athletes who were digging up dust for the palæstra, and said that they marvelled that men who had such a city had no slaves to dig the palæstra for them. Another Sybarite, coming to Lacedæmon and being invited to the phidition, sitting down on a wooden seat and eating with them, said that originally he had been surprised at hearing of the valor of the Lacedæmonians; but that now that he had seen the city, he thought that they in no respect surpassed other men, for that the greatest coward on earth would rather die a thousand times than live and endure such a life as theirs.

It is a custom among them that even their children up to the age when they are ranked among the ephebi, should wear purple gowns and curls braided with gold. It is a custom also with them to breed in their houses little manikins and dwarfs, as Timon says, who are called by some people stilpones, and also little Maltese dogs, which follow them even to the gymnasia. . . .

Furthermore the Sybarites used to wear garments made of Milesian wool, and from this custom arose a great friendship between the two cities, as Timæus relates. For of the inhabitants of Italy the Milesians gave the preference to the Etruscans, and of foreigners to the Ionians because they were devoted to luxury. But the cavalry of the Sybarites, in number more than 5000, used to march in procession in saffron-colored robes over their breastplates; and in summer their young men used to go away to the caves of the Lusiades nymphs, and live there in all kinds of luxury.

Whenever the rich men of Sybaris left the city for the country, although they always travelled in carriages, they used to consume three days in a day's journey. Some of the roads which led to their villas in the country were covered all over with awnings; and a great many of them had cellars near the sea, into which their wine was brought by canals from the country. Some of it was exported and some brought to the city in boats. They celebrate many public festivals, and they honor with golden crowns those who display great magnificence on such occasions, and proclaim their names at public sacrifices and games, announcing not only the general good will of such people toward the city but also the great magnificence they had displayed in the feasts. On these occasions they even crown those cooks who have served up the most exquisite dishes. Among the Sybarites there were found baths in which, while lying down, people were steamed with warm vapors. . . . Laughing at those who left their country to travel in foreign lands, they themselves used to boast that they had grown old without ever having crossed the bridges which led over their frontier rivers.

It seems to me, however, that besides the fact of their riches, the natural character of their country — since there are no harbors on their coasts and since in consequence nearly all the produce of their land is consumed by the inhabitants themselves — and to some extent also an oracle of God has excited them all to luxury and has caused them to live in practices of most immoderate dissoluteness. Further, their city lies in a hollow, and in summer is liable to excess of cold both morning and evening; but in the middle of the day the heat is intolerable, so that the majority of the inhabitants believe that the rivers contribute a great deal to their health. On this account it has been said that an inhabitant of Sybaris who wishes not to die before his time ought never to see the sun rise or set. . . .

(Phylarchus, *Histories*, xxv, quoted by Athenæus xii. 20)

Phylarchus was a Greek historian who wrote in great detail an account of the period from the expedition of Pyrrhus against Peloponnese to the death of king Cleomenes of Sparta, 272–220 B.C., in twenty-eight books. His trustworthiness is impugned by Polybius, ii. 56, and by Plutarch, *Themistocles*, 32; *Aratus*, 38. He was especially inclined to digression with a view to entertaining his readers and to giving them moral instruction. For the fragments of his work, see Müller, *Frag. hist. græc.* I. pp. 334–58. See also Christ, *Griech. Lit.* II. 161 *sq.*

Phylarchus states that the Sybarites, giving loose rein to luxury, made a law that women might be invited to banquets, and that those who intended to invite them to sacred festivities must make preparation a year beforehand, in order that they might have all that time to provide themselves with garments and other ornaments in a manner worthy of the occasion, and so might come to the banquet to which they were invited. If, too, any confectioner or cook invented any peculiar and excellent dish, no other artist was allowed to make it for a year. But he alone who invented it was entitled to all the profit to be derived from the manufacture of it for that time, in order that others might be induced to labor at excelling in such pursuits. In the same way it was provided that those who sold eels were not to be liable to pay a tax, nor those who caught them. In the same way the laws exempted from all burdens those who dyed the marine purple and those who imported it.

57. The Mines of Siphnos

(Herodotus iii. 57)

The Samians who had fought against Polycrates, when they knew that the Lacedæmonians were about to forsake them, left Samos themselves, and sailed to Siphnos. They happened to be in want of money; and the Siphnians at that time were at the height of their greatness, no islanders having so much wealth as they. There were mines of gold and silver in their country, and of so rich a yield, that from a tithe of the ores the Siphnians furnished out a treasury at Delphi which was on a par with the richest there. What the mines yielded was divided year by year among the citizens. At the time when they formed the treasury, the Siphnians consulted the oracle, and asked whether their good things would remain to them many years. The prophetess made answer as follows: —

"When the Prytaneis' seat shines white in the island of Siphnos,
White-browed all the forum — need then of a true seer's wisdom —
Danger will threat from a wooden host, and a herald in scarlet."

Now about this time the forum of the Siphnians and their town-hall (prytaneum) had been adorned with Parian marble.

58. The Mines of Thasos

(Herodotus vi. 46)

The year after these events, Darius received information from certain neighbors of the Thasians that those islanders were making preparations for revolt; he therefore sent a herald, and bade them dismantle their walls, and bring all their ships to Abdêra. The Thasians, at the time when Histiæus the Milesian made his attack upon them, had resolved that, as their income was very great, they would apply their wealth to building ships of war, and surrounding their city with another and a stronger wall. Their revenue was derived partly from their possessions upon the mainland, partly from the mines which they owned. They were masters of the gold-mines at Scaptê-Hylê, the yearly produce of which amounted in all to eighty talents. Their mines in Thasos yielded less, but still were so far prolific that, besides being entirely free from land-tax, they had a surplus income, derived from the two sources of their territory on the mainland and their mines, in common years of two hundred, and in the best years of three hundred talents.

BIBLIOGRAPHY

The range of sources for this subject is sufficiently indicated by the selections. The topics are covered by Botsford, *Hellenic History*, chs. viii, ix;

Beloch, *Griech. Gesch.* I. 265–346, 402–46. The subject is lightly treated by Mahaffy, J. P., *Social Life in Greece from Homer to Menander*, chs. iv, v. The works on Greek literature, religion, and philosophy treat their appropriate aspects of the subject. More special are Wildbrandt, M., "Die politische und sociale Bedeutung der attischen Geschlechter vor Solon," in *Philol.* supplb. VII (1898). 133–228; Glotz, G., *La solidarité de la famille dans le droit criminel en Grèce* (Paris, 1904); *Études sociales et juridiques sur l'antiquité grecque* (Paris, 1906). On the economic history of the period, in addition to Beloch, see the earlier chapters of Guiraud, P., *La propriété foncière en Grèce* (Paris, 1893); Francotte, H., *L'Industrie dans la Grèce ancienne* (2 vols., Brussels, 1900).

For other works on society and economy, see ch. xiv.

CHAPTER VI

GENERAL POLITICAL CONDITIONS

During the period 479–404 B.C.

59. Aristeides and the Founding of the Absolute Democracy

(Aristotle, *Constitution of the Athenians*, 24. Translated by G. W. B.)

For the earlier chapters of this treatise, see nos. 27–30. The reforms of Cleisthenes had so accentuated the popular features of the constitution that from his time the government of Athens may be called a democracy though of a strongly conservative character. Conservative elements were (1) the prevalence of country life, which kept the masses from continual participation in public affairs, (2) the want of pay for public services, which practically debarred the poorer classes from the offices. By introducing pay for various public services Aristeides encouraged the concentration of the population within the City, and founded the absolute democracy; *cf.* Plutarch, *Aristeides*, 25. Afterward Ephialtes and Pericles still further democratized the constitution along the lines drawn by Aristeides; Arist. *Const. Ath.* 25, 27, 41.

Afterward [1] as (the citizens of) the state had acquired confidence, and a great quantity of money had accumulated, he (Aristeides) advised them to lay hold on the leadership,[2] and to come in from the country and live in the City,[3] assuring them that there would be a livelihood for all, — some serving in the army, others in garrisons, others attending to administrative work,[4] — and that thus they would secure the leadership.[5] Adopting this policy and usurping

[1] After the battle of Salamis, 480 B.C.

[2] The leadership of the Delian confederacy; no. 67 *sqq.*

[3] Merely the beginning of this concentration took place in the lifetime of Aristeides; for at the outbreak of the Peloponnesian war the majority of Athenians still lived in the country; Thucydides ii. 14–16. It is clear, however, that in this chapter Aristotle is speaking mainly of the results, rather than of the beginnings, of the policy initiated by Aristeides.

[4] Evidently the policy of Aristeides was to introduce pay for both military and civil services.

[5] Here is an indication that the development of the democracy and of imperialism went hand in hand.

the imperial power, they began to treat their allies more despotically, with the exception of the Chians, Lesbians, and Samians, whom they retained as guards of their empire, leaving them their own constitutions and the dependencies which they severally chanced to rule. Thus they established for the multitude an abundant supply of provisions, as Aristeides had pointed out; for it resulted that from the tributes and the taxes more than twenty thousand men derived their support.

There were 6000 jurors, 1600 archers, and besides them 1200 cavalry, 500 councillors, 500 guards of the dockyards; in the city moreover 50 guardsmen, about 700 men in domestic offices, and about 700 (?) [1] men in the offices beyond the border. Afterward, too, when they engaged in the (Peloponnesian) war, there were 2500 heavy infantry,[2] 20 guard-ships, and the other ships which carried the guards [3] appointed by lot, 2000 in all; furthermore those maintained in the prytaneum, the orphans, and the guards of the prisons. All these persons obtained their living from the public funds.

60. The Old Juror Madly Loves his Work

(Aristophanes, *Wasps*, 87–135)

An old juror has devoted himself to his daily task with so much spirit that he is in danger of losing his wits. His adult son hopes to cure him of his strange malady by confining him at home behind bolts and bars. The following account of this procedure is given by Xanthias, a household slave. The *Wasps*, from which the following extracts are taken, was presented at Athens in the Lenæan festival of the year 422.

I'll tell you the disease old master has.
He is a lawcourt-lover, no man like him.

[1] It is reasonable to suspect that this number is merely a dittography of the preceding, 700, in place either of some smaller number or perhaps of some phrase which has been lost beyond recovery.

[2] That number was kept permanently under arms, in addition to special expeditions, for which pay had to be provided; *cf.* Cavaignac, *Études sur l'histoire financière d'Athènes au Ve siècle*, 115 *sqq*.

[3] Recent editors have changed φόρους, "tributes," to φρούρους. "guards." The tributes were regularly brought in by the allies themselves, arrears only being collected by Athenian fleets. The ships here referred to probably had the task of transporting the garrisons to places where they were needed.

Judging is what he dotes on, and he weeps
Unless he sits on the front bench of all.
At night he gets no sleep, no, not one grain;
Or if he doze the tiniest speck, his soul
Flutters in dreams about the water-clock.[1]
So used is he to holding votes, he wakes
With thumb and first two fingers closed,[2] as one
That offers incense on a new moon's day.
If on a gate is written *Lovely Demus*,[3]
Meaning the son of Pyrilamp, he goes
And writes beside it, *Lovely Verdict-Box*.
The cock which crew from eventide, he said,
Was tampered with, he knew, to call him late, —
Bribed by officials whose accounts were due.
Supper scarce done, he clamors for his shoes,
Hurries ere daybreak to the Court, and sleeps
Stuck like a limpet to the doorpost there.
So sour he is, the long condemning line
He marks for all, then homeward, like a bee
Laden with wax beneath his finger-nails.[4]

Lest he lack votes, he keeps, to judge withal,
A private pebble-beach [5] secure within.
Such is his frenzy, and the more you chide him
The more he judges; so with bolts and bars
We guard him straitly that he stir not out.
For ill the young man brooks the sire's disease.
And first he tried by soft emollient words

[1] Water-clock, clepsydra (κλεψύδρα), was used for measuring the amount of time allowed to the speakers, and was therefore one of the most prominent features of the court room.

[2] As though he were holding the pebble, ballot, ready to cast.

[3] It was a habit of the lover to write the name of his beloved on gates and walls. Demus, son of Pyrilampes, was a noted beauty.

[4] In a considerable class of cases the law permitted the prosecutor to propose a penalty. The defendant could then propose a lighter penalty, and the jurors had to decide between the two. A short mark on a waxen tablet, used in such cases as a ballot, indicated the lighter penalty and a longer mark the heavier. The sour juror always made the long mark, digging his nails deeply into the wax.

[5] See note 2.

To win him over, not to don his cloak
Or walk abroad; but never a jot he yielded.
He washed and cleansed him then; but never a jot.
A Corybant [1] next he made him, but old master,
Timbrel and all, into the New Court bursts
And there sits judging. So when these rites failed,
We cross the strait, and in Ægina place him,
To sleep the night inside Asclepius' temple; [2]
Lo! with the dawn he stands at the Court rails!
Then after that we let him out no more.
But he! he dodged along the pipes and gutters,
And so made off; we block up every cranny,
Stopping and stuffing them with clouts of rag:
Quick he drove pegs into the wall, and clambered
Up like an old jackdaw, and so hopped out.
Now then we compass all the house with nets,
Spreading them round, and mew him safe within.
Well, sirs, Philocleon is the old man's name;
Ay truly; and the son's, Bdelycleon: [3]
A wondrous high-and-mighty mannered man.

(Aristophanes, *Wasps*, 214–78)

Bdelycleon, the son, and Sosias, another slave, are outside the house on guard. They especially fear that when the rest of the jurors, swarming in from the country, pass the house, they will contrive somehow to free their caged comrade. The description of these old men trudging through the night along the rough, muddy roads, some accompanied by their sons carrying lanterns, is a striking feature of life at Athens in those times. Particularly it is to be noticed that the jurors here referred to are all old men, and are from country homes.

BDELYCLEON . . . In a little while
His fellow-justices will come this way
Calling him up.
SOSIAS. Why, sir, 'tis twilight now.

[1] Corybant, priest of Cybele, worshiped with noisy music and wild excitement.

[2] For a passage illustrating incubation in a temple of Asclepius, see no. 78.

[3] Philocleon signifies "Lover of Cleon," the famous demagogue; Bdelycleon means "Hater of Cleon."

BDEL. Why then, by Zeus, they are very late to-day.
Soon after midnight is their usual time
To come here carrying lights, and warbling tunes
Sidono-Phrynich-beautiful-antique,[1]
Wherewith they call him out.

SOS. And if they come,
Had we not better pelt them with some stones?

BDEL. Pelt them, you rogue! You might as well provoke
A nest of wasps[2] as anger these old men.
Each wears beside his loins a deadly sting,
Wherewith they smite, and on with yells and cries
They leap, and strike at you, like sparks of fire.

SOS. Tut, never trouble, give me but some stones,
I'll chase the biggest wasps-nest of them all.

CHORUS OF JURORS —

Step out, step out, my comrades stout: no loitering, Comias, pound along,
You're shirking now, you used, I vow, to pull as tough as leathern thong;
Yet now, with ease, Charinades, can walk a brisker pace than you.
Come, every dear and tried compeer, come, quickly come, ere morning break,
And as you go, be sure to throw the light around on every side;
Lest somewhere nigh a stone may lie, and we therefrom be damnified.

BOY. O father, father, here's some mud! look sharp or in you'll go.

CHOR. Pick up a stick and trim the wick,[3] a better light to show.

BOY. Nay father, with my finger thus I choose to trim the lamp.

CHOR. How dare you rout the wick about, you little wasteful scamp,

[1] Phrynichus, a dramatic poet, was an older contemporary of Æschylus. There was much song and little dialogue in his plays, and evidently he delighted in compounding words, as did Æschylus.

[2] The Chorus of jurors were dressed to represent wasps, hence the name of the comedy.

[3] The lantern was a vessel containing olive oil, in which floated a wick. Outside the larger towns of Greece the same kind of lamp is still in use.

And that with oil so scarce? But no, it don't disturb your quiet,
However dear the oil may be, when I have got to buy it.

BOY. If with your knuckles once again you 'monish us, I swear
We'll douse the light and take to flight, and leave you floundering there.
Then wading on without the lamp in darkness, I'll be bound
You'll stir and splash the mud about, like snipes in marshy ground.

CHOR. Ah, greater men than you, my boy, 'tis often mine to beat.
But, bless me, this is filth indeed I feel beneath my feet;
Ay, and within four days from this, or sooner, it is plain,
God will send down upon our town a fresh supply of rain.
So dense and thick around the wick these thieves[1] collect and gather,
And that's, as everybody knows, a sign of heavy weather.
Well, well, 'tis useful for the fruits, and all the backward trees,
To have a timely fall of rain, and eke a good north breeze.
But how is this?[2] Our friend not here! How comes it he's so slack?
By Zeus, he never used to be at all a hanger-back.
He always marched before us all, on legal cares intent,
And some old tune of Phrynichus he warbled as he went.
O he's a wonder for the songs! Come, comrades, one and all,
Come stand around the house and sing, its master forth to call.
If once he hears me tuning up, I know it won't be long
Before he comes creep, creeping out, from pleasure at the song.

How is it our friend is not here to receive us?
Why comes he not forth from his dwelling?
Can it be that he's had the misfortune to lose
His one pair of shoes:
Or striking his toe in the dark, by the grievous
Contusion is lamed, and his ankle inflamed?

[1] Thieves (μύκητες), fungous growths on the wick, caused by the heaviness of the atmosphere. The roads are now bad enough but will be worse after that rain; but the fields and trees need it.

[2] They halt in the road and look toward Philocleon's house.

(Aristophanes, *Wasps*, 291–317)

The following conversation between the boy and his father indicates the straitened condition of the small farmer at this time. His fields had been ravaged by the enemy, and he had nothing but his juror's fee to depend upon for the daily food of his family.

BOY. Father, if a boon I pray,
Will you grant it, father, eh?
CHOR. Certainly I will, my son.
Tell me what you'd have me buy.
Dibs,[1] my son? Hey, my son?
Dibs it is undoubtedly.
BOY. Dibs, my father! No, my father!
Figs! for they are sweeter far.
CHOR. You be hanged first: yet you shall not
Have them, monkey, when you are.
BOY. Then, my father, woe betide you! Not another step I'll guide you.
CHOR. Is it not enough that I
With this paltry pay must buy
Fuel, bread, and sauce for three?
Must I needs buy figs for thee!
BOY. Father, if the Archon say
That the court won't sit to-day,
Tell me truly, father mine,
Have we wherewithal to dine?
O my father, should not we
Then in "Straits of Hellê"[2] be?
CHOR. Out upon it! Out upon it!
Then indeed, I should not know
For a little bit of supper
Whither in this world to go.
BOY. Why, my mother, didst thou breed me, giving nothing else to feed me,
But a store of legal woe?

[1] Dibs, knucklebones, commonly played by children.

[2] Straits of Hellê; the boy means to say that they will be in straits, but the word reminds him of a poetic phrase, which he proceeds to utter, though it makes mere nonsense.

CHOR. Empty scrip! O empty show,
Bootless, fruitless ornament!
BOY. O! O! Woe! Woe!
Ours to sorrow and lament.

(*Ibid.* 548–614)

As the action of the comedy develops, Philocleon, the father, proposes to discourse on the enviable features of the juror's position, while his son, Bdelycleon, takes note of the points he makes.

PHILOCLEON. Away, away, like a racer gay, I start at once from the head of the lists,
To prove that no kinglier power than ours in any part of the world exists.
Is there any creature on earth more blest, more feared and petted from day to day,
Or that leads a happier, pleasanter life, than a Justice of Athens, though old and gray?
For first when rising from bed in the morn, to the criminal Court betimes I trudge,
Great six-foot fellows are there at the rails, in anxious haste to salute their judge.
And the delicate hand which has dipped so deep in the public purse, he claps into mine,
And he bows before me and makes his prayer, and softens his voice to a pitiful whine;
'O pity me, pity me, Sir,' he cries, 'if you ever indulged your longing for pelf,
When you managed the mess on a far campaign, or served some office of state yourself.'
The man would never have heard my name, if he had not been tried and acquitted before.
BDELYCLEON (*Writing*). I'll take a note of the point you make that 'suppliant fellows your grace implore.'
PHIL. So when they have begged and implored me enough, and my angry temper is wiped away,
I enter in and take my seat, and then I do none of the things I say.

I hear them utter all sorts of cries, designed expressly to win my grace,
What won't they utter, what won't they urge, to coax a Justice who tries their case?
Some vow they are needy and friendless men, and over their poverty wail and whine,
And reckon up hardships, false and true, till he makes them out to be equal to mine.
Some tell us a legend of days gone by, or a joke from Æsop witty and sage,
Or jest and banter to make me laugh, that so I may doff my terrible rage.
And if all this fails, and I stand unmoved, he leads by the hand his little ones near,
He brings his girls and he brings his boys; and I, the Judge, am composed to hear.
They huddle together with piteous bleats; while trembling above them he prays to me,
Prays as to a God his accounts to pass, to give him a quittance, and leave him free.
'If thou lovest a bleating male of the flock, O lend thine ear to this boy of mine;
Or pity the sweet little delicate girl, if thy soul delights in the squeaking of swine.'
So then we relax the pitch of our wrath, and screw it down to a peg more low.
Is *this* not a fine dominion of mine, a derision of wealth with its pride and show?

BDEL. (*Writing*). A second point for my note-book that, 'a derision of wealth with its pride and show.' . . .

PHIL. But the nicest and pleasantest part of it all is this, which I'd wholly forgotten to say,
'Tis when with my fee in my wallet I come, returning home at the close of the day,
O then what a welcome I get for its sake; my daughter, the darling, is foremost of all,
And she washes my feet and anoints them with care, and above them she stoops and a kiss lets fall,

Till at last by the pretty Papas of her tongue she angles withal my three-obol away.
Then my dear little wife, she sets on the board nice manchets of bread in a tempting array,
And cosily taking a seat by my side, with loving entreaty constrains me to feed;
'I beseech you taste this, I implore you try that.' This, this I delight in, and ne'er may I need
To look to yourself and your pantler, a scrub, who, whenever I ask him my breakfast to set,
Keeps grumbling and murmuring under his breath.

61. The Relative Value of the Three Principal Forms of Government

(Herodotus iii. 80–82)

In the age of Pericles and of Herodotus the Greeks began for the first time to take a lively interest in discussing the principles of government — a study which finally led to the creation of Political Science. The following passage contains the earliest known comparison of monarchy, oligarchy, and democracy. Although Herodotus puts it in the mouths of certain Persian grandees shortly before the accession of Darius, 521 B.C., there can be no doubt that the ideas were Greek, and that in the lifetime of the historian discussions of the kind were novel.

80. And now when five days were gone, and the hubbub had settled down, the conspirators[1] met together to consult about the situation of affairs. At this meeting speeches were made, to which many of the Greeks give no credence, but they were made nevertheless. Otanes recommended that the management of public affairs should be entrusted to the whole nation. "To me," he said, "it seems advisable that we should no longer have a single man to rule over us — the rule of one is neither good nor pleasant. Ye cannot have forgotten to what lengths Cambyses went in his haughty tyranny, and the haughtiness of the Magi ye have yourselves ex-

[1] They were the grandees above mentioned. The conspiracy had been for the slaying of a certain Magian who had usurped the Persian throne after the death of Cambyses. Of those who were present three men, Otanes, Megabyzus, and Darius, engaged in the discussion.

perienced. How indeed is it possible that monarchy should be a well-adjusted thing, when it allows a man to do as he likes without being answerable? Such license is enough to stir strange and unwonted thoughts in the heart of the worthiest of men. Give a person this power, and straightway his manifold good things puff him up with pride, while envy is so natural to human kind that it cannot but arise in him. But pride and envy together include all wickedness — both of them leading on to deeds of savage violence. True it is that kings, possessing as they do all that heart can desire, ought to be void of envy; but the contrary is seen in their conduct toward the citizens. They are jealous of the most virtuous among their subjects, and wish their death; while they take delight in the meanest and basest, being ever ready to listen to the tales of slanderers. A king, besides, is beyond all other men inconsistent with himself. Pay him court in moderation, and he is angry because you do not show him more profound respect; show him profound respect, and he is offended again, because (as he says) you fawn on him. But the worst of all is that he sets aside the laws of the land, puts men to death without trial, and subjects women to violence. The rule of the many, on the other hand, has, in the first place, the fairest of names, to wit, *isonomy;*[1] and further it is free from all those outrages which a king is wont to commit. There, places are given by lot, the magistrate is answerable for what he does, and measures rest with the commonalty. I vote, therefore, that we do away with monarchy, and raise the people to power. For the people are all in all."

81. Such were the sentiments of Otanes. Megabyzus spoke next, and advised the setting up of an oligarchy: — "In all that Otanes has said to persuade you to put down monarchy," he observed, "I fully concur; but his recommendation that we should call the people to power seems to me not the best advice. For there is nothing so void of understanding, nothing so full of wantonness as the unwieldy rabble. It were folly not to be borne, for men, while seeking to escape the wantonness of a tyrant, to give themselves up to the wantonness of a rude unbridled mob. The tyrant, in all his doings, at least knows what he is about, but a mob is al-

[1] Isonomy, equality before the law.

together devoid of knowledge; for how should there be any knowledge in a rabble, untaught, and with no natural sense of what is right and fit? It rushes wildly into state affairs with all the fury of a stream swollen in the winter, and confuses everything. Let the enemies of the Persians be ruled by democracies; but let us choose out from the citizens a certain number of the worthiest, and put the government into their hands. For thus both we ourselves shall be among the governors, and with power entrusted to the best men, it is likely that the best counsels will prevail in the state."

82. This was the advice which Megabyzus gave, and after him Darius came forward, and spoke as follows: — "All that Megabyzus said against democracy was well said, I think; but about oligarchy he did not speak advisedly; for take these three forms of government — democracy, oligarchy, and monarchy — and let them each be at their best, I maintain that monarchy far surpasses the other two. What government can possibly be better than that of the very best man in the whole state? The counsels of such a man are like himself, and so he governs the mass of the people to their heart's content; while at the same time his measures against evil-doers are kept more secret than in other states. Contrariwise, in oligarchies, where men vie with each other in the service of the commonwealth, fierce enmities are apt to arise between man and man, each wishing to be leader, and to carry his own measures; whence violent quarrels come, which lead to open strife, often ending in bloodshed. Then monarchy is sure to follow; and this result, too, shows how far that rule surpasses all others. Again, in a democracy it is impossible but that there will be malpractices; these malpractices, however, do not lead to enmities, but to close friendships, which are formed among those engaged in them, who must hold well together to carry on their villainies. Thus things go on until a man stands forth as champion of the commonalty, and puts down the evil-doers. Straightway the author of so great a service is admired by all, and from being admired soon comes to be appointed king; so that here too it is plain that monarchy is the best government. Lastly, to sum up all in a word, whence, I ask, was it that we got the freedom which we enjoy? — did democracy give it us, or oligarchy or a monarch? As a single man recovered our freedom for us, my sentence

is that we keep to the rule of one. Even apart from this, we ought not to change the laws of our forefathers when they work fairly; for to do so is not well."

62. Strictures on the Athenian Democracy

(*Polity of the Athenians*, by an unknown author. The translation of Dakyns, *Works of Xenophon*, has been revised, on the basis of a comparison of the Greek text, by E. G. S.)

In the introduction to the preceding selection reference has been made to the dawning interest in the principles of government. One of the lines along which political thought was advancing was the criticism of existing constitutions. An example is the treatise here given, which has come down to us among the works of Xenophon, but which is certainly earlier than any of his writings. Evidently it was composed early in the Peloponnesian war, about 425 or 424. The real author, unknown by name, is aptly styled "Old Oligarch" by Zimmern, *Greek Commonwealth*, 444. The work itself is evidence that the author was a man of mature years, experience, and judgment, who set forth the blemishes of democracy usually with truth, however hostile his spirit, and always with clearness and logic. His pamphlet should be studied along with the *Funeral Oration* of Pericles, as the two documents balance and correct each other.

Naturally we are repelled by the tone of the pamphlet, by the author's narrow, unsympathetic treatment of common people, slaves, and aliens — by his total lack of humanity, his complete absorption in the welfare of his narrow class. He cannot entertain a thought of compromise; the only alternative to democracy is the rule of his own class and the enslavement of the masses.

It is interesting to the student of political science as the earliest known political treatise in any language, while to anyone investigating the history and the society of that age it is an invaluable source of information. Notable is the author's interest in economic conditions. Because of its unusual importance the entire document is printed below.

I. 1. Now, as concerning the Polity of the Athenians, and the type or manner of constitution which they have chosen, I praise it not, in so far as the very choice involves the welfare of the baser folk as opposed to that of the better class. I repeat, I withhold my praise so far; but, given the fact that this is the type agreed upon, I propose to show that they set about its preservation in the right way; and that those other transactions in connection with it, which are looked upon as blunders by the rest of the Hellenic world, are the reverse.

2. In the first place, I maintain, it is only just that the poorer classes and the People of Athens should have the advantage over the men of birth and wealth, seeing that it is the people who row the vessels, and put round the city her girdle of power. For the steersman, the boatswain, the commanders of fifty, the lookout-man at the prow, the shipwright — these are the people who engird the city with power far rather than her heavy infantry and men of birth and quality. This being the case, it seems only just that offices of state should be thrown open to every one both by the lot and by the show of hands,[1] and that the right of speech should belong to any citizen who likes, without restriction. 3. Further, there are many of these offices which, according as they are in good or in bad hands, are a source of safety or of danger to the People and in these the People prudently abstain from sharing; as, for instance, they do not think it incumbent on themselves to share in the drawing of lots for general or commander of cavalry. The sovereign People recognize the fact that in foregoing the personal exercise of these offices and leaving them to the control of the more competent citizens, they secure the balance of advantage to themselves. It is only those departments of government which bring emolument and assist the private households that the People care to keep in their own hands.[2]

4. In the next place, in regard to what some people are puzzled to explain — the fact that everywhere greater consideration is shown to the base, to poor people and to common folk, than to persons of good quality, — so far from being a matter of surprise, this, as can be shown, is the keystone of the preservation of the democracy. It is these poor people, this common folk, this riff-raff, whose prosperity, combined with the growth of their numbers, enhance the democracy. Whereas a shifting of fortune to the advantage of the wealthy and the better classes implies the establishment on the part of the commonalty of a strong power in opposition to itself. 5. In fact, all the world over the cream of society is in

[1] The ordinary method of electing officials who were not appointed by lot. Voting in the law courts, on the other hand, was by ballot.

[2] The democratic theory was that for most offices the Athenians were all sufficiently qualified, but that for certain magistracies special qualifications were necessary. The former were filled by lot, the latter by election.

opposition to the democracy. Naturally, since the smallest amount of intemperance and injustice, together with the highest scrupulousness in the pursuit of excellence, is to be found in the ranks of the better class, while within the ranks of the People will be found the greatest amount of ignorance, disorderliness and rascality,[1] — poverty acting as a strong incentive to base conduct, not to speak of lack of education and ignorance, traceable to the want of means which afflicts some portions of mankind.

6. The objection may be raised that it was a mistake to allow the universal right of speech and a seat in council. These privileges should have been reserved for the cleverest, the flower of the community. But here again it will be found that they are acting with wise deliberation in granting to even the baser sort the right of speech, for supposing only the better people might speak, or sit in council, blessings would fall to the lot of those like themselves, but to the commonalty the reverse of blessings. Whereas now, any one who likes, any base fellow, may get up and discover something to the advantage of himself and his equals. 7. It may be retorted: "And what sort of advantage either for himself or for the People can such a fellow be expected to discern?" The answer is, that in their judgment the ignorance and the baseness of this fellow, together with his good will, are worth a great deal more to them than your superior person's virtue and wisdom, coupled with aversion. 8. What it comes to, therefore, is that a state founded upon such institutions will not be the best state; but, given a democracy, these are the right means to secure its preservation. The People, it must be borne in mind, do not demand that the city should be well governed and themselves slaves. They desire to be free and to be masters. As to bad legislation, they do not concern themselves about that. In fact, what you believe to be poor legislation is the very source of the People's strength and freedom. 9. But if you seek for good laws, in the first place you will see the cleverest members of the community laying down the laws for the rest. And in the next place, the better class will curb and chastise

[1] The view here offered is rejected, and the opposite view maintained, by Socrates, in Xenophon, *Memorabilia*, iii. 5. 19. He asserts — and there is no reason for doubting it — that the poor were far more obedient to authority than the knights and the heavy infantry.

the lower orders; the better class will deliberate in behalf of the state, and not suffer men in fits of madness to sit in council, or to speak or vote in the assembly. No doubt; but under the weight of such blessings the People would in a very short time be reduced to slavery.

10. Another point is the extraordinary amount of license granted to slaves and resident aliens at Athens, where a blow is illegal, and a slave will not step aside to let you pass him in the street. I will explain the reason of this peculiar custom. Supposing it were legal for a slave to be beaten by a free citizen, or for a resident alien or freedman to be beaten by a citizen, it would frequently happen that an Athenian might be mistaken for a slave or an alien and receive a beating; since the Athenian People are not better clothed than the slave or alien, nor in personal appearance is there any superiority. 11. Or if the fact itself that slaves in Athens are allowed to indulge in luxury, and indeed in some cases to live magnificently, be found astonishing, this too, it can be shown, is done of set purpose. Where we have a naval power dependent upon wealth, we must perforce be slaves to our slaves, in order that we may get in our slave-rents, and let the real slave go free. Where you have wealthy slaves it ceases to be advantageous that my slave should stand in awe of you. In Lacedæmon my slave does stand in awe of you. But if your slave is in awe of me, the chances are he will give away his own money to avoid running a risk in his own person. 12. It is for this reason then that we have established an equality of speech between our slaves and free men; and again between our resident aliens and full citizens, because the city stands in need of her resident aliens to meet the requirements of such a multiplicity of arts and for the purposes of her navy. That is, I repeat, the justification of the equality conferred upon our resident aliens.

13. Citizens devoting their time to gymnastics and to the cultivation of music are not to be found in Athens; the sovereign People have dissolved their power,[1] not from any disbelief in the

[1] This statement is not true, and is partly contradicted by what follows. It is natural, however, for the oligarch to imagine that the democratization of athletics was equivalent to their abolition, especially in view of the fact that in general the democracy did not pursue athletics and prepare for the great national games with the zeal of the aristocracy.

beauty and honor of such training, but recognising the fact that these are things the cultivation of which is beyond their power. On the same principle, in the case of the choregia, the gymnasiarchy, and the trierarchy, the fact is recognised that it is the rich man who trains the chorus, and the People, for whom the chorus is trained; it is the rich man who is trierarch or gymnasiarch,[1] and the People that profit by their labors. In fact, what the People deem proper is to make wages by singing and running and dancing and manning the vessels but only in order that they may be the gainer, while the rich are made poorer. Thus too in the courts of justice, justice is not more an object of concern to the jurymen than what touches personal advantage.[2]

14. To speak next of the allies, and in reference to the point that emissaries from Athens come out and, according to common opinion, calumniate and vent their hatred upon the better sort of people, this is done on the principle that the ruler cannot help being hated by those whom he rules; but that if wealth and respectability are to wield power in the subject cities, the empire of the Athenian People has but a short lease of existence. This explains why the better people are punished with infamy, robbed of their money, driven from their homes, and put to death, while the baser sort are promoted to honor.[3] On the other hand, the better Athenians throw their ægis over the better class in the allied cities. And why? Because they recognise that it is to the interest of their own class at all times to protect the best element in the cities. 15. It may be urged that if it comes to strength and power, the real strength of Athens lies in the capacity of her allies to contribute their money quota. But to the democratic mind it appears a higher advantage still for the individual Athenian to get hold of the wealth of the allies, leaving them only enough to live upon and to cultivate their estates, but powerless to harbor treacherous designs.[4]

16. Again, it is looked upon as a mistaken policy on the part of

[1] On these liturgies, expensive public services performed unpaid by the wealthy, see Botsford, *Hellenic History*, ch. xii.

[2] On the jurors see no. 60.

[3] On the character of the Delian confederacy as a democratic alliance, see Botsford, *Hellenic History*, ch. xiv.

[4] This statement is absolutely untrue; under Athenian rule the allies greatly increased in wealth and prosperity; Botsford, *loc. cit.*

the Athenian democracy to compel her allies to voyage to Athens in order to have their cases tried. On the other hand, it is easy to reckon up what a number of advantages the Athenian People derive from the practice impugned. In the first place, there is the steady receipt of salaries throughout the year derived from the court fees. Next, it enables them to manage the affairs of the allied states while seated at home without the expense of naval expeditions. Thirdly, they thus preserve the partisans of the democracy, and ruin her opponents in the law courts. Whereas, supposing the several allied states tried their cases at home, being inspired by hostility to Athens, they would destroy those of their own citizens whose friendship to the Athenian People was most marked. 17. But besides all this the democracy derives the following advantages from hearing the cases of her allies in Athens. In the first place, the one per cent levied in Peiræus is an advantage to the state;[1] again, the owner of a house for a number of families[2] does better, and so, too, the owner of a pair of beasts, or of slaves to be let out for hire. 18. Again, heralds and criers are a class of people who fare better owing to the sojourn of the allies at Athens. Further still, supposing the allies had not to resort to Athens for the hearing of cases, only those of the Athenians who sail out to them would be held in honor, such as the general, or trierarch, or ambassador; whereas now every single individual among the allies is forced to pay flattery to the People of Athens because he knows that he must betake himself to Athens and lose or win his case at the bar, not of any stray set of judges, but of the sovereign People themselves, such being the law and custom at Athens. He is compelled to behave as a suppliant in the courts of justice, and when some juryman comes into court, to grasp his hand. For this reason, therefore, the allies find themselves more and more in the position of slaves to the democracy of Athens.

19. Furthermore, owing to the possession of property beyond the limits of Attica, and the exercise of magistracies which take them into regions beyond the frontier, they and their attendants have insensibly acquired the art of navigation. A man who is perpetually voyaging is forced to handle the oar, he and his slave alike,

[1] This was the amount of duty levied on imports and exports.

[2] Συνοικία.

and to learn the terms familiar in seamanship. 20. Hence a stock of skilful navigators is produced, bred upon a wide experience of voyaging and practice. They have learnt their business, some in piloting a small craft, others a merchant vessel, whilst others have been drafted off from these activities for service on a ship-of-war. So that the majority of them are able to row the moment they set foot on board a vessel, having been in a state of preliminary practice all their lives.

II. 1. As to the heavy infantry, an arm the deficiency of which at Athens is well recognized, this is how the matter stands. They recognize the fact that, in reference to the hostile power, they are themselves inferior, and must be, even if their heavy infantry were more numerous. But relatively to the allies, who pay the tribute and are quite strong on land, they are even satisfied to have the hoplite element carry on the government, if they (the Athenians) are stronger than the allies. 2. Apart from all else, to a certain extent fortune must be held responsible for the actual condition. The subjects of a power which is dominant by land have it open to them to form *one* commonwealth from several small states and fight with all their forces gathered into a compact union. But with the subjects of a naval power it is different. As far as they are groups of islanders, it is impossible for their states to meet together for united action; for the sea lies between them, and the dominant power is master of the sea. And even if it were possible for them to assemble in some single island unobserved, they will only (do so to) perish by famine. 3. And as to the states subject to Athens which are not islanders, but situated on the continent, the larger are held in check by apprehension, and the small ones absolutely by want, since there is no state in existence which does not depend upon imports and exports, and these she will forfeit if she does not lend a willing ear to those who are masters by sea. 4. In the next place, a power dominant by sea can do certain things which a land power is debarred from doing; as, for instance, ravage the territory of a superior, since it is always possible to coast along to some point, where either there is no hostile force to deal with or merely a small body; and in case of an advance in force on the part of the enemy they can take to their ships and sail away.[1] Such a performance is

[1] Such was the policy of Pericles in the Peloponnesian war; Thucydides ii. 23.

attended with less difficulty than that experienced by the relieving force on land. 5. Again, it is open to a power so dominating by sea to leave its own territory and sail off on as long a voyage as you please, whereas the land power cannot place more than a few days' journey between itself and its own territory, for marches are slow affairs; and it is not possible for an army on the march to have food supplies to last for any great length of time. Such an army must either march through friendly territory or it must force a way by victory in battle. The voyager meanwhile has it in his power to disembark at any point where he finds himself in superior force, or, at the worst, to coast by until he reaches either a friendly district or an enemy too weak to resist. 6. Again, those diseases to which the fruits of the earth are liable as visitations from Zeus fall severely on a land power, but are scarcely felt by the naval power, for such sicknesses do not visit the whole earth everywhere at once. Thus the ruler of the sea can get in supplies from a thriving district. 7. If one may descend to more trifling particulars, it is to this same lordship of the sea that the Athenians owe the discovery, in the first place, of many of the luxuries of life through intercourse with other countries. Thus it is that the choice things of Sicily and Italy, of Cyprus and Egypt and Lydia, of Pontus, of Peloponnese, or wheresoever else it be, are all swept, as it were, into one center, and all owing, as I say, to their maritime empire. 8. Again, in process of listening to every form of speech, they have selected for themselves this from one place and that from another. Hence while the rest of the Hellenes employ each pretty much their own peculiar mode of speech, habit of life, and style of dress, the Athenians have adopted a composite type, to which all sections of Hellas and the foreigner alike, have contributed.

9. As regards sacrifices and temples and festivals and sacred enclosures, the Attic Democracy sees that it is not possible for every poor citizen to do sacrifice and hold festival, or to set up temples and to inhabit a large and beautiful city. But it has hit upon a means of meeting the difficulty. They sacrifice — that is, the whole state sacrifices — at the public cost a large number of victims; but it is the Attic Democracy that keeps holiday and distributes the victims by lot amongst its members. 10. Rich men have in some cases private gymnasia and baths with dressing-rooms, but

the People take care to have built at the public cost a number of palæstras, dressing-rooms, and bathing establishments for their own special use, and the mob gets the benefit of the majority of these luxuries rather than the select few or the well-to-do.

11. As to wealth, the Athenians are exceptionally placed with regard to Hellenic and foreign communities alike, in their ability to hold it. For given that some state or other is rich in timber for shipbuilding, where is it to find a market for the product except by persuading the ruler of the sea? Or suppose the wealth of some state or other to consist of iron, or may be of bronze, or of hemp, where will it find a market except by permission of the supreme maritime power? Yet these are the very things, you see, which I need for my ships. Timber I must have from one, and from another iron, from a third bronze, from a fourth hemp, from a fifth wax, etc. 12. Besides they will not suffer our antagonists in these parts to carry these products elsewhither, or they will cease to use[1] the sea. Accordingly I, without one stroke of labor, from land possess all these good things, thanks to my supremacy on the sea; whilst not a single other state possesses as much as two of them; not timber, for instance, and hemp together, has the same city, but where hemp is abundant, the soil will be light and devoid of timber. And in the same way bronze and iron will not be products of the same city. The same rule holds for the rest, never two, or at best three, in one state, but one thing here and another thing there. 13. Moreover, above and beyond what has been said, the coastline of all the mainland presents either some jutting promontory, or adjacent island, or narrow strait of some sort, so that those who are masters of the sea can come to moorings at one of these points and inflict injury on the inhabitants of the mainland.

14. There is just one thing which the Athenians lack. Supposing they were the inhabitants of an island, and were still as now rulers of the sea, they would have had it in their power to inflict whatever mischief they liked, and to suffer no evil in return (as long as they kept command of the sea), neither the ravaging of their territory nor the expectation of an enemy's approach. At present the farming portion of the community and the wealthy landowners are ready to cringe before the enemy overmuch, whilst the

[1] Another reading is ἢ οὗ χρήσονται τῇ θαλάττῃ "or where they shall use the sea."

People, knowing full well that, come what may, not one stock or stone of their property will suffer, nothing will be cut down, nothing burnt, live in freedom from alarm, without fawning at the enemy's approach. 15. Besides this, there is another fear from which they would have been exempt in an island home — the apprehension of the city's being at any time betrayed by a handful of men and the gates thrown open, and an enemy bursting suddenly in. How could such incidents have taken place if an island had been their home? Again, had they inhabited an island there would have been no stirring of sedition against the people; whereas at present, in the event of a rising, those who set it on foot would base their hopes of success on the introduction of an enemy by land. But a people inhabiting an island would be free from all anxiety on that score. 16. Since, however, they did not chance to inhabit an island from the first, what they actually do is this — they deposit their property in the islands, trusting to their command of the sea, and they suffer the soil of Attica to be ravaged without a sigh. To expend pity on that, they know, would be to deprive themselves of other blessings still more precious.

17. Further, states oligarchically governed are forced to ratify their alliances and solemn oaths in a substantial fashion, and if they fail to abide by their treaties, the offence, by whomsoever committed, lies nominally at the door of the oligarchs who entered upon the contract. But in the case of engagements entered into by a democracy it is open to the People to throw the blame on the single individual who spoke in favor of some measure, or who put it to the vote, and to enter a denial for the rest of the citizens, averring that one was not present, or did not approve of the terms of the agreement. Inquiries are made in a full meeting of the People, and should any of these things be disapproved of, the demus has devised already innumerable excuses to avoid doing whatever they do not wish. If too any mischief should spring out of any deliberations of the assembly, the People charge that a handful of men acting against the interests of the citizens have ruined the state. But if any good result ensue, they, the People, at once take the credit of that to themselves.

18. In the same spirit it is not allowed to caricature on the comic stage or otherwise libel the People, because they do not care to hear

themselves ill spoken of. But if any one has a desire to satirize his neighbor, he has full leave to do so. And this because they are well aware that, as a general rule, the person caricatured does not belong to the People, or the masses. He is more likely to be some wealthy or well-born person, or man of means and influence. In fact, but few poor people and of the popular stamp incur the comic lash, or if they do, they have brought it on themselves by excessive love of meddling or some covetous self-seeking at the expense of the People, so that no particular annoyance is felt at seeing such folk satirized.

19. What I venture to assert is therefore that the People of Athens have no difficulty in recognizing which of their citizens are of the better sort and which the opposite. Recognizing, accordingly, those who are serviceable and advantageous to themselves, even though they be base, the People love them; but the good folk they are disposed the rather to hate. This excellence of theirs, the People hold, is not ingrained in their nature for any good to itself, but rather for its injury. In direct opposition to this, there are some persons who, being born of the People, are yet by natural instinct not commoners. 20. For my part I pardon the People their democracy, as indeed it is pardonable in any one to do good to himself. But the man who, not being himself one of the People, prefers to live in a state democratically governed rather than in an oligarchical state takes steps to commit wrong. He knows that a bad man has a better chance of slipping through the fingers of justice in a democratic than in an oligarchical state.

III. 1. I repeat that my position concerning the polity of the Athenians is this: the type of polity is not to my taste, but given that a democratic form of government has been agreed upon, they do seem to me to go the right way to preserve the democracy by the adoption of the particular type which I have set forth.

But there are other objections brought, as I am aware, against the Athenians by certain people, and to this effect: It not seldom happens, they tell us, that a man is unable to transact a piece of business with the council or the People, even if he sit waiting a whole year. Now this does happen at Athens, and for no other reason save that, owing to the immense mass of affairs, they are unable to work off all the business on hand and dismiss the applicants. 2. How in the world should they be able, considering in the first place, that they, the Athenians, have more festivals to celebrate than any other state throughout the length and breadth of Hellas? During these festivals necessarily the transaction of any sort of affairs of state is still more out of the question. In the next place, only consider the number of cases they have to decide, — private suits and public causes and scrutinies of accounts, etc. — more than the whole of the rest of mankind put together; while the council has multifarious points to advise upon concerning peace and war, concerning ways and means, concerning the framing and passing of laws, and concerning the thousand and one matters affecting the state perpetually occurring, and endless questions touching the allies, besides the receipt of the tribute, the superintendence of dockyards and temples, etc. I ask again, can any one find it at all surprising that, with all these affairs on their hands, they are unequal to attending to the business of all the world?

3. But some people tell us that if the applicant will only address himself to the council or the People with a fee in his hand, he will have his business done. For my part I would agree with these persons that a good many things are accomplished at Athens by dint of money; and I will add that a good many more still might be done, if the money flowed still more freely and from more pockets. One thing, however, I know full well, that as to transacting with every one of these applicants all he wants, the state could not do it, not even if all the gold and silver in the world were the inducement offered.

4. Here are some of the cases which have to be decided on. Some one fails to fit out his ship: judgment must be given. Another puts up a building on a piece of public land: again judgment must be given. Or to take another class of cases: adjudication has to be made between the choregi for the Dionysia, the Thargelia, the Panathenæa year after year. [And again in behalf of the gymnasiarchs a similar adjudication for the Panathenæa, the Prometheia, and the Hephæstia, also year after year.][1] Also as between the trierarchs, four hundred of whom are appointed each year; of these, too, any who choose must have their cases adjudicated on, year after year. But that is not all. There are various magis-

[1] Probably spurious. On the liturgies, see p. 226, n. 1, *supra*. In the distribution of liturgies many contentions arose as to who were liable.

trates to examine and approve and decide between; there are orphans whose status must be examined; and guardians of prisoners to appoint. 5. These, be it borne in mind, are all matters of yearly occurrence; while at intervals there are exemptions and abstentions from military service which call for adjudication, or in connection with some extraordinary misdemeanor, some case of outrage and violence of an exceptional character, or some charge of impiety. A whole list of others I simply omit; I am content to have named the most important part with the exception of the assessments of tribute which occur, as a rule, at intervals of five years.

I put it to you, then: can any one suppose that all or any of these disputes may dispense with adjudication? If so, will any one say which ought, and which ought not to be adjudicated on, there and then? 6. If, on the other hand, we are forced to admit that these are all fair cases for adjudication, it follows of necessity that they should be decided during the twelve-month; since even now the boards of judges sitting right through the year are powerless to stay the tide of evildoing by reason of the multitude of the people.

7. So far so good. "But," some one will say, "try the cases you certainly must, but lessen the number of the jurors." Yet if so, it follows of necessity that unless the number of courts themselves are diminished, there will be only a few jurors sitting in each court, with the further consequence that in dealing with so small a body of jurors it will be easier for a litigant to present an invulnerable front to the court, and to bribe the whole body, to the great detriment of justice.

8. But besides this we cannot escape the conclusion that the Athenians have their festivals to keep, during which the courts cannot sit. As a matter of fact these festivals are twice as numerous as those of any other people. However I will reckon them as merely equal to those of the state which has the fewest.

This being so, I maintain that it is not possible for business affairs at Athens to stand on any very different footing from the present, except to some slight extent, by adding here and deducting there. Any large modification is out of the question, short of curtailing the democracy itself. 9. No doubt many expedients might be discovered for improving the constitution, but if the problems be to discover some adequate means of making it better while at the same time the democracy is to remain intact, I say it is not easy to do this, except, as I have just stated, to the extent of some trifling addition here or deduction there.

10. There is another point in which it is sometimes felt that the Athenians are ill advised, in their adoption, namely, of the less respectable party, in those states divided by faction. But they do this advisedly. If they chose the more respectable, they would not be choosing those who held convictions identical with their own; for there is no state in which the best element is friendly to the people. It is the worst element which in every state favors the democracy — on the principle that like favors like. The case is simple enough. The Athenians choose what is most akin to themselves. 11. Also on every occasion on which they have attempted to side with the better classes, it has not fared well with them, but within a short interval the democratic party has been enslaved, as for instance in Bœotia;[1] or, as when they chose the aristocrats of the Milesians, and within a short time these nobles revolted[2] and cut the people to pieces; or, as when they chose the Lacedæmonians as against the Messenians,[3] and within a short time the Lacedæmonians subjugated the Messenians and went to war against Athens.

12. I seem to overhear a retort, "No one, of course, has been deprived of his civil rights at Athens unjustly." My answer is, that there are some who are unjustly deprived of their civil rights, though the cases are certainly rare. But it will take more than a few to attack the democracy at Athens. 13. You may consider it an established fact that it is not the man who has lost his civil rights justly who takes the matter to heart, but the victims, if any, of injustice. Yet how in the world can any one imagine that many are in a state of civil disability at Athens, where the People and the holders of office are one and the same? It is from iniquitous exercise of office, from iniquity exhibited either in speech or action, and the like circumstances, that citizens are punished with deprivation

[1] After the battle of Tanagra, 457. This passage is discussed by Botsford, in *Pol. Sci. Quart.* xxv (1910). 281–3.

[2] The Lesbian revolt took place in 428 (Thuc. iii. 2 *sqq.*), shortly before the composition of this oligarchic treatise.

[3] The author here refers to the aid brought by Cimon to the Lacedæmonians who were besieging the helots on Mount Ithome, 462; Thucydides i. 102; Plutarch, *Cimon*, 16; Aristophanes, *Lysistrate*, 1143; Botsford, *Hellenic History*, ch. xii.

of civil rights in Athens. Due reflection on these matters will serve to dispel the notion that there is any danger at Athens from persons visited with disfranchisement.

63. The First Ideal Constitution

(*The Constitution* of Hippodamus of Miletus, summarized and commented upon by Aristotle, *Politics*, ii. 8, 1267 a *sq.* Jowett, verified by E. G. S.)

The two selections last given represent the beginnings of political thought in the criticism and comparison of existing forms of government. Another line of political study, beginning nearly at the same time and running parallel, was the creation of ideal constitutions. The first constitution of the kind was that of Hippodamus, a contemporary of Pericles. As a civil engineer he had planned the cities of Peiræus and Thurii (Italy); see Botsford, *Hellenic History*, ch. xvii.

ch. 8. 1. Hippodamus, son of Euryphon, a native of Miletus, the same who invented the art of planning cities, and who also laid out Peiræus, was a strange man, whose fondness for distinction led him into a general eccentricity of life, which made some think him affected; for he would wear flowing hair and expensive ornaments; and yet he dressed himself in the same cheap warm garment both in winter and in summer. Besides aspiring to be an adept in the knowledge of nature, he was the first person not a statesman who made inquiries about the best form of government.

2. The city of Hippodamus was composed of 10,000 citizens divided into three parts, — one of artisans, one of husbandmen, and a third of armed defenders of the state. 3. He also divided the land into three parts, one sacred, one public, the third private. The first was set apart to maintain the customary worship of the gods, the second was to support the warriors, the third was the property of the husbandman. 4. He also divided his laws into three classes, and no more; for he maintained that there are three subjects of lawsuits, — insult, injury, and homicide. He likewise instituted a single final court of appeal, to which all cases seeming to have been improperly decided might be referred; this court he formed of elders chosen for the purpose. 5. He was further of the opinion that the decisions of the courts ought not to be given by the use of a voting pebble, but that every one should have a tablet on

which he might not only write a simple condemnation, or leave the tablet blank for a simple acquittal; but, if he partly acquitted and partly condemned, he was to distinguish accordingly. To the existing law he objected that it obliged the judges to be guilty of perjury, whichever way they voted. 6. He also enacted that those who discovered anything for the good of the state should be rewarded; and he provided that the children of citizens who died in battle should be maintained at the public expense, as if such an enactment had never been heard of before; yet it actually exists at Athens[1] and in other places.

7. As to the magistrates, he would have them all elected by the people, — that is, by the three classes already mentioned, and those who were elected were to watch over the interests of the public, of strangers, and of orphans. These are the most striking points in the constitution of Hippodamus. There is not much else.

The first of these proposals to which objection may be taken, is the threefold division of the citizens. 8. The artisans, the husbandmen, and the warriors, all have a share in the government. But the husbandmen have no arms, and the artisans neither arms nor land, and therefore they become all but slaves of the warrior class. 9. That they should share in all the offices is an impossibility; for generals and the guardians of the citizens, and nearly all the principal magistrates, must be taken from the class of those who carry arms. Yet if the two other classes have no share in the government, how can they be loyal citizens? It may be said that those who have arms must necessarily be masters of both the other classes, but this is not so easily accomplished unless they are numerous. 10. If however they are, why should the other classes share in the government at all, or have power to appoint magistrates? Artisans there must be; for they are wanted in every city, and they can live by their craft, as elsewhere; and the husbandmen, too, if they really provided the warriors with food, might fairly have a share in the government. But in the republic of Hippodamus they are supposed to have land of their own, which they cultivate for their private benefit. 11. Again, as to this common land out of which the soldiers are maintained, if they are themselves to be the cultivators of it, the warrior class will be identical with the husband-

[1] See Thuc. ii. 46 (*Funeral Oration* of Pericles); no. 64.

men, although the legislator intended to make a distinction between them. If, again, there are to be other cultivators distinct both from the husbandmen, who have land of their own, and from the warriors, they will make a fourth class, which has no place in the state and no share in anything. 12. Or if the same persons are to cultivate their own lands and those of the public as well, they will have a difficulty in supplying the quantity of produce which will maintain two households: and why in this case should there be any division, for they might find food themselves and give to the warriors from the same lots? There is surely a great confusion in all this.

13. Neither is the law to be commended which says that the judges, when a simple issue is laid before them, should distinguish in their judgment; for the judge is thus converted into an arbitrator. Now, in an arbitration, although the arbitrators are many, they confer with one another about the decision, and therefore they can distinguish; but in courts of law this is impossible; and in fact most legislators take pains to prevent the judges from holding any communication with one another. 14. Again, will there not be confusion if the judge thinks that damages should be given, but not so much as the suitor demands? He asks, say, for twenty minæ, and the judge allows him ten minæ, or one judge more and another less; one five, another four minæ. In this way they will go on apportioning the damages, and some will grant the whole and others nothing. 15. How is the final reckoning to be taken? Again, no one who votes for a simple acquittal or condemnation is compelled to perjure himself, if the indictment is quite simple and in right form; for the judge who acquits does not decide that the defendant owes nothing, but that he does not owe the twenty minæ. He only is guilty of perjury who thinks that the defendant ought not to pay twenty minæ, and yet condemns him.

16. To reward those who discover anything which is useful to the state is a proposal which has a specious sound, but cannot safely be enacted by law; for it may encourage informers, and perhaps even lead to political commotions. This question involves another. It has been doubted whether it is or is not expedient to make any changes in the laws of a country, even if another law be better. 17. Now if all changes are inexpedient, we can hardly assent to the

proposal of Hippodamus; for under pretence of doing a public service, a man may introduce measures which are really destructive to the laws or to the constitution. But since we have touched upon this subject, (18) perhaps we had better go a little into detail; for as I was saying, there is a difference of opinion, and it may sometimes seem desirable to make changes. Such changes in the other arts and sciences have certainly been beneficial; medicine, for example, and gymnastic and every other art and science have departed from traditional usage. If accordingly politics be an art, change must be necessary in this as in any other art. 19. The need of improvement is shown by the fact that old customs are exceedingly simple and barbarous. For the ancient Hellenes went about armed, and bought their wives of each other. 20. The remains of ancient laws which have come down to us are quite absurd; for example, at Cymê there is a law about murder, to the effect that if the accuser produce a certain number of witnesses from among his own kinsmen, the accused shall be held guilty.

64. Athenian Character and Ideals

(Pericles, *Funeral Oration*, in Thucydides ii. 35–46. Jowett, revised by E. G. S.)

Pericles, who brought his community to a summit of civilization never before reached by the human race, expressed in his own public life the noblest aspirations of his age. No one could doubt the competence of this man of clear, penetrating vision to interpret the character and ideals of his people. This task he sets before himself in the *Funeral Oration* delivered over those who fell in the first year of the great war with Peloponnesus, 431. As given by Thucydides, the essential ideas are those of the statesman, but the style is certainly that of the historian (p. 29 *supra*), who in inserting this oration in his narrative after the close of the war, undoubtedly colored even the thought with somber hues from his city's overthrow in 404. However the credit may be divided between Pericles and Thucydides, the speech is certainly one of the most precious documents which treat of the history of civilization. See Zimmern, *Greek Commonwealth*, a large part of which is avowedly a commentary on this document. For a briefer interpretation in the same spirit, see Ferguson, *Greek Imperialism*, lect. ii.

35. Most of those who have spoken here before me have commended the lawgiver who added this oration to our other funeral customs; it seemed to them a worthy thing that such an honor

should be given at their burial to the dead who have fallen on the field of battle. But I should have preferred that, when men's deeds have been brave, they should be honored in deed only, and with such an honor as this public funeral, which you are now witnessing. Then the reputation of many would not have been imperilled by the eloquence or want of eloquence of one, and their virtues believed or not as he spoke well or ill. For it is difficult to say neither too little nor too much; and even moderation is apt not to give the impression of truthfulness. The friend of the dead who knows the facts is likely to think that the words of the speaker fall short of his knowledge and of his wishes; another who is not so well informed, when he hears of anything which surpasses his own powers, will be envious and will suspect exaggeration. Mankind are tolerant of the praises of others so long as each hearer thinks that he can do as well or nearly as well himself; but when the speaker rises above him, jealousy is aroused and he begins to be incredulous. However, since our ancestors have set the seal of their approval upon the practice, I must obey, and to the utmost of my power shall endeavor to satisfy the wishes and beliefs of all who hear me.

36. I will speak first of our ancestors, for it is right and becoming that now, when we are lamenting the dead, a tribute should be paid to their memory. There has never been a time when they did not inhabit this land, which by their valor they have handed down from generation to generation, and we have received from them a free state. But if they were worthy of praise, still more were our fathers, who added to their inheritance, and after many a struggle transmitted to us, their sons, this great empire. And we ourselves assembled here to-day, who are still most of us in the vigor of life, have chiefly done the work of improvement, and have richly endowed our city with all things; so that she is sufficient for herself both in peace and war.[1] Of the military exploits by which our various possessions were acquired, or of the energy with which we or our fathers drove back the tide of war, Hellenic or Barbarian,

[1] Because of the insecurity of commerce in Hellenic times, and of the dangers which continually threatened the communications of every city-state with the outside world, the general policy of statesmen was to make their communities as self-sufficing as possible.

I will not speak; for the tale would be long and is familiar to you. But before I praise the dead, I should like to point out by what principles of action we rose to power, and under what institutions and through what manner of life our empire became great. For I conceive that such thoughts are not unsuited to the occasion, and that this numerous assembly of citizens and strangers may profitably listen to them.

37. Our form of government does not enter into rivalry with the institutions of others. We do not copy our neighbors, but are an example to them. It is true that we are called a democracy, for the administration is in the hands of the many and not of the few. But while the law secures equal justice to all alike in their private disputes, the claim of excellence is also recognized; and when a citizen is in any way distinguished, he is preferred to the public service, not as a matter of privilege, but as the reward of merit. Neither is poverty a bar, but a man may benefit his country whatever be the obscurity of his condition. There is no exclusiveness in our public life, and in our private intercourse we are not suspicious of one another, nor angry with our neighbor if he does what he likes; we do not put on sour looks at him which, though harmless, are not pleasant. While we are thus unconstrained in our private intercourse, a spirit of reverence pervades our public acts; we are prevented from doing wrong by respect for authority and for the laws, having an especial regard to those which are ordained for the protection of the injured as well as to those unwritten laws which bring upon the transgressor of them the reprobation of the general sentiment.

38. And we have not forgotten to provide for our weary spirits many relaxations from toil; we have regular games and sacrifices throughout the year; at home the style of our life is refined; and the delight which we daily feel in all these things helps to banish sadness. Because of the greatness of our city the fruits of the whole earth flow in upon us; so that we enjoy the goods of other countries as freely as of our own.

39. Then, again, our military training is in many respects superior to that of our adversaries. Our city is thrown open to the world, and we never expel a foreigner, or prevent him from seeing or learning anything of which the secret, if revealed to an enemy,

might profit him.[1] We rely not upon management or trickery, but upon our own hearts and hands. And in the matter of education, whereas they from early youth are always undergoing laborious exercises which are to make them brave, we live at ease, and yet are equally ready to face the perils which they face. And here is the proof. The Lacedæmonians come into Attica not by themselves, but with their whole confederacy following; we go alone into a neighbor's country; and although our opponents are fighting for their homes and we on a foreign soil, we have seldom any difficulty in overcoming them. Our enemies have never yet felt our united strength; the care of a navy divides our attention, and on land we are obliged to send our own citizens everywhere. But they, if they meet and defeat a part of our army, are as proud as if they had routed us all, and when defeated they pretend to have been vanquished by us all.

If, then, we prefer to meet danger with a light heart but without laborious training, and with a courage which is gained by habit and not enforced by law, are we not greatly the gainers? Since we do not anticipate the pain, although, when the hour comes, we can be as brave as those who never allow themselves to rest; and thus too our city is equally admirable in peace and in war. 40. For we are lovers of the beautiful, yet simple in our tastes, and we cultivate the mind without loss of manliness. Wealth we employ, not for talk and ostentation, but when there is a real use for it. To avow poverty with us is no disgrace; the true disgrace is in doing nothing to avoid it. An Athenian citizen does not neglect the state because he takes care of his own household; and even those of us who are engaged in business have a very fair idea of politics. We alone regard a man who takes no interest in public affairs, not as a harmless but as a useless character; and if few of us are originators, we are all sound judges of a policy. The great impediment to action is, in our opinion, not discussion, but the want of that knowledge which is gained by discussion preparatory to action. For we have a peculiar power of thinking before we act and of acting too, whereas other men are courageous from ignorance but hesitate upon reflection. Further, they are surely to be esteemed the bravest spirits who, having the

[1] In contrasting the Athenians with "others," Pericles has especially the Lacedæmonians in mind.

clearest sense both of the pains and pleasures of life, do not on that account shrink from danger. In doing good, again, we are unlike others; we make our friends by conferring, not by receiving, favors. Now he who confers a favor is the firmer friend, because he would fain by kindness keep alive the memory of an obligation; but the recipient is colder in his feelings, because he knows that in requiting another's generosity he will not be winning gratitude but only paying a debt. We alone do good to our neighbors not upon a calculation of interest, but in the confidence of freedom and in a frank and fearless spirit. 41. To sum up: I say that Athens is the school of Hellas, and that the individual Athenian in his own person seems to have the power of adapting himself to the most varied forms of action with the utmost versatility and grace. This is no passing and idle word, but truth and fact; and the assertion is verified by the position to which these qualities have raised the state. For in the hour of trial Athens alone among her contemporaries is superior to the report of her. No enemy who comes against her is indignant at the reverses which he sustains at the hands of such a city; no subject complains that his masters are unworthy of him. It is true, too, that we shall assuredly not be without witnesses; there are mighty monuments of our power which will make us the wonder of this and of succeeding ages; we shall not need the praises of Homer or any other panegyrist whose poetry may please for the moment, although his representation of the facts will not bear the light of day. For we have compelled every land and every sea to open a path for our valor, and have everywhere planted eternal memorials of our friendship and of our enmity. Such is the city for whose sake these men nobly fought and died; they could not bear the thought that she might be taken from them; and every one of us who survive should gladly toil on her behalf.

42. I have dwelt upon the greatness of Athens because I want to show you that we are contending for a higher prize than those who enjoy none of these privileges, and to establish by manifest proof the merit of these men whom I am now commemorating. Their loftiest praise has been already spoken. For in magnifying the city I have magnified them, and men like them whose virtues made her glorious. Of how few Hellenes can it be said as of them, that

their deeds when weighed in the balance have been found equal to their fame! Methinks that a death such as theirs has been gives the true measure of a man's worth; it may be the first revelation of his virtues, but is at any rate their final seal. For even those who come short in other ways may justly plead the valor with which they have fought for their country; they have blotted out the evil with the good, and have benefited the state more by their public services than they have injured her by their private actions. None of these men were enervated by wealth or hesitated to resign the pleasures of life; none of them put off the evil day in the hope, natural to poverty, that a man, though poor, may one day become rich. But deeming that the punishment of their enemies was sweeter than any of these things, and that they could fall in no nobler cause, they determined at the hazard of their lives to be honorably avenged, and to leave the rest. They resigned to hope their unknown chance of happiness; but in the face of death they resolved to rely upon themselves alone. And when the moment came they were minded to resist and suffer, rather than to fly and save their lives; they ran away from the word of dishonor, but on the battle-field their feet stood fast, and in an instant, at the height of their fortune, they passed away from the scene, not of their fear, but of their glory.

43. Such was the end of these men; they were worthy of Athens, and the living need not desire to have a more heroic spirit, although they may pray for a less fatal issue. The value of such a spirit is not to be expressed in words. Any one can discourse to you for ever about the advantages of a brave defence which you know already. But instead of listening to him I would have you day by day fix your eyes upon the greatness of Athens, until you become filled with the love of her; and when you are impressed by the spectacle of her glory, reflect that this empire has been acquired by men who knew their duty and had the courage to do it, who in the hour of conflict had the fear of dishonor always present to them, and who, if ever they failed in an enterprise, would not allow their virtues to be lost to their country, but freely gave their lives to her as the fairest offering which they could present at her feast. The sacrifice which they collectively made was individually repaid to them; for they received again each one for himself a praise which

grows not old, and the noblest of all sepulchers — I speak not of that in which their remains are laid, but of that in which their glory survives, and is proclaimed always and on every fitting occasion both in word and deed. For the whole earth is the sepulcher of famous men; not only are they commemorated by columns and inscriptions in their own country, but in foreign lands there dwells also an unwritten memorial of them, graven not on stone but in the hearts of men. Make them your examples; and esteeming courage to be freedom and freedom to be happiness, do not weigh too nicely the perils of war. The unfortunate who has no hope of a change for the better has less reason to throw away his life than the prosperous who, if he survive, is always liable to a change for the worse, and to whom any accidental fall makes the most serious difference. To a man of spirit, cowardice and disaster coming together are far more bitter than death striking him unperceived at a time when he is full of courage and animated by the general hope.

44. Wherefore I do not now commiserate the parents of the dead who stand here; I would rather comfort them. You know that your life has been passed amid manifold vicissitudes; and that they may be deemed fortunate who have gained most honor, whether an honorable death like theirs, or an honorable sorrow like yours, and whose days have been so ordered that the term of their happiness is likewise the term of their life. I know how hard it is to make you feel this, when the good fortune of others will too often remind you of the gladness which once lightened your hearts. Sorrow is felt at the want of those blessings, not which a man never knew, but which were a part of his life before they were taken from him. Some of you are of an age at which they may hope to have other children, and they ought to bear their sorrow better; not only will the children who may hereafter be born make them forget their own lost ones, but the city will be doubly a gainer. She will not be left desolate, and she will be safer. For a man's counsel cannot have equal weight or worth, when he alone has no children to risk in the general danger. To those of you who have passed their prime, I say: "Congratulate yourselves that you have been happy during the greater part of your days; remember that your life of sorrow will not last long, and be comforted by the glory of those

who are gone. For the love of honor alone is ever young, and not riches, as some say, but honor is the delight of men when they are old and useless.

45. To you who are the sons and brothers of the departed, I see that the struggle to emulate them will be an arduous one. For all men praise the dead, and however preëminent your virtue may be, hardly will you be thought, I do not say to equal, but even to approach them. The living have their rivals and detractors, but when a man is out of the way, the honor and good-will which he receives is unalloyed. And if I am to speak of womanly virtues to those of you who will henceforth be widows, let me sum them up in one short admonition: To a woman not to show more weakness than is natural to her sex is a great glory, and not to be talked about for good or for evil among men.

46. I have paid the required tribute, in obedience to the law, making use of such fitting words as I had. The tribute of deeds has been paid in part; for the dead have been honorably interred, and it remains only that their children should be maintained at the public charge until they are grown up: this is the solid prize with which, as with a garland, Athens crowns her sons living and dead, after a struggle like theirs. For where the rewards of virtue are greatest, there the noblest citizens are enlisted in the service of the state. And now, when you have duly lamented, every one his own dead, you may depart.

65. Athenian and Lacedæmonian Policy and Character Contrasted

(*Speech* of Corinthian deputies in the Peloponnesian Congress at Sparta, 432, as given by Thucydides i. 68–71. Jowett, revised, on the basis of a comparison of the Greek text, by E. G. S.)

This selection is placed with those which immediately precede, to represent, in the conflict of feelings and of interests which resulted in the Peloponnesian war, a view hostile to Athens. The Corinthian speech and the reply of the Athenians given immediately afterward by Thucydides 1. 72–8, but not included in this volume, are masterpieces of pure political reasoning, and they set forth, not merely the political status and the underlying sentiment in the leading states as they were before the outbreak of the Peloponnesian war, but also involve a retrospect of the political development of the Ægean world as it passed through the half century which elapsed since Salamis and Platæa.

68. The spirit of trust, Lacedæmonians, which animates your own political and social life, makes you distrust others who, like ourselves, have something unpleasant to say, and this temper of mind, though favorable to moderation, too often leaves you in ignorance of what is going on outside your own country. Time after time we have warned you of the mischief which the Athenians would do to us; but instead of taking our words to heart, you chose to suspect that we only spoke from interested motives. And this is the reason why you have summoned these allies here to Sparta too late, — not before but after the injury has been inflicted, and when we are smarting under the sense of it. Of all persons who has a better right to speak than ourselves, who have the heaviest accusations to make, outraged as we are by the Athenians, and neglected by you? If the crimes which they are committing against Hellas were being done in a corner, then you might be ignorant, and we should have to inform you of them: but now, what need of many words? Some of us, as you see, have already been enslaved; they are at this moment intriguing against others, notably against allies of ours; and long ago they had made all their preparations in expectation of war. Else why did they seduce from her allegiance Corcyra, which they still hold in defiance of us, and why are they blockading Potidæa, — the latter a most advantageous post for the command of the Thracian peninsula, the former a great naval power which might have assisted the Peloponnesians?[1]

69. And the blame of all this rests on you; for you originally allowed them to fortify their city after the Persian War,[2] and afterwards to build their Long Walls;[3] and to this hour you have gone on depriving of liberty not only those enslaved by them but are now beginning to take it away even from your own allies. For the true enslaver of a people is he who can put an end to their slavery but has no care about it; and all the more, if he be reputed the champion of liberty in Hellas. — And barely now have we met in a congress and not even yet on the basis of a clear situation. By this

[1] Athens had recently made a defensive alliance with Corcyra, a colony of Corinth. Potidæa, another colony of Corinth, had long been a tributary member of the Athenian empire but had recently revolted. The Athenians accordingly were attempting by blockade to reduce the city. See Thucydides i. 24 *sqq.*; Bury, *History of Greece*, ch. x. § 1; Botsford, *Hellenic History*, ch. xvii (*init.*).

[2] See Thucydides i. 90–92.

[3] The walls connecting Athens with Peiræus; Thuc. i. 107.

time we ought to have been considering, not whether we are wronged, but how we are to be revenged. The aggressor is not now threatening, but advancing; he has made up his mind, while we are resolved about nothing. And we know too well by what road and how little by little the Athenians move upon their neighbors. While they think that you are too dull to observe them, they are more careful, but when they perceive that you with full knowledge overlook their aggressions, they will strike and not spare. Of all Hellenes, Lacedæmonians, you are the only people who keep at rest warding off (an enemy) not with your active power but with delay: and you are the only people who do not destroy the increase of your foes in the beginning but when it has grown to fulness. How came you to be considered safe? That reputation of yours was never justified by facts. We all know that the Persian made his way from the ends of the earth against Peloponnesus before you encountered him in a worthy manner; and now you are blind to the doings of the Athenians, who are not at a distance as he was, but close at hand. Instead of attacking your enemy, you wait to be attacked, and take the chances of a struggle which has been deferred until his power is doubled. And you know that the Barbarian miscarried chiefly through his own error; and that we have oftener been delivered from these very Athenians by blunders of their own, than by aid from you. Some have already been ruined by the hopes which you inspired in them; for so entirely did they trust you that they took no precautions themselves. These things we say in no accusing or hostile spirit — let that be understood — but by way of expostulation. For men expostulate with erring friends, they bring accusation against enemies who have done them a wrong.

70. Still we have a right to find fault with our neighbors, if any one ever had. There are important interests at stake to which, as far as we can see, you are insensible. You have never considered what manner of men are these Athenians with whom you will have to fight, and how utterly unlike yourselves. They are ready to resort to novel devices, equally quick in the conception and in the execution of every new plan; while you are conservative — careful only to keep what you have, originating nothing, and in execution achieving not even what is urgently necessary. Again they are

bold beyond their strength; they run risks which prudence would condemn; and in critical situations they are full of hope. Whereas it is your way to have your action fall short of your strength and of your conviction to put faith not even in sound things: when calamities come upon you, to think that you will never be delivered from them. They are impetuous, and you are dilatory; they are always abroad, and you are always at home. For they hope to gain something by leaving their homes; but you are afraid that any new enterprise may impair what you have already. When conquerors, they pursue their victory to the utmost; when defeated, they fall back the least. In behalf of their commonwealth they make use of the physical service of men who are complete strangers to Athens; while the directing mind is in supreme degree Athens' own.[1] When they do not carry out an intention which they have formed, they seem to have sustained a personal bereavement; when an enterprise succeeds, they have gained but an instalment of what is to come; if they fail, however, they at once conceive new hopes and so fill up the void. With them alone to hope is to have, for they lose not a moment in the execution of an idea. This is the life-long task, full of danger and toil, which they are always imposing upon themselves. None enjoy their good things less, because they are always engaged in acquisition. To do their duty is their only holiday, and they deem the quiet of inaction to be as disagreeable as the most laborious occupation. Therefore if a man should say of them, in a word, that they were born neither to have peace themselves nor to allow peace to other men, he would simply speak the truth.

71. In the face of such an enemy, Lacedæmonians, you procrastinate and you do not believe that peace is most enduring to those who use their preparation for just action, but are clearly minded not to yield if they be wronged, whereas justice with you seems to consist in giving no annoyance to others and in defending yourselves only against positive injury. But this policy would hardly be successful, even if your neighbors were like yourselves; and in the present case, as we pointed out just now, your ways compared with theirs are

[1] Jowett's rendering is quite different: "Their bodies they devote to their country as though they belonged to other men; their true self is their mind, which is most truly their own when employed in her service."

old-fashioned. Furthermore, as in the arts, so also in politics, the new must always prevail over the old. In settled times the traditions of government should be observed: but when circumstances are changing and men are compelled to meet them, much additional devising is required. The Athenians have had a wider experience, and therefore the administration of their state has adopted novelties in a greater degree than yours. But here let your procrastination end; send an army at once into Attica and assist especially the Potidæans, to whom your word is pledged. Do not allow friends and kindred to fall into the hands of their worst enemies; nor drive us in despair to seek the alliance of others; in taking such a course we should be doing nothing wrong either before the gods who are the witnesses of our oaths, or before men whose eyes are upon us. For the true breakers of treaties are not those who, when forsaken, turn to others, but those who forsake allies whom they have sworn to defend. We will remain your friends if you choose to bestir yourselves; for we should be guilty of an impiety if we deserted you without cause; and we shall not easily find allies equally congenial to us. Take heed then: you have inherited from your fathers the leadership of Peloponnesus; see that her greatness suffers no diminution at your hands.

66. The Revolution at Corcyra, 427; the Morals of Political Seditions

(Thucydides iii. 81–3. Jowett, revised, on the basis of a comparison of the Greek text, by E. G. S.)

Shortly before the events mentioned in the following selection the oligarchs of Corcyra had seized the government, put down the democracy, and murdered the leading men among their opponents; Busolt, *Griech. Gesch.* III. 1040 *sqq.* Hearing soon afterward that a Peloponnesian fleet was sailing to the support of the oligarchy, the Athenians despatched Eurymedon with sixty triremes to Corcyra for the protection of their own interests in that island; Thuc. iii. 80. After devastating the country, the Peloponnesians, on the approach of the Athenian fleet, withdrew, leaving the Corcyræan oligarchs in the lurch.

The relentless keenness, the depth, and the undoubted truth of this analysis of the motives and the character of political factions, which not only undermined the foundations of right conduct, but even distorted the terms and phrases of current judgment, make the passage here quoted one of the most remarkable in the history of literature.

81. The Peloponnesians set out that very night on their way home, keeping close to the land, and transporting the ships over the Leucadian isthmus, that they might not be seen sailing round. When the Corcyræans perceived that the Athenian fleet was approaching, while that of the enemy disappeared, they took the Messenian troops, who had hitherto been outside the walls, into the city, and ordered the ships which they had manned to sail round into the Hyllaic harbor. These vessels proceeded on their way. Meanwhile they killed any of their enemies whom they caught in the city. On the arrival of the ships they disembarked those whom they had induced to go on board, and despatched them; they also went to the temple of Hera, and persuading about fifty of the suppliants to stand their trial, condemned them all to death.[1] The majority of the suppliants would not come out, and when they saw what was going on, destroyed one another in the enclosure of the temple where they were, except a few who hung themselves on trees, or put an end to their own lives in any other way which they could. During the seven days, too, while Eurymedon after his arrival remained with his sixty ships, the Corcyræans continued slaughtering those of their fellow-citizens whom they deemed their enemies; they professed to punish them for their designs against the democracy, but in fact some were killed from motives of personal enmity, and some because money was owing to them, by the hands of their debtors. Every form of death was to be seen, and as is wont to be the case in such a crisis, there was nothing that did not come to pass, and in fact there was more than ever.[2] For the father slew the son, and the suppliants were torn from the temples and slain near them; some of them were even walled up in the temple of Dionysus, and there perished.

82. To such extremes of cruelty did revolution go; and this seemed to be the worst of revolutions, because it was the first. For afterward even the whole Hellenic world was stirred in civil disorder: in every city the chiefs of the democracy and of the oligarchy were struggling, the one to bring in the Athenians, the other the

[1] Here the democrats, regaining the upper hand and looking to Athenian support, began to retaliate upon the oligarchs.

[2] This statement is hyperbolical; the author means to express the unusual character of the proceedings.

Lacedæmonians. Now in time of peace, men would have had no excuse for introducing either, and would not be ready to do so, but when they were at war and both sides could easily obtain allies to the hurt of their enemies and the advantage of themselves, the dissatisfied party were only too ready to invoke foreign aid. Thus revolution brought upon the cities of Hellas many terrible calamities, such as have been and always will be while human nature remains the same, but which are more or less aggravated and differ in character with every new combination of circumstances. In peace and prosperity both states and individuals are actuated by higher motives, because they do not fall under the dominion of imperious necessities; but war, which takes away the comfortable provision of daily life, is a hard master, and tends to assimilate the wrathful excitement of the many to the prevailing situation.[1]

When troubles had once begun in the cities, those who followed carried the revolutionary spirit further and further, and determined, by the ingenuity of their enterprise and the atrocity of their revenges, to outdo the report of all who had preceded them. The meaning of words had no longer the same relation to things, but was changed by them as they thought proper. Reckless daring was held to be loyal courage; prudent delay was specious cowardice; moderation was the disguise of unmanly weakness; to be thoughtful in meeting every issue was inactivity. Frantic energy was the true quality of a man. A conspirator who wanted to be safe was a recreant in disguise. The lover of violence was always trusted, and his opponent suspected. He who succeeded in a plot was deemed knowing, but a still greater master in craft was he who detected one. On the other hand, he who plotted from the first to have nothing to do with plots was a breaker up of his faction and a poltroon who was afraid of the enemy. In a word, he who could outstrip another in a bad action was applauded, and so was he who encouraged to evil one who had no idea of it. The tie of party was stronger than the tie of blood, because a partisan was more ready to dare without asking why. In fact party associations are not based upon any established law, nor do they seek the public good; they are founded in defiance of the laws and from self-interest. The seal

[1] πρὸς τὰ παρόντα τὰς ὀργὰς τῶν πολλῶν ὁμοιοῖ; the translation of this clause here given is more precise than that of Jowett.

of good faith was not divine law but fellowship in crime. If an enemy when he was in the ascendant offered fair words, the opposite party received them not in a generous spirit, but with a jealous watchfulness of his actions. Revenge was dearer than self-preservation. Any agreements sworn to by either party, when they could do nothing else, were binding for the moment only, when they had no strength from other sources. But he who on a favorable opportunity first took courage and struck at his enemy when he saw him undefended, had greater pleasure in a perfidious than he would have had in an open act of revenge. He congratulated himself that he had taken the safer course, and also that he had overreached his enemy and gained the prize of superior ability. In general, the dishonest more easily gain credit for cleverness than the simple for goodness; men take a pride in the one, but are ashamed of the other.

The cause of all these evils was the love of power, originating in avarice and ambition, and the party-spirit which is engendered by them when men are fairly embarked in a contest. For the leaders on either side used specious names, the one party professing to uphold the constitutional equality of the many, the other the wisdom of an aristocracy, while they made the public interests, to which in name they were devoted, in reality their prize. Striving in every way to overcome each other, they committed the most monstrous crimes; yet even they were surpassed by the magnitude of their revenges which they pursued to the very utmost, neither party observing any definite limits either of justice or public expediency, but both alike making the caprice of the moment their law. Either by the help of an unrighteous sentence, or grasping power with a strong hand, they were eager to satiate the love of victory[1] of the moment. Neither faction cared for religion; but any specious pretence which succeeded in effecting some odious purpose was greatly lauded. And the citizens who held an intermediate position fell a prey to both sides; either they were disliked because they held aloof, or men were jealous of their surviving.

83. Thus revolution gave birth to every form of wickedness in Hellas. The simplicity which is so large an element in a noble

[1] τὴν αὐτίκα φιλονικίαν ἐκπιμπλάναι (Stahl's text).

nature was laughed to scorn and disappeared. An attitude of perfidious antagonism everywhere prevailed; for there was no word binding enough, nor oath terrible enough to reconcile enemies. Each man was strong only in the conviction that nothing was secure; he had to look to his own safety, and could not afford to trust others. Inferior intellects generally succeeded best. For aware of their own deficiencies, and fearing the capacity of their opponents, for whom they were no match in powers of speech, and whose subtle wits were likely to anticipate them in contriving evil, they struck boldly and at once. But the clever sort, presuming in their arrogance that they would be aware in time, and disdaining to act when they could think, were taken off their guard and easily destroyed.

BIBLIOGRAPHY

Botsford, *Hellenic History*, chs. xii–xix; Ferguson, *Greek Imperialism*, 23 *sqq.*; Bury, chs. viii–xi; Holm, II. chs. vi–xxviii; Abbott, *Greece*, II. ch. vi to end of vol. III; *Pericles and the Golden Age of Athens;* Curtius, bk. III. ch. ii–bk. IV. ch. v; Grote, chs. xliv–lxv; Freeman, *History of Sicily*.

Zimmern, A. E., *Greek Commonwealth* (see Contents); Grundy, G. B., *Thucydides and the History of his Age* (London, 1911); "Population and Policy of Sparta in the Fifth Century," in *Journ. Hell. St.* XXVIII (1908). 77–96.

Meyer, *Gesch. d. Alt.* III. 418 to end of vol. IV; Beloch, *Griech. Gesch.* II. 1. 74 to end of pt.; *Attische Politik seit Perikles* (Leipzig, 1884); Busolt, *Griech. Gesch.* III entire; Cavaignac, E., *Histoire de l'antiquité,* II (Paris, 1913). 1–234; *Études sur l'histoire financière d'Athènes au Ve siècle* (Paris, 1908).

Whibley, L., *Political Parties at Athens in the Time of the Peloponnesian War* (Cambridge: University Press, 1889); Croiset, M., *Aristophanes and the Political Parties at Athens*, trans. by J. Loeb (Macmillan, 1909); Stawell, F. M., "Pericles and Cleon in Thucydides," in *Class. Quart.* II (1908). 41–6; Gilbert, G., *Beiträge zur inneren Geschichte Athens im Zeitalter des Peloponnesischen Krieges* (Leipzig, 1877); Nestle, W., "Politik und Aufklärung in Griechenland im Ausgang des V. Jahrhunderts v. Chr." in *N. Jahrb.* XXIV (1903). 1–22.

CHAPTER VII

THE CONFEDERACY OF DELOS AND THE ATHENIAN EMPIRE

478–404 B.C.

67. The First Step Toward Confederation

(Herodotus ix. 106)

In 479 a land force of Hellenes won the great battle of Platæa, Bœotia. Meanwhile their fleet crossed to Asia Minor, where the crews landed and won an equally splendid victory over the Persians intrenched at Mycale, a promontory on the Ionian coast. The subsequent movement of the victors is well told by Herodotus in the following passage.

Having set fire to the wall and the ships, they sailed away; and when they came to Samos, the Hellenes deliberated about removing the inhabitants of Ionia, and considered where they ought to settle them in those parts of Hellas of which they had command, leaving Ionia to the Barbarians: for they considered it impossible for them to be always stationed as guards to protect the Ionians, and unless they did protect them in this way, they had no hope that the Ionians would escape with impunity from the Persians. It seemed good, therefore, to those of the Peloponnesians who were in authority that they should remove the inhabitants of the trading ports which belonged to those peoples of Hellas who had taken the side of the Medes, and give that land to the Ionians to dwell in. The Athenians, however, did not think it good that the inhabitants of Ionia should be removed at all, nor that the Peloponnesians should consult about Athenian colonies; and as they vehemently resisted the proposal, the Peloponnesians gave way. The result was, accordingly, that they joined as allies to their league the Samians, Chians, Lesbians, and the other islanders who chanced to be serving with the Hellenes, binding them by pledge and by oaths to remain faithful and not withdraw from the league.

"Those in authority," here mentioned, were King Leotychidas of Lacedæmon and the ephors who accompanied him, whereas the chief admiral of the Athenians was Xanthippus, father of Pericles. The arbitrary transplanting of an entire people from one region to another was an Oriental custom totally foreign to Hellenic ideas. In repudiating it the Athenians were actuated, not only by their feeling of kinship with the Ionians, but also by their ambition to build up an alliance of their own. While mentioning the admission of the Samians and other islanders to the general Hellenic league, Herodotus leaves the reader to infer the important fact that, at the same time, the Athenians entered into close relations of friendship and alliance with the Ionians, perhaps also with other Asiatic Greeks. This was the slight beginning of a union which afterward developed into the Confederacy of Delos.

68. Organization of the Confederacy

(Thucydides i. 95–6)

The Lacedæmonians, however, might long have retained the naval command, had they possessed a competent admiral. During the siege of Byzantium by the Hellenes and after its fall, Pausanias, the Lacedæmonian commander, treated the Ionians, Lesbians, and other newly acquired allies with such arrogance and brutality as to drive them to open rebellion. They turned for leadership to Aristeides, Cimon, and the other generals in command of the Athenian contingent. Pausanias was recalled, and after another vain attempt to supply the Hellenes with an admiral, the Lacedæmonians yielded the naval leadership to Athens (Thuc. i. 95; Arist. *Const. Ath.* 23; Plut. *Arist.* 23).

Henceforth the Lacedæmonians sent out no more commanders, for they were afraid that those whom they appointed would be corrupted, as they had found to be the case with Pausanias; they had had enough of the Persian war; and they thought that the Athenians were fully able to lead, and at that time believed them to be their friends.

Thus the Athenians by the good-will of the allies, who detested Pausanias, obtained the leadership. They immediately fixed which of the cities should supply money and which of them ships for the war against the Barbarians, the avowed object being to compensate themselves and the allies for their losses by devastating the King's country. Then was first instituted at Athens the office of Hellenic

Treasurers,[1] who received the tribute, for so the impost was termed. The amount was originally fixed at 460 talents. The island of Delos was the treasury, and the meetings of the allies were held in the temple.[2]

(Plutarch, *Aristeides*, 23; *cf.* Aristotle, *Constitution of the Athenians*, 23; for other sources, see Hill, *Sources for Greek History*, pp. 5–11)

As they (the allies) wished each city to be assessed for a reasonable contribution, they asked the Athenians to appoint Aristeides to visit each city, learn the extent of its territory and revenues, and fix upon the amount which each was capable of contributing according to its means. Although he was in possession of such great power — the whole of Hellas[3] having, as it were, given itself up to be dealt with at his discretion — yet he laid down his office a poorer man than when he accepted it, but having completed his assessment to the satisfaction of all.[4] As the ancients used to tell of the blessedness of the golden age, even so did the states of Hellas honor the assessment of Aristeides, calling the time when it was made, fortunate and blessed for Hellas.

[1] There were ten Hellenic Treasurers (Ἑλληνοταμίαι), one elected from each of the ten Attic tribes; *CIA*. i. no. 259 *sqq.*; *cf.* 188. Naturally while the treasury remained in Delos, they were located there. The president of the federal council was also an Athenian, while Athenian generals served as commanders-in-chief of the federal army and navy.

[2] The temple of Apollo, the seat of an Ionian (so-called Delian) amphictyony, which reached the height of its splendor in the eighth and seventh centuries; see the Homeric *Hymn to the Delian Apollo;* Thuc. iii. 104. In the winter of 426–5 the Athenians purified the island, and revived the amphictyonic festival; Thuc. *loc. cit.* While the amphictyony served as a religious basis of the new union, the political and military organization of the latter was patterned, with important modifications, after the Peloponnesian league.

[3] This is a greatly exaggerated statement; at this time the Confederacy included but a part of the island and coast region of the Ægean Sea.

[4] Craterus, a generally trustworthy historian, stated (Plut. *Arist.* 26) that a certain Athenian, Diophantus of Amphitrope, obtained a verdict against Aristeides on the charge of his having been bribed by the Ionians to make their assessment less than their proportional due, and that, unable to pay the fine of fifty talents, the condemned statesman ended his days in exile. Although Aristeides may not have been guilty of the crime, there is considerable evidence that in his own lifetime he did not enjoy the universal reputation for absolute probity which centuries later he acquired among moralists and rhetoricians.

69. Commercial Treaty with Phaselis

(*Inscr. græc.* II. no. 11; Hicks and Hill, no. 36. Translated by G. W. B.)

Under the arrangements above described Athens proceeded to make treaties with individual states of the Confederacy to regulate her commercial relations with them. Among the earliest of these agreements is the treaty with Phaselis preserved in an inscription. Phaselis was a Dorian colony on the Lycian coast, and was annexed to the Delian Confederacy in that campaign of Cimon which culminated in the battle of the Eurymedon, 468 (Thuc. i. 100; Plut. *Cim.* 12). From this document we learn that a similar treaty had already been concluded with Chios.

1. Be it resolved by the Boulê and the Demus. Acamantis was the prytanizing tribe. Onasippus was secretary. ...des was chairman. Leon moved the resolution:[1] —

2. That there be engraved the decree for the Phaselitans, to the effect that if there shall be made at Athens a contract with any of the Phaselitans, the suits arising from it shall be tried at Athens before the polemarch — just as is done in the case of the Chians[2] — and nowhere else.

3. That suits arising from other kinds of contracts under treaty are to be settled with the Phaselitans in the same way as in the treaty with the Chians; and the reference of such cases to arbitrators is hereby abolished.[3]

[1] This is the usual heading (prescript) of an Athenian decree (ψήφισμα). The Boulê is the Council of Five Hundred; the Demus, "commons," is the people in assembly (ἐκκλησία). The ten tribal delegations took their turns in acting as an administrative and legislative committee, each for a tenth of the year. The fifty delegates on duty for the time being were termed prytaneis, "foremen" (or "the prytanizing tribe," as here), and the period of their duty was, accordingly, termed a prytany. The chairman of the prytaneis was also chairman of the entire boulê and of the assembly. On the Five Hundred and the assembly, see Gilbert, *Const. Antiq.* 265 *sqq.*

[2] Reference to the Chians is due not only to the fact that the treaty with Chios was earlier, and served therefore as a model for all similar treaties, but also to the fact that it was the Chians who persuaded Phaselis to enter the Confederacy (Plut. *Cim.* 12). Chios was not only free but among the most favored of the allies; and this article of the treaty accorded with general Greek usage.

[3] Unfortunately, as the treaty with Chios has not been preserved, we do not know what the arrangements were for this class of suits. Doubtless, however, they were complex; a contract made between a Phaselitan and an Athenian at Phaselis was probably actionable in that city; if the Athenian resided, for instance, at Chios and the contract was made there, it may have been actionable at Chios, etc.

The clause relating to arbitrators is a conjectural reading. If the passage is correctly restored, it has reference to the choice of arbitrators from a disinterested state; see Hesychius, ἔκκλητοι δίκαι· αἱ ἐπὶ ξένης λεγόμεναι, καὶ οὐκ ἐν τῇ πόλει.

4. That if the magistrate[1] receive against any of the Phaselitans one of the cases which belong elsewhere, and the Phaselitan be condemned in the suit to pay, the suit shall be invalid.

5. That if the magistrate shall be shown to have violated this decree, he shall be liable to a fine of 1000 drachmas, to be consecrated to Athena.

6. That the secretary of the boulê inscribe this decree on a stone pillar and place it on the Acropolis at the expense of the Phaselitans.

70. The Transformation of the Confederacy into an Athenian Empire

(Thucydides i. 97–99)

At first the allies were independent and deliberated in a common assembly under the leadership of Athens. But in the interval between the Persian and the Peloponnesian wars, by their military success and by policy in dealing with the Barbarian, with their own rebellious allies, and with the Peloponnesians who from time to time crossed their path, the Athenians made immense strides in power. . . .

The Naxians revolted, and the Athenians made war against them and reduced them by blockade. This was the first of the allied cities which was enslaved contrary to Hellenic law; the turn of the others came later.

The causes which led to the defection of the allies were various, the principal being their neglect to pay the tribute or to furnish ships, and in some cases, failure of military service. For the Athenians were exacting and oppressive, using coercive measures toward men who were neither willing nor accustomed to work hard. For various reasons, too, they soon began to prove less agreeable leaders than at first. They no longer fought upon an equality with the rest of the confederates, and they had no difficulty in reducing them when they revolted. Now the allies brought all this misfortune upon themselves; for the majority of them disliked

[1] The magistrate (ἄρχων) mentioned here and in the following article is necessarily the polemarch.

military service and absence from home; hence they agreed to contribute a regular sum of money instead of ships. In this way the Athenian navy was proportionally increased, while the allies themselves were always untrained and unprepared for war when they revolted.

71. The Constitution of Erythræ

(*Inscr. Græc.* I. 9; Hicks and Hill, no. 32; Ditt. 8; trans. by C. J. O.)

The independence of a Greek city consisted essentially of two rights: (1) to enter freely into relations of war, peace, and alliance with other states, (2) to have whatever form of government it pleased. Gradually Athens deprived her allies of these rights, and imposed on them democratic constitutions. Under the new arrangements they varied greatly in the degree of their subjection to Athens; particularly these constitutions, or charters, limited the judicial power of the respective states and prescribed what cases were to be sent to Athens for trial. The constitution of Erythræ, issued about 450, was found on a large block of marble near the Erechtheum, on the Acropolis. Unfortunately the marble has been lost, but a somewhat mutilated copy of the inscription is extant. Busolt, *Griech. Gesch.* III. 235 *sqq.*; other references, Hicks and Hill, p. 46.

1. (*A few letters only are left of the prescript.*) [1]

2. The Erythræans [2] shall bring to the Greater Panathenæa [3] offerings worth not less than three minas. The ten Commissioners of the Sacrifices shall distribute the meat among those of the Erythræans who are present, a drachma's worth to each. If the sacrificial animals are acceptable, but are not worth three minas as above stated, the Cattle-Buyers shall purchase oxen for sacrifice and the account shall be charged to the demus of the Erythræans; and anyone so desiring may feast upon the meat.

3. There shall be a council of the Erythræans, filled by lot, and

[1] For examples of the opening formula (prescript), see nos. 69, 72.

[2] Erythræ, an Ionian city on the Asiatic coast opposite Chios, was one of the original members of the Confederacy. In general on this city, see Pauly-Wissowa, *Real-Encycl.* VI. 575 *sqq.*

[3] The Panathenæa, a festival of all the Athenians in honor of their guardian goddess, was held annually in July. From the time of Peisistratus every fourth-year festival of this name was celebrated with especial splendor, and was known accordingly as the Greater Panathenæa. It is significant that the members of the empire were sharers in the same worship, and further that Athenian imperialism tended to substitute Athena for Apollo as the protecting deity of the empire.

consisting of one hundred and twenty men. A man so appointed shall undergo scrutiny [1] before the council, and it shall not be lawful for anyone under thirty years of age to be a councillor. Those who are disqualified shall be liable to prosecution and shall not be councillors within four years. The council shall be drawn by lot and established at present by the overseers [2] and the commandant of the garrison,[3] in future by the council (in office) and the commandant.

4. Each of those who are to be councillors at Erythræ shall, before entering office, swear by Zeus and Apollo and Demeter, imprecating destruction upon himself and upon his children if he commits perjury; and he shall swear the oath upon the burning sacrifices. The councillors in office shall compel the performance of these things; and if they fail to do so, they may be fined 1000 drachmæ or whatever sum the Erythræan people may decree for them to pay. The councillors shall swear in the following terms:

5. I will be councillor as well and truly as I am able for the people of the Erythræans and of the Athenians and of the Allies. And I will not revolt against the commonwealth of the Athenians, or against the Allies of the Athenians, either of my own accord or at the will of another. Neither will I desert them, either of my own accord or at the will of another. Neither will I receive back, either of my own accord or at the will of another, any one of those who fled to the Medes, except with the sanction of the Athenians and of the (Erythræan) people. Neither will I drive away any who are remaining, except with the sanction of the Athenians and of the people.

6. If any Erythræan shall kill another Erythræan, let him be put to death. If anyone shall be condemned to perpetual banishment, let him be banished [at the same time?] from the (territory

[1] Scrutiny (δοκιμασία), an examination into the character and qualification of officials, at Athens and elsewhere in Hellas, before entering upon their public duties.

[2] Overseers (ἐπίσκοποι) were a board of civil officials sent by Athens to various dependent states. Along with the commandant of the garrison they took care that the state pursued a policy of loyalty toward Athens. On this magistracy, see Pauly-Wissowa, *Real-Encycl.* VI. 199.

[3] In some states, as at Erythræ, permanent garrisons were established (*cf.* Isoc. *Areop.* 64), and in such a case the commandant exercised civil as well as military functions; *cf.* Busolt, *Griech. Gesch.* III. 226 and notes.

of the) Athenian alliance, and let his property be confiscated by the Erythræans. If anyone is convicted of attempting to betray the city of the Erythræans to the tyrants,[1] let him be put to death [with impunity], both himself(?) and his children, unless his children are shown to be [favorably] disposed towards the Erythræan people and that of the Athenians. The children, after surrendering the property of one convicted, shall receive one half of it back, and the other half shall be confiscated. The same shall be the case if anyone is convicted of attempting to betray the Athenian people or the garrison at Erythræ.[2] (*The rest of the inscription is fragmentary.*)

72. The Constitution of Chalcis

(*Inscr. græc.* I. Supplem. 1. no. 27 a; Hicks and Hill, no. 40; Ditt. no. 17 and Add. vol. ii. p. 807; for other references, see Hicks and Hill, p. 63; trans. by C. J. O.)

In 446 Eubœa revolted against Athens but was subdued in the autumn of the same year. In punishment for the massacre of Athenian prisoners the people of Histiæa were expelled and their territory was occupied by colonists from Athens. The rest of the island submitted under an agreement (Thuc. i. 114) which fixed the general status of the cities. This convention was supplemented by decrees which in greater detail regulated the constitutions of the several states and their relations with Athens. The document given below is a decree of the kind for settling the affairs of Chalcis. On this city in general, see Pauly-Wissowa, *Real-Encycl.* III. 2078 *sqq.*

1. Be it resolved by the Boulê and the Demus.[3] Antiochis was the prytanizing tribe. Dracontides was chairman. Diognetus moved the resolution: —

That the council and the jurors[4] of the Athenians shall swear the oath in the following terms: "I will not expel the Chalcidians

[1] This reference to the tyrants is obscure. The oligarchy of the Basilidæ had given way to democracy in far earlier time (Arist. *Polit.* viii. 5. 4, 1305 b. 18), which, so far as we know, was not overthrown by a tyrant.

[2] The restoration of the last clause, by Dittenberger, is uncertain.

[3] *Cf.* no. 69; literally, "It seemed good to the Boulê and the Demus."

[4] The council here meant is the Council of Five Hundred, as in the decree concerning the Erythræans; no. 71. There were in Athens 6000 jurors drawn by lot from the citizens above thirty years of age, and serving for the year; Arist. *Const. Ath.* 24, 63; Gilbert, *Const. Antiq.* 391 *sqq.* Interesting is their participation, as here, in interstate affairs.

from Chalcis or destroy their city;[1] and I will not punish any private citizen with loss of civil rights or with exile or give judgment of arrest or of death or of confiscation of goods against him without a trial, except by (authority of) the Athenian people;[2] and I will not put to vote[3] (a motion) against either the community or any private citizen (of Chalcis), when a summons has not been issued against them; and if an embassy comes, I will introduce it to the council and the people within ten days, when I am prytanis, to the best of my ability; and I will maintain these things for the Chalcidians, if they are obedient to the Athenian people."

An embassy from Chalcis shall administer the oath to the Athenians with the help of the Commissioners of Oaths, and shall register (the names of) those who swear it. Let the Generals see to it that all swear.

2. The Chalcidians shall swear in the following terms:[4] "I will not revolt against the Athenian people by any art or device, either in word or in deed, and I will not follow one who undertakes to revolt; and if anyone incites to revolt, I will denounce him to the Athenians. And I will pay the tribute to the Athenians, as I may induce them (to assess it).[5] And I will be to them as good and true an ally as I can; and I will aid and succor the Athenian people, if anyone wrongs the Athenian people; and I will be obedient to the Athenian people."

3. All the men of Chalcis who are of age shall swear; and if anyone shall not swear, he shall lose his civil rights; his property shall be confiscated, and a tenth of it shall be consecrated to Olympian Zeus.[6] An Athenian embassy shall go to Chalcis and administer the oath with the help of the Commissioners of Oaths in Chalcis, and shall register (the names of) the Chalcidians who swear.

4. Anticles moved (the further resolution): —

With good fortune to the Athenians, — the Athenians and the

[1] After the expulsion of the Histiæans the remaining inhabitants of Eubœa must have appreciated this guarantee.

[2] Demus of the Athenians, — the people in assembly.

[3] This reference is to the prytaneis and their president; no. 69, n. 1.

[4] *Cf.* the oath of the Erythræan councillors in the decree above given; no. 69.

[5] In relation to the assessment of the tribute the allies had merely the right of petition, as here indicated.

[6] Worshiped at Chalcis; see *infra*.

Chalcidians shall take the oath on the same terms as the Athenian people decreed for the Eretrians.[1] Let the Generals see to it that this be done as soon as possible. The people shall choose immediately five men to go to Chalcis and administer the oath. Concerning the hostages the reply shall be made to the Chalcidians that for the present the Athenians are pleased to abide by what they have decreed, but when it shall please them, they will take counsel and will make an arrangement as may seem proper for the Athenians and the Chalcidians. The aliens resident in Chalcis, except those who are taxed in Athens and any to whom exemption has been granted by the Athenian people, shall be taxed in Chalcis like the Chalcidians themselves.

5. The Secretary of the council shall record this decree and the oath on a stone stele and shall place them on the Acropolis at Athens,[2] at the expense of the Chalcidians; and the council of the Chalcidians shall record and place them in the temple of Olympian Zeus at Chalcis. — Such shall be the decree regarding the Chalcidians; but furthermore three men, whom the council shall choose from its members, shall, in company with Hierocles,[3] offer as soon as possible the sacrifices (demanded) by the oracles concerning Eubœa. Let the Generals assist in seeing that the sacrifices are offered as soon as possible, and let them furnish the money therefor.

6. Archestratus moved as an amendment to (the motion of) Anticles: —

The Chalcidians may inflict punishments upon their own citizens at Chalcis just as the Athenians (do on theirs) at Athens, excepting exile, death, or loss of civil rights, concerning which there shall be an appeal to Athens to the court of the Thesmothetæ[4] ac-

[1] Neighbors of the Chalcidians in Eubœa. The decree containing this oath is not extant.

[2] Reference is necessarily to the inscription here translated. It was found on the Acropolis in 1876.

[3] Hierocles was evidently the seer who accompanied the Athenian army to Eubœa, according to Hellenic custom. He was afterward ridiculed by Aristophanes, *Peace*, 1046 *sq*.

[4] Thesmothetæ, the six so-called junior archons. They had the public documents in their keeping, and in their judicial capacity they enjoyed especially cognizance of cases affecting the integrity of the laws and of agreements with other states; Arist. *Const. Ath.* 3, 48, 59. Busolt, *Griech. Gesch.* III. 230 and n. 1, interprets this passage to signify, not an appeal to the court of the Thesmothetæ, but a reference of the case to it in the first instance.

cording to the decree of the people. Concerning the guarding of Eubœa the Generals shall see to the best of their ability that it be for the greatest advantage of the Athenians.

73. Athenian Decree for the Colonization of Brea, in Thrace

(*Inscr. græc.* I. no. 31; Hicks and Hill, no. 41; Ditt. no. 19; trans. by C. J. O.)

Pericles followed systematically the policy of founding colonies of Athenians chiefly within the empire. "He sent out 1000 settlers to the Chersonese, 500 to Naxos, half as many to Andros, 1000 to dwell among the Thracian tribe of the Bisaltæ, and others to the new colony in Italy . . . named Thurii. By these means he relieved the state of numerous idle agitators, assisted the needy, and overawed the allies of Athens by placing his colonies near them to watch their behavior"; Plut. *Per.* 11. His objects are well stated by Plutarch. This passage may contain a reference to Brea, founded by Pericles in Thrace. The date of the decree of founding must be 446 or not materially later; Busolt *Griech. Gesch.* III. 417. This inscription is valuable as the only one extant which treats of the founding of a Greek colony.

A. (*The beginning is lost.*)

7. . . . If he does import,[1] the person who has brought the information or the indictment shall take [the goods(?)] in pledge. The [leaders of the colonists] shall provide [flocks of goats], as many as they shall deem sufficient, for the offering of auspicious sacrifices on behalf of the colony. [Ten men] shall be chosen as surveyors, one from each tribe, and these shall assign [the land]. Democlides shall have full power to establish the colony according to the best of his ability.

2. The sacred demesnes that have been set apart[2] shall be left as they are, and no others shall be consecrated. (The colonists) shall contribute an ox[3] and [a suit of armor] for the Greater Panathenæa and a phallus for the Dionysia.[4] If anyone shall attack the land of the colonists, the cities[5] shall render aid as [vigorously] as

[1] Evidently a prohibition of smuggling has preceded.

[2] The sanctuaries of the former Thracian inhabitants are meant.

[3] This contribution to the great quadrennial festival was obligatory upon all the Athenian colonies, *cf.* the scholiast on Aristophanes, *Clouds*, 386.

[4] The Greater, or City, Dionysia, held every year in March.

[5] *I.e.*, the Athenian confederacy.

possible, according to the statute that was passed in the secretaryship of . . . regarding the [cities] of Thrace.

3. These provisions shall be inscribed upon a stele and placed on the Acropolis, and the colonists shall [furnish] the stele at their own [expense]. If anyone shall put to vote a motion contrary to (the provisions of) the stele, or shall speak (against them) as a public orator, or shall [attempt] to incite (others) to rescind or annul any portion of the decree, he shall [lose his civil rights] both he himself and his children, and his property shall be confiscated, one tenth of it to the Goddess (Athena); except that the colonists themselves may make [requests in their own behalf].

4. Those of the soldiers [1] who shall enroll themselves [as prospective colonists], shall be at Brea [as colonists] within thirty days after they have reached [Athens]. The colony shall be led forth within thirty days. Æschines shall follow and pay over the money.[2]

B. Phantocles moved as an amendment to the motion of Democlides regarding the colony to Brea: —

5. The prytaneis of (the tribe) Erechtheïs [3] shall introduce Phantocles to the council at the first session. The colonists to go to Brea shall be from the thetes [4] and the zeugitæ.

[1] Perhaps those who were campaigning in Eubœa in 446 B.C.

[2] For the expenses of the journey.

[3] Evidently the tribe that was to hold the following prytany.

[4] The thetes were the lowest of the four classes into which the Athenians were divided according to the amount of their property. The zeugitæ, who were the class next to the lowest, comprised those who were liable to service in the heavy infantry. Originally the estimate was made on the basis of produce from rural estates free from encumbrance (Arist. *Const. Ath.* 7), but before the age of Pericles an assessment in money had been substituted.

74. Two Tribute Lists

(The extant tribute lists will be found in *Inscr. græc.* I. nos. 226–72. *Cf.* also Supplem. 1; as far as 432 B.C., in Hill, *Sources for Greek History* (Oxford, 1897), ch. ii. (A) is from *Inscr. græc.* I. no. 244; Hill, *op. cit.* ch. ii. no. 19; Hicks and Hill, *Greek Hist. Inscr.* no. 48. It is taken from the list for 436–5 B.C. (B) is from the list of the year 425, "put together out of thirty fragments found at various times on the Acropolis." It is given also by Hill, *op. cit.* p. 14, no. 72; Hicks and Hill, *op. cit.* no. 64. In this inscription the island list alone is sufficiently complete to warrant reproduction. Translated by C. J. O.)

The sum total of the contributions — generally termed tributes — to be paid by the members of the Delian Confederacy was originally fixed, 478 B.C., by Aristeides at 460 talents (Thuc. i. 96; Arist. *Const. Ath.* 23. 5; Plut. *Arist.* 24). The cities were re-assessed every four years; but for a long time little variation was made from this norm, even after the Confederacy had been enlarged by the addition of many new members. Probably in 454–3, certainly not later than that date, the treasury was transferred from Delos to Athens. This event marks, better than any other, the completion of the gradual process of transforming the Confederacy into an Athenian empire. From this date begins a series of quota lists, imperfectly preserved in inscriptions, detailing, not as a rule the actual contributions paid by the several allies, but the offerings to Athena made from these respective sums. As the goddess received a sixtieth part of the tribute, a mina from every talent, it is a simple matter to compute from these lists the contributions of the individual states. In the following extracts from these inscriptions (A) is an example of such a list of offerings, the amounts of tribute, given in the third column, being calculated by multiplying the numbers in the second column by sixty. The extract designated as (B) is from the only extant inscription which gives directly the amount of assessment.

In 447–6 began an effort to arrange the states in local groups, and four years afterward the empire was definitely organized in the following tribute districts, Ionian, Hellespontine, Thracian, Carian, and Island. After 439 B.C. the Ionian and Carian tributes were combined under one heading, and the number of districts was thus reduced to four. Before the Peloponnesian war the Island district, to which alone the following extracts have reference, comprised the Cyclades, Eubœa, Lemnos, Imbros, and Ægina, the number of tribute-paying states being twenty-three or twenty-four. In the assessment of 425–4 the names of the Lemnian cities and of Imbros must have stood in the portion of the inscription now lost; and Ægina, which was occupied by Athenian colonists in 431 (Thuc. ii. 27), is omitted. The islands of Melos and Thera, on the other hand, are added; and a number of small towns, which had previously been taxed with their larger neighbors, were made distinct tributaries. It will be seen, too, from a comparison of the figures in (A) and (B), that on the average the several assessments were more than doubled. This increase is generally credited by scholars to the ambitious war policy of Cleon. While granting this interpretation in part, we must bear in mind that the wealth of the states had vastly increased since the assessment of Aristeides (*cf.* Isoc. *Paneg.* 103; Plut. *Cim.* 11), that money was now far more plentiful, and that its purchasing power had correspondingly declined. It was just, therefore, that the contributions should be increased, though perhaps not doubled. The author of the decree — *ψήφισμα* — which brought about this change was Cleonymus. On the increase, see Busolt, *Griech. Gesch.* III. 1117 *sqq.*; *Philologus*, XLI (1882). 688–92.

THE LISTS

(A) From the quota list of 436–5 B.C.

In the term of the nineteenth board,[1] of which Philetærus, son of Theodectus, . . . was secretary, Dionysius being (chief) Hellenotamias. . . .

(*Here follows the quota of the Ionian tribute.*)

Island Tribute

The People Of	*Quota Paid to Athena*[3]	*Calculated Amount of Tribute*
Seriphos		
Chalcis [2]	[3]00 drachmæ	(3 talents)
Ceos	400 drachmæ	(4 talents)
Tenos	300 drachmæ	(3 talents)
Naxos	666⅔ drachmæ	(6⅔ talents)
Myconos		
Andros	600 drachmæ	(6 talents)
Siphnos	300 drachmæ	(3 talents)
Syros	25 drachmæ	(¼ talent)
Styra [2]		
Eretria [2]	[3]00 drachmæ	(3 talents)
Grynchæ [2]	(1000 drachmæ)	10 talents
Rhenæa	(300 drachmæ)	3 talents
Athenæ [2]	(2000 drachmæ)	20 talents
Dium of Cenæum [2]	(2000 drachmæ)	20 talents
Ios	(3000 drachmæ)	(30) talents
Ægina	[more than] 300 talents	(more than 3 talents)

[1] The board of Hellenic treasurers is probably here meant, not that of the auditors, who reckoned the offering of the sixtieth part.

[2] Concerning the places in Eubœa mentioned in these lists see Geyer, *Topographie und Geschichte der Insel Euboia*, Part I (Berlin, 1903), *passim.*

[3] These figures are restored from a fragment of another tribute list, probably for the year 439–438, published by Köhler in *Hermes*, XXXI (1896), 142 *sq.*

(*Ten lines are wanting. Then follow the quotas of the Hellespontine and of the Thracian tribute, then a heading* "Self-assessing cities,"[1] *with eleven quotas, then another heading,* "Cities which were enrolled to pay tribute on the motion of private citizens,"[2] *with six quotas among which is that of the* Diacrians of Chalcis, 13⅓ drachmæ (800 dr.).)

(B) From the assessment of tribute in 425–4 B.C.

The tribute was assessed as follows upon the cities by the council of which Pleistias was the first secretary, [and by the court (?)] in the archonship of Stratocles[3] and in the term of the introducers[4] whose [secretary was . . .]

Island Tribute

The People Of	*Assessment*
Paros	30 talents
Naxos	15 talents
Andros	15 talents
Melos[5]	15 talents
Siphnos	9 talents
Eretria[6]	15 talents
Thera[7]	5 talents
Ceos	10 talents
Carystus[6]	5 talents
Chalcis[6]	10 talents
Cythnos	6 talents
Tenos	10 talents
Styra[6]	2 talents
Myconos	
Seriphos	
Ios	
Dium[6]	
Athenæ[6]	1 talent
Syros	1 talent
Grynchæ[6]	2000 drachmæ
Rhenæa	1000 drachmæ
Diacrians of Chalcis[6]	2000 drachmæ

[1] *Cf.* Busolt, *Griech. Gesch.* III. 207, n. 4.

[2] *Cf. Ibid.*, 210, n. 1.

[3] In 425–424 B.C.

[4] Officials who presided at the trial of cases that had to be decided within a month.

[5] Though the Melians were assessed as tributaries, they never acknowledged the supremacy of Athens until they were overcome and destroyed in 416–415; *cf.* Thucydides, iii. 91; v. 84, 116.

[6] Concerning the places in Eubœa mentioned in these lists see Geyer, *Topographie und Geschichte der Insel Euboia*, Part I (Berlin, 1903). *passim.*

[7] Thera was not subject to Athens at the beginning of the Peloponnesian war; *cf.* Thuc. ii. 2.

The People Of	*Assessment*
Anaphe	1000 drachmæ
Ceria, 10½ dr.[1]	
Pholegandros	2000 drachmæ
Belbina [2]	300 drachmæ
Cimolos	1000 drachmæ
Sicinos	1000 drachmæ
Posideum	100 drachmæ
Diacrians in Eubœa [3]	1⅓ talents
[Hephæstia (?)] in Eubœa [3]	4 talents

(*The remainder of the assessment of the Island tribute is lost in* (B). *Then follow fragments of the assessments of the Ionian, the Hellespontine, and the Thracian tribute respectively. At the bottom of the inscription is the line "Sum total,* [500 +] 460 + . . . *Talents.*" [4])

75. Athenian Decrees in Honor of the Democrats of Samos

(Hicks and Hill, no. 81; Ditt. nos. 56, 57; Michel, *Recueil*, no. 80; Szanto, *Griech. Bürgerrecht*, 95 *sq*. Translated by C. J. O.)

The Athenians rarely granted citizenship to aliens. In 427, however, after the destruction of Platæa they conferred the citizenship on all the survivors who could prove that they were Platæans and friendly to the Athenian state (Busolt, *Griech. Gesch*. III. 1038). This was thus far the most striking example of their liberality. After the Sicilian disaster there was talk of admitting to the state all loyal metics and all the allies of Ionian speech (Aristoph. *Lysist.* 571 *sqq.*) but such discussion bore no fruit, and in fact it was then too late to save the empire by concessions of that nature (*cf.* Thuc. viii. 48. 5). When the allies heard of the Athenian defeat at Ægospotami (405), all revolted excepting the Samians, who remained loyal chiefly through fear of the oligarchs whom they had banished. Putting to death, therefore, a number of oligarchs who still remained in the island, the Samians sent two embassies to Athens to report what they had done and to assure her of their continued loyalty (Xen. *Hell*. ii. 2. 6). Thereupon the Athenians passed the first of the following decrees.

[1] Possibly the small island now called Karos near Naxos. The peculiar position of the figures may indicate that the town paid merely Athena's sixtieth in lieu of the full assessment.

[2] An islet at the entrance of the Saronic Gulf, now Hagios Georgios.

[3] Concerning the places in Eubœa mentioned in these lists see Geyer, *Topographie und Geschichte der Insel Euboia*, Part I (Berlin, 1903), *passim*.

[4] If this figure is correct, and the tributaries paid in full, the annual revenue under the increased assessment was over $1,000,000.

A. FIRST DECREE

Cephisophon of Pæania was secretary.[1] *For the Samians who sided with the Athenian people.*

1. Be it resolved by the Boulê and the Demus. Cecropis was the prytanizing tribe. Polymnis of Euonymon was secretary. Alexias was archon.[2] Nicophon of Athmonon was chairman. Cleisophus and his fellow-prytaneis moved the resolution:

To commend both the former and the present embassy of the Samians as well as the council, the generals, and the rest of the Samians, inasmuch as they are good and true men and are ready to do whatsoever good they can; furthermore (to approve) their acts,[3] because they seem to have done right by the Athenians and the Samians.

2. Whereas also they have benefited the Athenians and are now making much of them and are proposing good measures, be it resolved by the Boulê and the Demus: —

That the Samians shall be Athenians, using such form of government as they themselves may desire; and according to their own suggestion, a joint consultation concerning the remaining points, with a view to making this arrangement most satisfactory to both parties, shall be held upon the conclusion of peace.[4] They shall use their own laws and be autonomous; and in other respects they shall act according to the oaths and the agreements entered into by the Athenians and the Samians; and with regard to the misunderstandings that may arise between them, both parties shall grant and receive legal recourse according to the existing compacts.[5]

3. If by reason of the war, any pressing question concerning the right of citizenship shall arise sooner, then, according to the suggestion of the embassy, they shall consult and act as may seem to be best in view of the circumstances. If peace is concluded, the pres-

[1] When, as here, decrees passed at different times were engraved together, the name of the latest secretary appears in the title.

[2] 405–404 B.C.

[3] Reference is doubtless to their massacre of oligarchs; see introduction to the decree.

[4] With the Peloponnesians. It was made in 404, but the Samians were not included.

[5] Συμβολάς — treaties, generally regulating commercial and other relations, and providing for the settlement of cases at law arising from such relations.

ent[1] inhabitants of Samos shall share in it upon the same terms as the Athenians; but if it is necessary to carry on the war, they shall make preparations in concert with the generals to the best of their ability. If the Athenians send an embassy to any quarter, those who are present from Samos may join in it by sending someone if they wish, and they may offer whatever good advice they can.

4. The triremes that are at Samos[2] shall be given to the Samians to repair and to use as they please. The names of the captains (trierarchs)[3] to whom these ships belonged shall be reported by the ambassadors to the secretary of the boulê and to the generals; and if the trierarchs are charged in the records of the treasury [with any indebtedness] on account of their receipt of the triremes, the dock wardens shall [cancel it all] wheresoever found, and shall reclaim the tackle for the treasury [as soon as possible and] compel those who have any of it to return [it in full].

5. [Proposal of Cleisophus and his] fellow-prytaneis as an amendment to that of the boulê; — [The grant shall be made to those of the Samians] who have come, as they themselves request, and they shall be assigned [immediately to demes and to] tribes[4] in ten divisions. Passage shall be provided [for the ambassadors by the generals] as soon as possible. Eumachus and [all the other Samians who have come with Eumachus] shall be commended for being [good and true toward the Athenians], and Eumachus shall be invited to dine in the Prytaneum[5] on the morrow. The secretary of the boulê together with the generals shall record the decree upon a stone pillar and shall place it on the Acropolis, and the Hellenic Treasurers[6] shall give the money therefor. It shall be recorded at Samos in the same way at the expense of the Samians.

[1] Provision was hereby made to exclude the oligarchs then in exile.

[2] Twenty Athenian triremes had been left at Samos (Diod. xiii. 104. 2).

[3] The trierarch (captain of a trireme) was responsible to the state for his ship during his year of command, and was obliged to return it, or deliver it to his successor, unimpaired; hence the need of this provision to exonerate the captains when their ships were turned over to the Samians.

[4] Compare the language of the decree admitting the Platæans to citizenship in 427; Pseudo-Demosth. lix. 104: "The Platæans shall be assigned to demes and to tribes."

[5] The City Hall, containing the sacred hearth of the community, and the tables at which certain officials, together with guests honored by the state, dined at public expense.

[6] This board, mentioned here for the last time, was abolished at the close of the war.

Unfortunately the terms of the agreement could not be carried out; for in the spring of 404 Athens was compelled to surrender to the Peloponnesians; and soon afterward Lysander conquered Samos (Xen. *Hell.* ii. 3. 6). Expelled from their homes, the Samian democrats found refuge in the Ionian cities on the coast of Asia Minor. The next year, 403, when on the point of sending a petition to Sparta, these exiles invoked the good offices of the Athenians, who by the terms of a second decree, given below, complied with the request and also confirmed the favors granted in the earlier decree.

B. SECOND DECREE

1. Be it resolved by the boulê and the demus. Pandionis was the prytanizing tribe. Agyrrhius of Collytus was secretary. Eucleides was archon.[1] Callias of Oa was chairman. Cephisophon moved the resolution: —

To commend the Samians inasmuch as they are good and true men toward the Athenians, and to ratify all that the Athenian people have previously decreed for the Samian people.

2. [The Samians may send] to Lacedæmon, as they themselves urge, whomsoever [they wish; and since] they entreat the Athenians to join in the negotiations, there shall be chosen additional [ambassadors, and these shall join] with the Samians in effecting whatever good they can, [and shall consult in common with] them.[2] Furthermore, the Athenians commend the people of Ephesus and Notium[3] [inasmuch as they readily received] the Samians who were in exile. The Samian embassy shall be introduced to (the assembly of) the people to transact business, if they shall have need of anything, and the embassy shall be invited to dine in the Prytaneum on the morrow.

3. Cephisophon moved as an amendment to the proposal of the boulê: — Be it decreed by the Athenian people that the previous decree concerning the Samians be ratified, as the boulê reported to the demus in its proposal, and that the Samian embassy be invited to dine in the Prytaneum on the morrow.

BIBLIOGRAPHY

This subject is included in all histories of Greece (*cf.* p. 61 *supra*) and in all works on the constitutional history and the public antiquities of the Greeks.

[1] 403–402 B.C.

[2] The restoration of this passage by Hicks is conjectural but gives the general sense.

[3] A town on the coast a few miles north of Ephesus.

See also Herzog, E., *Zur Verwaltungsgeschichte des attischen Staats* (Tübingen, 1897). On the tribute, see Bannier, W., "Die Tributeinnahmeordnung des attischen Staates," in *Rhein. Mus.* LIV (1899). 544–54; Pedroli, "I tributi degli alleati d'Atene," in Beloch, *Studi di Storia antica*, I (1891). 101–207; Busolt, G., *Griech. Gesch.* III. 192–222. On the coinage, Gardner, P., "Coinage of the Athenian Empire," in *Journ. Hell. St.* XXXIII (1913). 147–88. On jurisdiction, see Goodwin, W. W., Δίκαι ἀπὸ συμβόλων καὶ Δίκαι συμβολαῖαι in *Am. Journ. Philol.* I (1880). 4–16; Stahl, *De sociorum atheniensium iudiciis* (Münster, 1881); Morris, C. D., "Jurisdiction of Athenians over their Allies," in *Am. Journ. Philol.* V (1884). 298 *sqq.*; Meyer and Schömann, *Der attische Process* (2d ed., Berlin, 1883–1887), 994–1006; Gilbert, G., *Const. Antiq.* 429–34; Phillipson, C., *International Law and Custom of Ancient Greece and Rome*, I. 198–209; Meyer, E., *Gesch. des Alt.* III. 496–500; Busolt, G., *Griech. Gesch.* III. 230–36; Weber, H., "Attisches Processrecht in den attischen Seebundesstaaten," in *Stud. zur Gesch. und Kultur des Alt.* I. 5 (1908).

CHAPTER VIII

PRIVATE AND CRIMINAL LAW

In the Period 479–404

IN this chapter the private law of the fifth century is represented by the Laws of Gortyn, and criminal law by the Draconian Law concerning Homicide, as republished in 409.

76. THE LAWS OF GORTYN

In Greek tradition Crete was an early home of law. The scanty notices of Cretan law preserved in literature refer mainly to public law; and the discovery in the nineteenth century of a Gortynian code, in the form of a mural inscription, has given us for the first time a clear view of some portions at least of Cretan private law. This code deals fully with family relations and with inheritance; less fully with tools; slightly with property outside of the household relations; slightly, too, with contracts; but it contains no criminal law or criminal procedure. This inscription is the largest document of Greek law in existence. It is to be noted, however, that many fragments of other Gortynian laws have been found, some of which are edited and translated in Kohler und Ziebarth, *Stadtrecht von Gortyn* (Göttingen, 1912), now the best treatment of the subject in general. From these fragments we may justly infer that the inscription now under consideration formed but a small fraction of a great Gortynian code.

This document itself recognizes the existence of earlier law, not repeated but still in force, — particularly in the phrase, "as has been written," or "as is the established statute." In the opinion of Bürchner, Pauly-Wissowa, *Real-Encycl.* VII (1912). 1669, the oldest extant legislation of Gortyn belongs to the sixth century, followed by a period of revision or reformation in the fifth century, to which the present document belongs. References to "kettles" and "tripods" as standards of value led the earlier commentators to the conclusion that these laws preceded the period of coinage. More recently Svoronos, *Journal internat. d'archéol. numismat.* IX (1906). 217 *sq.*, has made it clear that the figures of these articles were stamped upon silver coins of Gortyn and other Cretan cities, and that accordingly without doubt the laws refer to the coins rather than to the articles. See also De Sanctis, *Monumenti Antichi*, XVIII. 303 *sq.* From various considerations it appears highly probably that these laws were enacted about the middle of the fifth century; *cf.* Kohler and Ziebarth, *op. cit.* p. vi *sq.*

The most salient tendencies of the reformation represented by the document are the restriction of self-help and the betterment of the legal position of women. "They receive rights of inheritance, which they probably had not before; and because they now have these rights, gifts to them and dowries are limited. The power to dispose of women's property is restricted, in their favor, as against husbands, fathers, sons and uncles; and here for the first time, perhaps, a way is opened to heiresses to escape, by a sacrifice of a part of their property, from the burdensome compulsion to marry near kinsmen." It is a curious fact that at a time when the Athenians were repressing the social freedom of women, the Cretans were giving them larger liberties and rights. Interesting, too, is the admirable status of the class of persons described as "serfs." Various features of the statute make it akin to Indo-European rather than to Oriental usage.

A new importance has been given to Hellenic law by the discovery of papyri which prove its continued existence in parts of the Roman empire. Briefly, Hellenic law is of vast importance to the student, not merely of jurisprudence, but also of ancient culture.

The translation which follows was originally made by Professor Augustus C. Merriam of Columbia University, published in the *American Journal of Archæology*, II. (1886). 24–45 (*cf.* I. 350 *sqq.*). Professor Munroe Smith has compared it with the German versions of Bücheler (Bücheler und Zitelmann, *Das Recht von Gortyn* (1885), and Lewy, H., *Altes Stadtrecht von Gortyn* (1885), and has contributed annotations. Finally the translation has been revised, on the basis of the improved text of Kohler and Ziebarth, *op. cit.*, by E. G. S.

THE GODS ! [1]

I. *Suit for the ownership of a slave or of one so claimed.*[2] — Whoever intends to bring suit in relation to a free man or a slave, shall not take action by seizure before trial;[3] but if he do seize him, let the judge fine him 10 staters for the free man, 5 for the slave, because he seizes him, and let him adjudge that he shall release him within three days. But if he do not release him, let the judge sentence him to a stater for a free man, a drachma[4] for a slave, each

[1] By this formula the gods are invoked to protect and bless the enactment. It is often prefixed to documents.

[2] The divisions and headings here given are the translator's. Of the abbreviations used below, B refers to the edition of Bücheler and Zitelmann; L to that of Lewy; M.S. to Professor Munroe Smith.

[3] "Before judgment" (L).

[4] As the Æginetan standard prevailed (Head, *Historia numorum*, 457) the drachma approximately equaled 25 cents. A stater was two drachmas.

day until he shall have released him; and according to the time (of non-payment)[1] the judge shall decide, confirming it by oath. But if he should deny that he made the seizure, the judge shall render decision with confirmatory oath, unless a witness testify.

But if one party contend that he is a free man, the other that he is a slave, those who testify that he is free shall be preferred. And if they contend about a slave, each declaring that he is his, if a witness testify, the judge shall decide according to the witness; but if they testify either for both parties or for neither of the two, the judge shall render his decision by oath.

If the one who holds (the person in question) lose the suit, he shall set the free man at liberty within 5 days, and the slave he shall deliver in hand; and if he do not set at liberty or deliver in hand, let the judge pronounce that (the successful party) shall have judgment against him in 50 staters for the free man and a stater each day till he sets him free, and for the slave 10 staters and a drachma each day till he delivers him in hand. But if the judge shall have sentenced him to a fine, within a year thrice the amount or less shall be exacted, but not more; and according to the time[2] the judge shall decide, confirming it by oath.

But if the slave on account of whom (the defendant) was defeated take refuge in a temple (the defendant), summoning (the plaintiff) in the presence of two witnesses of age and free, shall point out (the slave) at the temple, wherever he may be a suppliant, either himself or another in his behalf; but if he do not issue the summons or do not point out, he shall pay what is written. And if he do not return him, even within the year, he shall pay in addition the sums one-fold. But if he die while the suit is progressing, he shall pay his value one-fold.

And if one, while cosmos,[3] (so) seize a man, or another for him while he is cosmos, when he has retired from office the case shall be tried, and if (the delinquent) be convicted he shall pay what is written from the day he made the seizure.

[1] "And as regards the time," *i.e.*, the period of disobedience (B).

[2] "As regards the time" (see note above).

[3] The chief magistrates were ten cosmi, "Keepers of Order," who commanded in war, exercised judicial and general administrative functions, and enforced discipline among the citizens; Botsford, *Hellenic History*, ch. vi. § 1.

For one seizing the person in the possession of the defeated party, and the (slave) that has been mortgaged, there shall be no penalty.

II. *Rape and assault.* — If one commit rape on a free man or woman, he shall pay 100 staters, and if on (the son or daughter) of an *apetairos*[1] 10, and if a slave on a free man or woman he shall pay double, and if a free man on a male or female serf[2] 5 drachmas, and if a serf on a male or female serf, 5 staters. If one debauch a female house-slave by force he shall pay 2 staters, but if one already debauched, in the daytime an obol, but if at night 2 obols; and the slave shall have preference in taking the oath.

If one tries to seduce a free woman, under the tutelage of her relative, he shall pay 10 staters, if a witness testify.

III. *Adultery.* — If one be taken in adultery with a free woman in her father's, or in her brother's, or in her husband's house, he shall pay 100 staters, but if in another's house, 50; and with the wife of an apetairos, 10; but if a slave with a free woman, he shall pay double, but if a slave with a slave's wife, 5.

And let (the captor) give notice in the presence of three witnesses to the relatives of the man taken, that they shall ransom him within 5 days, and to the master of the slave in the presence of two witnesses. But if one do not ransom him, it shall be in the power of the captors to do with him as they will. But if he assert that the other has enslaved him, in the case of 50 staters or more, the captor himself with four others shall swear, each calling down curses on himself, and in the case of the apetairos, (the captor) himself with two others, and in case of the domestic, the master himself and another, that he took him in adultery, and did not enslave him.

IV. *Divorce.* — If a husband and wife be divorced, she shall have her own property that she came with to her husband, and the half of the income if it be from her own property, and whatever she has woven, the half, whatever it may be, and 5 staters, if her hus-

[1] Apetairos, one who did not belong to a hetæria, or association of fully privileged citizens. The apetairos seems to have been personally free but politically dependent, somewhat like the Lacedæmonian periœcus.

[2] The serf (*οἰκεύς*, German *Häusler*) was somewhat like the Laconian helot, but enjoyed a far better legal position. With his family he tilled a piece of ground belonging to his lord, occupying a farm house, whence the name of the class. The serf is often contrasted with the slave, who lived in the house of the lord in the city, and performed domestic service.

band be the cause of her dismissal; but if the husband deny that he was the cause, the judge shall decide, confirming his decision by oath. But if she carry away anything else belonging to her husband, she shall pay 5 staters and the thing itself, whatever she carries, and whatever she has purloined she shall return the thing itself; but of whatsoever she makes denial the judge shall decide: the woman shall take her oath of denial by Artemis, who stands next to the Amyclæan (Apollo),[1] the archer-goddess. And whatever anyone may take away from her after she has made her oath of denial, he shall pay 5 staters and the thing itself. If an unrelated person assist in removing (the effects) he shall pay 10 staters and the amount two fold of whatever the judge swears that he assisted in removing.

V. *Rights of the widow.*—If a man die, leaving children, if his wife wish she may marry, taking her own property and further whatever her husband may have given her, according to what is written, in the presence of 3 witnesses of age and free. But if she carry away anything belonging to her children she shall be answerable. And if he leave her childless, she shall have her own property and whatever she has woven, the half, and of the produce on hand in possession of the heirs, a portion, and whatever her husband has given her as is written. But if she should carry away anything else she shall be answerable.

If a wife should die childless, (the husband) shall return to her heirs her property, and whatever she has woven within, the half, and of the produce, if it be from her own property, the half.

If a husband or wife wish to give *komistra*,[2] (it shall be) either clothing or 12 staters, or something worth 12 staters, but not more.

If a female serf be separated from a male serf while alive or in case of his death, she shall have her own property, but if she carry away anything else she shall be answerable.

VI. *Children born after divorce.*—If a woman bear a child while living apart from her husband (after divorce), she shall have it conveyed to the husband at his house, in the presence of 3 witnesses; and if he do not receive the child, it shall be in the power of the mother either to bring up or expose,[3] and the relatives and the

[1] The reading is that of B.

[2] *Komistra*, gifts (of regard or affection).

[3] Ἀποθέμεν.

witnesses shall have preference in taking the oath as to whether they carried it. And if a female serf bear a child while living apart, she shall carry it to the master of the man who married her, in the presence of 2 witnesses. And if he do not receive it, the child shall be in the power of the master of the female serf. But if she should marry the same man again before the end of the year, the child shall be in the power of the master of the male serf and the one who carried it and the witnesses shall have preference in taking the oath. If a woman living apart should cast away her child before she has presented it as written, she shall pay, for a free child, 50 staters, for a slave, 25, if she be convicted. But if the man have no house to which she may carry it, or she do not see him, if she expose her child, there shall be no penalty. If a female serf should conceive and bear without being married, the child shall be in the power of the master of the father; but if the father be not living, it shall be in the power of the masters of the brothers.

VII. *Division of property among children.* — The father shall have power over his children and the division of the property, and the mother over her property. As long as they live, it shall not be necessary to make a division. But if any one (of the children) should be condemned to pay a fine, his portion may be divided off to him who has been condemned to pay a fine, as is written. But if a (father) die, the houses in the city and whatever there is in the houses in which a serf residing in the country does not live, and the sheep and larger animals which do not belong to the serf, shall belong to the sons; but all the rest of the property shall be divided fairly, and the sons, how many soever there be, shall receive two parts each, and the daughters, how many soever there be, one part each. The mother's property also shall be divided, in case she dies, as is written for the father's. And if there should be no property but a house, the daughters shall receive their share as is written. And if a father while living may wish to give to his married daughter, let him give according to what is written, but not more. But to which daughter he gave before or promised, she shall have this, but shall not receive anything further in the distribution. If a woman have no property, either by gift from father or brother, or by promise, or received by inheritance as (was written) when the

Æthalean *startos*[1] — Cyllus and his colleagues — ruled as cosmi, such shall receive their portion; but, against those (who received) before, there shall not be ground for action.

VIII. *Heirs at law.* — If a man or woman die, if there be children, or grandchildren or great-grandchildren, they shall have the property; but if there be none of these and there be brothers of the deceased and children or grandchildren from the brothers, they shall have the property; but if there be none of these, but sisters of the deceased, and children from these, or children from the children, they shall have the property; but if there be none of these, to whomsover it belongs where there may be property, these shall receive it. But if there should be no relations of the *klaros*,[2] whoever be the body designated by lot, these shall have the property.

IX. *Partition of property.* — And if (of) the relatives some may wish to divide the property and others not, the judge shall decide; and all the property shall be in the power of those who wish to divide, until they make the division. And if after the judge has rendered his decision, anyone enter by force, or drive or carry off anything, he shall pay 10 staters and double the thing in question. And of perishable objects and crops and clothing and ornaments and furniture, if the sons do not wish to make a division, the judge under oath shall decide with a view to matters in litigation. If further when dividing the property, they cannot agree about the division, they shall offer the property for sale, and having sold it to him who offers most, let them share each his just due of the values received. And while they are dividing the property witnesses shall be present, of age and freemen, three or more. If a father give to a daughter, (let the procedure be) the same.

X. *Property rights of the family.* — As long as a father lives, no one shall purchase any of his property from a son, or take it on

[1] The startos is one of the puzzles of Cretan public life. Evidence is furnished by Kohler and Ziebarth, *op. cit.* 47 *sq.*, that it was closely related to the hetæria, that it had a military character, and was perhaps a military company drawn from the hetæria. Its relation with the cosmi is not clear. The text here seems to indicate that the cosmi were drawn from the starti in rotation.

[2] Klaros is evidently a group of kinsmen wider than the family and the near kin above enumerated; it is substantially the genos, gens, whose members have a right to inherit in failure of the near kin.

mortgage; but whatever the son himself may have acquired or obtained by inheritance, he may sell if he will; nor shall the father sell or promise the property of his children, whatever they have themselves acquired or succeeded to,[1] nor the husband that of his wife, nor the son that of the mother. And if any one should purchase, or take on mortgage, or accept a promise, otherwise than as written in these writings, the property shall still belong to the mother and the wife, and the one who sold or mortgaged or promised shall pay to the one who bought, or accepted the mortgage or promise, two-fold, and if he shall have caused any other loss, he shall pay one-fold in addition; but as regards transactions under earlier laws, there shall be no ground for action. If however the defendant shall contend in court, in relation to the matter about which they are disputing, that it does not belong to the mother or the wife, the case shall be adjudicated as is proper before the judge, as each thing is written.

If a mother die leaving children, the father shall be trustee of the mother's property,[2] but he shall not sell or mortgage unless the children assent, being of age; and if any one should otherwise purchase or take on mortgage, the property shall (still) belong to the children; and to the purchaser or mortgagee the seller or mortgagor shall pay two-fold the value, and if he shall have caused any other loss, one-fold. But if he wed another wife, the children shall have control of the mother's property.

XI. *Ransomed prisoners.* — If any one be brought out of misfortune from sojourn abroad (where he has been) held by force,[3] and one have released him at his desire, he shall be in the power of the one who released him until he pay what is proper; but if they do not agree upon the amount, or he did not himself request (the other) to release him, the judge shall decide with a view to the matters in controversy.

XII. *Miscegenation.* — [If a slave (?)] going to a free woman shall wed her, the children shall be free; but if the free woman to a slave, the children shall be slaves; and if from the same mother

[1] The Cretan father accordingly had less right to the *peculium* of children than had the Roman father.

[2] "The father shall have control of the mother's property" (B and L).

[3] "If anyone has been brought out of duress abroad by reason of alienage" (B).

free and slave children be born, if the mother die and there be property, the free children shall have it; but if free children should not be born of her, her relatives shall succeed to the property.

XIII. *Responsibility for the acts of a slave.* — If a person should purchase a slave from the market-place, and should not complete the transaction within 60 days, in case he shall have done any wrong before (the 60 days have expired) or after, there shall be ground for action against the one who has acquired him.

XIV. *Rights and obligations of heiresses.* — The heiress shall marry the brother of her father, the eldest of those living; and if there be more heiresses and brothers of the father, they shall marry the eldest in succession.[1] But if there be no brothers of the father, but sons from his brothers, she shall marry the first one from the eldest (brother);[2] and if there be more heiresses and sons from brothers, they shall marry the sons of the eldest in succession. The pertinent relative shall have one heiress, but not more.

As long as the pertinent relative or the heiress is too young to marry, the heiress shall have the house, if there be one, but the pertinent relative shall receive half of the income of all the property. And if the pertinent relative be still under age (under 17) but above puberty, and the heiress also, but he do not wish to marry her, all the property and the income shall belong to the heiress, until he marry her. But if he, being of age (above 17), do not wish to marry the heiress, now of proper age and willing to marry him, the relatives of the heiress shall bring the matter to trial, and the judge shall order him to marry her within two months; and if he do not marry as is written, she with all the property shall wed the next in succession, if there be another: but if there be none, she may marry any one of the tribe whom she wishes, who may demand her hand.

And if she, being of age to marry, do not wish to marry the pertinent relative, or the pertinent relative be too young and the heiress do not wish to wait, the heiress shall have the house, if there be one in the city, and whatever there is in the house, but sharing half of the remaining property, she may marry another,

[1] That is, each heiress in succession shall marry the next eldest uncle (M.S.).

[2] She is to marry the eldest son of the eldest brother of her father.

whomsoever she wish of her tribe demanding her hand; and they shall portion off (the half) of the property to the first one.

If the heiress should have no kinsmen within the limits prescribed, holding all the property she may marry any one of the tribe she wishes. But if no one of the tribe desire to marry her, the relatives of the heiress shall proclaim throughout the tribe, "Does no one wish to marry her?" and if any one will marry her, (it shall be) within the 30 days, as they shall have declared; and if not, she shall wed another, whomsoever she may be able to.

If she become an heiress after her father or brother shall have given her in marriage, in case she do not wish to marry the one to whom they gave her, though he be willing, if she have borne children, partitioning (with him) the property as is written, she shall wed another of the tribe; but if she have no children, with all the property she shall marry the pertinent relative if there be one, but if not, as is written.

In case a husband should die leaving children to an heiress, if she wish, let her wed any one of the tribe she may be able to, but it is not compulsory. If the deceased should leave no children, she shall marry the pertinent relative as is written. If the one to whom it falls to marry the heiress should not be in the country, and the heiress be of age to marry, she shall wed the (next) in succession as is written. She shall be an heiress if she have no father, or brother from the same father; and the father's relatives shall have control of the income of the property, and share half the proceeds, as long as she is unmarriageable. In case there be no pertinent relative while she is unmarriageable, the heiress shall have possession of the property and the income, and as long as she is unmarriageable she shall be brought up among her mother's relatives. And if any one should marry an heiress, while it is written otherwise, the pertinent relatives shall institute an investigation before the cosmi.

If any one dying leave an heiress, either she herself or in her behalf the father's or mother's relatives may mortgage or sell some of the estate and the sale and mortgage shall be legal, — but if in another way some one were to purchase the estate or secure a mortgage of the heiress's estate,[1] the property shall (still) belong

[1] This reading is based on the restored text of Kohler and Ziebarth.

to the heiress, and the seller or mortgagor if he be convicted,[1] shall pay double to the buyer or mortgagee; and if there be any further loss, he shall pay an equivalent besides, as these writings are written; but in case of previous[2] transactions, there shall not be ground for action. But, if the defendant should contend, in relation to the thing about which they are disputing, that it does not belong to the heiress, let the judge under oath decide; and if he should gain his case, to the effect that it does not belong to the heiress, suit (for ownership) shall be tried, where it is pertinent, according as each thing is written.

XV. *Actions in special cases.* — If a person should die who has become a surety, or lost a suit, or owes a loan, or has defrauded any one, or has entered into an agreement, or another (hold like relations) toward him, the case shall be reviewed before the close of the year, and the judge shall decide according to the testimony; if indeed the case be renewed in relation to a judgment, the judge and the clerk of the court,[3] if he be alive and a citizen, and the witnesses who are the pertinent ones (shall testify); while in a case of surety, and loans, and fraud, and agreement, the heirs shall testify as witnesses; but if they refuse, let the judge under oath pass upon their case and declare that (their opponents) have judgment against the witnesses in the amount in question. If a son should become surety while his father is living, he shall be held, himself and the property which he owns.

If any one have a dispute about a venture abroad, or do not reimburse one who has contributed to such a venture, should witnesses of age testify, — 3 in a case of 100 staters or more, 2 in a case of less down to 10 staters, 1 for still less, — let the judge decide according to the testimony; but if witnesses do not depose, in case the contracting party comes, whichever of the two courses the complainant may choose, either to make oath of denial, or . . . (*nine lines lacking*).

XVI. *Legality of gifts.* — A son may give to a mother or a

[1] Better "if decision is rendered against him." The buyer or mortgagee has committed no crime; the decision simply takes the property from him, leaving him redress against the seller or mortgagor (M.S.).

[2] That is, previous to the establishment of this rule (M.S.).

[3] *Mnamon*, recorder.

husband to a wife 100 staters or less, but not more; if he should give more, the pertinent relatives shall have the property, (only) paying the money if they wish.

If any one owing money, or under obligation for damages,[1] or during the progress of a suit, should give away anything, unless the rest of his property be equal to the obligation, the gift shall be null and void.

One shall not buy a man while mortgaged until the mortgagor release him, nor one in dispute, nor accept him (as a gift), nor accept a promise or mortgage upon him; and if one should do any one of these things, it shall be void if 2 witnesses should testify.

XVII. *Adoption.* — Adoption may take place whence one will; and the declaration shall be made in the market-place, when the citizens are gathered,[2] from the stone from which proclamations are made. And let the adopter give to his hetæria[3] a roast sacrifice and a can of wine. And if he (the adopted) receive all the property and there be no legitimate children, he shall fulfil all the divine and human obligations of his adoptive father, and receive as is written for legitimate children; but if he be not willing to do as is written, the kinsmen shall have the property. If there be legitimate children of the adoptive father, the adopted son shall receive with the males just as the females receive from the brothers. If however there be no males, but females, the adopted son shall have an equal share, and it shall not be compulsory upon him to pay the obligations of the adopter and accept the property which the adopter leaves, for the adopted son shall succeed to no more (than an equal share with the daughters).[4] If the adopted son should die without leaving legitimate children, the property shall return to the pertinent relatives of the adopter. If the adopter wish, he may renounce him (the adopted son) in the market-place, from the stone from which proclamations are made, when the citizens are gathered.

[1] "Or adjudged a debtor" (B and L). The meaning of this passage seems to be that if one owes money on a judgment, or if a suit for money has been brought against him, any gift in fraud of the judgment creditor or of the plaintiff is voidable (M.S.).

[2] *Cf.* the *adrogatio* in older Roman law.

[3] An association of citizens corresponding somewhat to the phratry, brotherhood, of other Greek states.

[4] "To more (than his share of property and obligations) the adopted son shall not succeed" (B and L).

And he shall deposit ten staters with the court, and the clerk of the court shall pay it to the person renounced as a parting gift of hospitality. A woman shall not adopt, nor a person under puberty. These things shall (now) be transacted as he (the legislator) has written these writings; but in previous cases, however one hold (property), whether by adoption or from an adopted son, it shall not be further subject to a legal claim.

XVIII. *Supplemental provisions.* — If one take action by seizure against a man before trial, (the defendant) shall always receive him under his surety.[1]

Whatever is written for the judge to decide according to witnesses or by oath of denial, he shall decide as is written,[2] but touching other matters shall decide under oath according to matters in controversy.

If a person die owing money or having a judgment against him, if those who are next of right to receive the property desire, they can pay the damages in behalf of the deceased, and the money to whom it is owing, and then have the property; but if they do not wish to do so, the property shall belong to those who have won the suit or to those to whom the money is owing, and there shall be no other loss to the heirs-at-law. The property of the father may be seized in behalf of the father, as also the mother's in behalf of the mother.

If a wife be separated from her husband, in case the judge decide upon the oath,[3] let her take the oath of denial within 20 days in the presence of the judge. Whatever he charges let the beginner of the suit announce to the woman and the judge and the clerk of the court, 4 days before in the presence of witnesses. . . . (*Sixteen lines are lacking.*)

If a son have given property to his mother, or a husband to his wife, as was written before these writings, it shall not be illegal; but hereafter gifts shall be made as here written.

If heiresses have no orphan judges while they are not of full maturity, they shall be treated as is written. And where, in de-

1 "(The man seized) is always to be protected" (B). "Against the person making the seizure opposition is to be raised whenever possible" (Zitelmann).

2 "In other cases he shall decide the points in controversy upon his oath" (B and L).

3 That is, if the judge decides that she is to take an oath (M.S.).

fault of a pertinent relative or orphan judges (public guardians) an heiress is brought up in her mother's house, the father's and mother's relatives that have been described shall manage the property and the income as they can best increase them until she marry. And she shall marry at 12 years or older.

77. Athenian Decree Ordering the Publication of Draco's Law of Homicide

(*Inscr. græc.* I. no. 61; Hicks and Hill, no. 78; Dareste, Haussoullier et Reinach, *Recueil des inscriptions juridiques grecques*, II. 1–24 (fullest restorations and commentary); Ditt. I. no. 52; Roberts and Gardner, *Greek Epigraphy*, II. no. 25. Translated by C. J. O.)

To the oligarchy of the Four Hundred succeeded the government, theoretically of the Five Thousand, practically of those who were able to equip themselves for service in the heavy infantry (411 B.C.; Botsford, *Hellenic History*, ch. xix). In the following year, however, the brilliant victory of Alcibiades off Cyzicus encouraged Athens to reëstablish the democracy. This movement was accompanied by unusual legislative activity. The Athenians appointed (410) a board of Anagrapheis (Ἀναγραφεῖς), Recorders of Law, whose duty was to eliminate inconsistencies from the code and to engrave anew the individual statutes. From Lysias, xxx, it appears that they continued in office six years and that they abused their power in their own financial interest. A part of the legislative activity of these years was the enactment of a decree for limiting the power of the council of Five Hundred and for determining its relation to the Assembly and probably to the Heliastic courts. The inscription (*Inscr. græc.* I. 57) is badly mutilated, but additional information may be gathered from Aristotle, *Const. Ath.* 45.

The decree, however, with which we are here concerned is an order of the Five Hundred and the Assembly to the anagrapheis above mentioned to receive from the basileus ("king," or as modern writers generally say, "king archon"), and to engrave anew on a stone, the law of Draco concerning homicide. It had originally been published in 621, and probably contained provisions applying to wilful murder as well as to other degrees of homicide. The present document, however, does not contain the article on murder in the first degree. The problem involved is exceedingly difficult; but the most satisfactory solution seems to be the assumption that Solon abolished that article and substituted a provision of his own. This supposition best accounts for the fact that nowhere in his legislation did Draco mention the Areopagites, who had cognizance in cases of wilful murder, but throughout his law of homicide referred only to the ephetæ (Plutarch, *Solon*, 19). In other words, the antiquarians, from whom Plutarch directly or indirectly drew his knowledge of this subject, had not seen the original law of Draco but only the revision — perhaps the document given below.

The text of the inscription is fragmentary, and can only be restored in part with the aid of Demosthenes xxiii (*Against Aristocrates*) and xliii (*Concerning Macartatus*), our most valuable sources for the general subject. See also Arist. *Const. Ath.* 57. On the laws of Draco and the revision of 409–8, see Meyer, *Gesch. des Alt.* II. 573–9; Busolt, *Griech. Gesch.* II. 225–43; III. 1538, n. 3; Gilbert, *Const. Antiq.* 379 *sqq.*; "Beiträge zur Entwicklungsgeschichte des griechischen Gerichtsverfahrens," in *Jahrbücher für class. Philologie*, Supplb. XXIII (1897). 443–536; Botsford, *Development of the Athenian Constitution*, 146 *sqq.*

DIOGNETUS OF PHREARRHOE WAS SECRETARY: DIOCLES WAS ARCHON[1]

Be it resolved by the Boulê and the Demus. (The tribe of) Acamantis held the prytany; Diognetus was secretary; Euthydicus was chairman; Xenophanes offered the resolution: —

That the *Anagrapheis*[2] (Recorders of the Laws) shall receive from the basileus[3] the law of Draco concerning murder, and shall record it, with the help of the secretary of the council, upon a stone stele and shall place it [in front of] the King's Porch.[4] The poletæ[5] shall let the contract according to law, and the hellenotamiæ[6] shall give the money.

First Table.[7] And[8] if anyone shall kill another without pre-

[1] 409–8 B.C.

[2] Anagrapheis, see introduction to this document.

[3] Basileus (Βασιλεύς), "king," or "king archon," originally the monarch of Athens but now a member of the board of nine archons; Arist. *Const. Ath.* 3.

[4] On the King's Porch, see Botsford, *Hellenic History*, ch. xiii. The laws of Solon were likewise set up in this building; Aristotle, *Const. Ath.* 7.

[5] Poletæ, commissioners attending to the sale of public goods, the letting of public contracts, etc.

[6] No. 68, n. 1.

[7] The word here translated by "table" is axon, a revolving pillar faced with four rectangular tablets, on which the law was originally written. It is doubtful whether the law is quoted directly from the "first table" of Draco or was incorporated into the first table of Solon's code.

[8] This word shows that the opening provisions of the original law of Draco are not quoted — a fact which helps substantiate the view that the original law contained an article on wilful murder. Below are collected some of the principal passages relating to murder in the first degree: —

1. Demosthenes xxiii. 24: "It is written in the law that the Council has cognizance

meditation, [he shall be exiled.] The kings[1] shall administer justice on a charge of murder or [if anyone charges another with contriving it (?)] and the *ephetæ*[2] shall decide. If there is a father or a brother or sons, all shall forgive,[3] or else the opposition of one shall prevail; [if there are no] such persons, the relatives as far as the degree of first cousin [may forgive, if all of them] are willing, after swearing the oath. If there is not any one of these persons and the homicide was involuntary and the fifty-one ephetæ decide that it was involuntary, the slayer shall be admitted (to the country) by ten members of the phratry,[4] if they are willing. These persons shall be chosen by

of murder and wounding with premeditation and arson and poisoning if anyone by administering it kills (another)."

2. Aristotle, *Const. Ath.* 57. 3: "Prosecutions for homicide and wounding, if anyone wilfully kills or wounds, are tried on the Areopagus, and for poisoning, if anyone kills by administering it, and for arson. These cases alone the boulê tries."

3. Dem. xxiii. 67 *sq.*: "You all know surely that on the Areopagus, where the law grants and commands that there shall be trials for murder, in the first place the one who charges another with having committed such a crime must take an oath, imprecating destruction upon himself and his kin (genos) and family; and it is no ordinary oath which he will take but one that no person swears in any other matter: he must stand on the vitals of a boar and ram and bull slain by fitting persons and at fitting times, so that with regard both to the time and the officiating persons the requirements of religious law have been met. Afterward the one who has sworn such an oath is not yet believed; but if he shall be convicted of falsehood, he will fasten the guilt of perjury on his children and his kin, and will gain no advantage by it. But if it shall appear that his accusation is just, and he shall convict the other of having perpetrated the murder, not even thus will he become the master of the convicted person, but the laws and the authorities concerned shall have power over the latter; he has it in his power to see the guilty person suffer the penalty imposed by the law and nothing more. These are the things that fall to the prosecutor; the accused, on the other hand, must take the oath in like manner; and after making the first pleading may retire into exile, and neither the prosecutor nor the judges nor any one else can prevent it." *Cf.* also Pollux viii. 117; Pausanias i. 28. 5; Lysias iii. 46. If the accused decides to take his trial, the punishment in case of conviction is death with the confiscation of property; Antiphon v (*On the Murder of Herodes*), 10; Lysias iii. 38.

[1] The question as to who these kings were is under controversy. The most likely view is that the four tribe kings assisted the "king archon" in the presidency of the court.

[2] A court of fifty-one jurors who were chosen from the nobility and were above fifty years of age. Before the fourth century they had cognizance of all cases of homicide excepting wilful murder, which came before the Areopagites. The origin of the court and the reason for the number are unknown.

[3] This formal act of reconciliation permitted the slayer, who was in exile, to return to his country.

[4] An association of citizens with their wives and children which was both religious and civic. The chief public function of the association was to maintain the racial

the fifty-one from those of noble birth.[1] This ordinance shall be applicable also to those who have committed homicide previously.[2] The warning[3] to the slayer shall be given, in the market-place, by the relatives nearer than the degree of first cousin, but first cousins and sons of first cousins and sons-in-law[4] and fathers-in-law and members of the phratry shall aid in the prosecution.

(*Then follow several lines which cannot be restored.*)

If anyone shall kill the murderer[5] or cause him to be slain while he is keeping away from the market-place on the frontier, from (public) games, and from amphictyonic sanctuaries,[6] such a person shall be subject to the same penalties as one who has killed an Athenian, and the decision shall rest with the ephetæ. It shall be allowable to kill or arrest murderers in our own country, but not to mistreat them or to take a ransom, under penalty of paying double the amount of the damage. (*The next line is lost.*)

If anyone shall kill another in self-defence[7] . . . if the homicide is involuntary, the kings shall try the case on a charge of murder, and the ephetæ shall decide. [One who has killed a slave shall be subject to trial for murder in the same way as one who has killed] a free man. If anyone in his own defence shall kill on the spot one who is forcibly and unlawfully plundering, the homicide shall not be punished. (*The remaining ten lines cannot be restored.*)

purity of the citizens by excluding all of alien blood, and to care for the civic interests of the children of citizens from the time of their introduction into the association to the enrolment of youths in the deme registers and the marriage of girls.

[1] This undoubtedly is the original meaning of the word ἀριστίνδην; it is evident that at least from the time of Draco the phratries comprised both nobles and commons. In the fifth century, however, it probably had reference to precedence in respectability as determined by the ephetæ.

[2] As the present document was not a new law, there was no injustice in this provision.

[3] As a polluted person the slayer was formally interdicted from the market-place, the sanctuaries, and religious ceremonies.

[4] The Greek word (gambros, γαμβρός) may also include brothers-in-law.

[5] This section refers to the case of one who has been convicted of accidental homicide and has gone into exile; *cf.* Demosthenes xxiii. 37–41.

[6] In the fifth century the principal amphictyony was that of Delphi. The Delian amphictyony, which had flourished in the eighth and seventh centuries, had declined; but an effort was made by the Athenians in the fifth century to revive it.

[7] Literally, "kill one who has made a beginning of unjust hands."

BIBLIOGRAPHY

On the Gortynian laws, in addition to the works mentioned in the introduction, see Bernhöft, Fr., "Das Gesetz von Gortyn," in *Zeitschr. f. vergleichende Rechtswissenschaft*, VI. 281–304, 430–40; Lipsius, H., *Zum Recht von Gortyn* (Teubner); Bürchner, "Gortyn," in Pauly-Wissowa, *Real-Encycl.* VII (1912) 1665–71 (with references to recent studies in the subject).

On Greek law, and particularly Attic law, see Telfy, I. B., *Corpus iuris attici* (Leipzig, 1868), a collection of laws; Meier, M. H. E., and Schömann, G. F., *Der attische Process*, revised by Lipsius, J. H., 2 vols. (Berlin: Calvary, 1883–1887); Lipsius, *Das attische Recht und Rechtsverfahren mit Benutzung des 'Attischen Process' von Meier und Schömann*, 2 vols. (Leipzig: Reissland, 1905–1908); Beauchet, L., *L'Histoire du droit privê de la rêpublique athênienne*, 4 vols. (Paris, 1897), the most useful work for the student of general Greek history; Gilbert, G., "Beiträge zur Entwicklungsgeschichte des griechischen Gerichtsverfahrens," in *Jahrb. für Cl. Philol.* Supplb. XXIII (1897). 445–536; *Constitutional Antiquities of Sparta and Athens*, 376–416; Swoboda, H., "Beiträge zur griechischen Rechtsgeschichte," in *Zeitschrift der Savigny-Stiftung für Rechtsgeschichte*, XXVI (1905). 149–280; Szanto, E., *Ausgewählte Abhandlungen* (Tübingen: Mohr, 1906), including various studies in Greek law; Bonner, R. J., *Evidence in Athenian Courts* (Chicago, 1905), dissertation.

Minor studies are Allen, J. T., "On Secrecy in Voting in the Athenian Courts in the Fifth Century B.C.," in *Class. Rev.* XVIII (1904). 456–8; Arvanitopoullos, A., Ζητήματα τοῦ Ἀττικοῦ δικαίου II. Περὶ τῶν εὐθυνῶν (Athens, 1900); Brehier, L., *De græcorum iudiciorum origine* (Paris, 1899); Bonner, R. J., "Did Women testify in Homicide Cases in Athens," in *Class. Philol.* I (1906). 127–32; Caillemer, E., "Études sur les antiquités juridiques d'Athènes," etc., in *Ass. pour . . . Études grecques*, XII (1878). 184–200; Dareste, R., "Le droit criminel athénien," *ib.* XII. 29–47; Francotte, H., "L'antidosis," etc., *Mêm. acad. roy. des sciences*, etc., LI (Brussels, 1895); Goldstaub, M., *De ἀδείας notione et usu in iure attico* (Breslauer Philol. Abhdl., 1889); Goligher, W. A., "Isæus and Attic Law," in *Hermathena* XIV (1907). 183–204; "Antidosis," *ib.* 481–515; Headlam, J. W., "On the Πρόκλησις εἰς βάσανον in Attic Law," in *Class. Rev.* VII (1893). 1–5, slave torture; Hille, G. E. van, *De testamentis in iure attico* (Amsterdam, 1898), dissert.; Körte, A., "Zum attischen Erbrecht," in *Philol.* LXV (1906). 388–96; Lögberg, L. E., *Animadversiones de actione παρανόμων* (Upsala, 1898), dissert.; Thalheim, Th., *Zu den Rechtsaltertümern* (Hirschberg, 1894), program; Partsch, J., *Griechisches Burgschaftsrecht* (Teubner, 1909); Welsing, C., *De inquilinorum et peregrinorum apud Athenienses iudiciis* (Monast. Guestf., 1887); program; Ziebarth, E., *De iureiurando in iure græco quæstiones* (Göttingen, 1892), dissert.; "Der Fluch im griechischen Recht," in *Hermes*, XXX (1895). 609–28; Hirzel, R., *Themis, Dike und Verwandtes* (Leipzig, 1907).

CHAPTER IX

MEDICAL SCIENCE

In the Fifth Century B.C.

A. Superstition

THE progress of the healing art is here illustrated by a selection from Aristophanes, *Plutus*, describing incubation as it was practised from early times through the fifth century and long afterward, and by a few selections from Hippocrates, the most famous physician of the ancient world.

78. INCUBATION

(Aristophanes, *Plutus*, 659 *sqq.*)

Liberty is here taken in inserting a passage from an early fourth-century comedy to illustrate fifth-century conditions. The fact is, however, that in a custom of this kind little change was made from one century to another. Plutus, god of wealth, is blind; consequently he distributes his gifts with little discrimination, often bestowing much upon the unworthy, leaving little or nothing for the good. Vexed at this state of affairs, a certain Athenian of moderate means resolves to take Plutus to a temple of Asclepius to have him cured of his blindness. In this visit the Athenian is accompanied by his slave Cario, who afterward tells the story of the incubation to his master's wife. The selection is not only amusing but highly instructive.

CARIO. Then to the precincts of the God we went.
There on the altar honey-cakes and bakemeats
Were offered, food for the Hephæstian flame.
There laid we Wealth[1] as custom bids; and we
Each for himself stitched up a pallet near.

WIFE. Were there no others waiting to be healed?

CAR. Neoclides was, for one; the purblind man,
Who in his thefts out-shoots the keenest-eyed.[2]

[1] That is, Plutus, god of wealth.

[2] It was a part of his profession to pretend that he was purblind.

And many others, sick with every form
Of ailment. Soon the temple servitor
Put out the lights and bade us fall asleep,[1]
Nor stir nor speak, whatever noise we heard.
So down we lay in orderly repose.
And I could catch no slumber, not one wink,
Struck by a nice tureen of broth which stood
A little distance from an old wife's head,
Whereto I marvellously longed to creep.
Then, glancing upward, I behold the priest
Whipping the cheese-cakes and the figs from off
The holy table; thence he coasted round
To every altar, spying what was left.
And everything he found he consecrated
Into a sort of sack; so I, concluding
This was the right and proper thing to do,
Arose at once to tackle that tureen.

WIFE. Unhappy man! Did you not fear the God?

CAR. Indeed, I did, lest he should cut in first,
Garlands and all, and capture my tureen.
For so the priest forewarned me he might do.
Then the old lady, when my steps she heard,
Reached out a stealthy hand; I gave a hiss,
And mouthed it gently like a sacred snake.
Back flies her hand; she draws her coverlets
More tightly round her, and beneath them lies
In deadly terror like a frightened cat.
Then of the broth I gobbled down a lot
Till I could eat no more, and then I stopped.

WIFE. Did not the God approach you? CAR. Not till later.

* * * * * * *

So then alarmed, I muffled up my head,
Whilst he[2] went round with calm and quiet tread,

[1] The idea was that the god would approach the patient and heal him while asleep in the temple — hence the word incubation.

[2] Cario naturally supposes that the god went about among the patients to administer to their maladies. In fact there were connected with every temple of Asclepius physicians, who attended to this function, while giving the god credit. It was in these places that medical science developed.

To every patient, scanning each disease.
Then by his side a servant placed a stone
Pestle and mortar, and a medicine chest.
WIFE. A stone one? CAR. Hang it, not the medicine chest.
WIFE. How saw you this, you villain, when your head,
You said just now, was muffled? CAR. Through my cloak.
Full many a peep-hole has that cloak, I trow.

* * * * * * *

Then after this, he sat him down by Wealth,
And first he felt the patient's head and next
Taking a linen napkin, clean and white,
Wiped both his lids, and all round them, dry;
Then Panaceia, with a scarlet cloth
Covered his face and head; then the God clucked,
And out there issued from the holy shrine
Two great enormous serpents. WIFE. Good heavens!
CAR. And underneath the scarlet cloth they crept
And licked his eyelids, as it seemed to me;
And mistress dear, before you could have drunk
Of wine ten goblets, Wealth arose and saw.

B. The Condition of the Medical Science and Profession

(Selections from the works of Hippocrates; from the edition by E. Littré in 10 vols., Paris, 1839–1862. Translated by E. G. S.)

While in the fifth century the masses still believed in expelling diseases by charms and prayer, or by visits to the shrines of Asclepius, the medical profession had eliminated magic and every form of superstition from theory and practice, and stood on the solid ground of scientific observation and experiment. As stated above, medical science developed in these temples. The physicians in the Asclepieion of Cos were reputed the most skilful in Greece; and among them by far the most famous was Hippocrates (460–377). In fact he was the first to abandon for good and all the mysticism and superstition of the shrines and to make his profession scientific. With keen and sober faculties trained by careful observation and experience he connected the gift of didactic exposition. Plato (*Protagoras* 311 b) represents him as sojourning at Athens and giving instruction in his profession. Like his compatriot Herodotus, he traveled widely and closely observed everything which had a bearing on his department of knowledge. Like Herodotus he adopted the Ionic dialect for his writings, probably, too, for the lectures given by him in various parts of the

Hellenic world. His style, particularly the quaint simplicity in the arrangement of clauses, reminds us of Herodotus. The brevity of his *Aphorisms* approaches the margin of harshness.

This physician has created many abiding terms, such as chronic, acute, crisis. A great part of the works of Galen consists of a commentary on the master. Although his life and services must have broken into the old Asclepiad habits, such places as the great Asclepieion at Epidaurus do not seem to have felt through his influence any diminution of credit or of popular support. The most eminent modern editor of his works is Littré mentioned above. In this splendid edition a combination of rigid philological precision with generous and comprehensive interest in the technical and professional significance of every theme impresses even the cursory reader. See also Ilberg, J., "Die Erforschung der griechischen Heilkunde," in *N. Jahrbücher*, I (1908). 585 *sqq.*

Hippocrates laid great stress on physical environment, on wind, water, climate, temperature, soil, and sea. His contrast between Asiatics and Europeans, based upon physical as well as political conditions, is valuable to the student of ancient civilization. The *Oath* discloses the manner in which the science and art of medicine were guarded and handed down within a guild, and expresses the high moral ideal of the profession.

79. Aphorisms of Hippocrates

I. 1. Life is brief, but art is long, the emergency swift, the test deceptive, and judgment difficult. It is necessary not only to be in readiness oneself to do what is needful, but the patient too must be in such readiness and the attendants and outward circumstances all must concur.

2. In the disturbances of the bowels and vomitings, namely those which are spontaneous, if those organs which ought to be purged, are purged, the former are useful and (the patients) bear them easily; but if not, the opposite is the result. One must take into consideration also the given country, season, time of life, and diseases in which evacuations are indicated or not indicated.

3. In professional athletes the excellence of physical fitness carried to the extreme is dangerous, if such athletes be in the latter stage of their career; for they cannot remain at the same point nor keep at rest; and not being at rest, they cannot advance to any further improvement: it remains therefore that any change must be for the worse. On this account it is advantageous to reduce the high point of athletic form without delay, in order that the body may gain a beginning of reparation through more generous diet;

nor should the reduction of weight be carried to the uttermost point, for it is dangerous, but this reduction must be adjusted to the constitution of the given person about to undergo it. Likewise evacuations carried to excess are dangerous, and in turn the process of reparations by a generous diet (when the given body has been at that low stage) is dangerous.

II. 1. A disease, in which sleep causes pain, is fatal; but if sleep is helpful (that disease) is not fatal.

2. Where sleep terminates delirium, it is beneficial.

3. Both sleep and waking, when they exceed measure, are harmful.

4. Not free eating, nor fasting, nor anything else is good provided it exceeds the limits of Nature.

5. Fits of exhaustion that come of themselves indicate some disease.

6. All those who while suffering in some part of their body are in the main not conscious of the pain, these are in a state of mental alienation.

7. Bodies which have been running down a long time one must but slowly restore by nourishing them again, and consume but little time in restoring those whose reduction has consumed but little time.

8. If a patient, after a disease, does not gain any strength through taking nourishment, it is a sign that he eats more than he should; but if he remains weak because he takes no nourishment, then one must know that a purging is required. . . .

11. It is easier to (restore health) with liquid nourishment than with solid.

12. Those elements in diseases which are left after the crisis, are wont to cause relapses. . . .

19. In the case of acute diseases prediction, neither of a fatal termination nor of recovery, is entirely safe. . . .

23. Acute diseases reach a crisis in fourteen days.

24. The fourth day is that which gives indication of the first seven; the eighth is the beginning of the second week, the eleventh is the day which permits judgment, for this is the fourth of the second week; and again the seventeenth is a day permitting vision, for this is fourth from the fourteenth and seventh from the eleventh.

III. 1. It is particularly the changes of the seasons which beget diseases and *within* the seasons the drastic changes either of cold or heat, and the rest thus by the same principle.

2. Some constitutions are well or ill adapted for summer, others for winter.

3. Some diseases in their essence have a favorable bearing on other diseases; others an evil, and some ages have such a relation as to seasons, places, or diets.

4. Whenever in the seasons within the same day at one time heat, at another cold arises, one must expect autumnal diseases.

5. Winds from the south cause obstruction to hearing, a mist over the eyes, headache, torpor, prostration; whenever this wind prevails they (the sick) suffer such things in their various diseases. But when the wind is from the north, (there occur) cough, sore throat, constipation, difficulty of water coupled with ague, pain in the sides and in the chest; whenever this (wind) prevails, such things one must expect in the diseases.

6. Whenever summer resembles spring, one must expect many perspirations in the fevers. . . .

8. In settled periods, seasonable products are produced in a seasonable way, while diseases are normal and easy of diagnosis; but in the unsettled (seasons) (diseases) are abnormal and difficult of diagnosis.

9. In autumn diseases are most acute and most fatal on the whole; spring is the most salubrious and least fatal.

80. The Oath of Hippocrates

(Littré, iv. 628)

I swear by Apollo the Healer and Asclepius and Hygeia (Health) and Panaceia (all-healing) and all the gods and goddesses, making them witnesses, that I will fulfil this oath of mine and written agreement to the best of my power and judgment; that I will esteem him who taught me this art equal with my own parents, and let him share in my substance, and contribute to him when he is in debt, and judge his sons as my brothers and teach them this art if they wish to learn it, without pay and written contract, to let them share in delivery and lecture and all the remaining doctrine both to mine own sons and those of him who taught me and to the pupils who have been enrolled by contract and sworn by the physicians' oath, and to none other. And the forms of diet I shall select for the benefit of the patients to the best of my ability and judgment, and refrain from injury and injustice. I shall give to no one any deadly drug on request, nor give such counsel, nor shall I give to any woman a pessary to bring on a miscarriage.

In a chaste and a spotless fashion shall I maintain my life and my art. I shall not perform any surgical operation on those suffering from the stone, nor shall I give place to men who make a practice thereof. Into all the houses which I shall enter I shall enter for the benefit of the sufferers, being beyond all wrongdoing voluntary and destructive. . . . Whatever in my practice I either see or hear, — or even outside of my practice in connection with the life of human beings, which should never be uttered outside, I shall hold my peace thereon, convinced that such things ought not to be spoken. As for me, if I keep this oath and not break it, may it be my lot to profit both in life and art in my reputation with all men for always, and if I transgress and commit perjury, may (I suffer) the opposite of these things.

81. Airs, Waters, and Places

1. Whoever desires rightly to inquire into the medical art, must do this: first he must consider the seasons of the year, what each can accomplish, for they have no resemblance, but they differ much themselves from themselves and in their mutations, and then the hot and cold winds; most of all, what is common to all men, and what is local to each land. It is necessary also to consider the properties of the waters, for just as these differ in their body and weight, so also the influence of each differs much. So that, when one arrives in a city of which one has no experience, he must reflect upon its situation, how it lies both as to winds and as to the rising of the sun. For the same influence is not potent in that which lies toward the north and that which lies toward the south, nor in that which lies toward the west (has a western exposure). These things he must consider as nicely as possible, and concerning the waters how they are and whether (the people of a given community) use marshy and soft or hard water that comes from high and

rocky sources, or salty and bitter; and as for the soil, whether it is bare and unwatered, or wooded and well-watered, or whether it lies in a hollow and exposed to the winds, or whether high and cold; and as to the diet which they like, whether they are fond of drinking and take breakfasts and are incapable of bearing fatigue, or fond of exercise and hardships, and are hearty eaters and sparing in drink.

12. I desire to point out concerning Asia and Europe, how far they differ from one another, both as a whole and as to the forms of the races, because they do differ, and do not resemble one another at all. About the whole of it there would be an extensive discourse, but about the greatest points and those involving the greatest difference, I shall say how it seems to me. Asia I claim differs very much from Europe as to the physical properties of all — both plants and human beings; for everything grows much fairer and larger in Asia; one country (Asia) is milder than the other, the customs of the men are milder and better-tempered. The reason is the blending of the seasons, situated in the central point between the risings of the sun, toward the East, and further away from the cold: it permits (or furnishes) growth and mildness most of all whenever nothing dominates in a drastic manner, but equal distribution holds sway over everything. In Asia however it is so not everywhere equally, but in all that territory which lies midway between the hot and the cold, this is the most fruitful and has the finest growth of trees; it has the clearest atmosphere and enjoys the finest waters both from the sky and from the earth. For neither has it been excessively burned out by the heat, nor is it parched by droughts and rainlessness nor roughly dealt with by cold; and since it is moistened also by many rains and snow, it is likely that many things there gain their full maturity of growth, both whatever spring from seeds and whatever plant the earth itself gives forth of itself: the fruits which men use, cultivating out of the wild growth and transplanting in a suitable fashion. The animals raised there are likely to be of generous stature and particularly to bear offspring very frequently and to rear very handsomely. And as for men, they are easily reared and very handsome in appearance, and very large of size, and differ very little from one another as to form and stature; and it is likely that this country is nearest to the vernal type in its nature and the moderation of the seasons. But

fortitude and endurance and hardiness and courage could not well be produced in such a nature — whether of the same race or of others — but pleasure must needs hold sway.

16. As regards the lack of courage of the men and lack of virility, that the Asiatics are more unwarlike than the Europeans and milder of character, — of this the seasons are chiefly the cause, making not any great mutations, either in the direction of hot and cold, but so as to resemble each other.

For there occur no shocks of intelligence, nor any drastic shift in the physical body from which it is likely that anger might be roused, and (these) should have a greater share of thoughtlessness and spirited disposition than those remaining always in the same (frame). For it is the universal changes which rouse the mentality of men and do not permit them to remain quiet. For these reasons the Asiatic race seems to me to be lacking in vigor, and furthermore on account of the laws. For the most parts of Asia are ruled by kings. Now where men have not power over themselves, nor are autonomous, but are under absolute rulers, their concern is *not* to train themselves for war, but how *not* to seem to be fitted for fighting. For the dangers are not similar. It is likely that some through necessity should go to war and suffer hardships and die on behalf of their masters, being away from children and wife and the rest of their friends, and whatever useful and courageous deeds they do, it is their *sovereigns* that grow and increase from them. As for dangers and death, that is what *they* reap themselves; and the land must needs be made desolate both by the enemy and through the cessation of work. So that even if one is manly and spirited by nature, his mental trend is bound to be diverted by the political character of things. A great proof of this is the following: all the Greeks and Barbarians in Asia who are not under absolute sway but self-governing, and endure hardships for their own advantage, these are the most warlike of all, for it is for themselves that they encounter dangers, and of their valor they carry off the prizes themselves, and of cowardice the penalty likewise. And you will find also that the Asiatics differ from one another, some being braver, and others more inferior: the reasons for these things are the changes of the seasons, as I have said before. And about those in Asia it is so.

BIBLIOGRAPHY

Complete works of Hippocrates with translation and medical commentary, in French, by Littré, E., 10 vols.; by Kühlewein, H., 2 vols. (Leipzig, 1894, 1902); *De natura hominis*, ed. by Mewaldt, J., Helmreich, G., and Westenberger, J. (Teubner, 1914); *The Genuine Works*, translated by Adams, F., 2 vols. (New York: Wood, 1891). For studies in Hippocrates, see Kühlewein, H., "Beiträge zur Geschichte und Beurteilung der hippokratischen Schriften," in *Philol.* XLII (1884). 119–33; Gomperz, Th., "Die hippokratische Frage," etc., *ib.* LXX (1911). 213–41; Diels, H., "Hippokratische Forschungen," in *Hermes*, XLV (1910). 125–50; XLVI. 269–85; XLVIII. 378–407; Ilberg, J., "Die Erforschung der griech. Heilkunde," in *N. Jahrb.* XI (1908). 585–602; "Aus Galens Praxis," etc., *ib.* VIII. 276–312; Wellmann, M., "Zur Geschichte der Medicin im Altertum," in *Hermes*, XLVII (1912). 1–17; Smith, F. R., "The Oath of Hippocrates," in *Johns Hopkins Hospital Bull.* III. no. 21. A *Corpus medicorum græcorum* (Teubner) has been under way for some years; *cf.* Diels, H., "Ueber das neue Corpus medicorum," in *N. Jahrb.* X (1907). 722–6. For other recent literature on medicine, see *Jahresb.* 1912.

See also Hamilton, M., *Incubation or the Cure of Diseases in Pagan Temples and Christian Churches* (London, 1906); Lefort, Th., "Notes sur le culte d'Asklepios: Nature de l'incubation dans ce culte," in *Musée Belge*, X (1906). 21–37; Jones, W. H. S., *Malaria and Greek History*, etc. (Manchester, 1909); Rid, H., *Klimalehre der alten Griechen nach den Geographica Strabos* (Kaiserslautern, 1904); Schellenberg, O., *Studien zur Klimatologie Griechenlands: Temperatur, Niederschläge, Bewölkung* (Leipzig, 1908).

CHAPTER X

ASPECTS OF HELLENIC SOCIETY

In the Period 479–404 B.C.

82. Through Tribulation to Glory

(Pindar, Second *Olympian*)

Although the happy outcome of the war with Persia gave a great impetus to democracy (Botsford, *Hellenic History*, ch. xii), the aristocratic spirit was still strong. Its best literary representative was Pindar (p. 32). The passages from his poems given below have been chosen, not so much for their literary excellence, as for their general intelligibility and for their usefulness in illustrating the social ideas and conditions of the age. The second Olympian was composed for the celebration of the chariot race won by Theron, tyrant of Acragas, in 476. The pedigree and the myth contained in the poem begin with Cadmus, founder and first king of Thebes. Among his children were a son, Polydorus, and the daughters, Semele and Ino. Semele and Zeus were the parents of the man-god Dionysus. Utterly consumed by a thunderbolt of Zeus as jealous Hera had contrived, the mother was nevertheless granted immortality and a life of blessedness among the gods. Ino, after manifold sufferings brought upon her by Hera's anger, leaped into the sea and became a water goddess. A miserable fate befel the male line. Laïus, grandson of Polydorus, was unwittingly slain by his own son, Œdipus. In time the Erinys (Fury) of Laïus brought Œdipus to ruin, and incited his sons, Eteocles and Polyneices, to civil war, in which each died by the other's hand. The fate of this family is the subject of many a tragedy. A son of Polyneices and his wife Argeia, daughter of Adrastus, king of Argos, was Thersander, whose descendants "went successively to Sparta, to Thera, to Rhodes, and finally to Acragas — evidently a roving, and doubtless a quarrelsome race" (Gildersleeve). One of them, Emmenes, or Emmenides, was father of Ænesidamus and grandfather of Theron and Xenocrates, hence these two brothers are called Emmenidæ. Usurping the government of Acragas, Theron ruled magnificently and on the whole wisely.

"In the opening of the second Olympian, Pindar himself points out the threefold chord that runs through the ode. . . . When he asks, 'What god, what hero, what man shall we celebrate?' he means to celebrate all three, and god, hero, and man recur throughout: the god helping, the hero toiling, the man achieving. God is the disposer, the hero the leader, and the man the follower. The man, the Olympian victor, must walk in the footsteps of the greater victor, must endure hardness as the hero endured hardness, in order that he may have a reward, as the hero had his reward, by the favor of God. This is a poem for one who stands on the solemn verge beyond which lies immortal, heroic life. But we must not read a funeral sermon into it, and we must notice how the poet counteracts the grave tone of the poem by the final herald cry, in which he magnifies his own office and champions the old king." (Gildersleeve, *Pindar*, 41 *sq.*)

Lords of the Lute, my Songs, what god, what hero, or what man are we to celebrate? Verily of Zeus is Pisa the abode, of Heracles the Olympian feast was founded from the chief spoils of war, and Theron's name[1] must we proclaim for his victory with the four-horse car, a righteous and god-fearing host, the stay of Acragas, of famous sires the flower, a savior of the state.

They after long toils bravely borne took by the river's side[2] a sacred dwelling place, and became the eye of Sicily, and a life of good luck clave to them, bringing them wealth and honor to crown their inborn worth.

O son of Cronos and Rhea, lord of Olympus' seat, and of the chief of games and of Alpheus'[3] ford, for joy in these my songs guard ever graciously their native fields for their sons that shall come after them.

Now of deeds done whether they be right or wrong, not even Time the father of all can make undone the accomplishment, yet with happy fortune forgetfulness may come. For by high delights an alien pain is quelled and dieth, when the decree of God sendeth happiness to grow aloft and widely.[4]

This word is true, too, concerning Cadmus' fair-throned daughters, whose misfortunes were great, yet their sore grief fell before greater good. Amid the Olympians long-haired Semele still liveth, albeit she perished in the thunder's roar, and Pallas cherisheth her

[1] *I.e.*, the god, hero, and man whom he has in mind are Zeus, Heracles, and Theron, respectively.

[2] The river Acragas, on which the city of the same name was founded.

[3] The river on which Olympia is situated.

[4] Pindar here presents the doctrine that misfortune bravely borne is rewarded by happiness; he illustrates this principle with the following myths.

ever, and father Zeus exceedingly, and her son, the ivy-bearing god.[1] Into the sea, too, they say that to Ino, among the sea-maids of Nereus, life incorruptible hath been ordained for evermore.

Ay but to mortals the day of death is certain never, neither at what time we shall see in calm the end of one of the Sun's children, the Days, with good thitherto unfailing; now this way and now that run currents bringing joys or toils to men.[2]

Thus Destiny, which from their fathers holdeth the happy fortune of this race, together with prosperity heaven-sent, bringeth ever at some other time bitter reverse: from the day when Laïus was slain by his destined son[3] who met him on the road and made fulfilment of the oracle spoken of old at Pytho. Then swift Erinys, when she saw it, slew by each other's hand his warlike sons; yet after Polyneices fell, Thersander lived after him and won honor in the Second Strife[4] and in the fights of war, a savior scion to the Adrastid house.

From him they have beginning of their race: meet it is that Ænesidamus receive our hymn of triumph on the lyre. For at Olympia he himself received a prize and at Pytho, and at the Isthmus to his brother of no less a lot did kindred Graces bring crowns for the twelve rounds of the four-horse chariot-race.[5]

Victory setteth free the essayer from the struggle's griefs, yea and the wealth that a noble nature hath made glorious bringeth power for this and that, putting into the heart of man a deep and eager mood, a star far seen, a light wherein a man shall trust,[6] if but the holder thereof knoweth the things that shall be, how that of all who die the guilty souls pay penalty, for all the sins sinned in

[1] For this and the following myths, see Introduction. The ivy-bearing god is Dionysus.

[2] *Cf.* the Third *Pythian:* "The immortals deal to men two ill things for one good. The foolish cannot bear them with steadfastness but the good only, putting the fair side forward."

[3] Œdipus, see Introduction.

[4] A later attack made upon Thebes under Argive leadership.

[5] In these odes it was customary to celebrate not only the present victor, but also others of his family who had won similar fame.

[6] The inspiration to noble deeds that comes from wealth combined with excellent character is here indicated. As great wealth and unwonted success, however, tend to insolence and lawlessness, one who possesses these gifts should be guided to moderation through fear of punishment and hope of reward after death. The view of future life which follows originated with the Orphists; see Botsford, *Hellenic History*, ch. ix.

this realm of Zeus One judgeth under earth, pronouncing sentence by unloved constraint.

But evenly ever in sunlight night and day an unlaborious life the good receive, neither with violent hand vex they the earth nor the waters of the sea, in that new world; but with the honored of the gods, whosoever had pleasure in keeping of oaths, they possess a tearless life; but the other part suffer pain too dire to look upon.

Then whosoever have been of good courage to the abiding steadfast thrice on either side of death and have refrained their souls from all iniquity, travel the road of Zeus unto the tower of Cronos: there round the islands of the blest the Ocean-breezes blow, and golden flowers are glowing, some from the land on trees of splendor, and some the water feedeth, with wreaths whereof they entwine their hands: so ordereth Rhadamanthus' just decree, whom at his right hand hath ever the father Cronos, husband of Rhea, throned above all worlds.

Peleus and Cadmus are counted of that company; and the mother of Achilles, when her prayer had moved the heart of Zeus, bare thither her son, even him who overthrew Hector, Troy's unbending invincible pillar, even him who gave Cycnus[1] to death and the Ethiop son of the Morning.[2]

Many swift arrows have I beneath my bended arm within my quiver, arrows that have a voice for the wise, but for the multitude they need interpreters. His art is true who of his nature hath knowledge; they who have but learnt, strong in the multitude of words, are but as crows that chatter vain things in strife against the divine bird of Zeus.[3]

Come bend thy bow on the mark, O my soul — at whom again are we to launch our shafts of honor from a friendly mind? At Acragas will I take aim, and will proclaim and swear it with a mind of truth, that for a hundred years no city hath brought forth a man of mind more prone to well-doing toward friends or of more liberal mood than Theron.

[1] Cycnus, though born invulnerable, was strangled to death by Achilles.

[2] Memnon, son of Tithonus, king of the Ethiopians, and of Eos, "Morning," was also slain at Troy by Achilles.

[3] Pindar, the poet of inborn genius, is the eagle, whereas his rivals, including perhaps Bacchylides, men of training merely, are as crows.

Yet praise is overtaken of distaste, wherewith is no justice, but from covetous men it cometh, and is fain to babble against and darken the good man's noble deeds.[1]

The sea-sand none hath numbered; and the joys that Theron hath given to others — who shall declare the tale thereof?

83. God and Blood

(Pindar, Tenth *Pythian*)

This poem is in honor of Hippocleas of Pelinnæum (or Pelinna), Thessaly, winner in the double-stadium foot race of boys. The Aleuadæ, ruling family of Larisa, to whom possibly the winner belonged, engaged Pindar to compose the poem. The Aleuadæ were descendants of Perseus through Heracles; hence the pedigree and the myth which occupy so large a place in the Ode. It is said that the poet was at this time (502) but twenty years of age. In this early manhood he was perhaps even more thoroughly aristocratic than later in life; the language is relatively simple; but the genius of the poet is evident.

Happy is Lacedæmon, blessed is Thessaly: in both there reigneth a race sprung from one sire, from Heracles bravest in the fight.[2] What vaunt is this unseasonable? Nay, now, but Pytho calleth me, and Pelinnæum, and the sons of Aleuas[3] who would fain lead forth the loud voices of a choir of men in honor of Hippocleas.

For now hath he tasted the joy of games, and to the host of the dwellers round about hath the valley beneath Parnassus proclaimed him best among the boys who ran the double race.

O Apollo, sweet is the end when men attain thereto, and the beginning availeth more when it is speeded of a god. Surely of thy devising were his deeds: and this his inborn valor hath trodden in the footsteps of his father twice victor at Olympia in panoply of war-affronting arms;[4] moreover the games in the deep meadow beneath Cirrha's cliff gave victory to the fleet feet of Phricias.[5]

May good luck follow them, so that even in after days the

[1] Undoubtedly there was great popular discontent in Acragas and Syracuse, during the later years of Theron and Hieron, against both rulers. Their successors were speedily overthrown, whereupon both states established republics.

[2] Both were ruled by Heracleidæ.

[3] The Aleuadæ: see Introduction.

[4] See p. 305, note 5 *supra*.

[5] Apparently his father's horse which gained a victory at Pytho.

splendor of their wealth shall bloom. Of the pleasant things of Hellas they have no scanty portion to their lot; may they happen on no envious repentings of the gods.[1] A god's heart, it may be, is painless ever; but happy and a theme of poet's song is that man who for his valiance of hands or feet the chiefest prizes hath by strength and courage won, and in his lifetime seen his young son by good hap attaining to the Pythian crown. Never indeed shall he climb the brazen heaven, but whatsoever splendors we of mortal race may reach, through such he hath free course even to the utmost harborage. But neither by taking ship, neither by any travel on foot, to the Hyperborean folk shalt thou find the wondrous way.[2]

Yet of old the chieftain Perseus entered into their houses and feasted among them, when that he had lighted on them as they were sacrificing ample hecatombs of asses to their gods. For ever in their feasts and hymns hath Apollo especial joy, and laugheth to see the braying ramp of the strange beasts. Nor is the Muse a stranger to their lives, but everywhere are stirring to and fro dances of maidens and shrill noise of pipes: and binding golden bay-leaves in their hair, they make them merry cheer. Nor pestilence nor wasting eld approaches that hallowed race: they toil not neither do they fight, and dwell unharmed of cruel Nemesis.

In the eagerness of his valiant heart went of old the son of Danaë,[3] for that Athena led him on his way, unto the company of that blessed folk. Also he slew the Gorgon and bare home her head with serpent tresses decked, to the island folk a stony death. I ween there is no marvel impossible if gods have wrought thereto.

Let go the oar, and quickly let drive into the earth an anchor from the prow, to save us from the rocky reef, for the glory of my song of praise flitteth like a honey-bee from tale to tale.

I have hope that when the folk of Ephyra[4] pour forth my sweet strains by Peneus'[5] side, yet more glorious shall I make their Hippocleas for his crowns and by my songs among his fellows and his elders, and I will make him possess the minds of the young maidens.

[1] The common Greek idea that the gods were envious of good fortune is here implied.

[2] A reflection, often repeated in manifold form, on the limitations of man.

[3] Perseus, whose journey to the Hyperboreans is here detailed.

[4] Ephyra, afterward Crannon, a city of Thessaly.

[5] Peneus, the chief river of Thessaly, on which the victor's city was situated.

For various longings stir secretly the minds of various men; yet each if he attain to the thing he striveth for will hold his eager desire for the time present to him, but what a year shall bring forth, none shall foreknow by any sign.

My trust is in the kindly courtesy of my host Thorax,[1] of him who to speed my fortune hath yoked this four-horse car of the Pierides, as friend for friend, and willing guide for guide.

As gold to him that trieth it by a touch-stone, so is a true soul known.

His noble brethren also will we praise, for that they exalt and make great the Thessalians' commonwealth.[2] For in the hands of good men lieth the good piloting of the cities wherein their fathers ruled.

84. Victory and Fame by the Grace of God

(Pindar, Sixth *Nemean*)

This ode is in honor of Alcimidas of Ægina, winner in the boys' wrestling match. The pedigree of the victor was as follows: Agesimachus, Socleides, Praxidamas, Theon, Alcimidas; they belonged to the Bassid clan, descendants of Æacus, the hero-founder of Ægina.

One race there is of men and one of gods, but from one mother draw we both our breath,[3] yet is the strength of us diverse altogether, for the race of man is as naught, but the brazen heaven abideth, a habitation steadfast unto everlasting.

Yet withal have we somewhat in us like unto the immortals' bodily shape or mighty mind, albeit we know not what course hath Destiny marked out for us to run, neither in the daytime, neither in the night.

And now doth Alcimidas give proof that it is with his kindred as with fruitful fields; for they in turn now yield to man his yearly bread upon the plains, and now again they pause, and gather back their strength.[4]

[1] The Aleuad magnate who had engaged Pindar to write the ode.

[2] The kinsmen of the young athlete belonged to the ruling class.

[3] A more democratic idea than we should expect of Pindar. In his usual opinion the aristocratic families are sprung on one side from the gods, and hence are of a race superior to common men.

[4] The doctrine of heredity here set forth, that the preëminent virtue of a great

From the pleasant meeting-places of Nemea hath the athlete boy come back, who following the ordinance of Zeus hath now approved him no baffled hunter in his wrestling-quest, and hath guided his feet by the footprints of Praximadas, his father's father, of whose blood he sprang.

For Praximadas also by his Olympian victory first won the olive wreath from Alpheus for the Æacidæ, and five times being crowned at Isthmus, and at Nemea thrice, he took away thereby the obscurity of Socleides, who was the eldest of the sons of Agesimachus.

For these three warriors attained unto the topmost height of prowess, of all who essayed the games, and by grace of God to no other house hath the boxing-match given keeping of so many crowns in this inmost place of all Hellas. I deem that though my speech be of high sound, I yet shall hit the mark, as it were an archer shooting from a bow.

Come, Muse, direct thou upon this house a gale of glorious song; for after that men are vanished away, the minstrel's story taketh up their noble acts, whereof is no lack to the Bassid clan; old in story is the race and they carry cargo of home-made renown, able to deliver unto the Muses' husbandmen rich matter of song in honor of their lofty deeds.

For at sacred Pytho in like wise did a scion of the same stock overcome, with the thong of the boxer bound about his hand, even Callias in whom were well-pleased the children of Leto [1] of the golden distaff, and beside Castaly in the evening his name burnt bright when the glad sounds of the Graces rose.

Also the Bridge [2] of the untiring sea did honor unto Creontidas at the triennal sacrifice of bulls by the neighbor states in the holy place of Poseidon; and once did the herb of the lion shadow his brows for a victory won beneath the shadeless primal hills of Phlius.

Wide avenues of glory are there on every side for chroniclers to draw nigh to do honor unto this isle: for supreme occasion have

family is repeated in alternate generations, Pindar illustrates by the circumstance that the Greeks allowed their arable land to lie fallow in alternate years. The athletic history of the victor's family which follows is evidence of the principle. For the pedigree, see introductory note.

[1] Apollo and Artemis.

[2] *I.e.*, the Isthmus of Corinth, where games were held in honor of Poseidon.

the children of Æacus given them by the showing forth of mighty feats.

Over land and beyond the sea is their name flown forth from afar: even unto the Ethiopians it sprang forth, for that Memnon came not home: for bitter was the battle that Achilles made against him, having descended from his chariot upon the earth, what time by his fierce spear's point he slew the son of the bright Morn.

And herein found they of old time a way wherein to drive their car; and I too follow with my burden of song: and all men's minds, they say, are stirred the most by whatsoever wave at the instant rolleth nearest to the mainsheet of the ship.

On willing shoulders bear I this double load, and am come a messenger to proclaim this honor won in the games that men call holy to be the five and twentieth that the noble house of Alcimidas hath shown forth: yet were two wreaths in the Olympian games beside the precinct of Cronion denied to thee, boy, and to Polytimidas, by the fall of the lot.

Peer of the dolphin hurrying through the brine — such would I call Melesias [1] by whom thy hands and strength were guided, as a chariot by the charioteer.

85. Cimon and Pericles, as seen by an Aristocratic Contemporary

(Ion of Chios, *Journeys*, quoted by Plutarch)

Ion of Chios, a contemporary of Cimon and Pericles, died in 421 or shortly before that date (Aristoph. *Peace*, 835 with schol.). In addition to dramas and various other forms of poetry, he wrote a work entitled *Journeys* (Ἐπιδημίαι), which, had it been preserved, would have been most interesting and valuable to us for the light it threw on the character of the great men with whom the author came into personal touch, and on the social conditions of his age. As it is, we are obliged to depend upon the meager excerpts from the work quoted by Plutarch and Athenæus (Müller, *Fragmenta historicorum græcorum*, II. 46 *sqq.*). During his stay at Athens this aristocrat and enthusiastic admirer of Sparta naturally gravitated to Cimon and his circle, but was repelled by the austerity of Pericles. On this author in general, see Müller, *op. cit.* II. 44–6; Schöll, Fr., in *Rhein. Mus.* XXXII (1877). 145 *sqq.*; Busolt, *Griech. Gesch.* III. 4–6; Christ, *Griech. Lit.* I. 369.

[1] The trainer of Alcidimas.

The following passages, though brief, are useful as contemporary glimpses of eminent men and social conditions in the greatest age of Greece, and at the same time they give an idea of one class of sources from which Plutarch drew material for his immortal biographies.

(Plutarch, *Cimon*, 9)

Ion tells us that when quite a boy he came from Chios to Athens, and met Cimon at dinner in the house of Laomedon. After dinner he (Cimon) was asked to sing, and he sang well. The guests all praised him, and said that he was a more clever man than Themistocles: for Themistocles was wont to say that he did not know how to sing or to play the lyre, but that he knew how to make a state great and rich.[1] Afterward the conversation turned upon Cimon's exploits, and each mentioned what he thought the most important. Thereupon Cimon himself described what he considered to be the cleverest thing he had ever done. After the capture of Sestos and Byzantium by the Athenians and their allies, there were a great number of Persians taken captive, whom the allies desired Cimon to divide among them.[2] He placed the prisoners on one side and all their clothes and jewellery on the other, and offered the allies their choice between the two. When they complained that he had made an unequal division, he bade them take whichever they pleased, assuring them that the Athenians would willingly take whichever part they rejected. By the advice of Herophytus of Samos, who urged them to take the property of the Persians, rather than the Persians themselves, the allies chose the clothes and jewels. Hereupon Cimon was thought to have made a most ridiculous division of the spoil, as the allies went swaggering about with gold bracelets, armlets, and necklaces, dressed in Median robes of rich purple, while the Athenians possessed only the naked persons of men who were altogether unfit for labor. Shortly afterward, however, the friends and relatives

[1] Another contemporary, Stesimbrotus of Thasos, who knew Cimon personally, "tells us that he was never taught music or any of the other usual accomplishments of a Greek gentleman" (Plut. *Cim.* 4). Under these circumstances it is quite possible that Themistocles showed better taste in keeping quiet than Cimon in singing.

[2] One object of the Delian Confederacy was to gain wealth by the plunder of Persian territory (no. 68). The passage throws light on the division of spoil between Athens and her allies, and on the treatment of prisoners.

of the prisoners came down to the Athenian camp from Phrygia and Lydia, and ransomed each captive for great sums of money; so that Cimon was able to give his fleet four months' pay [1] and also remit a large sum to Athens from the money paid for their ransom.

(Plut. *op. cit.* 5)

Ion the poet tells us that he was not an ill-looking man, but tall and with a thick curly head of hair.

In the debate between Ephialtes and Cimon in the Athenian popular assembly as to whether aid should be sent the Spartans against the revolted helots, Cimon favored the Spartan cause in the memorable words which Ion may himself have heard.

(Plut. *op. cit.* 16)

Ion the historian has preserved the argument which had most effect upon the Athenians, and says that Cimon besought them not to look on and see Hellas lame of one foot and Athens pulling without her yokemate.[2]

(Plut. *Pericles*, 5)

The poet Ion asserts that Pericles was overbearing and insolent in conversation, and that his pride had in it a great deal of contempt for others,[3] while he praises Cimon's civil, sensible, and polished address.

All the following passage is probably from Ion; the latter part of it certainly is.

(Plut. *op. cit.* 28)

After the reduction of Samos, Pericles returned to Athens, where he buried magnificently those who had fallen in the war, and was much admired for the funeral oration which, as is customary, was spoken by him over the graves of his countrymen.

[1] The pay of the sailor at this time was undoubtedly two obols, or about six cents, daily; Botsford, *Hellenic History*, ch. xii.

[2] In this debate, 462, Cimon won, and himself conducted the aid, consisting of a force of 4000 heavy infantry, to Peloponnese. The words quoted illustrate the direct, unpolished but forceful oratory of Cimon.

[3] Evidently Ion was thoroughly prejudiced against Pericles, and could not speak of him in a fair spirit. This passage and the following give a hint of the kind of opposition which throughout his public career Pericles had to face.

When he descended from the speaker's stand, the women greeted him, crowning him with garlands and ribbons like a victorious athlete; but Elpinice, drawing near him, said, "A fine exploit, truly, Pericles, and well worthy of a wreath, to lose many of our brave fellow-citizens, not in fighting with Persians or Phœnicians as my brother Cimon did, but in ruining a city of men of our own blood and our own allies." [1] At these words of Elpinice, Pericles merely smiled and repeated the verse of Archilochus: —

Too old art thou for rich perfumes.

Ion says that his victory over the Samians wonderfully flattered his vanity. Agamemnon, he was wont to boast, required ten years for taking a barbarian city, but he in nine months had made himself master of the first and most powerful city in Ionia.

86. The Country People in the Peloponnesian War

(Aristophanes, *Peace*, 632–52)

Hermes. Then your laboring population, flocking in from vale and plain,[2]
Never dreamed that, like the others, they themselves were sold for gain.
But as having lost their grape-stones, and desiring figs to get,
Everyone his wrapt attention on the public speakers set;
These beheld you poor and famished, lacking all your home supplies,
Straight they pitch-forked out the Goddess,[3] scouting her with yells and cries,

[1] In addition to this passage there are other indications that during the age of Cimon and the earlier career of Pericles women were socially freer and more influential than they afterward became. On this point and on the social conditions in general which these excerpts from Ion illustrate, see Botsford, *Hellenic History*, ch. xiii.

[2] On the opening of the Peloponnesian war the policy of Pericles was to bring the entire country population of Attica into the city for protection, and to permit their lands to be ravaged by the enemy (Thuc. ii. 13–17). "The others," referred to in the following line, were the Laconians, mentioned above by Aristophanes: Athenians and Laconians alike, he declares, were duped by demagogues into voting for the war. Then having lost their grapes and other subsistence, and desiring gifts of food from the state, the Attic farmers blindly followed these same evil-minded speakers.

[3] Eirene, the goddess Peace.

Whenso'er (for much she loved you) back she turned with wistful eyes.
Then with suits they vexed and harassed your substantial rich allies,
Whispering in your ear, "The fellow leans to Brasidas," [1] and you
Like a pack of hounds in chorus on the quivering victim flew.
Yea, the City, sick and pallid, shivering with disease [2] and fright,
Any calumny they cast her, ate with ravenous appetite.
Till at last your friends, perceiving whence their heavy wounds arose,
Stopped with gold the mouths of speakers, who were such disastrous foes:
Thus the scoundrels throve and prospered; whilst distracted Hellas came
Unobserved to wrack and ruin; but the fellow most to blame
Was a tanner.[3]

TRYGÆUS. Softly, softly, Hermes, master, say not so;
Let the man remain in silence, whereso'er he is, below;
For the man is ours no longer; he is all your own, you know;
Wherefore whatso'er you call him,
Knave and slave while yet amongst us,
Wrangler, jangler, false accuser,
Troubler, Muddler, All-Confuser,
You will all these names be calling
One who now is yours alone.

87. The Military Officers are Unfair toward the Farmers

(*Op. cit.* 1179–90)

CHORUS OF PEASANTS. Ah, but when at home they're [4] stationed, things that can't be borne they do,
Making up the lists unfairly, striking out and putting down

[1] Certain allies were harassed by prosecutions on the suspicion that they sympathized with the Lacedæmonian general Brasidas, while he was operating in Chalcidice and Thrace.

[2] The great plague described by Thucydides ii. 47–53.

[3] Cleon, killed in battle with Brasidas in 422, hence a dweller with Hermes in the realm of Hades.

[4] "They" were the taxiarchs, colonels of the ten tribal regiments.

Names at random. 'Tis to-morrow that the soldiers leave the town;
One poor wretch has bought no victuals, for he knew not that he must go
Till he on Pandion's [1] statue spied the list and found 'twas so,
Reading there his name inserted; off he scuds with aspect wry.
This is how they treat the farmers, but the burghers certainly
Somewhat better: godless wretches, rogues with neither shame nor — shield,[2]
Who one day, if God be willing, strict accounts to me shall yield.
For they've wronged me much and sorely:
Very lions in the City,
Very foxes in the fight.

88. If Peace would only Come

(*Op. cit.* 346–57)

Chorus of Peasants. Oh, that it were yet my fortune those delightful days to see!
Woes enough I've had to bear,
Sorry pallets, trouble, care,
Such as fell to Phormion's [3] share;
I would never more thereafter so morose and bitter be,
Nor a judge so stubborn-hearted, unrelenting, and severe; [4]
You shall find me yielding then,
Quite a tender youth again,
When these weary times depart.
Long enough we've undergone
Toils and sorrows many a one,
Worn and spent and sick at heart,
From Lyceum to Lyceum, trudging on with shield and spear.[5]

[1] Pandion, one of the ten tribal heroes, whose statues stood near the market-place. Public notices, including conscription lists of soldiers, were posted there. Before setting out, each soldier had to provide himself with three days' rations.

[2] It is hinted that the taxiarchs through cowardice have abandoned their shields in battle — the greatest disgrace that could befall a Greek.

[3] A famous naval officer of Athens in the earlier part of the war.

[4] They refer to their function as jurors, of whom there were six thousand. Noteworthy is their reputation for severity.

[5] The Lyceum, an enclosure sacred to Apollo outside the city, had been adorned

89. When Peace Comes

(*Op. cit.* 339–45)

Then will be the time for laughing,
Shouting out in jovial glee,
Sailing, sleeping, feasting, quaffing,
All the public sights to see.
Then the cottabus [1] be playing,
Then be hip-hip-hip-hurrahing,
Pass the day and pass the night
Like a regular Sybarite.

(*Op. cit.* 539–49)

Hermes. And look there,
See how the reconciled cities greet and blend
In peaceful intercourse, and laugh for joy;
And that, too, though their eyes are swollen and blackened,
And all cling fast to cupping instruments.
Trygæus. Yes, and survey the audience; by their looks
You can discern their trades.[2] Herm. O dear! O dear!
Don't you observe that man that makes the crests
Tearing his hair? And yon's a pitchfork-seller.
Fie! How he fillips the sword-cutler there.
Tryg. And see how pleased the sickle-maker looks,
Joking and poking the spear-burnisher.

(*Op. cit.* 435–53)

Trygæus. And as we pour we'll pray. O happy morn,
Be thou the source of every joy to Hellas!
And O may he who labors well to-day
Be never forced to bear a shield again!
Chorus. No; may he spend his happy days in peace,
Stirring the fire, his mistress at his side.

with fountains, trees, and buildings. There the youths took military exercise, and there during the war, as this passage implies, the recruits had their training.

[1] A favorite game among the Greeks.

[2] Interest in the sale of arms and ambition for military distinction, as indicated in this passage and in the following, were as strong motives to war in ancient times as they are at present.

TRYG. If there be any that delights in war,
King Dionysus, may he never cease
Picking out spearheads from his funny-bones.

CHOR. If any, seeking to be made a Captain,
Hates to see Peace return, O may he ever
Fare in his battles like Cleonymus.[1]

TRYG. If any merchant, selling spears or shields,
Would fain have battles, to improve his trade,
May he be seized by thieves and eat raw barley.

CHOR. If any would-be General won't assist us,
Or any slave preparing to desert,
May he be flogged and broken on the wheel.
But on ourselves all joy: hip, hip, hurrah!

TRYG. Don't talk of being hipped—hurrah's the word to-day.

CHOR. Hurrah, hurrah, hurrah's the word to-day!

(*Op. cit.* 1128–37)

What a pleasure, what a treasure,
What a great delight to me,
From the cheese and from the onions,
From the helmet to be free.
For I can't enjoy a battle
And I love to pass my days
With my wine and boon companions
Round the merry, merry blaze,
When the logs are dry and seasoned,
And the fire is burning bright,
And I roast the pease and chestnuts
In the embers all alight.

90. BACK TO THE COUNTRY

(*Op. cit.* 551–81)

TRYGÆUS. O yes, O yes! the farmers all may go
Back to their homes, farm implements and all.
You can leave your darts behind you; yea, for sword and spear
shall cease.

[1] Often ridiculed as a coward by Aristophanes.

All things all around are teeming with the mellow gifts of Peace;
Shout you pæans, march away to labor in your fields to-day.

CHORUS. Day most welcome to the farmers and to all the just and true,
Now I see you, I am eager once again my vines to view,
And the fig-trees which I planted in my boyhood's early prime,
I would fain salute and visit after such a weary time.
First, then, comrades, to the Goddess be our grateful prayers addressed,
Who has freed us from the Gorgons[1] and the fear-inspiring crest.
Next a little salt provision fit for country uses buy,
Then with merry expedition homeward to the fields we'll hie.

HERMES. O Poseidon! fair their order, sweet their serried ranks to see:
Right and tight, like rounded biscuits, or a thronged festivity.

TRYG. Yes, by Zeus! the well-armed mattock seems to sparkle as we gaze,
And the burnished pitchforks glitter in the sun's delightful rays.
Very famously with those will they clear the vineyard rows.
So that I myself am eager homeward to my farm to go,
Breaking up the little furrows, long-neglected, with the hoe.

Think of all the thousand pleasures,
Comrades, which to Peace we owe,
All the life of ease and comfort
Which she gave us long ago;
Figs and olives, wine and myrtles,
Luscious fruits preserved and dried,
Banks of fragrant violets, blowing
By the crystal fountain's side;
Scenes for which our hearts are yearning,
Joys that we have missed so long —
— Comrades, here is Peace returning,
Greet her back with dance and song!

[1] A common device for a shield.

91. Mayfair

(*Op. cit.* 887–904)

Theoria — "Festival," here translated "Mayfair." Trygæus speaks, introducing a personification of Mayfair to the Council: —

Councillors! Magistrates! behold Mayfair!
And O remember what a deal of fun
That word implies; what pastimes and what feasts!
See here's a famous kitchen chest she brings;
'Tis blacked a little; for in times of Peace
The jovial Council kept its saucepans there.
Take her and welcome her with joy; and then
To-morrow morning let the sports begin:
Then we'll enjoy the Fair in every fashion,
With boxing matches and with wrestling bouts,
And tricks and games, while striplings soused in oil
Try the pancration,[1] fist and leg combined.
Then the third day from this we'll hold the races,
The eager jockeys riding; the great cars
Puffing and blowing through the lists, till dashed
Full on some turning-post, they reel and fall
Over and over; everywhere you see
The hapless drivers wallowing on the plain.[2]

92. On a Rainy Day

(*Op. cit.* 1140–58)

Chorus of Peasants. Ah, there's nothing half so sweet as when the seed is in the ground,
God a gracious rain is sending, and a neighbor saunters round.
"O Comarchides," he hails me; "How shall we enjoy the hours?"
"Drinking seems to suit my fancy, what with these benignant showers.

[1] A contest consisting of boxing and wrestling.

[2] For a vivid account of a chariot race, see Sophocles, *Electra*, 696 *sqq.*, quoted in Botsford, *Source-Book of Ancient History*, 189–91.

Therefore let three quarts, my mistress, of your kidney-beans be fried,
Mix them nicely up with barley, and your choicest figs provide;
Syra, run and shout to Manes, call him in without delay,
'Tis no time to stand and dawdle pruning out the vines to-day,
Nor to break the clods about them, now the ground is soaking through.
Bring me out from home the fieldfare, bring me out the siskins [1] two;
Then there ought to be some beestings, four good plates of hare beside,
(Hah! unless the cat purloined them yesterday at eventide;
Something scuffled in the pantry, something made a noise and fuss;)
If you find them, one's for father, bring the other three to us.
Ask Æschinades to send us myrtle branches green and strong;
Bid Charinades attend us, shouting as you pass along.
Then we'll sit and drink together,
God the while refreshing, blessing
All the labors of our hands."

93. The Public Slave in the Temple of the Delphian Apollo

(Euripides, *Ion*, 36 *sqq.*)

Often illegitimate children as well as those of poor parents were exposed in a public place, where they either died or were taken up by passersby, occasionally to be adopted but more frequently to be reduced to slavery. In myth Creusa, daughter of Erechtheus, an early king of Athens, secretly bore to Apollo a son, Ion, whom the mother exposed in a wicker basket in the cave of Agraulus, in the northern declivity of the Acropolis. At the request of Apollo, Hermes rescued the child and carrying him to Delphi, placed him on the threshold of the shrine of Apollo. The rest of the story is told in the following passage remarkable for the beautiful description of Delphi, its references to Athens, and the light it throws on the almost enviable life of a public slave in a temple like that of Apollo.

HERMES. To do my brother Loxias a service, I took up the woven basket and bore it off, and at the threshold of the shrine

[1] Fieldfare, a species of thrush; siskin, a species of finch.

I have laid the babe, after opening the lid of the wicker cradle that the child might be seen. But just as the Sun-God was starting forth to run his course, a priestess chanced to enter the God's shrine; and when her eyes lit upon the tender babe, she thought it strange that any Delphian maid should dare cast her illegitimate child down at the temple of the God; wherefore her purpose was to remove him beyond the altar, but from pity she renounced her cruel thought; and the God to help his child did second her pity to save the babe from being cast out. She took him, accordingly, and brought him up, but knew not that Phœbus was his sire, nor of the mother that bare him, nor yet did the child know his parents. While yet he was a child, around the altar that fed him he would ramble at his play, but when he came to man's estate, the Delphians made him Treasurer of the God and Steward of all his store, and found him true. Till the present day, therefore, he leads a holy life in the God's temple. Meantime Creusa, mother of this youth, is married to Xuthus. . . . After many years of wedded life he and Creusa are still childless; wherefore they come to this oracle of Apollo in their desire of offspring. To this end is Loxias guiding their destiny nor hath it escaped his ken, as some suppose. For when Xuthus enters this shrine, the God will give him his own son and declare that Xuthus is the sire, that so the boy may come to his mother's home and be acknowledged by Creusa, while the marriage of Loxias remains a secret, and the child obtains his rights; and he shall cause him, throughout all the breadth of Hellas, to be called Ion, founder of the realm in Asia. . . .

Ion. Lo! the Sun-God is e'en now turning toward earth his chariot-car resplendent; before yon fire the stars retire to night's mysterious gloom from forth the firmament; the peaks of Parnassus, where no man may set foot, are all ablaze, and hail the car of day for mortal's service. To Phœbus' roof mounts up the smoke of myrrh, offering of the desert. There on the holy tripod sits the Delphian priestess, chanting to the ears of Hellas, in numbers loud, whate'er Apollo doth proclaim. Ye Delphians, votaries of Phœbus, away to Castalia's gushing fount as silver clear, and when you have bathed you in waters pure, enter the shrine; and keep your lips in holy silence that it may be well. Be careful to utter words of good omen amongst yourselves to those who wish to consult the oracle; while I, with laurel sprays and sacred wreaths and drops of water sprinkled o'er the floor, will purify the entrance to the shrine of Phœbus — my task each day from childhood's hour. With my bow will I put to flight the flocks of feathered fowls that harm his sacred offerings; for here in Phœbus's shrine, which nurtured me, I minister, an orphan, fatherless and motherless . . .

Enter chorus of maid servants of Creusa, queen of the Athenians; the members speak individually, admiring the paintings or sculptured decorations of the temple.

CHORUS 1. It is not in holy Athens only that there are courts of the Gods with fine colonnades, and the worship of Apollo, guardian of highways; but here, too, at the shrine of Loxias, son of Latona, shines the lovely eye of day on faces twain.

CHORUS 2. Just look at this! here is the son of Zeus killing with his golden scimitar the watersnake of Lerna.[1] Do look at him my friend!

CHORUS 1. Yes, I see. And close to him stands another with a blazing torch uplifted; who is he? Can this be the warrior Iolaüs,[2] whose story is told on my embroidery, who shares with the son of Zeus his labors, and helps him in the moil?

CHORUS 3. O but look at this! a man mounted on a winged horse, killing a fire-breathing monster with three bodies.[3]

CHORUS 1. I am turning my eyes in every direction. Behold the rout of the giants carved on these walls of stone.

CHORUS 4. Yes, yes, good friends, I am looking.

CHORUS 5. Dost see her [4] standing over Enceladus, brandishing her shield with the Gorgon's head?

CHORUS 6. I see Pallas, my own Goddess.

CHORUS 7. Again, dost thou see the massy thunderbolt all aflame in the far-darting hands of Zeus?

CHORUS 8. I do; 'tis blasting with its flame Mimas,[5] that deadly foe.

[1] Lerna, a place near Argos where Heracles killed the Hydra, here described as a watersnake.

[2] Iolaüs, a kinsman and faithful comrade of Heracles.

[3] Bellerophon killing the Chimæra.

[4] Athena (Pallas) standing triumphant over the giant Enceladus.

[5] Mimas, a giant, killed by a thunderbolt as here described.

CHORUS 9. Bromius,[1] too, the God of revelry, is slaying another of the sons of Earth with his thyrsus of ivy, never meant for battle.

CHORUS 1. Thou that art stationed by this fane, to thee I do address me; may we pass the threshold of these vaults with our fair white feet?

ION. Nay, ye must not, stranger ladies.

CHORUS 10. May I ask thee about something I have heard?

ION. What wouldst thou ask?

CHORUS 11. Is it true that the temple of Phœbus stands upon the centre of the world?

ION. Aye, there it stands with garlands decked and gorgeous all around.

CHORUS 12. E'en so the legend saith.

ION. If ye have offered a sacrificial cake before the shrine and have aught ye wish to ask Phœbus, approach the altar; but enter not the inmost sanctuary, save ye have sacrificed sheep.

CHORUS 13. I understand; but we have no mind to trespass against the God's law; the pictures here without will entertain us.

ION. Feast your eyes on all ye may.

CHORUS 14. My mistress gave me leave to see these vaulted chambers.

ION. Whose handmaids do ye avow yourselves?

CHORUS 15. The temple where Pallas dwells is the nursing-home of my lords. But lo! here is she of whom thou askest.

Creusa enters, and in a long conversation with Ion reveals her anxiety for the son she has borne to Apollo. Thereupon Ion, when left alone, calls Apollo to account for his misconduct. The Gods ought to obey the laws they have established for mankind.

ION. Why doth this stranger lady hint dark reproaches against the God unceasingly? . . . Maybe because she is hiding something needing secrecy? Yet what have I to do with the daughter of Erechtheus? She is naught to me. No, I will go to the laver, and from golden ewers sprinkle the holy water. Yet I must warn Phœbus of what is happening to him; he wrongs a maid and proves unfaithful to her, and after secretly becoming the parent of a son leaves him to die. O Phœbus, do not so, but as thou art supreme,

[1] Bromius, Dionysus.

follow in virtue's track; for whosoever of mortal men transgresses, him the Gods punish. How, then, can it be just that you should enact your laws for men, and yourselves incur the charge of breaking them? Now I will put this case, though it will never happen. Wert thou, were Poseidon, and Zeus, lord of Heaven, to make atonement to mankind for every act of lawless love, ye would empty your temples in paying fines for your misdeeds. For when ye pursue pleasure in preference to the claims of prudence, ye act unjustly; no longer is it fair to call men wicked, if we are imitating the evil deeds of Gods, but rather are those who give us such examples.

After a time Xuthus enters; and, directed by Apollo to claim Ion as his son, he invites the young man to accompany him to Athens, there to enter public life with a view to succeeding to the throne. The reply of Ion indicates some of the obstacles in the way of a new man's success in Athenian politics, and by contrast the blessedness of the life of a slave in office at Apollo's shrine.

ION. . . . Athens, I am told — that glorious city of a native race — owns no aliens;[1] therefore I shall force my entrance there under a twofold disadvantage, — as an alien's son and base-born as I am. Branded with this reproach, while as yet I am unsupported, I shall get the name of a mere nobody, a son of nobodies; and if I win my way to the highest place in the state, and seek to be someone, I shall be hated by those who have no influence, for superiority is galling; while amongst men of worth who could show their wisdom but are silent, and take no interest in politics, I shall incur ridicule and be thought a fool for not keeping quiet in such a fault-finding city. Again, if I win a name among the men of mark who are engaged in politics, still more will jealous votes bar my progress; for thus, father, it is ever wont to be: they who have the city's ear, and have already made their mark, are most bitter against all rivals. Again if I, a stranger, come to a home that knows me not, and to that childless wife who before had thee as partner of her sorrow, but now will feel the bitterness of having to bear her fortune all alone — how, I ask, shall I not fairly earn her hatred, when I take my stand beside thee; while she, still childless, sees thy dear pledge with bitter eyes; and then

[1] Athens rarely granted the citizenship to aliens.

thou have to choose between deserting me and regarding her, or honoring me and utterly confounding thy home? How many a murder, and death by deadly drugs, have wives devised for husbands! Besides I pity that wife of thine, father, with her childless old age beginning; she little deserves to pine in barrenness, a daughter of a noble race.

That princely state we fondly praise is pleasant to the eye; but yet in its mansions sorrow lurks; for who is happy or by fortune blest that has to live his life in fear of violence, with many a sidelong glance? Rather would I live among the common folk and taste their bliss, than be a tyrant who delights in making evil men his friends, and hates the good in terror of his life. Perchance wilt thou tell me, 'Gold outweighs all these evils, and wealth is sweet.' I have no wish to be abused for holding tightly to my pelf, nor yet to have the trouble of it. Be mine a moderate fortune free from annoyance! Now hear the blessings, father, that here were mine; first leisure, man's chiefest joy, with but moderate trouble; no villain ever drove me from my path, and that is a grievance hard to bear, to make room and give way to sorry knaves. My duty was to pray unto the Gods, or with mortal men converse, a minister to their joys, not to their sorrows. And I was ever dismissing one company of guests, while another took their place, so that from the charm of novelty I was always welcome. That honesty which men must pray for, even against their will, custom and nature did conspire to plant in me in the sight of Phœbus. Now when I think on this, I deem that I am better here than there, father. So let me live on here, for 'tis an equal charm to joy in high estate or in a humble fortune find a pleasure.

94. Origin of Various Social Customs

(Critias, quoted by Athenæus i. 50. Translated by E. G. S.)

The cottabus[1] is from Sicilian soil, a feat of excellence, which we establish as the mark for hurling remnant drops of wine; and then the Sicilian carriage in beauty and in costliness is preëmi-

[1] The object of this game, which was very popular at banquets, was to throw in a high curve at a mark the last few drops of the wine-cup without spilling any of it. Illustrations are found in vase paintings.

nent. . . . The armchair is from Thessaly, most luxurious seat for limbs; but for the couch of rest chiefly possess distinction both Miletus and Chios, the sea-town of Œnopion.[1] Of Tuscan craft is foremost the cup of hammered gold, and everything of bronze, all that adorns the home in every need.[2] Phœnicians devised the letters that preserve discourse;[3] Thebes was the first to join together the carriage chair; and cargo-bearing boats the Carians, stewards of the sea. But she who did invent the child of wheel and earth and oven, most famous pottery, useful dispenser in the household, 'twas she who did establish a fair trophy at Marathon.[4]

(*Idem*, quoted by Athen. x. 41. Translated by E. G. S.)

This is the usage at Sparta and practice established, that (all) should drink from the same winebearing cup, nor make a gift of drinking healths in citing (friends) by name, nor pass it toward the right within the brotherhood (thiasos) . . .

[A Lydian hand of Asian origin invented goblets,][5] and passing healths toward the right, and calling out by naming him to whom one desires to drink a health. Then starting with such draughts, they loose their tongues to stories shameful, they enfeeble more their bodies; upon the eye doth settle blinding darkness; oblivion melts away the memory of the mind. Intelligence fails; like slaves they have licentious manners — upon them falls expenditure that ruins house and home.

But the lads of Lacedæmon drink so much only as carries every mind to gladsome hope, to kindly cheer and talk and measured mirth. Such drinking is useful for the body and for the mind and store; well to the doings of Aphrodite and to sleep — the port of toil — it is adjusted, and to the Goddess Health, most charming to mankind, and to Self-Restraint, next door to Piety.

[1] Œnopion, son of Dionysus, led a company of Cretans to colonize Chios, according to Pausanias vii. 4. 8.

[2] From the contents of Etruscan tombs, as well as from various literary sources, we learn that the Etruscans were famous for their bronze wares.

[3] It is now believed that the Phœnicians derived the elements of the alphabet, in whole or part, from the Minoan Cretans; Evans, *Scripta Minoa*, I. 77 *sqq.*

[4] Athenæus remarks: "In fact the pottery of Athens is deservedly praised"; *loc. cit.*

[5] This line is bracketed by Kaibel. The word ἄγγεα literally "pails," probably means large drinking cups, goblets. The excessive drinking of the Lydians is contrasted with the Lacedæmonian moderation. Critias was a great admirer of Sparta.

95. The Wonderful Powers of Man

(Sophocles, *Antigone*, 332–75)

Wonders are many, and none is more wonderful than man; the power that crosses the white sea, driven by the stormy south-wind, making a path under surges that threaten to engulf him; and Earth, the eldest of the gods, the immortal, the unwearied, doth he wear, turning the soil with the offspring of horses, as the ploughs go to and fro from year to year.

And the light-hearted race of birds, and the tribes of savage beasts, and the sea-brood of the deep, he snares in the meshes of his woven toils, he leads captive, man excellent in wit. And he masters by his arts the beast whose lair is in the wilds, who roams the hills; he tames the horse of shaggy mane, he puts the yoke upon its neck, he tames the tireless mountain bull.

And speech and swift-winged thought and all the moods that mould a state, hath he taught himself; and how to flee the arrows of the frost, when 'tis hard lodging under the clear sky, and the arrows of the rushing rain; yea, he hath resource for all; without resource he meets nothing that must come; only against Death shall he call for aid in vain; but from baffling maladies he hath devised escapes.[1]

Cunning beyond fancy's dream is the fertile skill which brings him now to evil, now to good. When he honors the laws of the land, and that justice which he hath sworn by the gods to uphold, proudly stands his city; no city hath he who for his rashness dwells with sin. Never may he share my hearth, never think my thoughts, who doth these things!

96. Woman's Self-Sacrifice

(Euripides, *Alcestis*, 280–368)

In the age of Pericles the tendency was to limit the social freedom of Athenian women and to confine them as much as possible to the home. Doubtless the great majority of women met this demand upon them in the spirit of self-sacrifice best shown in Alcestis, whom Euripides presented on the stage in 438.

[1] On the progress of medical science, see nos. 79–81.

Admetus, a Thessalian lord, is doomed to die unless he can find a substitute. After he has vainly besought his friends and kinsfolk, including his father and mother, to go down to Hades' realm in his place, his wife Alcestis willingly offers to die that he may live, coward and weakling as he is. Especially interesting, too, in the following passage is the sentiment regarding a second marriage.

Alcestis. Admetus, lo! thou seest how it is with me; to thee I fain would tell my wishes ere I die. Thee I set before myself, and instead of living have ensured thy life, and so I die, though I need not have died for thee, but might have taken for my husband whom I would of the Thessalians, and have had a home blessed with royal power; reft of thee, with my children orphans, I cared not to live, nor, though crowned with youth's fair gifts, wherein I used to joy, did I grudge them. Yet the father that begat thee, the mother that bare thee, gave thee up, though they had reached a time of life when to die were well, so saving thee their child, and winning noble death. For thou wert their only son, nor had they any hope, when thou wert dead, of other offspring. And I should have lived and thou the remnant of our days, nor wouldst thou have wept thy wife's loss, nor have had an orphan family. But some god hath caused these things to be even as they are. Enough! Remember thou the gratitude due to me for this; yea, for I shall never ask thee for an adequate return, for naught is prized more highly than our life; but just is my request, as thou thyself must say, since I no less than thou dost love these children, if so be thou thinkest aright. Be content to let them rule my house, and do not marry a new wife to be a stepmother to these children, for she from jealousy, if so she be a woman worse than me, will stretch out her hand against the children of our union. Then do not this, I beseech thee. For the stepmother that succeeds, hateth children of a former match, cruel as the viper's are her tender mercies. A son, 'tis true, hath in his sire a tower of strength, [to whom he speaks and has his answer back];[1] but thou, my daughter, how shall thy maidenhood be passed in honor? What shall thy experience be of thy father's wife? She may fasten on thee some foul report in thy youthful bloom, and frustrate thy marriage. Never shall thy mother lead thee to the bridal bed, nor by her presence in thy

[1] This line is probably spurious.

travail hearten thee, my child, when a mother's kindness triumphs over all. No, for I must die; and lo! this evil cometh to me not to-morrow nor yet on the third day of the month, but in a moment shall I be counted among the souls that are no more. Fare ye well, be happy; and thou, husband, canst boast thou hadst a peerless wife, and you, children, that you had such a one for mother.

Chorus. Take heart; I do not hesitate to answer for him; he will perform all this, unless his mind should go astray.

Adm. It shall be so, fear not it shall; alive thou wert the only wife I had, and dead thou shalt, none else, be called mine; no Thessalian maid shall ever take thy place and call me lord; not though she spring from lineage high, nor though besides she be the fairest of her sex. Of children I have enough; god grant I may in them be blessed, for in thee has it been otherwise. No year-long mourning will I keep for thee, but all my life through, lady; loathing the mother that bare me, and hating my father, for they were friends in word but not in deed. But thou didst give thy dearest for my life and save it. May I not then mourn to lose a wife like thee? And I will put an end to revelry, to social gathering over the wine, forego the festal crown and music which once reigned in my halls. For nevermore will I touch the lyre nor lift my soul in song to the Lydian flute, for thou hast taken with thee all my joy in life. . . . Thou wilt come to me in dreams and gladden me. For sweet it is to see our friends, come they when they will, e'en by night.

Had I the tongue, the tuneful voice of Orpheus to charm Demeter's daughter or her husband by my lay and bring thee back from Hades, I had gone down, nor Pluto's hound, nor Charon, ferryman of souls, whose hand is on the oar, had held me back, till to the light I had restored thee alive. At least do thou await me there, against the hour I die, prepare a home for me to be my true wife still. For in this same cedar coffin I will bid these children lay me with thee and stretch my limbs by thine; for never even in death may I be severed from thee, alone found faithful of them all.

(*Op. cit.* 895–1005; Way)

The following passage appreciates the worth of Alcestis who has sacrificed herself to save her husband, and expresses some interesting thoughts on future life and on the resistless power of Necessity.

ADMETUS [1]

O long grief and pain,
For beloved ones passed!
Why didst thou restrain,
When myself I had cast
Down into her grave, with the noblest to lie peace-lulled at the last?
Not one soul, but two
Had been Hades' prey,
Souls utterly true
United for aye,
Which together o'er waves of the underworld-mere had passed this day.

CHORUS [2]

Of my kin was there one,
And the life's light failed
In his halls of a son,
One meet to be wailed,
His only beloved; howbeit the manhood within him prevailed;
And the ills heaven-sent
As a man did he bear,
Though by this was he bent
Unto silvered hair,
Far on in life's path, without son for his remnant of weakness to care.

ADMETUS [3]

Oh how can I tread
Thy threshold, fair home?

[1] Admetus regrets that he had been prevented from dying with his wife, to whom he was devotedly attached.

[2] The Chorus gives him an example of patient resignation, with the implication that he ought to be instructed by it.

[3] Here Admetus contrasts the present desolation of his home with its happiness on the day when he brought into it his bride with festal gaiety. Thereupon the Chorus, changing their manner of consolation, rebukes him sternly though pityingly: with a great price indeed he has gained his object.

How shelter mine head
'Neath thy roof, now the doom
Of my fate's dice changeth? — ah me, what change upon all things is come!
For with torches aflame
Of the Pelian pine,
And with bride-song I came
In thy hour divine,
Upbearing the hand of a wife — thine hand, O darling mine!
Followed revellers, raising
Acclaim: ever broke
From the lips of them praising,
Of the dead as they spoke,
And of me, how the noble, the children of kings, Love joined near his yoke.
But for bridal song
Is the wail of the dead,
And, for white-robed throne,
Black vesture hath led
Me to halls where the ghost of delight lieth couched on a desolate bed.

CHORUS

To the trance of thy bliss
Sudden anguish was brought.
Never lesson like this
To thine heart had been taught:
Yet thy life hast thou won, and thy soul hast delivered from death: is it naught?
Thy wife hath departed:
Love tender and true
Hath she left; stricken-hearted,
Wherein is this new?
Hath death not unyoked from the chariot of Love full many ere you?

ADMETUS

Friends I account the fortune of my wife
Happier than mine, albeit it seem not so.
For naught of grief shall touch her any more.

But I, unmeet to live, my doom outrun,
Shall drag out bitter days: I know it now.
How shall I bear to enter this my home?
Speaking to whom, and having speech of whom,
Shall I find joy of entering? — whither turn me?
The solitude within shall drive me forth,
Whenso I see my wife's couch tenantless,
And seats whereon she sat, and 'neath the roof,
All foul the floor; when on my knees my babes
Falling shall weep their mother, servants moan
The peerless mistress from the mansion lost.
All this within: but from the world without
Me shall Thessalian bridals chase, and throngs
Where women gossip — oh I shall not bear
On these young matrons like my wife to look!
And whatsoever foe I have shall scoff:
'Lo there who basely liveth — dared not die,
But whom he wedded gave, a coward's ransom,
And 'scaped from Hades. Count ye him a man?
He hates his parents, though himself was loth
To die!' Such ill report, besides my griefs,
Shall mine be. Ah what honor is mine to live,
O friends, in evil fame, in evil plight?

CHORUS [1]

I have mused on the words of the wise,
  Of the mighty in song;
I have lifted mine heart to the skies,
I have searched all truth with mine eyes;
  But none more strong
Than Fate have I found: there is naught
  In the tablets of Thrace,
Neither drugs whereof Orpheus taught,

[1] Failing in every effort to console Admetus, the Chorus, in a splendid Ode, addresses Necessity (in the translation "Fate"), the Goddess unworshiped by man, who rules the human race, without whose aid even Zeus could not accomplish his purpose. Interesting is the last paragraph, which gives the departed Alcestis a character like that of the mediæval saint.

Nor in all that Apollo brought
To Asclepius' race,
When the herbs of healing he severed, and out of their anguish delivered
The pain distraught.

There is none other Goddess beside
To the altars of whom
No man draweth near, nor hath cried
To her image, nor victim hath died,
Averting her doom.
O Goddess, more mighty for ill
Come not upon me
Than in days overpast; for his will
Even Zeus may in no wise fulfil
Unholpen of thee.
Steel is molten as water before thee, but never relenting came o'er thee,
Who art ruthless still.

Thee, friend, hath the Goddess gripped: from her hands never wrestler hath slipped.
Yet be strong to endure: never mourning shall bring our beloved returning

From the nethergloom up to the light.
Yea, the heroes of Gods begotten,
They fade into darkness, forgotten
In death's chill night.
Dear was she in days ere we lost her,
Dear yet, though she lie with the dead.
None nobler shall Earth-mother foster
Than the wife of thy bed.

Not as mounds of the dead which have died, so account we the tomb of thy bride;
But oh, let the worship and honor that we render to Gods rest upon her:
Unto her let the wayfarer pray.

As he treadeth the pathway that trendeth
Aside from the highway, and bendeth
At her shrine, he shall say:
'Her life for her lord's was given;
With the blest now abides she on high.
Hail, Queen, show us grace from thy heaven!'
Even so shall they cry.

97. Sorrows of a Wife

(Euripides, *Medeia*, 204–66)

Having come to Corinth with his wife Medeia and his two sons, Jason has repudiated his wife and has married the daughter of the Corinthian king. Medeia, full of sorrow for her misfortune and of hatred for Jason, approaches with a bitter cry. The Chorus of sympathetic Corinthian women speak among themselves of her sad plight, after which she addresses them.

Chorus. I heard a bitter cry of lamentation! loudly, bitterly she calls on the traitor of her marriage bed, her perfidious spouse; by grievous wrongs oppressed she invokes Themis,[1] bride of Zeus, witness of oaths, who brought her unto Hellas, the land that fronts the strand of Asia,[2] o'er the sea by night through ocean's boundless gate.

Medeia. From the house I have come forth, Corinthian ladies, for fear lest ye be blaming me; for well I know that amongst men many by showing pride have got them an ill name and a reputation for indifference, both those who shun men's gaze and those who move among the stranger crowd, and likewise they who choose a quiet walk in life. For there is no just discernment in the eyes of men, for they, or ever they have surely learnt their neighbor's heart, loathe him at first sight, though never wronged by him; and so a stranger most of all should adopt a city's views;[3] nor do I commend that citizen, who, in the stubbornness of his heart, from churlishness resents the city's will.

[1] Themis, divine legislator, was especially protector of the marriage tie, desecrated by Jason.

[2] Medeia was a foreigner, from Colchis, a city on the eastern coast of the Black Sea.

[3] Throughout Greek literature are many references to the hard lot of the alien resident; *cf.* no. 93. Those of Attica, however, were well protected, and stood on a social level with the citizens.

But on me hath fallen this unforeseen disaster, and sapped my life; ruined am I, and long to resign the boon of existence, kind friends, and die. For he who was all the world to me, as well thou knowest, hath turned out the veriest villain, my own husband. Of all things that have life and sense we women are the most hapless creatures; first must we buy a husband at an exorbitant price, and o'er ourselves a tyrant set which is an evil worse than the first; and herein lies a most important issue, whether our choice be good or bad. For divorce is discreditable to women, nor can we disown our lords. Next must the wife, coming as she does to ways and customs new, since she hath not learned the lesson in her home, have a diviner's eye to see how best to treat the partner of her life. If haply we perform these tasks with thoroughness and tact, and the husband live with us, without resenting the yoke, our life is a happy one; if not, 'twere best to die. But when a man is vexed with what he finds indoors, he goeth forth and rids his soul of its disgust, betaking him to some friend or comrade of like age; whilst we must needs regard his single self.[1]

And yet they say we live secure at home, while they are at the wars — with their sorry reasoning; for I would gladly take my stand in battle array three times o'er, than once give birth. But enough! this language suits not thee as it does me; thou hast a city here, a father's house, some joy in life, and friends to share thy thoughts; but I am destitute, without a city, and therefore scorned by my husband, a captive I from a foreign shore, with no mother, brother, or kinsman in whom to find a new haven of refuge from this calamity.[2] Wherefore this one boon and only this I wish to win from thee, — thy silence, if haply I can some way or other devise to avenge me on my husband for this cruel treatment, and on the man who gave to him his daughter, and on her who is his wife. For though a woman be timorous enough in all else, and as regards courage, a coward at the mere sight of steel, yet in the moment she finds her honor wronged, no heart is filled with deadlier thoughts than hers. . . .

[1] Though Athenian women of the higher classes could visit one another, they had far less liberty than the men to move about through the city.

[2] Usually the father or brother was ready to give refuge and protection to a woman abused by her husband; of this fact the Attic orators furnish many illustrations.

(*Op. cit.* 807–08; Way)

Let none account me impotent or weak,
Or spiritless! — O nay, in other sort,
Grim to my foes, and kindly to my friends.
Most glorious is the life of such as I.[1]

98. Children a Great Care

(Euripides, *Medeia*, 1081–1115)

Chorus. Oft ere now have I pursued subtler themes and have faced graver issues than woman's sex should seek to probe; but then e'en we aspire to culture, which dwells with us to teach us wisdom; I say not all; for small is the class amongst women — one maybe shalt thou find mid many — that is not incapable of culture. And amongst mortals I do assert that they who are wholly without experience and have never had children far surpass in happiness those who are parents. The childless, because they have never proved whether children grow to be a blessing or curse to men, are removed from all share in many troubles; whilst those who have a sweet race of children growing up in their houses do wear away, as I perceive, their whole life through; first with the thought how they may train them up in virtue, next how they shall leave their sons the means to live; and after all this 'tis far from clear whether on good or bad children they bestow their toil. But one last crowning woe for every mortal man I will now name; suppose that they have found sufficient means to live, and seen their children grow to man's estate and walk in virtue's path, still if fortune so befall, comes death and bears the children's bodies off to Hades. Can it be any profit to the gods to heap upon us mortal men, beside our other woes, this further grief for children lost, a grief surpassing all?

[1] It can readily be seen that Medeia was made of sterner stuff than were most Hellenic women; Botsford, *Hellenic History*, ch. xx.

99. An Unequal Match and its Results

(Aristophanes, *Clouds*, 41–72)

Strepsiades, a well-to-do but uncultured farmer, marries a noble lady, niece of Megacles of the mighty Alcmeonid gens. The incompatibility of this wedded pair, their quarrel over the naming of their first son, and the prodigality of the latter when he becomes a young man and a knight, are set forth in the following lines.

Strepsiades. Oh that that love-broker[1] who put me on to marry your mother — beshrew her — had perished first! For a rustic lot was mine — a most delightful life — full of slovenry, unaffrighted by bugs, carelessly diffused — a life full-fraught with honey-bees and droves and olive-cakes; and then I had to ally me to the niece of Megacles, son of Megacles — a rural fellow to a city-bred madam, a proud and mincing peat, a very Cœsyra[2] incarnate, wedded and abode with her, I with the reek about me of must, of fig-cakes, of wool — in a word, of affluence, while she was all myrrh and fragrance and soft caresses, spendthrift ways, gormandising epicurism, and worse.[3] . . .

Afterward, then, when this son of ours was born, to me and to my worthy mistress, we forthwith at brain-buffets fell about his name: she wanted some horsey tag — something with hippus in it — Xanthippus or Charippus or Callippides; while I was for naming him after his thrifty grandfather, Pheidonides.[4] For a while accordingly we kept at jars but at length we compromised on Pheidippides.[5] Now she was for making a dandy of this son of ours; 'Twill be a brave day,' quoth she, 'when a man full-

[1] Professional match-makers were common in ancient Athens.

[2] Cœsyra, said to have been a fashionable lady of Eretria who had married into the Alcmeonid gens.

[3] "And worse," a general expression for the specific but untranslatable epithets of the text.

[4] Usually the eldest son was named after the paternal grandfather. But in case the wife was of higher rank than the husband, as here, she commonly chose the name from her own family. The ending hippus ("horse") is indicative of knightly rank. Xanthippus, Charippus, etc., are names of men of the upper class. Pheidonides signifies "son of Thrift," or "Thrifty-son," and could only belong to the middle or poorer class.

[5] Pheidippides has some such meaning as "son of a sparer of horses," applied ironically to this spendthrift young knight.

grown, you shall drive your car to the citadel, in a festal robe, like Megacles.' 'Nay rather,' said I, 'when you shall drive your goats from the scaur, in a greasy fell, like your father.'

(*Op. cit.* 12–40)

The scene of the following passage is a bedroom; Pheidippides, the son, now in early manhood, is talking in his sleep, while the father is kept awake by the worry of his debts.

STREPS. (*Tossing about in bed*). I'm so nettled and stung by these expenses and stable bills and debts — thanks to this son of mine. But he, curled darling, jaunts up and down, and drives his four-in-hand, and dreams of horses. Meanwhile on me ruin speeds apace, as I watch the moon bring on the day of doom, for the interests mount up.[1] (*Jumping up.*) What, boy! light the lamp and fetch me my table-book that I may read the rubrics of my debts, and make up the audit of the interest. Let me see how much I really owe. '*To Pasias fifty minas.*' [2] Why fifty minas to Pasias? What did I spend it on? 'Twas for the stone horse — a murrain on it! I wish a stone had knocked out my eye ere I had seen him.

PHEIDIPPIDES (*In sleep*). Philon,[3] you're cheating; keep to your own track.

STREPS. Ah, this is the cause of my ruin; he dreams of the turf, — e'en in the watches of the night.

PHEID. How many courses will the war-cars run?

STREPS. 'Courses!' A pretty course you make me, your father, run. (*Turning to his ledger.*) But after Pasias, within whose danger do I stand? '*Twelve minas to Amynias*' — for pelting car and a brace of wheels.

PHEID. Give the horse a good roll and lead him home.

STREPS. O foolish youth, you have rolled me out of my estate; for I have been cast in suits, and others are demanding surety for the interest.

PHEID. (*Awakening*). Father, pray why are you so peevish, and toss about the whole night?

[1] Interest was payable at the end of the month.

[2] Mina, about $18.00.

[3] Philon, probably a rival in the race.

STREPS. A bailiff [1] from the bed-clothes is biting me.

PHEID. Suffer me, good sir, to sleep a little.

STREPS. Sleep on then; but be assured that all these debts will turn upon your head.

100. PROGRAM OF WOMEN FOR THE BETTER GOVERNMENT OF ATHENS

(Aristophanes, *Lysistrate*, 486–597)

The *Lysistrate*, from which the following passage has been quoted, is interesting as the first-known piece of literature which treats of "woman's rights." Aristophanes proposes, between jest and earnest, that the women of Athens should assume the reins of government, make peace with the Peloponnesians, join the allies on equal terms with the Athenians in "one mighty political aggregate," and improve the administration in various ways. It is a great credit to the women that these enlightened ideas should be attributed to them. The women have seized the Acropolis, whereupon the Proboulos (p. 346, n. 3) approaches them and talks with their leaders about their intentions.

PROBOULOS. Foremost and first I should wish to inquire of them,
what is this silly disturbance about?
Why have ye ventured to seize the Acropolis,
locking the gates and barring us out?
LYS. Keeping the silver securely in custody,
lest for its sake ye continue the war.
PROB. What, is the war for the sake of the silver, then?
LYS. Yes; and all other disputes that there are.
Why is Peisander [2] forever embroiling us,
Why do the rest of our officers feel
Always a pleasure in strife and disturbances?
Simply to gain an occasion to steal.
Act as they please for the future, the treasury
Never a penny shall yield them, I vow.
PROB. How, may I ask, will you hinder their getting it?
LYS. We will ourselves be the treasurers now.

[1] Bailiff, demarch (δήμαρχος), chief magistrate of a township or deme, whose jurisdiction included suits for the collection of debts.

[2] Peisander, one of the foremost politicians of the time and among the chief promoters of the oligarchic revolution of that year.

PROB. You, women, you be the treasurers? LYS. Certainly.
Ah, you esteem us unable, perchance!
Are we not skilled in domestic economy,
do we not manage the household finance?
PROB. Oh, that is different. LYS. Why is it different?
PROB. This is required for the fighting, my dear.
LYS. Yes, but the fighting itself isn't requisite.
PROB. Only, without it, we're ruined, I fear.
LYS. We will deliver you. PROB. You will deliver us!
LYS. Truly we will. PROB. What a capital notion!
LYS. Whether you like it or not, we'll deliver you.
PROB. Impudent hussy! LYS. You seem in commotion.
Nevertheless we will do as we promise you.
PROB. That were a terrible shame, by Demeter.
LYS. Friend, we must save you. PROB. But how if I wish it not?
LYS. That will but make our resolve the completer.
PROB. Fools! what on earth can possess you to meddle with matters of war, and matters of peace?
LYS. Well, I will tell you the reason. PROB. And speedily,
else you will rue it. LYS. Then listen, and cease
Clutching and clenching your fingers so angrily;
keep yourself peaceable. PROB. Hanged if I can;
Such is the rage that I feel at your impudence.
STRATYLLIS. Then it is *you* that will rue it, my man.
PROB. Croak your own fate, you ill-omened antiquity.
(*To Lys.*) *You* be the spokeswoman, lady. LYS. I will.
Think of our old moderation and gentleness,
think how we bore with your pranks, and were still,
All through the days of your former pugnacity,
all through the war that is over and spent;
Not that (be sure) we approved of your policy;
never our griefs you allowed us to vent.
Well we perceived your mistakes and mismanagement,
Often at home on our housekeeping cares,
Often we heard of some foolish proposal you
made for conducting the public affairs.
Then would we question you mildly and pleasantly,
inwardly grieving, but outwardly gay;

'Husband how goes it abroad?' we would ask of him;
 'what have ye done in assembly to-day?
What would ye write on the side of the Treaty stone?'
 Husband says angrily, 'What's that to you?
You, hold your tongue!' And I held it accordingly.
 STRAT. That is a thing I *never* would do!
PROB. Madam, if you hadn't, you'd soon have repented it.
 LYS. Therefore I held it, and spake not a word.
Soon of another tremendous absurdity,
 wider and worse than the former we heard.
'Husband,' I say, with a tender solicitude,
 'Why have ye passed such a foolish decree?'
Vicious, moodily, glaring askance at me,
 'Stick to your spinning, my mistress,' says he,
'Else you will speedily find it the worse for you,
 War is the care and the business of men!'
PROB. Zeus, 'twas a worthy reply, and an excellent!
 LYS. What! you unfortunate, shall we not then,
Then, when we see you perplexed and incompetent,
 shall we not tender advice to the state?
So when aloud in the streets and the thoroughfares
 sadly we heard you bewailing of late,
'Is there a Man to defend and deliver us?'
 'No,' says another, 'there's none in the land;'
Then by the Women assembled in conference
 jointly a great Revolution was planned,
Hellas to save from her grief and perplexity.
 Where is the use of a longer delay?
Shift for the future our parts and our characters;
 you, as the women, in silence obey;
We, as the men, will harangue and provide for you;
 then shall the state be triumphant again,
Then shall we do what is best for the citizens.
 PROB. Women to do what is best for the men!
That were a shameful reproach and unbearable!
 LYS. Silence, old gentleman. PROB. Silence, for ***you?***
Stop for a wench with a wimple enfolding her?
 No, by the Powers, may I *die* if I do!

LYS. Do not, my pretty one, do not I pray,
Suffer my wimple to stand in the way.
Here take it, and wear it, and gracefully tie it,
Enfolding it over your head and be quiet.
Now to your task.
CALLONICE. Here is an excellent spindle to pull.
MYRRHINA. Here is a basket for carding the wool.
LYS. Now to your task.
Haricots chawing up, petticoats drawing up,
Off to your carding, your combing and trimming,
War is the care and the business of women.
LYS. First we will stop the disorderly crew,
Soldiers in arms promenading and marketing.
STRAT. Yea, by the divine Aphrodite, 'tis true.
LYS. Now in the market you see them like Corybants,[1]
jangling about with their armor of mail.
Fiercely they stalk in the midst of the crockery,
sternly parade by the cabbage and kail.
PROB. Right, for a soldier should always be soldierly!
LYS. Troth, 'tis a mighty ridiculous jest,
Watching them haggle for shrimps in the market-place,
grimly accoutred with shield and with crest.
STRAT. Lately I witnessed a captain of cavalry,
proudly the while on his charger he sat,
Witnessed him, soldierly, buying an omelet,
stowing it all in his cavalry hat.
Comes like a Tereus,[2] a Thracian irregular,
shaking his dart and his target to boot;
Off runs a shop-girl, appalled at the sight of him,
down he sits soldierly, gobbles her fruit.
PROB. You, I presume, could adroitly and gingerly
settle this intricate, tangled concern:
You in a trice could relieve our perplexities.
LYS. Certainly. PROB. How? Permit me to learn.
LYS. Just as a woman with nimble dexterity,
thus with her hands disentangles a skein,

[1] Corybants (Corybantes), priests of Cybele, danced tumultuously in armor.
[2] Tereus, a mythical king of Thrace, changed by the gods into a hoopoo.

Hither and thither her spindle unravels it,
    drawing it out, and pulling it plain.
So would this weary Hellenic entanglement
    soon be resolved by our womanly care,
So would our embassies neatly unravel it,
    drawing it here and pulling it there.
PROB. Wonderful, marvellous feats, not a doubt of it,
    you with your skeins and your spindles can show;
Fools! do you really expect to unravel a
    terrible war like a bundle of tow?
LYS. Ah, if you could only manage your politics
    just in the way that we deal with a fleece!
PROB. Tell us the recipe. LYS. First in the washing-tub
    plunge it, and scour it, and cleanse it from grease,
Purging away all the filth and the nastiness;
    then on the table expand it and lay,
Beating out all that is worthless and mischievous,
    picking the burrs and the thistles away.
Next for the clubs, the cabals, and the coteries,
    banding unrighteously, office to win,
Treat them as clots in the wool, and dissever them,
    lopping the heads that are forming within.
Then you should card it, and comb it, and mingle it,
    all in one Basket of love and of unity,
Citizens, visitors, strangers, and sojourners,
    all the entire, undivided community.
Know you a fellow in debt to the Treasury?
    Mingle him merrily in with the rest.
Also remember the cities our colonies,
    outlying states in the east and the west,
Scattered about to a distance surrounding us,
    these are our shreds and our fragments of wool;
These to one mighty political aggregate
    tenderly, carefully, gather and pull,
Twining them all in one thread of good fellowship;
    thence a magnificent bobbin to spin,
Weaving a garment of comfort and dignity,
    worthily wrapping the People therein.

PROB. Heard any ever the like of their impudence,
those who have nothing to do with the war,
Preaching of bobbins, and beatings, and washing-tubs.
LYS. Nothing to do with it, wretch that you are!
We are the people who feel it the keenliest,
doubly on us the affliction is cast;
Where are the sons that we sent to your battlefields?
PROB. Silence! a truce to the ills that are past.
LYS. Then in the glory and grace of our womanhood
all in the May and the morning of life,
Lo, we are sitting forlorn and disconsolate,
what has a soldier to do with a wife?
We might endure it, but ah! for the younger ones,
still in their maiden apartments they stay,
Waiting the husband that never approaches them,
watching the years that are gliding away.
PROB. Men, I suppose, have their youth everlastingly.
LYS. Nay, but it isn't the same with a man:
Grey though he be when he comes from the battlefield,
still if he wishes to marry he can.
Brief is the spring and the flower of our womanhood,
once let it slip, and it comes not again;
Sit as we may with our spells and our auguries,
never a husband will marry us then.

101. WOMEN LOVE PERSONAL ADORNMENTS

(Euripides, *Medeia*, 156–66)

Repudiated by her husband Jason, Medeia sends a poisoned robe and crown to his new bride, who before the poison begins to work finds great pleasure in their beauty.

Soon as she saw the ornaments, she no longer held out, but yielded to her lord in all;[1] and ere the father and his sons were far from the palace gone, she took the broidered robe, and put it

[1] The request here implied, conveyed through Jason from Medeia, was that their sons might not be compelled to accompany their mother into exile, but might be cared for in Corinth; it was Medeia's excuse for sending the gifts.

on, and set the golden crown about her tresses, arranging her hair at her bright mirror,[1] with many a happy smile at her breathless counterfeit. Then rising from her seat, she passed across the chamber, tripping lightly on her fair white foot, exulting in the gift, with many a glance at her uplifted ankle.

(Aristophanes, *Lysistrate*, 399–423)

In the following selection from the *Lysistrate*, acted at Athens in 411, the Chorus of Men and the Proboulos, member of the Committee of Public Safety, denounce the effrontery of their wives, who have deserted their homes and seized the Acropolis in order to force the men to peace with the Peloponnesians. The opinion of the magistrate is that the men have brought all this trouble upon themselves by pampering their wives with excessive attentions.

Chorus of Men. What if you heard their insolence to-day,
Their vile, outrageous goings-on? And look,
See how they've drenched and soused us from their pitchers,
Till we can ring out water from our clothes.[2]
Proboulos.[3] Ay, by Poseidon, and it serves us right.
'Tis all our fault; they'll never know their place,
These pampered women, whilst we spoil them so.
Hear how we talk in every workman's shop.
'Goldsmith,' says one, 'this necklace that you made,
My gay young wife was dancing yester-eve,
And lost, sweet soul, the fastening of the clasp;
Do please reset it, Goldsmith.' Or again,
'O Shoemaker, my wife's new sandal pinches
Her little toe, the tender, delicate child,

[1] The mirror was of polished metal. Many examples of beautifully chased Etruscan mirrors have been preserved.

[2] The men have attempted to storm the citadel held by the women, but have been repulsed by a phalanx of pitcher-bearers.

[3] Proboulos; after the Sicilian disaster the first step toward the establishment of oligarchy was taken by the appointment of ten probouli, for 412–11, to be elected annually one from each tribe. They were to take the place of the prytaneis (see no. 69, n. 1) in determining the measures to be brought before the assembly. They were also to supervise the finances and attend to the equipment of the fleet. The board might well be described as a Committee of Public Safety. Though the age qualification was fixed at forty years, the members were in fact far older men. Aristophanes represents the typical proboulos as fussy and meddlesome but inefficient; *cf.* 594 *sqq.*; Thuc. viii. 1; Aristotle, *Const. Ath.* 29. 2; Suidas, *s.v.* Πρόβουλοι.

Make it fit easier, please.' — Hence all this nonsense!
Yea, things have reached a pretty pass, indeed,
When I, the State's Director, wanting money
To purchase oar-blades, find the Treasury gates
Shut in my face by these preposterous women.

BIBLIOGRAPHY

For recent literature on social and private life, see Blümner, H., in *Jahresb.* CLXIII (1913). 1–83. See also Abrahams, E. B., *Greek Dress* (London, 1908); Bechtel, F., *Attische Frauennamen*, etc. (Göttingen, 1902); Becker, *Charicles*, trans. by Metcalfe, F. (Longmans, 1895); Benecke, E. F. M., *Antimachus of Colophon and the Position of Women in Greek Poetry* (London, 1896); Blümner, H., *Leben und Sitten der Griechen*, 3 vols. (Leipzig, 1887); *Home Life of the Ancient Greeks*, trans. by Zimmern, A. (Cassel, 1893); Braunstein, O., *Die politische Wirksamkeit der griechischen Frau* (Leipzig, 1911); Bryant, A. A., "Boyhood and Youth in the Days of Aristophanes," in *Harv. St. in Class. Philol.* XVIII (1907). 73–122; Carroll, M., *Woman: in All Ages and in All Countries*, I: *Greek Women* (Phila., 1907); "The Athens of Aristophanes," in *Studies in Honor of Gildersleeve* (Baltimore, 1902), 241 *sqq.*; Cesaresco, E. M., *Outdoor Life in Greek and Roman Poets* (Macmillan, 1911); Clerc. M., *Les métèques athéniens* (Paris, 1893); "Condition des étrangères domiciliés dans les différentes cités grecques," in *Rev. des universités du midi*, IV (1898). 1–32, 153–80, 249–75; Donaldson, J., *Woman; her Position and Influence in Ancient Greece*, etc. (Longmans, 1907); Ferriman, Z. D., *Home Life in Hellas* (Mills and Boon, 1910), modern conditions; Gothein, M., "Der griechische Garten," in *Ath. Mitt.* XXXIV (1909). 100 *sqq.*; Guhl, E. K., and Koner, W., *Life of the Greeks and Romans* (from 3d German ed., London, 1889); Guiraud, P., *La vie privée et la vie publique des Grecs* (3d ed., Paris, 1901); Gulick, C. B., *Life of the Ancient Greeks* (Appleton, 1902); Haley, H. W., "Social and Domestic Position of Women in Aristophanes," in *Harv. St. in Class. Philol.* I (1890). 159–86; Lorimer, H. L., "The Country Cart of Ancient Greece," in *Journ. Hell. St.* XXIII (1903). 132 *sqq.*; Mahaffy, J. P., *Social Life in Greece from Homer to Menander* (Macmillan, 1883); Miller, W., *Greek Life in Town and Country* (London, 1905); Pöhlmann, R. v., *Geschichte der sozialen Frage und des Sozialismus der antiken Welt*, 2 vols. (Munich, 1912); Poland, F., *Geschichte des griech. Vereinswesens* (Teubner, 1909); Ransom, C. L., *Studies in Ancient Furniture; Couches and Beds of the Greeks, Etruscans, and Romans* (Chicago: University Press, 1905); Roper, A. G., *Ancient Eugenics* (Oxford: Blackwell, 1913); Savage, C. A., "The Athenian in his Relations to the State," in *Studies in Honor of Gildersleeve* (Baltimore, 1902), 87 *sqq.*; Schreiber, G. T., *Atlas of Classical Antiquities*, ed. by Anderson, W. C. F. (London, 1895); St. John, J. A., *History of the Manners and Customs of Ancient Greece*, 3 vols. (London, 1842); Sudhoff, K., *Aus dem antiken Badewesen* (Berlin, 1910); Sundwall, J., "Epigraphische Beiträge zur sozialpolitischen Geschichte Athens im Zeitalter des Demosthenes," in *Klio: Beiträge zur alt. Gesch.* Ergzb. I. 4 (1906); Tod, M. N., "Statute of an Attic Thiasos," in *Ann. Brit. School at Ath.* XIII (1906–7). 328–38; Tucker, T. G., *Life in Ancient Athens* (Macmillan, 1906); Wägner, W., *Hellas: das Land und Volk der alten Griechen*, 2 vols. (6th ed., Leipzig, 1886); Ward, C. O., *The Ancient Lowly*, 2 vols. (Chicago: Kerr, 1910); Wilamowitz-Moellendorff, U. v., *Staat und Gesellschaft der Griechen und Römer* (Teubner, 1910); Wolf, H., *Geschichte des antiken Sozialismus* (Gütersloh, 1909).

CHAPTER XI

RELIGION

In the Period 479–404 B.C.

THIS chapter comprises a group of inscriptions of the fifth century whose primary interest is religious. At the same time, however, they afford information on various other topics.

102. IMPRECATIONS OF THE TEIANS AGAINST EVIL DOERS

(*CIG.* 3044; Hicks and Hill, no. 23; Michel, *Recueil*, no. 1318; Roberts, I. no. 142; Collitz-Bechtel, *SGDI*. III. 2. no. 5632; trans. by C. J. O.)

This inscription was found near the site of ancient Teos, on the coast of Asia Minor south of Smyrna. Of the two stelæ on which it was written, only the former (A) is now known to be extant. From the character of the alphabet and the references to piracy and the barbarians the document may be assigned to the period of insecurity intervening between the defeat of the Persians at Mycale and the admission of Teos to the Delian Confederacy — to about 475 B.C. Strange to us, but quite common in early Greece, is the use of the curse for the enforcement of regulations; *cf.* Plut. *Sol.* 24; Isoc. *Paneg.* 157; Schömann, *Griechische Altertümer*, II. 254; Ziebarth, in *Hermes*, XXX (1895). 57 *sqq.*; see further Hicks and Hill, p. 27 *sq.*

(A) If anyone should prepare harmful drugs against the Teians as a community or against a private citizen, let him perish, both himself and his kin. If anyone should prevent the importation of grain into the Teian territory, by art or device, by sea or by land, or should reject it after it has been imported, let him perish, both himself and his kin.

(B) (*Opening lines lost.*) If anyone should [disobey (?)] a Euthynos[1] or a supreme magistrate[2] of the Teians or should rebel against

[1] Euthynos (Εὔθυνος) in Teos was probably an officer who executed the penalties imposed by the courts, wholly different therefore from the functionary of the same name at Athens, who was an auditor; Pauly-Wissowa, *Real-Encycl.* VI. 1517. For another view, see Hicks and Hill, p. 28.

[2] Aisymnetes (Αἰσυμνήτης) an extraordinary magistrate in some Hellenic states, elected by the people and vested with a power somewhat like that of the Roman dictator; Pauly-Wissowa, *Real-Encycl.* I. 1088–91.

the supreme magistrate, let him perish, both himself and his kin. If anyone in future, while supreme magistrate in Teos or in the Teian territory, should put to death illegally [an innocent man or say that he has betrayed] the city and the territory of the Teians, or should betray the men [in the island or on the sea or those who have come to the aid of the commonwealth of the Teians],[1] or if he should practise highway robbery or harbor highway robbers or practise piracy or harbor pirates with knowledge, when they are plundering in the Teian territory or on the sea, or if he should knowingly plot any evil concerning the commonwealth of the Teians either with Greeks or with barbarians, let him perish, both himself and his kin. If any persons, while office-holders,[2] should not pronounce the imprecation to the best of their ability during sessions of the assembly, at the Anthesteria,[3] the festival of Heracles, and that of Zeus, let them be subject to the imprecation. If anyone shall break the stelæ on which the imprecation is written, or shall cut away the lettering, or shall remove them, let him perish, both himself and his kin.

103. Athenian Decree Concerning the Temple and the Priestess of Athena Nike

(Hicks and Hill, no. 37; Roberts and Gardner, no. 4; trans. by G. W. B.)

This inscription provides for the building of a shrine which is undoubtedly to be identified with the beautiful little temple of "Wingless Victory." The document belongs to 450–447. Callicrates, who drew up the plan, was also one of the architects of the Parthenon, begun about the same time. The inscription is interesting for the light it throws, not only upon the construction of temples of the kind, but also upon the salaries and perquisites of priestesses.

First Side of the Stele

...cus moved the resolution: That a priestess be established for Athena Nike, who shall be a citizen, born of citizen parents, taken from the whole body of Athenian women (thus qualified). That the shrine shall be furnished with a door, according as Calli-

[1] This reading follows the suggestion of Haussoullier, adopted by Michel, *Recueil*, no. 1318, but the reading is very uncertain.

[2] Office-holders, timuchi (Τιμοῦχοι) were probably the ordinary annual magistrates, suspended on the election of an aisymnetes.

[3] A festival celebrated in February in honor of Dionysus.

crates shall draw up the specifications. That the commissioners of sales[1] shall let the contract in the prytany of the tribe Leontis. That the priestess shall have a living of fifty drachmae together with the legs and hides of the public sacrificial animals. That the temple and a stone altar be erected according to the specifications of Callicrates.

Hestiæus further moved: That a committee of three men be elected from the boulê, and that they shall assist Callicrates in drawing up the specifications, and present to the boulê their judgment on the letting of the contract; and that the prytaneis report to the demus. . . .

Second Side

Be it resolved by the Boulê and the Demus. Ægeis was the prytanizing tribe. Neocleides was secretary. Agnodemus was chairman. Callias moved the resolution: That the Colacretæ,[2] who may be in office in the month [Poseideon[3]], shall pay to the priestess of Athena Nike the fifty drachmæ, recorded on the stele, to the priestess of Athena Nike. . . .

104. Additional Decree on the Same Subject

(Roberts and Gardner, no. 6; Ditt. I. no. 16)

. . . The Acropolis . . . to build, so that no runaway slave or sneakthief may gain entrance. Callicrates shall draw up the specifications for it, and the commissioners of sales shall prepare to let the contract as advantageously and as inexpensively as possible. They shall see that it be ready within sixty days. The guards shall be three archers drawn from the prytanizing tribe.[4]

[1] Poletæ, whose duty in general was to let out state contracts.

[2] Originally the Colacretæ had been the chief treasurers of the state, but their importance had shrunk with the institution of various other finance officials; *cf.* Meyer, *Forsch.* II. 136 *sq.*

[3] Corresponds roughly with December. For a list of the Attic months with their English equivalents, see Gulick, *Life of the Ancient Greeks*, 241.

[4] It is evident that these guards were citizens (*cf.* Wernicke, in *Hermes*, XXVI. 51 *sqq.*). The ordinary policemen of Athens, however, were public slaves, brought originally from Scythia, and known therefore as Scythian archers. They were introduced in the sixth century; *cf.* Walters, *Ancient Pottery*, II. 176 (illustration).

105. Athenian Decree Concerning the Repayment of Sums Borrowed from the Treasuries of the Gods

(Hicks and Hill, no. 49; Ditt. I. no. 21; Roberts and Gardner, II. no. 10; Böckh, *Staatshaushaltung der Athener*, II. 42–8 (text, translation, and commentary); trans. by C. J. O.)

This inscription is on a marble slab, formerly part of the altar of a Greek church but now in the Louvre. It belongs most probably to 435–4.

At this time the Athenians had attained to a high degree of prosperity. Notwithstanding large sums expended on temples and other public works, accumulations in the state treasury had enabled them in recent years to repay 3000 talents formerly borrowed from the treasury of Athena. It is noteworthy that among ancient Hellenic states there was no system of public credit or of public debt, such as burdens every modern state, county, and municipality; but in time of need the government could borrow from a temple. As religion was a part of the state, such loans were merely a transfer of funds from one department to another, to be returned should circumstances permit. Accumulations in temples, accordingly, constituted a reserve fund for the state. In addition to the repayment of sums borrowed from Athena, the government was now in a position to return certain smaller sums drawn in like manner from the funds of other gods. The decree here translated provides for the latter transaction. The money so paid, however, was to constitute the beginning of a new treasury, to be placed under the charge of Treasurers of the Other Gods, drawn by lot, as were the Treasurers of Athena, from the highest property class (the pentacosiomedimni). The style of the inscription proves that it was not engraved till some fifteen years after the date of enactment above given. See further on the document, Busolt, *Griech. Gesch.* III. 562–5; Meyer, *Forsch.* II. 88 *sqq.*; Cavaignac, *L'Histoire financière d'Athènes au Ve siècle*, 104 *sqq.*

Be it resolved by the Boulê and the Demus. Cecropis was the prytanizing tribe. Mnesitheus was secretary. Eupeithes was chairman. Callias moved the resolution.

That the moneys owed shall be repaid to the gods, since there have been brought up into the Acropolis for Athena the three thousand talents[1] in our own coin, as had been voted. The repayment shall be made from the moneys which have been voted for repaying the gods; namely, the sums now in the hands of the

[1] This was the sum recently paid Athena in liquidation of the debt due her by the state. At $1100 to the talent it would amount to $3,300,000. About this time the total amount of money stored in the treasuries on the Acropolis was 9700 talents, an immense reserve for a Greek state. Before the opening of the Peloponnesian war the erection of temples and other public works had reduced it to 6000 talents; Thuc. ii. 13.

Hellenic Treasurers,[1] the remainder that belongs to these funds, and the proceeds of the tithe,[2] when it shall have been farmed out. The thirty accountants[3] now in office shall audit with exactness the sums due to the gods, and the boulê shall have full power[4] to convoke the accountants. The prytaneis, together with the (whole) boulê, shall repay the moneys and shall cancel (the indebtedness) upon making payment, searching for the tablets and the account books and whatever other records there may be. The priests, the commissioners of sacrifices, and any other person who has knowledge, shall be obliged to produce the records. Treasurers[5] of these funds shall be taken by lot at the same time as the other magistrates and upon the same terms as the Treasurers of the Sacred Funds of Athena. They shall deposit the funds of the gods, so far as is possible and allowable, in the Opisthodomos[6] on the Acropolis, and they shall join with the Treasurers of Athena in opening and closing and sealing the doors of the Opisthodomos. The funds (received) from the present treasurers and the superintendents and the commissioners of sacrifices in the temples, who have the management at present, shall be counted and weighed out in the presence of the boulê on the Acropolis by the Treasurers to be appointed, and these

[1] Hellenotamiæ were the imperial treasurers, in charge of the fund made up of tributes from the allies.

[2] Probably a rent of ten per cent on public lands let by the state to private persons.

[3] Logistæ (λογισταί), a board filled by lot, to whom all public accounts had to be submitted.

[4] This the boulê could do on its own responsibility, without consulting the assembly of citizens.

[5] Hereby was instituted the office of Treasurers of the Other Gods (see introduction). Like the Treasurers of Athena they were doubtless ten in number, and were taken by lot from members of the highest property class. For a fragment of their account for the year 429–8, see *Inscr. græc.* I. nos. 194, 195, where, however, only five names appear.

[6] Opisthodomos (Ὀπισθόδομος), "Rear Chamber," applying to the rear chamber of a temple. Some scholars have supposed that the Opisthodomos here mentioned was the rear chamber of the Parthenon; but a careful examination of the sources proves that view untenable. Certain scholars, accordingly, have taken the ground that the term has reference to the back part of the old Athena temple, north of the Parthenon, and contend that this part, consisting of three rooms, was rebuilt as a Treasury after the Persian war. The most complete defense of this view is given by J. W. White, *Harvard Studies in Classical Philology*, VI (1895). Another view, represented by Judeich, *Topographie von Athen*, 230, which regards the Opisthodomos as a building to the west of the Parthenon, erected about 454 as an imperial Treasury, seems to have less evidence in the sources.

officers shall receive the funds from the persons now in office and shall record them all on a single stele, both the amounts belonging to each of the gods respectively and the sum total, the silver and the gold separately. And in future the Treasurers for the time being shall make record upon a stele and shall account to the auditors for the funds at hand and for those accruing to the gods, and for whatever is expended during the year. They shall submit to examination,[1]—and shall render their account from Panathenæa to Panathenæa,[2] like the Treasurers of Athena. The Treasurers shall place on the Acropolis the stelæ on which they record the sacred funds. When the moneys shall have been repaid to the gods, the surplus shall be used for the dockyard and the fortifications.

106. The Athenian Decree for Regulating the Offerings of First Fruits to the Goddesses of Eleusis

(*Inscr. græc.* I. Supplem. no. 27 b, p. 59; Ditt. no. 20; Prott and Ziehen, *Leges græcorum sacræ*, pt. II (Leipzig, 1906), p. 19 *sqq.*; Foucart, in *Bulletin de correspondance hellénique*, IV (1880). 229 *sqq.*; trans. by C. J. O.)

One of the aims of Pericles was to use religion as a means of securing to Athens a recognized leadership in Hellenic affairs. Such was his project for the restoration of temples destroyed by the Persian invader (Plut. *Per.* 17). If, as seems probable, the decree given in *Inscr. græc.* I. no. 1; Supplem. p. 3, 133, belongs to the time shortly following 460 (Busolt, *Griech. Gesch.* III. 473), we may infer that he wished to apply the Eleusinian worship to that end. He had all the greater hope for success in this policy because of the fact that the Eleusinian cult had already extended far beyond the borders of Attica—*e.g.*, to Sicily (Athenæus ix. 17, 374 d). To a somewhat later period—evidently to a time of peace, perhaps 444–436—belongs the following decree (Busolt, *op. cit.* III. 474 and n. 2), which regulates the offering of first fruits to the Goddesses Twain of Eleusis on the part of the Athenians and their allies, and invites all other Hellenes to participate.

Be it resolved by the Boulê and the Demus. Cecropis was the prytanizing tribe. Timoteles was secretary.[3] Cycneas was chair-

[1] Euthyna (Εὔθυνα), a general investigation to which outgoing officials were subjected and more thorough than formal accounting.

[2] That is, their term begins with the Panathenaic festival (July), and not with the civil year.

[3] At this time a new secretary of the boulê was appointed for each prytany.

man. The commissioners of legislation[1] drafted (the statute) in the following terms:

The Athenians shall offer first fruits from the harvest to the Two Goddesses[2] according to ancestral custom and the oracle from Delphi:[3] namely, from every hundred *medimni* of barley not less than one sixth of a medimnus,[4] and from every hundred medimni of wheat not less than one twelfth of a medimnus. If anyone has a harvest of greater, or of equal, or of less amount, he shall offer the first fruits in the same proportion. The demarchs[5] shall collect the offering by demes and shall bring it to Eleusis, to the commissioners of sacrifices. Three corn pits shall be constructed according to ancestral custom, wherever the commissioners of sacrifices and the architect may think proper, with the money of the Two Goddesses; and the commissioners shall store therein the grain that they may receive from the demarchs. The allies[6] also shall offer first fruits on the same terms, and the cities shall choose collectors of the grain, according as they may think that the grain will best be collected. When it is collected, they shall send it to Athens, and those who take it shall bring it to Eleusis to the commissioners of sacrifices at Eleusis; and if the commissioners shall not accept it within five days after announcement and tender are made by the men of the city from which the grain comes, they shall be fined a thousand drachmæ[7] apiece. They shall accept it from the demarchs also on the same terms. Let the council choose heralds and send them to the cities to announce the [present] decree of the people, (and let it do so) for the present occasion as soon as possible,

[1] Syngrapheis (Συγγραφεῖς), a committee appointed to draw up a comprehensive law.

[2] Demeter and Persephone (Corê), in whose worship the Eleusinian mysteries were celebrated.

[3] *Cf.* Isocrates, *Paneg.* 31 (composed 390–380): "Most of the cities sent us every year offerings of the first fruits of grain in remembrance of our ancient benefactions; and the Pythia (the priestess of Apollo at Delphi) has often enjoined the neglectful to contribute their tithes of the harvest, and to show toward our city the conduct prescribed by ancestral usage"; see also the scholiast on Aristoph. *Plutus*, 1054.

[4] A medimnus was about 1½ bu.; a sixth would therefore be about a peck.

[5] Demarch (δήμαρχος), chief officer of the deme, or township. Attica was divided into considerably more than a hundred demes.

[6] The states of the Delian Confederacy and Athenian empire.

[7] A drachma was about eighteen cents.

and in future whenever it thinks best. Let both the hierophant and the torch-bearer at the celebration of the Mysteries [1] bid the Greeks offer first fruits from the harvest according to the ancestral custom and the oracle from Delphi. Let them (the commissioners) write upon a tablet both the amount of grain received from the demarchs according to demes and that received from the cities according to cities, and let them place (a tablet) in the Eleusinion [2] at Eleusis and in the council-hall. The council shall send word also to all the other Greek cities, wheresoever in its opinion it may be possible to send, by men who shall tell them how the Athenians and the allies offer first fruits, and who, without commanding them, shall urge them to offer if they so desire according to the ancestral custom and the oracle from Delphi. The commissioners of sacrifices shall receive (offerings) on the same terms from these cities also, if anyone brings (offerings). They (the commissioners) shall sacrifice from the sacred porridge according as the Eumolpidæ [3] shall direct, and, from (the proceeds of) the barley and the wheat, an ox and two other animals [4] with gilded horns to each of the Two Goddesses, a full-grown sheep to Triptolemus and the God and the Goddess and Eubulus [5] severally, and an ox with gilded horns to Athena. The commissioners shall sell the remainder of the barley and of the wheat and, together with the council, shall make and dedicate offerings to the Two Goddesses, such as shall seem good to the Athenian people, and they shall inscribe upon the offerings the fact that they were dedicated from (the proceeds of) the first fruits of the harvest and the name of the Greeks who offered the first fruits. And may those who do thus have many blessings and good and abundant harvests, provided that they do not wrong the Athenians or the city of the Athenians or the Two Goddesses.

[1] Celebrated annually at Eleusis in September. About that time the contributions of grain were probably brought to Eleusis; *cf.* A. Mommsen, *Feste der Stadt Athen* (Leipzig, 1898), 192–5.

[2] The temple of Eleusis. Dittenberger, however, would transpose the following words so as to read: "in the Eleusinion (a sanctuary at Athens) and at Eleusis in the council-hall."

[3] A gens (an association of families assumed to be of one kin) who had the function of regulating the Eleusinian ceremonial.

[4] Literally, "a triad headed by an ox" — an ox, a ram, and a he-goat.

[5] On these divinities, see Farnell, *Cults of the Greek States*, III (Oxford, 1907). 135 *sq.*, 144 *sq.*

Lampon[1] moved as an amendment to the statute concerning the offering of the first fruits of the harvest to the Two Goddesses: The secretary of the council shall record the statute and the following decree on two stone stelæ and shall place one of them in the sanctuary at Eleusis and the other on the Acropolis. The poletæ[2] shall let the contract for the stelæ, and the colacretæ[3] shall give the money therefor. These provisions concerning the offering of the first fruits of the harvest to the Two Goddesses shall be recorded upon the stelæ; but furthermore the new archon shall intercalate the month Hecatombæon.[4] The king archon[5] shall mark the bounds of the sanctuaries in the Pelargicum,[6] and in future altars shall not be set up in the Pelargicum without (the authority of) the council and the people. Neither shall the stones be quarried from the Pelargicum nor shall earth or stone be taken thence. If anyone shall violate any of these provisions, he shall pay (a fine of) five hundred drachmæ, and the king archon shall denounce him to the council. Lampon shall draft a statute concerning the offering of the first fruits of oil and shall exhibit it to the council in the ninth prytany, and the council shall of necessity bring it before the people.

107. The Construction of the Erechtheum

A. Condition of the Material in 409–8 B.C.

(*Inscr. græc.* I. 322. Translated by E. G. S.)

In 409–8, shortly after the restoration of the absolute democracy (no. 77, introduction) the Athenians resumed work on the Erechtheum, on the Acropolis, a temple second only to the Parthenon in beauty. We do not know when it had been begun, whether after the peace of Nicias, 421, or possibly before

[1] An influential soothsayer, often mentioned by writers of comedy in that age.

[2] See no. 103, n. 1.

[3] See no. 103, n. 2.

[4] In order to adjust the lunar months of the Attic calendar to the seasons, an extra month was inserted every second or third year by the head Archon, usually after the sixth month in midwinter. The insertion of an extra Hecatombæon (July) in this case seems to have been for the purpose of allowing more time for the sending of the contributions.

[5] The chief religious official.

[6] A precinct at the western extremity of the Acropolis, by the gateway of the original fortifications; *cf.* Judeich, *Topographie von Athen*, 107 *sqq.* For the "taboo" upon it see Thucydides, ii. 17.

the outbreak of the Peloponnesian war; D'Ooge, *Acropolis*, 196. It was devoted to Athena Polias — guardian of the city — whose statue was a log rudely carved in human form, and to Erechtheus, a hero-king of Athens; see Botsford, *Hellenic History*, ch. xx. The following passage comprises a few items excerpted from a lengthy report to the government on the condition of the material for the Erechtheum, at the time of the resumption of its construction, drawn up by the committee of supervisors for the building of that temple.

The Committee of Supervisors [1] of the temple on the Acropolis, in which is the ancient cult statue,[2] Brosunes of Cephisia, Chariades of Argyle, Diodes of Cephisia, the chief architect Philocles of Acharnæ, Etearchus of Cydathenaion the secretary, recorded the following works of the temple in the condition in which they took them over in accordance with a resolution of the demus — (comprising material) finished and half-wrought — in the archonship of Diocles, when the tribe Cecropis held the first prytany, in the term of that boulê [3] in which Nicophanes of Marathon was first to serve as secretary.

Of the temple we took over the following (material) half-wrought: —

At the corner near the Cecropion [4] —

4 blocks not set, 4 feet in length, 2 feet in width, 3½ in thickness.

1 'armpit' piece, 4 feet in length, 3 feet in width, 1½ feet in thickness.

5 blocks of toplayer, 4 feet in length, 3 feet in width, 1½ feet in thickness.

1 angle block, 7 feet in length, 4 feet in width, 1½ feet in thickness.

1 curved stone not set, corresponding to the toplayer blocks, 10 feet in length, 1½ feet in height. . . .

Of the columns at the wall on the side of the Pandroseion; [5] of (half-done material): —

[1] Ἐπιστάται, the committee appointed to supervise the construction of the building. The names of the supervisors follow.

[2] This was the wooden statue mentioned in the introduction. Individuals are distinguished by their demes (townships).

[3] On demus, prytany, and boulê, see no. 69, n. 1.

[4] Cecropion, shrine of Cecrops, hero-king of Athens. It stood near the southwest corner of the Erechtheum; D'Ooge, *Acropolis*, 216 *sqq.*

[5] As the only wall columns connected with the Erechtheum were on the west, it follows that the Pandroseion, shrine of Pandrosos, daughter of Cecrops, was on that side; *cf.* D'Ooge, *loc. cit.*

4 pieces of columns in position uncut for 1½ feet of each column from the inner anthemion.[1]

It is necessary to set in addition a volute at the inside of the south wall.

The following are unpolished and not fluted: —

The wall on the inside of the south wing is not polished except that one in the portico near the Cecropion.

The upright blocks are unpolished, the outside ones all around, except those in the portico contiguous to the Cecropion.

All the rounded base mouldings are unfluted; the columns all unfluted except the one at the wall; the entire foundation around is unfluted; parts of the inner wall are unpolished. . . .

In the façade which is at the portal: —

(We found) the altar of the sacrificing priest unset; the cross-beams (of the roof) and tie-beams unset (not firmly set).

At the façade near the Cecropion: —

It is necessary to work the roofstones (3) lying on the maidens,[2] on their upper surfaces, for a length of 13 feet, a width of 5.

The bronze ornaments on the architraves ought to be wrought to completion.

Items of stone completely wrought which are on the ground: —

11 blocks, 4 feet in length, 2 feet in width, 1½ feet in thickness.

1 'armpit' block 4 feet in length, 3 feet in width, of a thickness of 1½ feet. . . .

Facing the wall at the Pandroseion, a length of 7½ feet, width of 3½ feet, half-wrought in smooth work.

1 length of 6 feet, width of 3 feet and 1 palm, thickness of 5 palms, at the wall facing the Pandroseion; five feet of this part did not have the bead-work carved in.

6 pieces of pediment, those from the colonnade, 7½ feet in length, 3½ feet in width, 1 foot in thickness — half-wrought. . . .

4 doors of stone 8 feet long and a palm; 2½ feet wide; of these parts the rest have been completed, but the black stones should be inserted in the rails (of the doors): —

[1] For the architectural terms used in this inscription, see Fowler and Wheeler, *Greek Archæology*, and Tarbell, *History of Greek Art* (indices).

[2] These are the famous statues of maidens (Caryatids) in the south porch.

The console [1] for the space above the eastern door, half-done.
3 for the altar of the sacrificing priest, of Pentelic marble, 4 feet in length, 2 feet high, and 2 feet and 1 palm in thickness. . . .

108. Construction of the Erechtheum

B. Account of Expenses for Work and Material

(*Inscr. græc.* I. no. 324. Translated by E. G. S.)

The following selection is made up of items excerpted from the account of expenditures on the construction of the Erechtheum for the year 408. The inscription is so mutilated that we cannot determine the sum total of expenditures. The value of the document lies chiefly in the information it affords regarding the social classes of laborers, their wages, and the cost of certain materials. The Athenian citizen is distinguished by the name of his deme, as "*Aresæchmus of Agryle*"; rarely by the name of his father and that of his deme. The metic (alien resident) is described as residing in a deme, as "*Manis residing in Collytus.*" The name of the slave is followed by that of the master in the genitive case, as "*Cerdon (slave) of Axiopeithes*"; see Francotte, *L'Industrie dans la Grèce*, I. 204, n. 2. Francotte has thus calculated that of eighty-one men engaged in the work, twenty-four were citizens, forty metics, and seventeen slaves. There are many besides who cannot be classified; but from the proportions given we can see that the citizens, though on the verge of famine, were not favored, and that the greater part of the work was done by free hands. It is clear, too, that the supervisors engaged either individuals or extremely small groups, as a man and his co-worker, a master with a slave or two; in other words, labor was not capitalized. A most remarkable fact is that slave, metic, and citizen, underling and architect received the same daily wage of one drachma.

* * * * * * *

For completing roof: to the men who brought on the rounded plank and the others for each seat:

To Manis residing in Collytus	1 drachma.
To Crœsus residing in Scambonidæ	1 dr.
To Andreas residing in Melite	1 dr.
To Prepon residing in Agryle	1 dr.

* * * * * * *

To the six men who took down the scaffolding from the columns of the façade

To Teucrus residing in Cydathenaion [2] 1 dr.

[1] Roberts and Gardner.

[2] Evidently the workmen thus far mentioned were metics; see introduction.

To Cerdon (slave) of Axiopeithes [1] 1 dr.

* * * * * * *

To the men who did the scaffolding for the encaustic artists under the roof:

To Manis residing in Collytus 4 dr.

* * * * * * *

Total for underworkers 84 dr. 5½ obols.

To the sawyers working day by day, 16 days for 2 men, 1 dr. per day per man

To Radius residing in Collytus and his co-worker 32 dr.

To sawyers working by the day, for third period of twelve days, wooden laths for the roofs, for seven days, 1 dr. per day (each) for two men

To Radius residing in Collytus and his co-worker 14 days.

Total for the sawyers 46 dr.

For the encaustic painters:

To the one who made the encaustic cymatium which is on the inner architrave, 5 obols per foot.[2]

* * * * * * *

Total to encaustic painters 30 dr.

To goldsmiths (lit. gold pourers):

We further gave to him who gilded bronze figures what was due of the preceding prytany,[3] that of Oeneis.

* * * * * * *

To the architect Archilochus of Agryle 37 dr.[4]

To the underclerk Pyrgion 30 dr. 5 obols.

Total for wages 67 dr. 5 obols.

Total for entire expenditure 1790 dr. 3½ obols.

In the seventh prytany, that of the tribe of Leontis:

Received from the treasurers of the Goddesses,[5] from Aresæchmus and his fellow-officials, 4302 dr. 1 obol.

[1] For the fact that this workman was a slave, see introduction.

[2] Here we notice that some of the artists were paid according to the amount of work accomplished.

[3] It is clear that these accounts were kept according to prytanies, a prytany being a tenth of the year; see no. 69, n. 1. Each prytany was named after the tribe whose delegation in the council constituted the prytaneis (supreme administrative committee) for the time being.

[4] As this prytany doubtless included 37 days, we learn here that the architect received only a drachma a day, the same as a common laborer. From the item below it is not necessary to suppose that the underclerk received less, as he may have worked fewer days.

[5] On the Treasurers of the Goddess (Athena), see no. 105, introduction.

Expenditure; purchases: . . .

Phyromachus of Cephisia, the youth by the breastplate 60 dr.

Praxias residing in Melite, the horse and the figure appearing behind, turning the horse round 120 dr.

* * * * * * *

Phyromachus of Cephisia, the man leaning on the staff, the one next to the altar 60 dr.

Iasos of Collytus, the woman whom the young girl has embraced 80 dr.

Total for the making of religious figures 3315 dr.

Received 4302 dr. Expenditure the same.

In the Pandionis, the eighth prytany:

Received from the Treasurers of the Goddess, Aresæchmus and his fellow-officials 1239 dr. 1 ob.

Expenditure; purchases:

2 planks (wooden tablets) on which we are entering the account; each 1 dr.[1] 2 dr.

The stone-work account: for fluting the columns on the east side, those by the third altar from the altar of Dione:

Ameiniades residing in Cœle 18 dr.

(In another prytany)

* * * * * * *

Expenditure; purchases:

2 pieces of papyrus were purchased, on which we entered the copies (of the accounts) 2 dr. 4 obols.

4 tablets 4 dr.

Gold was purchased for the bronzes, leaves 165 dr. 1 obol.

Each leaf at 1 dr., from Adonis residing in Melite 166 dr.

Lead was purchased, 2 talents, for the clamping of the small figures, from Sostratus, residing in Melite[2] 10 dr.

Gold, 2 leaves, was purchased to gild the 'eyes' of the column, from Adonis residing in Melite 2 dr.

Total of purchases 189 dr. 1 obol.

For stone-work: for fluting pillars toward the east, those by the altar. That by the altar of Dione:

Laossus of Alopece, Philon of Erchia, Parmenon slave of Laossus, Carion slave of Laossus.[3] . . .

[1] It appears that the clerk kept the running accounts on wooden tablets, which were copied on papyrus, as is stated below; and the accounts as finally approved were engraved on stone, which alone has been preserved.

[2] It is an interesting fact that this merchant and another, Adonis, mentioned immediately above, were both metics. In these transactions there seems to have been no idea of giving native Athenians the preference.

[3] Here is an interesting combination of workmen: the citizen Laossus with two slaves has worked by the side of another citizen, Philon, in fluting certain pillars.

109. The Completed Erechtheum and the Worship of Athena

(Pausanias i. 26)

There is also a building called the Erechtheum. Before the entrance is an altar of Supreme Zeus, where they sacrifice no living thing; but they lay cakes on it, and having done so they are forbidden by custom to make use of wine. Inside of the building are altars: one of Poseidon, on which they sacrifice also to Erechtheus in obedience to an oracle; one of the hero Butes; and one of Hephæstus. On the walls are paintings of the family of the Butads.[1] Within, for the building is double, there is sea-water in a well. This is not surprising, for the same thing may be seen in inland places, as at Aphrodisias in Caria. But what is remarkable about this well is that, when the south wind has been blowing, the well gives forth a sound of waves; and there is the shape of a trident in the rock. These things are said to have been the evidence produced by Poseidon in support of his claim to the country.

The rest of the city and the whole land are equally sacred to Athena; for although the worship of other gods is established in the townships, the inhabitants none the less hold Athena in honor. But the object which was universally deemed the holy of holies many years before the union of the townships, is an image of Athena in what is now called the Acropolis, but what was then called the city. The legend is that the image fell from heaven, but whether this was so or not I will not inquire. As to this I shall not give an opinion, whether it was so or not. Callimachus made a golden lamp for the goddess. When they fill this lamp with oil, it lasts a whole year, although it burns continually night and day.

There are various other indications in this inscription that citizens, metics, and slaves worked side by side on the same architectural piece. It is interesting, too, that slaves could do as delicate artistic work as citizens or metics.

[1] The Butads, who after the time of Cleisthenes called themselves Eteobutadæ, to distinguish themselves as members of a noble clan from the Butad demesmen, were hereditary priests of Poseidon; Töpffer, J., *Attische Genealogie* (Berlin, 1889). 113 *sqq*.

110. Law of the City of Iulis in Ceos for Regulating Funerals

(*Inscr. græc.* XII. no. 593; Ditt. II. no. 877; Michel, *Recueil*, no. 398 A; Dareste-Haussoullier-Reinach, *Recueil des inscriptions juridiques grecques*, I (1891). 10–17; Buck, *Greek Dialects*, II. no. 8; and especially Prott and Ziehen, *Leges Græcorum Sacræ*, II. 1. 260–67, including an elaborate commentary. Translated by C. J. O.)

This inscription, found at Iulis on the island of Ceos, belongs on philological grounds to the last quarter of the fifth century (425–400); but the fundamental laws contained in it must be far older. They were either simply republished or more probably revised in some points. Sumptuary regulations, directed against extravagant and ostentatious funeral ceremonies, were common in ancient Hellenic states, and were ascribed to various eminent lawgivers, notably to Solon; Cicero, *De Legibus*, ii. 59–66; Plutarch, *Solon*, 20 *sq.* For the most part, however, we have only scattered allusions to the subject in ancient authors, and this stringent law of Iulis is valuable as a connected though brief account of Hellenic burial customs, in addition to its mention of curious superstitions. The similar ordinance of the Labyadæ at Delphi (Ditt. II. no. 438 C; Michel, no. 995 C) should be compared; and for a general view of the subject, see Rohde, *Psyche* (4th ed. Tübingen, 1907). I. 216–58.

The following (are the) laws regarding the departed. They shall bury [1] the dead person in the following manner: in three pieces of white cloth,[2] namely, a sheet, a garment, and a coverlet — it shall also be permitted to use fewer — all three not to exceed one hundred drachmæ [3] in value. They shall bear him forth on a bed with wedge-shaped feet,[4] and shall not cover the . . .[5] with the cloths. They shall take to the tomb not more than three choes of wine and not more than one chous of olive oil; [6] and they shall take the vessels away with them. They shall carry the dead person (with his face) covered,[7] observing silence as far as the tomb. They shall perform the preliminary sacrifice [8] according to ancestral

[1] The Greek word thaptein (θάπτειν), which may be used of either interment or cremation, seems here to signify all the funeral rites.

[2] Cloth in which the body is to be wrapped.

[3] Drachma, about 18 cents. The entire cost therefore is not to exceed $18.

[4] *I.e.*, unornamented.

[5] Both the reading and the interpretation of the word here omitted are uncertain.

[6] About nine quarts of wine and three of oil.

[7] So as to avoid polluting the streets of the city and the light of day.

[8] Probably a sacrifice offered in the grave itself before the burial; Prott and Ziehen, *op. cit.* II. 264 *sq.*

custom. They shall take the bed and the coverings [1] home from the tomb. On the following day a free person shall sprinkle the house with sea water first,[2] and then all the rooms(?) [3] with hyssop.[4] When the house has been sprinkled throughout, it shall be pure, and they shall offer sacrifices upon the hearth.

The women who go to the funeral shall not(?) [5] go away from the tomb before the men.

They shall not perform rites on the thirtieth day [6] for the dead person. They shall not place a cup beneath the bed, nor pour out the water, nor shall they carry the sweepings to the tomb.[7]

Wherever a person dies, no women shall go to the house after the body is borne forth, except those who are polluted (by the death), namely, the mother, the wife, sisters and daughters, and not more than five women besides them; also children of daughters and of cousins (are polluted), but no one else.[8] Those who are polluted, after washing themselves . . . by pouring water, shall be pure.

(*The remainder is lost.*)

III. Worship of the Dead at Athens

(Sophocles, *Electra*, 404–500)

The following passage offers further information on the relations between the kinsmen and their dead, as represented in Attic tragedy. Noteworthy is the belief that the spirit of the deceased father, when duly invoked, will come from the tomb to aid his daughter against enemies.

[1] Probably the sheet and coverlet already mentioned.

[2] *Cf.* Euripides, *Iphigeneia in Tauris*, 1193: "The sea washes away all the ills of men."

[3] So Prott and Ziehen. Buck would restore thus: "And then a slave shall step in (and shall sprinkle the house)."

[4] For the use of hyssop in purifications, see *Leviticus* xiv. 49–53.

[5] The insertion of the word is very doubtful.

[6] At Athens a memorial feast was held thirty days after the funeral; *cf.* Rohde, *Psyche*, I. 233, n. 3.

[7] These superstitions are not mentioned by ancient writers, but may be compared with similar practices among the modern Greeks and the German peasantry; *Cf.* Prott and Ziehen, *op. cit.* II. 265 *sqq.*

[8] The sense of this passage is slightly confused, but it seems to mean that the relatives as far as the fifth degree are rendered impure, but only five women from their number, in addition to the immediate family, shall join in the lamentations.

Clytemnestra, queen of Argos, has murdered her husband Agamemnon, and now lives in dread of punishment for the crime. Frightened by a dream, she sends her daughter Chrysothemis with a sacrifice to offer at the tomb of the slain king. Electra, another daughter, meets Chrysothemis on the way, and the following conversation takes place.

CHRYSOTHEMIS. Then I will go forth upon mine errand.

ELECTRA. And whither goest thou? To whom bearest thou these offerings?

CHR. Our mother sends me with funeral libations for our sire.

EL. How sayest thou? For her deadliest foe?

CHR. Slain by her own hand — so thou wouldest say.

EL. What friend hath persuaded her? Whose wish was this?

CHR. The cause, I think, was some dread vision of the night.

EL. Gods of our house! be ye with me — now at last!

CHR. Dost thou find any encouragement in this terror?

EL. If thou wouldest tell me the vision, then I could answer.

CHR. Nay, I can tell but little of the story.

EL. Tell what thou canst; a little word hath often marred, or made men's fortunes.

CHR. 'Tis said that she beheld our sire, restored to the sunlight, at her side once more; then he took the scepter, — once his own, but now borne by Ægisthus, — and planted it at the hearth; and thence a fruitful bough sprang upward, wherewith the whole land of Mycenæ was overshadowed.[1] Such was the tale that I heard told by one who was present when she declared her dream to the Sun-god. More than this I know not, — save that she sent me by reason of that fear. So by the gods of our house I beseech thee, hearken to me, and be not ruined by folly! For if thou repel me now, thou wilt come back to seek me in thy trouble.

EL. Nay, dear sister, let none of these things in thy hands touch the tomb; for neither custom nor piety allows thee to dedicate gifts nor bring libations to our sire from a hateful wife. No — to the winds with them; or bury them deep in the earth, where none of them shall ever come near his place of rest; but, when she dies, let her find these treasures laid up for her below.

And were she not the most hardened of all women, she would

[1] This omen foretells the growth of her son Orestes, now an exile, to manhood and his succession to the throne of his father.

never have sought to pour these offerings of enmity on the grave of him whom she slew. Think now if it is likely that the dead in the tomb shall take these honors kindly at her hand, who ruthlessly slew him, like a foeman, and mangled him, and for ablution wiped off the bloodstains on his head? Canst thou believe that these things which thou bringest will absolve her of the murder?

It is not possible. No, these things cast aside; give him rather a lock cut from thine own tresses, and on my part, hapless that I am, — scant gifts these, but my best, — this hair, not glossy with unguents, and this girdle, decked with no rich ornament. Then fall down and pray that he himself may come in kindness from the world below, to aid us against our foes; and that the young Orestes may live to set his foot upon his enemies in victorious might, that henceforth we may crown our father's tomb with wealthier hands than those which grace it now.

I think, indeed, I think that he also had some part in sending her these appalling dreams; still, sister, do this service, to help thyself and me, and him, that most beloved of all men, who rests in the realm of Hades, thy sire and mine.

Chorus. The maiden counsels piously; and thou, friend, wilt do her bidding.

Chr. I will. When a duty is clear, reason forbids that two voices shall contend, and claims the hastening of the deed. Only, when I attempt this task, aid me with your silence, I entreat you, my friends; for should my mother hear of it, methinks I shall yet have cause to rue my venture.

Ch. If I am not an erring seer and one who fails in wisdom, Justice, that hath sent the presage, will come, triumphant in her righteous strength, — will come ere long, my child, to avenge. There is courage in my heart, through those new tidings of the dream that breathes comfort. Not forgetful is thy sire, the lord of Hellas; not forgetful is the two-edged axe of bronze that struck the blow of old, and slew him with foul cruelty.

The Erinys [1] of untiring feet, who is lurking in her dread ambush, will come as with the march and with the might of a great host. For wicked ones have been fired with passion that hurried

[1] Erinys, the avenging Fury of the slain man; she will soon punish the murderess.

them to a forbidden bed, to accursed bridals, to a marriage stained with guilt of blood. Therefore am I sure that the portent will not fail to bring woe upon the partners in crime. Verily mortals cannot read the future in fearful dreams or oracles, if this vision of the night find not due fulfilment.

112. Colonus and its Religious Associations

(Sophocles, *Œdipus of Colonus*, 668–719)

Colonus was a deme (township) of Attica, about a mile and a quarter northwest of Athens, and not far from the Academy. It was the birthplace of Sophocles. In that age Greece was well watered, and Colonus was most beautiful, as this description shows, though it is now desolate.

The passage is included in this chapter to illustrate the religious associations which clustered even about places not distinguished for famous shrines. At the same time it is evidence of the marvelous beauty of the place and of the poet's appreciation of the loveliness of nature.

Stranger,[1] in this land of goodly steeds thou hast come to earth's fairest home, even to our white Colonus; where the nightingale, a constant guest, trills her clear note in the covert of green glades, dwelling among the wine-dark ivy and the god's inviolate bowers, rich in berries and fruit, unvisited by sun, unvexed by wind of any storm; where the reveller Dionysus ever walks the ground, companion of the nymphs that nursed him.

And fed of heavenly dew, the narcissus blooms morn by morn, with fair clusters, crown of the great Goddesses[2] from of yore; and the crocus blooms with golden beam. Nor fail the sleepless founts whence the waters of Cephissus wander, but each day with stainless tide he moveth over the plains of the land's swelling bosom, for the giving of quick increase; nor hath the Muses' choir abhorred this place, nor Aphrodite of the golden rein.

And a thing there is such as I know not by fame on Asian ground, or as ever born in the great Dorian isle of Pelops, — a growth unconquered, self-renewing, a terror to the spears of foemen, a growth which mightily flourishes in this land, — the gray-

[1] The stranger is Œdipus, who wandering in exile is now approaching Colonus. The speaker is the Chorus, composed of the elders of Colonus.

[2] Demeter and her daughter Persephone.

leafed olive, nurturer of children. Youth shall not mar it by the ravage of his hand, nor any one who dwells with old age; for the sleepless eye of the Morian Zeus[1] beholds it, and the gray-eyed Athena.

And another praise have I to tell for this the city of our mother, the gift of a great god, a glory of the land most high; the might of horses, the might of young horses, the might of the sea.

For thou, son of Cronos, our Lord Poseidon,[2] hast throned her in this pride, since in these roads first thou didst show forth the curb that cures the rage of steeds. And the shapely oar, apt to men's hands, hath a wondrous speed on the brine, following the hundred-footed Nereids.

113. The Gods are Man's Invention

(Critias, *Sisyphus;* Nauck. Frag. p. 771 *sq.* Translated by E. G. S.)

The author is the famous leader of the "Thirty" who governed Athens with terror and violence for a short time after the close of the Peloponnesian war. Though his talent was remarkably versatile, he lacked moral character, wanting even the generous impulses of the friend of his youth, Alcibiades. The following passage from his *Sisyphus* is a bolder denial of the existence of the gods than anything that can be found in Euripides; See Botsford, *Hellenic History*, ch. xx.

A time once existed when unordered was the life of men, and kindred to the beasts — a life enslaved to brute force, when no reward existed for the good, nor for the bad was wrought chastisement. Then, methinks, did men establish laws as means of punishment, that Justice might be autocrat . . . and have Insolence for slave; and penalty was meted out to any who transgressed. When the laws restrained them openly from doing deeds of force, but secretly they did them, then, methinks, some man, adroit and wise, conceived the notion of devising gods for mankind, that awe might be for the bad, even if secretly they should perform or say or think (some evil). Thence he did introduce divinity: that there is a Supernal Being flourishing with life imperishable, and mind, hearing and seeing and thinking, and attending to these things and

[1] Zeus Morios, guardian of the sacred olives (μορίαι) of the Academy, a public garden near by.

[2] Poseidon, god of the sea and of horses, had a shrine here.

bearing divine nature, who will hear all that is spoken among mortals and will perceive all that is enacted. Even if in silence thou some evil plannest, this will not escape the gods. For faculty of thought . . . abides in them. These sayings uttering, he did bring forward doctrine winsome, greatly blinding truth with fraudulent discourse. The gods, he said, dwelt in that place by mention whereof he would most terrify mankind — the region whence he knew men had their fears; benefactions, too, (they had) for their life of toil from circular movement above, where he discerned the thunderbolts, and terrible reports of thunder and the gleaming stars of heaven, the fair and varied work of Time, the knowing architect, whence gleams the fiery mass of shining orb, and drenching rain issues upon the earth. Such fears he stationed around about mankind; with awe beset and cleverly he housed the power supernal and in befitting place; thus he extinguished lawlessness with fears. . . . In such wise, I believe, did some one first persuade the mortals that there was a race of supernal beings.[1]

BIBLIOGRAPHY

Prott, J. de, and Ziehen, L., *Leges græcorum sacræ e titulis collectæ*, I, II. 1 (Leipzig, 1896–1906); Dinsmoor, W. B., "Attic Building Accounts," in *Am. Journ. Arch.* XVII (1913). 53–80, 242–65, 371–98; Elderkin, G. W., *Problems in Periclean Buildings* (Princeton University Press, 1912); Dörpfeld, W., "Zu den Bauwerken Athens," in *Ath. Mitt.* XXXV (1910). 39–72; Caskey, L. D., "Die Baurechnung des Erechtheion für das Jahr 409–08 v. Chr.," *ib.* XXXVI. 317–43; Goodyear, H., *Greek Refinements: Study in Temperamental Architecture* (London, 1912).

The following titles are given as an aid to the general study of Greek religion. Adams, J., *Religious Teachers of Greece.* Gifford Lects. (Edinburgh, 1908); Bischoff, E. F., "Kauf und Verkauf von Priesterthümern bei den Griechen," in *Rhein. Mus.* LIV (1899). 9–18; Caird, E., *Evolution of Theology in the Greek Philosophers*, 2 vols. (Glasgow, 1904); Campbell, L., *Religion in Greek Literature* (Longmans, 1898); Cumont, F., *Astrology and Religion among the Greeks and Romans* (Putnam, 1912); Decharme, P., *La critique des traditions religieuses chez les Grecs*, etc. (Paris, 1904); Farnell, L. R., *Cults of the Greek States*, 5 vols. (Clarendon Press, 1898–1909); *Higher Aspects of Greek Religion.* Hibbert Lects. (Scribner, 1912); Gardner, E. A., *Religion and Art in Ancient Greece* (Harper, 1910); Gardner, E. N., *Greek Athletic Sports and Festivals* (Macmillan, 1910); Gilbert, O., *Griechische Religionsphilosophie* (Leipzig,

[1] The entire passage is here presented, the lacunæ in the text being indicated in the usual way.

1911); Gruppe, P. O., *Griechische Mythologie und Religionsgeschichte*, 2 vols. (Munich, 1906); Hamilton, M., *Incubation; or the Cure of Disease in Pagan Temples and Christian Churches* (London, 1906); Harrison, J. E., *Prolegomena to the Study of Greek Religion* (Cambridge, 1903); *Themis: a Study of the Social Origins of Greek Religion* (Cambridge, 1912); *Ancient Art and Ritual* (Holt: University Library); Holderman, E. S., *A Study of the Greek Priestess*. Diss. (Chicago: University Press, 1913); Halliday, W. R., *Greek Divination: a Study of its Methods and Principles* (Macmillan, 1913); Kern, O., *Ueber die Anfänge der hellenischen Religion* (Berlin, 1902); Lang, A., *Myth, Ritual, and Religion* (Longmans, 1887); Mommsen, A., *Feste der Stadt Athen im Altertum* (Teubner, 1898); Moore, G. F., *History of Religions*, I. chs. xvii–xx; Murray, G., *Four Stages of Greek Religion* (Columbia University Press, 1912); Philios, M. D., *Eleusis: her Mysteries, Ruins, and Museums* (Appleton, 1906); Reitzenstein, R. A., *Die hellenistischen Mysterienreligionen*, etc. (Teubner, 1910); Rouse, W. H. D., *Greek Votive Offerings* (Cambridge, 1902); Wheeler, B. I., *Dionysos and Immortality* (Houghton Mifflin, 1899).

CHAPTER XII

HELLENIC INTERSTATE RELATIONS

During the Period 404–337

CHAPTERS xii–xv illustrate various activities of the Hellenes during the period extending from the close of the Peloponnesian war, 404, to the formation of the Hellenic federation under Philip of Macedon in 337, the year following the battle of Chæroneia.

114. IDEAL HELLENIC RELATIONS

(Plato, *Republic*, 470 *sq.*)

The principal speaker in this dialogue, as elsewhere in Plato, is Socrates.

Neither shall we offer up arms at the temples of the gods, least of all the arms of Hellenes, if we care to maintain good feeling with other Hellenes; and indeed, we have reason to fear that the offering of spoils taken from kinsmen may be a pollution unless commanded by the god himself?

Very true.

Again, as to the devastation of Hellenic territory or the burning of houses, what is to be the practice?

May I have the pleasure, he said, of hearing your opinion?

Both should be forbidden, in my judgment; I would take the annual produce and no more. Shall I tell you why?

Pray do.

Why, you see, there is a difference in the names 'discord' and 'war,' and I imagine that there is also a difference in their natures; the one is expressive of what is internal and domestic, the other of what is foreign and external; and the first of the two is termed discord, and only the second, war.

That is a very proper distinction, he replied.

And may I not observe with equal propriety that the Hellenic race is all united together by ties of blood and friendship, and alien and strange to the barbarians?

Very good, he said.

And therefore when Hellenes fight with barbarians and barbarians with Hellenes, they will be described by us as being at war when they fight, and by nature enemies, and this kind of antagonism should be called war; but when Hellenes fight with one another we shall say that Hellas is then in a state of disorder and discord, they being by nature friends; and such enmity is to be called discord.

I agree.

Consider then, I said, when that which we have acknowledged to be discord occurs, and a city is divided, if both parties destroy the lands and burn the houses of one another, how wicked does the strife appear! No true lover of his country would bring himself to tear in pieces his own nurse and mother. There might be reason in the conqueror depriving the conquered of their harvest, but still they would have the idea of peace in their hearts and would not mean to go on fighting for ever.

Yes, he said, that is a better temper than the other.

And will not the city, which you are founding, be an Hellenic city?

It ought to be, he replied.

Then will not the citizens be good and civilized?

Yes, very civilized.

And will they not be lovers of Hellas, and think of Hellas as their own land, and share in the common temples?

Most certainly.

And any difference which arises among them will be regarded by them as discord only — a quarrel among friends, which is not to be called a war?

Certainly not.

Then they will quarrel as those who intend some day to be reconciled?

Certainly.

They will use friendly correction, but will not enslave or destroy their opponents; they will be correctors, not enemies?

Just so.

And as they are Hellenes themselves they will not devastate Hellas, nor will they burn houses nor ever suppose that the whole population of a city — men, women, and children — are equally their enemies, for they know that the guilt of war is always confined to a few persons and that the many are their friends. And for all these reasons they will be unwilling to waste their lands, and raze their houses; their enmity to them will only last until the many innocent sufferers have compelled the guilty few to give satisfaction?

I agree, he said, that our citizens should thus deal with their Hellenic enemies; and with barbarians as the Hellenes now deal with one another.

115. Monetary Union between Mytilene and Phocæa, Early Fourth Century

(Hicks and Hill, no. 94; Buck, *Greek Dialects*, II. no. 21. Translated by C. J. O.)

This inscription was found on a block which was built into a house at Mytilene, but which has now disappeared. The subject is evidently an agreement between Mytilene, on the island of Lesbos, and the neighboring city of Phocæa on the mainland, to the effect that the two cities should issue a common coinage, alternating year by year; *cf.* Wroth, *Catalogue of the Greek Coins of Troas, Æolis, and Lesbos*, pp. lxv–lxvii and 156–8. From the coins themselves we learn that the metal used was electrum, a natural or artificial alloy of gold with silver, and that the denominations were staters and "sixths," the latter weighing about 39 grains. Although this inscription, as indicated by the style of writing, belongs to the early part of the fourth century, the original agreement between the two cities may have been far earlier, for these coins were issued as early as 480. It is interesting to note that, in spite of the severe penalties for adulteration, the Phocæan coinage had a bad reputation and was not received in full value by other cities; Hill, *Hdb. of Greek and Roman Coins* (London, 1899), 70. On the general subject of monetary unions, of which this inscription furnishes the best example, *ibid.* 103–6; Head, *Historia Numorum* (Oxford, 1911), p. lxxxiii *sq.*

(*The first part of the inscription is lost.*)

If the two cities . . . shall write anything upon the [stele or erase anything], such change shall be effectual. One who [debases] the gold coinage[1] shall be liable to both cities. The judges shall be,

[1] That is, a careless or dishonest director of the mint. Noteworthy is the fact that the director, not the state, was responsible. We notice, also, that though the metal is in fact electrum, the coinage is officially termed gold.

in the case of one who [coins] at Mytilene, all the magistrates of Mytilene for a majority of the court; and at Phocæa all the magistrates of Phocæa for a majority of the court. The trial shall be within six months after the termination of the year.[1] If he is convicted of purposely making the alloyed gold too base,[2] he shall be punished with death; if he is acquitted of doing wrong purposely, the court shall determine what he shall suffer or pay; but the city shall be exempt from responsibility and from loss. The people of Mytilene drew the lot to mint first. (This agreement shall be in effect) beginning (with the term of) the prytanis succeeding Colonus (at Mytilene) and the successor of Aristarchus at Phocæa.[3]

116. The Relation of Larisa, Thessaly, to Macedon and to Sparta, about 400 B.C.

(Pseudo-Herodes Atticus, *On the Constitution* — Περὶ Πολιτείας Translated by E. G. S.)

This curious document, which has come down to us under the name of Herodes (Atticus), 101–177 A.D., is in Codex Burneianus, no. 95, of the British Museum, following the sophistic declamations of Gorgias, Alcidamas, and Lesbonax. It began to attract the attention of historians in 1893, when Köhler, U., *Sitzb. Berl. Akad.* XXVI. 489–507, set forth its value for the political relations of Thessaly at the close of the fifth century B.C. In his judgment Herodes, whom he accepts as the author, drew his historical material from Thrasymachus of Chalcedon, *On the Larisæans* — Περὶ Λαρισαίων. Beloch, *Griech. Gesch.* II (1897). 132, n. 2, advancing a step farther, decided the treatise to have been the work of a sophist resident in Larisa, or perhaps rather a native sophist, of about 400. Meyer, *Gesch. des Alt.* V (1902). 56 *sq.*, following Beloch, entertains no doubt that it is the work of a Larisæan. As far as the date is concerned, this view is accepted by Drerup, E., "[Ἡρώδου] Περὶ Πολιτείας: ein politisches Pamphlet aus Athen 404 vor Chr.," in *Gesch. u. Kult. des Alt.* II. 1 (1908), who, however, prefers to consider the writer an Athenian of the school of Theramenes. In any event the author shows a far better acquaintance with the details of the Greek political situation about 400 B.C. than could be credited to any sophist of the Christian era. The early date is favored, too, by the style. In the judgment of the present translator, it is too little polished, too inadequate on the score of formal perfection, often too awkward with its labored rather than bril-

[1] The year during which the accused director held office.

[2] Literally, "mixing the gold too weak," a metaphor from the mixing of wine with water.

[3] *I.e.*, with the beginning of the next official year.

liant antitheses, to be the work of a late sophist; and the language is not archaizing but distinctly archaic. Although the dialect is not Æolic but pure Attic, this circumstance need not hinder our believing it to have been addressed to a Thessalian community, even by a Thessalian; for Gorgias of Chalcidic Leontini composed orations in Attic, and Isocrates addressed the Doric Dionysius and the Macedonian Philip in the same dialect. In favor of the early date, see also Nestle, W., *N. Jahrb.* VI (1903). 191 *sqq.* (who claims Thrasymachus of Chalcedon as author); Pöhlmann, *Griech. Gesch.* (4th ed. 1909). 182, n. 4; Ferguson, *Greek Imperialism*, 20 *sq.*; Costanzi, V., in *Studi italiani di filologia classica*, VII (1899). 137–59. For the conservative view, Schmid, W., *Rhein. Mus.* LIX (1904). 512–24; Wilamowitz-Moellendorff, U. v., in *Kultur der Gegenwart*, I. 8 (1905). 149 *sq.*; Adcock and Knox, in *Klio*, XIII (1913). 249–57 (whose contention is that the document does not precisely fit the political situation at any point of time in the neighborhood of 400 B.C., and that the language is not early Greek, or even good Greek of any period).

The translation of the entire document is given below, partly because of its unusual nature, and partly because of its inaccessibility to the general student of Greek affairs. The peculiar style is rendered literally into English in so far as it does not put an excessive strain upon the language. The best treatment of the entire subject is by Drerup, *op. cit.*, whose article includes the text with an introduction and an elaborate commentary.

(1) I must first explain that it is necessary to speak about the present matter [1] to men of this age and not to much younger per-

[1] For an appreciation of this document a few general facts regarding the political history of Thessaly, and its condition about 400 B.C., are necessary. First it is to be noted that neither Thessaly nor Larisa is mentioned by name; and it is only from allusions in the pamphlet that scholars have been able to identify as Larisa the city-state to which it was addressed. They have noticed that its territory borders upon Macedon (§ 25) and that the nearest neighbors on the Hellenic side are the Phocians (28). The description of the country (14 *sq.*) as the largest and most productive of Hellas, the reference to its oligarchic governments (30), and to its attitude in the Persian war (22 *sq.*) point unmistakably to Thessaly; *cf.* Drerup, in *Gesch. u. Kult. des Alt.* II. 1. 87 *sq.* It is known further that about 400 Thessaly was ruled by a few great city-states, of which Pelasgiotis under Larisa lay nearest to Macedon. For these reasons there can be no doubt that the Larisæans were the people to whom the pamphlet appealed.

Toward the end of the sixth century the Aleuadæ, a noble family of Larisa, united all Thessaly under their royal sway (Hdt. vii. 6). They sided with the Persian invaders, whereas the commons sympathized with the patriot cause (Hdt. vii. 172–4). After the war the unity was broken and Thessaly fell into great confusion. In Larisa, as elsewhere, were factions of the Few and the Many in deadly strife with one another (*cf.* Thuc. ii. 22. 3, 431 B.C.). On their conflict hinged the history of the state, not only in its domestic affairs, but in its relations with outsiders. This fact is kept in the foreground throughout the present document. Taking advantage of seditions, Archelaüs, king of Macedon, 413–399, aimed to make himself master of Thessaly. The Few, in their strife with the Many, had invited his aid (§ 9). He had invaded

sons. That it is seemly to be silent when one has something to say, I neither can learn from another nor do I find it so myself. (2) For concerning another matter one might be able to censure those who speak, charging them with futility or with meddlesomeness, namely, that they were not acquainted with the facts in the case before them; but in affairs relating to the war [1] all have an interest in common; and most necessary and pertinent it is that men in these stages of life [2] should know and speak about them. They to whom the danger comes most nearly home should most necessarily be concerned about it; and they upon whom it is laid to be concerned should most certainly ascertain the facts.[3] (3) For speaking I find much need, but for holding my peace I see no excuse. It was my desire that you yourselves, together with the Gods, should be the causes of your own blessings. If however it is this about which you are delaying, and if it is sweet to you to owe your success to others, it seems to me that whatever takes place is due to the care of one of the Gods. (4) All that you ought to have brought about by persuading with money and by risking with your bodies, Fortune has accomplished for you without trouble or money, so that your own adversaries willingly pay you the penalty. First, then, I shall teach you that it is well to follow those who propose war, and next that it is necessary.

(5) For we were able to perceive the forces that were naturally hostile to this country, and perceiving in advance before suffering,

Larisa, and, in coöperation with his partisans, had perpetrated a horrible massacre of the commons (16–18). His permanent gain was the occupation of the Perrhæbian territory, which, at least a generation earlier, Larisa had forcibly annexed (6).

In the Peloponnesian war Archelaüs had sympathized with Athens. It was natural, then, that the Lacedæmonians should feel unfriendly toward him. When therefore they invited Larisa to join the Hellenic league, the writer composed this pamphlet, in the form of an address, to persuade the Larisæans to accept the terms, chiefly on the ground that it would guarantee protection from their northern enemy. The author was evidently a sophist, rather than a practical statesman. His *Oration* is like those of Isocrates in general character and purpose, though narrower in scope and relatively crude in style and thought.

[1] The question before the assembly was whether Larisa should join the Hellenic league, a step which was liable to involve them in war with King Archelaüs of Macedon.

[2] Particularly men of military age, taking part in the assembly.

[3] Notice the heavy, labored movement of the style here and throughout the document. The author seems a pioneer of prose, feeling his way with great difficulty through an unknown field.

we would be on our guard, rendering their affairs weak in every way and our own affairs stronger than theirs, understanding that whatever is by nature hostile keeps quiet through inability to inflict evil. (6) But now from what has happened we have our instruction — that this man [1] will never be our friend nor will there be any reconciliation between him and us. For not being injured by us but wishing to inflict injury, is he our adversary. He holds a territory which our fathers acquired and handed down to us,[2] which on account of our weakness he will hold, and on account of our power will reluctantly restore. (7) This is one pretext for his ill-will toward us. Another is that Greek commonwealths are satisfied to preserve their own power for their descendants, while for autocrats [3] this does not suffice, but they always need, in addition, to subjugate the richest (of their neighbors). (8) Now it is our conviction that we should not suffer this misfortune ourselves and should also prevent others from suffering it. Hence that man has a grudge against us, desiring the hopes of those who trust in us to fail. Beginning then with a single device,[4] he believes he will overcome us and those whom we are preventing him from ruling. (9) These things we were formerly permitted to conjecture but now clearly to experience in fact. Any means which gave him a chance to conquer community and territory did not escape him when he saw us in civil disruption; but in alliance with the Few (the aristocracy) he did not hesitate to assail all these people (here assembled).[5] (10) He knew when he came that should he attack the Few he would accomplish nothing that he wished; for by beating down the weaker party in joint warfare he would

[1] King Archelaüs; see 376, n. 1.

[2] Undoubtedly the territory of the Perrhæbians, lying between Pelasgiotis and Macedon, a region conquered by Larisa and more recently taken from that city by Macedon; see 376, n. 1.

[3] Τυράννοις, "tyrants." In fact he was a king; but the author applies to him the opprobrious title in order to rouse hatred against him. The contrast between the grasping nature of despots and the peaceful disposition of city-states is without historical foundation.

[4] Evidently his device is to side with one of the factions found in every Thessalian state.

[5] That is, he joined with the Few against the Many. The latter are represented in the assembly which the author is, in imagination, addressing. The government about 400 was no longer a narrow oligarchy. On the other hand, it was not a democracy, as it did not include the laborers, penestæ.

by no means gain sway over the more numerous, as they would have been able to ward him off; but if he were to subjugate the Many in alliance with the Few, he believed he would easily have them all in his power.[1] Thus he naturally wishes us to be in civil disruption.[2] If these things are profitable to him, you must believe, too, that he will do them. (11) To what extent his advantage is our misfortune, look ye, comparing it with the weightiest of other things. Now we all agree that war is the greatest of evils in proportion as peace is of blessings. Civil disruption, however, exceeds war in the degree that war exceeds peace. For in a foreign war they die while saving their country, but in civil strife while destroying it, so that not even those who have done the slaying have good repute; (12) because in warring on others we fight in behalf of our friends; in conquering foreigners we acquire others as friends; but in conquering our own countrymen we are deprived even of the friends that exist. The seizure of territory, the destruction of property, the delight of enemies and the consequent disaster of friends, it is tedious to recount in detail. (13) When one begins such things, it is not easy to be rid of them, for no reconciliation [3] can be found. Men are not annoyed when neighbors have civil broils; the weaker, that they may escape subjugation; the equal, that they may become stronger; and the strong, that they may rule the more easily. (14) Of these facts I think it unnecessary to look for evidence elsewhere; for we are a proof to others. For possessing the largest territory of the Hellenes, and one which can furnish most products not only to the inhabitants but also to neighbors, we do not appear to be richer than those who export from us, since they accumulate products for themselves, but we spend them on foreigners,[4] making the common property personal,

[1] The reasons are here given why he sided with the aristocrats against the commons. The "weaker" are the aristocrats.

[2] It is by civil strife that he has gained his power, and by civil strife he expects to keep the upper hand. He has not given continued support to the Few, and the Many at present control the government.

[3] The translator prefers to emend *διάλογον* to *διαλλαγήν*.

[4] *Τοῖς παροίκοις*, evidently aliens who have taken up their residence in the Thessalian towns for commercial objects. Agriculturally the country was the richest in the peninsula but was wholly backward in economy. As there was no accumulation of native capital adequate to the needs of the expanding trade, it was inevitable that the country should be commercially exploited by other Greeks.

and that of private persons common. (15) Now is it not outrageous to support at common expense those who do not deliver the commonwealth to us as a common possession? Furthermore, though possessing a territory best adapted to warding off invaders, and a country which furnishes native allies and horses,[1] not only do we thereby check [2] those who wish to injure us, but we even bring in those who will defend us, persuading them with money,[3] and we guard ourselves against strangers, but at the same time the power of the country is despised and we are ourselves a laughing-stock.[4] (16) The man who is responsible for all these ills and for many others you yourselves saw when he was present — the man who made before all such a display that no one is so hard or such a hater of mankind that he could describe it without tears.[5] For what one of the greatest evils did not come to pass? Did not children and women and aged fathers become witnesses of deaths, some of fathers, some of husbands, some of children, some of those who passed away in their own arms, others destroyed by the hands of the foe? (17) And houses razed and property taken away? And what was most terrible of all, whenever one who shared in the same worship, and performed the same sacred rites,[6] and was a member of the same tribe — whom it behoved to repel according to the law, but not lawlessly to destroy — when even to old men old age appeared a misfortune, and to orphans in like manner? (18) The man, then, who was responsible for these calamities, ought we not to injure when we can, repelling those who were his aid, avenging the dead, and lamenting with the bereaved? Not only is it so great an advantage that we will get satisfaction for the past but that, offering this as an example, we will teach others not to consider our disharmony a piece of sheer luck nor to plot against us in alliance with our own countrymen.

[1] Thessaly was the best country in Greece for rearing horses.

[2] The translator emends διαλύομεν to κωλύομεν.

[3] Mercenaries are thus described.

[4] That is, through the interference of Archelaüs as a result of civil broils.

[5] Invited by the aristocrats, Archelaüs had intervened, and in company with his partisans had perpetrated a horrible massacre described below; *cf.* 376, n. 1.

[6] Ὁ ταῦτα δρῶν should perhaps be ὁ τὰ αὐτὰ δρῶν, "who chances to be doing the same things," the connection seemingly indicating that reference is to the performance of sacred rites.

If this result is achieved, I am hopeful that we will have no more civil strife, when plotters are not aided by allies from abroad. (19) Thus it is *well* for us voluntarily to agree to join in war with those who summon us; but that it is *necessary* we must now examine.[1] Archelaüs did not march against the Peloponnesians along with the Athenians, nor did he stop the former when they wished to go through his territory,[2] nor did he furnish them (the Athenians) funds against the others,[3] nor is there any pretext for hostility except that he was unwilling to join them in war against the Athenians, but kept quiet. (20) Since therefore the Peloponnesians have an adequate pretext for deeming as enemies those who did not support them in the war, let us be on our guard lest they on the same pretext make war on us, if being summoned we shall be unwilling to join the Peloponnesians in war, for he was not injured by the Athenians at all.[4] (21) What argument, then, is left to us? Is it that we were not injured? We shall teach them to do just what he did; for it is not wrong if he who did it is no wrong-doer.[5] Shall we say, then, that we are wronged but unwilling to avenge ourselves? Much cowardice indeed we shall arouse in those who wish to injure us.[6] (22) But are we willing though unable? Who then will not despise our power, if, having the Hellenes as allies,

[1] In the preceding paragraphs the writer has been urging the advantage of a league with the Lacedæmonians in a war against Macedon. He will now consider the necessity of such a union.

[2] The only Peloponnesian march of the kind known to us was the expedition of Brasidas in 424 (Thuc. iv. 78). Though at that time Perdiccas, not Archelaüs, was king, the principle alone is important. Notwithstanding the opinion of the writer, this permission was a breach of neutrality in favor of the Lacedæmonians.

[3] This statement is untrue. After the Sicilian disaster Archelaüs supplied Athens with ship timber (Thuc. viii. 4. 1; Andoc. ii. 11; Xen. Hell. vi. 1. 11), and in return was aided by an Athenian force (Diod. xiii. 49. 1). It is to be noted that Archelaüs was a great admirer and patron of Athenian literary men and artists; *cf.* Drerup, *op. cit.* 98 and n. 3. There was accordingly a far greater pretext for war than the writer states.

[4] The argument is that we must either join with the Peloponnesians against Archelaüs or ourselves incur the danger of being assailed by the Peloponnesians. The latter are in fact so sensitive that they are making war upon Archelaüs because he did not join them against the Athenians, even though this king had suffered no wrong at the hands of the Athenians. The argument is too finely spun to be appreciated at first glance.

[5] That is, if we excuse ourselves from the war on the ground that Archelaüs has not harmed us, we shall teach the Peloponnesians to treat us just as Archelaüs has.

[6] This is, of course, ironical.

we shall not even thus be able to repel our enemies? The greatest consideration is, if we shall incur for a second time from the Greeks the accusation that we did not join in the war against the Persians, and secondly the one now announced.[1] (23) As to the former, we had an adequate excuse: in behalf of ourselves we were willing to share their danger; for it would have been on more equitable terms (to fight here) than to abandon our country and struggle in defence of theirs.[2] Now, however, what shall we say? For they have themselves arrived, willing to face danger in behalf of us and of our country. (24) Is it not outrageous, too, if we along with the Greeks are not to be counted in with the Hellenic coalition? How great a thing it is, this man himself has made clear; for though eager and willing to give money even to the Greeks to become their ally, he could not bring it about.[3] His conduct is a fair sign of two conditions: that it is a good thing (to join the coalition) and that it is difficult. To any one who objects to my view such is my argument. (25) I have already heard something said which is to me sufficient proof of the soundness of the view I hold against my political opponents.[4] If what they have said is true, there is no need of fear. (26) They say in fact that Archelaüs is powerful and that he, not the Peloponnesians, is our neighbor. Him we might keep at bay, if we wished, but not the Peloponnesians. Their idea is that it is better for us to have civil broils among ourselves than be slaves to others. If I saw that there was any need of choosing one of the two alternatives, I should deliberate as to which of the two I ought to take; but the restful alternative I find is connected with the Peloponnesians. (27) I marvel also at those

[1] That is, if we do not now join with the Greeks in war against this foreigner, we shall again be reproached with having deserted them in that war and again on this similar occasion.

[2] The writer means that in the Persian invasion the Thessalians would have fought against the foreigner had they been supported in their own country by the Hellenes. In the present instance the Hellenic forces are on the ground, ready to help them.

[3] It seems clear that Archelaüs had recently asked for admission to the Hellenic league but had been refused. It is clear, too, from the general context that at the time of the composition of this pamphlet practically all Hellas, with the exception of Larisa, was in the Hellenic alliance under Lacedæmonian leadership. That could only have been after the downfall of Athens, 404.

[4] The opponents of the speaker (writer) favored friendship with Archelaüs and opposed alliance with the Peloponnesians.

who set matters over against matters; for they do not compare similar things with similar; in the first place, what issues from him we know already, but the actions of the others we merely surmise. One thing we did suffer, but the other we do not know whether we will suffer. Is it reasonable, then, to refrain from anger at what has happened and to fear what is merely surmised? (28) From what precedents ought we to dread future events? Do we not see the nearest of our neighbors among the Greeks, the Phocians, free, and those contiguous to them, the Bœotians, neither paying tribute nor any of the Lacedæmonians holding sway there, and further away, the Corinthians independent and governing their own, and near them the Achæans, neither more numerous than we nor dwelling in more numerous commonwealths, and the Eleians, and those of Tegea, and the other Arcadians, who are neighbors? (29) No one has ever found a Spartan ruling there or here, but everywhere, as we know, laws and governments are in operation, and these states enjoy the common revenues in common.[1]

(30) But perhaps some one may say: they everywhere establish oligarchy. Yes, such a form of government as we, long wishing and yearning for, having seen for a short time, have been deprived of, if indeed we ought to call those governments oligarchies in comparison with the forms in operation here. For where is there so small a community in which one third of the citizens are excluded from political life? (31) All those who have neither arms nor any other force to govern by were deprived of the franchise, not by the Lacedæmonians, but by fate. Deprived were they for a long time, till there came a change in the constitution. These things we have had with us. I believe that not even in our prayers would we pray to be otherwise governed; but it is not reasonable that, while furnishing such examples, we should ourselves be in dread —

[1] The favorable view of the Spartan supremacy was possible only in the period shortly following the close of the war, perhaps after the fall of the Thirty at Athens and of the decarchies in the Ægean cities; for the Lacedæmonians soon began to show themselves tyrannical, and the allies began accordingly to chafe under the tyranny; Botsford, *Hellenic History*, ch. xxi. These circumstances would favor 404, or perhaps rather 403, as the date of the pamphlet. Naturally a political pleader could not be depended upon to state the exact facts in a given situation, to the impairment of his own cause. Adcock and Knox, in *Klio*, XIII. 249–57, have set too high a standard for mortal politicians or even for mortal sophists.

examples whose non-occurrence, rather than whose occurrence, would be a grievous thing.[1]

(32) As for the Lacedæmonians, it is not in their natural disposition to attack us; for they dwell far from us and are unprepared to assail our territory. For in what we are strongest they are not a little inferior.[2] In the first place it is improbable that they are plotting against us; and again, if they undertake it, they will be discovered; and if we discover it in advance, we shall not neglect them. (33) If this argument, too, is offered, that Archelaüs has some of our children, and on account of the children it is impossible to join in the war, in the first place we ought to wonder at the man who would make mention of ten children but says nothing about the common interest or the community. The advantage of all he takes away but about the few he makes his point. If it were necessary that the children should suffer something, it would not be strange to say it; but it is now clear that by overpowering him we shall gain the children at the same time; so that if we involve him in difficulties,[3] we shall easily recover the children.

(34) My discourse bids you beat off the wrong-doer, avenge the dead, gratify their kinsfolk, receive fate, be allies to the Hellenes and foes to the barbarians,[4] trust those who benefit us and hold no dread of those who are not friends, consider as enemies those who wrong us and as friends those who defend us, and in addition, hold our insight more decisive than our conjectures. (35) This is my thesis; but for my opponents, who will go to that limit of audacity, their argument is the opposite: to endure when wronged, to benefit the wrong-doer, to flee from those who wish to benefit, to distrust friends, to trust enemies, to dread what is far away, to

[1] The writer strongly favors a government in which the franchise is held by those who have property qualifications for the heavy infantry, and contends that the Lacedæmonians are supporting that form of constitution among their allies. From this political view of the writer, however, we cannot, with Drerup, deduce the conclusion that the writer was an Athenian of the school of Theramenes.

[2] That is, in cavalry.

[3] The reading *ἀφελόντες τῶν ἐκεινουκακῶν* makes no sense whatever, and it is difficult to say how it should be emended. The translation here given, "if we involve him in difficulties," is a guess at the meaning.

[4] It is noteworthy that the Hellenes of this time regarded the Macedonians as barbarians.

overlook what is close at hand, (36) and then not to become allies of the Hellenes but of the barbarians, and they our most bitter enemies; furthermore, to permit the dead to die unavenged and their relatives to be dishonored, to bring it about that there shall be no government or laws or justice. (37) Such we must say is the thesis of those who speak against my contention. Following them, you will not miss the results to which they lead; but if you receive the alliance with eagerness, we shall obtain satisfaction for what we suffered; and for the future we shall not suffer such things.

117. Constitution of the Bœotian League

(Oxyrhynchus *Hellenica*, xi, in Grenfell and Hunt, *Oxyrhynchus Papyri*, V (1908). Translated by Grenfell and Hunt)

The question as to the authorship of this *Hellenica* is touched upon in ch. i of the present volume. The most valuable part of the recovered fragment is the chapter translated below, which throws a new and valuable light on the constitution of the Bœotian league during the latter part of the fifth century and the beginning of the fourth. The year which the author refers to definitely is 395. For commentary, see Bonner, R. J., in *Class. Journ.* V (1910). 353–9; in *Class. Philol.* V (1910). 405–17; Botsford, G. W., in *Pol. Sci. Quart.* XXV (1910). 271–96; see also Bibliography at the close of the chapter.

In the summer[1] the Bœotians and Phocians went to war. Their enmity was chiefly caused by a party at Thebes; for not many years previously the Bœotians had entered into a state of discord. The condition of Bœotia at that time was as follows. There were then appointed in each of the cities four *boulai*, of which not all the citizens were allowed to become members, but only those who possessed a certain amount of money; of these boulai each one in turn held a preliminary sitting and deliberation about matters of policy, and made proposals to the other three, and a resolution adopted by all became valid. Their individual affairs they continued to manage in that fashion, while the arrangement of the Bœotian league was this. The whole population of the country was divided into eleven units, and each of these provided one Bœotarch, as follows. The Thebans contributed four,

[1] The year 395.

two for the city and two for Platæa, Scolus, Erythræ, Scaphæ, and the other towns which formerly were members of one state with the Platæans, but at that time were subject to Thebes. Two Bœotarchs were provided by the inhabitants of Orchomenus and Hysiæ, and two by the inhabitants of Thespiæ with Eutresis and Thisbæ, one by the inhabitants of Tanagra, and another by the inhabitants of Haliartus, Lebadeia, and Coroneia, each of these cities sending him in turn; in the same way one came from Acræphion, Copæ, and Chæroneia. Such was the proportion in which the chief magistrates were appointed by the different units, which also provided sixty *bouleutæ* for every Bœotarch, and themselves defrayed their daily expenses. Each unit was, moreover, under the obligation to supply a corps of approximately a thousand hoplites and a hundred horsemen. To speak generally, it was in proportion to the distribution of their magistrates that they enjoyed the privileges of the league, made their contributions, sent judges, and took part in everything whether good or bad. This nation then as a whole had this form of polity, and the general assemblies of the Bœotians used to meet in the Cadmeia.

118. Political Factions at Thebes

(Ox. *Hell.* xii. The same translators)

The selection given below is useful, not only for a view of the internal affairs of Thebes on the eve of the Corinthian war, but even more for the new light thrown upon the relation of that city to Athens in the Peloponnesian war and upon the economic condition of Attica in the same period.

At Thebes the best and most notable of the citizens were, as I have already stated, divided against each other, one faction being led by Ismenias, Antitheus, and Androclidas, the other by Leontiades, Asias, and Corrantadas. The political party of Leontiades sided with the Lacedæmonians, while that of Ismenias was accused of Atticizing, because it favored the Athenian democracy when the latter was exiled.[1] Ismenias' party, however, was not concerned for the Athenians but . . . Such being the condition of

[1] Reference is to the exiles under the Thirty, 404–403; Botsford, *Hellenic History*, ch. xxi.

affairs at Thebes, and each of the two factions being powerful, many people from the cities throughout Bœotia then came forward and joined one or the other of them. At that time, and for a short period previously, the party of Ismenias and Androclides was the stronger both at Thebes itself and in the boulê of the Bœotians; but formerly that of Asias and Leontiades was in the ascendant for a considerable period and (had complete control of?) the city. For when the Lacedæmonians in the war with the Athenians were occupying Deceleia [1] and collected a large concourse of their allies, this party prevailed over their opponents both by reason of the proximity of the Lacedæmonians and because the latter were instrumental in conferring great benefits upon the city. The Thebans made a great advance in the direction of complete prosperity as soon as war between the Athenians and Lacedæmonians began; for when the Athenians commenced to threaten(?) Bœotia, the inhabitants of Erythræ, Scaphæ, Scolus, Aulis, Schœnus, and Potniæ, and many other similar places which had no walls, congregated at Thebes, thus doubling the size of the city. But it nevertheless came to prosper in a much higher degree when the Thebans in conjunction with the Lacedæmonians fortified Deceleia against the Athenians; for they took over the prisoners and all the other spoils of the war at a small price, and as they inhabited the neighboring country, carried off to their homes all the furnishing material in Attica, beginning with the wood and tiles of the houses. The country of the Athenians at that time had been the most lavishly furnished in Greece, for it had suffered but slight injury from the Lacedæmonians in the former invasions, and had been adorned and elaborated with so much extravagance that . . . Such was the condition of Thebes and Bœotia.

119. The Olynthian Confederacy

(Xenophon, *Hellenica*, v. 2. 11–19)

The embassy mentioned in this excerpt belongs to the year 383. The selection is offered because of the remarkable character of the confederacy of which it treats. See Freeman, *History of Federal Government*, I. 190–97; Grote, *History of Greece*, X. 50 *sqq.*; Botsford, *Hellenic History*, ch. xxi.

[1] In the later years of the war; *op. cit.* ch. xix.

Now from yet another quarter ambassadors arrived in Lacedæmon; that is to say, from Acanthus and Apollonia, the two largest and most important states of the Olynthian confederacy. The ephors, after learning from them the object of their visit, presented them to the assembly and the allies, in presence of whom Cleigenes of Acanthus made a speech to this effect:

"Men of Lacedæmon and of the allied states," he said, "are you aware of a silent but portentous growth within the bosom of Hellas? Few here need be told that for size and importance Olynthus now stands at the head of the Thracian cities. But are you aware that the citizens of Olynthus have already brought over several states by the bribe of joint citizenship and common laws; that they have forcibly annexed some of the larger states; and that, so encouraged, they have taken in hand further to free the cities of Macedon from Amyntas[1] the king of the Macedonians; that, as soon as their immediate neighbors had shown compliance, they proceeded to attack larger and more distant communities; so much so, that when we started to come hither, we left them masters not only of many other places, but of Pella itself, the capital of Macedon? Amyntas, we saw plainly, must ere long withdraw from his cities, was in fact already but a name, an outcast from Macedon.

"The Olynthians have actually sent to ourselves and to the men of Apollonia a joint embassy, warning us of their intention to attack us if we refuse to present ourselves at Olynthus with a military contingent.[2] Now, for our part, men of Lacedæmon, we desire nothing better than to abide by our ancestral laws and institutions, to be free and independent citizens:[3] but if aid from without

[1] Archelaüs, the able and unscrupulous king of Macedon mentioned in no. 116, was assassinated in 399. After several short reigns which ended violently, Amyntas, a member of the royal family but not a descendant of Archelaüs, succeeded to the throne. This man, noted for his success in unifying Macedon, and still more as the father of Philip and the grandfather of Alexander, reigned interruptedly twenty-four years, 393–369; *cf.* Grote, *op. cit.* x. 45–9. At the time of the Chalcidic embassy to Sparta, described in the present excerpt, the fortunes of Amyntas were at a low ebb; he was obliged to yield his capital, Pella, to Olynthus and came near being driven from his kingdom.

[2] That is, the Olynthians were planning to force these two cities into the league.

[3] This was the sentiment of every Hellenic city — a longing for absolute political isolation.

is going to fail us, we too must follow the rest and coalesce with the Olynthians. Why, even now they muster no less than eight hundred heavy infantry (?) [1] and a considerably larger body of light infantry, while their cavalry, when we have joined them, will exceed a thousand men. At the date of our departure we left embassies from Athens and Bœotia in Olynthus, and we were told that the Olynthians themselves had passed a formal resolution to return the compliment. They were to send an embassy on their side to the aforesaid states to treat of an alliance.[2] And yet, if the power of the Athenians and the Thebans is to be further increased by such an accession of strength, look to it," the speaker added, "whether hereafter you will find things so easy to manage in that quarter.

"They hold Potidæa, the key to the isthmus Pallene, and therefore, you can well believe, they can command the states within that peninsula. If you want any further proof of the abject terror of those states, you have it in the fact that notwithstanding the bitter hatred which they bear to Olynthus, not one of them has dared to send ambassadors along with us to apprise you of these matters.[3]

"Reflect how you can reconcile your anxiety to prevent the unification of Bœotia [4] with your neglect to hinder the solidifying of a far larger power — a power destined, moreover, to become formidable not on land only, but by sea. For what is to stop it when the soil itself supplies timber for shipbuilding, and there are rich revenues derived from numerous harbors and commercial centers? [5] — it can not but be that abundance of food and abun-

[1] The smallness of this number is utterly disproportionate to the number of cavalry, to the actual strength of the league, as known from other circumstances, and to the general tone of the context. Though it is evidently corrupt, we have no sure means of emending it; "eight thousand" is a mere possibility.

[2] Remarkable is the intense diplomatic and military aggressiveness of the new league.

[3] In a situation of this kind we should not too confidently rely upon the speaker for his statement as to the feelings of others. The refusal of other cities to join the embassy may have been due to friendship for Olynthus.

[4] It was at this time that, in fear of the growing power of Thebes in Bœotia, the Lacedæmonians violently seized the acropolis of that city, and forced upon it an oligarchy devoted to Sparta.

[5] The speaker here calls attention to the economic advantages of the Chalcidic

dance of population will go hand in hand. Nor have we yet reached the limits of Olynthian expansion; there are their neighbors to be thought of — the kingless or independent Thracians. These are already to-day the devoted servants of Olynthus, and when it comes to their being actually under her, that means at once another vast accession of strength to her. With the Thracians in her train, the gold mines of Pangæus will stretch out to her the hand of welcome.[1]

"In making these assertions we are but uttering remarks ten thousand times repeated in the democracy of Olynthus. Furthermore as to their confident spirit, who shall attempt to describe it? It is God, for aught I know, who, with the growth of a new capacity, gives increase also to the proud thoughts and vast designs of humanity. For ourselves, men of Lacedæmon and of the allied states, our task is completed. We have played our parts in announcing to you how things stand there. To you it is left to determine whether what we have described is worthy of your concern. One only thing further you ought to recognize: the power we have spoken of as great is not as yet invincible, for those states which are involuntary participators in the citizenship of Olynthus will, in prospect of any rival power appearing in the field, speedily fall away. On the other hand, let them be once closely knit and welded together by the privileges of intermarriage and reciprocal rights of holding property in land — which have already become enactments; let them discover that it is a gain to them to follow in the wake of conquerors (just as the Arcadians, for instance, find it profitable to march in your ranks, whereby they save their own property and pillage their neighbor's); let these things come to pass, and perhaps you may find the knot no longer so easy to unloose." [2]

towns; they exported ship timber, which commanded a high price throughout Hellas, and they were the medium of commercial intercourse between the Mediterranean world and Macedon. It was chiefly these circumstances which led Philip, son of Amyntas, to annex the coast region to his kingdom.

[1] These gold mines afterward yielded Philip a thousand talents a year.

[2] From the words of these ambassadors, who were enemies of Olynthus, we infer that this city was building up a league on a principle broader and more generous than Hellas had known before — a principle so fair and attractive that a community once adjusted to membership had no desire of withdrawing. Clearly the citizens of one community had the rights of intermarriage, commerce, and landholding in every other. The union approached nearly to a state, in which the cities were municipalities.

120. The Founding of the Second Athenian Confederacy, 377 B.C.

(*Inscr. græc.* II. 17, editio minor, 1913, no. 43; Hicks and Hill, no. 101; Ditt. I. no. 80; Roberts and Gardner, *Greek Epigraphy*, II. no. 32. Translated by C. J. O.)

This inscription has been pieced together from twenty fragments found at Athens. It is of cardinal importance as the best authority for the early history of the so-called Second Athenian Confederacy, the greatest step toward federation voluntarily taken by the Greek states in the fourth century. This league, composed chiefly of maritime states under the leadership of Athens, was formed in 378–377, to check the aggressions of Lacedæmon, and endured, though with diminishing effectiveness, till the beginning of Macedonian supremacy, 338. The decree here given, passed by the Athenians in 377, recognizes the confederacy as already existing, and is principally concerned with reaffirming the independence and the privileges of the allies, who may well have feared that Athens might have attempted the restoration of her former empire. The list of states inscribed after the decree not only informs us of the extent of the confederacy, but also enables us to trace its growth as far as the year 373. The account of the founding and early history of the union given by Diodorus, xv. 28 *sqq.* — the chief literary source — may be compared. See also Marshall, F. H., *The Second Athenian Confederacy* (Cambridge, 1905), chs. ii, iii, where the results of recent investigation are summarized.

IN THE ARCHONSHIP OF NAUSINICUS. CALLIBIUS, SON OF CEPHISOPHON, OF PÆANIA, WAS SECRETARY

In the seventh prytany,[1] that of (the tribe) Hippothontis, it hath pleased the council and the people, — Charinus of Athmonon presided; Aristoteles made the motion: —

That, with good fortune to the Athenians and their allies, and in order that the Lacedæmonians may allow the Greeks to live in quiet, free and autonomous, and to possess their respective territories in security[2] . . . be it decreed by the people: —

That if any of the Greeks or of the barbarians dwelling on the mainland[3] or of the islanders, except such as are subjects of the

[1] February or March, 377.

[2] The three lines following, which probably contained a still more unfavorable characterization of the Lacedæmonians, were erased in ancient times, perhaps in 370–369, when Athens and Sparta were friendly.

[3] Thracians, Macedonians, and Epeirotes are meant.

King,[1] wish to be allies of the Athenians and of their allies, they may become such while preserving their freedom and autonomy, using the form of government that they desire, without either admitting a garrison or receiving a commandant or paying tribute,[2] and upon the same terms as the Chians,[3] the Thebans, and the other allies. In favor of those who make an alliance with the Athenians and with the allies, the (Athenian) people shall release all the Athenians' landed possessions,[4] whether public or private, that may chance to be in the territory of those who make the alliance; and [the Athenians] shall give assurances to this effect. If with regard to the cities that make the alliance with the Athenians, there chance to be at Athens inscriptions of a prejudicial character,[5] the council holding office for the time being shall have authority to destroy them. From the date of the archonship of Nausinicus it shall not be allowable for any Athenian, either in behalf of the state or as a private person, to acquire either a house or a piece of land in the territories of the allies, whether by purchase or by mortgage, or in any other way. If anyone shall undertake to purchase or acquire or take property on mortgage, in any way whatsoever, any ally who wishes may lay an information against him before the delegates of the allies;[6] and the delegates, after

[1] This provision is inserted in recognition of the peace of Antalcidas, 387–386 B.C., by the terms of which the Hellenic cities in Asia Minor were made subject to the Persian king.

[2] Unlike the confederacy in the previous century; *cf.* the decrees regarding Erythræ and Chalcis, nos. 71, 72.

[3] Chios was the first state to enter the alliance; *cf.* the list *infra*, and Diodorus xv. 28. 3.

[4] These words, though of general application, are especially designed to prevent a return to the practice of forcible colonization by the Athenians (the system of cleruchies), which under the former confederacy had proved so irritating to the allies.

[5] *I.e.*, copies of land grants made by the allied states, treaties confirming such rights, etc.

[6] *Cf.* Diod. *l.c.*: "The (Athenian) people . . . assembled a joint congress (synedrion) of all the allies; and delegates (synedroi) were appointed for each city. It was ordained by a joint resolution that the congress should sit at Athens, and that each city, the small and the great alike, should be entitled to one vote." The congress of allies and the Athenian assembly had coördinate and independent authority; *cf.* Marshall, *op. cit.* 22 *sq.* and note that throughout this document the "Athenians" and the "allies" are distinguished. In other words, the system comprised two equal powers, (1) the Athenians, (2) the allies, and was governed by two equal coördinate parliaments, the Athenian assembly and the congress composed of delegates from all the

selling the property, shall give one half (of the proceeds) to the informer, and the other half shall belong to the common fund of the allies. If anyone shall go to war against the members of the alliance, whether by land or by sea, the Athenians and the allies shall give aid to the party attacked, both by land and by sea, with all their might, according to their ability. If anyone, whether magistrate or private citizen, shall propose or put to vote a motion contrary to this decree with the effect of annulling any of the provisions of this decree, he himself shall incur loss of civil rights, and his property shall be confiscated, one tenth of it for the Goddess (Athena); and he shall be tried before the Athenians and the allies [1] on the charge of destroying the alliance. The punishment shall be death or banishment from the domain of the Athenians and the allies; and if he is sentenced to death, he shall not be buried in Attica or in the territory of the allies. The secretary of the council shall inscribe this decree on a stone stele and shall place it by (the statue of) Zeus the Deliverer.[2] The money for inscribing the stele, sixty drachmas, shall be given by the treasurers of the Goddess from the fund of ten talents.[3] There shall be inscribed on this stele the names both of the cities now in the alliance and of any that may join it. Furthermore, the people shall choose immediately three envoys to go to Thebes and, so far as they can, to induce the Thebans to take good measures.[4]

The following were chosen: Aristoteles of Marathon,[5] Pyrrhander of Anaphlystus, Thrasybulus of Collytus.

The following cities [6] are allies of the Athenians: —

allies though not from Athens. A resolution adopted by the two parliaments was binding upon the system.

[1] This may possibly refer to a joint court of Athenians and allies; *cf.* Marshall, *op. cit.* 35–7.

[2] On the west side of the Athenian market place; Judeich, *Top. von Athen*, 302.

[3] A reserve fund, which, owing to a lack of ready money, may have been borrowed from the treasury of Athena.

[4] As the Thebans have already been mentioned among the allies, this embassy must have had another object than that of attaching this people to the confederacy.

[5] The mover of the decree.

[6] For the situation of these towns — instead of which the Greek text gives the names of the inhabitants — see the map in Marshall, *op. cit.* 1. Diodorus, xv. 30. 2, informs us that seventy cities joined the alliance. For the historical details, see Dittenberger's notes and Marshall, *op. cit.* ch. iii.

Chios,[1] Tenedos[3]
Mytilene[1]
Methymna[1]
Rhodes,[1] Poeëssa[3]
Byzantium[1]
Perinthus[2]
Peparethos[2]
Sciathos[2]
Maronea[2]
Dion[3]
Paros,[3] O ...
Athenæ,[3] P ...

Thebes[1]
Chalcis[2]
Eretria[2]
Arethusa[2]
Carystus[2]
Icos[2]
Pall ...

(*Here follows a fragment of another motion made by Aristoteles.*)

(*On the left face of the stone the following names*[4] *are written in a single column*):

The democracy[5] of Corcyra, Abdera, Thasos, the Chalcidians in Thrace, Ænus, Samothrace, Dicæopolis, the Acarnanians, Pronni in Cephallenia, Alcetas,[6] Neoptolemus, [Jason],[7] Andros, Tenos, Hestiæa, Myconos, Antissa, Eresus, Astræus, Iulis in Ceos, Carthæa, Coresus, Elæus, Amorgos, Selymbria, Siphnos, Sicinos, Dion in Thrace, Neapolis, the democracy of Zacynthus living in Nellus.[8]

[1] These cities were allies at the time of the adoption of the decree, and their names were then inscribed, with the possible exception of Thebes.

[2] These cities, the names of which are inscribed by two different hands, joined the alliance in 377.

[3] These cities probably joined after the battle of Naxos in the autumn of 376.

[4] All these names except the last are inscribed by the same hand; but the allies first mentioned (up to Jason) seem to have joined in 375–374, and those from Andros to Neapolis in 373. Kirchner, *Inscr. græc.* II, ed. minor, 1913, p. 28, would date all in 375–374.

[5] This expression seems to indicate that the oligarchical and democratic factions were then at variance.

[6] King of the Molossians, Neoptolemus being his son.

[7] The name has purposely been erased but was probably that of Jason, tyrant of Pheræ, Thessaly, who was friendly to Athens in 375, but fell away before 371.

[8] This faction, which had possession of a fort on Mount Nellus, was enrolled in the alliance in 372; Marshall, *op. cit.* 66; but *cf.* Kirchner, *supra.*

The formation of this alliance secured comparative peace to the Ægean islands and afforded them an opportunity to regain the prosperity they had lost through recent wars.

121. Admission of Methymna to the Confederacy, 377 B.C.

(*Inscr. græc.* II. 5. no. 18 b, editio minor, no. 42; Hicks and Hill, no. 103; Ditt. no. 82; Scala, R. von, *Staatsverträge,* I. no. 140. Translated by G. W. B.)

This inscription is on a marble stele found on the Athenian Acropolis. Methymna, already in alliance with Athens, desired to become a member of the new confederacy. The procedure in admitting this state was undoubtedly followed in other cases. First the state sent an embassy to Athens with a request for admission. If the request was granted, the name of the community was enrolled in the list (see preceding number). Thereupon three oaths were taken: the first by the embassy of the state in the presence of the congress of allies and of the Athenian generals and hipparchs, next by the three groups of functionaries last mentioned; and finally by a committee of the applying state before a board consisting of one Athenian and a commission of the congress. After these oaths were taken, the city was recognized as a member; *cf.* Pistorius, H., *Beiträge zur Geschichte von Lesbos*, etc. (Bonn, 1913). 37 *sq.*

The oath is given in the number next following.

(Be it resolved by the Council and the People. The tribe) . . . is held the prytany. Call... of Alopece was secretary. Simon... ius was chairman. Astyphilus moved the resolution:

Concerning the matters on which the Methymnæans speak — inasmuch as the Methymnæans are allies and friends of the city of the Athenians — in order that they may have an alliance also with the other allies of the Athenians, let the secretary of the council enroll them in the same way that the other allies have been enrolled. Also let the embassy of the Methymnæans swear before the delegates of the allies and before the generals and hipparchs the same oath which the rest of the allies have taken. Then let the delegates of the allies and the generals and hipparchs swear in the same terms before the Methymnæans.[1] Next let Æsimus and 'the delegates on the ships' [2] see to it that the magistrates of the Methymnæans take the oath in the same manner as the rest of the allies. Furthermore, let the community of the

[1] Here necessarily the ambassadors from Methymna are meant.

[2] Æsimus was the representative of Athens who accompanied the congressional committee known as the "delegates on the ships" to receive the oath from the applying allies. "The delegates on the ships" were a standing committee, and received their name from their continual voyaging among the islands of the Ægean for the purpose of receiving new members.

Methymnæans be commended, and their ambassadors be invited to dinner.[1]

122. Oaths of the Allies

(*Inscr. græc.* II. 5. 49 b. Translated by E. G. S.)

The selection below is taken from the treaty which admitted Corcyra to the Confederacy in 377. The oaths are preceded by a statement that the alliance is to last forever: "Let there be an alliance of the Corcyræans and Athenians forever. If any one in war shall invade the country of the Corcyræans, . . . let the Athenians bring aid," etc.

I shall give aid to the people of the Corcyræans with all my strength to the best of my ability, if any one for the purpose of war, either by land or by sea, go against the territory of the Corcyræans, in accordance with whatever notification the Corcyræans shall send; and as concerning war and peace, I shall act in accordance with whatever may seem good to the full body of the allies,[2] and other things I shall do[3] in accordance with the resolutions of the allies. These things I shall do, so help me Zeus and Apollo and Demeter. To me, if I keep my oath, may there be many blessings; if not, the opposite.

I shall give aid to the people of the Athenians with all my strength to the best of my ability, if any one for the purpose of war, either by land or by sea, go against the territory of the Athenians, in accordance with whatever notification the Athenians shall send; and as concerning war and peace, I shall act in accordance with whatever may seem good to the full body of the allies, and other things I shall do in accordance with the resolutions of the Athenians and the allies. These things I shall do, so help me Zeus and Apollo and Demeter. To me, if I keep my oath, may there be many blessings; if not, the opposite.[4]

[1] Ἐπὶ ξένια, the hospitality due to honored guests. In addition to the state dinner in the Prytaneum, they were regularly invited to front seats in the theater and a prominent place in such festivals as occurred during their stay in Athens.

[2] The congress in full session is here meant.

[3] That is, all other things involved in the relations between the contracting parties.

[4] The obligations contained in these oaths we may regard as typical of the defensive alliances of that period.

123. Athenian Monopoly of Red Ochre produced in Ceos, 360–350 B.C.

(*Inscr. græc.* II. no. 546; Hicks and Hill, no. 137; Roberts and Gardner, *Greek Epigraphy*, II. no. 71. Translated by C. J. O.)

This inscription, found on the Acropolis of Athens, contains decrees of three towns of Ceos. The opening portion, now lost, must have included an Athenian decree regarding the appointment of the commissioners named at the close. From the position of the Cean decrees that are preserved it seems probable that they had been passed as the result of previous negotiations, and that the commission here named was to see to their enforcement. The regulations, the general purport of which is plain in spite of the mutilation of the inscription, give an interesting view of an ancient trade monopoly and of the domineering policy of Athens toward her weaker allies in the fourth century. In spite of her promises on the founding of the Confederacy (see no. 120) she could not resist the temptation to turn the league to her own advantage as soon as she found herself in a commanding position. The island of Ceos, nearest of the Cyclades to Athens, was noted for its red ochre, or ruddle (μίλτος; *cf.* Theophrastus, *De lapidibus*, 52), which was used both in medicine and in the arts. Athens, therefore, by controlling the supply of this raw material, secured an advantage for her manufactures. On account of the writing, the inscription is assigned to the middle of the fourth century, probably not long after 363, when the Cean towns, which had seceded from the Confederacy, were reduced by force; *cf.* Hicks and Hill, no. 118.

(*Only a few fragments remain of the decree of Carthæa.*) (*Decree of Coresus.*) Theogenes moved: — Be it resolved by the council and the people of Coresus, with regard to the message of the Athenian commissioners, that red ochre shall be exported to Athens only . . . as was formerly the case. In order to enforce the decrees . . . [of the Athenians] and the Coresians regarding red ochre, it shall be exported in a ship which the [1] . . . shall assign, and not in any other ship. The producers shall pay as freight an obol [on each talent [2] to the shipowners]. If anyone shall export it in another ship, he shall be subject [to the provisions of the law(?)]. This decree shall be inscribed upon a stone stele and placed [in the temple] of Apollo, and the law, as it was formerly, shall be in force. A charge (of violating the law) shall be brought

[1] Perhaps the astynomi mentioned below.

[2] *I.e.*, $\frac{1}{36000}$.

before the *astynomi*,[1] who shall refer it to the vote of the court within [thirty] days. The bringer of the information or of the charge [2] shall have the half (of the cargo); but if the bringer of the charge is a slave, he shall, if he belongs to the exporters, receive his freedom and have [three fourths?] (of the cargo); if he belongs to someone else, he shall receive his freedom. . . . Both the bringer of an information and the bringer of a charge shall also have the right of appeal to Athens.[3] Whatever other decrees the Athenians may make regarding the supervision of (the trade in) red ochre shall be in force (at Coresus) when brought hither. The duty of one fiftieth [4] shall be paid to the collectors by the [importers]. The Athenians shall be invited to dine in the Prytaneum on the morrow.

(*The decree of Iulis is here omitted as it contains substantially the same terms as the preceding.*)

(*Names of the Athenian commissioners.*) The following were chosen: Andron of Cerameicus, Lysias (*or* Lysiades), of . . ., . . . of Phlya, Euphrosynus of Pæania.

124. Athenian Decree in Honor of Dionysius I of Syracuse

(*Inscr. græc.* II. no. 51, editio minor, 1913, no. 103; Hicks and Hill, no. 108; Ditt. I. no. 89; also Köhler, "Die griechische Politik Dionysius des Älteren," in *Ath. Mitt.* I (1876). 1–26. Translated by C. J. O.)

This document throws an interesting light upon the relations of Dionysius I, tyrant of Syracuse, 405–367 B.C., with the states of peninsular Hellas. As a friend of Sparta he had been opposed to Athens during the greater part of his rule, although there is a fragment of an Athenian decree in his honor belonging to 394–393 (Hicks and Hill, no. 91); but when Sparta and Athens were drawn together after the battle of Leuctra, 371, it was natural that the latter state should enter into relations with Dionysius, at that time the ruler of the most

[1] These officials, who at Athens had charge of the public highways (Aristotle, *Const. Ath.* 50), must have been also port wardens at Coresus.

[2] An information (Greek *phasis*) had to be prosecuted by the informer himself; a charge (Greek *endeixis*) might be prosecuted by the public authorities; so that even a slave could bring it; *cf.* Ziebarth, in *Hermes*, XXXII (1897). 609–28, and especially 612 *sq.*

[3] Or possibly, "shall have the right to bring the suit at Athens."

[4] Probably the duty of two per cent collected by Athens on all exports and imports.

powerful state in the Hellenic world. The particular reason for his sending an embassy to Athens in 368 and for the honors conferred on him can only be conjectured; but as he is known to have assisted the Spartans and their allies with troops on two occasions (Xenophon, *Hellenica*, vii. 1. 20, 28), either in 369 and 368, or in 368 and 367, it is probable that the decree has reference to one of these expeditions. Early in 367 a formal alliance was concluded between Athens and Dionysius (see Hicks and Hill, no. 112), but it was rendered ineffectual by his death a few months later.

In the archonship of Lysistratus, in the tenth[1] prytany, that of [Erechtheis], when Execestus, son of [Pæonides (?)], of Azenia, was secretary, the proëdros[2] who put the question was Evangelus[3] . . . Pandius moved the resolution: —

That with regard to the message of the ambassadors from Dionysius, be it resolved by the council: —

That with regard to the letters sent by Dionysius concerning the building of the temple[4] and the peace,[5] the allies[6] shall bring before the people whatever resolution may seem best to them in their deliberations; and that the proëdri after inviting the allies, shall introduce the ambassadors to the people at the next assembly, and shall include their message in the business of the day, and shall also communicate the proposal of the council to the people, to the effect that it pleases the council:[7] —

To commend Dionysius, the archon[8] of Sicily, and his sons Dionysius and Hermocritus, inasmuch as they are good and true men toward the Athenian people and the allies, and aid the King's

[1] June–July, 368.

[2] From the early part of the fourth century nine proëdri ("managers") were appointed by lot to supervise each meeting of the assembly, and their president was named in the heading of decrees instead of the president of the prytaneis.

[3] In the obliterated line two wreaths may have been carved.

[4] The temple of Apollo at Delphi, which had been at least partially destroyed by fire or earthquake in 373–372; *cf.* Ditt. I. no. 93; Jacoby, *Marmor Parium* (Berlin, 1904), 18, 119.

[5] If the peace congress at Delphi (Xen. *Hell.* vii. 1. 27) was held in 368, as is generally assumed, the embassy of Dionysius was probably connected with it. Niese, however, in his "Beiträge zur griech. Geschichte," in *Hermes*, XXXIX (1904). 84–132, especially 88–93, 125–8, assigns the congress to the following year.

[6] *I.e.*, the delegates from the cities of the Athenian confederacy, who held their sessions at Athens; *cf.* no. 120.

[7] The following bill, though in form only a resolution of the council, must have been accepted *verbatim* by the assembly.

[8] The official title of Dionysius in the Athenian decrees, "ruler," "chief magistrate."

Peace,[1] which was made by the Athenians and the Lacedæmonians and the rest of the Hellenes; and to send to Dionysius the crown (already) decreed to him by the people, and to crown each of the sons of Dionysius with a golden crown of the value of one thousand drachmas on account of their loyalty and their friendliness; and that Dionysius and his sons shall be Athenian citizens, they themselves and their descendants, (and shall belong) to the tribe and the deme and the phratry that they wish. The prytaneis of (the tribe) Erechtheis shall refer this matter to the vote of the people . . .

(*The remainder of the inscription is fragmentary.*)

125. Decree of Amphipolis Ordering the Banishment of Two Partisans of Athens

(Hicks and Hill, no. 125; Ditt. I. 113; Buck, *Greek Dialects,* II. no. 12. Translated by C. J. O.)

This inscription was found near the site of ancient Amphipolis. The town, which was situated on the border of Macedon and Thrace near the mouth of the river Strymon (now Struma), was originally a colony of Athens, but had maintained its independence many years, until it was annexed by Philip of Macedon, 357 B.C. The decree contained in the inscription must be assigned to the latter part of this year; for the Stratocles whose banishment is ordered is undoubtedly the Stratocles who went as ambassador to the Athenians to urge them to take possession of Amphipolis; Demosthenes, *Olynthiac Oration,* i. 8. The Athenians, however, refused; for they relied on the promise of Philip, who, instead of restoring the town to them, had the opponents of his rule sent into exile; Diodorus xvi. 8. This inscription, therefore, though in form the decree of a free city, is in reality one of the earliest monuments of the Macedonian supremacy.

It hath pleased the people: that Philo and Stratocles shall be banished from Amphipolis and from the land of the Amphipolitans forever, both they themselves and their children; and, if they are captured anywhere, they shall be treated as public enemies and may be put to death with impunity.[2] Their property shall be confiscated and the tenth part shall be consecrated to Apollo and

[1] The peace of Antalcidas, 387–386; see Botsford, *Hellenic History*, ch. xxi.

[2] *I.e.*, they are not merely exiled, but outlawed as well.

to Strymon.[1] The prefects [2] shall inscribe their names on a stone stele. If anyone shall demand another vote upon this decree or shall harbor these men by any art or device whatsoever, his property shall be confiscated and he himself shall be banished from Amphipolis forever.

126. Philip's War upon Olynthus

(Demosthenes, *Olynthiac Oration*, II. Kennedy, revised by E. G. S.)

Philip, who came to the throne of Macedon in 359, devoted himself (1) to the consolidation of his own kingdom from a loose aggregate of primitive tribes to a highly centralized monarchy, (2) to the formation of a more efficient army than Europe had known before, (3) to the extension of his supremacy not only over neighboring tribes of barbarians, but also over peninsular Hellas. The first object of his foreign policy was to get possession of the coast towns, in order to gain access to the sea. It was for this purpose that he seized Amphipolis, as mentioned in the preceding selection. His failure to restore it to Athens as promised involved him in a war with that country, 357–346. During the greater part of this period the war existed in name and in feeling only, though at times there were actual hostilities. Meanwhile Philip busied himself with the extension of his power over Thessaly and Thrace. For a time Olynthus with her Chalcidic allies (see no. 125) was friendly with him and hostile to Athens; but at length when the Olynthians found themselves menaced by the growing power and insolence of Philip, they became his enemies and called on Athens for an alliance and immediate aid. The act of Philip which precipitated this war was his demand for the surrender of his half-brother Arrhidæus, who had fled to Olynthus to escape Philip's wrath. The Olynthians, true to their religious obligation, refused to deliver the suppliant, whereupon Philip began war, 349. It was during the year 349–348 that Demosthenes delivered his three *Olynthiac Orations*, urging the Athenians to send strong forces at once to the support of Olynthus. Dionysius of Halicarnassus concluded that the oration numbered the second was in reality spoken first, and this view was accepted by Grote, *History of Greece*, XI. 327; see also Blass, *Attische Beredsamkeit*, III. 1. 268 *sqq*. This is the oration given below. It is valuable for the political situation of that time.

THE SECOND OLYNTHIAC

(1) On many occasions, men of Athens, one may see the kindness of the gods to this country manifested, but most signally, I think, on the present. That here are men prepared for a war

[1] The god of the river of the same name.

[2] Greek prostatæ, officials whose function is unknown.

with Philip, possessed of a neighboring territory and some power, and (what is most important) so fixed in their hostility, as to regard any accommodation with him as insecure, and even ruinous to their country; this really appears like an extraordinary act of divine beneficence. (2) It must then be our care, Athenians, that we are not more unkind to ourselves than circumstances have been; as it would be a foul, a most foul reproach, to have abandoned not only cities and places that once belonged to us, but also the allies and emergencies provided by fortune.

(3) To dilate, Athenians, on Philip's power, and by such discourse to incite you to your duty, I think improper: and why? Because all that may be said on that score involves matter of glory for him, and misconduct on our part. The more he has transcended his repute, the more is he universally admired; you, as you have used your advantages unworthily, have incurred the greater disgrace. (4) This topic, then, I shall pass over. Indeed, Athenians, a correct observer will find the source of his greatness here, and not in himself. But of measures for which those who have managed the government in his interest, deserve his gratitude and your vengeance, I see no occasion to speak now. Other things are open to me, which it concerns you all to know, and which must, on a due examination, Athenians, reflect great disgrace on Philip. To these will I address myself.

(5) To call him perjured and treacherous, without showing what he has done, might justly be termed idle abuse. But to go through all his actions and convict him on the basis of the same, will take, as it happens, but a short time, and is expedient, I think for two reasons: first, that his baseness may appear in its true light; secondly, that they, whose terror imagines Philip to be invincible, may see he has run through all the artifices by which he rose to greatness, and his affairs have reached their very termination. (6) I myself, men of Athens, should most assuredly have regarded Philip to be an object of fear and admiration, had I seen him exalted by honorable conduct; but actually observing and considering, I find that in the beginning when certain persons drove away the Olynthians from here, who desired a conference with us, by saying that he was going to surrender Amphipolis, and to execute the secret article once so much harped upon; afterward

he got the friendship of the Olynthians, by taking Potidæa from you, wronging you, his former allies, and delivering it to them; and lastly now the Thessalians, by promising to surrender Magnesia, and to undertake the Phocian war on their behalf.[1] In short, none who have dealt with him has he not fooled. He has risen by conciliating and cajoling the weakness of every people in turn who knew him not. (8) As, therefore, by such means he grew great when each people imagined he would advance their interest, so ought he by the same means to be pulled down again when the selfish aim of his whole policy is exposed.[2] To this crisis, O Athenians, are Philip's affairs come; or let any man stand forward and prove to me, or rather to you, that my assertions are false, or that men whom Philip has once overreached will trust him hereafter, or that the Thessalians who have been degraded into servitude would not gladly become free.

(9) But if any among you, though agreeing in these statements, thinks that by force Philip will maintain his power, by having occupied forts and havens and the like, this is a mistake. True, when a coalition subsists by good-will, and all parties to the war have a common interest, men are willing to coöperate and bear hardships and persevere. But when one has grown strong, like Philip, by rapacity and artifice, on the first pretext, the slightest reverse, all is overturned and broken up. (10) Impossible is it, — impossible, Athenians, — to acquire a solid power by injustice and perjury and falsehood. Such things last for once, or for a short period; maybe, they blossom fairly with hope; but

[1] During her ascendancy, 371–362, Thebes had built up a strong federation in central Greece. Among the allies which she held by force only was Phocis. Soon after the battle of Mantineia, 362, which was in effect a defeat for Thebes, Phocis renounced her allegiance. To regain her power Thebes persuaded the Amphictyonic council to fine certain leading Phocians for sacrilege against the Delphic Apollo. Phocis resisted, and thus the so-called Sacred War began, 356. With the aid of the Delphic treasury the Phocians hired mercenaries, more than held their own against Thebes, and invaded Thessaly. Philip, taking the side of the Thessalians, succeeded finally in defeating the Phocians and in driving them from Thessaly. It was chiefly by these means that he acquired supremacy over that country.

[2] The argument is that his successes have been due chiefly to the conduct of the Hellenes themselves, cajoled into friendship or alliance by his false promises. Thus far the orator is right. He reasons further that if the Hellenes, at length aware of his character, should join in resisting him, they would succeed. This, we may say, is possible though not certain, so great had the power of Philip already become.

in time they are discovered and collapse. As a house, a ship, or the like, ought to have the lower part firmest, so in human conduct, I ween, the principle and foundation should be just and true. But this is not so in Philip's conduct.

(11) I say then, we should at once aid the Olynthians (the best and quickest way that can be suggested will please me most), and send an embassy to the Thessalians, to inform some of our measures, and to stir up the rest; for they have now voted to demand Pagasæ, and remonstrate about Magnesia. (12) But look to this, Athenians, that our envoys shall not only make speeches, but have some real proof that we have gone forth as becomes our country, and are engaged in action. All speech without action appears vain and idle, but especially that of our commonwealth; as the more we are thought to excel therein, the more is speaking distrusted by all. (13) You must show yourselves greatly reformed, greatly changed, contributing, serving personally, acting promptly, if indeed any one is to pay attention to you. If ye will perform these duties properly and becomingly, Athenians, not only will it appear that Philip's alliances are weak and precarious, but the poor state of his native empire and power will be revealed.

(14) To speak roundly, the Macedonian power, state, and empire are very well as a help, as it was for you in Timotheus' time against the Olynthians; likewise for them against Potidæa the conjunction was important; and lately it aided the Thessalians in their broils and troubles against the regnant house: and the accession of any power, however small, is undoubtedly useful. But the Macedonian state is feeble of itself, and full of defects. (15) The very operations which seem to constitute Philip's greatness, his war and his expeditions, have made it more insecure than it was originally. Think not, Athenians, that Philip and his subjects have the same likings. He desires glory, makes that his passion, is ready for any consequence of adventure and peril, (16) preferring to a life of safety the honor of achieving what no Macedonian king ever did before. But they have no share in the glorious result; ever harassed by these excursions up and down, they suffer and toil incessantly, allowed no leisure for their employments or private concerns, unable even to dispose of their hard earnings, the markets of the country being closed on account

of war. (17) By this then it may easily be seen, how the Macedonians in general are disposed to Philip. His mercenaries and guards, indeed, have the reputation of admirable and well-trained soldiers; as I heard from one who had been in the country, a man incapable of falsehood, they are no better than others. (18) For if there be any among them experienced in battles and campaigns, Philip is jealous of such men and drives them away, he says, wishing to keep the glory of all actions to himself;[1] his jealousy (among other failings) being excessive. Or if any man be generally temperate and virtuous, unable to bear Philip's daily intemperances, drunkenness, and indecencies, he is pushed aside and accounted nobody.[2] (19) The rest about him are brigands and parasites, and men of that character, who will get drunk and perform dances which I scruple to name before you. My information is undoubtedly true; for persons whom all scouted here as worse rascals than mountebanks, Callias the town-slave and the like of him, antic-jesters, and composers of ribald songs to lampoon their companions, such persons Philip esteems and keeps about him. (20) Small matters these may be thought, Athenians, but to the wise they are strong indications of his way of thinking and his wrongheadedness. Success perhaps throws a shade over them now; prosperity is a famous hider of such blemishes; but on any miscarriage they will be fully exposed. And this (trust me, Athenians) will appear in no long time, if the gods so will and you determine. (21) For as in the human body, a man in health feels not partial ailments, but when some illness occurs, every element of physical wellbeing is stirred from its composure, whether it be a rupture or a sprain or anything else unsound; so with states and monarchs, whilst they wage external war, their weaknesses are undiscerned by most men, but the tug of a frontier war betrays all.

(22) If any of you think Philip a formidable opponent, because they see he is fortunate, such reasoning is prudent, Athenians. Fortune has indeed a great preponderance — nay, is everything in human affairs. Not but that, if I had the choice, I should prefer our fortune to Philip's, would you but moderately perform your

[1] In this matter Demosthenes was misinformed; Philip appreciated those who served him ably.

[2] There seems to have been truth in this statement; see no. 167.

duty. For I see you have many more claims to the divine favor than he has. But in fact we sit doing nothing; (23) and a man who is himself idle cannot require even his friends to act for him, much less the gods. No wonder then that he, marching and toiling in person, present on all occasions, neglecting no time or reason, prevails over us delaying and voting and inquiring. I marvel not at that; the contrary would have been marvellous if we, doing none of the duties of war, had beaten one doing them all. (24) But this surprises me, that formerly, Athenians, you resisted the Lacedæmonians for the rights of Greece, and rejecting many opportunities of selfish gain to secure the rights of others, expended your property in contributions, and bore the brunt of the battle; yet now you are loth to serve, slow to contribute in defence of your own possessions, and, though you have often saved the other communities of Greece collectively and individually, under your own losses you sit still. (25) This surprises me, and one thing more, Athenians; that not one of you can reckon, how long your war with Philip has lasted, and what you have been doing while the time has passed. You surely know, that while you have been delaying, expecting others to act, accusing, and passing judgment on one another, expecting again, doing much the same as ye so do now, all the time has passed away. (26) Then are ye so senseless, Athenians, as to imagine that the same measures, which have brought the country from a prosperous to a poor condition, will bring it from a poor to a prosperous? Unreasonable were this and unnatural; for all things are easier kept than gotten. The war now has left us nothing to keep; we have all to get and the work must be done by ourselves. (27) I say then you must contribute money, serve in person with alacrity, accuse no one, till you have gained your objects; then, judging from facts, honor the deserving, punish offenders; for you cannot harshly scrutinize the conduct of others, unless you have done what is right yourselves. (28) Why, think you, do all the generals whom you commission avoid this war, and seek wars of their own? (for of the generals too must a little truth be told). Because here the prizes of the war are yours; for example, if Amphipolis be taken, you will immediately recover it; the commanders have all the risk and no reward. But in the other case the risks are less, and the gains belong to the commanders and soldiers: Lampsacus, Sigeum, the vessels which they plunder. (29) So they proceed to secure their several interests; you, when you look at the bad state of your affairs, bring the generals to trial; but when they get a hearing and plead these necessities, you acquit them. The result is that, while you are quarreling and divided, some holding one opinion, some another, the commonwealth goes wrong. Formerly, Athenians, you had divisions for taxes; now you have divisions for politics. There is an orator presiding on either side, a general under him, and three hundred men who will do the shouting;[1] the rest of you are attached some to the one party and some to the other. (30) This you must leave off; be yourselves again; establish a general liberty of speech, deliberation, and action. If some are appointed to command as with autocratic authority, some to be compelled to be ship-captains, tax-payers, soldiers, others only to vote against them, and help in nothing besides, no duty will be seasonably performed; the aggrieved parties will in each case fail you, and you will have to punish them instead of your enemies. (31) I say, in short, you must all fairly contribute, according to each man's ability; take your turns of service till you have all been afield; give every speaker a hearing and adopt the best counsel; then not only will you praise the speaker at the moment, but yourselves afterward, when the universal condition of things is improved.[2]

127. The Condition of Hellas about 346, and Philip's Great Opportunity

(Isocrates, *Philippus*)

The effort of Demosthenes, expressed in the preceding selection, failed. The Athenians gave the Olynthians little aid. Philip conquered Olynthus and the allies who remained faithful to her. These cities he destroyed, and sold the inhabitants into slavery, 348. Two years later Athens concluded with

[1] See Calhoun, *Athenian Clubs in Politics and Litigation*, a work which has acquired an international reputation.

[2] One of the facts most noticeable in this speech is the lack of military spirit and political ambition in the Athenians. Although they were still willing to defend their country when attacked, they had lost all zest for fighting to defend distant possessions. Demosthenes here and elsewhere attempts to inspire them with their old military ardor. Although he met with a certain degree of success, it came too late and was insufficient.

him a treaty known as the peace of Philocrates, after the Athenian who moved the resolution. In this year Philip, as champion of the Delphic amphictyony, crushed the Phocians, destroyed their cities, scattered the inhabitants in villages, and imposed upon them an annual tax for the repayment of the treasury taken from Delphi. At this time he was master of a great part of Greece, and the terror of his name filled the cities that were still free. In every city were his partisans who worked for his interest. In some cases they may have been moved by farsightedness, a conviction that Philip's lordship over Hellas would be best for the country's interests. In other cases they were bribed or were actuated by fear. Isocrates, who formerly in his *Panegyricus* had proposed a union of all Hellas under the joint leadership of Sparta and Athens against Persia, now looked to Philip for this leadership. The works of Isocrates are especially important in view of the fact that Ed. Meyer, von Pöhlmann, and other modern scholars look upon him as the truest interpreter of the social and political conditions of his age.

(2) Seeing that the war in which you and this state were involved concerning Amphipolis [1] was producing many evils, I (at that time) essayed the task [2] of using concerning that city and its territory arguments bearing no resemblance to those which were in the mouths of your friends or the orators among us, but as far as possible removed from their line of thought. (3) They were inciting you to the war, by appealing to your passions; I on the contrary expressed no opinion at all on disputed matters, but devoted my attention to the argument which of all others I supposed most likely to produce peace, urging that both of you were mistaken in your judgment of affairs, and that while you, Philip, were fighting in furtherance of our interests, our state was fighting in support of your power, — that it was to your advantage that we should possess the territory in dispute, and to ours not to acquire it by any means whatever.[3] (4) The opinion of my pupils,[4]

[1] This war between Philip and Athens is referred to in the introduction to no. 126. It began in 357 and closed with the treaty of Philocrates in 346, shortly before the writing of the *Philippus*.

[2] Before the peace of Philocrates (see note *supra*) Isocrates was engaged in the preparation of an address to Philip on the relation between him and Athens. From § 7 it appears that the epistle was not yet complete when the treaty was signed. From this and other sources we see how slowly and, we might say, painfully Isocrates labored on his writings. The tenor of this unfinished letter Isocrates describes in § 2 *sqq*.

[3] His argument as here outlined was highly sophistical, and could have had little effect on Philip, had the letter been completed and sent to him.

[4] Among the pupils of Isocrates were young men from the most eminent families in Hellas. Their ideas therefore had some degree of weight in forming public opinion.

too, as to my treatment of this question was such as to lead no one of them to praise the argument or the style for accuracy and clearness, as some are wont to do, but to cause them to admire the truth of the matter expressed,[1] (5) and to consider that the only way for you to cease on either side from your rivalry was for you, Philip, to be convinced that the friendship of our state would be worth more to you than the revenues accruing from Amphipolis,[2] and for our state to be able to recognize the policy of avoiding the kind of colonies which have brought ruin four or five times over on those domiciled in them, and of looking for places lying far from neighbors with a capacity for ruling, and near those who have become accustomed to slavery, such as the place to which the Lacedæmonians have sent the Cyreneans;[3] (6) and further, you should recognize that a verbal renunciation of this territory to us will enable you in reality to become master of it, and also to earn our goodwill; for all the colonists that we send within reach of your power will be so many hostages of friendship for you from us. Our people, too, should be taught that if we take Amphipolis, we shall be compelled to observe the same kind of friendliness to your policy for the sake of the inhabitants of that place, that we had to observe toward Amadocus[4] of old for the sake of those who tilled the soil of Chersonese. (7) By the use of many arguments of this character I caused all who heard them to hope that, after my discourse had been circulated,[5] you would conclude the war, change your

[1] In the case of Isocrates it is always a question whether the rhetorician or the thinker has the upper hand; here he claims that in the judgment of his pupils the thought was better than the style.

[2] No amount of argument could bring Philip to this view; to his ambitious policy it was all-important to incorporate in his kingdom the coast cities, so as to make Macedon a maritime state. Isocrates fails to recognize this fact. Further, though Philip valued the goodwill of Athens, as he afterward showed, that consideration could not hinder him from pursuing his own independent policy of expansion.

[3] This statement involves a criticism on Athens for having colonized Amphipolis. At the time of that settlement, however, the condition of the surrounding region was very different; Macedon was still insignificant.

[4] Amadocus was a Thracian chief in the vicinity of Chersonese. Early in the fourth century Athens entered into relations of friendship with him in order better to safeguard the interests of the Athenian colony in Chersonese.

[5] Undoubtedly Isocrates had many copies of his *Orations* (in reality essays) and *Epistles* made and circulated among his pupils, friends, and influential men of Hellas. The effect of the epistle under consideration, therefore, would come not only directly to Philip but also indirectly, through the force of public opinion.

opinions, and adopt some common policy for your mutual good.[1] Whether they were foolish or sensible in thinking thus, they are the proper persons to bear the responsibility; but while I was engaged in this business, you anticipated me by making peace before my discourse was finally completed, and in that you were wise; for it were better that peace should be concluded in any way whatever [2] than that we should be exposed to the evils arising in consequence of the war. (8) Rejoicing then at the resolution to which you had come concerning peace, and thinking that they would be to your advantage, and to that of all the rest of Hellas as well as to ours, I was unable to divert my thoughts from what was connected with it, but was in such a frame of mind that I set to work to consider at once how to give permanence to what we had achieved and to prevent our state from again, after a short interval, desiring other wars; [3] (9) an examination of these questions in my own mind led me to the conclusion that there was no other way for her to live in quiet, except by the determination of the leading states to make up their mutual quarrels and to carry the war into Asia, and by their resolving to win from the barbarians the selfish advantages which they now look for at the expense of the Hellenes. This is the policy I had already advised in my *Panegyric* discourse.[4]

(10) On these reflections, thinking that I could never find a subject nobler than this, or one of more general application or more conducive to the interests of us all, I was moved to write upon it again, not in any ignorance of my own deficiencies, but knowing that this discourse was not suited to one of my age,[5] but required a man in the prime of life and with powers far beyond those of

[1] The mutual advantage of Philip and Athens.

[2] This was the peace of Philocrates, 346, referred to above. It seems that Isocrates was for "peace at any price!" Some agreed with him, whereas many, among them Demosthenes, were determined upon maintaining for their city an independent interstate policy.

[3] At this time the line was sharply drawn between the Macedonian and anti-Macedonian parties at Athens. The latter looked upon the peace merely as an opportunity to prepare for war.

[4] The *Panegyricus*, the ablest of all the writings of Isocrates, was published in 380. In it he advocated a union of all the Hellenes under the joint leadership of Athens and Sparta against Persia; *cf.* Botsford, *Hellenic History*, ch. xxi.

[5] Isocrates was now ninety years old.

other men. (11) I am aware, too, that it is difficult to utter two discourses on the same subject in any fashion that can be tolerated, especially if the one first published has been written in such a manner that it is imitated and admired even more by our detractors than by our most extravagant eulogists.[1] (12) Nevertheless, overlooking these disabilities, I have become so ambitious in old age that I resolved to combine with the observations I should address to you some hints to those who have worked with me, and to make it clear that to trouble the Great Festivals with oratory, and to speak to the crowds who come together there, is to speak without an audience. Speeches of this kind are as ineffectual as laws and constitutions written out by the sophists.[2] (13) Those who wish, on the contrary, to do some practical good instead of idly trifling, and those who think they have formed ideas of value to the community, must leave others to figure at the Festivals, and must take a champion for their cause from among those who are powerful in speech and action and who have great reputations, if (that is to say) anyone is to pay attention to them.[3] (14) Knowing these things, I elected to address my discourse to you, not making this choice to win your favor, although, it is true, I should consider it of great importance to speak in a manner acceptable to you, but it was not to this end that I directed my thoughts. In fact I saw that all other men of repute were living under the rule of states and laws, without power to do anything but obey orders, and moreover were far too weak for the enterprise which I shall propose, (15) while to you alone had fortune given full power to send ambassadors to whomsoever you chose and to receive them from whomsoever you pleased,[4] and to say whatever you should

[1] Here he refers to the fact that the general subject of his present discourse is the same as that of the *Panegyricus:* the union of the Hellenes for a war against Persia is common to both, though the leadership is different.

[2] This is a confession that his *Panegyricus* has had little effect. For the first ideal constitution, such as Isocrates has in mind, see no. 63. Plato's *Republic* is the most famous constitution of the kind.

[3] Both Plato and Isocrates (see § 81 omitted from this selection) had appealed in some such way to Dionysius, tyrant of Syracuse, but without result.

[4] From this passage it appears that Isocrates supposed that the relations between Philip and Hellas would be conducted through embassies merely; he nowhere gives evidence of an idea of institutional relationship such as was actually established; see no. 128.

deem it expedient to say, and further that you were the possessor to a greater degree than any man in Hellas of wealth and power, the only two things in existence which can both persuade and compel; things, too, which I think will be required by the enterprise which I am going to propose. (16) My intention is to advise you to take the lead both in securing the harmony of Hellas and in conducting the expedition against the barbarians; and persuasion is expedient with Greeks and force useful with the barbarians.[1] Such, then, is the general scope of my discourse. . . .

Some of his friends urge that Isocrates is too old for the task of advising Philip, who is himself too wise to need counsel, and who has also the advantages mentioned below.

(19) Further, he has at his side the most competent men in Macedon, who though unversed in other matters, probably understand his interests at least better than you (Isocrates) do. Moreover, you will also find many of the Hellenes living in that country, men not devoid of reputation or good sense, but men by the help of whose counsels he has not diminished the power of his throne, but has achieved things worth praying for. (20) What is wanting to complete his success? Has he not caused the Thessalians, whose rule formerly extended over Macedon, to be so friendly disposed to him that they, one and all, have more confidence in him than in their compatriots?[2] Further, as to the cities of that locality, has he not either won them over by kindness to alliance with him, or when they grievously vexed him, has he not reduced them to ruins? (21) Has he not overthrown the Magnesians and the Perrhæbians and the Pæonians, and brought them all into subjection, become lord and master of the Illyrians excepting those who live on the shores of the Adriatic, and placed the whole of Thrace under despots of his own choosing?[3] . . .

[1] Isocrates expects Philip in his relations with the Hellenes to use persuasion only; compulsion was to be reserved for barbarians. In this matter he was thoroughly mistaken.

[2] It was to such internal dissensions, leading to the calling in of outsiders, that the Greeks lost their freedom, having to surrender it partially to the Macedonians and afterward fully to the Romans.

[3] The conduct of Philip up to this point ought to have convinced Isocrates of Philip's readiness to use force against Hellas, and to make himself master of free Hellenic cities which he was willing to spare from ruin.

In spite of friends Isocrates persists in his purpose to compose a letter of advice to Philip.

(30) I will now direct my remarks to the subject itself. My idea is that, while neglecting none of your private interests, you ought to try to effect a reconciliation between Argos, Sparta, Thebes, and our state; for if you are able to bring these states together, you will have no difficulty in causing the other commonwealths to agree; (31) for they are all under the influence of those I have mentioned, and when in fear they take refuge with one or another of those states, from which they draw their succor. If therefore you can persuade four states only to be wise, you will release the others also from many evils.

(32) Now you will feel that there is no one of these commonwealths that you should despise, if you trace back their conduct toward your ancestors;[1] for you will find that each one is to be credited with much friendship and great kindnesses toward your house. Argos is your fatherland, for which it is right for you to have as much regard as for your own parents.[2] The Thebans honor the founder[3] of your race with processions and with sacrifices more than all the other gods. (33) The Lacedæmonians have bestowed on his descendants both royalty and leadership for all time; and our state, say those whom we trust in matters of ancient history, contributed to win immortality for Heracles and deliverance for his children. . . .

The conditions above mentioned are a ground for friendship between Philip and the four commonwealths respectively. Isocrates next proceeds to discuss the possibility of a general Hellenic reconciliation.

(39) Someone will perhaps venture to oppose what I have said, on the ground that I am endeavoring to induce you to under-

[1] Down to this time the citing of mythical antecedents formed part of the polite language of diplomacy, and naturally Isocrates indulges in the practice. Although Philip may have been pleased by this reference to his ancestors, he certainly was not influenced by it.

[2] Undoubtedly the story that the founder of the reigning Macedonian dynasty was a genuine Greek, a colonist from Argos and descendant of Heracles, was composed by one of the many Greek *literati* who had enjoyed a happy existence at the court of the Macedonian kings. In the same way they made up stories and extended pedigrees to connect the origins of Rome with their own people.

[3] Heracles.

take an impossible task. "The Argives," he may say, "can never be friends with the Lacedæmonians, or the Lacedæmonians with the Thebans, nor in a word can those who have always been accustomed to seek their selfish interests ever cast in their lot with one another." (40) I think, however, that nothing of this kind could have been effected when our state, or again when Lacedæmon, held supremacy in Hellas; for either of them could easily have prevented what was going forward; but now I no longer have the same opinion of them; for I know that they have all been brought to a level by their misfortunes, so that I think they will greatly prefer the benefits of union to the selfish advantages of their former policy.

(41) Then again I admit that there is no one else who could reconcile these states, but to you no such undertaking is difficult; for I see that you have accomplished many things which others considered hopeless and beyond expectation, so that it would not be strange if you alone should be capable of effecting this union. . . .

To prove that the Hellenic states are capable of harmony, Isocrates cites their union against Persia at the time of the invasion of Xerxes, 480 B.C.

(46) Now I think the best way for you to learn whether these commonwealths are disposed to peace or to war among themselves would be for me to give an account, not merely in general terms, nor yet too much in detail, of the chief features of their present condition.[1] First let us consider the position of the Lacedæmonians.

(47) These people, not so long ago the rulers of Hellas by land and sea, suffered such a reversal of fortune when defeated in the battle of Leuctra,[2] that they were deprived of the supremacy over Hellas, and lost such men among them as chose to die rather than live in subjection to those whose masters they formerly were. (48) Furthermore, they had to look on and see all the Peloponnesians who formerly followed in their train against the rest of Hellas, joining the Thebans in invading their country, against whom they were compelled to fight, not in the country for the harvest, but in the midst of their city, even at the seat of government, to

[1] The brief account of contemporary Greece which follows is true and instructive.
[2] 371 B.C.

save their wives and children, — a struggle in which failure would have been immediate destruction, while victory has not released them from their miseries. (49) They were subjected to war by their neighbors, distrusted by all the Peloponnesians, and hated by the majority of Hellenes. They are robbed and harried night and day by their own slaves,[1] and no time passes but they are either making expeditions or fighting battles, or helping their perishing fellow-countrymen. (50) The greatest of their woes, however, is this: they continue in dread lest the Thebans should settle their quarrel with the Phocians,[2] come against them again, and involve them in greater disasters than those they have already incurred.

How can one fail to suppose that men in such a position would gladly see negotiations for peace presided over by a man of consideration, able to bring to a close the wars which threaten them?

(51) The Argives, moreover, you will find to be in some respects in a like condition with those we have mentioned, and in other respects worse off than they; for ever since they have occupied their city they have been engaged in war with their neighbors, as the Lacedæmonians have, but with this difference, that the foes of the Lacedæmonians were weaker than themselves, those of the Argives stronger. Everyone will admit that this is the greatest misfortune. They have been so unfortunate in war that almost every year they have stood by to see their territory ravaged and laid waste. (52) But the worst of all is to come; whenever their enemies cease from injuring them, they themselves put to death the most distinguished and wealthy of their citizens, and feel more pleasure in doing these deeds than any other people feel in slaying their enemies.[3] The reason of their living in such a state of con-

[1] The helots.

[2] Isocrates refers to the Sacred War, which the Delphic Amphictyony, particularly its most powerful member Thebes, had been waging against Phocis since 356. At the time of the writing of this letter to Philip it seems that the fate of the Phocians had not yet been determined upon, or at least was still unknown to the writer (see introduction *supra*). Sparta had sympathized with the Phocians and had given them a little aid.

[3] The writer may have especially in mind the sedition that occurred in Argos shortly after the battle of Leuctra, 371. The democrats, who controlled the government, learning of an oligarchic conspiracy, put to death thirty of the leading plotters. Then arming themselves with clubs, the populace rose up against the wealthier class, and beat to death twelve hundred, or possibly fifteen hundred. This massacre was called scytalism, cudgeling; Diodorus xv. 57 *sq.* Grote, *History of Greece*, x. 199–201.

fusion is no other than war; and if you put an end to it, you will not only release them from these miseries, but you will also cause them to be better advised in their general conduct.

(53) The condition of the Thebans even you are acquainted with.[1] After having won a splendid victory and gained great glory from it, through failure to make good use of their success they are no better situated than are those who were defeated and unsuccessful. For they had hardly overcome their enemies, when, neglecting everything, they proceeded to annoy the Peloponnesian states, ventured to reduce Thessaly to slavery, threatened their neighbors the Megarians, robbed our state of a portion of its territory, laid waste Eubœa, and began to send triremes to Byzantium as if they were going to be lords of land and sea. (54) Finally they carried war against the Phocians with the intention of mastering their cities in a short time, occupying the whole of the surrounding region, and overcoming the Delphic treasures by the contributions they could levy upon their own resources. None of these hopes were realized; instead of having taken the cities of the Phocians, they have lost their own, and they inflicted less injury upon their enemies by invading their country than they suffer themselves in returning to their own; (55) for in Phocis they killed some of the mercenaries, to whom death is more profitable than life, but on their way home they lost the most distinguished of their own citizens, and those most ready to die for their country. Their affairs have come to such a pass that, from hoping that all Hellas would be at their feet, they now rest on you their hopes for their own preservation. I think therefore that they, too, will speedily do what you urge and advise.

(56) It would still have remained for me to speak about our own state, had she not wisely made peace before the others. Now I think she would even contend in support of your policy, especially if she can feel that you are settling these matters with a view to the campaign against the barbarians. . . .

(68) Consider now the fitness of devoting yourself mainly to enterprises of the kind, in which by success you will place your

[1] The idea that Philip knew the condition of the Thebans but not that of the other Hellenes is wholly mistaken; he probably understood the situation of Hellas far better than Isocrates.

reputation in competition with the first and the foremost, and if you fail in your expectation, you will at least win the goodwill of Hellas, the acquisition of which is a far nobler thing than the forcible capture of many Greek cities. For such achievements bring envy and illwill and much evil speaking, but the course which I have advised involves none of these things. Nay if some god should give you the choice of the kind of pursuit and occupation in which you would long to pass your life, you would choose no other, if you took my advice, in preference to this. (69) For not only will you be deemed happy by others, but you will recognize your own bliss. What indeed could surpass the happiness of your position, when from the greatest states the men of most renown are come as ambassadors to your throne, and you take counsel with them about the common welfare,[1] for which no other man will appear to have entertained such thought; (70) when further the whole of Hellas is on tiptoe in regard to the proposals you may make, and no one is indifferent as to what is decided upon at your court, but some make inquiries concerning the state of affairs, others pray to Heaven that you may not fail to obtain the object of your desires, while others are afraid that something may happen to you before you have accomplished your undertaking? (71) If you should succeed, you would have a right to be proud, and could not help feeling highly delighted all your life in the knowledge that you had been at the head of so great an undertaking. . . .

Next Isocrates takes up several matters of less importance. Perhaps the most interesting point omitted from §§ 72–95 is the statement that Philip had many enemies in Hellas, who assert that his real intention is to make himself master of the Greeks (§ 73 *sqq.*). Isocrates repudiates the idea as foolish, alleging that a descendant of Heracles, the greatest benefactor of Hellas, could not think of injuring a people whom his ancestor had so befriended. He then considers the expeditions of Cyrus the Younger and Agesilaus into Asia, and aims to show that Philip has far greater chances of success.

(96) Further, you will find as many soldiers as you desire in readiness; for such is the condition of Hellas that it is easier to get together a larger and better force from wanderers than from

[1] The function Philip is to perform in relation to Greece is that of giving advice through embassies; see 411, n. 4 *supra*.

settled inhabitants. In those times, on the contrary, there were no hired forces, so that, when compelled to raise mercenaries from the towns, they spent more on presents to those who levied them than on the actual pay of the soldiers.[1] . . .

Isocrates now proceeds to give proof of the weakness of Persia and of the feasibility of her conquest. Afterward he discusses the policy of the Macedonian dynasty, beginning with its supposed founder Caranus, in relation to Hellas.

(106) Your father [2] was on friendly terms with all these states, to which I advise you to give your attention; and the founder (Caranus) of your empire, whose aspirations were higher than those of his own countrymen, and who desired undivided authority, did not adopt the same course of action as others whose projects were equally ambitious. (107) While they endeavored to gain this exalted position by causing strife, disturbance and bloodshed in their cities, he left Hellas alone altogether and devoted himself to establishing his kingdom in Macedon; for he knew that the Hellenes were not accustomed to put up with monarchies while the rest were unable to order their life aright without such a form of government.[3] (108) The result was that owing to his peculiar views on these subjects, his rule was one of quite a different character than the rest; for he alone among the Hellenes claimed rule over a people not of kindred race,[4] and alone was able to escape the dangers that beset monarchy. For we should find that amongst the Hellenes, those who have managed to acquire such an authority have not only been destroyed themselves, but that their race has been utterly blotted out from amongst mankind,[5] while he not

[1] It is implied here, and from other indications it seems to be true, that the number of Greeks available for mercenary purposes had increased since the expedition of Cyrus the Younger, 401; see Botsford, *Hellenic History*, ch. xxv.

[2] King Amyntas; Botsford, *op. cit.* ch. xxiv.

[3] The ascription of these ideas to Caranus, it need hardly be said, is pure fiction. The passage, however, is highly important in showing Isocrates' idea of the future relation of Philip to Hellas; he was by no means to be a monarch.

[4] Here Isocrates expresses the opinion that the Macedonians were not racially akin to the Hellenes; and this was the prevalent view during his lifetime. There can be no doubt, however, that they belonged to the Hellenic race, and that they spoke a dialect which the Greeks could understand, naturally with difficulty; see Beloch, *Griech. Gesch.* III. 1. 1–9, with references.

[5] The writer has in mind the tyrannic dynasties of Hellas, all of which were short-lived. In this passage he draws no distinction between legitimate monarchy and tyranny.

only passed his own life in happiness and prosperity, but bequeathed to his children the same honors as he himself enjoyed. . . .

Isocrates then returns to Heracles, the mythical ancestor of Philip, and extols at length the virtues of that hero and especially his goodwill and beneficence to Hellas (109–112). He sets before Philip this example for imitation in character and conduct, that the king of Macedon may be filled with the same mildness and love of mankind, the same desire to do good service to the Hellenes,[1] and to imitate the Olympian gods, who have showered their blessings upon mankind, and in reward have received temples and altars from the beneficiaries of their bounty (113–17). After this digression the writer returns to some of the practical aspects of the campaign against Persia.

(119) You might learn from many instances that this is the manner in which you ought to act, but above all from the fortunes of Jason.[2] Without having achieved anything like yourself, he gained the highest renown, not from his deeds but from his utterances; for he spoke as if he intended to cross over from the continent and to make war upon the King. (120) Since Jason, then, increased his power to such an extent merely by words, what opinion must we think all will have of you, if you do this in reality, and endeavor if possible to destroy the whole kingdom, or if not, to take away from it as much territory as possible, to separate from it Asia from Cilicia to Sinope, as some describe this region, and in addition to build cities through the district, and to send thither as colonists those who are now wanderers from want of their daily bread, and who harass all whom they meet?[3] (121) For if we do not put a stop to their massing together by providing them with sufficient to live upon, they will imperceptibly become so numerous

[1] The teachers of Hellas had long been accustomed to use the heroes of old as patterns of virtue; in fact they had idealized these heroes to that end; Botsford, *Hellenic History*, ch. xiii.

[2] Jason was tyrant of Pheræ, Thessaly, at the time of the battle of Leuctra, 371. For his power and his projects, see Grote, *History of Greece*, x. 138 *sqq.*, 189 *sq.*, 195–8.

[3] Isocrates has in mind the conquest of the entire Persian empire, or at least of Asia Minor, and the colonization of the conquered territory with the superfluous Hellenic population. Precisely how far Philip intended to carry out this program we do not know. The fact, however, that it was executed to the full by Alexander may be taken as evidence of the statesmanlike thought of the writer.

As indicated by the notes above, it is clear that in many matters the judgment of Isocrates was sound, whereas on other important points, particularly in his idealization of the character of Philip and his future relations with Hellas, the ideas of the writer seem almost childish.

that they will be as great a cause of alarm to the Hellenes as are the barbarians. . . .

(154) It remains to summarize what I have said before, that in as few words as possible you may understand the chief point of my advice. I say that you ought to be the benefactor of the Hellenes, the king of Macedon, and the ruler over as many barbarians as possible. If you succeed in these matters, all will be grateful to you, the Hellenes by reason of advantages enjoyed, the Macedonians if you govern them like a king and not like a despot, the rest of mankind if they are freed by you from barbarian sway and gain the protection of Hellas. . . .

128. Oath of Alliance and List of the States of the Hellenic Confederacy Formed under Philip of Macedon in 337

(Hicks and Hill, no. 154; *Inscr. græc.* II. editio minor (1913), no. 236. Translated by C. J. O.)

These two fragments were discovered separately at Athens. The first (*Inscr. græc.* II. no. 160) was published by Dittenberger, (*Syl.* I. no. 149) according to the restoration made by Wilhelm, A., *Archaeologisch-epigraphische Mittheilungen aus Oesterreich-Ungarn*, XVII (1894). 35–7. The second (*Inscr. græc.* II. no. 184; Ditt. I. no. 159) was formerly thought to belong to another inscription, and was supposed to refer to the Lamian war, 323–322 B.C., on account of its similarity to the catalogue of allies given by Diodorus, xviii. 11. 1–2. After Wilhelm discovered the connection between the two fragments, they were published together by Hicks and Hill, as indicated above. Since that time the inscription has been discussed, and the subject-matter interpreted, in great detail, by Wilhelm, in *Sitzb. Wien. Akad.* CLXV (1911). pt. 6. It is important as a record of the Greek confederacy organized by Philip at Corinth in the winter of 338–337 (cf. Schäfer, *Demosth. u. seine Zeit*, III. 51–7) and renewed by Alexander late in 336 (*op. cit.* III. 97 *sq.*). From the fragmentary list of the allied states we learn that northern Greece was included in the confederacy, a fact for which there was previously no direct evidence; *cf.* Beloch, *Griech. Gesch.* II. 573, n. 2. The most important revelation of this document, however, is the fact that the numbers of deputies furnished by the allies were proportioned to their respective populations, as was the case with the Bœotian federation; see no. 117 *supra* and Ferguson, *Greek Imperialism*, 28 *sq.*

(*First fragment, much mutilated.*) . . . And I will not bear arms for the purpose of injury against any of those that abide by the oaths, either by land or by sea. I will not seize for the purpose of war a city or fort (*or* place) or harbor belonging to any of those that share in the peace, by any art or device whatever. I will not overthrow the kingship of Philip and his descendants or the governments existing in the respective states at the time when they swore the oaths regarding the peace.[1] I will do nothing contrary to this treaty either in person or by allowing another, in so far as I can prevent; and if any one shall commit any violation of the agreement, I will give aid to those who need it at the time, according as they may demand. I will make war upon him who violates the general peace, according as it may be required of me and the commander-in-chief may order.[2] . . .

(*The second fragment is a part of the list of the allied states with the number of votes which they possessed in the congress.*)

. . . the . . ., 5;
. . . the Thessalians,[3] 10;
. . . the . . ., 2;
. . . the Elimiotæ (?),[4] 1 (?);
. . . the Thasians,[5] 2;
. . . the . . ., 2; the Ambraciotæ,[6] . . .;
. . . (the . . .) of Thrace and
. . . the Phocians, 3; the Locrians, 3;
. . . the Œtæans[7] and the Malians[7] and
. . . the Agræans[8] and the Dolopes,[9] 5;
. . . the Perrhæbi,[10] 2;
. . . Zacynthus and Cephallenia, 3.

(*End of list.*)

BIBLIOGRAPHY

On the interstate relations of the fourth century, see the histories of Greece by Grote, Curtius, Bury, Holm, and Beloch; also Schömann, G. F., *Griechische Altertümer*, II. bk. iv; Scala, R. von, *Die Staatsverträge des Altertums* (Leipzig, 1898); Hitzig, H. F., "Altgriechische Staatsverträge über Rechtshilfe," in

[1] *Cf.* Pseudo-Demosthenes, *On the Agreement with Alexander* (XVII). 10: "For it is provided that, if any persons shall overthrow the governments in the respective states at the time when they swore the oaths regarding the peace, such persons shall be enemies of all those who share in the peace."

[2] Greek hegemon, the title of the Macedonian king as general-in-chief of the allied forces.

[3] *I.e.*, the inhabitants of central Thessaly.

[4] North of Thessaly.

[5] Perhaps joined with the inhabitants of the neighboring island of Samothrace.

[6] Of Ambracia in southern Epirus.

[7] On the southern border of Thessaly.

[8] Of northern Ætolia.

[9] In southwestern Thessaly.

[10] In northern Thessaly.

Festgabe für Regelsberger (Zurich, 1907), 1–70; Burle, E., *Essai historique sur le développement de la notion de droit naturel dans l'antiquité grecque* (Trevoux, 1908); Holtzendorff, F. von, and Rivier, A., *Introduction au droit des gens* (1891), I. ch. ii; Bortolucci, J., "De iure gentium criminali apud Græcos," in *Rivista di storia antica* (Padua), 1905, pp. 421–35; Bonucci, A., *La legge comune nel pensiero greco* (Perugia, 1903); Barth, B., *De Græcorum asylis* (Strassburg, 1887); a Columbia University doctorate dissertation on ancient sanctuary by C. Huth is nearing completion; Phillipson, C., *International Law and Customs of Ancient Greece and Rome*, 2 vols. (Macmillan, 1911); Kaerst, J., "Die Entwickelung der Vertragstheorie im Altertum," in *Zeitschr. für Politik*, II (1909). 305–38; Schöll, R., *Die Anfänge einer politischen Litteratur bei den Griechen*, Festrede Münch. Akad. (1890); Clerc, M., *Les métèques athéniens: Étude sur la condition légale, la situation morale et le rôle social et économique des étrangers domiciliés à Athènes* (Paris, 1893); "De la condition des étrangers domiciliés dans les différentes cités grecques," in *Revue des universités du midi*, IV (1898). 1–32, 153–80, 249–74; Freeman, E. A., *History of Federal Government in Greece and Italy*, I (London, 1893); Sonne, E., *De arbitris externis, quos Græci adhibuerunt ad lites et intestinas et peregrinas componendas quæstiones epigraphicæ* (Göttingen, 1888); Berard, V., *De arbitrio inter liberas Græcorum civitates* (Paris, 1894); Westermann, W. L., "Interstate Arbitration in Antiquity," in *Class. Journ.* II (1906–07). 197 *sqq.*; Raeder, A., *L'arbitrage international chez les Hellènes* (Putnam, 1912); Tod, M. N., *International Arbitration amongst the Greeks* (Oxford: Clarendon Press, 1913); Kahrstedt, U., *Forschungen zur Geschichte des ausgehenden fünften und des vierten Jahrhunderts* (Weidmann, 1910); Kessler, *Isokrates und die panhellenische Idee* (Paderborn, 1911); Meyer, E., "Isokrates' zweiter Brief an Philipp und Demosthenes' zweite Philippika," in *Sitz. Berl. Akad.* 1909. pt. i. 758–79; Kaerst, J., "Der korinthische Bund," in *Rhein. Mus.* LII (1897). 519–56; Köhler, U., "Die Eroberung Asiens durch Alexander den Grossen und der Korinthische Bund," in *Sitz. Berl. Akad.* 1898. pp. 120–34.

CHAPTER XIII

THE STATE

In the Period 404–337 B.C.

In this chapter are gathered materials for illustrating the relation of the state to the citizen, state regulation of social and economic conditions, and the character and relative value of various forms of democracy and oligarchy.

129. A Public-spirited Citizen

(Isæus vii. *Concerning the Inheritance of Apollodorus*, 39–42. Translated by G. W. B.)

The speaker claims that Apollodorus in his right mind and in due form adopted him as heir. His claim is contested by several adversaries, among whom is Pronapes. The passage below is typical of the appeal made to the jury — the demand for a favorable verdict on the ground of services rendered in the past by the litigant and his kinsmen, and the promise of further services in case of a favorable decision. In general the jury seems to have been swayed more by a consideration of the character and usefulness of the parties to the trial than by the letter of the law.

Apollodorus himself did not, like Pronapes, have his property assessed at a small value; but as a member of the knightly class he took upon himself the duty of holding office.[1] He did not seek violent possession of other men's property nor fancied it no business of his to benefit you,[2] but rendering his whole estate visible to you, he patriotically carried out all your orders and tried to live in such wise that no harm could come from him or his own, thinking it right to spend upon himself but a moderate amount and to place the rest at the disposal of the state that it might have enough to meet expenses. With these resources what liturgy did

[1] The knightly, or hippic, class, was the next to the wealthiest of the four property classes continuing from before the time of Solon (Botsford, *Hellenic History*, ch. vii. § 2 *sq.*). To what offices the knights alone were eligible is unknown.

[2] "You," the jurors, are identified with the whole body of citizens and with the state.

he not perform, or what war-tax did he not help contribute among the foremost of the citizens?[1] Or what duty did he evade? he who won a victory in a boys' chorus, in which a memorial of his public spirit is the tripod standing there. Now what ought to be the conduct of a sober citizen? Was it not his duty, where others were wont violently to seize property not their own, to do nothing of the kind but to attempt to secure his own? and where the city needs money, to contribute among the foremost and not to conceal his possessions? Such a man was he, in return for which conduct it would be just for you to grant him this favor — leaving his own judgment to be master of his estate.[2] As to me, too, so far as my early age permitted, you will find me neither base nor useless. I have taken part in military campaigns for the state; I attend to whatever is ordered, for that is the task of men of my age. On the ground of these services it would be reasonable of you to exercise a foresight in our interest, particularly as these adversaries have seized an estate worth five talents and capable of performing the trierarchy, and have sold it and rendered it masterless, whereas we have already performed liturgies, and will continue to perform them, if you will approve the intention of Apollodorus by granting us this inheritance.

130. State Aid to the Disabled

(Lysias xxiv. *Concerning the Cripple*, 6–8, 15–17, 22 *sq.* Translated by G. W. B.)

A certain cripple has been receiving an allowance of one obol (about three cents) daily from the state. Another citizen brings before the Council the charge that he does not deserve it, (1) because he is really of sound body, (2) because he has a trade, (3) because he associates with rich men, and must therefore be well-to-do, (4) because he is a man of bad character, violent, insolent, and of loose morals, (5) because his shop is the resort of evil men. The excerpts given below have a varied interest.

My father left me nothing, and I ceased to support my mother only three years ago when she died, and my children are not yet old enough to support me. I have a trade which brings me scant returns, which I now carry on with great difficulty, and am unable

[1] On the liturgies, see Botsford, *Hellenic History*, ch. xii.

[2] That is, approving of his adoption of a son.

to find any one to take it off my hands. I have no income besides this (allowance), and if you take it from me, I shall run the risk of falling into the direst straits. . . . It would be unreasonable, Council, if when my misfortune was single I should receive this dole but should be deprived of it when old age and diseases and their attendant evils have been added to my lot. . . .

(My adversary) asserts that I am insolent and violent and possessed of an excessively unbridled temper, as though he could only speak the truth if he used terrible words, and could not do so if he used only mild words and abstained from exaggeration. But I fancy, Council, that you know well how to distinguish between men whose part it is to be insolent and men to whom such a thing is unbecoming. It is not reasonable that the poor and the desperately needy should be insolent; that rather falls to the lot of those who possess far more than a competence; nor the disabled in body but those rather who trust to their physical strength; nor those who have far advanced in age, but the young and the possessors of youthful dispositions. For the wealthy with their money purchase exemption from the danger of punishment,[1] whereas the poor are forced to sobriety by their present need. . . .

Do not because of this man (my accuser) deprive me of the only part or lot in my country that fortune has granted me. . . . For since, Council, the deity (Daimon) has debarred us from the highest offices, the state has voted us this money, considering that the chances of good and ill are common to all.[2] How then should I not be the most wretched of all men, if through my misfortune I should be deprived of the noblest and greatest things, and then through my accuser should lose what the state has bestowed in its forethought for men who are situated as I am?

[1] Here we get the point of view of the poor man — that wealth is a shield against prosecution. Had more needy Greeks thus spoken to us, we should probably have had material to counterbalance the charge that the wealthy were often condemned that their property might fall to the state and be paid out to the jurors as fees; *cf.* p. 466 and n. 2.

[2] This is a peculiar theory, that as the state cannot bestow office upon the poor and the crippled, it is under obligation to grant them a money allowance as a substitute.

131. State Regulation of the Grain Trade

(Lysias xxii. *Against the Grain-Dealers.* Translated by E. G. S.)

One of the first objects of an Athenian statesman was to provide for an adequate supply of imported grain, seeing that the country produced scarcely half the amount needed for consumption. Two-thirds of every cargo brought to Peiræus had to be sold in the country; the rest might be carried farther. State regulations were established to prevent cornering the market and unreasonable profits of dealers. Among the regulations was one which forbade a profit of more than an obol to the basket, phormos, holding about a medimnus, *i.e.*, a bushel and a half. It was ordered further that no one should buy more than fifty phormi at a time. To enforce these regulations a board of Grain Inspectors (Σιτοφύλακες, Sitophylaces) was instituted. Death was the penalty for the violation of these laws.

The case represented by the subjoined oration is made clear by the document itself. From this source, and from many others, we infer that the Hellenic state took far greater care of the citizens in general than does any modern state, in which any such care would be resented as an interference with business.

(1) Many have approached me, gentlemen of the jury, wondering that I attacked the grain dealers in the Council and saying that if you were ever so convinced of their acting wrongfully, you would none the less consider those who compose addresses about them, to be blackmailers. Why then I have been constrained to accuse them, I wish to explain first.

(2) When the prytaneis reported to the Council about them, the members were so enraged at them, that some said they ought to hand them over to the Eleven without trial and punish them with death. But thinking it awful that the Council should fall into the habit of doing such things, I arose and said that it seemed best to me to try the grain dealers according to the law, considering that if they have done what is worthy of death, you will none the less arrive at a just verdict; but if they are no wrong doers, they ought not to perish without trial . . . (3) And when the Council was convinced thereof they undertook to calumniate me, saying that I am making these discourses in order to save the grain dealers.[1] As pertains to the Council then, I made my actual defence when

[1] Charges against these grain dealers were first brought into the Council, many members of which were for putting the accused to death without trial. The present speaker, however, persuaded that body to allow the case to come before an ordinary court. That resolution prevailed; and the present oration was delivered before a jury in accusation.

they had the trial; for while the others were keeping quiet, I arose and accused them and made it clear to all, that I did not speak in behalf of them but supported the established laws. (4) I began therefore because I feared the charges; and I consider it disgraceful to cease before you give about it whatever verdict you desire.

(5) First, stand up and tell me, are you a metic?[1] "Yes." And are you a metic with the expectation of obeying the laws of the commonwealth, or of doing what you like? "Of obeying." Do you deserve anything else but death, if you have done anything contrary to the laws — any act on which the death-penalty is set? "I do not." Answer me then, whether you admit having bought up more grain than fifty phormi, which the law allows? "I bought it up under orders of the officials."

(6) If then he demonstrates, gentlemen of the jury, that a statute exists, which orders the grain dealers to buy up the grain in case the officials order them to do so, acquit him; but if not, it is just that you should find him guilty. For we presented to you the statute which prohibits anyone in the commonwealth from buying up more grain than fifty phormi.[2]

(7) This charge then, gentlemen of the jury, ought to be sufficient, since this man admits that he bought it up, but the law appears as prohibiting that, and you have sworn to give your verdict according to the laws. It is necessary, however, to speak more at length about them. (8) When these men shifted the blame upon the grain inspectors, we called upon the latter and interrogated them. Two of them said they knew nothing of the matter, but Anytus explained that last winter when grain was high, and when these men bid up the price against one another, and fought among themselves, he had advised them to cease wrangling, thinking it advantageous to you who bought from them, that they should make their purchases at as fair a figure as possible: for it was necessary for them to sell at a rise of no more than one obol. (9) That he did not order them to buy up and store away, but not to outbid one another in the buying, I shall produce Anytus himself as witness, and that this man made these statements in the term of the former

[1] Metic, alien resident. Much of the trade was in the hands of this class.

[2] Phormi, see introduction.

Council, but the accused appear as having formed a corner in the time of the present Council.[1]

(10) That they bought up the grain without an order of the officials, you have heard; and I hold that if their statements about these things are ever so true, they will not produce a defence of themselves, but will accuse these officials; for where statutes are specifically written, why should not the penalty be paid both by those who do not obey (the statutes) and those who bid them act contrary to the same? (11) But, gentlemen of the jury, I think they will not resort to this plea; yet perhaps they will say, as they did in the Council, that they bought up the grain from devotion to the community, in order to sell it to you at as fair a price as possible. I will, however, bring before you a very great and very lucid proof that they lie. (12) For they ought, if indeed it was for your sake that they did these things, to appear selling at the same price for many days, until the grain which they had bought up, failed them, whereas in fact sometimes in the course of the same day they sold it one drachma higher, just as though they had bought it up at the rate of a single *medimnus*.[2] And for these facts I shall offer you witnesses. . . .

(13) It seems outrageous to me, if whenever a tax is to be paid, of which all are bound to have knowledge, they are unwilling but allege poverty as a pretext, yet in a matter in which death is set as a penalty and it is profitable for them to escape notice, they say they committed these illegal acts from devotion to you. Still you all know that it behooves these men least of all to make such statements. For their advantage is the opposite to that of others: their gains are largest when upon the arrival of some bad news they sell their grain to the community at a high figure. (14) So gladly therefore do they see your troubles that some of them they ascertain earlier than others, and some they invent themselves, either that the ships in the Black Sea have perished, or while sailing out were captured by the Lacedæmonians, or that the harbors are closed, or that the truce is about to be cancelled, and they have

[1] A Council held office one year; the trouble regarding these grain merchants began therefore in the preceding year.

[2] Medimnus, see introduction.

advanced to that point of enmity toward you, that they plot against you in precisely the same emergencies in which the public enemy do. (15) For when you happen to be most in want of grain, they grab it and are unwilling to sell, and you may be well satisfied to buy from them at any price whatever and take your leave of them, so that sometimes when there is peace we are reduced to a state of siege by them.

(16) For this reason the community long ago came to such a determination about their cunning and evil-mindedness that over all the other wares you appointed the marketmasters as guardians, but for this craft alone, separately, you appoint grain inspectors by lot; and ofttimes you imposed upon them, citizens though they were, the most severe penalties, because they were unable to master the scoundrellism of these dealers. What then should the malefactors themselves suffer at your hands, when you even put to death those who are not able to maintain a watch over them?

(17) You ought to ponder on the fact that it is impossible for you to acquit them. For if you shall find them guiltless when they themselves admit that they made a combination against the importers, you will seem to plot against the skippers who come here. If they make some other defence, no one could find fault with those who acquitted them; for it lies with you to give credence to whichsoever of the two sides you choose; but in the actual situation how would you not seem to act outrageously if you are to let go scotfree the men who confess that they have been acting illegally?

(18) Remember, gentlemen of the jury, that you have condemned to death many men already who were subject to this charge and furnished witnesses, deeming more reliable the statements of the accusers. Why would it not be strange, if while sitting in judgment on the same misdemeanors you are eager to impose penalty on those who make denial? (19) In fact, gentlemen of the jury, I think it is clear to all that the contests about such things happen to be of the widest concern in common to every one in the community, so that they are going to discover what opinion you entertain about them, thinking, if you condemn them to death, the others will be more seemly; but if you let them go scotfree, you will have voted them ample immunity to do what they like.

(20) But it is necessary, gentlemen of the jury, to chastise them

not only for the sake of the past, but also as an example for the future; for as things now are, they will be hardly endurable. And consider that in consequence of this vocation very many already have stood trial for their life; and so great are the emoluments which they derive from it that they prefer to risk their life every day rather than cease to draw from you unjust profits. (21) And indeed not even if they entreat you and supplicate, would you justly pity them, but much rather the citizens who perished on account of their wickedness, and the importers against whom they made a combination. The importers you will gratify and cheer, if you impose a penalty on the dealers. Otherwise what opinion do you think they will have, when they learn that you acquitted the retailers who admitted plotting against the skippers?

(22) I do not know what I should say further; for concerning other evildoers one must learn from the prosecutors at the time of trial, but the wickedness of these men you all know. If then you shall condemn them, you will act justly and you will buy grain cheaper; otherwise, dearer.

132. A Plan for Increasing the Revenues of Athens

(Xenophon, *Ways and Means*. Dakyns, revised by E. G. S.)

In ancient times no doubt was expressed as to the authenticity of this work. Among modern scholars, however, there are some who wish to remove it from the list of Xenophon's genuine writings on the supposition, (1) that according to internal evidence it was composed as late as 346, and therefore after Xenophon's death; (2) that the views expressed in the treatise were repugnant to the author's well-known convictions. Others argue on the contrary that internal evidence points to 355 as the date of composition. In favor of its authenticity we may say further that the style seems to be that of Xenophon, and that it was perfectly possible for Xenophon in old age to modify his political and social views. If then we accept the pamphlet as a genuine work of Xenophon, it is in place to notice the powerful influence of fourth-century socialism upon the intellectual class, to extort such concessions from a pronounced conservative. The entire pamphlet is here presented, partly because of the light which it throws upon the economic resources of Athens at that time and partly because of its unique ideas, which though utterly impracticable, cannot help attracting at least the curiosity of all who are interested in social history.

I. (1) For myself I hold to the opinion that the qualities of the men in charge of the government, whatever they be, are reproduced in the character of the constitutions themselves.

It has been maintained of certain leading statesmen in Athens that they know, as well as the rest of mankind, what is just, but that, owing to the pressure of poverty on the masses, a certain measure of injustice in their dealing with the allied states could not be avoided. I set myself therefore to discover whether by any manner of means it were possible for the citizens of Athens to be supported solely from the soil of Attica itself, which would obviously be the most equitable solution. For if so, herein lay, as I believed, the antidote at once to their own poverty and to the feeling of suspicion with which they are regarded by the rest of Hellas. (2) I had no sooner begun my investigation than one fact presented itself clearly to my mind, which is that the country itself is made by nature to provide the amplest resources. And with a view to establishing the truth of this initial proposition I will describe the physical features of Attica.

(3) In the first place, the extraordinary mildness of the climate is proved by the actual products of the soil. Numerous plants which in many parts of the world appear as stunted leafless growths are here fruit-bearing. As with the soil, so too with the sea indenting our coasts, the varied productivity of which is exceptionally great. Again with regard to those boons which the gods bestow on man in the seasons, one and all they commence very early and end very late in this land.[1] (4) Nor is the supremacy of Attica shown only in those products which year after year flourish and grow old, but the land contains treasures of a more perennial kind. Within its folds lies imbedded by nature an unstinted store of marble, out of which are chiselled temples and altars of rarest beauty and the most comely images of worship for the gods. This marble, moreover, is an object of desire to many foreigners, Hellenes and barbarians alike. (5) Then there is land which, although it yields no fruit to the sower, needs only to be mined in order to feed many times more mouths than it could as corn-land. Doubtless we owe it to a divine dispensation that our land is veined with silver; if we consider how many neighboring states lie round us by

[1] These remarks on the productivity of the soil of Attica are significant in view of the fairly grounded opinion that it was inferior to the average soil of Hellas. Notwithstanding the ravages of the Peloponnesian war and the later growth of industry, there can be no doubt that intelligent farming was still profitable; *cf.* 499 and n. 1.

land and sea and yet into none of them does a single thinnest vein of silver penetrate.

(6) Further it would be scarcely irrational to maintain that the city of Athens lies at the navel, not of Hellas merely, but of the habitable world. So true is it that the farther we remove from Athens the greater the extreme of heat or cold to be encountered; or to use another illustration, the traveller who desires to traverse the confines of Hellas from end to end will find that, whether he voyages by sea or by land, he is describing a circle, the centre of which is Athens. (7) Once more, this land though not literally sea-girt has all the advantages of an island, being accessible to every wind that blows, and can invite to its bosom or waft from its shore all products, since it is peninsular; whilst by land it is the emporium of many markets, as being a portion of the continent.

(8) Lastly, whilst the majority of states have barbarian neighbors, the source of many troubles, Athens has as her next-door neighbors civilized states which are themselves far remote from the barbarians.

II. (1) All these advantages, to repeat what I have said, may, I believe, be traced primarily to the soil and position of Attica itself. But these native blessings may be added to: in the first place, by a careful handling of our resident alien population. For my part, I can hardly conceive of a more splendid source of revenue than lies open in this direction. Here you have a self-supporting class of residents conferring large benefits upon the state, and instead of receiving payment themselves, contributing on the contrary to the gain of the exchequer by the sojourners' tax. (2) Nor under the term of careful handling do I demand more than the removal of obligations which, while they confer no benefit on the state, have an air of inflicting various disabilities on the resident aliens. I would further relieve them from the obligation of serving as hoplites side by side with the citizens proper; since beside the personal risk, which is great, the trouble of quitting trades and homesteads is no trifle. (3) Incidentally the state itself would be benefited by this exemption, if the citizens were more in the habit of campaigning with one another,[1] rather than shoulder to shoulder

[1] The dislike of the Athenians for military service is one of the most significant factors of their political history during the fourth century.

with Lydians, Phrygians, Syrians, and barbarians from all quarters of the world, who form the staple of our resident alien class. (4) Besides the advantage of so weeding the ranks, it would add a positive lustre to our city, were it admitted that the men of Athens, her sons, have reliance on themselves alone for their battles rather than on foreigners. (5) I think, too, if we were to give to the alien residents a share in the other things which it is honorable to bestow a share in, and in the right of cavalry service, we should render them more loyal and at the same time render the city stronger and greater.

(6) In the next place, seeing that there are at present numerous building sites within the city walls as yet devoid of houses,[1] supposing the state were to make free grants of such land to foreigners for building purposes in cases where there could be no doubt as to the respectability of the applicant, if I am not mistaken, the result of such a measure will be that a larger number of persons, and of a better class, will be attracted to Athens as a place of residence. (7) Lastly, if we could bring ourselves to appoint, as a new government office, a board of guardians of foreign residents like our Guardians of Orphans, with special privileges assigned to those guardians who should show on their books the greatest number of resident aliens, — such a measure would tend to improve the goodwill of the class in question, and in all probability all people without a city of their own would aspire to the status of foreign residents in Athens, and so further increase the revenues of the city.

III. (1) At this point I propose to offer some remarks in proof of the attraction and advantages of Athens as a center of commercial enterprise. In the first place, it will hardly be denied that we possess the finest and safest harborage for shipping, where vessels of all sorts can come to moorings and be laid up in absolute security as far as stress of weather is concerned. (2) But farther than that, in most states the trader is under the necessity of lading his vessel with some merchandise or other in exchange for his cargo, since the current coin has no circulation beyond the frontier. But at

[1] The total citizen population of Attica was less in the fourth than in the fifth century, and the tendency of business men and of artisans was to gather in Peiræus, leaving Athens with a dwindling population. Aliens could not acquire land in Attica without especial permission.

Athens he has a choice; he can either in return for his wares export a variety of goods, such as human beings seek after, or if he does not desire to take goods in exchange for goods, he has simply to export silver, and he cannot have a more excellent freight to export, since wheresoever he likes to sell it, he everywhere realizes more than his capital investment. (3) Or again, supposing prizes were offered to the market officials for equitable and speedy settlements of points in dispute, to enable any one so wishing to proceed on his voyage without hindrance, the result would be that far more merchants would trade with us and with greater satisfaction.

(4) It would indeed be a good and noble institution to pay special marks of honor, such as the privilege of the front seat, to merchants and shipowners, and on occasion to invite to hospitable entertainment those who, through something notable in the quality of ship or merchandise, may claim to have done the state a service. The recipients of these honors would be devoted to us as friends, not only under the incentive of gain, but of distinction also. (5) Now the greater the number of people attracted to Athens either as visitors or as residents, clearly the greater the development of imports and exports. More goods will be sent out of the country, there will be more buying and selling, with a consequent influx of money in the shape of rents to individuals and dues and customs to the state exchequer. (6) To secure this augmentation of the revenues, mark you, not the outlay of one single penny; nothing is needed beyond one or two philanthropic measures and certain details of supervision.

With regard to the other sources of revenue which I contemplate, I admit, it is different. For them I recognize the necessity of a capital to begin with. (7) I am not, however, without good hope that the citizens of this state will contribute heartily to such an object, when I reflect on the large sums subscribed by the state on various late occasions, as, for instance, when reinforcements were sent to the Arcadians under the command of Lysistratus,[1] and again at the date of the generalship of Hegesileos.[2] (8) I am well aware that ships of war are frequently despatched and that too although it is uncertain whether the venture will be for the

[1] This expedition was made in 366; Xen. *Hell.* vii. 4. 3.

[2] In 362; Xen. *Hell.* vii. 5. 15.

better or for the worse, and the only certainty is that the contributor will not recover the sum subscribed nor have any further share in the object for which he gave his contribution.

(9) For a sound investment I know of nothing comparable with the initial outlay to form this fund. Any one whose contribution amounts to ten minæ may look forward to a return as high as he would get on bottomry, of nearly one-fifth, as the recipient of three obols a day.[1] The contributor of five minæ will on the same principle get more than a third, (10) while the majority of Athenians will get more than cent per cent on their contribution. That is to say, a subscription of one mina will put the subscriber in possession of nearly double that sum, and that, moreover, without setting foot outside Athens, which, as far as human affairs go, is as sound and durable a security as possible. (11) Moreover I am of opinion that if the names of contributors were to be inscribed as benefactors for all time, many foreigners would be induced to contribute, and possibly not a few states, in their desire to obtain the right of inscription; indeed I anticipate that some kings, princes and satraps would display a keen desire to share in such a favor.

(12) To come to the point: were such a capital once furnished, it would be a magnificent plan to build lodging-houses for the benefit of shipmasters in the neighborhood of the harbors, in addition to those which exist; and again on the same principle, if suitable places of meeting for merchants — for the purposes of buying and selling — and thirdly, (13) if public lodging-houses and stores for vending goods, were fitted up for retail dealers in Peiræus and the city, they would at once be an ornament to the state and a fertile source of revenue. (14) Also it seems to me it would be a good thing to try to see if, on the principle on which at present the state possesses public warships, it would not be possible to secure public merchant vessels to be let out on the security of guarantors just like any other public property. If the plan were found feasible, this public merchant navy would be a large source of extra revenue.

[1] The idea is that every Athenian will receive three obols daily, whatever he subscribes. One who contributes ten minas, or 1000 drachmas, will receive for the year 3 × 360 obols, or 1080 obols, which equals 180 drachmas. That is, his return will be 18 per cent. The contributor of half that sum will receive double the rate of interest, and so on.

IV. (1) I come to a new topic. I am persuaded that the establishment of the silver mines on a proper footing would be followed by a large increase of wealth apart from other sources of revenue. I should like, therefore, for the benefit of those who may be ignorant, to point out what the capacity of these mines really is. You will then be in a position to decide how to turn them to better account. (2) It is clear, I presume, to every one that these mines have for a very long time been in active operation; at any rate no one will venture to fix the date at which they first began to be worked. Now in spite of the fact that the silver ore has been dug and carried out for so long a time, I would ask you to note that the mounds of rubbish so shovelled out are but a fractional portion of the series of hillocks containing veins of silver, and as yet unquarried. (3) Nor is the silver-bearing region gradually becoming circumscribed. On the contrary, it is evidently extending in wider area from year to year. That is to say, during the period in which the greatest number of workers have been employed within the mines, no hand was ever stopped for want of work to do. Rather, at any given moment, the work to be done was more than enough for the hands employed. (4) Thus it is today with the owners of slaves working in the mines; no one dreams of reducing the number of his hands. On the contrary, the object is perpetually to acquire as many additional hands as the owner possibly can. The fact is that with few hands to dig and search, the find of treasure will be small, but with an increase of labor the discovery of the ore itself is more than proportionally increased. So much so that of all operations with which I am acquainted, this is the only one in which no sort of jealousy is felt at a further development of the industry. (5) I may go a step farther: every proprietor of a farm will be able to tell you exactly how many yoke of oxen are sufficient for the estate, and how many farm hands. To send into the field more than the exact number requisite every farmer would consider a dead loss. But in silver mining [operations] the universal complaint is the short supply of hands. Indeed there is no analogy between this and other industries. (6) With an increase in the number of bronze-workers articles of bronze may become so cheap that the bronze-workers are ruined. And so again with ironfounders. Or again, in a plethoric condition of the corn and wine market these fruits of the soil will be so depreciated in value that the particular husbandries cease to be remunerative, and many a farmer will give up his tillage of the soil and betake himself to the business of a merchant, or of a shopkeeper, to banking or money-lending.[1] But the converse is the case in the working of silver; there the larger the quantity of ore discovered and the greater the amount of silver extracted, the greater the number of persons ready to engage in the operation. (7) One more illustration: take the case of movable property. No one when he has got sufficient furniture for his house dreams of making further purchases on this head, but of silver no one ever yet possessed so much that he was forced to cry "enough." On the contrary, if ever anybody does become possessed of an immoderate amount he finds as much pleasure in digging a hole in the ground and hoarding it as in the actual employment of it. (8) And from a wider point of view; when a state is prosperous there is nothing which people so much desire as silver. The men want money to expend on beautiful armor and fine horses, and houses, and sumptuous outfittings of all sorts. The women betake themselves to expensive apparel and ornaments of gold. (9) Or when states are sick, either through barrenness of corn and other fruits or through war, the demand for current coin is even more imperative (whilst the ground lies unproductive), to pay for necessaries or military aid. (10) Furthermore if it be asserted that gold is after all just as useful as silver, without gainsaying the proposition I may note this fact about gold, that, with a sudden influx of this metal, it is the gold itself which is depreciated whilst causing at the same time a rise in the value of silver.

(11) The facts given above are, I think, conclusive. They encourage us not only to introduce as much human labor as possible into the mines, but to extend the scale of operation within, by increase of plant, etc., in full assurance that there is no danger either of the ore itself being exhausted or of silver becoming depreciated.[2] In advancing these views I am merely following a pre-

[1] This was precisely the tendency of the farming population of Attica at the time when this pamphlet was being written; the cheapness of imported grain and the attractions of an expanding city economy were drawing many agriculturists from their fields.

[2] On both these points the writer is wholly wrong: in fact the amount of silver remaining in the mines was then very limited, and further the production of unlimited

cedent set me by the state herself. (12) So it seems to me, since the state permits any foreigner who desires it to undertake mining operations on a footing of equality with her own citizens.

(13) But to make my meaning clearer on the question of maintenance, I will at this point explain in detail how the silver mines may be furnished and extended so as to render them much more useful to the state. Only I would premise that I claim no sort of admiration for anything which I am about to say, as though I had hit upon some recondite discovery. Since half of what I have to say is at the present moment patent to the eyes of all of us, and as to what belongs to past history, if we are to believe the testimony of our fathers, things were then much of a piece with what is going on now. (14) No, what is really marvellous is that the state, with the fact of so many private persons growing wealthy at her expense and under her very eyes, should have failed to imitate them. It is an old story, trite enough to those of us who have cared to attend to it, how once on a time Nicias,[1] the son of Niceratus, owned a thousand men in the silver mines, whom he let out to Sosias, a Thracian, on the following terms. Sosias was to pay him a net obol a day, without charge or deduction, for every slave of the thousand, and be responsible for keeping up the number perpetually at that figure. (15) So again Hipponicus had six hundred slaves let out on the same principle, which brought him in a net mina a day without charge or deduction. Then there was Philemonides, with three hundred, bringing him in half a mina, and others doubtless there were, making profits in proportion to their respective resources and capital. (16) But there is no need to revert to ancient history. At the present moment there are hundreds of human beings in the mines let out on the same principle. (17) Supposing therefore that my proposal were carried into effect, the only novelty in it is that, just as the individual in acquiring the ownership of a gang of slaves finds himself at once provided with a permanent source of income, so the state, in like fashion, should possess herself of a body of public slaves, to the number, say, of three for every

quantities would have greatly depreciated the value. The depreciation of gold, which he mentions just above, ought to have taught him better.

[1] Nicias, the famous Athenian general in the Peloponnesian war; Botsford, *Hellenic History*, chs. xviii, xix.

Athenian citizen. (18) As to the feasibility of our proposals, I challenge any one whom it may concern to test the scheme point by point, and to give his verdict.

With regard to the price then of the men themselves, it is obvious that the public treasury is in a better position to provide funds than any private individual. What can be easier than for the Council to invite by public proclamation all whom it may concern to bring their slaves, and to buy up those produced? (19) Assuming the purchase to be effected, is it credible that people will hesitate to hire from the state rather than from the private owner, and actually on the same terms? People have at all events no hesitation at present in hiring consecrated grounds, sacred victims, houses, etc., or in purchasing the right of farming taxes from the state. (20) To ensure the preservation of the purchased property, the treasury can take the same securities precisely from the lessee as it does from those who purchase the right of farming its taxes. In fact fraudulent dealing is easier on the part of the man who has purchased such a right than of a man who hires slaves; (21) for it is not easy to see how the misappropriation of public money is to be detected, when it differs in no way from private money. It will however take a clever thief to make off with these slaves, marked as they will be with the public stamp, and in face of a heavy penalty attached at once to the sale and exportation of them. Up to this point then it would appear feasible enough for the state to acquire property in men and to keep a safe watch over them.

(22) But with reference to an opposite objection which may present itself to the mind of some one; what guarantee is there that, along with the increase in the supply of laborers, there will be a corresponding demand for their services on the part of contractors? It may be reassuring to note, first of all, that many of those who have already embarked on mining operations will be anxious to increase their staff of laborers by hiring some of these public slaves, for they have a large capital at stake; and again, many of the actual laborers now engaged are growing old; and secondly, there are many others, Athenians and foreigners alike, who, though unwilling and indeed incapable of working physically in the mines, will be glad enough to earn a livelihood by their wits as superintendents.

(23) Let it be granted, however, that at first a nucleus of twelve hundred slaves is formed. It is hardly too sanguine a supposition that out of the profits alone, within five or six years this number may be increased to at least six thousand. Again, out of that number of six thousand — supposing each slave to bring in an obol a day clear of all expenses — we get a revenue of sixty talents a year. (24) Supposing further twenty talents out of this sum laid out on the purchase of more slaves, there will be forty talents left for the state to apply to any other purpose it may find advisable. By the time the round number of ten thousand is reached, the yearly income will amount to a hundred talents. (25) As a matter of fact, the state will receive much more than these figures represent, as any one here will bear me witness who can remember what the dues derived from slaves realized before the troubles at Deceleia.[1] Testimony to the same effect is borne by the fact, that in spite of the countless number of human beings employed in the silver mines within the whole period, the mines present exactly the same appearance today as they did within the recollection of our forefathers. (26) Once more, everything that is taking place today tends to prove that, whatever the number of slaves employed, you will never have more than the works can easily absorb. The miners find no limit of depth in sinking shafts or laterally in piercing galleries. (27) To open cuttings in new directions today is just as possible as it was in former times. In fact no one can take on himself to say whether there is more silver ore in the regions already cut into, or in those where the pick has not yet struck. (28) Well then, it may be asked, why is it that there is not the same rush to make new cuttings now as in former times? The answer is, because the people concerned with the mines are poorer nowadays. The attempt to restart operations, renew plant, and the like, is of recent date, and any one who ventures to open up a new area runs a considerable risk. (29) Supposing he hits upon a productive field, he becomes a rich man, but supposing he draws a blank, he loses the whole of his outlay; and that is a danger which people of the present time are shy of facing.

(30) It is a difficulty, but it is one on which, I believe, I can offer some practical advice. I have a plan to suggest which will

[1] In the last years of the Peloponnesian war; Botsford, *Hellenic History*, ch. xix.

reduce to a minimum the risk of opening up new cuttings. The citizens of Athens are divided, as we all know, into ten tribes.[1] Let the state then assign to each of these ten tribes an equal number of slaves, and let the tribes agree to associate their fortunes and proceed to open new cuttings. What will happen? Any single tribe hitting upon a productive lode will be the means of discovering what is advantageous to all. (31) Or supposing two or three, or possibly the half of them, hit upon a lode, clearly these several operations will proportionally be more remunerative still. That the whole ten will fail is not at all in accordance with what we should expect from the history of the past. (32) It is possible of course for private persons to combine in the same way, and share their fortunes and minimize their risks. Nor need you apprehend, sirs, that a state mining company, established on this principle, will prove a thorn in the side of the private owner, or the private owner prove injurious to the state. But rather like allies who render each other stronger the more they combine, so in these silver mines, the greater number of companies at work the larger the riches they will discover and carry off.

(33) This then is a statement, as far as I can make it clear, of the method by which, with the proper state organization, every Athenian may be supplied with ample maintenance at the public expense. (34) Possibly some of you may be calculating that the capital requisite will be enormous. They may doubt if a sufficient sum will ever be subscribed to meet the needs. All I can say is, even so, do not despond. (35) It is not as if it were necessary that every feature of the scheme should be carried out at once or else there is to be no advantage in it at all. On the contrary, whatever number of houses are erected, or ships built, or slaves purchased, or the like, these portions will begin to pay at once. (36) In fact, the bit-by-bit method of proceeding will be more advantageous than a simultaneous carrying into effect of the whole plan, to this extent: if we set about erecting buildings wholesale we shall make a more expensive and worse job of it than if we finish them off gradually. Again, if we set about bidding for hundreds of slaves at once, we shall be forced to purchase an inferior type at a higher

[1] On the tribal organization of the citizens by Cleisthenes, see Aristotle, *Const. Ath.* 21 (no. 30); Botsford, *Hellenic History*, ch. vi. § 5.

cost. (37) On the other hand, if we proceed tentatively, as we find ourselves able, we can complete any well-devised attempt at our leisure, and, in case of any obvious failure, take warning and not repeat it. (38) Again, if everything were to be carried out at once, it is we, sirs, who must make the whole provision at our expense, whereas if part were proceeded with and part stood over, the portion of revenue in hand will help to furnish what is necessary to go on with.

(39) But to come now to what every one probably will regard as a really grave danger, lest the state may become possessed of an over-large number of slaves, with the result that the works will be overstocked. That again is an apprehension which we may escape if we are careful not to put into the works more hands from year to year than the works themselves demand. (40) Thus I am persuaded that the easiest method of carrying out this scheme, as a whole, is also the best. If, however, you are persuaded that, owing to the extraordinary property taxes to which you have been subjected during the present war,[1] you will not be equal to any further contributions at present, what you should do is this: during the current year resolve to carry on the financial administration of the state within the limits of a sum equivalent to that which your dues realized before the peace. That done, you are at liberty to take any surplus sum, whether directly traceable to peace itself, or to the more courteous treatment of our resident aliens and traders, or to the growth of the imports and exports, coincident with the collecting together of large masses of human beings, or to an augmentation of harbor and market dues: this surplus, I say, however derived, you should take and invest so as to bring in the greatest revenue.

(41) Again, if there is an apprehension on the part of any that the whole scheme will crumble into nothing on the first outbreak of war, I would only beg these alarmists to note that, under the condition of things which we propose to bring about, war will have more terrors for the attacking party than for this state. (42) What possession, I should like to know, can be more serviceable for war

[1] If this pamphlet was written in 355, as is generally supposed, the war referred to was the Social war, 357–354, in which Athens lost her more important allies; Beloch, *Griech. Gesch.* II. 313–19.

than that of men? Think of the many ships which they will be capable of manning on public service. Think of the number who will serve on land as infantry and will bear hard upon the enemy. Only we must treat them with courtesy. (43) For myself, my calculation is that even in the event of war, we shall be quite able to keep a firm hold of the silver mines. I may take it, we have in the neighborhood of the mines certain fortresses — one on the southern slope in Anaphlystus; and we have another on the northern side in Thoricus, the two being about seven and a half miles apart. (44) Suppose then a third breastwork were to be placed between these two, on the highest point of Besa, that would enable the operatives to collect into one out of all the fortresses, and at the first perception of a hostile movement it would only be a short distance for each to retire into safety. (45) In the event of an enemy advancing in large numbers they might certainly make off with whatever corn or wine or cattle they found outside. Even if they did get hold of the silver ore, it would be little better to them than a heap of stones. (46) But how is an enemy ever to march upon the mines in force? The nearest state, Megara, is distant, I take it, a good deal over sixty miles; and the next closest, Thebes, a good deal nearer seventy. (47) Supposing then an enemy to advance from some such point to attack the mines, he cannot avoid passing Athens; and presuming his force to be small, we may expect him to be annihilated by our cavalry and frontier police. I say, presuming his force to be small, since to march with anything like a large force, and thereby leave his own territory denuded of troops, would be a startling achievement. Why, the fortified city of Athens will be much closer to the states of the attacking parties than they themselves will be by the time they have got to the mines. (48) But for the sake of argument, let us suppose an enemy to have arrived in the neighborhood of Laurium; how is he going to stop there without provisions? To go out in search of supplies with a detachment of his force would imply risk, both for the foraging party and for those who have to do the fighting; whilst, if they are driven to do so in force each time, they may call themselves besiegers, but they will be practically in a state of siege themselves.

(49) It is not the income derived from the slaves alone to which we look to help the state toward the effective maintenance of her

citizens, but with the growth and concentration of a dense population in the mining district various sources of revenue would accrue, whether from the market at Sunium, or from the various state buildings in connection with the silver mines, from furnaces and all the rest. (50) We must expect a thickly populated city to spring up here, if organized in the way proposed, and plots of land will become as valuable to owners out there as they are to those who possess them in the neighborhood of the capital.

(51) If at this point I may assume my proposals to have been carried into effect, I think I can promise, not only that our city will be relieved from a financial strain, but that she will make a great stride in orderliness and in tactical organization; she will grow in martial spirit and readiness for war. (52) I anticipate that those who are under orders to go through gymnastic training will devote themselves with a new zeal to the details of the training school, now that they will receive a large maintenance while under the orders of the trainer in the torch race. So again those on garrison duty in the various fortresses, those enrolled as peltasts, or again as frontier police to protect the rural districts, one and all will carry out their respective duties more ardently when the maintenance appropriate to these several functions is duly forthcoming.

V. (1) If it is evident that, in order to get the full benefit of all these sources of state revenue, peace is an indispensable condition, — if that is plain, I say, the question suggests itself, would it not be worth while to appoint a board to act as guardians of peace? Since no doubt the election of such a magistracy would enhance the charm of this city in the eyes of the whole world, and add largely to the number of our visitors. (2) But if any one is disposed to take the view, that by adopting a persistent peace policy, this city will be shorn of her power, that her glory will dwindle and her good name be forgotten throughout the length and breadth of Hellas, the view so taken by our friends here is in my poor judgment somewhat unreasonable. For they are surely the happy states; they, in popular language, are most fortune-favored, which endure in peace the longest season. And of all states Athens is pre-eminently adapted by nature to flourish and wax strong in peace. (3) The while she abides in peace she cannot fail to exercise an attractive force on all. From the mariner and the merchant upward, all seek her, flocking they come; the wealthy dealers in corn and wine and oil, the owner of many cattle. Not these only, but the man who depends upon his wits, whose skill is to do business and make gain out of money and its employment. (4) Here another crowd, artificers of all sorts, artists and artisans, professors of wisdom, philosophers, and poets, with those who exhibit and popularize their works. Next a new train of pleasure-seekers, eager to feast on everything sacred or secular, which may captivate and charm eye and ear. Or once again, where are all those who seek to effect a rapid sale or purchase of a thousand commodities to find what they want, if not at Athens?

(5) If there is no desire to gainsay these views — only that certain people, in their wish to recover that headship which was once the pride of our city, are persuaded that the accomplishment of their hopes is to be found, not in peace but in war, I beg them to reflect on some matters of history, and to begin at the beginning, the Median war. (6) Was it by high-handed violence, or as benefactors of Hellenes, that we obtained the headship of the naval forces, and the trusteeship of the treasury of Hellas? Again, when through the too cruel exercise of her presidency, as men thought, Athens was deprived of her empire, is it not the case that even in those days, as soon as we held aloof from injustice we were once more reinstated by the islanders, of their own free will, as presidents of the naval force? (7) Nay, did not the very Thebans, in return for certain benefits, grant to us Athenians to exercise leadership over them? And at another date the Lacedæmonians suffered us Athenians to arrange the terms of hegemony at our discretion, not as driven to such submission, but in requital of kindly treatment. (8) Again today, owing to the chaos which reigns in Hellas, if I mistake not, an opportunity has fallen to this city of winning back our fellow-Hellenes without pain or peril or expense of any sort. It is given to us to try to harmonize states which are at war with one another: it is given to us to reconcile the differences of rival factions within those states themselves, wherever existing.

(9) Make it but evident that we are minded to preserve the independence of the Delphic shrine in its primitive integrity, not

by joining in any way but by the moral force of embassies throughout the length and breadth of Hellas, — and I for one shall not be astonished if you find our brother Hellenes of one sentiment and eager under seal of solemn oaths to proceed against those, whoever they may be, who shall seek to step into the place vacated by the Phocians[1] and to occupy the sacred shrine. (10) Make it but evident that you intend to establish a general peace by land and sea, and if I mistake not, your efforts will find a response in the hearts of all. There is no man but will pray for the salvation of Athens next to that of his own fatherland. (11) Again, is any one persuaded that, looking solely to riches and money-making, the state may find war more profitable than peace? If so, I cannot conceive a better method of deciding that question than to allow the mind to revert to the past history of the state and to note well the sequence of events. (12) He will discover that in times long gone by, during a period of peace, vast wealth was stored up in the Acropolis, the whole of which was lavishly expended during a subsequent period of war. He will perceive, if he examines closely, that even at the present time we are suffering from its ill effects. Countless sources of revenues have failed; or if they have still flowed in, they have been lavishly expended on a multiplicity of things. Whereas now that peace is established by sea, our revenues have expanded and the citizens of Athens have it in their power to turn them to account as they like best.

(13) If you turn on me with the question, "Do you really mean that even in the event of unjust attacks upon our city on the part of any, we are still resolutely to observe peace toward that offender?" I answer distinctly, No! On the contrary, I maintain that we shall all the more promptly retaliate on such aggression in proportion as we have done no wrong to any one ourselves, for that will be to rob the aggressor of his allies.

VI. (1) If none of these proposals be impracticable or even difficult of execution; if rather by giving them effect we may conciliate further the friendship of Hellas, whilst we strengthen our

[1] The author refers to the Sacred war, which closed in 346 with the expulsion of the Phocians from the Amphictyonic league. Some have thought therefore that this treatise must have been composed after that date; but perhaps the writer is merely looking forward to the end of the war.

own administration and increase our fame; if by the same means the people shall be provided with the necessaries of life, and our rich men be relieved of expenditure on war; if with the large surplus to be counted on, we are in a position to conduct our festivals on an even grander scale than heretofore, to restore our temples, to rebuild our forts and docks, and to reinstate in their ancient privileges our priests, our senators, our magistrates, and our knights — surely it were but reasonable to enter upon this project speedily, so that we too, even in our own day, may witness the unclouded dawn of prosperity in store for our city.

(2) But if you are agreed to carry out this plan, there is one further counsel which I would urge upon you. Send to Dodona and to Delphi, I would beg you, and consult the will of Heaven whether such provision and such a policy on our part be truly to the interest of Athens both for the present and for the time to come. (3) If the consent of Heaven be thus obtained, we ought then, I say, to put a further question: whose special favor among the gods shall we seek to secure with a view to the happier execution of these measures? [1]

In accordance with that answer, let us offer a sacrifice of happy omen to the deities so named, and commence the work; for if these transactions be so carried out with the will of God, have we not the right to prognosticate some further advance in the path of political progress for this whole state?

133. The Political Capacity of Women

(Plato, *Republic*, 451–7)

Toward the close of the fifth century at Athens some members of the intellectual class began to talk of the political capacity of women, and even to suggest that they might be given the suffrage. To some extent this idea must have interested the public, to have called for the presentation of Aristophanes, *Lysistrate* (no. 100). While ridiculing the idea in his usual manner, Aristophanes invests it with a considerable sympathy. Early in the fourth century (389, or, according to some, 392) he presented his *Ecclesiazusæ*, which treats satirically of "woman's rights," and the communism of wives and of property. Although there can be no doubt that such views were then agitated in intellectual circles, we have no reason for believing that Aristophanes was attacking

[1] This advice to seek the wisdom of the oracle and the blessings of the gods is in the true Xenophontic spirit.

Plato, whose *Republic* was certainly not composed earlier than the decade 380–370; Christ, *Griech. Lit.* I. 646. The view presented by "Socrates" in the dialogue below is in all earnest.

For men born and educated like our citizens, the only way, in my opinion, of arriving at a right conclusion about the possession and use of women and children is to follow the path on which we originally started, when we said that the men were to be the guardians and watchdogs of the herd.

True.

Let us further suppose the birth and education of our women to be subject to similar or nearly similar regulations; then we shall see whether the result accords with our design.

What do you mean?

What I mean may be put into the form of a question, I said: Are dogs divided into hes and shes, or do they both share equally in hunting and in keeping watch and in the other duties of dogs? or do we entrust to the males the entire and exclusive care of the flocks, while we leave the females at home, under the idea that the bearing and suckling of their puppies is labor enough for them?

No, he said, they share alike; the only difference between them is that the males are stronger and the females weaker.

But can you use different animals for the same purpose, unless they are bred and fed in the same way?

You cannot.

Then if women are to have the same duties as men, they must have the same nurture and education?

Yes.

The education which was assigned to the men was music and gymnastic?

Yes.

Then women must be taught music and gymnastic and also the art of war, which they must practice like the men? . . .

Can you mention any pursuit of mankind in which the male sex has not all these gifts and qualities in a higher degree than the female? Need I waste time in speaking of the art of weaving, and the management of pancakes and preserves, in which womankind does really appear great, and in which for her to be beaten by a man is of all things the most absurd?

You are quite right, he replied, in maintaining the general inferiority of the female sex: although many women are in many things superior to many men, yet on the whole what you say is true.

And if so, my friend, I said, there is no special faculty of administration in a state which a woman has because she is a woman, or which a man has by virtue of his sex, but the gifts of nature are alike diffused in both; all the pursuits of men are the pursuits of women also, but in all of them a woman is inferior to a man.

Very true.

Then are we to impose all our enactments on men and none of them on women?

That will never do.

One woman has a gift of healing, another not; one is a musician, and another has no music in her nature?

Very true.

And one woman has a turn for gymnastic and military exercises, and another is unwarlike and hates gymnastics?

Certainly.

And one woman is a philosopher, and another is an enemy of philosophy; one has spirit, and another is without spirit?

That is also true.

Then one woman will have the temper of a guardian, and another not. Was not the selection of the male guardians determined by differences of this sort?

Yes.

Men and women alike possess the qualities which make a guardian; they differ only in their comparative strength or weakness.

Obviously.

And those women who have such qualities are to be selected as the companions and colleagues of men who have similar qualities and whom they resemble in capacity and character?

Very true.

Then ought not the same natures to have the same pursuits?

They ought.

Then, as we were saying before, there is nothing unnatural in assigning music and gymnastic to the wives of the guardians — to that point we come round again.

Certainly not.

The law which we then enacted was agreeable to nature, and therefore not an impossibility or mere aspiration; and the contrary practice, which prevails at present, is in reality a violation of nature.

That appears to be true.

We had to consider first, whether our proposals were possible, and secondly whether they were the most beneficial?

Yes.

And the possibility has been acknowledged?

Yes.

The very great benefit has next to be established?

Quite so.

You will admit that the same education which makes a man a good guardian will make a woman a good guardian; for their original nature is the same?

Yes.

I should like to ask you a question.

What is it?

Would you say that all men are equal in excellence, or is one man better than another?

The latter.

And in the commonwealth which we were founding do you conceive the guardians who have been brought up on our model system to be more perfect men, or the cobblers whose education has been cobbling?

What a ridiculous question!

You have answered me, I replied: Well, and may we not further say that our guardians are the best of citizens?

By far the best.

And will not their wives be the best women?

Yes, by far the best.

And can there be anything better for the interests of the state than that the men and women of a State should be as good as possible?

There can be nothing better.

And this is what the arts of music and gymnastic, when present in such a manner as we have described, will accomplish?

Certainly.

Then we have made an enactment not only possible but in the highest degree beneficial to the state?

True.[1] . . .

The law, I said, which is the sequel of this and of all that has preceded, is to the following effect, — that the wives of our guardians are to be common, and their children are to be common, and no parent is to know his own child, nor any child his parent.[2]

134. The Muckraker *versus* the Patriot

(Plato, *Protagoras*, 346)

Bad men, when their parents or country have any defects, look on them with malignant joy, and find fault with them and expose and denounce them to others, under the idea that the rest of mankind will be less likely to take themselves to task and accuse them of neglect; and they blame their defects far more than they deserve, in order that the odium which is necessarily incurred by them may be increased; but the good man dissembles his feelings, and constrains himself to praise them; and if they have wronged him and he is angry, he pacifies his anger and is reconciled, and compels himself to praise his own flesh and blood.

135. A Critique of the Statesmen of Athens

(Plato, *Gorgias*, 515–19)

It is well known that Plato had no sympathy with democracy; and in the subjoined passage he denounces the statesmen of Athens both past and present. His contention is that a statesman ought to improve the moral character of his people, and within the few years of his career to make them so virtuous that the great majority will appreciate his services and render him due gratitude. If they fail in this respect, if they turn against him and fine him or ostracize him, as they did in the case of Cimon, Themistocles, and Pericles, the statesman has only himself to blame. It is hardly necessary to add that Plato thus imposes upon the statesman an utterly impossible task.

[1] The part here omitted, though interesting, is too long for inclusion in this volume.

[2] With the view of Plato regarding the qualitative equality of women with men we may contrast that of Xenophon, *Economicus* (no. 154). In the judgment of Xenophon women are the equals of men (each sex has its points of superiority to the other), but they are unlike in nature. It is clear that in this treatise Xenophon is consciously opposing the doctrine of those who, like Plato, contend for the qualitative equality of the sexes.

Socrates. Now, my friend, as you are already beginning to be a public character, and are admonishing and reproaching me for not being one, suppose that we ask a few questions of one another. Tell me, then, Callicles, how about making any of the citizens better? Was there ever a man who was once vicious or unjust or intemperate or foolish, and became by the help of Callicles good and noble? Was there ever such a man, whether citizen or stranger, slave or freeman? Tell me, Callicles, if a person were to ask these questions of you, what would you answer? Whom would you say that you had improved by your conversation? There may have been good deeds of this sort which were done by you as a private person, before you came forward in public. Will you not answer?

Callicles. You are contentious, Socrates.

Soc. Nay, I ask you, not from a love of contention, but because I really want to know in what way you think that affairs should be administered among us — whether, when you come to the administration of them, you have any other aim but the improvement of the citizens? Have we not already admitted many times over that such is the duty of a public man? Nay, we have surely said so; for if you will not answer for yourself I must answer for you. But if this is what the good man ought to effect for the benefit of his own state, allow me to recall to you the names of those whom you were just now mentioning, Pericles, Cimon, Miltiades, and Themistocles, and ask whether you still think that they were good citizens.

Cal. I do.

Soc. But if they were good, then clearly each of them must have made the citizens better instead of worse?

Cal. Yes.[1]

Soc. Therefore when Pericles first began to speak in the assembly, the Athenians were not so good as when he spoke last?

Cal. Very likely.

Soc. Nay, my friend, 'likely' is not the word; for if he was a good citizen, the inference is certain.

[1] Callicles loses his case by his too hasty admission: in fact the primary object of the state cannot be the moral regeneration of the citizens; that end, if it is to be achieved, must be reached by other agencies, as the family, social intercourse, education, and the church.

Cal. And what difference does that make?

Soc. None; only I should like further to know whether the Athenians are supposed to have been made better by Pericles, or on the contrary to have been corrupted by him; for I hear that he was the first who gave the people pay,[1] and made them idle and cowardly, and encouraged them in love of talk and of money.

Cal. You heard that, Socrates, from the laconizing set who bruise their ears.

Soc. But what I am going to tell you now is not mere hearsay, but well known both to you and to me: that at first Pericles was glorious and his character unimpeached by any verdict of the Athenians — this was during the time when they were not so good — yet afterward, when they had been made good and gentle by him, at the very end of his life, they convicted him of theft and almost put him to death, clearly under the notion that he was a malefactor.

Cal. Well, how does that prove Pericles' badness?

Soc. Why, surely, you would say that he was a bad manager of asses or horses or oxen, who had received them originally neither kicking nor butting nor biting him, and implanted in them all these savage tricks? Would he not be a bad manager of any animals who received them gentle, and made them fiercer than they were when he received them? What do you say?

Cal. I will do you the favor of saying yes.

Soc. And will you also do me the favor of saying whether man is an animal?

Cal. Certainly he is.

Soc. And was not Pericles a shepherd of men?

Cal. Yes.

Soc. And if he was a good political shepherd, ought not the animals who were his subjects, as we were just now acknowledging, to have become more just, and not more unjust?[2]

Cal. Quite right.

[1] Pay for naval and military service, also probably for some civil services, was introduced by Aristeides; for jury service, by Pericles; Botsford, *Hellenic History*, chs. xii, xv.

[2] Here again Socrates favors an utterly erroneous theory: it is a simple thing for a man to train animals to certain tricks or habits but altogether a different matter to reform as many human beings, not to speak of the population of an entire state.

Soc. And are not just men gentle, as Homer says? — or are you of another mind?

Cal. I agree.

Soc. And yet he really did make them more savage than he received them, and their savageness was shown toward himself; which he must have been very far from desiring.

Cal. Do you want me to agree with you?

Soc. Yes, if I seem to you to speak the truth.

Cal. Granted then.

Soc. And if they were more savage, must they not have been more unjust and inferior?

Cal. Granted again.

Soc. Then upon this view, Pericles was not a good statesman?

Cal. That is, upon your view.

Soc. Nay, the view is yours, after what you have admitted. Take the case of Cimon again. Did not the very persons whom he was serving ostracize [1] him, in order that they might not hear his voice for ten years? And they did just the same to Themistocles, adding the penalty of exile; and they voted that Miltiades, the hero of Marathon, should be thrown into the pit of death, and he was only saved by the prytanis.[2] And yet, if they had really been good men, as you say, these things would never have happened to them. For the good charioteers are not those who at first keep their place, and then, when they have broken in their horses, and themselves become better charioteers, are thrown out — that is not the way either in charioteering or in any other profession. What do you think?

Cal. I should think not.

Soc. Well, but if so, the truth is as I have already said, that in the Athenian state no one has ever shown himself to be a good statesman. You admitted that this was true of our present statesmen, but not true of former ones, and you preferred them to the others; yet they have turned out to be no better than our present ones. If therefore they were rhetoricians, they did not use the true art

[1] On ostracism, see no. 31; Botsford, *Hellenic History*, ch. vii; Gilbert, *Constitutional Antiquities of Sparta and Athens*, 309.

[2] President, the individual drawn by lot from the fifty prytaneis to act as president of the prytaneis, of the entire council, and of the assembly. On the prytaneis, see Botsford, *Hellenic History*, ch. vii.

of rhetoric or of flattery, or they would not have fallen out of favor.

CAL. But surely, Socrates, no living man ever came near any one of them in his achievements.

SOC. O, my dear friend, I say nothing against them regarded as the serving-men of the state; and I do think that they were certainly more serviceable than those who are living now, and better able to gratify the wishes of the state. But as to transforming those desires and not allowing them to have their own way, and using the powers which they had, whether of persuasion or of force, in the improvement of their fellow citizens, which is the prime object of the truly good citizen, I do not see that in these respects they were a whit superior to our present statesmen, although I do admit that they were more clever at providing ships and walls and docks and all that. . . .

You praise the men who feasted the citizens and satisfied their desires, and the people say that they have made the city great, not seeing that the swollen and ulcerated condition of the state is to be attributed to these elder statesmen; for they have filled the city full of harbors and docks and walls and revenues and all that, and have left no room for justice and temperance. When therefore the crisis of the disorder comes, the people will blame the advisers of the hour, and applaud Themistocles and Cimon and Pericles, who are the real authors of their calamities; and if you are not careful, they may assail you and my friend Alcibiades, when they are losing not only their new acquisitions but also their original possessions — not that you are the authors of these misfortunes of theirs, although you may perhaps be accessories to them. A foolish ado is always being made, as I see and am told, now as of old, about our statesmen. When the state treats any of them as malefactors, I observe that there is a great uproar and indignation at the supposed wrong that is done to them; "after all their many services to the state, that they should unjustly perish" — so the tale runs. But the cry is all a falsehood; for no statesman ever could be unjustly put to death by the city of which he is the head.[1]

[1] By the same argument Socrates could have been proved useless for his inability to reform Alcibiades and Critias, and these pupils might have justly punished him for his failure.

136. A Reason for Caution in the Bestowal of Citizenship

(Aristotle, *Politics*, v. 3. 11–13, 1303 a)

The illiberality of Greek states in the admission of aliens to the citizenship has generally been set down as strangely shortsighted. In the subjoined excerpt Aristotle gives a reason for such caution. From it we learn that the question involves a consideration, not only of the character of the state but also of the compatibility of the persons to be admitted. Generally the latter were so difficult of social and political assimilation that the admission of any large number proved disastrous to the state. In early Italy conditions were different; and in modern times they are so utterly dissimilar that it is impossible for us without great effort to appreciate the attitude of the Greek state.

Another cause of revolution is difference of races which do not at once acquire a common spirit; for a state is not the growth of a day, neither is it a multitude brought together by accident. Hence the reception of strangers in colonies, either at the time of their foundation or afterward, has generally produced revolution; for example, the Achæans who joined the Trœzenians in the foundation of Sybaris, being the more numerous, afterward expelled them; hence the curse fell upon Sybaris. At Thurii the Sybarites quarrelled with their fellow-colonists; thinking that the land belonged to them, they wanted too much of it, and were driven out. At Byzantium the new colonists were detected in a conspiracy, and were expelled by force of arms; the people of Antissa, who had received the Chian exiles, fought with them and drove them out; and the Zancleans, after having received the Samians, were driven by them out of their own city. The citizens of Apollonia on the Euxine, after the introduction of a fresh body of colonists, had a revolution; the Syracusans, after the expulsion of their tyrants, having admitted strangers and mercenaries to the rights of citizenship, quarrelled and came to blows; the people of Amphipolis, having received Chalcidian colonists, were nearly all expelled by them.

137. The Kind of Equality underlying Oligarchy and Democracy Respectively

(Aristotle, *Politics*, v. 1. 12–15, 1301 b *sq.*)

In the period now under consideration kingship had long disappeared from the progressive states of Hellas. Tyranny was less common than it had been in the seventh and sixth centuries, and was always temporary. Few traces of aristocracy remained. The prevailing forms of government, accordingly, were oligarchy and democracy. These are the two forms of government therefore which require illustration in the present chapter.

Each of these two forms of government is based on a peculiar idea of equality.

Equality is of two kinds, numerical and proportional. By the first I mean sameness or equality in number or size; by the second, equality of ratios. For example, the excess of three over two is equal to the excess of two over one; whereas four exceeds two in the same ratio in which two exceeds one; for two is the same part of four that one is of two, namely, the half. As I was saying before, men agree about justice in the abstract, but they differ about proportion:[1] some think that if they are equal in any respect they are equal absolutely; others that if they are unequal in any respect, they are unequal in all. Hence there are two principal forms of government, democracy and oligarchy;[2] for good birth and virtue are rare, but wealth and numbers are more common. In what city shall we find a hundred persons of good birth and of virtue?[3] whereas the poor everywhere abound. That a state should be ordered simply and wholly according to either kind of equality is not a good thing; the proof is that such forms of government never last. They are originally based on a mistake, and as they begin badly, cannot fail to end badly. The inference is that both kinds of equality should be employed, numerical in some cases and proportionate in others.

[1] *Cf. Politics*, v. 1. 2.

[2] On the "mixed constitution" Aristotle writes as follows (ii. 6. 17 *sq.* 1265 b *sq.*): "Some say that the best constitution is a combination of all existing forms, and they praise the Lacedæmonian because it is made up of oligarchy, monarchy, and democracy — the king forming the monarchy, the council of elders the oligarchy, while the democratic element is represented by the ephors; for the ephors are selected by the people. . . . They are near the truth who combine many forms; for the state is better which is made up of more numerous elements." Thus the ideal of a mixed constitution, existing before Aristotle, was accepted by him.

[3] The Greek word for virtue (ἀρετή), as Aristotle uses it, is much broader than the idea of moral excellence; it signifies rather capacity or ability combined with moral excellence. It was in this sense only that there could have been so few as a hundred men of virtue in a large community.

138. The Principal Forms of Government and their Perversions

(Aristotle, *Politics*, iii. 7. 1–5, 1279 a *sq.*)

We have next to consider how many forms of government there are, and what they are; and in the first place what are the true forms, for when they are determined, the perversions of them will at once be apparent. The words 'constitution' and 'form of government' have the same meaning;[1] and the government, which is the supreme authority in states, must be in the hands of one, or of the few or of many. The true forms of government therefore are those in which the one or the few or the many govern with a view to the common interest; but governments which rule with a view to the private interest, whether of the one or of the few or of the many, are perversions.[2] For citizens, if they are truly citizens, ought to participate in the advantages of the state. Of forms of government in which one rules we call that which regards the common interest kingship or royalty; that in which more than one, but not many, rule, aristocracy; and it is so called, either because the rulers are the best men, or because they have at heart the best interests of the state and of the citizens. When however the citizens at large administer the state for the common interest, the government is called by the generic name *politeia* (constitution, polity). There is a reason for this use of language. One man or a few may excel in virtue; but of virtue there are many kinds; and as the number increases it becomes more difficult for them to attain perfection in every kind, though they may in military virtue, for this quality is found in the masses. Hence in a politeia the fighting men have the supreme power, and those who possess arms are the citizens.[3]

[1] The words here used are πολιτεία and πολίτευμα respectively.

[2] Such ethical distinctions are no longer held; the truth is now recognized that no man or political party, when unrestrained by constitutional checks and by the force of public opinion, can be trusted to conduct the government in the common interest.

[3] Here is implied the theory that originally there were few men of virtue capacity in a state, and that as the number increased, the government expanded to an aristocracy and then to a politeia. With the latter constitutional change the idea of civic virtue narrowed to military capacity. In Aristotle's opinion the politeia was a form of government in which those qualified for heavy-infantry service enjoyed the franchise, as in Athens before Solon, and again for a brief period after the fall of the Four Hundred.

Of the forms mentioned above, the perversions are as follows: of royalty, tyranny; of aristocracy, oligarchy; of politeia, democracy. For tyranny is a kind of monarchy which has in view the interest of the monarch only; oligarchy has in view the interest of the wealthy; democracy, of the needy; none of them the common good of all.

139. Prevalence of Oligarchy and Democracy

(Aristotle, *Politics*, iv. 11. 16–19, 1296 a *sq.*)

Before coming to the passage given below Aristotle calls attention to the middle class — the people of moderate wealth — as the chief element of stability in a state.

These considerations will help us understand why most governments are either democratical or oligarchical. The reason is that the middle class is seldom numerous in them, and whichever party, whether the rich or the common people, transgresses the mean and predominates, draws the government to itself, and thus arises either oligarchy or democracy. There is another reason — the poor and the rich quarrel with one another, and whichever side gets the better, instead of establishing a just or popular government, regards political supremacy as the prize of victory, and the one party sets up a democracy and the other an oligarchy. Both the parties which had the supremacy in Hellas looked only to the interest of their own form of government, and established in states, the one democracies, the other oligarchies; they thought of their own advantage, of the public not at all.[1] . . . It has now become a habit among the citizens of states, not even to care about equality; all men are seeking for dominion, or if conquered, are willing to submit.

140. Laudable and Blameworthy Forms of Democracy and of Oligarchy

(Aristotle, *Politics*, v. 9. 7–15, 1309 a *sq.*)

Those who think that all virtue is to be found in their own party principles push matters to extremes; they do not consider that disproportion destroys a state. A nose which varies from the ideal of

[1] Here he is thinking of Athens and Lacedæmon respectively in the preceding century.

straightness to a hook or a snub may still be of very good shape and agreeable to the eye; but if the excess be very great, all symmetry is lost, and the nose at last ceases to be a nose at all on account of some excess in one direction or defect in the other; and this is true of every other part of the human body. The same law of proportion equally holds in states. Oligarchy or democracy, although a departure from the most perfect form, may be at the same time a good enough government; but if any one attempts to push the principles of either to an extreme, he will begin by spoiling the government and end by having none at all.[1] The legislator and the statesman ought therefore to know what democratical measures save and what destroy a democracy, and what oligarchical measures save or destroy an oligarchy. For neither the one nor the other can exist or continue to exist unless both rich and poor are included in it. If equality of property is introduced, the state must of necessity take another form; for when by laws carried to excess one or other element in the state is ruined, the constitution is ruined.[2]

There is an error common both to oligarchies and to democracies: in the latter the demagogues,[3] when the multitude are above the law, are always cutting the city in two by quarrels with the rich, whereas they should always profess to be maintaining their cause; just as in oligarchies, the oligarchs should profess to maintain the cause of the people, and should take oaths the opposite of those which they now take. For there are cities in which they swear: "I will be an enemy to the people, and will devise all the harm against them which I can;" but they ought to exhibit and to entertain the very opposite feeling; in the form of their oath there should be an express declaration: "I will do no wrong to the people."

But of all the things which I have mentioned, that which most

[1] In brief, Aristotle totally condemns neither oligarchy nor democracy, but only the extreme forms of each; both forms of government are blameworthy in the degree that they approach the extreme.

[2] Throughout the *Politics*, Aristotle constantly calls attention to the necessity of governmental checks and balances, not only in the organization of the constitution, but also in the proportion of the social classes.

[3] It is a noteworthy fact that Aristotle nowhere blames the masses for the evils of democracy, but fastens the fault upon the demagogues. This attitude of mind, here suggested, is illustrated in his treatment of political education a few lines below, and still further in selection no. 143.

contributes to the permanence of constitutions is the adaptation of education to the form of government, and yet in our own day this principle is neglected. The best laws, though sanctioned by every citizen of the state, will be of no avail unless the young are trained by habit and education in the spirit of the constitution: if the laws are democratical, democratically, or oligarchically if the laws are oligarchical. For there may be a want of self-discipline in states as well as in individuals. Now to have been educated in the spirit of the constitution, is not to perform the actions in which oligarchs or democrats delight, but those by which the existence of a democracy or an oligarchy is made possible. Whereas among ourselves the sons of the ruling class in an oligarchy live in luxury, but the sons of the poor are hardened by exercise and toil, and hence they are both more inclined and better able to make a revolution. In democracies of the more extreme type also there has arisen a false idea of freedom which is contradictory to the true interests of the state. For two principles are characteristic of democracy, the government of the majority and freedom. Men think that what is just is equal; and that equality is the supremacy of the popular will; and that freedom and equality mean the doing what a man likes. In such democracies every one lives as he pleases, or in the words of Euripides, 'according to his fancy.' But this is all wrong; men should not think it slavery to live according to the rule of the constitution; for it is their salvation.

141. Growth of Democracy

(Aristotle, *Politics*, iii. 15. 12, 1286 b)

Aristotle understands very clearly that there was a constitutional development of Hellas from the earliest times to the fourth century. It was due (1) to the increase of wealth and its distribution among an increasing number of citizens, (2) to the spread of virtue (intelligence, capacity) among the citizens, (3) to the deterioration of the parties successively in power. It was thus that kingship developed into an aristocracy. From that stage he traces the growth of democracy in the following passage.

The ruling class (aristocracy) soon deteriorated and enriched themselves out of the public treasury. Riches became the path to honor, and thus oligarchies grew up. These governments passed into tyrannies and tyrannies into democracies; for the love of gain in the ruling classes was always tending to diminish their number, and so to strengthen the masses, who in the end set upon their masters and established democracies. Since cities have increased in size, no other form of government appears to be any longer possible.

(*Ibid.* iv. 6. 5 *sq.*, 1293 a)

In our own day, when cities have far outgrown their original size, and their revenues have increased, all the citizens have a share in the government through the great preponderance of their numbers; and they all, including the poor who receive pay and therefore have leisure to exercise their rights, share in the administration. In fact when they are paid, the common people have the most leisure, for they are not hindered by the care of their property, which often fetters the rich, who are thereby prevented from taking part in the assembly or in the courts;[1] hence the state is governed by the poor, who are a majority, and not by the laws.

142. Agricultural and Pastoral Democracies

(Aristotle, *Politics*, vi. 4. 1–15, 1318 b *sq.*)

All democracies are not to be treated alike, to be equally praised or condemned. There are among the various forms many degrees of excellence or the reverse. The more nearly a democracy approaches the politeia, the better it is. In iv. 4. 22–6, 1292 b *sq.* Aristotle enumerates five kinds of democracy. Of four kinds he approves, as they are all under the laws; but the fifth form is that in which not the laws but the multitude rule, in which the law is superseded by decrees. This is a condition of affairs brought about by demagogues, and of this form only he disapproves.

Again (iv. 14. 3–7, 1298 a) he classifies democracy on the basis of the extent to which the people participate in the deliberative function. Thus arise four forms of democracy, the last being that in which all the people are consulted on all subjects. This form he denounces. Furthermore (iv. 6. 1–6, 1292 b *sq.*) he enumerates four classes of democracy based on the matter of revenues.

[1] The author here refers to a bourgeoisie, largely composed of men from the poorer classes, including even some freedmen, who had enriched themselves through fortunate business operations, and who cared more for their wealth, and for the comforts it brought, than for the state. In like manner there was a considerable class, including even eupatrids, addicted to gambling and sensual pleasures. There had grown up, too, a smaller but more influential class wholly devoted to intellectual pleasures, including philosophers and other literary men. All these people alike, for their several individualistic reasons, held aloof from politics, and thus contributed to the growth of extreme democracy, and ultimately to the decay of the city-state.

Under the first three forms, as there is a lack of revenue, the people have to work for a living; and the offices, being unpaid, are filled by the well-to-do only. The constitution therefore, though democratic in name, is in fact a government by the competent. These three forms are earlier stages of growth, developing into the form described in no. 141. The most approved forms of democracy are described in the selection here given.

Of the four forms of democracy, as was said in the previous discussion, the best is that which comes first in order; it is also the oldest of them all.[1] I am speaking of them according to the natural classification of their inhabitants. For the best material of democracy is an agricultural population. There is no difficulty in forming a democracy where the mass of the people live by agriculture or by pasturing cattle. Being poor, they have no leisure, and therefore do not often attend the assembly; and not having the necessaries of life, they are always at work, and do not covet the property of others. In fact they find their employment pleasanter than the cares of government or office where no great gains can be made from them, for the many are more desirous of gain than of honor. A proof is that even the ancient tyrannies were patiently endured by them, as they still endure oligarchies, if they are allowed to work and are not deprived of their property; for some of them quickly grow rich and the others are well enough off. Moreover they have the power of electing the magistrates and of calling them to account; their ambition, if they have any, is thus satisfied. In some democracies, although they do not all share in the appointment to offices, except through representatives elected in turn out of the whole people, as at Mantineia, yet if they have the power of deliberating, the many are contented.[2] Even this form of government may be regarded as a democracy, and was such at Mantineia. Hence it is both expedient and customary in such a democracy that all should elect to offices, and conduct scrutinies,[3] and sit in the law-courts, but that the great offices should be filled by election and from persons having a qualification: the greater requiring a greater

[1] This principle of age holds for industrial states like Athens. There were, however, wide agricultural and pastoral areas, including Arcadia, Achæa, Ætolia, Acarnania, Thessaly, etc., in which, as late as the time of Aristotle, such a form of democracy either existed or could be formed.

[2] This passage is a tribute to the moderation of the masses.

[3] Εὐθύνειν, to call a magistrate to account after the expiration of his office.

qualification, or if there be no offices for which a qualification is required, then those who are marked out by special ability should be appointed. Under such a form of government the citizens are sure to be ruled well; for the offices will always be held by the best persons; the people are willing enough to elect them and are not jealous of the good. The good and the notables will then be satisfied, for they will not be governed by men who are their inferiors; and the persons elected will rule justly, because others will call them to account. Every man should be responsible to others, nor should any one be allowed to do just as he pleases; for where absolute freedom is permitted there is nothing to restrain the evil which is inherent in every man. The principle of responsibility, however, secures that which is the greatest good in states; the right persons rule and are prevented from doing wrong, and the people have their due. It is evident that this is the best kind of democracy, and why? because the people are of a certain quality. The ancient laws of many states which aimed at making the people husbandmen were excellent. They provided either that no one should possess more than a certain amount of land, or that if he did, the land should not be within a certain distance from the town or the acropolis.[1] Formerly in many states there was a law forbidding any one to sell his original allotment of land. There is a similar law attributed to Oxylus, which is to the effect that there should be a certain portion of every man's property on which he could not borrow money. A useful correction to the evil of which I am speaking would be the law of the Aphytæans,[2] who although they are numerous and do not possess much land, are all husbandmen. For their properties are reckoned in the census not entire, but only in such small portions that even the poor may have more than the amount required.

Next best to an agricultural population, and in many respects similar, are a pastoral people, who live by their flocks. They are the best trained for war, robust in body and able to camp out. The people of whom other democracies consist are far inferior to them, for their life is inferior; there is no room for moral excellence in any

[1] The nearer a man lived to the city, the greater his opportunity to attend the assembly and other political functions. If therefore a few should be permitted to monopolize the land in the neighborhood of the city, they would to that extent be depriving the masses of their opportunity to participate in civic rights.

[2] People of Aphytis, a Hellenic city of Chalcidice.

of their employments, whether they are mechanics or traders or laborers. Besides, people of the latter classes can readily come to the assembly, because they are continually moving about in the city and in the market place; whereas husbandmen are scattered over the country and do not meet or equally feel the want of assembling together. Where the territory extends to a distance from the city, there is no difficulty in making an excellent democracy or politeia; for the people are compelled to live in the country; and even if there is a town population, the assembly ought not to meet when the country people cannot come. We have thus explained how the first and best form of democracy should be constituted; it is clear that the other or inferior forms will deviate in regular order, and that the population which is excluded will at each stage be of a lower kind.[1]

143. Extreme Democracy

(Aristotle, *Politics*, vi. 4. 15 to 5. 11, 1319 b–1320 b)

In the following excerpt Aristotle gives the characteristics of extreme democracy and suggests remedies for its evils. Noteworthy is his optimism; though the constitutions of many city-states are defective, he entertains no doubt that they may be made good by the application of reasonable remedies.

The last form of democracy, that in which all share alike, is one which cannot be borne by all states, and will not last long, unless well regulated by laws and customs. The more general causes which tend to destroy this or other kinds of government have now been pretty fully considered. In order to constitute such a democracy and strengthen the people, the leaders have been in the habit of including as many as they can, and making citizens not only of those who are legitimate, but even of the illegitimate, and of those who have only one parent a citizen, whether father or mother; for nothing of this sort comes amiss to such a democracy.[2] This is the way in which demagogues proceed. Whereas the right thing would be to make no more additions when the number of the com-

[1] The lower the form of democracy the poorer will be the quality of the population excluded from the franchise.

[2] Here Aristotle approves of the narrow, exclusive policy followed by Athens and many other Hellenic states in relation to the bestowal of the citizenship upon aliens or semi-aliens. The reason given in this case is the danger of upsetting the social balance. In the excerpt no. 136 he gives another reason for preferring the exclusive policy.

monalty exceeds that of the notables or of the middle class, — beyond this not to go. When in excess of this point the state becomes disorderly, and the notables become excited and impatient of the democracy, as in the insurrection at Cyrene; for no notice is taken of a little evil, but when it increases, it strikes the eye. Measures like those which Cleisthenes passed when he wanted to increase the power of the democracy at Athens, or such as were taken by the founders of popular government at Cyrene, are useful in the extreme form of democracy. Fresh tribes and brotherhoods should be established;[1] the private rites of families should be restricted and converted into public ones; in short, every contrivance should be adopted which will mingle the citizens with one another and get rid of old connections. Again, the measures which are taken by tyrants appear all of them to be democratic; such, for instance, as the licence permitted to slaves (which may be to a certain extent advantageous) and also that of women and children, and the allowing everybody to live as he likes. Such a government will have many supporters, for most persons would rather live in a disorderly than in a sober manner.

The mere establishment of a democracy is not the only or principal business of the legislator, or of those who wish to create such a state, for any state, however badly constituted, may last one, two, or three days; a far greater difficulty is the preservation of it. The legislator should therefore endeavor to have a firm foundation according to the principles already laid down concerning the preservation and destruction of states; he should guard against the destructive elements, and should make laws, whether written or unwritten, which will contain all the preservatives of states. He must not think the truly democratical or oligarchical measure to be that which will give the greatest amount of democracy or oligarchy, but that which will make them last longest. The demagogues of our own day often get property confiscated in the law-courts in order to please the people.[2] But those who have the wel-

[1] It is difficult to say whether in this passage Aristotle wishes to affirm that new phratries, as well as new tribes, were instituted by Cleisthenes; *cf.* Aristotle, *Const. Ath.* 21, no. 30 *supra*. It seems most likely that he left the old citizens their original phratries and created new phratries for the new citizens.

[2] The important question is whether in a democracy, like that of Athens, a jury ever condemned an innocent man in order to confiscate his property. No individual

fare of the state at heart should counteract them, and make a law that the property of the condemned which goes into the treasury should not be public but sacred. Thus offenders will be as much afraid, for they will be punished all the same, and the people, having nothing to gain, will not be so ready to condemn the accused. Care should also be taken that state trials are as few as possible, and heavy penalties should be inflicted on those who bring groundless accusations; for it is the practice to indict, not members of the popular party, but the notables, although the citizens ought to be all equally attached to the state, or at any rate should not regard their rulers as enemies.

Now since in the last and worst form of democracy the citizens are very numerous, and can hardly be made to assemble unless they are paid, and to pay them when there are no revenues presses hardly upon the notables (for the money must be obtained by a property-tax and confiscations and corrupt practices of the courts, things which have before now overthrown many democracies); where, I say, there are no revenues, the government should hold few assemblies, and the law-courts should consist of many persons, but sit for a few days only. This system has two advantages: first, the rich do not bear the expense, even although they are unpaid themselves when the poor are paid; and secondly, causes are better tried, for wealthy persons, although they do not like to be long absent from their own affairs, do not mind going for a few days to the law-courts. Where there are revenues the demagogues should not be allowed after their manner to distribute the surplus; the poor are always receiving and always wanting more and more, for such help is like water poured into a leaky cask. Yet the true friend of the people should see that they be not too poor, for extreme poverty lowers the character of the democracy; measures should also be taken which will give them lasting prosperity; and as this is equally the interest of all classes, the proceeds of the public revenues should be accumulated and distributed among them, if pos-

case of the kind has ever been mentioned. Such injustice may occasionally have been inflicted. This however is no ground for the total condemnation of Greek democracy. In some modern courts the wealthy have a great advantage over the poor; in others the soldiers outrage the civilians. If we are to judge Hellenic institutions by our ideals, it is only fair to ascertain also how far modern institutions fall short of the same standards.

sible, in such quantities as may enable them to purchase a little farm, or, at any rate, make a beginning in trade and husbandry. And if this benevolence cannot be extended to all, money should be distributed in turn according to tribes or other divisions, and in the meantime the rich should pay the fee for the attendance of the poor at the necessary assemblies; and should in return be excused from useless public services. By administering the state in this spirit the Carthaginians retain the affections of the people; their policy is from time to time to send some of them into their dependent towns, where they grow rich. It is also worthy of a generous and sensible nobility to divide the poor amongst them, and give them the means of going to work. The example of the people of Tarentum is also well-deserving of imitation, for by sharing the use of their own property with the poor, they gain their good-will.[1] Moreover they divide all their offices into two classes, one half of them being elected by vote, the other by lot; the latter, that the people may participate in them, and the former, that the state may be better administered. A like result may be gained by dividing the same offices, so as to have two classes of magistrates, one appointed by lot, the other by vote.

BIBLIOGRAPHY

I. The State and Political Tendencies. — For the 'theory of the state,' forms of government, and the like, see bibliography under Plato and Aristotle, ch. i. § xi. For the character and activities of the various states of the fourth century, see the pertinent chapters of the larger histories of Greece, especially those of Grote, Holm, and Beloch. The organization and administration of states are treated of more specifically in the works on constitution and antiquities. Under this heading see Schömann, *Griechische Altertümer*, I. (4th ed. rev. by Lipsius); Gilbert, *Constitutional Antiquities of Sparta and Athens;* Greenidge, A. H. J., *Handbook of Greek Constitutional History;* Thumser, V., *Griechische Staatsaltertümer* (Frieburg, 1892, in Hermann's *Lehrbuch der griech. Antiquitäten*); Swoboda, H., *Griechische Staatsaltertümer* (Tübingen, 1913, also in Hermann's *Lehrb.*); Wilamowitz-Moellendorff, von, and Niese, B., *Staat und Gesellschaft der Griechen und Römer* (Teubner, 1910); Francotte, H., "La polis grecque," in *Stud. z. Gesch. u. Kult. des Alt.* I. 3–4 (1907); *Mélanges du droit public grec* (Liège, 1910), a collection of essays on various aspects of the subject; "Formation des villes, des états," etc., in *Acad. roy. Belg.* 1901. pp.

[1] It is noteworthy that Aristotle approves of state aid to the needy, but insists that it must be so granted as to place the beneficiary in a position to help himself.

949–1012; Kornemann, E., "Stadtstaat und Flächenstaat des Altertums in ihren Wechselbeziehungen," in *N. Jahrb.* XI (1908). 233–53. On the socialistic tendencies of government, see Pöhlmann, R. von, *Geschichte der sozialen Frage und des Sozialismus in der antiken Welt*, 2 vols. (Munich, 1912), an excessively pessimistic view, counteracted by a study of actual conditons, as by Sundwall, J., "Epigraphische Beiträge zur sozialpolitischen Geschichte Athens im Zeitalter des Demosthenes," in *Klio: Beiträge zur alten Geschichte.* Ergzb. I. 4 (1906); and Haussoullier, B., *La vie municipale en Attique* (Paris: Thorin, 1884). For a brief review of the tendencies of domestic politics during this century, see Botsford, *Hellenic History*, ch. xxvi. See further Whibley, L., *Greek Oligarchies* (London: Methuen, 1896); Baron, Ch., "La candidature politique chez les Athéniens," in *Rev. des ét. gr.* XIV (1901). 372–99; Calhoun, G. M., *Athenian Clubs in Politics and Litigation* (University of Texas, 1913), an especially meritorious work; Hartel, W. A., *Studien über attisches Staatsrecht und Urkundenwesen* (Vienna, 1878); Swoboda, H., *Die griech. Volksbeschlüsse* (Leipzig, 1890); Szanto, E., *Ausgewählte Abhandlungen* (Tübingen, 1906).

II. Economy and Finance. — Riezler, K., *Ueber Finanzen und Monopole im alten Griechenland* (Berlin, 1907); Böckh, A., *Staatshaushaltung der Athener*, 2 vols. (3d. ed. rev. by M. Fränkel, Berlin: Reimer, 1886); Guiraud, P., *Études économiques sur l'antiquité* (Paris: Hachette, 1905); *La propriété foncière en Grèce jusqu'à la conquête romaine* (Paris, 1893); *Main d'œuvre dans l'ancienne Grèce* (Paris, 1900); Francotte, H., *Les finances des cités grecques* (Paris: Champion, 1909); "L'administration financière des cités grecques," in *Acad. roy. Belg. des Sciences*, LXIII. pt. vi (1903); "Le pain à bon marché et le pain gratuit dans les cités grecques," in *Mélanges Nicole* (Geneva, 1905), 135–57; *L'industrie dans la Grèce ancienne*, 2 vols. (Brussels, 1900), a standard work; Büchsenschütz, B., *Besitz und Erwerb im griech. Altertume* (Halle, 1869); *Die Hauptstätten des Gewerbfleisses im klassischen Altertume* (Leipzig, 1869); Blümner, H., *Technologie und Terminologie der Gewerbe und Künste bei Griechen und Römern* (2d ed., vol. I only has come to the notice of the editor, Teubner, 1912); Borguet, E., *L'administration financière du sanctuaire pythique au IVe siècle avant J.-C.* (Paris, 1905); Head, B. V., *Historia numorum: A Manual of Greek Numismatics* (Oxford: Clarendon Press, 1911); Hill, G. F., *Handbook of Greek and Roman Coins* (Macmillan, 1899); *Historical Greek Coins* (Macmillan, 1906); Gardner, P., "Gold Coinage of Asia before Alexander the Great," in *Proceedings of the British Academy*, III (1907–08). 107–38.

Speck, E., *Handelsgeschichte des Altertums*, 2 vols. (Leipzig, 1900, 1901) vol. I: "Greece," drawn from secondary sources; Lindsay, W. S., *History of Merchant Shipping and Ancient Commerce*, 4 vols. (London: 1874–1876), vol. I; Georgiades, A. S., *Les portes de la Grèce dans l'antiquité qui subsistent encore aujourd'hui* (Athens, 1907), exhaustive, valuable; Ardaillon, E., *Les mines du Laurion dans l'antiquité* (Paris, 1897); Wallon, H. A., *Histoire de l'esclavage dans l'antiquité*, 3 vols. (Paris, 1847), useful though old; Meyer, E., *Die Sklaverei im Altertum* (Dresden, 1898); Silverio, O., *Untersuchungen zur Geschichte der attischen Staatssklaven* (Munich, 1900), Program; Szanto, E.,

Ausgewählte Abhandlungen (Tübingen, 1906), various economic studies; Ziebarth, E., *Das griechische Vereinswesen* (Leipzig, 1896); Poland, F., *Geschichte des griech. Vereinswesens* (Leipzig, 1909); Beloch, J., *Die Bevölkerung der griech. u. röm. Welt* (Leipzig, 1886); "Die Volkszahl als Faktor und Gradmesser der historischen Entwickelung," in *Hist. Zeitschr.* CXI (1913). 321–37; Cavaignac, E., "La population du Peloponnèse aux Ve et IVe siècles," in *Klio* XII (1912). 261–80.

CHAPTER XIV

SOCIAL CONDITIONS

In the Period 404–337 B.C.

144. Regulations of the Phratry of the Demotionidæ

(Ditt. II. no. 439; Michel, *Recueil*, no. 961; Dareste-Haussoullier-Reinach, *Recueil*, II (1904). 199–227; Tarbell, in *Am. Journ. Arch.* V (1889). 135–53; *cf.* Von Schoeffer, in Pauly-Wissowa, *Real-Encycl.* V. 194–202; Von Wilamowitz-Moellendorff, *Aristoteles und Athen*, II. 259–79. Translated by C. J. O.)

This inscription, found on the site of ancient Deceleia, a deme in northern Attica, contains three decrees of the phratry of the Demotionidæ for regulating the admission of new members, and is our chief source of information concerning the organization and functions of the Athenian phratry for the fifth and fourth centuries. In the early days of the state the phratries had been subdivisions of the four Ionic tribes. Their members were bound together by the tie of kinship, as the name phrater ("brother") implies. Their functions were political as well as religious and social. After the reforms of Cleisthenes (508) their political importance declined. It was still necessary, however, that every Athenian should belong to a phratry; hence it was customary to admit children to the phratry of their father, such admission being held as evidence of their legitimacy and their right to the citizenship; in other words, the chief remaining political function of the phratry was that of watching over the citizenship of children — of boys till their enrolment in the deme register, and of girls till their marriage. The admission took place at the distinctive festival of the phratry, termed Apaturia. In the most probable view of the case, girls and boys were presented at the Apaturia next following their birth, and on this occasion the sacrifice designated as *meion* was offered by the presenter. When the boy became a youth, he was enrolled, and another sacrifice, the *koureion*, was offered. The girl was not enrolled; but at marriage her husband presented her to his phrateres, on which occasion he offered the *gamelia*, most probably a sacrifice in which his phrateres participated; see Töpffer, in Pauly-Wissowa, *Real-Encycl.* I. 2672–80.

It is clear that in organization the phratries differed widely from one another, as the state left them free to adopt whatever constitutions they desired. Often the nucleus of a phratry was a gens, *genos*, which naturally held the religious leadership. In the Demotionidæ the leadership fell to the "house of the Deceleians," the character of which is under controversy. The phrateres were divided into small groups, apparently of near kin, termed *thiasoi*.

The general rules governing the phratry were doubtless laid down in its fundamental law; and the decrees contained in this inscription have to do merely with a revision of the procedure to be followed particularly in admissions. Greater strictness was the aim; for during the last years of the Peloponnesian war many unqualified persons had been put upon the list of citizens, and the affairs of the Demotionidæ must have been extremely deranged through the occupation of Deceleia, their local center, by a Peloponnesian garrison, 413–404. The decree of Hierocles, passed 396–5, provided accordingly that there should be a formal decision (*diadikasia*) in the case of those who had been admitted irregularly; and also for the purpose of preventing fraud, that thereafter a year should elapse between the presentation of the candidate and the voting upon him. In case of an appeal by the presenter of the child, the "house of the Deceleians" was to support the case of the phratry. The decree of Nicodemus, which must have been passed soon afterward, has the appearance of ignoring this body and of substituting a preliminary vote by the members of the presenter's thiasos, to be followed immediately by a vote of the whole body of phrateres. The third decree, that of Menexenus, must be at least half a century later, as indicated by the character of the writing; and so far as it is preserved, it simply provides for the posting of the candidates' names. Though some matters of detail relating to the phratry are still obscure, the entire inscription clearly reveals to us the essential character of the institution as protector of the purity of citizenship.

ZEUS PHRATRIOS [1]

1. The priest Theodorus, son of Euphantides, had the stele inscribed and erected.

There shall be given to the priest, as perquisites of the sacrifices: from the *meion*[2] a thigh, a side, and an ear (of the victim), and three obols in money; from the *koureion* a thigh, a side, and an ear, a flat cake containing a *chœnix*[3] measure, a half *chous* of wine, and a drachma in money.

[1] The guardian deity of the association, with whom Athena Phratria was often joined. This superscription implied that the stele and its document were sacred to the god.

[2] *Meion*, the "lesser" sacrifice, is explained in the introduction above, as is also the *koureion*, "youth's" sacrifice, which occurs in the text immediately below; *cf.* Prott and Ziehen, *Leg. græc. sac.* II. 1. 69 *sq.* Others maintain that children were presented but once, and distinguish the *meion* and *koureion* as sacrifices for girls and boys respectively; see also Schömann, *Griech. Alt.* II. 574–6 with notes.

[3] *Chœnix*, about a quart; *chous*, immediately following, about three pints.

The following resolutions were passed by the phrateres, when Phormion was archon [1] of the Athenians and Pantacles of Oeon was phratriarch.[2]

Hierocles moved: With regard to all those who have not yet been voted upon according to the law of the Demotionidæ,[3] the phrateres shall proceed to a vote immediately, pledging themselves in the name of Zeus Phratrios, and taking their ballots from off the altar. If it is decided that a person without the proper qualifications [4] has been introduced (into the phratry), the priest and the phratriarch shall erase his name from the register kept among the Demotionidæ and from the copy. The introducer of the person rejected shall be fined one hundred drachmas, which shall be devoted to Zeus Phratrios; and the priest and the phratriarch shall collect this money or themselves be liable for it. In future the voting (upon the candidate) shall take place in the year following that in which the sacrifice of the *koureion* has been offered, and on the day of the Apaturia [5] known as the *koureotis;* [6] and the ballots shall be taken from off the altar. If any of those who may be rejected shall desire to appeal to the Demotionidæ, they shall have the right; and the house of the Deceleians [7] shall choose five men over thirty years of age as counsel to oppose the appeal. These men shall swear before the phratriarch and the priest that they will

[1] 396–5 B.C.

[2] The chief officer of the phratry, some of whose functions are made clear by this document. There were phratries with two officers of this title.

[3] This phratry took its name from a legendary hero Demotion; Von Wilamowitz-Moellendorff, *Arist. u. Ath.* II. 278 *sq.*; "Demotionidæ," in Pauly-Wissowa, *Real-Encycl.* V. 194–202.

[4] Literally, "without being a phrater."

[5] A festival common to all the Ionians, including the Athenians (Hdt. i. 147), celebrated in Attica for three, or four, days in the month Pyanepsion (October-November).

[6] "Day of the koureion."

[7] It has been maintained by Töpffer, *Attische Genealogie*, 289, that there was a gens (γένος) of the Deceleians, which claimed descent from the local hero Decelos (Hdt. ix. 73), and hence was doubtless eupatrid. According to another view the "house of the Deceleians" was merely an association of certain thiasoi of the phratry; *cf.* especially Schöll, *Sitzb. Münch. Akad.* 1889, ii. 19; Milchhöfer, in Pauly-Wissowa, *Real-Encycl.* IV. 2425. A hasty reading would lead us to believe that the power of this "house" was limited by the first decree, which granted an appeal to the whole phratry, and abolished by the second, which gave the first vote to the thiasotes. It is possible, however, that an application for a second hearing before the Demotionidæ is intended, and that the privilege of the Deceleians to provide advocates was not touched by the second decree.

advocate what is wholly upright, and that they will not allow anyone without the proper qualifications to be a member of the phratry.

2. An appellant who is rejected by the Demotionidæ shall be fined one thousand drachmas, which shall be devoted to Zeus Phratrios; and the priest [1] of the house of the Deceleians shall collect this money or himself be liable for it. Any other phrater who wishes may collect it for the common fund. These provisions shall be in force beginning with the archonship of Phormion. The phratriarch shall put the question concerning those who are to be voted upon year by year. If he does not put the question, he shall be fined five hundred drachmas, which shall be devoted to Zeus Phratrios; and the priest and any one else who wishes shall collect the money for the common fund.

In future the *meion* and the *koureion* victims shall be brought to the altar at Deceleia; and if the offerer does not sacrifice them upon the altar, he shall be fined fifty drachmas, which shall be devoted to Zeus Phratrios; and the priest shall collect this money or himself be liable for it, [except in case of pestilence or war (?)]. If any of these circumstances shall interfere, the *meion* and the *koureion* victims shall be brought to such place as the priest may advertise, said advertisement to be made five days [2] before the *dorpia*,[3] upon a whitened tablet not less than a span in breadth, in such quarter of the city as the Deceleians may frequent.[4] The priest shall have this decree and the (tariff of) sacrificial perquisites inscribed upon a stone stele before the altar in Deceleia at his own expense.

3. Nicodemus moved, as an amendment to the former decrees adopted concerning the presentation of children and the voting upon them: The three witnesses whom the presenter is required to furnish at the investigation shall be from his own thiasos,[5] bear-

[1] Apparently the same as the priest of the phratry.

[2] Four days by our system of exclusive reckoning.

[3] "Banquet Day," the first day of the festival.

[4] In this period the rendezvous of the Deceleians at Athens was "by the Hermæ" in the market place; Lysias xxiii. 3–15.

[5] A subdivision of the phratry, evidently containing but few households, undoubtedly of near kin. If the "house of the Deceleians" formed the eupatrid nucleus of the phratry, it would be natural to assume that the thiasoi contained the common members. The reason for the name is not clear. As outside the phratry the thiasos connects

ing witness in answer to the interrogatories and taking oath by Zeus Phratrios; and they shall lay hold of the altar when they bear witness and take oath. If there are not as many (as three) in the particular thiasos, the presenter shall furnish witnesses from the rest of the phrateres.

4. When the voting takes place, the phratriarch shall not refer the decision concerning the children to the whole body of phrateres, until the thiasotes of the candidate shall have voted secretly, taking their ballots from off the altar; and the phratriarch shall count their ballots before the whole body of phrateres present in the market place, and shall announce the result of the vote. If after the thiasotes have voted that the candidate is their fellow-phrater, the rest of the phrateres reject him, a fine of one hundred drachmas, to be devoted to Zeus Phratrios, shall be levied upon the thiasotes, excepting those of them who make open accusation or objection at the time of the vote.[1] If the thiasotes reject the candidate, and his presenter appeals to the whole body, and the whole body decides that he is a phrater, he shall be enrolled in the public registers. But if the whole body rejects him, his presenter shall be fined one hundred drachmas, which shall be devoted to Zeus Phratrios. If the thiasotes reject and the presenter does not appeal to the whole body, the rejection by the thiasotes shall stand. The thiasotes shall not vote together with the rest of the phrateres concerning children from their own thiasos.

The priest shall have this decree also inscribed upon the stone stele.

5. Oath of the witnesses upon the presentation of children: "I bear witness that the one whom he presents is his own legitimate son by his wedded wife, (and I swear) by Zeus Phratrios that this statement is true. May I have many blessings if I swear rightly, and the contrary if I swear falsely."

6. Menexenus moved: Be it resolved by the phrateres, as an amendment to the former decrees concerning the presentation of children, to the end that the phrateres may know those who are

itself especially with the worship of Dionysus, some have supposed that the creation of these societies within the phratry, at some unknown time in their history, signifies the entrance of Dionysus worship into the phratry.

[1] That is, in the discussion preceding the vote itself.

to be presented — that in the year next[1] to that in which the *koureion* is brought, a statement containing the name (of the candidate) with the father's name and the deme, and the mother's name, with her father's name and his deme, shall be given to the phratriarch. On receiving the statements, the phratriarch shall have them inscribed and exposed in such place as the Deceleians may frequent, and the priest likewise shall have them inscribed upon a whitened tablet and exposed in the sanctuary of Leto. This decree shall be inscribed upon the stele. . . .[2]

145. The Military Training of Athenian Youths

(Aristotle, *Constitution of Athens*, 42. Translated by G. W. B.)

Those have political rights whose parents are both Athenians.[3] They are enrolled among the demesmen at the age of eighteen.[4] At the time of their enrolment the demesmen under oath take a vote concerning them, first as to whether they have reached the legal age, and if they decide in the negative, the candidates return to the boys, secondly as to whether the candidate is free and of legal birth. In case they decide that he is not free, he has the right of appeal to a lawcourt, and the demesmen choose from their own number five men to act as accusers. If the court decides that he has been illegally enrolled, the state sells him into slavery; but if he wins, the demesmen are compelled to enroll him. Afterward the council examines those who have been enrolled, and if it decides that any one is younger than eighteen years, it fines the demesmen who enrolled him. When the youths (ephebi) have passed their examination, their fathers, assembling by tribes, take oath and elect from their tribesmen three persons above forty years of age whom they consider to be the best and most fitted

[1] The phrase is awkward, but must mean the year intervening between the sacrifice and the voting, as in the first decree.

[2] The paragraph numbering of this document is the present editor's.

[3] This regulation dates from 451; in former time it was only required that the father should be an Athenian, the more exclusive condition being introduced by a statute of Pericles. In the Peloponnesian war the law was greatly relaxed, but was reaffirmed by the restored democracy in 403.

[4] The meaning undoubtedly is "on the completion of the eighteenth year." The enrolment was in the deme register, ληξιαρχικὸν γραμματεῖον, which contained the names of all the adult male members of the deme.

to supervise the youths, and from them the popular assembly elects a moderator [1] for each tribe, and from the Athenians in general a commander [2] for the entire company.

These officials, assembling the youths, make a procession about the shrines and then proceed to Peiræus; some garrison Munichia [3] and others Acte. The assembly elects also two trainers for them and instructors who are to teach them to fight in heavy armor and to discharge the bow and javelin and catapult. Furthermore it furnishes each moderator with a drachma a day for provisions and the youths with four obols daily. Each moderator, receiving the allowance for his own tribesmen, buys provisions for them all, to be used at common meals, for they dine together according to tribes; and he looks after all other matters.

Thus they pass the first year. At the beginning of the second year an assembly is held in the theatre, where they exhibit their military attainments, and receive from the state a shield and spear. Then they make a circuit of the country and pass their time in the forts. Thus for two years they perform garrison duty, wearing military cloaks,[4] and are free from all public burdens. They neither sue nor are sued, that there may be no pretext for absence, except in case of an inheritance or a claim to an heiress [5] or in case of an hereditary right to a priesthood.[6] Having passed their two years, they at length associate with the rest of the citizens.[7]

[1] Moderator, sophronistes (σωφρονιστής).

[2] Commander, kosmete (κοσμητής).

[3] Munichia is a hill, acropolis, in the eastern peninsula of Peiræus; Acte, mentioned below, is the southwestern peninsula of the same city.

[4] The cloak here referred to was the chlamys; for an illustration, see Gulick, *Life of the Ancient Greeks*, 90.

[5] If the father died leaving no sons but a daughter only, she inherited the estate, and her nearest kinsmen had a legal right to marry her. The youth could absent himself from military training to claim an estate or the hand of an heiress to whom he was next of kin.

[6] Κἄν τινι κατὰ τὸ γένος ἱερωσύνη γίνηται, Kenyon translates: "or of any sacrificial ceremony connected with the clan of any individual." But ἱερωσύνη signifies priesthood; and any one acquainted with the legal language of the orators knows that κατὰ τὸ γένος has reference to degree of relationship, succession.

[7] This system of training is essentially a creation of the fourth century, and reached its full development in the administration of Lycurgus after the battle of Chæroneia (338); see Thalheim, in Pauly-Wissowa, *Real-Encycl.* V. 2737–41; Beloch, *Griech. Gesch.* II. 614 *sq.*

146. The Oath of the Ephebi

(Lycurgus, *Against Leocrates*, 75–89. Translated by E. G. S.)

The excerpt subjoined is taken from the only remaining speech of Lycurgus, mentioned in note 7 of the preceding selection. Leocrates had abandoned Athens after the battle of Chæroneia and had taken up his residence first at Rhodes and afterward at Megara. To patriots, such as Lycurgus and Demosthenes, this period seemed the most critical in the history of their country, when Athens stood in greatest need of support from every citizen. Naturally the political sense of the Athenians rated the conduct of Leocrates, not merely as exhibiting a lack of ordinary affection for his motherland, but as a species of treason comparable with our own idea of parricide.

It was probably while making the round of the temples that the ephebi, or youths in training (see selection above), took the oath of loyalty in the cave of Aglauros (Demosth. *On the Embassy*, 303; Stobæus, *Florilegium*, xliii. 48). The oath as given below is preserved in Stobæus. Though suspected by one or two modern scholars, it is now considered undoubtedly genuine; *cf.* Gilbert, *Const. Antiq.* 197–9; Thalheim, in Pauly-Wissowa, *Real-Encycl.* V. 2737–41.

Consider further in what manner you have instituted a custom regarding these things, and what sentiments you cherish. Though you are aware of the facts, it is fitting in addressing you, to review the subject. A eulogy of the commonwealth, by Athena, are the ancient laws and usages of those who from the beginning regulated these matters. If you heed their enactments, you will do the right and will seem to all mankind to be worthy of reverence and of the commonwealth. You have an oath which all the citizens swear when they are enrolled in the register of civil maturity [1] and become ephebi, neither to disgrace the sacred arms nor to abandon their place (in battle), but to come to the aid of their fatherland and to hand it down (to posterity) in improved condition. If Leocrates has sworn this oath, he has openly committed perjury, and not only has injured you but also has perpetrated an act of impiety against the Deity.[2] If however he has not taken the oath, he is at once revealed as a man who has deliberately prepared not to fulfil his duties at all, for which you should justly

[1] "Register of civil maturity" is perhaps the most exact translation of *ληξιαρχικὸν γραμματεῖον*, deme register, mentioned in a note of the selection immediately preceding. The idea contained in *ληξιαρχικόν* is that the enrolled youth had a right to manage his own estate: *τῶν λήξεων ἄρχειν*; Harpocration, *s. v.*

[2] Τὸ *θεῖον*, an abstract noun.

condemn him both in behalf of yourselves and in behalf of the Gods. Now I wish you to hear the oath. Read it, clerk.

THE OATH

I will not disgrace the sacred arms,[1] nor will I abandon the man next to me, whoever he may be. I will bring aid to the ritual of the state and to the holy duties both alone and in company with many. Moreover my native commonwealth I will not transmit lessened, but larger and better than I have received it. I will obey those who from time to time are judging; and the established statutes I will obey, and whatever other regulations the people shall enact unanimously. If any one shall attempt to destroy the statutes, I will not permit it, but will repel (such a person) both alone and with all. Furthermore I will honor the ancestral religion. Witnesses of these declarations (shall be) Aglauros, Enyalios, Zeus, Thallo, Auxo, Hegemónê.[2]

147. Dowries

(Isæus, *Orations*, ii. 3-5. Translated by G. W. B.)

This selection is to illustrate the right and duty of brothers to give their sisters in marriage and to provide them with suitable dowries.

Eponymus of Acharnæ, our father, gentlemen,[3] was a friend and intimate companion of Menecles. He had four children, two sons and two daughters. When father died, we gave the eldest sister in marriage, since she was of age,[4] to Leucolophus, bestowing on

[1] These are the shield and spear presented in the assembly, as described in the preceding selection.

[2] Aglauros, daughter of Cecrops, whose shrine was a cave in the northern declivity of the Acropolis, in which the oath was taken. Enyalios, an epithet of Ares, god of war. Thallo, "the Blossoming one," a deity related to the youthful age. Auxo, "Increase." Hegemónê, "Leadership."

[3] The jury are addressed as "gentlemen of the jury," or simply as "gentlemen," or as "Athenians."

[4] A girl however young could be contracted in marriage by her father or guardian, but the marriage of either sex could take place only after puberty. At Athens the legal age of a girl seems to have been the fifteenth year; cf. Demosth., *Against Aphobus*, i. 4 *sq.*; Xen. *Econ.* vii. 5. In other parts of the Greek world the age seems to have fallen as low as the thirteenth year; see Beauchet, *Histoire du droit privé de la république Athénienne*, I. 158 *sqq*.

her twenty minas as dowry. In the fourth or fifth year after that date, when our younger sister was scarcely of marriageable age, the former wife of Menecles died. After Menecles had performed for her the customary rites, he asked us for our sister, recalling the friendship between our father and himself, and stating how he was disposed toward us. Now as we knew that our father would have bestowed her upon no one more readily than upon him, we gave her to him, not without dowry as my opponent continually asserts, but with the same dowry that we gave to our elder sister. In this way, having formerly been friends, we became kinsmen. Moreover that Menecles received twenty minas as dowry for her, I wish first to offer the following testimony.

(Lysias, *Orations*, xix. 14–17. Translated by G. W. B.)

The grant of a dowry was legally advantageous to a wife and to her children in that it served as evidence of a legitimate marriage. As she could recover it in case of separation, it tended to make her marriage more stable. Although a dowerless wife was in these two respects placed at a disadvantage, it was considered generous and patriotic in a citizen to marry a poor dowerless girl. In the selection below the speaker takes credit for such meritorious conduct.

When he (my father) became of age, though it was possible for him to marry a woman with a large dowry, he took my mother with none at all, because she was the daughter of Xenophon,[1] son of Euripides, who not only in private had a reputation for uprightness, but whom too you deemed worthy to fill the office of general, as I hear. As to my sisters also, whereas certain very wealthy persons were willing to take them without dowries, he (my father) refused, because their reputation fell short of respectability; but he bestowed one upon Philomelus the Pæanian, who is generally considered better in character than in wealth, and the other upon a man who had been impoverished through no baseness of his own, namely, his nephew Phædrus [2] of Myrrhinus, with a dowry of forty minas, and afterward upon Aristophanes [3] with the same dowry.

[1] The Xenophon here mentioned served during the early years of the Peloponnesian war, and was killed by the enemy; Thuc. ii. 70, 79; Diod. xii. 45.

[2] It is believed that the Phædrus here mentioned is the person after whom the dialogue of Plato of that name is called.

[3] This Aristophanes devoted himself with great energy to public affairs; but for some unknown reason he and his father were put to death without trial, and their prop-

Moreover when it was permitted me to get a very large dowry, he advised me to take a smaller one under conditions such that I could know that I was to have orderly and sober relatives by marriage. I now have as wife accordingly the daughter of Critodemus of Alopecê, who was killed by the Lacedæmonians when the naval battle was fought in the Hellespont.[1] Well then, gentlemen of the jury, in case of a man who himself married a portionless wife and gave great dowries to his two daughters, but advised his son to take a wife with a small portion, is it not reasonable to believe in regard to him that it was not for the sake of money that he became a kinsman of these persons?

148. Evidence of Legitimate Descent

(Isæus viii. 15–17. Translated by G. W. B.)

Interesting is the great importance attaching to participation in common religious rites and customs.

It was on the assumption that we were children of his daughter that he never offered any sacrifice apart from us, but whether the religious service was great or small, we were everywhere present with him, and joined in the sacrifice. Furthermore we were not only invited to such ceremonies, but also he always brought us to the rural Dionysia,[2] and sitting by his side, we viewed the show, and took part with him in all festivities. When too he sacrificed to Zeus Ktesios,[3] in which solemnity he took especial interest and never brought to it any slave or unrelated freeman, but himself attended personally to everything, we shared with him in this service and aided him in preparing the sacrifice and in offering it; in brief we were associated with him in everything he did, and he prayed that health and wealth be granted us, as was reasonable on his part, being our grandfather. Yet if he did not

erty was confiscated. The brother-in-law of Aristophanes delivers before the court the speech, *On the Property of Aristophanes*, from which this excerpt is taken.

[1] The battle of Ægospotami, 405.

[2] The festival termed the smaller or rural Dionysia was held in the month of Poseideon (December–January) at the first tasting of the year's vintage. In the larger demes dramas were played by itinerant troups of actors.

[3] God of property, possession.

consider us sons of his daughter, he would have done not a single one of these things, but would have invited to his side this other man, who now claims to be his nephew. That these things are true, is most accurately known to my grandfather's slaves, whom my opponent refuses to hand over for torture.[1]

149. A Case of Adoption

(Isæus ii. 13–16, 36 *sq.* Translated by G. W. B.)

Next I wish to show you that the adoption was made in accordance with the laws. Read for me therefore the law itself which grants him permission to will his property as he pleases, if there are no male children.[2] For this reason, gentlemen, the legislator enacted this law, because he found it the only refuge from desolation and the only comfort in life to the childless, namely, the right to adopt whomsoever they choose. Seeing therefore that the laws granted him the right to adopt because of his childlessness, he adopted me, not by writing it in a will and at the point of death, gentlemen, as some other citizens do, nor in illness but in good health, sound mind and sense. Moreover having adopted me, he introduced me to his phrateres in the presence of these adversaries, and enrolled me among his demesmen and among his orgeones.[3] At that time these adversaries made no objection, to the effect that he was not in his right mind. Yet it would have been far better for them to persuade him while living, if they wished anything, than to insult him after death and to render his house desolate.

Furthermore he lived after the adoption not merely a year or

[1] Legally a slave could be subjected to torture for the purpose of extracting evidence. In the fourth century demands are often made for the torture of slaves, but they are invariably refused, at least so far as we can learn from the orators. It is clear that in this period humane feeling was far in advance of the law.

[2] In case there are daughters, but no sons, he may will his property as he pleases, always provided that the heirs take the daughters in marriage. If there are no children, he is absolutely free to dispose of his property as he wishes. The widow can claim no more than her dowry.

[3] On the introduction of a born son to the phratry, see no. 144. In a phratry which included a gens, the members of the gens were called gennetæ, and the non-members orgeones; Philochorus, frag. 94, Müller, *Frag. hist. græc.* I. 399. Most probably the thiasotes (no. 144) are to be identified with the orgeones.

two but twenty-three years; and in this time, long as it was, he did not in the slightest repent of what he had done, thanks to its being acknowledged by all that he had planned it rightly. To prove that I speak the truth, I shall bring before you his phrateres and orgeones and demesmen as witnesses of the adoption; but that it was permitted him to make the adoption, the law itself, according to which the adoption took place, will be read in evidence. . . .

I, the adopted son, cherished him while living — I and my wife, the daughter of Philonides here; and I gave my child his name [1] that the house might not remain nameless; and when he died, I buried him in a manner worthy of himself and me, and erected over his grave a beautiful tombstone,[2] and performed for him the third and the ninth day sacrifices [3] and all the other fitting ceremonials of his burial in the most beautiful way possible, so that all his demesmen commended what I did. But this adversary of mine, who blames him for having adopted a son, deprived him while living of the land that remained to him, and after his decease seeks to render him childless and nameless. Such is his character.

150. A Swarm of Heirs

(Isæus iv. 7–10. Translated by G. W. B.)

Nicostratus, absent from Athens eleven years as a mercenary, died in Ake, Phœnicia (Strabo xvi. 25). His ashes with two talents in money were sent home to Athens. Their arrival occasioned a comedy.

Who did not cut his hair when the two talents arrived from Ake? [4] Or who did not put on a black robe, with the idea that his grief would make him heir to the estate? How many kinsmen and sons claimed the estate of Nicostratus as a gift? Demosthenes [5] declared himself to be his nephew; but confuted by my adversaries, he withdrew. Then Telephus declared that Nicostratus had given all his property to him; but no long time afterward this

[1] It was customary to name the eldest son after the paternal grandfather.

[2] See Gardner, *Sculptured Tombs of Hellas*, for an excellent discussion of the subject, with many illustrations.

[3] Offerings made at the tomb on the third and ninth day after burial.

[4] Ake is the modern Acre.

[5] It is hardly necessary to say that this Demosthenes is unknown to us, and that no importance attaches to the individuals mentioned in this selection.

man too desisted. Next Ameiniades brought before the Archon a son for him, not yet three years old, and that too though Nicostratus had not been in Athens for eleven years. Pyrrhus of Lamptra, next in order, declared that the property had been devoted by Nicostratus to Athena, and had been given by him (Nicostratus) to himself (Pyrrhus).[1] Then Ctesias of Besa and Cranaûs first declared that they had obtained a judgment of a talent against Nicostratus; but finding themselves unable to prove this point, they pretended that he was their freedman; but not even thus did they sustain their declaration. These are the persons who first leaped upon the money of Nicostratus. At that time Chariades[2] made no claim at all; but afterward he not only came forward himself, but tried to foist the son of his mistress upon the deceased. His double object was to inherit the property and to make the son a citizen. But when he discovered that he should be confuted on the question of the relationship, he let fall the claim of the child, and laid by deposit a claim for himself on the basis of gift.

151. Treatment of a Poor Free Laborer

(Plato, *Euthyphron*, 4)

On the treatment of slaves in the fourth century, see no. 154. Doubtless a master was more inclined to deal gently with his slaves than with a day laborer, especially on an isolated farm where the hired man could not invoke the law. Although the Athenians were a remarkably humane people, cases like that described by Plato below doubtless occurred. The brutality of the proprietor, however, was to a great degree offset by the extremely sensitive conscience of the son. The conversation between this son, Euthyphron, and Socrates takes place at the King's Porch (Stoa Basileios), where the young man has come to bring before the "king" (archon) a prosecution against his father for the murder of the hired man.

Socrates. I suppose that the man whom your father killed was one of your relatives — clearly he was; for if he had been a stranger, you would never have thought of prosecuting him.[3]

[1] It is possible that Pyrrhus really claimed that the property had been so devoted with reservations in favor of himself, but Isæus has purposely misrepresented the case *ad absurdum*.

[2] Chariades is the adversary of the speaker and his brother in the present trial.

[3] Prosecutions for homicide were legally brought by the near kin in the order of their propinquity; see the Law of Draco, no. 77.

EUTHYPHRON. I am amused, Socrates, at your making a distinction between a relative and a non-relative; for surely the pollution [1] is the same in either case, if you knowingly associate with the murderer when you ought to clear yourself and him by proceeding against him. The real question is whether the slain man has been justly killed. If justly, then your duty is to let the matter alone; but if unjustly, then even if the murderer lives under the same roof with you and eats at the same table, proceed against him. In the present case the man who is dead was a poor dependent [2] of mine who worked for us as a field laborer on our farm in Naxos; and one day in a fit of drunken passion he got into a quarrel with one of our slaves and killed him. My father bound him hand and foot and threw him into a ditch, while he sent to Athens to ask of an exegete [3] what he should do with him. Meanwhile he never attended to him or took care about him, regarding him as a murderer. In fact he thought that no great harm would come even if he should die. That was indeed just what happened; for such was the effect of cold and hunger and chains upon him, that before the messenger returned from the exegete, he was dead. My father and family are now angry with me for taking the part of the murderer and prosecuting my father. They say that he did not kill him; and that if he did, the dead man was but a murderer and that I ought not to notice the deed, for that son is impious who prosecutes a father. These pleas show, Socrates, how little they know what the Deity thinks about piety and impiety.

152. THE CONTEMPT OF DEMOSTHENES FOR THE POVERTY OF HIS OPPONENT

(Demosthenes, *On the Crown*, 257–265. Translated by G. W. B.)

Ctesiphon, an Athenian citizen, had proposed that the Five Hundred and the Assembly vote Demosthenes a golden crown (wreath) as a token of appreciation of his good will to the state, manifested not only in his general public

[1] As here indicated, the Greeks considered the shedding of blood by violence a religious pollution, to be expiated by prosecution and accompanying ceremonies.

[2] Dependent (πελάτης, pelates). In this period no legal relation of the kind existed among the citizens, but the dependent may have been an alien.

[3] The exegetes were sacerdotal officers whose function was the interpretation of traditional religious usages; *cf.* Kern, in Pauly-Wissowa, *Real-Encycl.* VI. 1583 *sq.*

policy but particularly in his gifts of money for the improvement of the fortifications and for the fund devoted to the expenses of festivals. Thereupon Æschines, a political opponent, prosecuted Ctesiphon under the "Writ against Illegality" (γραφὴ παρανόμων). Though nominally Ctesiphon was brought to trial, the chief assault was made against Demosthenes as a man unworthy of such honor on the ground of either private or public conduct. The answering speech by Demosthenes in defense of his own character and policy is undoubtedly the greatest oration of the world's most famous orator. Most of its sentiments are beautiful and noble. The excerpt below, which bears quite a different character, has been chosen to present to view the chasm then widening between the rich and the poor. Incidentally it reveals the pitiable condition of the school-teacher.

It was my good fortune, Æschines, when I was a boy, to attend the schools that became my position, and to enjoy those possessions which one ought who is not to commit a shameful act through penury.[1] Then as I passed from childhood it was my lot to follow a line of conduct consistent with these earlier conditions, to act as choregus, to serve as trierarch, to contribute war taxes,[2] to fail in no line of social or public spirit, but to be useful alike to the state and to my friends. When further I resolved to enter public life, I chose such a policy that I was often crowned both by my fatherland and by many other Hellenes; such a policy that not even you, my enemy, dare deny that it was noble. Such was the fortune with which I lived my life, and though I could say much else about it, I pass that by, for I wish to avoid offending any one in the matters on which I pride myself.

But you, august man, who now spit upon others, consider what fortune you enjoyed, through which in boyhood you were reared in dire poverty, assisting your father in the school-room, grinding ink, sponging off the seats, and sweeping the room, occupying the post of a slave, not of a free lad. When, too, you became a man you were an acolyte of your mother in her initiations,[3] read-

[1] Demosthenes was the son of a wealthy manufacturer; see no. 156. The idea that poverty is a cause of crime was entertained by many of the noble and wealthy classes; *cf.* the view of the "Old Oligarch," no. 62.

[2] Expensive public services, performed by the wealthy citizens, were termed liturgies. On this subject, see Botsford, *Hellenic History*, ch. xii.

[3] The ceremony, ludicrously described by Demosthenes, is an initiation into a mystery cult imported from Phrygia or Thrace; *cf.* Botsford, *Hellenic History*, ch. xx; Moore, *History of Religions*, I. 456.

ing the books for her and getting ready the other ceremonial apparatus, at night covering the novitiates with fawn-skins, giving them drink from bowls, cleansing them and swabbing them off with clay and meal, lifting them up from the lustration and bidding them say, "I ESCAPED THE BAD, I FOUND THE BETTER," boasting of a capacity for howling louder than any other; in fact I believe him, for do not imagine that so loud a talker [1] could prove inferior in howling. By day you conducted through the streets the fair orgiasts crowned with wreaths of fennel and poplar, throttling the swollen-cheeked snakes and holding them over your head, while you shouted EUOI SABOI and danced to the tune of HYES ATTES, ATTES HYES, and are proclaimed Leader, Conductor, Chest-Bearer, Sieve-Bearer and the like by wrinkled hags, receiving as your pay for these services tarts, biscuits, and rolls, for which any one would certainly esteem himself and his fortune blessed.

Next when you were enrolled among your demesmen, I do not say by what means,[2] but when you were enrolled, forthwith you chose the noblest of occupations, that of scribe and servant of petty officials. Then when you were dismissed from this position, having yourself performed all the disgraceful things you now charge against others, you did not, by Heaven, by your subsequent life disgrace your earlier course of conduct, but hired yourself out to those ranting players, Simylus and Socrates, and in their company acted a third-rate part, gathering from other people's orchards, like a fruit-dealer, a store of figs, grapes, and olives,[3] and wounds too in greater abundance than from the plays themselves, in which you were struggling for your lives, since between you and the spectators there was a truceless, heraldless war, from which you suffered so many wounds that naturally now you taunt as cowards persons who have lacked such experience.

Passing over those doings of yours which might be charged to poverty, I shall proceed to accusations against your character. When it occurred to you to enter upon public life, you chose such

[1] As an orator Æschines was famous for his clear, powerful voice.

[2] Here is an insinuation that Æschines had no right to the citizenship but had himself enrolled by fraud.

[3] The spectators pelted the actors with fruit, which proved a greater source of profit to the players than was their ill-paid profession.

a policy that while your country prospered, you lived the life of a hare, fearing and trembling lest you might suffer a flogging for the crimes you were conscious of, but whenever the rest of the citizens were unfortunate, you have displayed your effrontery in the eyes of all. Yet he who has been emboldened by the slaughter of a thousand fellow-citizens — what punishment ought he to suffer at the hands of the living? [1] Although I could say much else about him, I pass it by; for I consider it proper to rehearse, not all his baseness and infamy, but so much as is not disgraceful for me to repeat.

Well then, Æschines, compare these two lives, yours and mine, with one another, calmly but not in bitterness, and ask these jurors which of the two fortunes each one of them would prefer. You taught reading; I attended school. You performed initiations; I was initiated. You danced; I was choregus. You were a public scribe; I a public orator. You were a third-rate actor; I a spectator at the play. You failed in your part, and I hissed you.

153. Attitude of Free Athenians toward Labor

(Xenophon, *Memorabilia*, ii. 7, 8)

The time of the conversation between Socrates and Aristarchus, given in § 7, was under the Thirty (Botsford, *Hellenic History*, ch. xxi), when economic as well as political conditions were extremely unfavorable. It is noteworthy that even in these times a man like Ceramon, with a few slaves, could do a profitable business. Interesting, too, is the fact that the women of well-to-do families were required to learn spinning, weaving, the making of clothes, and other household duties in order to be able to instruct and to superintend slaves.

In § 8 Eutherus is one of many Athenian citizens whose whole capital had been invested in the states of the allies, and who were therefore deprived of their all by the downfall of the Athenian empire, 404. That the position of manager of an estate should be looked upon as servile is utterly foreign to modern ideas. To be free, the Greek felt that he must not be held accountable to another for anything.

7. He (Socrates) had two ways of dealing with the difficulties of his friends; where ignorance was the cause, he tried to meet the trouble by a dose of common sense; or where want and pov-

[1] As a partisan of Philip and Alexander of Macedon, Æschines is here said to have profited by the success of the enemy and the misfortunes of his own country.

erty were to blame, by teaching them that they should assist one another according to their ability; and here I may mention certain incidents which occurred within my own knowledge. How, for instance, he chanced upon Aristarchus wearing the look of one who suffered from a fit of the "sullens," and thus accosted him: —

SOCRATES. You seem to have some trouble on your mind, Aristarchus; if so, you should share it with your friends. Perhaps together we might lighten the weight of it a little.

ARISTARCHUS. Yes, Socrates, I am in sore straits indeed. Ever since the party strife declared itself in the city, what with the rush of people to Peiræus and the wholesale banishments, I have been fairly at the mercy of my poor female relatives. Sisters, nieces, cousins, they all come flocking to me for protection. I have fourteen free-born souls, I tell you, under my single roof, and how are we to live? We can get nothing out of the soil — that is in the hands of the enemy; nothing from my house property, for there is scarcely a living soul left in the city; my furniture? no one will buy it; money? there is none to be borrowed — you would have a better chance to find it by looking for it on the road than to borrow it from a banker. Yes, Socrates, to stand by and see one's relatives die of hunger is hard indeed, and yet to feed so many at such a pinch impossible.

After he had listened to the story Socrates asked: How comes it that Ceramon, with so many mouths to feed, not only contrives to furnish himself and them with the necessaries of life, but to realize a handsome surplus, whilst you being in like plight are afraid that you will one and all perish of starvation for want of the necessaries of life?

AR. Why, bless you, do you not see he has only slaves and I have free-born souls to feed?

SOC. And which should you say were the better human beings, the free-born members of your household or Ceramon's slaves?

AR. The free souls under my roof without a doubt.

SOC. Is it not a shame, then, that he with his baser folk to back him should be in easy circumstances, while you and your far superior household are in difficulties?

AR. To be sure it is, when he has only a set of handicraftsmen to feed, and I my liberally-educated household.

Soc. What is a handicraftsman? Does not the term apply to all who can make any sort of useful product or commodity?

Ar. Certainly.

Soc. Barley-meal is a useful product, is it not?

Ar. Preëminently so.

Soc. And loaves of bread?

Ar. No less.

Soc. Well, and what do you say to cloaks for men and for women — tunics, mantles, vests?

Ar. Yes, they are all highly useful commodities.

Soc. Then your household do not know how to make any of them.

Ar. On the contrary, I believe they can make them all.

Soc. Then you are not aware that by means of the manufacture of one of these alone — his barley-meal store — Nausicydes not only maintains himself and his domestics, but many pigs and cattle besides, and realizes such large profits that he frequently contributes to the state benevolences; while there is Cyrebus, again, who out of a bread factory, more than maintains the whole of his establishment, and lives in the lap of luxury; and Demeas of Collytus gets a livelihood out of a cloak business, and Menon as a mantle-maker; and thus more than half the Megarians maintain themselves by the making of vests.

Ar. Bless me, yes! They have got a set of barbarian fellows, whom they purchase and keep, to manufacture by forced labor whatever takes their fancy. My kinswomen, I tell you, are free-born ladies.

Soc. Then, on the ground that they are free-born and your kinswomen, you think they ought to do nothing but eat and sleep? Or is it your opinion that people who live in this way — I speak of free-born people in general — lead happier lives, and are more to be congratulated, than those who give their time and attention to such useful arts of life as they are skilled in? Is this what you see in the world, that for the purpose of learning what it is well to know, and of recollecting the lessons taught, or with a view to health and strength of body, or for the sake of acquiring and preserving all that gives life its charm, idleness and inattention are found to be helpful, whilst work and study are simply a dead loss?

Pray, when those relatives of yours were taught what you tell me they know, did they learn it as barren information which they would never turn to practical account, or on the contrary, as something with which they were to be seriously concerned some day, and from which they were to reap solid advantage? Do human beings in general attain to well-tempered manhood by a course of idling, or by carefully attending to what will be of use? Which will help a man the more to grow in justice and uprightness, to be up and doing, or to sit with folded hands revolving the ways and means of existence? As things now stand, if I am not mistaken, there is no love lost between you. You cannot help feeling that they are costly to you, and they must see that you find them a burden. This is a perilous state of affairs, in which hatred and bitterness have every prospect of increasing whilst the preëxisting bond of affection is likely to be snapped.

But now, if you will only allow them free scope for their energies, when you come to see how useful they can be, you will grow quite fond of them, and they, when they perceive that they can please you, will cling to their benefactor warmly. Thus, with the memory of former kindnesses gratitude will increase; you will in consequence be knit in closer bonds of love and domesticity. If, indeed, they were called upon to do any shameful work, let them choose death rather than that; but now they know, it would seem, the very arts and accomplishments which are regarded as the loveliest and the most suitable for women; and the things which we know, any of us, are just those which we can best perform, that is to say, with ease and expedition; it is a joy to do them, and the result is beautiful. Do not hesitate then, to initiate your friends in what will bring advantage to them and you alike; probably they will gladly respond to your summons.

Ar. Well, upon my word, I like so well what you say, Socrates, that though hitherto I have not been disposed to borrow, knowing that when I had spent what I got I should not be in a condition to repay, I think I can now bring myself to do so in order to raise a fund for these works.

Thereupon a capital was provided; wools were purchased; the goodman's relatives set to work, and even whilst they breakfasted they worked, and on and on till work was ended and they supped. Smiles took the place of frowns; they no longer looked askance with suspicion, but full into each other's eyes with happiness. They loved their kinsman for his kindness to them. He became attached to them as helpmates; and the end of it all was, he came to Socrates and told him with delight how matters fared; "and now," he added, "they tax me with being the only drone in the house, who sit and eat the bread of idleness."

To which Socrates replied: Why do you not tell them the fable of the dog? Once on a time, so goes the story, when beasts could speak, the sheep said to their master, "What a marvel is this, master, that to us, your own sheep, who provide you with fleeces and lambs and cheese, you give nothing, save only what we may nibble off earth's bosom; but with this dog of yours, who provides you with nothing of the sort, you share the very meat out of your mouth." When the dog heard these words, he answered promptly, "Ay, in good sooth, for is it not I who keep you safe and sound, you sheep, so that you are not stolen by man nor harried by wolves; since, if I did not keep watch over you, you would not be able so much as to graze afield, fearing to be destroyed." And, so says the tale, the sheep had to admit that the dog was rightly preferred to themselves in honor. And so do you tell your flock yonder that like the dog in the fable you are their guardian and overseer, and it is thanks to you that they are protected from evil and evildoers, so that they work their work and live their lives in blissful security.[1]

8. At another time chancing upon an old friend (Eutherus) whom he had not seen for a long while, he greeted him thus: —

Soc. What quarter of the world do you hail from, Eutherus?

Eutherus. From abroad, just before the close of the war; but at present from the city itself. You see, since we have been denuded of our possessions across the frontier, and my father left

[1] From the attitude of Aristarchus at the opening of the conversation it is evident that labor had been tainted by slavery. This feeling is offset by the sentiment developed near the close of the conversation that those only who work have a right to eat; *cf.* Aristotle, *Rhetoric*, ii. 4. 8, 1381 a: "We honor the generous and brave and the just. Such we conceive to be those who do not live upon others; and such are they who live by labor — chiefly agriculturists, and chief among the agriculturists, the small farmers." As long as these sentiments prevailed, it was possible for free laborers to maintain their self-respect.

me nothing in Attica, I must needs bide at home, and provide myself with the necessaries of life by means of bodily toil, which seems preferable to begging from another, especially as I have no security on which to raise a loan.

Soc. And how long do you expect your body to be equal to providing the necessaries of life for hire?

Euth. Goodness knows, Socrates — not for long.

Soc. And when you find yourself an old man, expenses will not diminish and yet no one will care to pay you for the labor of your hands.

Euth. That is true.

Soc. Would it not be better then to apply yourself at once to such work as will stand you in good stead when you are old — that is, address yourself to some large proprietor who needs an assistant in managing his estate? By superintending his works, helping to get in his crops, and guarding his property in general, you will be a benefit to the estate and be benefited in return.[1]

Euth. I could not endure the yoke of slavery, Socrates!

Soc. And yet the heads of departments in a state are not regarded as adopting the badge of slavery because they manage the public property, but as having attained a higher dignity of freedom rather.

Euth. In a word, Socrates, the idea of being held to account to another is not at all to my taste.

Soc. And yet, Eutherus, it would be hard to find a work which did not involve some liability to account: in fact it is difficult to do anything without some mistake or other, and no less difficult, if you should succeed in doing it immaculately, to escape all unfriendly criticism. I wonder now whether you will find it easy to get through your present occupations entirely without reproach. No? Let me tell you what you should do. You should avoid censorious persons and attach yourself to the considerate and kindhearted, and in all your affairs accept with good grace what you can and decline what you feel you cannot do. Whatever it be, do it heart and soul, and make it your finest work. There lies the method at once to silence faultfinders and to minister help to your

[1] Positions of this kind, as shown by Xenophon, *Economicus*, were often filled by slaves, but it is clear from this passage that freemen, too, were employed in them.

own difficulties. Life will flow smoothly, risks will be diminished, provision against old age secured.

154. The Management of a Household

(Xenophon, *Economicus*. Dakyns, revised by E. G. S.)

The Greek word for economy, οἰκονομία, signifies "management of a household." In the fourth century as society developed a greater complexity, human activities became more specialized, and the increasing knowledge relating to the various activities was systematized and in many cases reduced to writing. In this way economy came into existence as a branch of science. The treatise of Xenophon entitled *Economicus*, "The Economist," is an example of economic science representative of the period under consideration. Much space is devoted to the same subject by Aristotle in his *Politics*. Another *Economicus*, wrongly ascribed to Aristotle, was composed by some person unknown to us, who however was a man of sound judgment and well acquainted with Hellenic affairs. The pseudo-Aristotelian treatise therefore is a source of great value.

Xenophon's *Economicus*, with which we are now dealing, is one of the most valuable contributions to the history of Hellenic civilization during the fourth century. In the excerpts given below the conversation is for a time between Socrates and Critobulus. The latter is evidently a politician, who devotes most of his time and money to winning supporters as well as to his actual public duties. As he totally neglects his estate, its value and productiveness remain stationary, and he is always in want of money. Occasionally an ancient writer and, to a far greater extent, scholars of to-day criticize the Greek democracy on the ground that it so burdened the wealthy as to make their life unendurable. The expenses imposed upon the wealthy were in fact considerable; but no Athenian family is known to have been financially ruined, or greatly damaged, by its public burdens; and Critobulus, a typical example, makes no complaint, for he seems to feel that he receives an equivalent for his outlay. Some fortunes were undermined by luxury, vice, and neglect; and on the other hand, careful attention to business seems to have been all that was necessary for the building up of prosperity.

Especially interesting is the subject of the principal excerpt — the place of the wife in the management of the household. Some thinkers of the age were of the opinion that there were no differences between women and men, that women should have the same education as men, and should follow the same occupations, even politics and war. This is the view urged in Plato's *Republic*, and ridiculed in Aristophanes' *Ecclesiazusæ*. Xenophon, on the contrary, was convinced that women, though the equals of men, were in important respects essentially different, and that there should accordingly be a division of labor — that the sphere of woman or of man was only a hemisphere. This view is charmingly presented.

I. I once heard him discuss the topic of economy after the following manner. Addressing Critobulus, he said: Tell me, Critobulus, is "economy," like the words "medicine," "carpentry," "building," "smithying," "metal-working," and so forth, the name of a particular kind of knowledge or science?

CRITOBULUS. Yes, I think so.

SOCRATES. And as, in the case of the arts just named, we can state the proper work or function of each, can we similarly state the proper work and function of economy?

CRIT. It must, I should think, be the business of the good economist at any rate to manage his own house or estate well.

SOC. And supposing another man's house to be entrusted to him, he would be able, if he chose, to manage it as skilfully as his own, would he not? since a man who is skilled in carpentry can work as well for another as for himself; and this ought to be equally true of the good economist?

CRIT. Yes, I think so, Socrates.

SOC. Then there is no reason why a proficient in this art, even if he does not happen to possess wealth of his own, should not be paid a salary for managing a house, just as he might be paid for building one?

CRIT. None at all; and a large salary he would be entitled to earn if, after paying the necessary expenses of the estate entrusted to him, he can create a surplus and improve the property.

SOC. Well and this word "house," what are we to understand by it? the domicile merely? or are we to include all a man's possessions outside the actual dwelling-place?

CRIT. Certainly, in my opinion at any rate, everything which a man has, even though some portion of it may lie in another part of the world from that in which he lives, forms part of his estate. . . .

CRIT. I want to talk about persons of high degree,[1] of right noble family some of them, to do them justice. These are the people I have in my mind's eye, gifted with, it may be, martial or, it may be, civil accomplishments, which however they refuse

[1] The passage beginning here is evidence that when the property of a well-to-do Athenian fell to ruin, the fault was his own, not the democracy's. Xenophon, it is to be noted, was anti-democratic, and his testimony is therefore all the more valuable.

to exercise, for the very reason, as I take it, that they have no masters over them.

Soc. No masters over them! but how can that be if, in spite of their prayers for prosperity and their desire to do what will bring them good, they are still so sorely hindered in the exercise of their wills by those that lord it over them?

Crit. And who, pray, are these lords that rule them and yet remain unseen?

Soc. Nay, not unseen; on the contrary, they are very visible. And what is more, they are the basest of the base, as you can hardly fail to note, if at least you believe idleness and effeminacy and restless negligence to be baseness. Then, too, there are other treacherous beldames giving themselves out to be innocent pleasures, to wit, dicings and profitless associations among men. These in the fulness of time appear in all their nakedness even to them that are deceived, showing themselves that they are after all but pains tricked out and decked with pleasures. These are they who have the dominion over those you speak of and quite hinder them from every good and useful work.

Crit. But there are others, Socrates, who are not hindered by these indolences — on the contrary, they have the most ardent disposition to exert themselves, and by every means to increase their revenues; but in spite of all, they wear out their substance and are involved in endless difficulties.

Soc. Yes, for they too are slaves, and harsh enough are their taskmasters; slaves are they to luxury and lechery, vice, intemperance and the winecup along with many a fond and ruinous ambition. These passions so cruelly lord it over the poor soul whom they have under their thrall, that so long as he is in the heyday of health and strong to labor, they compel him to fetch and carry and lay at their feet the fruit of his toils, and to spend it on their own heart's lusts; but so soon as he is seen to be incapable of further labor through old age, they leave him to his gray hairs and misery, and turn to seize on other victims. Ah! Critobulus, against these vices must we wage ceaseless war, for very freedom's sake, no less than if they were armed warriors endeavoring to make us their slaves. Nay, foemen in war, it must be granted, especially when of fair and noble type, have many times ere now proved benefactors to those they have enslaved. By dint of chastening, they have forced the vanquished to become the better men and to lead more tranquil lives in future. But these despotic queens never cease to plague and torment their victims in body and soul and substance till their sway is ended.

II. The conversation was resumed by Critobulus, and on this wise. He said: I think I take your meaning fully, Socrates, about these matters; and for myself, examining my heart, I am further satisfied, I have sufficient continence and self-command in those respects. If therefore you will only advise me what I am to do to improve my estate, I flatter myself I shall not be hindered by those despotic dames, as you call them. Come, do not hesitate; only tender me what good advice you can, and trust me I will follow it. But perhaps, Socrates, you have already passed sentence on us — we are rich enough already, and not in need of any further wealth?

Soc. It is to myself rather, if I may be included in your plural "we," that I should apply the remark. *I* am not in need of any further wealth, if you like. I am rich enough already, to be sure. But you, Critobulus, I look upon as singularly poor, and at times, upon my soul, I feel a downright compassion for you.

At this view of his case, Critobulus fell to laughing outright, retorting: And pray, Socrates, what in the name of fortune do you suppose our respective properties would fetch in the market, yours and mine?

If I could find a good purchaser, he answered, I suppose the whole of my effects, including the house in which I live, might very fairly realize five minæ. Yours, I am positively certain, would fetch at the lowest more than a hundred times that sum.[1]

Crit. With this estimate of our respective fortunes, can you still maintain that you have no need of further wealth, that it is rather I who am to be pitied for my poverty?

Soc. Yes, for my property is amply sufficient to meet my

[1] As a mina was about eighteen dollars, the estate of Socrates is here estimated at about ninety dollars. As he had served in the heavy infantry, he must have been a zeugite. It is true that the state equipped some thetes for heavy-infantry service at its own expense, but in that case it preferred younger men than Socrates must have been at the time of his campaigns. During his service his estate must have been valued at no less than ten minas; *cf.* Botsford, *Hellenic History*, ch. xx.

wants, whereas you, considering the parade you are fenced about with, and the reputation you must needs live up to, would be barely well off, I take it, if what you have already were multiplied by three.

CRIT. Pray, how may that be?

SOC. Why, first and foremost, I see you are called upon to offer many costly sacrifices, failing which, I take it, neither gods nor men would tolerate you; and, in the next place, you are bound to welcome numerous foreigners as guests, and to entertain them handsomely; thirdly, you must feast your fellow-citizens and ply them with all sorts of kindness, or else be cut adrift from your supporters. Furthermore, I perceive that even at present the state enjoins upon you various large contributions, such as the rearing of horses, the training of choruses, the superintendence of gymnastic schools, or the entertainment of great numbers of aliens in magnificent style;[1] while in the event of war you will, I am aware, have further obligations laid upon you in the shape of money to carry on the trierarchy,[2] and the payment of war taxes so onerous, you will find difficulty in supporting them. Remissness in respect of any of these charges will be visited upon you by the good citizens of Athens no less strictly than if they caught you stealing their own property. But worse than all, I see you fondling the notion that you are rich. Without a thought or care how to increase your revenue, your fancy lightly turns to thoughts of love, as if you had some special license to amuse yourself. . . . That is why I pity and compassionate you, fearing lest some irremediable mischief overtake you, and you find yourself in desperate straits. As for me, if I ever stood in need of anything, I am sure you know I have friends who would assist me. They would make some trifling contribution — trifling to themselves, I mean — and deluge my humble living with a flood of plenty. But your friends, albeit far better off than yourself, considering your respective styles of living, persist in looking to you for assistance.

[1] Critobulus was probably proxenus, consular representative, of some foreign state, and had therefore to entertain in magnificent style the representatives of that state when they visited Athens.

[2] On the trierarchy, choregia, and other liturgies, see Botsford, *Hellenic History*, ch. xii (with references).

CRIT. I cannot gainsay what you have spoken, Socrates; it is indeed high time that you were constituted my patronus, or I shall become in very truth a pitiable object. . . .

SOC. I had been struck with amazement, I remember, to observe on some occasion that where a set of people are engaged in identical operations, half of them are in absolute indigence and the other half roll in wealth. I bethought me, the history of the matter was worth investigation. Accordingly I set to work investigating, and I found that it all happened very naturally. Those who carried on their affairs in a haphazard manner I saw were punished by their losses; whilst those who kept their wits upon the stretch and paid attention I soon perceived to be rewarded by the greater ease and profit of their undertakings. It is to these I would recommend you to betake yourself. What say you? Learn of them; and unless the will of God oppose, I venture to say you will become as clever a man of business as one might hope to see. . . .

Or take, again, the instance of two farmers engaged in cultivating farms as like as possible. The one has never done asserting that agriculture has been his ruin, and is in the depth of despair; the other has all he needs in abundance and of the best, and how acquired? — by this same agriculture.[1] . . .

IV. The base mechanic arts, so called, have got a bad name; and what is more, are held in ill repute by civilized communities, and not unreasonably; seeing they are the ruin of the bodies of all concerned in them, workers and overseers alike, who are forced to remain in sitting postures and to hug the gloom, or else to crouch whole days confronting a furnace. Hand in hand with physical enervation follows apace an enfeebling of soul, while the demand which these base mechanic arts make on the time of those employed in them leaves them no leisure to devote to the claims of friendship and the state. How can such folk be other than sorry friends and

[1] It is an interesting fact that in the fourth century, when agricultural conditions were less favorable than they had been in the fifth, it was still possible for a farmer with intelligence and energy, not merely to maintain himself, but to accumulate property. Ischomachus made a fortune by buying up decadent farms, improving them, and selling them at a profit. Many abandoned their farms to engage in trade in Peiræus or the City, while on the other hand prosperous citizens were glad to invest their savings in land, because of its security, even though the profits were small.

ill defenders of the fatherland? So much so that in some states, especially those reputed to be warlike, no citizen is allowed to exercise any mechanical craft at all.[1]

Crit. Then which are the arts you would counsel us to engage in?

Soc. Well, we shall not be ashamed, I hope, to imitate the king of Persia? That monarch, it is said, regards amongst the noblest and most necessary pursuits two in particular, which are the arts of husbandry and war, and in these two he takes the strongest interest.[2] . . .

VI. Crit. I think I am fully persuaded as to the propriety of making agriculture the basis of life. I see it is altogether noblest, best and pleasantest so to do. But I should like to revert to your remark that you understood the reason why the tillage of one man brings him in an abundance of all he needs, while the operations of another fail to make husbandry a profitable employment. I would gladly hear from you an explanation of both these points, so that I may adopt the right and avoid the harmful course.

Soc. Well, Critobulus, suppose I narrate to you from the beginning how I came in contact with a man who of all men I ever met seemed to me to deserve the appellation of a gentleman. He was indeed a "beautiful and good" man.[3]

Crit. There is nothing I should better like to hear, since of all titles this is the one I covet most the right to bear.

Soc. Well, then, I will tell you how I came to subject him to my inquiry. It did not take me long to go the round of various good carpenters, good bronze-workers, painters, sculptors, and so forth. A brief period was sufficient for the contemplation of themselves and of their most admired works of art. But when it came to examining those who bore the high-sounding title "beautiful

[1] This view was held also by Plato and Aristotle, and in fact prevailed among both Greeks and Romans.

[2] While on the expedition into the Persian empire described in his *Anabasis* Xenophon had an opportunity to observe the interest of the Persian king in agriculture, and was, like Herodotus, sufficiently broad-minded to admit that the Greeks could take many profitable lessons of the Persians.

[3] The Greek phrase for the perfect gentleman is **καλὸς καὶ ἀγαθός,** literally "beautiful and good." The word for beautiful assumed an ethical coloring, as the Greeks were inclined to measure things by an esthetic standard.

and good," in order to ascertain what conduct on their part justified their adoption of this title, I found my soul eager with desire for intercourse with one of them; and first of all, seeing that the epithet "beautiful" was conjoined with that of "good," every beautiful person I saw, I must needs approach in my endeavor to discover, if haply I might somewhere see the quality of good adhering to the quality of beauty. But, after all, it was otherwise ordained. I soon enough seemed to discover that some of those who in their outward form were beautiful were in their inmost selves the veriest knaves. Accordingly I made up my mind to let go beauty, which appeals to the eye, and address myself to one of those "beautiful and good" people so entitled. And since I heard of Ischomachus as one who was so called by all the world, both men and women,[1] strangers and citizens alike, I set myself to make acquaintance with him.

VII. It chanced, one day I saw him seated in the portico of Zeus Eleutherios,[2] and as he appeared to be at leisure, I went up to him and, sitting down by his side, accosted him: How is this, Ischomachus? you seated here, you who are so little wont to be at leisure? As a rule, when I see you, you are doing something, or at any rate not sitting idle in the market-place.

Nor would you see me now so sitting, Socrates, he answered, but that I promised to meet some strangers, friends of mine, at this place.

And when you have no such business on hand, I said, where in heaven's name do you spend your time and how do you employ yourself? I will not conceal from you how anxious I am to learn from your own lips by what conduct you have earned for yourself the title "beautiful and good." It is not by spending your days indoors at home, I am sure; the whole habit of your body bears witness to a different sort of life.

Then Ischomachus, smiling at my question, but also, as it seemed to me, a little pleased to be asked what he had done to

[1] Incidentally Greek writers inform us that in fact the sexes were not so strictly separated as is generally believed. Many women of Athens had seen and admired Ischomachus.

[2] The portico of Zeus Eleutherios ("the Liberator"), bordering upon the market place, was a social resort.

earn the title "beautiful and good," made answer: Whether that is the title by which folk call me when they talk to you about me, I cannot say. All I know is, when they challenge me to exchange properties, or else to perform some service to the state instead of them, the fitting out of a trireme, or the training of a chorus, nobody thinks of asking for the beautiful and good gentleman, but it is plain Ischomachus, the son of So-and-so, upon whom the summons is served. But to answer your question, Socrates, he proceeded, I certainly do not spend my days indoors, if for no other reason, because my wife is quite capable of managing our domestic affairs without my aid.

Ah! said I, Ischomachus, that is just what I should like particularly to learn from you. Did you yourself educate your wife to be all that a wife should be, or when you received her from her father and mother was she already a proficient, well skilled to discharge the duties appropriate to a wife?

Well skilled! he replied. What proficiency was she likely to bring with her, when she was not quite fifteen at the time she wedded me, and during the whole period of her life had been most carefully brought up to see and hear as little as possible, and to ask the fewest questions? or do you not think one should be satisfied, if at marriage her whole experience consisted in knowing how to take the wool and make a dress, and seeing how her mother's handmaidens had their daily spinning-tasks assigned them? For, he added, as regards control of appetite and self-indulgence, she had received the soundest education, and that I take to be the most important matter in the bringing-up of man or woman.

Then all else, said I, you taught your wife yourself, Ischomachus, until you had made her capable of attending carefully to her appointed duties?

That did I not, replied he, until I had offered sacrifice, and prayed that I might teach and she might learn all that could conduce to the happiness of us twain.

Soc. And did your wife join in sacrifice and prayer to that effect?

Isch. Most certainly, with many a vow registered to heaven to become all she ought to be; and her whole manner showed that she would not be neglectful of what was taught her.

SOC. Pray narrate to me, Ischomchus, I beg of you, what you first essayed to teach her. To hear that story would please me more than any description of the most splendid gymnastic contest or horse-race you could give me.

ISCH. Why, Socrates, when after a time she had become accustomed to my hand, that is, was tamed sufficiently to play her part in a discussion, I put to her this question: "Did it ever strike you to consider, dear wife, what led me to choose you as my wife among all women, and your parents to entrust you to me of all men? It was certainly not from any difficulty that might beset either of us to find another mate. That I am sure is evident to you. No! it was with deliberate intent to discover, I for myself and your parents in behalf of you, the best partner of house and children we could find, that I sought you out; and your parents, acting to the best of their ability, made choice of me. If at some future time God grant us to have children born to us, we will take counsel together how best to bring them up, for that too will be a common interest, and a common blessing, if haply they shall live to fight our battles and we find in them hereafter support and succor when ourselves are old. But at present there is our house here, which belongs alike to both. It is common property, for all that I possess goes by my will into the common fund, and in the same way all that you deposited was placed by you to the common fund. We need not stop to calculate in figures which of us contributed most, but rather let us lay to heart this fact that whichever of us proves the better partner, he or she at once contributes what is most worth having."

Thus I addressed her, Socrates, and thus my wife made answer: "But how can I assist you? what is my ability? Nay, everything depends on you. My business, my mother told me, was to be sober-minded!"

"Most true, my wife," I replied, "and that is what my father said to me. But what is the proof of sober-mindedness in man or woman? Is it not so to behave that what they have of good may ever be at its best, and that new treasures from the same source of beauty and righteousness may be most amply added?"

"But what is there that I can do," my wife inquired, "which will help to increase our joint estate?"

"Assuredly," I answered, "you may strive to do as well as possible what Heaven has given you a natural gift for and which the law approves."

"And what may these things be?" she asked.

"To my mind they are not the things of least importance," I replied, "unless the things which the queen bee in her hive presides over are of slight importance to the bee community; for the gods, my wife, would seem to have exercised much care and judgment in compacting that twin-system which goes by the name of male and female, so as to secure the greatest possible advantage to the pair. Since no doubt the underlying principle of the bond is first and foremost to perpetuate through procreation the races of living creatures; and next, as the outcome of this bond, for human beings at any rate, a provision is made by which they may have sons and daughters to support them in old age.

"And again, the way of human beings, not being maintained like that of cattle in the open air, obviously demands roofed homesteads. But if these same human beings are to have anything to bring in under cover, some one to carry out these labors of the field under high heaven must be found them, since such operations as the breaking up of fallow with the plough, the sowing of seed, the planting of trees, the pasturing and herding of flocks, are one and all open-air employments on which the supply of products necessary to life depends.

"As soon as these products of the field are safely housed and under cover, new needs arise. There must be some one to guard the store and some one to perform such operations as imply the need of shelter. Shelter, for instance, is needed for the rearing of infant children; shelter is needed for the various processes of converting the fruits of earth into food, and in like manner for the fabrication of clothing out of wool.

"But whereas both of these, the indoor and the outdoor occupations alike, demand new toil and new attention, to meet the case," I added, "God made provision from the first by shaping, as it seems to me, the woman's nature for indoor and the man's for outdoor occupations. Man's body and soul He furnished with a greater capacity for enduring heat and cold, wayfaring and military marches, or, to repeat, He laid upon his shoulders the outdoor works.

"While in creating the body of woman with less capacity for these things, God would seem to have imposed on her the indoor works; and knowing that He had implanted in the woman and imposed upon her the nurture of new-born babes, He endowed her with a larger share of affection for the new-born child than He bestowed upon man. And since He had imposed on woman the guardianship of the things imported from without, God, in His wisdom, perceiving that a fearful spirit was no detriment to guardianship, endowed the woman with a larger measure of timidity than He bestowed on man. Knowing further that he to whom the outdoor works belonged would need to defend them against malign attack, He endowed the man in turn with a larger share of courage.

"And seeing that both alike feel the need of living and receiving, He set down memory and carefulness between them for their common use, so that you would find it hard to determine whether of the two, the male or the female, has the larger share of these. So, too, God set down between them for their common use the gift of self-control, where needed, adding only to that one of the twain, whether man or woman, which should prove the better, the power to be rewarded with a larger share of this perfection. For the very reason that their natures are not alike adapted to like ends, they stand in greater need of one another; and the married couple is made more useful to itself, the one fulfilling what the other lacks.

"Now, being well aware of this, my wife, and knowing well what things are laid upon us twain by God Himself, must we not strive to perform, each in the best way possible, our respective duties? Law, too, gives her consent — law and the usage of mankind, by sanctioning the wedlock of man and wife; and just as God ordained them to be partners in their children, so the law established their common ownership of house and estate. Custom, moreover, proclaims as beautiful those excellences of man and woman with which God gifted them at birth. Thus for a woman to bide tranquilly at home rather than roam abroad is no dishonor; but for a man to remain indoors, instead of devoting himself to outdoor pursuits, is a thing discreditable. But if a man does things contrary to the nature given by God, the chances are, such insubordination escapes not the eye of Heaven: he pays the penalty, whether of neglecting his own works, or of performing those appropriate to woman."

I added: " Just such works, if I mistake not, that same queen-bee we spoke of labors hard to perform, like yours, my wife, enjoined upon her by God Himself."

"And what sort of works are these?" she asked; "what has the queen-bee to do that she seems so like myself, or I like her in what I have to do!"

"Why," I answered, "she too stays in the hive and suffers not the other bees to idle. Those whose duty it is to work outside she sends forth to their labors; and all that each of them brings in, she notes and receives and stores against the day of need; but when the season for use has come, she distributes a just share to each. Again, it is she who presides over the fabric of choicely-woven cells within. She looks to it that warp and woof are wrought with speed and beauty. Under her guardian eye the brood of young is nursed and reared; but when the days of rearing are past and the young bees are ripe for work, she sends them out as colonists with one of the seed royal to be their leader."

"Shall I then have to do these things?" asked my wife.

"Yes," I answered, "you will need in the same way to stay indoors, despatching to their toils without those of your domestics whose work lies there. Over those whose appointed tasks are wrought indoors, it will be your duty to preside; yours to receive the stuffs brought in; yours to apportion part for daily use, and yours to make provision for the rest, to guard and garner it so that the outgoings destined for a year may not be expended in a month. It will be your duty, when the wools are introduced, to see that clothing is made for those who need; your duty also to see that the dried corn is rendered fit and serviceable for food.

"There is just one of all these occupations which devolve upon you," I added, "you may not find so altogether pleasing. Should any of our household fall sick, it will be your care to see and tend them to the recovery of their health."

"Nay," she answered, "that will be the pleasantest of tasks, if careful nursing may touch the springs of gratitude and leave them friendlier than heretofore."

And I, continued Ischomachus, was struck with admiration at her answer, and replied: "Thank you, my wife, it is through some such traits of forethought seen in their mistress-leader that the hearts of bees are won, and they are so loyally affectioned toward her that, if ever she abandon her hive, not one of them will dream of being left behind; but one and all must follow her."

And my wife made answer to me: "It would much astonish me did not these leaders' works, you speak of, point to you rather than to myself. Methinks mine would be a pretty guardianship and distribution of things indoors without your provident care to see that the importations from without were duly made."

"Just so," I answered, "and mine would be a pretty importation if there were no one to guard what I imported. Do you not see," I added, "how pitiful is the case of those unfortunates who pour water into their sieves for ever, as the story goes, and labor but in vain?"

"Pitiful enough, poor souls," she answered, "if that is what they do."

"But there are other cares, you know, and occupations," I answered, "which are yours by right, and these you will find agreeable. This, for instance: to take some maiden who knows naught of carding wool and to make her a proficient in the art, doubling her usefulness; or to receive another quite ignorant of housekeeping or of service, and to render her skilful, loyal, serviceable, till she is worth her weight in gold; or again, when occasion serves, you have it in your power to requite by kindness the well-behaved whose presence is a blessing to your house; or maybe to chasten the bad character, should such a one appear.[1] But the greatest joy of all will be to prove yourself my better;[2] to make me your faithful follower; knowing no dread lest as the years advance you

[1] The house of the wealthy Athenian was, so to speak, a manufacturing plant, which aimed to produce as much as possible of the material, clothing, food, etc., needed by the members of the household, slave and free. A large number of hands were employed. As the director of this establishment a woman exercised more administrative authority than is now generally conceded to her in the business world, where almost all supervision is entrusted to men.

[2] It was possible for the wife to be not only the equal of her husband but his superior. In the face of such facts, it is absurd to speak of the inferiority of Athenian women of this period.

should decline in honor in your household, but rather trusting that, though your hair turn grey, yet in proportion as you come to be a better helpmate to myself and to the children, a better guardian of our home, so will your honor increase throughout the household as mistress, wife, and mother, daily more dearly prized. Since," I added, "it is not through excellence of outward form, but by reason of the lustre of virtues shed forth upon the life of man, that increase is given to things beautiful and good."

That, Socrates, or something like that, as far as I may trust my memory, records the earliest conversation which I held with her.

155. A Dissolute Spendthrift

(Æschines, *Against Timarchus*, 95–99. Translated by E. G. S.)

Timarchus, a politician of Athens, was a supporter of the anti-Macedonian policy of Demosthenes and therefore an opponent of King Philip's Athenian friend Æschines. In planning the prosecution of Æschines on the charge of having been bribed by Philip in the recent Athenian negotiations with him, Demosthenes secured the coöperation of Timarchus. The latter, however, had incurred a reputation for extreme dissoluteness, immorality of the vilest nature, and spendthriftness. Now there was a law at Athens which debarred such men from public speaking. Æschines accordingly prosecuted Timarchus under this law (345 B.C.), in order to eliminate him as an accuser. The success of Æschines in the prosecution brought the political career of Timarchus to an ignoble end. The entire oration against Timarchus is a valuable source for social conditions at Athens. The passage translated below is especially instructive for the light it throws upon the possessions of a well-to-do Athenian of the age of Demosthenes, and for its presentation of a typical spendthrift, merely suggested in the preceding excerpt from Xenophon, *Economicus*. The ruin of estates was due to conduct here described rather than to governmental oppression; Blass, *Demosthenes' Genossen und Gegner*, 167 *sqq.*

(95) When this (property)[1] too had disappeared and had been squandered in gambling and gluttony . . . and his abominable and wicked nature always maintained the same appetites, and in an excess of incontinence imposed command upon command and dissipated wealth in his daily life, then he turned to consuming his paternal estate. (96) Thus not only did he eat it up, but if

[1] The property here referred to is described above as coming to his use through his connections with a certain Hegesander.

one may use the expression, he even drank it up. Not for a proper price did he alienate his several possessions, nor did he wait for the opportunity of gain or advantage, but he used to sell for whatever price a thing would bring, so strenuously did he pursue his pleasures. (97) His father had left him an estate from which another man might even have discharged the expensive and gratuitous public functions (liturgies),[1] but he could not even maintain it for his own advantage. He had a house behind the Acropolis,[2] another in the outlying district, in the deme[3] Sphettus; in the deme Alopecê another place, and in addition slaves who were skilled in the shoemaker's trade, nine or ten of them, each of whom brought this man an income of two obols[4] a day, and the foreman of the shop three obols; also a woman slave who understood how to weave the fibre of Amorgos,[5] and a man slave who was a broiderer. There were some, too, who owed him money, and besides he possessed personal property. (98) . . . The house in town he sold to Nausicrates the comic poet, and afterward Cleænetus the trainer of choruses bought it of Nausicrates for twenty minas. The estate in the country was sold to Mnesitheus of the deme Myrrhinus. It was a large farm, but fearfully run to weeds under the management of the accused. (99) As to the farm at Alopecê, which is eleven or twelve stadia distant from the walls (of Athens), when his mother entreated and begged him, as I learn, to let it alone and not sell it, but if nothing else, to leave it for her to be buried in, — for all that, even from this place he did not abstain, but this farm too he sold, for 2000 drachmas. Furthermore of the woman slaves and the domestic slaves he left not one, but has sold everything.

[1] On the liturgies, see Botsford, *Hellenic History*, ch. xii.

[2] "Behind the Acropolis" signifies north of the Acropolis, within the city. In plan Athens formed an irregular circle, or as we may say, a wheel, with the Acropolis as a hub. The present passage assumes, as seems to be the case, that the southern section was the residence quarter *par excellence*.

[3] Deme, township. Cleisthenes had divided Attica into more than a hundred demes. On this subject, see Von Schoeffer, Pauly-Wissowa, *Real-Encycl.* V. 1–131.

[4] An obol was about three cents; a mina, mentioned below, about eighteen dollars.

[5] Amorgos, a small island in the Ægean sea, southeast of Naxos. Its most famous product was a fine transparent cloth made of wool, or possibly of cotton; Mau and Hirschfeld, Pauly-Wissowa, *Real-Encycl.* I. 1875, 1876.

156. The Estate and the Legacy of Demosthenes, Father of Demosthenes the Orator

(Demosthenes, xxvii. 4–22; *Against Aphobus*, I. Translated by G. W. B.)

The circumstances under which this speech was delivered are detailed in the passage below. It belongs to the year 363, when Demosthenes was in his twentieth year. It was commonly believed by ancient literary critics that Isæus aided him in the preparation of the group of speeches against his unfaithful guardians. We are informed, too, that as a result of the first oration against Aphobus the jury gave its decision for the recovery of ten talents; but Aphobus obstructed the delivery of the property by further litigation. In the end though Demosthenes recovered little of his property, the reputation he gained in the preparation of these judicial orations and in the general management of his case established him at once as a professional speech-writer, and thus laid the foundation of his fortune.

The excerpt given below is a valuable source of information on fourth-century manufacturing, business investments, legacies, and related matters.

(4) Demosthenes, my father, gentlemen of the jury, died worth nearly fourteen talents. He left me at the age of seven and my sister at five, and our mother, who had brought into the house a dowry of fifty minas. In his plans for us when he was about to die, he entrusted this whole estate to my adversary Aphobus and to Demophon, son of Demon, who were his nephews, one by his brother and the other by his sister, and further to Therippides of Pæania, who was not related to him in blood but who had been a friend from boyhood. To him he gave seventy minas from my estate, to use the interest of it during the whole time until I should become of age, in order that he might not through covetousness injure my estate through any mismanagement. (5) To Demophon he gave my sister with a dowry of two talents, to be paid immediately, whereas to my present adversary he gave my mother in marriage with a dowry of eighty minas and in addition the use of my house and furniture. These dispositions he made with the idea that if he could bind my guardians still more closely to me, their guardianship over me would be the better exercised because of the nearer bond. (6) These men accordingly took their respective legacies from my estate; and assuming the management of the remaining property, they have continued ten years in their guardianship of me. Now at the close of this period they have

handed over to me the house and fourteen slaves and thirty minas in cash — amounting altogether to about seventy minas — but have withheld from me all the rest. (7) This, gentlemen of the jury, is a summary of the wrongs they have done me. That the amount of the property left was what I have stated, they themselves are my chief witnesses; for they assigned me to a symmory to pay a tax on five hundred drachmas for every twenty-five minas of my property, just as do Timotheus, son of Conon, and the wealthiest men in the state. It is better, however, that you should hear in detail what parts of my estate are unproductive and what parts yield an income and how much each part is worth. Having learned these particulars, you will see clearly that of all who have ever acted as guardians none have ever robbed their wards more openly and shamelessly than these men have robbed us. (8) To prove in the first place that they have placed this estimate on my property in the symmory for taxation I will furnish witnesses, and next that my father did not leave me a poor boy or in possession of an estate worth no more than seventy minas, but of such a value that these adversaries could not conceal its magnitude from the state. Take and read this evidence.

(*Testimony*)

(9) From these facts, therefore, the value of my estate is evident. It is worth fifteen talents, and the taxable value is three talents. On that amount did they think it right that I should be taxed. Furthermore if you listen you will learn more precisely about the estate. My father, gentlemen of the jury, left two workshops, each with no inconsiderable trade. One was a sword factory employing thirty-two or thirty-three slaves, most of whom were worth five and six minas apiece, and the rest not less than three minas each; from this plant my father used to receive a net annual income of thirty minas. The other shop was a sofa factory employing twenty couch-makers, mortgaged to my father for forty minas. This plant brought him a net annual income of twelve minas. He left also a talent in money let out on interest at a drachma (a month to the mina), from which the annual interest amounted to more than seven minas. (10) This was the productive capital which he left, the sum of the principal

being four talents and fifty minas, and the income from it being fifty minas each year. Besides these sums he left ivory and iron, which they were using in the shops, and wood for the sofas, worth as much as eighty minas; gall and bronze, too, bought for seventy minas; still further a house worth thirty minas and furniture and plate and gold jewels and garments and adornments of my mother worth in all a hundred minas, and eighty minas in cash within the house. (11) Thus much he left at home. On a maritime venture he had invested seventy minas with Xuthus; he had deposited twenty-four minas in Pasion's bank; six in the bank of Pylades; sixteen he had lent to Demomeles, son of Demon; small sums of two or three minas he had lent to various persons, amounting in all to about a talent. And the sum of these items amounts to more than eight talents and fifty minas. You will find by reckoning that the total value reaches fourteen talents.

(12) This, gentlemen of the jury, is the value of the estate left to us. The portion of it that has been stolen, the amount that each one individually has pilfered, the sums, too, which they are collectively withholding, it is impossible for me to detail in the time allowed me. But I must keep these sums distinct. The portions of my property which Demophon and Therippides are keeping, it will suffice to describe at the time when we shall bring prosecutions against them. The amount, however, which these men prove to be in the hands of my present adversary, which I know that he has taken, I will proceed immediately to describe to you. First the fact that he has the dowry of eighty minas I shall make evident to you, and shall then take up the other items as briefly as I can.

(13) Immediately after our father's death he entered our house and abode in it according to the terms of the will; and he took possession of my mother's gold jewellery and the plate that had been left. Thus he got property to the value of fifty minas; and further when the slaves were sold he received from Therippides and Demophon the value, to complete the dowry of eighty minas. (14) When he had recovered this amount, and was about to sail as trierarch to Corcyra, he left a written statement with Therippides that he had these items, and acknowledged that he had received the dowry. Of these facts, in the first place, Demophon

and Therippides, his colleagues in the guardianship, are witnesses; and further that he acknowledged possession of this amount Demochares of Leuconium, husband of my aunt, and many others have given testimony. For seeing that he did not provide my mother with a living though he had her dowry, and was unwilling to let the house, but insisted on sharing in the management of the property with the other guardians, Demochares had a talk with him on the subject. When my adversary heard these facts, he did not deny having the property or complain that he had not received it, but admitted it all, and said he had a little dispute with my mother regarding her gold trinkets, and would be ready, as soon as that was settled, to do in regard to the question of support and other matters whatever would be agreeable to me. (16) And yet if it shall be proved that he made this admission to Demochares and to all the others who were present, that he has received from Demophon and Therippides the value of the slaves to be counted toward the dowry, and has given to his fellow-guardians a receipt to the effect that he has possession of the dowry; if it shall be proved further that he has occupied the house from the very time when my father died, the fact thus being acknowledged in every point, will it not be clearly established that he recovered the dowry of eighty minas, notwithstanding his present impudent denial of it? To prove that I speak the truth, take and read the testimonies.

(*Testimonies*)

(17) Having received the dowry in this manner, he continued in possession of it. But as he failed to marry my mother, the law directs that he is liable to pay the dowry with interest at nine obols a month; but I shall reckon it at merely a drachma. There results, if anyone will add the principal to the interest for ten years, about three talents. (18) Now I am proving to you that, having thus received this money, he continues to hold it and has confessed the fact in the presence of so many witnesses. Receiving thirty minas besides as the income from the shop, he has attempted to defraud me of this money in the most impudent manner possible. My father left an income of thirty minas from this source; and after these men sold a half of the slaves, I ought to have received

the proportional income of fifteen minas. (19) Therippides, however, who supervised this business for seven years, rendered me an account for eleven minas a year, which is four minas less annually than ought to be calculated. But the defendant, who supervised it during the first two years, renders no account whatever of the profits, but alleges that at times the shop was idle, at other times he did not have charge of it, but that the foreman Milyas, our freedman, managed the shop, so that I ought to ask him for the account. Now if he shall offer any of these excuses, it will be easy to convict him of falsehood. (20) If accordingly he shall say that the business was suspended, he has himself given an account of expenses, not for the provisions of the workmen, but for the trade, — for ivory, for hilts of the swords, and for other material, with the understanding that the artisans were at work. Further he charges me with money paid to Therippides for the hire of three slaves whom he had employed in my shop. And yet if the work was suspended, Therippides ought not to have received wages for his slaves, and I ought not to be charged with these expenses. (21) If on the other hand he shall say that the shop was busy but there was no sale for the commodities, it is doubtless incumbent upon him to prove that he has delivered to me the products of the shop and to furnish witnesses in whose presence he made the delivery. (22) If however he shall make neither of these assertions, but shall allege that Milyas managed this whole business, how can he be believed when he says that he underwent the expenses, amounting to more than five hundred drachmas, and that this Milyas received the profit, if there were any? It seems to me reasonable to suppose that the very opposite has happened: if Milyas supervised the business, he probably paid the expenses and the defendant gathered in the profits; that is the likely thing if we must judge by the general character and the impudence of my adversary. Take these testimonies, then, and read them to the court. . . .

In the fourth century the citizens were grouped according to property into associations called symmories. When direct taxes were levied, which was only in case of war, the symmories of the wealthiest class, to which Demosthenes belonged, had to advance the whole sum and reimburse themselves from the taxes of the less wealthy. A drachma was about 18 cents, a mina was 100 drachmas, a talent 60 minas.

157. Pasion and Phormion

THE TWO MOST FAMOUS BANKERS OF ATHENS

(Demosthenes, *In Behalf of Phormion*. Translated by G. W. B.)

In ancient Greece the only banks which could in any sense be described as public were the temples. In earlier time states and individuals made deposits in them for safe-keeping, and in the course of the fifth and fourth centuries it became increasingly practicable for them to let out these deposits on interest — in other words, to engage in banking business. Private banks were a development from the money-changer's trade, which lay in the hands of slaves and freedmen; hence bankers, too, were often freedmen. The greatest banker of Athens was Pasion, a slave by birth, who learned the business in the firm of his masters (see text *infra*). Having received his freedom, he ultimately began business on his own responsibility. So great was his reputation for honesty that his credit was good for any amount throughout the Hellenic world. The method of banking was to receive deposits on interest, which were then invested on security of land or capital; letters of credit were issued; and sometimes the banker engaged personally in commercial transactions. From the subjoined selection it is clear that often two or more partners engaged in the business, although it should be borne in mind that business corporations were rare and were more or less temporary in character.

Pasion died 370–369, leaving a will, according to which his two sons Apollodorus and Pasicles inherited the greater part of the estate. Phormion, his freedman, was to marry the widow, who was given an ample dowry, and was to act as guardian of Pasicles, who was still a minor. Twenty years after the death of Pasion, 350–349, Apollodorus prosecuted Phormion to recover twenty talents. The speech excerpted below was in defense of Phormion at the trial. The form of defense was a paragraphê — an objection to the bringing of the prosecution, in this instance on the ground that (1) a settlement had already been made by arbitration and a release granted the defendant by the plaintiff, (2) that the claim, if any existed, had been outlawed by time. Necessarily the speech came at the very beginning of the trial. It was so convincing that the jury accepted the plea and the prosecution was quashed. The principal facts necessary for understanding the case are given in the selection. The speech is the most famous of all the private orations of Demosthenes (Blass, *Attische Beredsamkeit,* III. 1. 404). Only those passages are here given which throw light upon the banking business and upon the character of Pasion and Phormion. Other sources on banking are Demosthenes, *Against Stephanus*, I; Isocrates, *Trapeziticus*. See also Böckh, *Staatshaushaltung der Athener*, I. 159–61; Beloch, *Griech. Gesch.* II. 349–52.

Phormion's lack of ability in speaking because of inexperience [1] all of you know, gentlemen of the jury. It is necessary, therefore, for us, his friends, to relate for your information what we know, having often heard him recount these matters. Our object is that you with full knowledge, after correctly ascertaining the facts from us, may vote whatever is just and in accordance with your oaths. (2) We have adopted the paragraphê as our form of procedure, not with a view to confusing the issue by urging the statute of limitations,[2] but that if the defendant can prove that he has committed no wrong whatever, a cessation from trouble may be validated for him by you. Everything that with other people arranges and settles disputes without bringing them to trial before you Phormion has done.[3] (3) He has conferred great benefits on the plaintiff Apollodorus and has justly paid for, or handed over, everything of which he was left manager for the plaintiff, and afterward was released from all claims. Nevertheless, as you see, since the defendant is unable to endure this man's treatment, the latter has maliciously brought against him this suit for twenty talents. I shall endeavor therefore to narrate from the beginning all the transactions of the defendant with Pasion and Apollodorus in the briefest terms. From these facts I know well that the plaintiff's conduct will appear malicious, and that you, having heard these statements, will decide that the case is not actionable.

(4) In the first place you will hear read the articles of agreement, in accordance with which Pasion leased the bank and the shield-factory [4] to the defendant. Take therefore the agreement and the challenge [5] and the testimonies.

[1] The idea is that Phormion's life has been so straightforward as to keep him free from litigation and the practice of speaking before the courts. This is a common device of the orators for winning the sympathy of the jurors.

[2] The period of limitation was five years, during which the plaintiff should have urged his claim.

[3] This statement refers to the bringing of the dispute before arbitrators, a common custom at Athens. In this instance the arbitrators settled the dispute to the satisfaction of both parties, and Apollodorus gave Phormion a written discharge from all claims.

[4] After Pasion had freed Phormion, his slave, he leased to the latter his two branches of business here mentioned.

[5] In this instance the challenge (πρόκλησις) was the formal demand made by Phormion upon Apollodorus for the production of the documents of agreement; *cf.* Meyer und Schömann, *Attischer Process*, 871.

(*Articles of agreement, challenges, testimonies* [1])

These, then, are the articles of agreement by which Pasion leased the bank and the shield-factory to the defendant when the latter became his own master, men of Athens. It is necessary also for you to hear and learn in what way Pasion came to owe eleven talents to the bank. (5) It was not through want that he owed it but because of his enterprise in business; for the landed property of Pasion was worth about twenty talents, and in addition to this amount he had lent out more than fifty talents of his own.[2] Among these fifty talents there were eleven talents from the bank deposits productively invested. (6) The defendant accordingly when he took in lease this business of the bank and received the deposits, seeing that he had not yet been made a citizen by you, and would therefore be unable to recover the amounts lent by Pasion on lands and tenements,[3] — for these reasons he chose to have Pasion debtor to him for this sum rather than the others to whom the loans had been made. Hence it was that Pasion was recorded in the lease as owing the defendant eleven talents, just as the witnesses have testified before you.

(7) In what way the lease was made has been testified before you by the manager of the bank. Afterward, when Pasion fell ill, consider the terms of the will that he made. Take [4] the copy of the will and this challenge and these testimonies made by the persons with whom the will has been deposited.

[1] Generally, as in this instance, the documents have not been preserved with the speech. Alleged documents have often been made up by an ancient editor from the context.

[2] It is clear from what immediately follows that the sum here mentioned was not all surplus, but in part at least deposits. The lands mentioned above had probably been obtained by the foreclosure of mortgages.

[3] An alien could not acquire real estate in Attica, unless granted the right as a special favor. For that reason Phormion, before he became a citizen, could not force the collection of debts on the security of real estate. From this fact we can infer how valuable the citizenship must have been to a business man.

[4] This is an order to the clerk to take the documents and read them to the court. Testimonies had previously been written down and kept for the trial by the magistrate who presided over the court. Witnesses were present to assent to their depositions, but not to give further evidence or submit to cross-questioning.

(*Will, Challenge, Testimonies*)

(8) After Pasion had died, having left this will, Phormion the defendant married the widow as the will directed [1] and became guardian of the (minor) son. As the plaintiff, however, kept appropriating moneys belonging to the common estate, and thought it proper to spend these sums, the guardians reasoned among themselves that, if it should be necessary according to the will to deduct whatever he should spend from the common estate and then divide the remainder, there would in fact be nothing left to divide. For this reason they concluded in behalf of the boy to divide the property forthwith. (9) They made a division, accordingly, of all the estate except the part of which the defendant had taken a lease; and half the revenue from this amount they rendered regularly to the plaintiff. Up to this point how is it possible for him to make any complaint regarding the lease? He ought not to have waited till now but should have expressed his dissatisfaction at the very time. In fact it is impossible for him to deny that he received the rents which afterward became due. (10) When Pasicles became of age and the defendant was discharged from the lease, the plaintiff would not have given him a quittance of all claims, but would at that very time have made his demand, if the defendant owed anything further. To prove that I am speaking the truth, and that the plaintiff divided the estate with his brother when a minor, and that they gave the defendant a quittance of the lease [2] and of all other claims, take this testimony.

(*Testimony*)

(11) Immediately after they had discharged the defendant from the lease, men of Athens, they divided between them the bank and the shield-factory; and Apollodorus, making choice, preferred the shield-factory to the bank. Yet if he had had any private capital [3]

[1] It was a common custom for a man in his will to provide for the remarriage of his wife. This provision was made by Demosthenes, father of the orator; see no. 156.

[2] This quittance was given at the time of the arbitration mentioned above.

[3] The word here translated by "capital," below by "banking stock," is aphormê (ἀφορμή). Such capital differed from ordinary deposits without wholly losing the character of loans. Apollodorus claimed to have twenty talents invested in the bank, a part of which, however, must have been dividend. It was for the recovery of this

in the bank, why would he ever have chosen the factory rather than the bank? Certainly the revenue was not greater but less (the one brought in a talent, the other a hundred minas); nor was the business more agreeable, if indeed he had private capital in the bank. But he did not have it. Therefore he prudently chose the shield-factory; for one was without risk, the other brought a precarious income from other people's property.

(12) Many proofs could be brought forward in evidence that the claim of the plaintiff to banking stock is fraudulent; but in my opinion the most cogent of all evidence of his having received no banking stock is the fact that in the lease Pasion is recorded as owing money to the bank and not as having invested in banking stock, secondly the fact that at the division of the estate the plaintiff made no claim for such a thing, and thirdly, that when he afterward lent the same business to other persons for the same amount of money, it will be proved that he did not let in addition any private banking stock. (13) But surely if he had been deprived by the defendant of anything left by his father, it was his business to provide it from some other source and to hand it over to the lessees. To prove that I am telling the truth, and that he afterward leased (the bank) to Xenon, Euphræus, Euphron, and Callistratus,[1] and that he delivered to them no private banking stock, but leased to them the deposits and the business connected with them, read for me the deposition as to these matters and also as to the fact that he chose the shield-factory. . . .

(28) For my part I wonder, gentlemen of the jury, what in the world the plaintiff Apollodorus will attempt to say in reply to these arguments. Surely he has not supposed that you, seeing him altogether unharmed in property rights, will be angry because Phormion married his mother; for he is not unaware of the fact, nor has it escaped the attention either of him or of many of your number that Socrates the banker, when liberated from his masters,

amount that he brought the suit. Evidently he had no documentary evidence, and we do not know the form of document representing such banking capital.

[1] Here is an example of a partnership of four persons for taking a banking business in lease. Rarely were partnerships made for any other kind of business except for commercial enterprises. In the latter line of business they were usually for a single voyage out and return, whereas in banking they were necessarily of longer duration.

just as this man's father, gave his own wife to Satyrus, who had formerly been his slave. (29) Socles another banker gave his wife to Timodemus, who is still living but who was once his slave. Not only in our state, men of Athens, do persons engaged in this business follow this policy, but also in Ægina Strymodorus gave his wife to Hermæus, his own domestic, and after her death he gave his own daughter to the same person. In fact one would be able to mention many such cases. (30) But to you, men of Athens, who are citizens by descent,[1] it is fitting to prefer no sum of money however great to respectable birth, whereas men who receive the gift of citizenship from you or from other states, and who have been deemed worthy of these honors from their original good fortune in the transaction of business and in their acquisition of properties above the average, must hold to these advantages. Pasion your father, therefore, was not the first and only man to do such a thing, nor did he thereby do violence either to himself or to you his sons, but seeing that the only security to his business lay in his attaching the defendant to you by close ties, he gave the defendant his own wife and your mother. . . .

(43) Regarding the prosperity of Phormion and the idea that he got it from your father and all the matters on which you say you will make inquiry of him, you alone of all men that are, have the least right to call Phormion to account for the source of his possessions. The reason is that not even your father Pasion acquired his wealth by his own invention, nor received it as a heritage from his father, but while he was still with his masters, Antisthenes and Archestratus, in the banking business he gave proof of honesty and uprightness, and therefore won confidence. (44) To men occupied with merchandise and money-making it seems a wonderful thing that the same person should be diligent and honest. Now his masters did not hand over this quality to him but he was himself honest by nature. Nor did your father give this virtue to

[1] The word for "descent," and for "birth" immediately below, is genos (γένος) corresponding to the Latin gens. This is in fact the common meaning of the word in both languages. Noteworthy is the pride of descent in the Athenians as contrasted with the love of money in the men of alien or servile birth. The method of keeping the business going by marrying the foreman to the widow was characteristic of a class who cared more for money than for birth; and Apollodorus, who was merely the son of a freedman, had no reasonable ground for objecting to the custom.

the defendant, for he would have preferred to make you honest instead, had it been in his power. If you are ignorant of this fact that trustworthiness is the greatest asset in business life,[1] you must be ignorant of everything. Apart from these considerations Phormion has in many ways proved useful to your father and to you and to your business generally. . . .

158. A Loan from a Usurer for an Investment

(Alciphron, *Letters*, ii. 5; old eds. i. 26. Translated by G. W. B.)

Alciphron, a Greek writer, evidently imitated Lucian, and seems to have been a younger contemporary. Probably therefore he lived during the latter part of the second and the opening years of the third century A.D. From his hand we have four books of *Letters*, which treat of various phases of life. His material he drew in part from Lucian, in part from Attic comedy, middle and new, one of his sources in this field being Menander. The fact is recognized that, in so far as he touches upon historical events or the features of actual life, he represents conditions mainly of the fourth century B.C. After allowance is made for the medium of his knowledge, his work still remains a useful source for fourth-century life. The letters are attractive because of their delicate humor and their sympathetic, appreciative spirit. Evidently the writer was in close touch with the subjects treated. See Christ, *Griech. Lit.* II. 656–8; Schmid, "Alkiphron," in Pauly-Wissowa, *Real-Encycl.* I. 1548 (3) *sq.*

This translation is made from the edition of Schepers (Teubner, 1905).

AGELARCHIDES TO PYTHOLAUS

The usurers in the city, kind friend, are a great nuisance. I do not know what was the matter with me when I ought to have gone to you or some other of my country neighbors, at the time I was in need of money for purchasing a farm at Colonus. On that occasion a man of the city went with me to the house of Byrtius to introduce me to him. There I found an old man looking wrinkled and with brows contracted, holding in his hand an antique paper, rotted by time and half-eaten by moths and bugs. Forthwith he spoke to me in brusquest fashion, as though he considered talking a loss of time. But when my voucher said I wanted money, he asked how many talents. Then when I expressed surprise at his

[1] The wide and solid reputation of Pasion and Phormion for honesty was the very foundation of their success.

mention of so large a sum, he forthwith spat, and showed ill temper. Nevertheless he gave the money, demanded a note, required a heavy interest on the principal, and placed a mortgage on my house. A great nuisance indeed are these men who reckon with pebbles and crooked fingers. Never, ye spirits who watch over the farmers, never may it again be my lot to behold a wolf or a usurer!

159. The Farmer Takes to Commerce

(Alciphron, *Letters*, ii. 4; old eds. i. 25. Translated by G. W. B.)

EUPETALIS TO ELATION

As the earth repays me nothing equivalent to my toils, I have resolved to devote myself to the sea and the waves. Life and death are the common lot of us all, and there is no possibility of escape, even if a man should lock himself up in a little room and stay there. The day of fate is not idle, and we cannot escape payment when it is due. Life therefore does not hang upon such circumstances but is determined by Chance. Some on land have proved short-lived whereas upon the sea others have lived to a good old age.[1] Knowing full well that this is true, I am going on a voyage, and shall keep company with the winds and the waves. It is better to return from Bosporos and Propontis with new-earned wealth [2] than to stay in the border fields of Attica and complain of hunger and thirst.

160. The Farmer Boy Wants to Visit the City

(Alciphron, *Letters*, ii. 28; old eds. iii. 31. Translated by G. W. B.)

Never yet have I gone to the city, nor do I know what it is like, but wish to see this novel sight, and the inhabitants dwelling together within one (narrow) circuit, and to find out all the other

[1] The common opinion was that life at sea was especially exposed to perils; but this man, on deliberation, comes to a different conclusion.

[2] From this statement we infer that the writer intended to go, not as a mere sailor, but as a merchant. Generally the "border farms" were larger than the average; and if this man was the owner of a farm of this kind, he had the means of making a commercial investment.

ways in which city differs from country. If then you have any business that would take you to the city, come and take me with you. For I fancy that I ought to be learning something more, as the hair is beginning to grow on my chin. Who is better fitted to initiate me into the mysteries of that place than you who are going about a great deal of the time within its gates?

161. Glaucippe Disagrees with Her Father

(Alciphron, i. 11; old eds. iii. 1. Translated by G. W. B.)

GLAUCIPPE TO CHAROPE

I can no longer contain myself, mother, nor can I endure to marry the young man from Methymna, the pilot's son to whom my father betrothed me, since I saw the city youth at the Oschophoria,[1] when you sent me to the city at the time of that festival. He is beautiful, O beautiful, mother, and most sweet. He wears his hair in curls more charming than sea-moss; his smiles are fairer than the quiet sea, and the blue of his eyes is like the ocean when first lit up by the sun's rays. His whole countenance — one would say that the Graces, after bathing in the fount Argaphia, had left Orchomenus and were dancing on his cheeks. His lips he has tinged with roses taken from the bosom of Aphrodite. Either I must marry him, or in imitation of the Lesbian Sappho, will throw myself from the promontory, not of Leucas,[2] but of Peiræus.

CHAROPE TO GLAUCIPPE

You are mad, daughter dear, and entirely beside yourself. You need a dose of hellebore,[3] not the ordinary kind but the sort that comes from Phocian Anticyra; for you ought to feel a maidenly shame, but have cast off all modesty. Compose yourself and thrust

[1] A festival in which the young men, dressed in women's clothes, marched in procession carrying vine branches loaded with grapes.

[2] There was a story that Sappho ended her life in this way, for a similar reason. The story was probably an inference from one of her poems, and therefore a fiction. The fact that a poet often personated other characters has too often been lost sight of by critics.

[3] Hellebore was considered a cure for insanity. The text indicates that the best quality was supposed to be produced at Anticyra, on the southern coast of Phocis.

from your mind this mischief. For if your father should learn a word of this, he would without a moment's thought or hesitation throw you as food to the sea monsters.

162. Anti-fat Regulations at Sparta

(Agatharchides, *History of Europe*, xvi, xxvii, quoted by Athenæus, xii. 74)

Agatharchides of Cnidos was a Peripatetic philosopher who flourished in the latter part of the second century B.C. Among his works was a *History of Asia* in ten books and a *History of Europe* in ninety-four books. A summary of these histories is given by Photius, cod. 213. It is clear that his work was an important source for Diodorus Siculus. See Christ, *Griech. Lit.* II. 196 *sq.* The subjoined excerpt illustrates the careful attention which the Lacedæmonians continued to give during the fourth century to the development and preservation of the athletic type of citizen.

Agatharchides, in the sixteenth book of his *History of Europe*, says that Magas, who was king of Cyrene for fifty years, and who never had any wars but spent all his time in luxury, became toward the end of his life so immensely bulky and burdensome to himself that he was at last actually choked by his fat, from the inactivity of his body and the enormous quantity of food which he consumed. Among the Lacedæmonians, however, the same man relates, in the twenty-seventh book, that it is thought a proof of no ordinary infamy if any one is of an unmanly appearance, or if any one is at all inclined to have a large stomach; as the younger men are exhibited unclad before the ephors every ten days. The ephors used every day to take notice also of the clothes and bedding of the young men, and very properly. The cooks of Lacedæmon were employed solely on dressing meat plainly, and on nothing else. In his twenty-seventh book Agatharchides says, too, that the Lacedæmonians brought Nauclides, son of Polybiades, who was enormously fat in body and had grown of vast size through luxury, into the middle of the assembly. Then after Lysander had publicly reproached him as an effeminate voluptuary, they nearly banished him from the city, and threatened him that they would certainly do so if he did not reform his life. On this occasion Lysander said that Agesilaüs, when he was in the country near the Hellespont, making war against the barbarians, and saw the Asiatics expensively clothed but utterly useless in body, ordered all who had been taken captive to be stripped and sold by the auctioneer. After that he ordered their clothes to be sold without them, that the allies, knowing that they had to fight for a great prize against contemptible men, might advance with greater spirit against the enemy.

BIBLIOGRAPHY

Wägner, W., *Hellas: das Land und Volk der alten Griechen*, 2 vols. (6th ed., Leipzig, 1886), popular; Wilamowitz-Moellendorff, U. von, and Niese, B., *Staat und Gesellschaft der Griechen und Römer* (Teubner, 1910); Savage, C. A., "The Athenian in his Relations to the State," in *Studies in Honor of Gildersleeve* (Baltimore, 1902), 87 *sqq.*; Pöhlmann, R. von, *Geschichte der sozialen Frage und des Sozialismus in der antiken Welt*, 2 vols. (2d ed. of his *Socialismus und Kommunismus*, Munich, 1912); "Isokrates und das Problem der Demokratie," in *Münch. Akad.* 1913, Abhdl. 1; Wolf, H., *Geschichte des antiken Sozialismus* (Gütersloh; 1909), dissert.; Ward, C. O., *The Ancient Lowly*, 2 vols. (Chicago, 1910); Wallon, H. A., *Histoire de l'esclavage dans l'antiquité*, 3 vols. (2d ed., Paris, 1879), useful though old; Ciccotti, E., "Del numero degli schiavi nell' Attica," in *Reale istituto lombardo di scienze e lettere rendiconti*, 1897, pp. 655–73; Meyer, E., "Die Sklaverei im Altertum," in *Kleine Schriften*, 169–212; Foucart, P., *De libertorum condicione* (Paris, 1896); Strack, M. L., "Die Freigelassenen in ihrer Bedeutung für die Gesellschaft der Alten," in *Hist. Zeitschr.* CXI (1913). 1–28; Clerc, M., *Les métèques athéniens* (Paris, 1893); Braunstein, O., *Die politische Wirksamkeit der griechischen Frau* (Leipzig, 1911); Carroll, M., *Woman; in all Ages and in all Countries*, I (Phila.: Barrie, 1907); Donaldson, J., *Woman; her Position and Influence in Ancient Greece*, etc. (Longmans, 1907); Bechtel, F., *Die attischen Frauennamen nach ihrem System dargestellt* (Göttingen, 1902); St. John, J. A., *History of the Manners and Customs of Ancient Greece*, 3 vols. (1842), still useful; Baumeister, A., *Denkmäler des klassischen Altertums zur Erläuterung des Lebens der Griechen und Römer in Religion, Kunst, und Sitte* (Leipzig, 1885–88); Guhl, E. K., and Koner, W., *Life of the Greeks and Romans*, translated from the 3d German edition (London, 1889); Becker, *Charicles: the Private Life of the Ancient Greeks* (Longmans, 1895, reprint of an earlier translation); Falke, J. von, *Greece and Rome; their Life and Art*, translated by Browne, W. H. (Holt, 1886), elegantly illustrated; Blümner, H., *Leben und Sitten der Griechen*, 3 vols. (Leipzig, 1887), illustrated; *Home Life of the Ancient Greeks* (London, 1893); Müller, I. von, *Die griechischen Privataltertümer* (Munich, 1893); Guiraud, P., *La vie privée et la vie publique des Grecs* (3d. ed., Paris, 1902); Gulick, C. B., *Life of the Ancient Greeks* (Appleton, 1902); Miller, W., *Greek Life in Town and Country* (London, 1905); Tucker, T. G., *Life in Ancient Athens* (Macmillan, 1906); Mahaffy, J. P., *Social Life in Greece from Homer to Menander* (London, 1883); Roper, A. G.,

Ancient Eugenics (Oxford: Blackwell, 1913); Abrahams, E. B., *Greek Dress* (London: Murray, 1908); Ransom, C. L., *Studies in Ancient Furniture* (Chicago: University Press, 1905); Schreiber, G. T., *Atlas of Classical Antiquities* (London, 1895), valuable for the illustrations; Gothein, M., "Der griechische Garten," in *Ath. Mitt.* XXXIV (1909). 100 *sqq.*; Sudhoff, K., *Aus dem antiken Badewesen* (Berlin, 1910); Foucart, P. F., *Les associations religieuses chez le Grecs* (Paris, 1873), important; Ziebarth, E., *Das griechische Vereinswesen* (Leipzig, 1896); Poland, F., *Geschichte des griechischen Vereinswesens* (Leipzig, 1909), comprehensive; Burckhardt, J., *Griechische Kulturgeschichte*, ed. by Oeri, J. (3d ed., Berlin, 1898), drawn from secondary sources; Wundt, M., *Griechische Weltanschauungen* (1910); Jones, W. H. S., *Greek Morality in Relation to Institutions* (London, 1906). The histories of Greece by Grote, Curtius, Holm, and Beloch (see Index and Contents) necessarily treat of social conditions and tendencies. See also the relevant chapters in Meyer, E., *Geschichte des Altertums*, V, and Cavaignac, E., *Histoire dell' antiquitê*, II, III. For a review of recent literature, see Blümner, H., in *Jahresb.* CLXIII (1913). 1–83.

CHAPTER XV

PERSONAL CHARACTER, LITERARY CRITICISM, AND ART

In the Period 404–337 B.C.

163. Life and Style of Lysias

(Dionysius of Halicarnassus, *Appreciation of Lysias*, 1–7. Translated by G. W. B.)

The rhetorical works of Dionysius are among the greatest helps to an appreciation of the Greek writers of which they treat; at the same time they contain many references to biographical and historical events, and should therefore be classed among the historical sources. For that reason a short selection is here given, dealing with a subject in which the writer, a rhetorician of delicate taste and discrimination, was at his best.

1. Lysias, son of Cephalus, was born of Syracusan parents. His birthplace was Athens, at a time when his father was a metic there. At the age of fifteen he accompanied his two brothers to Thurii to take part in the colony which the Athenians and the rest of Hellas were sending to that place, twelve years prior to the Peloponnesian war.[1] There he remained as a citizen in the enjoyment of great prosperity till the disaster befell the Athenians in Sicily. After that misfortune, in a time of sedition, he was banished along with three hundred others, on the charge of sympathizing with Athens.

2. Returning to Athens in the archonship of Callias [2] at the age of forty-seven, as one would calculate, from that time he passed

[1] As the Peloponnesian war began in 431, the colony of Thurii was founded, according to Dionysius, in 443, the date usually accepted by modern scholars. Pais, *Ancient Italy*, 330 *sq.*, on the basis of other data, prefers 446. Following Dionysius, however, we arrive at 458 (Attic year 459–458) for the date of his birth. He may have gone to Thurii long after its founding, however, and this possibility leaves us at sea as to the date of his birth. Christ, *Griech. Lit.* I. 523, prefers 445 for his natal year and 429 for his migration to Thurii.

[2] 413–412 B.C.

his life at Athens. He wrote many speeches well adapted to the courts and the council and the assembly, and in addition panegyrics and amatory addresses, and letters, in which he eclipsed the fame both of earlier orators and of those who flourished in his own time. To few of his successors did he leave an opportunity for glory, inasmuch as he excelled in all the forms of discourse and by no means in those of inferior worth. Now what character of oratory he employed, what improvements he introduced, in what respect he excelled those who flourished in his own age, in what respect he was inferior, and what we ought to learn from him, I shall attempt to explain.

3. In style he is exceedingly pure and is the most perfect canon of Attic, not the archaic form used by Plato and Thucydides, but the form in vogue during his own age, as may be proved by the speeches of Andocides, of Critias and of many others; for in this quality which is the first and the controlling element in discourse, I mean purity of dialect, no one that followed ever surpassed him, and no great number possessed the capability of imitating him, save only Isocrates. In the use of words the latter seems to me to have shown himself next to Lysias the purest of all. This merit in the orator I find worthy of emulation and imitation, and I should urge it upon those who wish to write and to speak with purity to make him their model in this quality.

4. There was another merit in no respect less than this one, which many of the famous men of his time emulated but no one could show in a higher degree. What is this? It is the quality which expresses the meaning in words that are appropriate and common and in general use; for least of all would one find Lysias employing figurative speech. He is worthy of commendation not only on this ground but also because he makes a subject appear singular or lofty or important by the use of the most common terms, never resorting to poetic devices. His predecessors were not so reputed; but any who wished to add adornment to a topic wholly discarded the idiomatic and took refuge in poetic diction, employing many paraphrases and exaggerations and other poetic forms, along with obscure and alien words, unwonted combinations, overmastering every-day speech with novel diction. . . .

5. A third quality which I discover in this man is clearness,

not only in words but in the treatment of the subject matter. It is a certain practical clearness unknown to many writers. A proof is that many points in the style of Thucydides and Demosthenes, who were most skilled in the setting forth of facts, are difficult for us to make out and obscure and in need of an interpreter, whereas the diction of Lysias is all open and clear even to one far removed from classic writings. Now if clearness arose from a want of power, the quality would not be worthy of praise; but the fact is that this merit is displayed by the wealth of masterful words which he has in superabundance; so that his clearness is a merit to be emulated. Moreover the expression of ideas briefly, along with clearness, is naturally a difficult matter, that is, the union of these two qualities and their blending in moderation, which especially Lysias is seen to employ in no way inferior to others. . . .

6. Next to these virtues I find in Lysias another merit altogether wonderful, which Theophrastus says was invented by Thrasymachus. This may be true, for the latter seems to me to have preceded Lysias somewhat in time. I refer to the acme of the two men's lives. . . . I make no assertion, however, at the present time as to which invented the quality, but that Lysias surpassed in it, this point I would boldly affirm. Now what is this merit? It is the quality of style which compresses the ideas and sets them forth tersely, a merit most appropriate and necessary to judicial oratory and to every genuine contest. This quality few have imitated. Demosthenes, however, has excelled in it, not in the easy simple manner of Lysias, but elaborately and bitingly. I mention this point just as it occurs to me, but in regard to these matters I shall discourse at length when the occasion arises.

7. The style of Lysias possesses also great dramatic vividness. This is the power which subjects the things said to the feelings (of the hearers); it arises from grasping the facts in their proper order. One who pays attention to the words of Lysias cannot be so dull, so morose, so slow of mind, as to fail to see the details of the story as it unfolds and be present, so to speak, at the events which the orator is relating. . . .[1]

[1] The paragraph numbering is the present editor's.

164. Life of Demosthenes

(Pseudo-Plutarch, *Lives of the Ten Orators*, viii)

The following selection is also drawn from a rhetorician, whose name however is unknown to us. His work has been preserved among the *Moralia* of Plutarch. It seems clear that he drew his material chiefly from Dionysius of Halicarnassus and from Cæcilius of Calê Actê, Sicily, who stood next to Dionysius in the Augustan age as a rhetorician and critic; *cf.* Brzoska, in Pauly-Wissowa, *Real-Encycl.* III. 1174–88; Christ, *Griech, Lit.* II. 391. The work is our chief source for the biographies of the ten orators.

1. Demosthenes, the son of Demosthenes and of Cleobulê, daughter of Gylon, was a Pæanian by descent. He was left an orphan by his father, when he was but seven years old,[1] together with a sister of the age of five. Being kept by his mother during his minority, he went to school to Isocrates, as some say; but the generality are of opinion that he was a pupil of Isæus the Chalcidian, who lived at Athens and was a pupil of Isocrates. He imitated Thucydides and Plato, and some affirm that he more especially attended the school of Plato. Hegesias the Magnesian writes that he entreated his master's leave to go and hear Callistratus,[2] son of Ampædus of Aphidna, a noble orator and sometime commander of a troop of horse, who had dedicated an altar to Hermes Agoræus, and was to make an oration to the people. When he had heard him, he became devoted to oratory, and so long as he continued at Athens, he remained his disciple.

2. Callistratus, however, was soon banished to Thrace; and Demosthenes, growing more mature, joined with Isocrates and Plato. Afterward he took Isæus into his house, and for the space of four years labored very hard in his desire to imitate his orations. But Ctesibius in his book on Philosophy affirms that by the help of Callias of Syracuse he got the orations of Zoïlus of Amphipolis and by the assistance of Charicles the Carystian those also of Alcidamas, and devoted himself to the imitation of them.[3] When he

[1] Some of the circumstances of his early life, including the trouble with his guardians, is told by himself in an oration; see no. 156.

[2] Callistratus was the most eminent orator and statesman of Athens at that time; Holm, *History of Greece*, III. 176–8. He retired into exile and was succeeded by Aristophon mentioned below.

[3] Most of these statements regarding his relations to various authors and teachers are doubted by modern scholars. The idea of the rhetorician was to connect him as a

became of age in the year of Timocrates,[1] he called his tutors and guardians to account for their maladministration, in not allowing him what was fitting and requisite out of his estate. These guardians were three, Aphobus, Therippides, and Demophon (or Demeas), the last of whom, an uncle, he charged more severely than the other two. He prosecuted each of them in an action for ten talents, and won the cases, but did not exact of them what the law had given him, releasing some for money and others for favor.

3. When Aristophon by reason of his age could not hold office any longer, he was chosen choregus.[2] During the administration of this office Meidias the Anagyrasian struck him as he was ordering the dances in the theater. Thereupon Demosthenes sued him, but let fall the prosecution on the condition that Meidias should pay him three thousand drachmas.[3]

4. It is reported of him that while he was a youth, he confined himself to a cave and there studied his orations, and shaved half of his head that he might not be allured to divert himself from it;[4] and that he lay upon a very narrow bed, that he might awake and rise the sooner. Further because he could not well pronounce the letter R, he practiced upon it much that he might master it if possible. As he had the habit of moving his shoulder in an unseemly manner when he spoke, he remedied that defect by a spit (or as some say, by a sword) stuck in the ceiling just over his shoulder, that the fear of being pricked with it might break him of the unbecoming gesture. They report of him further that when he could declaim fairly, he had a sort of mirror made as large as himself, and used always in declaiming to look in that, to the end that he

pupil with as many contemporaries as possible in order to explain his prodigious success as an orator. There can hardly be a doubt, however, that he was aided by Isæus.

[1] 364–363 B.C. This author places his birth in 385–384, whereas Dionysius and some others give the year 381–380. The date of his birth, accordingly, has not been definitively ascertained.

[2] The author seems to have a wrong notion of the choregus. The latter was not a magistrate in the ordinary sense but a wealthy citizen who took his turn in performing the liturgy connected with the equipment and training of the dramatic chorus; cf. Botsford, *Hellenic History*, ch. xii. The year of this event was 347; *cf.* Christ, *Griech. Lit.* I. 551.

[3] Drachma, about 18 cents.

[4] This anecdote and those that follow are doubtful; they may be taken as historical impressions of the marvelous training to which Demosthenes subjected himself.

might see and correct what was amiss. He used likewise at certain times to go down to the shore at Phalerum, that, being accustomed to the surges and the noise of the waves, he might not be daunted by the clamors of the people, when he should declaim in public. Moreover being by nature short-winded, he gave Neoptolemus, a player, ten thousand drachmas to teach him to pronounce long sentences in one breath.

5. Afterward, betaking himself to the affairs of the state, and finding the people divided into two different factions,[1] one in favor of Philip and the other standing for the liberty and the rights of the people, he took part with those who opposed Philip, and always persuaded the citizens to help those who were in danger and trouble through Philip's oppression, taking for his companions in council Hypereides, Nausicles, Polyeuctus, and Diotimus. Then he drew the Thebans, Eubœans, Corcyræans, Corinthians, Bœotians, and many more into a league with the Athenians.[2]

6. As he was in the assembly one day and his memory failed him, his oration was hissed, which made him return home very heavy and melancholy. On this occasion he was met by Eunomus the Thriasian and was greatly comforted and encouraged by him. He was chiefly animated, however, by Andronicus the player, who told him that his orations were excellent but that he lacked in action, and thereupon rehearsed certain parts of the oration Demosthenes had delivered in that same assembly. Demosthenes gave good ear and credit to what he said, and betook himself for instruction to Andronicus. When accordingly he was afterward asked what was the first part of oratory, he answered, 'Action'; and which was the second, he replied, 'Action'; and which was the third, he still answered, 'Action.' At another time when declaiming publicly and using expressions too youthful for one of his years, he was laughed at and ridiculed by the comedians, Antiphanes and Timocles, who in derision used to repeat from him such phrases as the following: "By earth, by the fountains, by the rivers, by the floods!"

[1] The statement is not correct, as it was mainly Demosthenes himself who created the anti-Macedonian party.

[2] This statement refers to the coalition which he formed on the eve of the battle of Chæroneia, 338.

7. For having sworn thus in the presence of the people, he raised a tumult about him. He likewise used to swear by Asclepius, and accented the second syllable [1] through some mistake but afterward defended it; for this Asclepius, he said, was called ἤπιος, that is, a mild God. This also often caused him to be interrupted. All these shortcomings, however, he reformed in time, through association with Eubulides, the Milesian philosopher. Once when present at the Olympic games he heard Lamachus the Myrrhinæan sound the praises of Philip and of Alexander the Great, and decry the cowardice of the Thebans and Olynthians, whereupon he stood up in their defence against him, and from the ancient poets he proclaimed the great and noble achievements of the Thebans and Olynthians. So elegantly did he behave himself in this affair that he at once silenced Lamachus and made him convey himself out of the assembly. Even Philip himself, when he had heard what harangues Demosthenes made against him, replied that if he had heard him, he should have chosen him general in the war against himself (Philip). He used to compare the orations of Demosthenes to soldiers, for the force which they carried with them; but the orations of Isocrates he likened to fencers because of the theatrical delight that accompanied them.

8. When about thirty-seven years of age, reckoning from Dexitheus to Callimachus [2] (in whose time the Olynthians sent to beg aid of the Athenians against Philip, who was then making war upon them), he persuaded the Athenians to answer the request of Olynthus; but in the following year, in which Plato died,[3] Philip overthrew and destroyed the Olynthians. Xenophon also, the pupil of Socrates, had some knowledge of Demosthenes, either at his first rise, or at least when he was most famous; for he narrated the affairs of the Greeks as touching what happened at the battle of Mantineia in the year of Chariclides.[4] Some time previously Demosthenes overthrew his guardians in a suit he had brought against them in the year of Timocrates.

9. When Æschines, after his condemnation, fled from Athens

[1] The accent is properly on the last syllable, Ἀσκληπιός.

[2] The two dates are 385–384 and 349–348 respectively. [3] 348–347 B.C.

[4] 363–362 B.C. It is unlikely that Xenophon knew anything of Demosthenes. The reason here given is insufficient.

Demosthenes, hearing of it, took horse and rode after him. Apprized of this move, and fearing to be apprehended again, Æschines came to meet Demosthenes, fell at his feet, covered his face, and begged for mercy. Thereupon Demosthenes bade him stand up, be assured of his favor, and as a pledge of it, gave him a talent of silver.

10. He advised the people to maintain a company of mercenary soldiers in Thasos, and thither he sailed as captain of a trireme. Another time, when commissioned to buy grain, he was accused of defrauding the city, but cleared himself of the accusation and was acquitted. When Philip had seized upon Elateia, Demosthenes and others went out to battle at Chæroneia,[1] where he is said to have deserted the ranks. While fleeing away, he was caught by a bramble in his chiton behind, when turning about in haste and thinking an enemy had overtaken him, he cried out, "Save my life and say what shall be my ransom!"[2] On his shield he had engraven for his motto, "To Good Fortune." It was he who made the oration at the funeral of those who had been slain in that battle.

11. After these events he bent his whole care and study to the reparation of the city and its walls; and when chosen commissary for repairing the walls, besides the money expended from the public fund, he laid out of his own at least a hundred minas.[3] In addition he gave ten thousand drachmas to the festival fund; and taking ship, he sailed from coast to coast to collect money from the allies. For these services he was often crowned with golden crowns, namely on the motion of Demoteles, Aristonicus, and Hypereides, and afterward of Ctesiphon. The last decree came near being retracted, for Diodotus and Æschines endeavored to prove it contrary to the laws; but Demosthenes defended himself[4] so well against their allegations that he overcame all difficulties and that his enemies did not receive a fifth part of the votes of the jurors.[5]

[1] 338 B.C.

[2] Necessarily all the Athenians fled who were not killed or taken captive, Demosthenes among the others. It is unlikely, however, that any one took note of his remarks during the retreat.

[3] A mina is 100 drachmas, or about $18.

[4] In his oration *On the Crown* (*De Corona*), the most famous of all his speeches.

[5] In an indictment of the kind, for an illegal proposal (γραφὴ παρανόμων), the prosecutor who failed to obtain a fifth part of the votes was fined 1000 drachmas and

12. Afterward when Alexander the Great made his expedition into Asia, and Harpalus fled to Athens with a great sum of money, at first Demosthenes would not let him be entertained; but afterward when Harpalus landed and gave him a thousand darics,[1] he was of another mind. When the Athenians determined to give Harpalus up to Alexander, Demosthenes opposed it, proposing to deposit the money in the Acropolis, yet without declaring the amount to the people. Thereupon Harpalus declared that he had brought with him from Asia seven hundred talents, and that this sum had been deposited in the Acropolis. But only three hundred and fifty or a little more could be found, as Philochorus relates. But Harpalus broke out of the prison in which he was to be kept till someone should come from Alexander, and escaped to Crete — or as some will have it, to Tænaron in Laconia. On this occasion Demosthenes was accused of having received from him a sum of money and had failed therefore to give a true account of the sum delivered to him, or to impeach the negligence of the keepers. He was therefore judicially cited by Hypereides, Pytheus, Menesæchmus, Himeræus and Patrocles, who prosecuted him with such vigor as to cause him to be condemned by the council of the Areopagus.

13. On his conviction he went into exile, as he was unable to pay fivefold; for he was accused of having received thirty talents. Others say that he would not run the risk of a trial but went into exile before the day came. After this tempest was over, when the Athenians sent Polyeuctus to the commonwealth of Arcadia to draw it from the Macedonian alliance, he did not succeed. Demosthenes then came to his aid and reasoned so effectually that he easily prevailed. This success procured him so much credit and esteem that after a time a trireme was despatched to call him home again. The Athenians decreed, too, that whereas he owed the state thirty talents as a fine laid on him for the misdemeanor of which he was accused, he should be excused on condition of building in Peiræus an altar to Zeus the Deliverer. This decree was

disqualified from bringing accusations of the kind for the future. Æschines suffered thus for his failure; and fearing that he might now be prosecuted by the party of Demosthenes, he retired into exile, as stated by the text above.

[1] Daric, a Persian gold coin worth 20 drachmas, or about $3.60.

proposed by Demon, his near kinsman. When it had passed, he resumed the administration of affairs in the commonwealth. . . .

Next is given an account of the unsuccessful Hellenic war of independence after the death of Alexander. Demanded by the enemy, Demosthenes fled to the temple of Poseidon at Calauria, where he was pursued by Archias, an officer in the Macedonian service.

14. When Archias attempted to force him thence, the towns-men would not suffer it. Demosthenes told them that he did not flee to Calauria to save his life, but that he might convince the Macedonians of their violence committed even against the Gods themselves. Thereupon he called for a writing-tablet; and if we may credit Demetrius the Magnesian, on that he wrote a distich, which afterward the Athenians caused to be affixed to his statue: —

Orator mighty in spirit, if only thy strength had been equal,
Ares, of Macedon God, ne'er would have ruled over Greece.

(Literally, "Had your physical power equalled your intellect, Demosthenes, the Macedonian war-god would never had ruled over the Hellenes.")

15. This statue, made by Polyeuctus, is placed near the cloister where the altar of the Twelve Gods is erected. Some say this writing was found: "Demosthenes to Antipater, Greeting." Philochorus tells us that he died by drinking poison; and Satyrus the historian will have it that the pen was poisoned with which he wrote his epistle; and putting it into his mouth, he soon afterward died. Eratosthenes is of another opinion, that being in continual fear of the Macedonians, he wore a poisoned bracelet on his arm. Others say that he died by holding his breath; and lastly others say that he carried strong poison in his signet. He lived to the age of seventy, according to those who give the highest number — of sixty-seven according to other statements. He was in public life twenty-two years.

16. When king Philip died, Demosthenes appeared publicly in a splendid mantle, rejoicing at this death, although he but just before was mourning for his daughter. He assisted the Thebans likewise against Alexander, and animated all the other Greeks. Hence when Alexander had conquered Thebes, he demanded Demosthenes of the Athenians, threatening them if they refused to give him up. When Alexander went against Persia, and de-

manded ships of the Athenians, Demosthenes opposed it, saying, "Who can assure us that he will not use those ships we should send him against ourselves?"

17. He left behind him two sons by one wife, the daughter of Heliodorus, a leading citizen. He had but one daughter, who died unmarried, while a mere child. A sister, too, he had, who married Laches of Leuconoe, his kinsman, and to him bore Demochares, who proved inferior to none of his time in eloquence, conduct, and courage. His statue is still standing in the Prytaneum, the first on the right as you approach the altar, clothed with a mantle and girt with a sword, because in this habit he delivered an oration to the people, when Antipater[1] demanded of them their orators.

18. After some time the Athenians decreed sustenance should be given to the kindred of Demosthenes in the Prytaneum, and likewise set up a statue in his memory, when he was dead, in the market, in the year of Gorgias. These honors were paid him at the request of Demochares, his sister's son.[2]

165. Epaminondas

(Cornelius, *Nepos*)

Although Nepos is an inferior authority, the historian is obliged to make whatever use he can of all sources, exercising due discrimination as to the trustworthiness of his material. Doubtless the general picture of Epaminondas drawn by Nepos is correct, though the anecdotes given for the illustration of his character have little if any historical basis.

(1) Epaminondas was the son of Polymnis, and was born at Thebes. . . . (2) He was of an honorable family, though left poor by his ancestors; but he was so well-educated that no Theban was more so; for he was taught to play upon the harp, and to sing to the sound of its strings, by Dionysius, who was held in no less honor among musicians than Damon or Lamprus, whose names are well known; to play on the flutes by Olympiodorus; and to

[1] Antipater commanded the Macedonians in the so-called Lamian war — the brief and unsuccessful struggle of the Hellenes to shake off the Macedonian yoke after the death of Alexander. After crushing the Greeks, Antipater demanded that the orators who had incited the people to war be delivered up to him. Among these orators was Demosthenes, who thereupon fled from Athens, and met his death, 322, in the way described in the text above.

[2] The paragraph numbering is the present editor's.

dance by Calliphron. For his instructor in philosophy he had Lysis of Tarentum, a Pythagorean, to whom he was so devoted that, young as he was, he preferred the society of a grave and austere old man before that of all those of his own age; nor did he part with him until he so far excelled his fellow students in learning, that it might easily be perceived he would in like manner excel them all in other pursuits. These acquirements according to our habits are trifling,[1] and rather to be despised; but in Greece, at least in former times, they were a great subject for praise. After he grew up, and began to apply himself to gymnastic exercises, he studied not so much to increase his strength as the agility of his body;[2] for he thought that strength suited the purpose of wrestlers, but that agility conduced to excellence in war. He used to exercise himself very much, therefore, in running and wrestling, as long as he could grapple with his adversary and contend standing. But he spent most of his labor on martial exercises.

To the strength of body thus acquired, were added many good qualities of the mind; for he was modest, prudent, grave, wisely availing himself of opportunities, skilled in war, brave in action, and possessed of remarkable courage. He was so great a lover of truth that he would not tell a falsehood even in jest; he was also master of his passions, gentle in disposition, and patient to a wonderful degree, submitting to wrong not only from the people, but from his own friends; he was a remarkable keeper of secrets, a quality which is sometimes not less serviceable than eloquence; and he was an attentive listener to others, because he thought that by this means knowledge was most easily acquired. Whenever he came into a company, therefore, in which a discussion was going on concerning government, or a conversation was being held on any point in philosophy, he never went away till the discourse was brought to its conclusion. He bore poverty so easily that he received nothing from the state but glory. He did not avail himself of the means of his friends to maintain himself; but he often used his credit to relieve others,

[1] The Roman Nepos naturally expresses the sentiment of the society in which he lived.

[2] This aim was opposed to that which prevailed in his own country; the main object of Bœotian gymnastics was to develop strength rather than agility.

to such a degree that it might be thought all things were in common between him and his friends; for when any one of his countrymen had been taken by the enemy, or when the marriageable daughter of a friend could not be married for want of fortune, he used to call a council of his friends, and to prescribe how much each should give according to his means; and when he had made up the sum required, he brought the man who needed it to the contributors and made them pay it to the person himself, in order that he, into whose hands the sum passed, might know to whom he was indebted, and how much to each.

(4) His indifference to money was put to a proof by Diomedon of Cyzicus; for at the request of Artaxerxes he undertook to bribe Epaminondas. Diomedon accordingly came to Thebes with a large sum in gold; and by a present of five talents brought over Micythus, a young man for whom Epaminondas then had great affection, to further his views. Micythus went to Epaminondas, and told him the cause of Diomedon's coming. But Epaminondas in the presence of Diomedon said to him: "There is no need of money in the matter; for if what the king desires is for the good of the Thebans, I am ready to do it for nothing; but if otherwise, he has not gold and silver enough to move me, for I would not accept the riches of the world in exchange for my love of country. I do not wonder at you, who have made trial of me without knowing my character, and have thought me like yourself; and I forgive you. But quit the city at once, lest you corrupt others, though you have been unable to corrupt me. You, Micythus, give Diomedon his money; unless you do so immediately, I shall give you up to the magistrates." Diomedon then entreated that he might be allowed to depart in safety and carry away what he had brought. "That," replied Epaminondas, "I will grant you, and not for your sake but for my own, lest any one, if your money should be taken from you, should say that what I would not receive when offered me, had come into my possession after being taken out of yours." Epaminondas then asked Diomedon whither he wished to go, and when the latter replied, "To Athens," he gave him a guard that he might reach that city in safety. . . .

(5) He was also an able speaker, so that no Theban was a match for him in eloquence; nor was his language less pointed in

brief replies than elegant in continued discourse. He had for a traducer and opponent in managing the government a certain Menecleidas, also a native of Thebes, a man well skilled in speaking, at least for a Theban; for in that people is found more vigor of body than of mind. Seeing that Epaminondas was distinguished in military affairs, he used to advise the Thebans to prefer peace to war, in order that his services as general might not be required. Epaminondas in consequence said to him: "You deceive your countrymen in dissuading them from war, since under the name of peace you are bringing upon them slavery; for peace is procured by war, and they accordingly who would enjoy it long must be trained to war. If therefore, my countrymen, you wish to be leaders of Greece, you must devote yourselves to the camp, not to the palæstra. . . ."

(7) He was of a patient disposition, and ready to endure wrongs from his countrymen, because he thought it a species of impiety to show resentment towards his country. There are the following proofs. When the Thebans from some feeling of displeasure toward him refused to place him at the head of the army, a leader was chosen who was ignorant of war, by whose mismanagement a great multitude of soldiers was brought to such a condition that all were alarmed for their safety. They were confined within a narrow space and blocked up by the enemy, whereupon the energy of Epaminondas began to be in request, for he was there as a private among the soldiers. When they desired aid from him, he showed no recollection of the affront that had been put upon him, but brought the army safely home after releasing it from the blockade. Nor did he act in this manner once only but often.

The most remarkable instance was when he had led an army into Peloponnesus against the Lacedæmonians, and had two joined in command with him, of whom one was Pelopidas, a man of valor and activity. On this occasion, when through the accusations of their enemies they had all fallen under the displeasure of their countrymen, and their commission was in consequence taken from them and other commanders came to take their places, Epaminondas did not obey the order of the people, and persuaded his colleagues to follow his example, continuing to prosecute the war which he had undertaken; for he saw that unless he did so, the whole army would be lost through the incautiousness and ignorance of its leaders. But there was a law at Thebes, which punished any one with death who retained his command longer than he was legally appointed. Epaminondas, however, as he saw that this law had been made for the purpose of preserving the state, was unwilling to make it contribute to its ruin, and continued to exercise his command four months longer than the people had prescribed.

(8) When they returned home, his colleagues were impeached for this offence, and he gave them leave to lay all the blame upon him, and to maintain that it was through his means that they did not obey the law. As they were freed from danger by this defence, nobody thought Epaminondas would make any reply, because it was supposed he would have nothing to say. But he stood forth on the trial, denied nothing of what his adversaries laid to his charge, and admitted the truth of all that his colleagues had stated; nor did he refuse to submit to the penalty of the law; but he requested of his countrymen one favor, namely, that they would write the following in their judicial record of the sentence passed upon him: "Epaminondas was punished by the Thebans with death, because he obliged them to overthrow the Lacedæmonians at Leuctra, whom, before he was general, none of the Bœotians durst look upon in the field, and because he not only by one battle rescued Thebes from destruction, but also secured liberty for all Greece, and brought the power of both peoples to such a condition that the Thebans attacked Sparta, and the Lacedæmonians were content if they could save their lives; nor did he cease to prosecute the war till after restoring Messene, he shut up Sparta with a close siege." When he had said this, there burst forth a laugh from all present, with much merriment, and no one of the judges ventured to pass sentence upon him. Thus he came off from this trial for life with the greatest glory.

166. Philip of Macedon

(Justin, *Epitome of the Philippic Histories of Pompeius Trogus*, ix. 4, 5, 8)

Regarding the Roman epitomator Justinus nothing certain is known. Some are of the opinion that he lived under the Antonines, others in the third century A.D. Pompeius Trogus, whom he abridged, was a contemporary of Livy. He was by descent a Gaul, whose grandfather received the Roman citizenship through Pompey the Great. His *Philippic Histories* covered the whole course of human events from the earliest times to his own day. There can be no doubt that for the period represented by the subjoined excerpts Pompeius drew his material largely from the *Philippica* of Theopompus, a contemporary of Philip. Naturally it is impossible to say to what degree Justin reflects the opinions of his far-off original source. See Schanz, *Geschichte der römischen Literatur*, II. 1. 444–54; Peter, *Geschichtliche Literatur über die römische Kaiserzeit*, I. 118; II. 215 *sq.*, 224, 298 *sq.*

4. Philip's joy for this victory [1] was artfully concealed. He abstained from offering the usual sacrifices on that day; he did not smile at table, or mingle any diversions with the entertainment; he had no chaplets or perfumes; and as far as was in his power, he so managed his conquest that none might think of him as a conqueror. He desired that he should not be called king but general of Greece; and conducted himself with such prudence between his own secret joy on the one hand and the grief of the enemy on the other, that he neither appeared to his own subjects to rejoice, nor to the vanquished to insult them. To the Athenians, whom he had found to be his bitterest enemies, he sent back their prisoners without ransom, and gave up the bodies of the slain for burial, bidding them convey the relics of their dead to the sepulchres of their ancestors. He also sent Alexander, his son, with his friend Antipater to Athens, to establish peace and friendship with them.

The Thebans, however, he compelled to purchase their prisoners as well as the liberty of burying their dead. Some of the chief men of the city, too, he put to death; others he banished, seizing upon the property of them all. Afterward he reinstated in their country those that had been unjustly banished, of whom he made three hundred judges and governors of the city, before whom when the most eminent citizens were arraigned on this very charge, that of having banished them unjustly, they had such spirit that they all acknowledged their participation in the fact, and proved that it was better with the state when they were condemned than when they were restored. A wonderful instance of courage! They passed sentence, as far as they could, on those who had the disposal of them for life or death, and set at naught the pardon which their

[1] The battle of Chæroneia, 338.

enemies could give them; and as they could not avenge themselves by deeds, they manifested their boldness by spirit of words.

5. War being at an end in Greece, Philip directed deputies from all the states to be summoned to Corinth, to settle the condition of affairs. Here he fixed terms of peace for the whole of Greece, according to the merits of each city; and chose from them all a council, to form a senate as it were for the country.[1] But the Lacedæmonians, standing alone, showed contempt alike for the terms and the king. They regarded the state of things, which had not been agreed upon by the cities themselves, but had been forced upon them by a conqueror, as a state, not of peace, but of slavery. The number of troops to be furnished by each city was then determined, whether the king in case of being attacked was to be supported by their united force, or whether war was to be made on any other power under him as their general. In all these preparations for war it was not to be doubted that the kingdom of Persia was the object in view. The sum of the force was two hundred thousand infantry and fifteen thousand cavalry. Exclusive of this number there were also the army of Macedonia and the barbarians of the adjacent conquered nations. . . .

8. As a king he was more inclined to display in war than in entertainments; and his greatest riches were means for military operations. He was better at getting wealth than keeping it, and in consequence was always poor amidst his daily spoliations. Clemency and perfidy were equally valued by him; and no road to victory was, in his opinion, dishonorable. He was equally pleasing and treacherous in his address, promising more than he could perform. He was well qualified either for serious conversation or for jesting. He maintained friendship more with a view to interest than good faith. It was a common practice with him to pretend kindness where he hated, and to counterfeit dislike where he loved; to sow dissensions among friends, and try to gain favor from both sides. With such a disposition, his eloquence was very great, his language full of point and studied effect; so that neither did his facility fall short of his art, nor his invention of his facility, nor his art of his invention.

To Philip succeeded his son Alexander, a prince greater than his

[1] For the organization of the Hellenic league under Philip, see no. 128.

father in both his virtues and his vices. Each of the two had a different mode of conquering; the one prosecuted his wars with open force, the other with subtlety; the one delighted in deceiving his enemies, the other in boldly repulsing them. The one was more prudent in council, the other more noble in feeling. The father would dissemble his resentment, and often subdue it; when the son was provoked, there was neither delay nor bounds to his vengeance. They were both too fond of wine, but the ill effects of their intoxication were totally different; the father would rush from a banquet to face the enemy, cope with him, and rashly expose himself to dangers; the son vented his rage not upon his enemies but on his friends. A battle often sent Philip away wounded; Alexander often left a banquet stained with the blood of his companions. The one wished to reign with his friends, the other to reign over them. The one preferred to be loved, the other to be feared. To literature both gave equal attention. The father had more cunning, the son more honor. Philip was more staid in his words, Alexander in his actions. The son felt readier and nobler impulses to spare the conquered; the father showed no mercy even to his allies. The father was more inclined to frugality, the son to luxury. By the same course by which the father laid the foundations of the empire of the world, the son consummated the glory of conquering the whole world.

167. A Contemporary Estimate of Philip

(Theopompus, *Philippica*, i, xlix, quoted and criticised by Polybius, *Histories*, viii. 11 (Müller, *Fragmenta historicorum græcorum*, I. p. 282. 27))

In the beginning of his *Philippica* he said that what chiefly induced him to undertake it was the fact that Europe had never produced such a man as Philip son of Amyntas; and then immediately afterward, both in his preface and in the whole course of his history, he represents this king as so madly addicted to women that he did all in his power to ruin his own family by this inordinate passion, — as having behaved with the grossest unfairness and perfidy to his friends and allies; as having enslaved and treacherously seized a vast number of towns by force or fraud; and as having been besides so violently addicted to strong drink that he was often seen by his friends drunk in open day.

If, however, any one will take the trouble to read the opening passage of the forty-ninth book, he would be indeed astonished at this writer's extravagance. Besides his other strange statements he has ventured to write as follows (for I here subjoin his actual words); "If there was any man in all Greece or among the Barbarians whose character was licentious and shameless, he was invariably attracted to Philip's court in Macedon, and got the title of the 'King's companion.' For it was Philip's constant habit to reject those who lived respectably and were careful of their property; but to honor and promote those who were extravagant, and passed their lives in drinking and dicing. His influence accordingly tended not only to confirm them in these vices, but to make them proficients in every kind of rascality and lewdness. What vice or infamy did they not possess? What was there virtuous or of good report that they did not lack? Some of them, men as they were, were ever clean-shaven and smooth-skinned; and even bearded men did not shrink from mutual defilement. They took about with them two or three slaves of their lust, while submitting to the same shameful services themselves. The men whom they called 'companions' deserved a grosser name, and the title of soldier was but a cover to mercenary vice; for though blood-thirsty by nature, they were lascivious by habit. In a word, to make a long story short, especially as I have such a mass of matter to deal with, I believe that the so-called 'friends' and 'companions' of Philip were more bestial in nature and character than the Centaurs [1] who lived on Pelion, or the Læstrygones [2] who inhabited the Leontine plain, or in fact any other monsters whatever."

(Theopompus xlix, quoted by Athenæus iv. 62)

When Philip became master of great treasures, he did not spend them quickly, but threw them away and squandered them. Of all men that ever lived he was not only the worst manager himself, but all about him were so too. Absolutely not one of them had any idea of living properly or of managing his household with moderation. Of that condition he was himself the cause, being a most insatiable

[1] Here perhaps the writer has in mind the myth first told by Pindar, *Pyth.* ii. 78 *sqq.*

[2] A mythical race of cannibals located by the Greeks (*cf.* Homer, *Odyssey*, x. 119) in eastern Sicily on the plain of Leontini.

and extravagant man, doing everything in an off-hand manner, whether he was acquiring property or giving it away; for although he was a soldier, he was through pure laziness unable to count what he had coming in and what he spent. Then, too, his 'companions' were men collected together from all quarters; some came from his own country, some from Thessaly, and some from other parts of Hellas, not selected for excellence;[1] but if among either Greeks or Barbarians there was any licentious, impure, or avaricious man, he had almost every one of the same character assembled in Macedon, and they were all called friends of Philip. Even if any one came who was not entirely of that disposition, still under the influence of the life and manners of the Macedonians, he very soon became like the rest. The reason is that their wars and military expeditions and other great expenses encouraged them to be bold and to live, not in an orderly fashion, but with prodigality and like robbers.

(Polybius viii. 12)

Who would not disapprove of such bitterness and intemperance of language in a historian? It is not only because his words contradict his opening statement that he deserves stricture; but also because he has libelled the king and his friends; and still more because his falsehood is expressed in disgusting and unbecoming words. . . . When speaking of Philip and his friends a man ought to be on his guard, not so much against accusing them of effeminacy and want of courage, or still more of shameless immorality, but on the contrary, lest he should prove unequal to express their praises in a manner worthy of their manliness, indefatigable energy, and the general virtue of their character. It is notorious that by their energy and boldness they raised the Macedonian empire from a most insignificant monarchy to the first rank in reputation and extent.[2]

[1] At least it may be said in his favor that under him Macedon was absolutely open to all strangers who wished to enter, that all who desired received the citizenship, and those whom the king favored were promoted to office. In this respect his kingdom contrasted strangely with the Hellenic city-state.

[2] The criticism of Polybius is to a certain degree warranted; there can be no doubt that Theopompus took pleasure in depicting the vices of individuals, and that in doing so he indulged in exaggeration. In the main point, however, the argument of Polybius fails; Philip may well have been the ablest man who had thus far appeared in European history, and he certainly achieved all that Polybius says. In spite of ability

168. Achievements of Philip

(Arrian, *Anabasis of Alexander*, vii. 9)

Arrian was a writer of the second century A.D., but drew his material from authors who were with Alexander on his marches. The selection is an alleged speech of Alexander to his discontented Macedonian soldiers. Whether Alexander actually spoke these words we cannot say, but there is no doubt that they give a trustworthy summary of Philip's achievements.

He (Philip) found you (Macedonians) vagabonds and destitute of means, most of you clad in skins, feeding a few sheep up the mountain sides, for the protection of which you had to fight with small success against the Illyrians, Triballians, and the border Thracians. Instead of skins he gave you cloaks to wear, and from the mountains he led you down into the plains, and made you capable of fighting the neighboring barbarians, so that you were no longer compelled to preserve yourselves by trusting rather to the inaccessible strongholds than to your own valor. He made you colonists of cities, which he provided with useful laws and customs; and from being slaves and subjects, he made you rulers over those very barbarians by whom you yourselves, as well as your property, were previously liable to be carried off or ravaged. He added, too, the greater part of Thrace to Macedon, and by seizing the most conveniently situated places on the seacoast, he spread abundance over the land by commerce, and made the working of the mines a secure employment. He made you rulers over the Thessalians, of whom you had formerly been in mortal fear; and by humbling the nation of the Phocians he rendered the avenue into Greece broad and easy for you, instead of being narrow and difficult. The Athenians and Thebans, who were always lying in wait to attack the Macedonians, he humbled to such a degree, with my personal aid in the campaign, that instead of paying tribute to Athens and being in vassalage to Thebes, those states now obtain security for themselves by our assistance. He penetrated into Peloponnese; and after regulating

and achievement, however, he may have been essentially the man described by Theopompus — a man reckless of expense, addicted to drink and to worse vices, a despiser of the sober-minded among the Hellenes, and a lover of low wild company. What Polybius says would hold true in a civilized community, but he forgets that the Macedonians were barbarians, who revelled in vice, and that Philip had but a veneer of civilization.

its affairs, he was publicly declared commander in chief of all the rest of Greece in the expedition against the Persians, adding this glory not more to himself than to the commonwealth of the Macedonians.

169. Sculpture

(Pliny, *Natural History*, xxxiv. 9 *sq.* Jex-Blake, revised by E. G. S.)

The material given below for the illustration of the history of Hellenic art is from the *Natural History* of Pliny the Elder, who was killed in the eruption of Mount Vesuvius, in 79 A.D. As the selection is of such a character that it cannot be conveniently divided into parts and distributed among the various periods, the editor has taken the liberty of assigning it somewhat arbitrarily to the present chapter. The reader is to bear in mind that some of the material belongs to an earlier, some to a later, age, and that the general tone is Roman rather than Greek. See especially K. Jex-Blake, *The Elder Pliny's Chapters on the History of Art*, with commentary by E. Sellers.

The bronze most celebrated in early times was that of Delos; for as all nations resorted to the market of the island,[1] great care was bestowed on the manufacture of bronze. It was first employed for the feet and framework of couches, and afterward its use was extended to images of the Gods and figures of men and of animals.

Æginetan bronze was the next to become celebrated. Ægina was also an island; it had no mines but owed its reputation to the admirable alloys produced in its foundries.[2] A bronze bull, taken from Ægina, and now in the Cattle Market at Rome,[3] may stand for an example of Æginetan bronze and the Jupiter in the temple of Jupiter the Thunderer on the Capitol for an example of Delian bronze. Æginetan bronze was employed by Myron, and Delian by Polycleitus.[4] These two artists were contemporaries and fellow-pupils, who carried their rivalry even into their choice of a material. In Ægina it was the trays, at Tarentum the stems of candelabra which were especially elaborated, so that the efforts of several workshops combine to recommend these utensils. They are things

[1] In the Hellenistic age and in the earlier Roman period Delos was a considerable center of commerce; V. Schoeffer, in Pauly-Wissowa, *Real-Encycl.* IV. 2476 *sqq.*

[2] The bronze of Ægina was celebrated not so much for its quality as for the famous artists who wrought in this material; Sellers, note.

[3] The Forum Boarium; Tacitus, *Annals*, xii. 24. In general the works of art in Rome which Pliny mentions were brought as plunder from the Greek states.

[4] On Myron and Polycleitus, see no. 170.

without even a name except one which they borrow from the light of their candles, and yet we are not ashamed to give as much for them as the year's pay of a military tribune.

(*Ibid.* xxxiv. 36–41)

(36) Mummius filled all Rome with sculpture after his conquest of Achaia,[1] and yet I must add in his favor that he eventually died too poor to leave his daughter a dowry. The Luculli [2] too brought over a number of statues; seventy-three thousand are still to be seen at Rhodes, according to Mucianus,[3] who was three times consul, and it is supposed that at least as many still remain at Athens, Olympia and Delphi. (37) A detailed knowledge of all these is unattainable and would moreover serve no purpose; still I should like to touch on the most famous, and those which any particular circumstance has made noteworthy, and to name the illustrious artists.

Even the works of individual artists are too numerous to be catalogued; Lysippus,[4] for example, is said to have made fifteen hundred pieces of statuary, all of such merit that any one alone would bring him fame. Their number was discovered when his heir broke open his money-box after his death, for it was his custom to lay by a piece of gold out of the price he received for each statue.

(38) Art has made extraordinary progress, in technique first and afterward in audacity. As an example of successful technique I shall mention a figure representing neither god nor man. Before the last fire in the Capitol, caused by the soldiers of Vitellius, our own generation could see in the temple of Juno a bronze dog licking his wound. The wonderful workmanship and absolutely life-like treatment [5] are sufficiently proved not only by the sacred spot where the work was dedicated, but also by the unusual guarantee

[1] After his destruction of Corinth, 146, he sent shiploads of art, chiefly the plunder of that city, to Rome.

[2] Lucius Lucullus, consul in 74 B.C., the conqueror of Mithridates, and his brother Marcus; Sellers, note.

[3] C. Licinius Mucianus, a contemporary of Pliny the Elder, wrote a book of notes or observations on the works of art which he saw during a sojourn in western Asia Minor and the neighboring islands.

[4] A contemporary of Alexander the Great, the most famous sculptor of his age.

[5] Works of this kind, characterized by exaggerated realism, were a feature of the Hellenistic age.

demanded for it. No sum of money was considered equivalent; it was a public ordinance that they should pledge their lives for its safety.

(39) Of audacity countless instances can be given. For example, artists have conceived the idea of gigantic statues called colossi,[1] as tall as towers. Of this class is the Apollo in the Capitol, brought from Apollonia in Pontus by Marcus Lucullus. It is forty-five feet high, and cost five hundred talents. Another is the Jupiter dedicated in the field of Mars by Claudius Cæsar, which, however, is dwarfed by its proximity to the theatre of Pompey. (40) Yet another is the Zeus at Tarentum by Lysippus, which is forty cubits [2] in height, and is noteworthy because the weight is so nicely balanced that the colossus can, they say, be turned round by a touch of the hand, and yet cannot be overthrown by the wind. The artist is said to have provided against this possibility by placing a column a little way off, on the side where it was most necessary to break the violence of the wind. The size of the statue and the difficulty of transporting it prevented Fabius Verrucosus from touching it, although he brought the Heracles in the Capitol from Tarentum. (41) The most marvellous of all, however, is the statue of the Sun at Rhodes,[3] made by Chares of Lindus, a pupil of the Lysippus already mentioned. It was seventy cubits in height; and after standing fifty-six years, it was overthrown by an earthquake, but even as it lies on the ground it arouses wonder. Few men can clasp their arms about its thumb; its fingers are taller than most statues, and wide caverns gape within its broken limbs, while inside can be seen huge fragments of rock, originally used as weights to steady it. According to tradition its construction lasted twelve years, and cost three hundred talents, contributed by the Rhodians from the siege-train left with them by king Demetrius when he wearied of the siege of Rhodes.

[1] Statues exceeding the human standard of size were made from the earliest times, but these enormous works were a product of the late classical and Hellenistic ages.

[2] 58 feet.

[3] The colossus at Rhodes was reckoned among the "seven wonders" of the world. The idea that it stood with one foot on each of the moles that bordered the entrance to the harbor, while ships passed between its legs, is a medieval error; Sellers, note; C. Torr, *Rhodes in Ancient Times*, 96 *sq.* 70 cubits is equivalent to 102 feet.

170. The Famous Sculptors and their Works

(Pliny, *Natural History*, xxxiv. 53–84. Jex-Blake, revised by E. G. S.)

The following are among the more convenient and reliable manuals of Hellenic art. Tarbell, F. B., *History of Greek Art* (Macmillan, 1896); Fowler, H. N., and Wheeler, J. R., *Handbook of Greek Archæology* (Am. Bk. Co., 1909); Gardner, P., *Principles of Greek Art* (Macmillan, 1914); *Sculptured Tombs of Hellas* (Macmillan, 1896); Von Mach, E., *Greek Sculpture, Its Spirit and Principles* (Ginn, 1903); Gardner, E. A., *Handbook of Greek Sculpture* (Macmillan, 1896); *Six Greek Sculptors* (Scribner, 1910). The most valuable guide to the collections at Rome is Helbig, W., *Führer durch die öffentlichen Sammlungen klassischer Altertümer in Rom*, 2 vols., 3d ed. revised by Amelung and other eminent scholars (Teubner, 1912). By the use of these manuals the various artists mentioned in the subjoined excerpt may be identified and studied.

(53) I shall touch briefly on the great names, and group others under various heads. The most famous artists, although born at some distance of time from each other, still came into competition, since each had made a statue of an Amazon, to be dedicated in the temple of Artemis at Ephesus, when it was decided that the prize should be awarded to the one which the artists themselves, who were on the spot, declared to be the best. This proved to be the statue which each artist placed second to his own, namely that of Polycleitus. The statue of Pheidias was second, that of Cresilas third, Cydon's fourth, and Phradmon's fifth.

(54) Besides his Olympian Zeus, a work which has no rival, Pheidias made in ivory the Athena at Athens, which stands erect in the Parthenon. In bronze, besides the Amazon already mentioned, he made an Athena of such surpassing beauty that she was named the Fair (Forma).[1] He also made the Key-Bearer, another Athena which Æmilius Paullus dedicated at Rome in front of the temple of the Fortune of this Day,[2] two draped statues dedicated by Catulus in the same temple and a nude colossal statue. He is rightly held to have revealed the capabilities of sculpture and indicated its methods.

(55) Polycleitus of Sicyon was a pupil of Hageladas.[3] He made

[1] Also known as the Lemnian Athena; Paus. i. 28. 2.

[2] This Æmilius Paullus was the conqueror of Perseus at Pydna, 168. The temple of Fortune of this Day was on the Palatine Hill.

[3] Hageladas of Argos flourished in the sixth century, too early therefore to have been the master of Polycleitus. The connection was probably deduced from a noticeable influence.

an athlete binding the diadem about his head, which was famous for the sum of one hundred talents which it realized. This Diadumenos has been described as 'a man, yet a boy;' the Doryphoros, or 'Spear-Bearer' as 'a boy, yet a man.' He also made the statue which sculptors call the 'canon,' referring to it as a standard from which they can learn the first rules of their art. He is the only man who has been held to have embodied the principles of his art in a single work. He also made an athlete scraping himself, a nude figure advancing with a weapon, and two boys, also nude, playing with knuckle-bones, who are known as the Astragalizontes, and are now in the atrium of Imperator Titus. Many think that the faultless execution of this work has never been surpassed. (56) Other works of his are a Hermes which was at Lysimacheia; a Heracles at Rome; a Captain putting on his armor; and finally a portrait of Artemon, known by the name of Periphoretos ('Man in the Litter'). He is considered to have brought the scientific knowledge of statuary to perfection, and to have systematized the art of which Pheidias had revealed the possibilities. It was his peculiar characteristic to represent his figures standing on one leg. Varro, however, says that they are square and almost exactly after the same type.

(57) Myron was born at Eleutheræ,[1] and was also a pupil of Hageladas. He is best known by his heifer, thanks to the well-known verses written upon it, for people generally owe their reputations to the talent of others rather than to their own. He made, too, a dog and a Discobolos, or athlete hurling the discus, a Perseus, sawyers, a Satyr gazing with wonder at the pipes and Athena, winners in the five contests at Delphi, pancratiasts, and the Heracles which is near the Circus Maximus in the temple (ædes) of Pompey the Great. A poem by Erinna also tells us that he made the monument of a cicada and a locust. (58) He also made the Apollo which was taken from the Ephesians by the triumvir Antony, and restored to them by the deified Augustus, in obedience to a dream. Evidently he was the first to multiply truth;[2] he was more pro-

[1] On the Bœotian frontier of Attica.

[2] That is, he "widened the range of representation in art, inasmuch as he laid hold on moments disclosed by attentive observation of nature, but not utilized before"; quoted from Brunn by Sellers, note.

ductive than Polycleitus, and a more diligent observer of symmetry. Nevertheless he too cared only for the physical form, and did not express mental sensations, and his treatment of the hair continued to betray an archaic want of skill.

(59) Pythagoras of Rhegium in Italy surpassed Myron with the pancratiast placed at Delphi; with the same statue he also surpassed Leontiscus. Furthermore he made the statues of the runner Astylus and of a Libyan, which are to be seen at Olympia. For the same place he made the boy holding a tablet, and a nude male figure carrying apples. At Syracuse is a statue by him of a man limping, the pain of whose ulcer even the spectators seem to feel. He was the first to make the sinews and veins duly prominent, and to bestow greater pains upon the hair. (60) A second Pythagoras, a Samian, was in early life a painter. Near the Temple of the Fortune of the Day are seven nude figures by him, and an old man, which are praised. According to tradition his personal resemblance to the other Pythagoras was so strong that the two could be mistaken. It was the Rhegine Pythagoras, however, of whom Sostratus was the pupil and nephew.

(61) Duris declared that Lysippus of Sicyon was no man's pupil; that he was originally a coppersmith, and was encouraged to venture on a higher path by the words of Eupompus. That painter, when asked which of the earlier artists he followed, pointed to a crowd of people, and replied that nature should be imitated and not any artist. (62) Lysippus produced more works than any other artist, possessing, as I have said, a most prolific genius. Among them is the 'man scraping himself' (Apoxyomenos), which Marcus Agrippa dedicated in front of his baths. In this statue the princeps Tiberius took a marvellous delight, and though capable of self-control in the first years of his principate, he could not refrain from having the statue removed into his private chamber, substituting another in its place. The populace of Rome resented this so deeply that they raised an outcry in the theatre, demanding the restitution of the Apoxyomenos, to which the princeps was fain to yield, in spite of the passion he had conceived for the statue.

(63) Lysippus has also won fame by his drunken flute-player, his dogs and huntsmen, and above all by the four-horse chariot and the figure of the Sun made for the Rhodians. He also made a

number of portraits of Alexander the Great, beginning with one of him as a boy, which the princeps Nero, who was greatly charmed with the statue, ordered to be gilded. Then as this costly addition spoiled the beauty of the work, the gold was removed, and the statue was considered the more valuable without it, in spite of the scars on it and the incisions for fastening the gold. (64) Furthermore he made a statue of Hephæstion, the friend of Alexander the Great, which some ascribe to Polycleitus, although that artist lived almost a hundred years earlier. We have also from his hand an Alexander in a hunting group, which is consecrated at Delphi, a Satyr at Athens and a troop of Alexander's personal guard, in which all his friends' portraits are rendered with great fidelity. This group was transported to Rome by Metellus after the conquest of Macedonia.[1] By Lysippus too are various four-horse chariots. (65) His chief contributions to the art of sculpture are said to consist in his vivid rendering of the hair, in making the heads smaller than older artists had done, and the bodies slimmer and with less flesh, thus increasing the apparent height of the figures. There is no word in Latin for the canon of symmetry (symmetria) which he was so careful to preserve, bringing innovations which had never been thought of before into the square canon of the older artists, and he often said that the difference between himself and them was that they represented men as they were, and he as they appeared to be. His chief characteristic is extreme delicacy of execution even in the smallest details.

(66) He left artists of high reputation in his sons and pupils, Laippus, Boëdas, and above all Euthycrates. The latter however imitated not so much the refinement as the perseverance of his father, choosing to win approval by an austere rather than a lighter style of execution. In this manner he made for Delphi an admirable statue of Heracles, for Thespiæ an Alexander hunting, a group of the Thespiades, and a combat between horsemen, a statue of Trophonius with his oracular cave, several chariots with four horses, a horse carrying hunting prongs, and hunting dogs.

(67) His pupil was Teisicrates, also a native of Sicyon, who followed more closely the school of Lysippus, so that many of his works can hardly be distinguished from those of the master. Wit-

[1] 146 B.C.

ness his portrait of an old man at Thebes, of King Demetrius and of Peucestes, who saved Alexander's life and well deserves the honor of a statue.

(68) Those sculptors who have written treatises on the subject give high praise to Telephanes of Phocæa, who is otherwise unknown, since, they say, he lived in Thessaly, where his works remained unnoticed. These writers, however, adjudge him a place beside Polycleitus, Myron and Pythagoras, praising his statues of Larissa, of Spintharus, a winner in the five contests, and of Apollo. Others give a different reason for his comparative obscurity saying that he passed into the service of king Xerxes and of Darius.

(69) Praxiteles also, though more successful and consequently better known as a worker in marble, created admirable works in bronze; a rape of Persephone, the Catagousa ('Spinning Girl'), a Dionysus, a figure of Intoxication grouped with an admirable Satyr known among the Greeks as the 'Renowned,' and also the statues which stood in front of the temple of Felicity, and an Aphrodite which was destroyed when the temple was burned down in the principate of Claudius, the worthy peer of his famous marble Aphrodite. (70) Other works of his are the Stephanousa ('Woman presenting a Wreath'), the Pselioumenê ('Woman clasping a Bracelet on her Arm'), Opora (Autumn), and statues of Harmodius and Aristogeiton, Slayers of the Tyrant. These statues were carried off by Xerxes, king of the Persians, and restored to Athens by Alexander the Great after his conquest of Persia. He also made a young Apollo with an arrow watching a lizard as it creeps up, with the intent to slay it close at hand. This is known as the Sauroctonos ('Lizard-Slayer'). There are two statues by him expressing contrary emotions, a mourning matron and a rejoicing courtesan. The latter is believed to be Phryne. The sculptor's love may be read in the whole statue, and Phryne's satisfaction is depicted on her face.

(71) There is also a statue which testifies to the kindness of Praxiteles; for he made a charioteer for a four-horse chariot by Calamis, not wishing it to be thought that Calamis failed in the man after succeeding with the horses. Calamis made other four-horse and two-horse chariot groups with varying success, though

unrivalled in his horses. And yet, for it must not be thought that he was inferior to others in representing the human figure, no artist has better portrayed the poet Alcman.

(72) Alcamenes, a pupil of Pheidias, produced works in marble as well as a winner in the five contests in bronze, called the Enkrinomenos ('Undergoing the Test'). A pupil of Polycleitus, Aristeides, made chariots with four horses and with two. Amphicrates is famous for his Leaina ('Lioness'). This Leaina was a courtesan, intimate, through her playing on the lyre, with Harmodius and Aristogeiton, whose plot of assassination she refused to betray, though tortured to death by the tyrants. The Athenians were anxious to pay her honor, and yet unwilling to commemorate a courtesan by a statue. Accordingly they made a figure of the animal whose name she bore, and to indicate their reason for honoring her, they forbade the artist to give it a tongue. (73) Bryaxis made an Asclepius and a Seleucus; Boëdas a praying figure; Baton the Apollo and Hera which are in the temple of Concord at Rome; (74) Cresilas a wounded man at the point of death, whose face betrays how fast his blood is ebbing, and also an Olympian Pericles, worthy of the epithet. The marvel of his art is that it made famous men yet more famous. Cephisodorus made a wonderful Athena in the harbor of Athens, and in the same city, in the temple of Zeus the Saviour, an altar to which few are comparable. (75) Canachus made the nude Apollo, which is named the Lover and is in the temple of Didyma, of Æginetan bronze, and with it a stag so poised upon its feet that a thread can be drawn beneath them while the heel and toe alternately catch the ground, both parts working with a jointed mechanism in such a way that the impact suffices to make them spring backward and forward. He also made boys on racehorses. (*Then follow several less-known artists omitted from this selection*). . . .

(79) Lycius was a pupil of Myron. In the boy blowing a dying fire he created a work worthy of his master; further, he made statues of the Argonauts. The eagle of Leochares appears to know how precious a burden it is ravishing in Ganymede and to what master it bears him, and its talons hold the boy tenderly though his dress protects him. He also made a statue of Autolycus, who was victorious in the pancration and in whose honor Xenophon

wrote the *Banquet;* the celebrated Zeus with the thunderbolt in the Capitol, a work of supreme excellence; Apollo wearing the diadem; the slave-dealer Lyciscus and a boy, on whose face may be read the wily craft of the servile character. Lycius too made a woman burning perfumes. . . .

(81) Styppax of Cyprus is known by one statue only, the Splanchnoptes ('Roaster of Entrails'). This was a slave of Pericles the Olympian; he is roasting entrails and blowing hard on the fire to kindle it, till his cheeks swell. Seilanion cast a portrait of Apollodorus, who was also a sculptor, who often broke up a finished statue, being unable to reach the ideal he aimed at; from this circumstance he was called the 'Madman.' (82) This characteristic Seilanion rendered, and made his bronze, not a portrait of an individual, but of a figure of Vexation itself. He also made a famous Achilles and a trainer exercising his athletes.

Strongylion made the Amazon called Euknemos, from the beauty of its legs. It was because of this special feature that the princeps Nero carried the statue about with him in his train. He also made the boy which Brutus of Philippi loved, and rendered illustrious by his name. (83) Theodorus, the maker of the labyrinth at Samos, also cast a portrait of himself in bronze, famed as a wondrous likeness, and celebrated for the extreme delicacy of the workmanship. The right hand holds a file, while three fingers of the left hand support a tiny team of four horses, which is now at Præneste — so small that the team, marvellous to relate, with chariot and charioteer, could be covered by the wings of a fly which the artist made to accompany it. Xenocrates was a pupil of Teisicrates, or according to some authorities, of Euthycrates. He outdid both in the number of statues which he produced, and he also wrote books on his art.

(84) The battles of Attalus and Eumenes against the Gauls were represented by several artists, Isogonus, Pyromachus, Stratonicus and Antigonus, who also wrote books on his art.

Boëthus, though greater as a worker in silver, made a child hugging a goose till he throttles it.

The best of all the works I have mentioned have now been dedicated at Rome by the princeps Vespasian in the temple of Peace and in his other galleries, Nero having first brought them by the strong hand to Rome, and placed them in the apartments of the Golden House.

171. The Most Famous Painters and their Works

(Pliny, *Natural History*, xxxv. 15, 53–97. Jex-Blake, revised by E. G. S.)

(15) The origin of painting is obscure, and hardly falls within the scope of this work. The claim of the Egyptians to have discovered the art six thousand years before it reached Greece is obviously an idle boast,[1] while among the Greeks some say that it was first discovered at Sicyon, others at Corinth. All however agree that painting began with the outlining of a man's shadow. This was the first stage; in the second a single color was employed; and after the discovery of more elaborate methods this style, which is still in vogue, received the name of monochrome. . . .

(53) I now propose to mention the most famous painters as briefly as may be, for a detailed account would be inconsistent with the scheme of my work. It will therefore be enough if I give some artists only a passing notice, or name them in connection with others. But I must still make separate mention of the most renowned paintings, whether they be still in existence or whether they have perished. . . .

(57) Panænus, brother of Pheidias, painted the battle between the Athenians and Persians at Marathon.[2] So extensively were colors now used, so perfect had technique now become, that he is actually said to have given the real portraits of the commander on each side, of Miltiades, Callimachus and Cynægeirus among the Athenians, of Datis and Artaphrenes among the barbarians. (58) Nay more, competitions for painters were instituted at Corinth and Delphi in the time of Panænus, when in the first contest he tried for the prize against Timagoras of Chalcis, who conquered him — as we know from an old epigram by Timagoras himself — at the Pythian games — an evident proof that the chroniclers are wrong in their dates. Yet other painters became famous before the ninetieth Olympiad,[3] as for example, Polygnotus of Thasos, who first

[1] Though ridiculed by the Greeks, the claim of the Egyptians is now known to be substantially true.

[2] This picture is variously assigned to Panænus, Micon, and Polygnotus; Sellers, note.

[3] 420–417 B.C.

painted women with transparent garments and gave them head-dresses of various colors. This artist made a first serious contribution to the development of painting by opening the mouth, showing the teeth, and varying the stiff archaic effect of the features. (59) He painted the picture now in the Portico of Pompey and formerly in front of his Senate-Chamber, representing a warrior armed with a shield, about whom people argue whether he is ascending or descending. He also decorated the temple at Delphi, and at Athens the Painted Porch as it is called. For this work he took no money, while Micon, to whom part of the work was intrusted, accepted payment. The position he thus won for himself was all the greater, so much so that the Amphictyonic council, or national assembly of Hellas, decreed that he should be a public guest. There was another Micon, distinguished as the Younger, whose daughter Timaretê was also an artist.

(60) In the ninetieth Olympiad lived Aglaophon, Cephisodorus, Erillus, and Evenor, the father and master of the great artist Parrhasius, whom I shall mention in due time. They were all notable painters, yet they need not prevent my hastening on to the true luminaries of art, among whom the first to shine was Apollodorus of Athens in the ninety-third Olympiad.[1] He was the first to give his figures the appearance of reality, and he first bestowed true glory on the brush. He painted a priest at prayer, and an Aias struck by lightning, which is still to be seen at Pergamon. No picture of any of his predecessors really rivets the gaze. (61) It was he who opened the gates of art through which Zeuxis of Heracleia passed in the fourth year of the ninety-fifth Olympiad,[2] giving to the painter's brush (for of the brush alone I speak as yet) the full glory to which it already aspired. Zeuxis is erroneously placed by some in the eighty-ninth Olympiad;[3] it is evident that Demophilus of Himera and Neseus of Thasos were among his contemporaries, seeing that there is a controversy as to which of the two was his master. (62) In an epigram written against him by the Apollodorus whom I mentioned above, it is said that 'Zeuxis bore away with him the art he had stolen from his masters.' He amassed great wealth; and in order to make a parade of it at Olympia, he showed his name woven in golden letters into the embroideries of

[1] 408–405 B.C. [2] 397 B.C. [3] 424–421 B.C.

his garments. Afterward he began to make presents of his pictures, saying that they were beyond all price. In this way he gave his Alcmena to the city of Agrigentum and his Pan to Archelaus. He also painted a Penelope, in whom he embodied Virtue's self, and an athlete with whom he was so well pleased that he wrote beneath it the line thenceforward famous; (63) "Another may carp more easily than he may copy." He also painted a superb Zeus enthroned amid the assembled Gods, with the infant Heracles strangling the snakes in presence of his trembling mother Alcmena and of Amphitryon. (64) Zeuxis is criticised, however, as having exaggerated the heads and extremities of his figures. For the rest he bestowed such minute pains upon his work that before painting for the people of Agrigentum a picture to be dedicated in the temple on the Lacinian promontory, he inspected the girls of the city unclad, and chose out five, whose peculiar beauties he proposed to reproduce in his picture. He also painted monochromes in white. Timanthes, Androcydes, Eupompus and Parrhasius were contemporaries and rivals of Zeuxis.

(65) The story runs that Parrhasius and Zeuxis entered into competition, Zeuxis exhibiting a picture of some grapes so true to nature that the birds flew up to the wall of the stage. Parrhasius then displayed a picture of a linen curtain realistic to such a degree that Zeuxis, elated by the verdict of the birds, cried out that now at last his rival must draw the curtain and show his picture. On discovering the mistake he surrendered the prize to Parrhasius, admitting candidly that he had deceived the birds, while Parrhasius had deluded himself, a painter. (66) Afterward we learn that Zeuxis painted a boy carrying grapes, and when the birds flew down to settle on them, he was vexed with his own work, and came forward saying with like frankness: 'I have painted the grapes better than the boy; for had I been perfectly successful with the latter, the birds must have been afraid.' He also modeled certain terracottas which were the only works of art left in Ambracia when Fulvius Nobilior brought the statues of the Muses to Rome. The paintings in Rome by the hand of Zeuxis are: the Helen in the Portico of Philippus and the bound Marsyas in the temple of Concord.

(67) Parrhasius, a native of Ephesus, also made great contri-

butions to the progress of art. He first gave painting symmetry, and added vivacity to the features, daintiness to the hair, and comeliness to the mouth, while by the verdict of artists he is unrivalled in the rendering of outline. This is the highest subtlety attainable in painting. Merely to paint a figure in relief is no doubt a great achievement, yet many have succeeded thus far. But where an artist is rarely successful is in finding an outline which shall express the contours of the figure. (68) For the contour should appear to fold back, and so enclose the object as to give assurance of the parts behind, thus clearly suggesting even what it conceals. Preëminence in this respect is conceded to Parrhasius by Antigonus and Xenocrates, writers on painting, who indeed not only concede but insist upon it. Many other traces of his draughtsmanship remain both in pictures and on parchments, which are said to be instructive to artists. Still, if tried by his own standard, he fails in modeling. (69) He painted an ingenious personification of the Athenian 'Demos,' discovering it as a fickle, passionate, unjust, changeable, yet exorable, compassionate and pitiful, boastful, proud and humble, bold and cowardly, in a word, everything at once. He also painted the Theseus formerly in the Capitol at Rome, an admiral in armor, and Meleager, Heracles and Perseus in a picture at Rhodes, where it has thrice been set on fire by lightning without being destroyed, a miracle which increases our wonder. (70) Further, he painted a priest of Cybele — a picture of which the princeps Tiberius was fond, and which according to Deculo,[1] although valued at 6,000,000 sesterces, he placed in his private apartments. Moreover he painted a Thracian nurse with an infant in her arms; a portrait of Philiscus, Dionysus by the side of Virtue, two boys whose features express the confidence and the simplicity of their age, and a priest with a boy at his side holding a censer and a wreath. (71) Two other pictures by him are most famous, a hoplite in a race who seems to sweat as he runs, and a hoplite laying aside his arms, whose laboring breath we seem to hear. His picture of Æneias, Castor and Polydeuces is praised; so is his Telephus with Achilles, Agamemnon and Odysseus. He was a prolific artist but carried his success with an arrogance that none

[1] One of Pliny's sources; he lived under or shortly after Tiberius; *cf.* F. Münzer, *Beiträge zur Quellenkritik der Naturgeschichte des Plinius* (Berlin, 1897), 400 *sq.*

have equalled. He called himself the 'luxurious,' and said in another epigram that he was the prince of painting, that he had brought it to the highest point of perfection, and more than all, that he was of the seed of Apollo and had painted the Heracles of Lindos precisely as he had often seen him asleep.[1] (72) Hence it was that when he was defeated by a large majority of votes in a competition with Timanthes at Samos, the subject of his picture being Aias and the Award of the Arms, he said in the name of the hero that he was grieved at being worsted a second time by an unworthy rival. Further, he painted small pictures of licentious subjects, seeking relaxation in this wanton humor.[2]

(73) To return — Timanthes was a painter most curious in invention, for by him is that Iphigeneia, praised by the orators, whom he depicted standing by the altar ready for death. Having represented all the onlookers, and especially her father's brothers, as plunged in sorrow, and having thus exhausted every presentment of grief, he has veiled the face of her father, for which he had reserved no adequate expression. (74) There are other examples of his inventiveness; for instance, being desirous of emphasizing, even in a small picture, the huge size of a sleeping Cyclops, he painted some Satyrs at his side, measuring his thumb with a thyrsos. He is the only artist whose works always suggest more than is in the picture; and great as is his dexterity, his power of invention yet exceeds it. He also painted a hero, a picture in which he touched perfection, having comprehended in it the whole art of painting the male form. The picture is now at Rome in the temple of Peace.

(75) In this period Euxeinidas was the master of Aristeides, a famous artist, and Eupompus of Pamphilus, who in turn was the master of Apelles. We have by Eupompus a victor in an athletic contest holding a palm. So great was this artist's reputation that it occasioned a new division of the schools of painting. Before his time there had been two schools, known as the Helladic proper and the Asiatic; but now the Helladic was subdivided in his honor, and

[1] This anecdote and the epigrams mentioned above may be found in Athenæus xii. 62. The following especially he used to inscribe on his works:

Parrhasius, a most luxurious man,
And yet a follower of purest virtue,
Painted this work.

[2] *Cf.* Suetonius, *Tiberius*, 44.

thus the schools became three; the Ionic, the Sicyonian, and the Attic, Eupompus himself being a Sicyonian.

(76) By Pamphilus we have a family group, the victorious engagement of the Athenians at Phlius, and a picture of Odysseus on his raft. A Macedonian by birth, Pamphilus was the first painter who was thoroughly trained in every branch of learning, more particularly in arithmetic and geometry, without which, so he held, art could not be perfect. He taught no one for less than a talent — five hundred denarii [1] — a year — the fee paid him both by Apelles and by Melanthius. (77) It was owing to his influence that first at Sicyon, and afterward throughout Hellas, drawing, or rather painting, on tablets of boxwood was the earliest subject taught to freeborn boys, and that this art was accepted as the preliminary step toward a liberal education. At all events it was held in such honor that at all times the freeborn and afterward persons of distinction practised it, while by standing prohibition no slaves might ever acquire it; and this is why neither in painting nor in statuary are there any celebrated works by artists who had been slaves. . . .

(79) In the hundred and twelfth Olympiad [2] Apelles of Cos excelled all painters who came before or after him. He of himself perhaps contributed more to painting than all the others together; he wrote treatises, too, on the theory of his art. The grace of his genius remained quite unrivalled, although the very greatest painters were living at the time. He would admire their works, praising every beauty and yet observing that they failed in the grace, called *charis* in Greek, which was distinctly his own. Everything else they had attained; in this alone none equalled him. (80) He laid claim to another merit; while admiring a work of Protogenes that betrayed immense industry and the most anxious elaboration, he said that, though Protogenes was his equal or even his superior in everything, he yet surpassed that painter in one point — namely in knowing when to take his hand from a picture — a memorable saying, which shows that too much care may often be hurtful. His candor was equal to his genius; he acknowledged the superiority of Melanthius in the distribution of figures, and that of Ascle-

[1] In the time of Pliny a denarius was about 16 cents.

[2] 332–329 B.C.

piodorus in perspective arrangement, that is, in giving accurate distances between different objects.

(81) A neat story is told of him in connection with Protogenes, who was living at Rhodes. Thither Apelles sailed, eager to see the works of a man known to him only by reputation, and on his arrival immediately repaired to the studio. Protogenes was not at home, but a solitary old woman was keeping watch over a large panel placed on the easel. In answer to the questions of Apelles, she said that Protogenes was out and asked the name of the visitor. 'Here it is,' said Apelles, and snatching up a brush, he drew a line of great delicacy across the board. (82) On the return of Protogenes the old woman told him what had happened. When he had considered the delicate precision of the line, he at once declared that his visitor was Apelles, for no one else could have drawn anything so perfect. Then in another color he drew a second still finer line upon the first, and went away, bidding her show it to Apelles if he came again, and add that this was the man he was seeking. It fell out as he had expected: Apelles did return, and ashamed to be beaten, drew a third line of another color cutting the two first down their length and leaving no room for any further refinements. (83) Protogenes owned himself beaten and hurried down to the harbor to find his visitor. They agreed to hand down the painting just as it was to posterity, a marvel to all but especially to artists. It perished, I am told, in the first fire of the house of the Cæsars on the Palatine. Formerly we might look upon it; its wide surface disclosed nothing save lines which eluded the sight, and among the numerous works of excellent painters it was like a blank, and it was precisely this feature that lent it surpassing attraction and renown.

(84) Apelles further made it an unvarying rule never to spend a day, however busy, without drawing a line by way of practise; hence the proverb.[1] It was also his habit to exhibit his finished works to the passers-by in a balcony, and he would lie concealed behind the picture and listen to the faults that were found with it, regarding the public as more accurate critics than himself. (85) There is a story that when found fault with by a cobbler for putting one loop too few on the inner side of a sandal, he corrected the mistake. Elated by this, the cobbler next day proceeded to find fault

[1] The proverb is Nulla dies sine linea (No day without a line); Sellers, note.

with the leg, whereupon Apelles thrust out his head in a passion and bade the cobbler 'stick to his last,' a saying which has also passed into a proverb. . . .

(88) His portraits were such perfect likenesses that, incredible as it may sound, Apio the grammarian has left it on record that a physiognomist was able to tell from the portraits alone how long the sitter had to live or had already lived. (89) When in Alexander's train he had been on unfriendly terms with Ptolemy, during whose reign he was once driven into Alexandria by a violent storm. As Apelles appeared at a banquet, to which his rivals had maliciously induced the king's fool to invite him, Ptolemy flew into a passion, and pointing to his chamberlains bade him say from which of them he had received his invitation. Thereupon the painter, snatching up a charred stick from the hearth, traced on the wall a likeness whose first strokes the king at once recognized as the face of the fool.

(90) He also painted a portrait of king Antigonus, who was blind of one eye; and he was the first to devise a means of concealing the infirmity by presenting his profile, so that the absence of the eye would be attributed to the position of the sitter merely, not to a natural defect; for he gave only the part of the face which could be shown uninjured. There are among his works some pictures of dying people, though it were difficult to say which were best. (91) His Aphrodite rising from the sea was dedicated by the deified Augustus in the temple of his father Cæsar. She is known as the Anadyomenê, being like other works of the kind at once eclipsed yet rendered famous by the Greek epigrams written in her praise. When the lower part was damaged, no one could be found to restore it, and thus the very injury redounded to the glory of the artist. In time the panel of the picture fell to decay, and Nero when princeps substituted for it another picture by the hand of Dorotheus.

(92) Apelles had begun another Aphrodite at Cos, intending to surpass even the fame of his earlier achievement, but when only a part was finished envious death interposed, and no one was found to complete the outlines already traced. Further he painted, for twenty talents, in the temple of Artemis at Ephesus a portrait of Alexander holding a thunderbolt. The fingers seem to stand out

and the thunderbolt to project from the picture. The reader should remember that all this was done with four colors. For this picture he was paid in gold coins, reckoned not by number but by measure. (93) He painted too the train of a megabyzus, or priest of Artemis at Ephesus, Cleitus on horseback going out to battle, and the picture of a squire handing a helmet to one who asks for it. It were vain to enumerate the number of times he painted Alexander and Philip. At Samos we admire his Habron, at Rhodes his Menander king of Caria and his Antæus, at Alexandria his Gorgosthenes the tragic actor, at Rome Castor and Polydeuces with Victory and Alexander the Great, and also a figure of War with his hands bound behind his back, and Alexander riding in triumph in a chariot. (94) These two pictures had been placed in the most crowded parts of his Forum with the restraint of good taste by the deified Augustus; but the deified Claudius thought fit to cut out in both the face of Alexander and substitute that of Augustus.

The Heracles with averted face, in the temple of Diana, is also attributed to Apelles; by a triumph of art the picture seems not only to suggest, but actually to give the face. Moreover he painted a nude hero, a picture which challenges comparison with Nature herself. (95) A horse also exists, or did exist, painted for a competition, in which he appealed from the judgment of men to that of dumb beasts. When he saw that his rivals were likely to be placed above him through intrigue, he caused some horses to be brought in and showed them each picture in turn. They neighed only at the horse of Apelles, and this was invariably the case ever afterward, so that the test was applied purposely to afford a display of his skill. (96) He also painted Neoptolemus [1] on horseback fighting against the Persians, Archelaüs in a group with his wife and daughter, and a portrait of Antigonus in armor advancing with his horse. Skilled judges of painting prefer among all his works his equestrian portrait of Antigonus and his Artemis amid a band of girls offering sacrifice, a painting thought to have excelled the lines of Homer [2] that describe the same scene. Further, he painted the unpaintable, thunder for example, lightning and thunderbolts. . . .

[1] This Neoptolemus and the Archelaüs following were officers of Alexander the Great; Sellers, note.

[2] *Odyssey* vi. 102 *sqq*.

(97) All have profited by his innovations, though one of them could never be imitated; he used to give his pictures when finished a black glazing so thin that by sending back the light it could call forth a whitish color, while at the same time it afforded a protection from dust and dirt, only becoming visible itself on the closest inspection. In using this glazing one main purpose was to prevent the brilliance of the colors from offending the eyes — the effect was as when they are looked at through talc — and also that when seen at a distance, those which were excessively vivid might be toned down.[1]

[1] For an explanation of this rendering see Sellers, note.

CHAPTER XVI

ADMINISTRATION, INDUSTRY, AND EDUCATION IN THE HELLENISTIC KINGDOMS 337–30 B.C.

A. ALEXANDER AND THE GREEK CITIES

172. Letter of Alexander to the People of Chios (333–332 B.C.)

(Hicks and Hill, no. 158; Ditt., *Syll.* I. no. 150. Translated by W. L. W.)

When Alexander invaded Asia, 334 B.C., Macedon was already an imperial state, and his position was a double one: he was king of Macedon and hegemon (war-leader) of those Greek cities which had joined the league of the Hellenes established by Philip, his father, in the winter of 338–337 (no. 128). The Greek cities of the coast of Asia Minor, which were freed from Persia in the campaign of 334, added another and different element to the two already under Alexander's sway. His plans for the final disposition of these cities, also his intentions in regard to the extent and the character of the authority of the council of the Hellenic league, are foreshadowed in this letter.

The Persian admiral, Memnon, had occupied Chios in 333, and had established in power the oligarchic or Persian party, which had aided him in taking the city. Soon thereafter, probably in 332, the popular party handed the city over to the troops who were attempting to recapture it from the Persians. This letter was probably written immediately before the Macedonians retook the city. See Niese, B., *Geschichte der griechischen und makedonischen Staaten*, I. 37–40; Ferguson, *Greek Imperialism*, ch. iv.

When Dositheus was prytanis:[1] From Alexander to the demus of the Chians. The exiles from Chios are to return, all of them, and the form of government of Chios is to be a democracy. Law-givers[2] are to be chosen who shall write the laws and set them in order in such a way that nothing in them shall oppose the democracy or the return of the exiles. When arranged or written the laws are to be referred to Alexander.

[1] The prytanis was the leading magistrate of the Chians by whose name the year was officially designated; *cf.* Ditt., *Syll.* II. no. 570.

[2] A special committee. Called in Greek *νομογράφοι*.

The Chians are to furnish twenty triremes, with a full complement for them, and these are to sail so long as the rest of the naval force of the Hellenes shall sail with us.

Of those who betrayed the city to the barbarians, as many as may already have escaped, are to be exiled from all the cities which have shared in the peace, and they are to be considered as outlaws according to the decree of the Hellenes. As many as may be captured, are to be brought before the Council of the Hellenes for judgment.

If any difficulty arises between the restored exiles and those in the city, they are to receive judgment in this matter in our presence. Until the Chians shall be reconciled, a garrison is to be stationed among them from Alexander, the king, as many as may be necessary. And the Chians shall support this garrison.

173. Award made by the Argive Assembly in a Case of Arbitration (337–330 B.C.)

(Hicks and Hill, no. 150; Ditt., *Syll.* II. no. 428. Translated by W. L. W.)

The following award of the assembly of Argos is interesting as an example of Greek arbitration and for the light it throws upon the use of the Common Council of the Hellenic League by Philip or Alexander. The date can only lie within a few years after the establishment of the Hellenic League by Philip II in 338–337; see *Class. Journ.* II (1906–1907), 197 *sqq.*

IN GOD'S NAME ! [1]

The demus of the Argives has made the following decision in the case referred to it by the council of the Hellenes. The Cimolians and the Melians have agreed to abide by whatever decision the Argives might make regarding the islands. The judgment is that the islands Polyægas, Etereia, and Libeia [2] belong to the Cimolians. They have adjudged that the Cimolians have won their case. Leon was priest in the second boulê of the year; Poseidaon was secretary of the boulê; Perillus was assistant.

[1] Θεός, an abbreviated prayer often found at the beginning of inscriptions.

[2] These are small islands lying near Cimolos and Melos.

B. THE ROYAL DOMAINS IN ASIA UNDER ALEXANDER AND HIS SUCCESSORS

174. Edict of Alexander Regarding Priene and the Royal Domains in its Vicinity (334 b.c.)

(Hicks and Hill, no. 155; Ditt., *Or. græc. inscrs.* no. 1. Translated by W. L. W.)

When the westernmost portion of the Persian empire fell to Alexander by conquest, 334–333, a new administrative problem of vast importance was presented to the young king. This was the question of the handling of the royal domains of the Persian ruler. The elements at that time comprised within Alexander's sway may best be listed under four divisions, partly territorial and partly ethnic. They were the kingdom of Macedon, the Hellenic league, the Greek cities of Asia Minor, and the conquered Persian territory. To each of these elements Alexander stood in a peculiar relation; he was king of Macedon, hegemon of the Hellenic league, liberator of the Greek cities of Asia (he addresses them as king), and to the conquered population he was successor to the power and appurtenances of the Persian king. All this is shown in the present edict. The land about Priene was divided into the domain of that city-state, and the royal domain, which belonged by conquest to Alexander. The royal domains paid the *phoros*, tribute, the city-states a *syntaxis*, contribution, unless as here they were especially exempt. This was the beginning of the problem of the royal domains confronting Alexander and his successors.

EDICT OF KING ALEXANDER

Of those settled in Naulochon,[1] as many as are Prienians are to be autonomous and free, keeping their plots of ground and all their houses in the city[2] and their country property . . . (*two broken lines*). . . . And all the land round about I regard as my own,[3] and that they who dwell in these villages bear the tribute (*phoros*). I absolve the city of the Prienians from the contribution (*syntaxis*) and the guard for which. . . .

175. The Feudal Estates of the Persian Nobles

(Plutarch, *Eumenes,* 8. Translated by W. L. W.)

When Eumenes of Cardia, after defeating Craterus and Neoptolemus in Phrygia, 321, was preparing to defend his rights against the combined forces of the Macedonian generals, he found himself in financial straits. In order to

[1] Naulochon was the harbor of Priene, situated at the mouth of the Mæander river.

[2] This must refer to Priene, since Naulochon was not a city.

[3] The land round about is therefore χώρα βασιλική (royal domain), and distinct from the land belonging to the city-state of Priene, as does Naulochon.

keep the loyalty of his Macedonian troops, it was necessary to devise a method of paying them. The means he employed throws light upon the agrarian conditions then existing in Phrygia. A land-holding nobility evidently controlled great estates, and owned the peasants who tilled the soil, governing them from their *tetrapyrgiai*, 'four-turreted castles.' Eumenes had accepted the theory of Alexander that the domains of the conquered Persians were the spoils of the conqueror (no. 174). See Rostowzew, *Römisches Kolonat*, 253 *sq.*

He had promised to give the soldiers their pay within three days. He therefore sold them the farms and turreted castles in the country district with their peasants [1] and cattle. The captain of a Macedonian company or the officer of a foreign troop who bought these places captured them by siege, using war implements and siege engines furnished by Eumenes. Thereupon the soldiers divided each of the captured places proportionally according to the pay due them.

176. The Alienation of Royal Domains by the Successors of Alexander (306–303?)

(*Am. Journ. Arch.* XVI (1912). 12–82; Rostowzew, *Römisches Kolonat*, 248–53. Translated by Buckler and Robinson.)

This document is the record of a mortgage deed made out by a certain Mnesimachus to the treasury of the goddess Artemis, as represented by the priests of her temple at Sardis. The inscription was discovered in 1910 by the American archæologists, W. H. Buckler and D. M. Robinson, on one of the inner walls of the *opisthodomus*, or treasury, of the temple of Artemis. The circumstances which led to the mortgaging of these estates, which were evidently very large, can only be learned from the document itself. They are as follows:

At some period before the date of the mortgage Antigonus Monophthalmos, in control of Asia Minor with the title of king from 306 to 301, made a large grant of lands in Lydia to this Mnesimachus, for reasons which do not appear. This grant is probably to be placed before 306, since Antigonus was not addressed as king at the time when the grant was made (lines 1 and 2). Mnesimachus was compelled later to borrow 1325 gold staters from the treasury of Artemis. When the loan became due he was unable to pay the debt. He, therefore, mortgaged the estates which he had received from Antigonus, to the goddess Artemis under a form called πρᾶσις ἐπὶ λύσει, 'sale subject to redemption.' The limit of the period of redemption is lost through an erasure of a part of the inscription. The present inscription is a copy of the original

[1] The Greek word σώματα undoubtedly includes the serfs of these manorial estates as well as the slaves.

mortgage. It was inscribed on the temple wall most probably *after* the period of redemption was past. It therefore represents a title-deed to the property, which fell to the temple at the end of the period of redemption.

The document illustrates the attitude of Alexander's immediate successors toward the domain land of the former Persian kings. In western Asia the tendency followed by the Seleucids was to lessen these royal domains by gift or sale of large tracts to individuals or to city-states. The information that may be gleaned regarding the position of the peasants is one of the most important features of this selection.

Column I

. . . Chaireas [1] having made inquiry . . . and afterwards Antigonus awarded the estate to me. Whereas now the temple-wardens are demanding from me the gold lent on deposit and belonging to Artemis, but I have no funds wherewith to pay it to them, there are then the items of which the estate consists; to wit, the villages named as follows: Tobalmoura, a village in the Sardian plain on the Hill of Ilus, and as appurtenances thereto other villages also: Tandus, as it is called, and Kombdilipia; the rent payable by the said villages to the chiliarchy [2] of Pytheus . . . is fifty gold staters a year. There is also an allotment at Kinaroa near Tobalmoura. Its rent is three gold staters a year. There is also another village, Periasasostra, in the River District of Morstas; its rent payable to the chiliarchy of ... arius, is fifty-seven gold staters a year. There is also in the River District of Morstas an allotment at Nagrioa; its rent, payable to the chiliarchy of Sagarius, son of Coreis, is three gold staters and four gold obols. There is also another village in the district of Attouda called Ilus' village; its rent is three gold staters and three obols. Now from all the villages, and from the allotments and the dwelling-plots thereto appertaining, and from the serfs (τῶν λαῶν) with all their households and belongings, and from the wine-vessels and the dues rendered in money

[1] Who Chaireas was and the nature of his inquiry cannot be determined because of the mutilation of the inscription.

[2] The chiliarchies were subdivisions of the satrapy of Lydia, evidently financial in character. The chiliarchy of Pytheus adjoined and probably included the city of Sardis. The editors are inclined to differentiate the chiliarchy of ... arius, placing it in the eastern part of the Lydian satrapy, from that of Sagarius, which they place on the Phrygian border of Lydia. The only known Attouda lies on the Lydian-Phrygian border.

and in labor, and from the revenues of other kinds accruing from the villages and still more beside these when the division took place, Pytheus [1] and Adrastus [2] received as their separate property a farmstead at Tobalmoura; and outside the farmstead are the houses of the serfs and slaves, and two gardens requiring fifteen artabas [3] of seed, and at Periasasostra dwelling-plots requiring three artabas of seed, and gardens requiring three artabas of seed, as well as the slaves dwelling at that place: at Tobalmoura, Ephesus, son of Adrastus; Kadoas, son of Adrastus; Heraclides, son of Beletras; Tuius, son of Maneus the son of Caïcus; also those dwelling at Periasasostra, Kadoas son of Armanandes, Adrastus son of Maneus. . . .

Column 2

neither to me [nor to my heirs, nor . . .] . . . nor to anyone else any longer the right of redemption. Should any person lay claim to any of the villages or of the allotments or to the other things here specified in writing, I and my heirs will act as warrantors, and will oust the claimant. If, however, we shall fail so to act, or if we shall commit any breach of the contract hereby drawn up in respect to the villages and the allotments and the lands and all the slaves, these shall remain the property of Artemis, and the temple-wardens shall on account of the same conduct legal proceedings and obtain judgment against the claimants in any way that they may see fit; and I Mnesimachus and my heirs will pay to the treasury of Artemis 2650 gold staters; [4] and on account of the produce and of the fruits, should the temple-wardens receive no fruits in that year, we will further pay to the treasury of Artemis such sum in gold as the same may be worth; and the value of the buildings erected and of the lands brought under cultivation by Artemis, or of such other things as the temple-wardens may do, whatever the same may be worth, we will pay; and so long as we shall not have paid, the debt

[1] This Pytheus may be the chiliarch mentioned before. But the identity of the two is uncertain.

[2] This Adrastus must have been some important person, and cannot be identified with the father of the slaves mentioned below. The farmstead once owned by Pytheus and Adrastus is now listed in the property of Mnesimachus.

[3] The artaba was a unit of measure equaling about 55.8 liters. The measure here used was the Persian artaba.

[4] The Macedonian gold stater was worth about $4.70.

shall continue a deposit-loan owing by us till we shall have paid the whole amount. Should the king on account of Mnesimachus take away from Artemis the villages or the allotments or any of the other things mortgaged, then the principal in gold of the deposit-loan, namely the 1325 gold staters, we ourselves — I Mnesimachus and my heirs — will forthwith pay to the treasury of Artemis; and the value of the buildings erected and of the lands brought under cultivation by Artemis, whatever they may be worth, we will pay forthwith; and on account of the produce and the fruits, should they receive no fruits in that year, we will further pay to the treasury of Artemis such sum in gold as the same may be worth; and so long as we shall not have paid, the debt shall constitute a deposit-loan owing by me and my heirs until we shall have paid the whole to the treasury of Artemis; and so long as this still remains unpaid by us, execution shall be lawful.

177. Alienation of Royal Domains by the Seleucids

(Ditt. *Or. græc. inscrs.* no. 221. Translated by W. L. W.)

On this inscription see introduction to no. 176. The documents given under this heading illustrate the transfer of land from the Royal Domain to the Land Register of a city-state; see Droysen, *Geschichte des Hellenismus*, II. 2. 377; Haussoullier, in *Rev. de Philologie*, XXV (1901). 30 *sqq.*; Rostowzew, *Römisches Kolonat*, 247 *sqq.*

When a sale or gift occurred it was necessary that the transfer of the property be recorded upon the official registers containing the records and the plots of the Royal Domain. Since, for purposes of taxation, all the land must appear somewhere upon the state records, when any tract was to be sold or given away it became necessary to cancel that tract from the land register of the Royal Domain and transfer it to the land register of the city-state concerned. In other words, the great sources of revenue of the Seleucid state were two; namely, the phoros, or tribute, from the Royal Domains, and the taxes which came in from the city-states. The peasants and the land, therefore, must be found enrolled either upon the register of the Royal Domains or upon that of some city-state. When land was alienated by sale or gift from the Royal Domain, the buyer or the person receiving the land was usually permitted to assign the land and its serfs to any city-state which he desired. The land thereupon became a part of the city-state territory.

The following document contains three letters of Antiochus, king of Syria, in all probability Antiochus I (280–261 B.C.), addressed to Meleager, governor of the Hellespontine satrapy. In these letters Antiochus gives orders to Meleager to measure off to a certain Aristodicides, a portion of the Royal Domain in the neighborhood of Ilium. Aristodicides is permitted to register the land thus granted him in any one of a group of neighboring city-states. Of the several cities which were anxious to have this territory attached to their city-state domain, he had selected Ilium. Then Meleager sent copies of the three letters of the king to the people of Ilium, headed by a letter from himself to them (I). In this letter Meleager advises them to pay the customary honors to Aristodicides.

I. Meleager to the Boulê and the Demus of Ilium, greeting: Aristodicides of Assos has given me letters from the king, Antiochus, copies of which I have appended below for you. He also appeared in person before me and stated that many others also were discussing the matter with him and granting him a crown; and I also know this to be true, because certain of the cities have sent embassies to me. Despite this he said that he desired the land granted to him by the king, Antiochus, to be attached to your city, both because of the temple and because of his good-will toward you. What he then desires to receive from your city, he himself will declare to you. You would do well to vote him all the customary decrees of friendship and to make a copy, according as he may agree, and inscribe it on a stele [1] and set it up in the temple, in order that the agreements may remain secure for you for all time.

II. King Antiochus to Meleager, greeting: We have granted to Aristodicides of Assos two thousand plethra [2] of arable land, to be attached to the city of Ilium or of Scepsis. You, therefore, give orders to furnish to Aristodicides from the domain adjoining Gergitha or Scepsis, wherever you may judge best, the 2000 plethra of land, and attach it to the city of Ilium, or of Scepsis. Farewell.

III. King Antiochus to Meleager, greeting: Aristodicides of Assos has appeared before us asking that we give him Petra in the satrapy of the Hellespont, which Meleager [3] formerly held, and 1500 plethra of the arable land of the district of Petra and 2000 plethra more of arable land from that which borders upon the grant already made to him. And we have given Petra to him, unless it has already been given to another, and the land near Petra and

[1] A stele was a stone slab.

[2] A plethrum was a Greek unit of measure falling a little short of a quarter of an acre.

[3] This Meleager is a different man from the satrap of the Hellespontine satrapy to whom the letter is addressed.

2000 plethra more of arable land, because he has shown himself to have been our friend with all good will and eagerness. Do you therefore look to see whether this district has already been given to another, and, if not, transfer it and the land around it to Aristodicides; and give orders to have measured off and transferred to him 2000 plethra from the royal domain bordering upon the land formerly given to Aristodicides, and allow him to register it with whatsoever city he may desire of those in the district and in the alliance. We have given orders to Aristodicides to permit the Royal Peasants [1] of the district in which Petra lies, to dwell in Petra if they wish to do so for the sake of safety. Farewell.

IV. King Antiochus to Meleager, greeting.

Aristodicides has come to us, asserting that he has not even yet received the place Petra and the land belonging with it, regarding which we have formerly written a letter granting it to him, through the fact that it had already been alloted to the Athenæum,[2] the one at the harbor. And he has requested that, in place of the Petrite land an equal number of plethra be transferred to him, and that 2000 plethra more be granted him, to be registered with whatsoever city he may wish of those in our alliance, just as we wrote formerly. Seeing, then, that he is well-disposed and eager in our affairs we wish to be very careful of this man and have agreed to these things. He says that the part of the Petrite land granted to him was 1500 plethra. Give orders, therefore, to measure off and transfer to Aristodicides 2500 plethra of arable land, and, in place of that around Petra, 1500 plethra more of arable land from the Royal Domain bordering upon that given to him by us in the beginning. Permit Aristodicides, also, to register the land with whatsoever city he may wish of those in our alliance, just as we wrote in the former letter. Farewell.

[1] The Greek is *βασιλικοὶ λαοί*.

[2] The temple and precinct of the goddess Athena.

178. Alienation of Royal Domain by the Seleucids: Decree Recording the Sale of a Tract near Cyzicus (253 B.C.)

(Ditt. *Or. græc. inscrs.* no. 225. Translated by W. L. W.)

The following document is the record of a sale to Laodice, queen of Antiochus II, of a tract of the Royal Domain near Cyzicus. The upper portion of the stone is lost. It consisted, first, of the order of Nicomachus, œconomus of the Hellespontine satrapy, to the under-official, ... crates the hyparch, who is to see to it that this transfer is properly made. Below this order of Nicomachus stood the letter of Metrophanes, satrap of the Hellespontine satrapy, to Nicomachus, which contained a copy of the letter of King Antiochus II to Metrophanes. The inscription begins in the midst of the king's letter, III. Section IV is a copy of the official record by the hyparch, ... crates, of the transfer of the property. The actual steps taken in executing the sale occurred in the reverse order: 1. Sale by the king to Laodice; 2. the king writes to the satrap Metrophanes; 3. Metrophanes writes to Nicomachus, the œconomus, who has charge of the Royal Domains in the Hellespontine satrapy, sending a copy of the king's letter; 4. Nicomachus writes to an under official, the hyparch, who is in charge of the Royal Domain in the same satrapy, sending to him copies of Metrophanes' letter and the king's letter. 5. The hyparch adds to these three documents a copy of the record of sale and has them published in five places in accordance with the king's orders. Of these five copies of the correspondence our inscription is the one placed in the temple of Apollo at Didyma near Miletus.

When portions of the Royal Domain were granted away or alienated by sale, the tract was transferred to the register of some city-state. The laoi, or serfs, did not ordinarily become the serfs of the individual who received the land. With the land they were attached to some city-state and became serfs upon the books of that city-state. That fact does not appear clearly defined in this document, probably because Laodice was a member of the royal household and the royal prerogative of owning serfs seems to be permitted her. See *Rev. de Philol.* XXV (1901). 9 *sqq.*; Rostowzew, *Römisches Kolonat*, I. 243–53; *Klio*, 295–99, 424–26.

III . . . (Laodice has bought) the village of Pannos and whatever other (village) shall be formed later, and whatever places[1] fall within the territory, and the peasants (laoi) belonging to them, with their entire households and all their possessions together with the revenues of the fifty-ninth year,[2] for thirty talents of silver.

[1] The meaning of the word "places" (τόπους) is not clear. It seems to refer to the homesteads within the districts which are not in the village itself.

[2] This is the fifty-ninth year of the Seleucid era, which dates from the year 312 B.C., when Seleucus I established his power in Babylon.

Furthermore whatever laoi of this village have gone into other places belong to her on the understanding that she shall pay nothing into the royal treasury, and that she shall have the right to assign them to whatever city she may wish. Likewise those who have bought or received land from her shall have full possession of it, and shall attach it to whatever city-state they wish, unless Laodice happen to have attached it beforehand to a city; and in that case they shall have proprietary rights wheresoever the land has been attached by Laodice. As to the purchase price, we have ordered that it be paid into the military treasury in three payments, the first to be made in the month Audnæus [1] of the sixtieth year, the second in Xandicus, the third in the third month thereafter.

Give orders to hand over to Arrhidæus, who manages the estates of Laodice, the village and Baris [2] and the adjoining territory and the laoi with all their households and possessions, and to have the purchase booked in the royal archives at Sardis, and inscribed upon five stone stelæ. Order that one of these stones be set up at Ilium in the temple of Athena, the second in the temple of Samothrace, the third in the temple of Artemis in Ephesus, the fourth in Didyma in the temple of Apollo, the fifth in Sardis in the temple of Artemis. Give orders straightway to delimit the land and to mark it with terminal stones and to inscribe the boundaries upon the aforesaid stelæ. . . .

(*Three fragmentary lines*)

IV. There has been handed over to Arrhidæus, the overseer of the estates of Laodice by ... crates the hyparch, the village and Baris and the adjoining territory according to the order of Nicomachus, to which has been subjoined the letter from Metrophanes and the one from the king to him giving orders to mark off the territory. Upon the East, stretching from the territory of Zeleia to that of Cyzicus, the boundary line is the royal road, the old one, passing near the village of Pannos, above the village and Baris, the one pointed out by Menecratus, son of Bacchius, of the village of Pythes, and Daüs, son of Asaretus, and Medeus, son of Metrodorus, of the village of Pannos. It has been ploughed up by those living

[1] Audnæus and Xandicus are names of months in the Macedonian calendar.

[2] Baris, a town situated on the right bank of the Æsepus River.

around the place. From this along past the altar of Zeus which lies above Baris to where the tomb lies, on the right of the road. From this tomb the royal road is the boundary which traverses the Eupanese,[1] to the river Æsepus. Furthermore the territory has been marked off with stones following the boundaries indicated.

179. Agreement between the People of Pitana and Mytilene to submit to Arbitration a Boundary Dispute, and the Award made by the Pergamenes (middle of the second century B.C.)

(Ditt. *Or. græc. inscrs.* no. 335. Translated by W. L. W.)

As early as the seventh century B.C. the Greeks had already adopted the idea of arbitrating boundary questions and other disputes which arose between the different city-states. These must be regarded as real cases of interstate arbitration because the city-states concerned were, in the earlier period, politically independent and approximately equal in military strength. In the period after the formation of the Hellenic League their freedom of independent action was, of course, curtailed. Philip of Macedon and Alexander made a conscious and apparent attempt to have the numerous disputes of the Greek states settled by arbitral decisions, using the General Council of the Hellenic League in the work. Under the Hellenistic kings who succeeded Alexander, many of the Greek states retained complete freedom and others a measure of their old independence in their foreign relations. The Ætolian and Achæan Leagues acknowledged the principle and resorted to the use of arbitration. We may, therefore, regard the cases decided in that period as falling under the head of pure arbitration. With the advent of Rome and the ascendancy of the Roman senate in the affairs of the eastern Mediterranean the balance of power had so markedly shifted to the senate that it becomes increasingly difficult to determine where arbitration ends and dictation to inferior and semi-dependent powers begins. It is safe to say that real arbitration between the Greek city-states ceased after 146 B.C.

The following document is set together from twenty-five different fragments of a large stele of marble found in various places in the ruins of Pergamum. It deals with the arbitration of a dispute regarding the ownership of a large tract of land, situated on the mainland opposite Mytilene on the island of Lesbos. The document consists of three parts: I, the decree of the Pitanæans by which the dispute is referred for arbitration to a board of five arbitrators from Pergamum; II, a similar decree of the Mytilenæans; III, the award of the board of five arbitrators, containing an account of their investigation and a summary of the evidence presented by the Pitanæans, who won the decision.

[1] Eupanese is an unknown geographical term, possibly the name of a plain.

The forms of the letters prove that the document was inscribed about the middle of the second century B.C.

The summary of the evidence contains proof of the sale of the tract under dispute to the city-state of Pitana by Antiochus I from his Royal Domains.

I. Decree of the Pitanæans

The strategi[1] have published the following statement:—

The Pergamenes, our relatives and friends, well-disposed to our city from ancient times, have sent us a decree and an embassy regarding our outstanding differences with the Mytilenæans. The embassy consists of Bacchius son of Eudemus, Apollodorus son of Athenodorus, Diogenes son of Asclepiades, Megistermus son of Attalus, Scamon son of Asclapon. They have worked out together a plan for the removal of our differences . . . and the ambassadors, under this authority, have taken upon themselves much toil which is advantageous to both cities, and they have approached the task with a celerity and zeal worthy of the city which sent them out. Therefore it has seemed advisable to the assembly to pass a vote of thanks to the Pergamenes, the friends and relatives of our city, because not only in the present instance but also in the past they have shown a zealous friendship toward our people. . . .

(*The twelve following lines are too badly shattered to allow of translation or paraphrase. They contain a further declaration of the kindly relations between the Pergamenes and the Pitanæans.*)

. . . we choose them as arbitrators[2] of our differences, since the Mytilenæans also have agreed to select them as arbitrators. They shall be present at the place in the month called . . . in Pitana, and . . . by the Pergamenes, shall begin to take testimony and look at the matter from the standpoint of each party, shall report their award upon oath, and shall give a written declaration of their findings to each of the cities. Their decision is to be authoritative and not subject to alteration. Likewise also they shall inscribe upon a stele the agreements made, if accepted by both sides. And they shall also inscribe upon the stele the other boundaries there

[1] These are the highest magistrates in the city of Pitana.

[2] The Pergamenes had requested that Pitana and Mytilene should accept the embassy named above as the arbitrating board. That request is here granted by the Pitanæans.

which need to be defined, leaving nothing unfinished, on the ground that it does not pertain to them, not even if . . . But they shall decide everything alike, so that the causes of strife shall be entirely removed and no accusation or strife based upon difference of opinion shall be left. . . .

(*Five broken lines*)

. . . and to praise the ambassadors and invite them to a public banquet, and that the strategi are to see to it that these things are done.

II. Decree of the Mytilenæans

The boulê and assembly has taken action regarding the decree passed by the assembly of the Pergamenes, which their appointed ambassadors have given to us: Bacchius son of Eudemus, Apollodorus son of Athanodorus, Diogenes son of Asclepiades, Megistermus son of Attalus, Scapon son of Asclapon. In this decree they have made clear that . . .

(*The following nineteen lines are so broken as to be unintelligible.*)

. . . is given over to the same men as arbitrators of the matters in dispute, since the Pitanæans also have agreed to select them. They shall be present at the place in the month called . . . in Mytilene, and . . . by the Pergamenes, shall begin to take testimony and look at the matter from the standpoint of each party, shall report their award on oath, and shall give a written declaration of their findings to each of the cities. Their decision is to be authoritative and not subject to alteration. Likewise also they shall inscribe upon a stele the agreements made, if accepted by both sides. And they shall also inscribe upon the stele the other boundaries there which need to be defined, leaving nothing unfinished.

(*Seven lines which are badly broken*)

. . . to praise the ambassadors for making the visit to Mytilene with devotion to their task and in a manner worthy of those who sent them out. . . .

(*Three broken lines*)

. . . let the kings [1] invite them as guests to the Prytaneum [2] to

[1] These kings (βασιλέες) were a board of magistrates at Mytilene.

[2] A public building in which the prytany, or committee of the senate, held its meetings.

a public banquet. Likewise let the strategi bring in a motion regarding them within the period specified by law, that they are to be proxeni and citizens of our city.

III. Decree of the Pergamene Embassy

(*The first twenty lines are sadly broken. They contained a brief survey of the origin of the dispute and the empowering of the Pergamene embassy to act as a board of arbitration. The board of five first heard the statement of each party in the case. They then went out to examine the territory under dispute as is shown in the following passage.*)

. . . the one upon the ridge down to the stream, and as the road runs and the boundary stones lie to the road which bounds the territory of Pitana and the ——, and as the road runs and the boundary stones lie to the two rocks which . . . and from these to the meadow, as the boundary stone lies and the road leads to Asturene,[1] as the boundary stones lie to the road, and as the road leads and the boundary stones lie along past Asturene to the tomb near the road, called the tomb of Epicratus; and from this to the boundaries on the side toward Atarneus.[2] When all the differences had been removed, according to their agreement that not a single accusation or strife based upon difference of opinion should be left, and as they had declared in their decrees. . . . We went up to Pergamum . . . and swore the oath in the temple of the Dioscuri. . . .

(*The following ten lines are quite fragmentary. One line shows that the Pitanæans introduced evidence taken from the historians in presenting their case.*)

. . . and after this when Seleucus conquered Lysimachus in battle and his son Antiochus[3] received the royal power, Antiochus sold the plain to them (the Pitanæans) for 330 talents in addition to which he exacted 50 talents more. And they made written pledges regarding this transaction, Philetærus[4] also giving —ty talents to the Pitanæans in connection with this matter, as they proved from a stele set up in our city in the temple of Athena. They likewise

[1] A small town between Antandrus and Adramyttium on the south shore of the Adramyttian Gulf.

[2] A small town on the mainland opposite Lesbos.

[3] These are the two famous Diadochi, Seleucus I and Lysimachus, who was defeated and killed in a battle with Seleucus near the Hellespont in 281 B.C. Antiochus Soter succeeded his father Seleucus as king of Syria in that year.

[4] The eunuch who founded the power of Pergamum and died in 263 B.C.

proved that absolute possession and dominion over the territory had been conceded them also by the rulers through the documents upon the distribution of territory, showing this irrefutably from the stelæ set up in Ilium, Delos and Ephesus, upon which the letter of Antiochus regarding the possession of this territory is recorded in full. And they also furnished testimony to the effect that Eumenes,[1] when he assumed control of affairs, ratified the letter of Seleucus to the Pitanæans. In this letter, among other things, he wrote word for word, as follows: 'We also grant for all time the undisputed possession and complete dominion over this territory already agreed upon.' . . .

(*Of the remaining fifteen lines very few words are left. It is evident that the award was in favor of the Pitanæans.*) See Tod, *Greek International Arbitration;* Westermann, "Interstate Arbitration in Antiquity," in *Class. Journ.* II (1907). 197–211.

C. *GOVERNMENT OF EGYPT UNDER ALEXANDER, AND THE WHEAT MARKET*

180. Oppression of Cleomenes, Financial Governor of Egypt under Alexander

(Pseudo-Aristotle, *Economics,* 33. Translated by W. L. W.)

For ten years after it fell to Alexander Egypt was under the provisional government established by the young king. He won the sympathies of the Egyptian priesthood by showing a tactful toleration of the religious prejudices of the inhabitants. His use of the native nobility in the civil division of the provisional government must have helped him greatly in establishing his administration without serious friction. The system devised was threefold. The military government was under three leaders; two for the land troops and one for the navy. These were Macedonians or Greeks. The civil administration remained under the control of two nomarchs, the Egyptians Doloaspis and Petesis. The financial administration was centered in the hands of an able but unscrupulous Greek from Naucratis named Cleomenes. Owing to the fertility of Egypt this position was easily the most important of all, and Cleomenes, during the long absence of Alexander in the east, was able to assume and maintain the practical authority of a governor of Egypt. His greed of money led him into oppressions which alienated all classes of the Egyptians, especially the priesthood and the mercantile class. When Ptolemy I assumed control of Egypt as satrap immediately after the death of Alexander, the execution of Cleomenes (322 B.C.) won for him the support of the most powerful elements

[1] Eumenes was in control of affairs in Pergamum from 263 to 241 B.C.

in the state. The methods of extortion employed by Cleomenes are disclosed in the following extracts from Pseudo-Aristotle, Œconomica, 33, 1352 a. See Schäfer, *Demosthenes und seine Zeit* (2d ed.), III. 293 *sqq.*

When Cleomenes of Alexandria was satrap [1] of Egypt and a great famine raged in other countries, but only a moderate one in Egypt, Cleomenes put a stop to the export of grain. The nomarchs [2] asserted that they were unable to pay the tribute because they could not export the grain. Cleomenes therefore gave them the right to export, but placed a high price upon the grain, so that he received a high revenue, although little grain was exported, and put an end to the excuses of the nomarchs.

When Cleomenes was travelling by boat through the nome in which the crocodile is a god, one of his slaves was seized by a crocodile. Summoning the priests he stated that a wrong had been done him and that he wished to punish the crocodiles. So he gave orders to hunt them. In order that their god might not be subjected to insult the priests brought together all the money that they could collect and gave it to him, and so put an end to the affair.

When King Alexander bade Cleomenes build a city near Pharos [3] and locate there the market which had formerly been at the Canopic mouth of the Nile, Cleomenes sailed down the river to Canopus and went to the priests and the wealthy citizens and said that he had come there in order to settle them elsewhere. The priests and inhabitants of Canopus brought money and gave it to him in order to induce him to leave the market in their district. He took the money and sailed away. Later, when he was quite ready to begin the building, he sailed down again and demanded an immense sum from them, saying that it was a great advantage to him to have the market at the other place rather than at Canopus.

[1] When Alexander conquered Egypt in 332–331 B.C. it was under Persian sway, with a Persian governor at its head called a satrap. Cleomenes of Naucratis held the position of financial head of Egypt. The powers which he assumed while Alexander was in the eastern portion of the Persian Empire, gave him the position of an all-powerful governor. It is this position which the Greeks recognized under the false title of satrap.

[2] The leading administrative officials of the nomes. The division into nomes, and the officials called nomarchs are inheritances from the old Pharaonic rule.

[3] An island in the harbor of Alexandria upon which the famous lighthouse of Pharos was built under the first two Ptolemies.

When they said that they could not possibly pay the money, he took them away as colonists.

When grain was selling in the country at ten drachmas he summoned those engaged in the grain business and asked them at what price they were willing to sell to him. They responded that they would sell it at a lower price than that at which they sold to the retailers. He ordered them to deliver it to him at the same price at which they sold to the others. He then fixed the price of grain at thirty-two drachmas and disposed of it at that price.

He called the priests to him and said that the expenditure upon the temples throughout the country was very great, and that the number of temples and priests must therefore be decreased. The priests individually and in common gave him the sacred treasures, thinking that Cleomenes was in truth about to decrease the number and each one wishing that his own temple should be left and he himself remain its priest.

181. Methods and Effects of Cleomenes' Operations in Wheat

(Demosthenes, *Against Dionysodorus*, 7–10. Translated by W. L. W.)

The wheat manipulations of Cleomenes in Egypt were evidently conducted upon a large scale. For we know from the speech written by Demosthenes against Dionysodorus that men of the time who were conversant with questions of the grain trade considered Cleomenes partially responsible for the astounding rise in the price of grain at Athens in the years 330–326 B.C.

The following extract is taken from a speech written by Demosthenes in a suit instituted against one Dionysodorus for breach of contract. Two other Athenians had lent this Dionysodorus 3000 drachmas which he needed to finance a shipment of grain from Egypt to Athens. As security for the loan they received a mortgage upon the ship. Dionysodorus, however, did not have his cargo of wheat or his ship brought to Athens, but unloaded and sold at Rhodes. After the cargo had been disposed of, he attempted to make a settlement, agreeing to pay the loan with interest up to the time of the sale of the cargo at Rhodes. His creditors, the plaintiffs in this case, then sued him for the interest in full from the time when the loan was made until the time of the trial, a space of two years. See Köhler, in *Ath. Mitt.* VIII (1883). 211 *sqq.*

According to this contract (the one just read), gentlemen of the jury, Dionysodorus and his partner, Parmeniscus, received the money from us and sent the ship away to Egypt. Parmeniscus sailed with the ship, but Dionysodorus remained here.

For all of these men, gentlemen of the jury, — you should not be ignorant of this fact — were agents and accomplices of Cleomenes, who ruled in Egypt, and who has done no little harm he and his agents, to your city and even more to the rest of the Greeks by buying and selling and combining to fix the price of wheat. For some of them shipped the grain out of Egypt, others sailed to the marketing centers, others remained here and disposed of the grain which had been shipped. Then those who were located here sent letters to those who were abroad, keeping them in touch with the current prices so that they might send the grain here if the price were high, or sail to some other market if the price of grain were rather low. Chiefly through these letters and partnerships, gentlemen of the jury, the price of grain has been fixed.

Now when these men sent away their ship from here, the price of grain was fairly high. Therefore they agreed in the contract a proviso that they should sail to Athens and into no other market. After that, gentlemen of the jury, when the Sicilian grain fleet returned and the price of grain fell and their ship had arrived in Egypt, Dionysodorus sent a man to Rhodes to announce the fall in price to Parmeniscus, his partner, who was stationed there. For he knew with certainty that the ship must necessarily put in at Rhodes. There the matter ended. For Parmeniscus, his partner, when he received the letter sent to him by Dionysodorus and learned the current price of grain here, unloaded the grain at Rhodes and sold it there. They thereby showed their contempt for the contract, gentlemen of the jury, and the punishments to which these men themselves subscribed in case they should in any way violate the contract. And they showed their contempt for your laws, which expressly order the ship-masters and merchants to sail into the market agreed upon, and subject them, if they do not do so, to the heaviest fines.

182. Decree of the Council and Assembly at Athens Touching upon the Grain Supply

(Ditt. *Syll.* no. 152.; Köhler, in *Ath. Mitt.* VIII (1883). 211 *sqq.* Translated by W. L. W.)

Further light is thrown upon the effects of these manipulations and other conditions which conspired to send up the price of foodstuffs at Athens in the years 330–326 B.C., by a series of decrees of the Athenian senate and assembly which are given in translation below. Their purpose and content is clear. Much more difficult is the question of the order in which they were presented and their interrelation. II B, which appears first upon the stone, was the last in the series in point of time. Though there are five parts of the published decree, the senate and assembly actually handled the matter but twice.

The first action was taken shortly after the archonship of Aristophon, 330–329 B.C. During that administrative year Heraclides had shipped in the 3000 medimni[1] of grain and relieved the famine by selling it at five drachmas the medimnus. This generosity gives rise to the first decree I A, I B, I C, of which the final form (I C) appears first on the stone. Telemachus, who introduced the first motion, was not a member of the senate. Therefore he could not speak or introduce a motion in the senate. Consequently he made the preliminary motion in the assembly (I A) asking that the senate frame a decree and present it before the assembly. This was done by the senate upon the motion of Cephisodotus (I B). This *probouleuma*, however, contains a clause which permitted the assembly to confer additional honors upon Heraclides. When the senate's report (I B) came down to the assembly for action, Telemachus took advantage of the fact to add the matter regarding an ambassador to Dionysius, tyrant of Heraclea, who was to demand satisfaction for an injustice done to Heraclides (I C). With this addition the decree was adopted by the assembly.

The second decree (II A, II B) arose out of another philanthropic act of the same Heraclides, in the archonship of Euthycritus (328–327 B.C.). This was a gift to the city of 3000 drachmas for the purchase of grain. In consequence of this Phyleus, a senator, introduced a motion before the senate which was passed (II A). It came before the assembly and was there enacted as the will of the people (II B). To it was appended a provision for the publication of the entire business relating to Heraclides.

II B. May the gods grant it.

In the archonship of Anticles in the fifth prytany, that of the tribe Aigeïs, in which Antiphon, son of Corœbus, the Eleusinian, was secretary, in the eleventh month,[2] upon the thirty-fourth day of the prytany. For the proëdri[3] Philyllus the Eleusinian put the question. Demosthenes, son of Democles, of Lamptræ moved:

[1] The Attic medimnus was about one and one-half bushels.

[2] This is the eleventh month of the common or calendar year of twelve months.

[3] The proëdri (πρόεδροι) were a board of nine members of the boulê selected by lot by the chairman of the prytany (ἐπιστάτης) before each meeting of the assembly, one being chosen from each tribe except the prytanizing tribe. They were the intermediaries between the boulê and assembly. One of the proëdri, also selected by lot, became the chairman of the proëdri (ἐπιστάτης τῶν προέδρων) and was president of the assembly for that meeting. This system is not known before 378 B.C. *Cf.* Greenidge, *Greek Constitutional History*, p. 167.

Since Heraclides the Salaminian [1] has always acted with liberality toward and done whatever service he could to the people of Athens, and, formerly, in the time of the grain famine, first among the merchants sailing into the harbor, presented the city with 3000 medimni of wheat at five drachmas, and later, when the voluntary contributions occurred, gave in 3000 drachmas for the purchase of grain, and in other matters has always been well-disposed and liberal toward the people, the assembly has voted to praise Heraclides, son of Chariclides, the Salaminian, and to crown him with a golden crown because of his good-will and liberality toward the Athenian people; and that he is to be a proxenus [2] and well-doer of the Athenians, both he himself and his descendants, and that they are to have the right of possession of land and house according to the law; [3] and that they are to be subject to military service and the special property-tax along with Athenians; and that the secretary of the prytany is to have this decree and the other praises which have been accorded him [4] inscribed on a stone stele and set up upon the Acropolis; and that the treasurer is to grant for the inscribing of the stele thirty drachmas out of the funds being expended by the assembly upon the publishing of decrees.

I C. Telemachus son of Theangelus of Acharnæ moved:

Since Heraclides the Salaminian was the first of the merchants sailing into the harbor in the archonship of Aristophon to give grain to the people at five drachmas, the assembly has voted to praise Heraclides son of Chariclides the Salaminian and to crown him with a golden crown because of his liberality toward the Athenian people. And since his ship was brought to land by the Heracleans when he was sailing to Athens and his sails were seized by them, it is hereby decreed that one man be chosen from the Athenians at large as ambassador who shall go to Heraclea to Dionysius [5] and demand that he give back the sails and for the future do no

[1] Salamis on the island of Cyprus.

[2] An honorary title, usually coupled with the title of well-doer (εὐεργέτης) granted to aliens for especial services to the state. It implies that the recipient stands in a special relation of friendship with the city-state which confers the honor.

[3] The right of purchase and possession of real property, granted to aliens by these special decrees, was circumscribed by some general law.

[4] These "praises" are those recorded in I A B C and II A. See introduction.

[5] Dionysius was tyrant of Heraclea on the Pontus from 337 to 305 B.C.

injustice to any one who is sailing to Athens, and state that, by doing so, Dionysius will do what is right and will not fail in meeting with justice from the Athenian people. The treasurer of the people[1] is to give fifty drachmas for travelling expenses to the ambassador who is chosen, out of the money being expended by the assembly upon the publishing of decrees. Thebagenes the Eleusinian was selected as ambassador.

I A. Telemachus son of Theangelus of Acharnæ moved:

It is decreed by the assembly that the senate should frame a decree and present it to the first meeting of the ecclesia regarding Heraclides, by which he shall receive all possible benefit from the Athenian people.

I B. Cephisodotus son of Euarchidus of Acharnæ moved:

Regarding the order which the assembly has given to the senate to prepare a decree concerning Heraclides the Salaminian, the senate has voted as follows:

Since Heraclides sailed to Athens with grain and gave to the people 3000 medimni at five drachmas each, let the chairmen (proëdri) who happen to be in office bring Heraclides into the ecclesia before the people and attend to the matter, and present to the people as the opinion of the senate, that the senate has voted to praise Heraclides son of Chariclides, the Salaminian, and to crown him with a golden crown worth 500 drachmas; and that he have and receive all possible benefit, in order that others also may display their liberality in the knowledge that the senate honors and crowns those who act with liberality.

II A. Phyleus son of Pausanias of Œnoë moved:

Since Heraclides the Salaminian sailed to Athens with grain in the archonship of Aristophon and gave to the people 3000 medimni at five drachmas, and on this account the assembly voted that the senate prepare a decree that he be brought before the assembly that he might receive all possible benefit from the Athenian people; and since again, in the archonship of Euthycritus he gave 3000 drachmas for the purchase of grain, it has been voted

[1] ὁ ταμίας τοῦ δήμου. A finance official of Athens of the fourth century B.C. He made the payments for the expenditures ordered by the assembly, such as those for the publication of decrees, expenses of ambassadors, etc. The office was probably abolished in 310 B.C., as it does not appear in the documents published after that date.

by the senate that the chairmen who may be in office for the regular[1] ecclesia bring Heraclides before the people and attend to the matter and present to the people as the opinion of the senate that the senate has voted to praise Heraclides son of Chariclides the Salaminian and to crown him with a golden crown worth 500 drachmas; and that he is to have and receive from the people whatever benefit he seems worthy of, in order that others also may desire readily to confer benefits upon the senate and people, seeing that those acting liberally. . . .

(*Two broken lines*)

D. THE LAND SYSTEM IN PTOLEMAIC EGYPT

183. Reversion of a Land-Grant to the Crown on the Death of the Holder (243–242 B.C.)

(Jouguet, *Papyrus grecs*, no. 41; Wilcken, *Papyruskunde*, I. 2. no. 335. Translated by W. L. W.)

The papyri recently discovered in Egypt have given us an entirely new understanding of the fundamental economic and political fact which underlies the history and civilization of Egypt in the Hellenistic period. This fact is that there was no *private ownership of agricultural land* in Ptolemaic Egypt. The right of ownership in all cases rested with the king. A large part of this very fertile land along the Nile was worked directly by the government through farmers who stood in a special relation to the crown and formed a distinct class in the rural population of Egypt. They were called Royal Cultivators (*βασιλικοὶ γεωργοί*) and the land thus leased by the state directly to small farmers was classified as Royal Land (*γῆ βασιλική*).

A second large division of the state's lands was called Land under Grant (*γῆ ἐν ἀφέσει*). This included 1, the lands opeıated by the temples, or Sacred Land (*γῆ ἱερά*); 2, Land under Gift (*γῆ ἐν δωρεᾳ*), or land assigned to favorites and nobles who enjoyed the usufruct, but did not have the right of ownership or administration over the cultivators upon their land; 3, Cleruch Land (*γῆ κληρουχική*), or land assigned to soldiers in active service. Upon these soldiers rested the burden of cultivating the land and paying in a portion of the produce to the state through its officials.

The following document is a letter from one official to another regarding the confiscation of an allotment of cleruch land because of the death of the

[1] *Εἰς τὴν κυρίαν ἐκκλησίαν*. There were four regular meetings in each prytany. The first of these was distinguished as the *κυρία ἐκκλησία*, or sometimes as the *πρώτη ἐκκλησία*. According to law, matters of the grain supply were to come before this meeting. See Aristotle, *Const. Ath.* 43. 4.

cleruch. Ammonius and Aristarchus are evidently official scribes, the former being of higher rank than the latter. The letter is dated in the fifth year of Ptolemy Euergetes I. The document shows clearly that the cleruch land belonged to the state.

Ammonius to Aristarchus, greeting. Artemidorus, agent of Stratius, has written to us announcing the death of one of those who held allotments near Pharbaitha,[1] an epilarch [2] of the mercenary cavalry, Theodorus, son of Phantocles, the Selymbrian,[3] of the detachment of Eteoneus. Take back, therefore, his allotment into the Royal Treasury (*βασιλικόν*), and regarding the produce [4] see to it that it is all brought into the Royal Treasury since the accounting is in your hands. Keep your health.

Year 5,[5] Pharmouthi 18th [6]

184. The Cleruch Allotments become Heritable (218–217 B.C.)

(Jouguet, *Pap. grecs*, no. 4; Wilcken, *Papyruskunde*, I. 2. no. 336. Translated by W. L. W.)

That the military allotments belonged to the Crown is evident from the foregoing document. It is also to be noted in this connection that these allotments were never, in the wills which come from the Ptolemaic period, made over by legal testament from father to son. The right of private ownership, therefore, did not develop under the Ptolemies. The *right of possession*, however, tended to become hereditary if the father at his death left a son who might take up the military duties which went with the allotment. But the ownership of the land by the Crown is emphasized by the fact that the property is taken in charge for the Basilikon upon the father's death and must be reassigned to the son. The document marks an important step in the process of the development of inherited allotments.

The entire correspondence evidently comes from the bureau of Stratocles and Lamiscus, who are two officials of equal powers in charge of the arrangements for military allotments (syntaxis officials). The first two groups of

[1] A village, known in the Ptolemaic and Roman periods, of the Fayum district.

[2] An officer of low rank in the Ptolemaic cavalry.

[3] From the Thracian city of Selymbria on the Propontis. The Thracians were well represented in the armies of the Ptolemies.

[4] When the allotments (κλῆροι) were taken back by the state, all the annual produce reverted to the state.

[5] The year five of the reign of Ptolemy III Euergetes I.

[6] Pharmouthi is the Egyptian month corresponding to March 27th–April 25th in our calendar.

letters (I and II) are letters written *from* their bureau, group III was written *to* their bureau. The officials who play a part in this complicated system of public accounts appear to stand in the following relation:

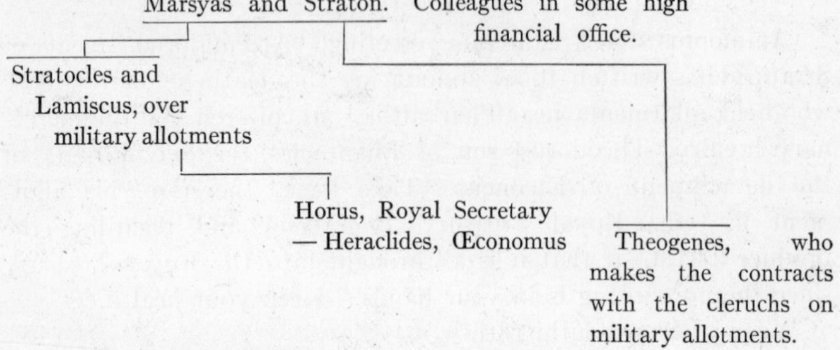

The two names, Hedulus and Dexandrus, seem to be those of two cleruchs (land-leasing soldiers) who had died. In I C arrangements are made so that the "produce" which the sub-lessees of the dead adjutant would have paid to him, may be taken over by the Basilikon. Also in II B the officials are giving orders that the government may get all the proceeds of the sale of wine from the allotments of the dead adjutant, until the allotment shall be reassigned. The object of the letter III B seems to be to acquaint the lower official, Theogenes, with the fact that the allotment had been reassigned by Lamiscus. What effect this would have upon the previous orders to Theogenes (I C) we cannot tell, because the end of the papyrus is missing.

I a. I have appended for you a copy of the letter written by Marsyas to us, that you may note its contents. Year 5,[1] Appellæus 7th, Pachon 7th.[2]

b. Marsyas to Stratocles and Lamiscus greeting. We have appended for you a copy of the letter to Theogenes, that you may act in accordance with its instructions. Year 5, Hyperberetæus 28th, Phamenoth[3] 29th.

c. To Theogenes. I have appended . . . the ex-epimeletes[4] of the year 5, Gorpiæus —, Mecheir —, . . . the allotments, all

[1] The year five of the reign of Ptolemy IV Philopator.

[2] Apellæus is a Macedonian month, Pachon the Egyptian month corresponding to April 26–May 25. In the third century B.C. the Macedonian calendar and Egyptian calendar had not been brought into harmony. Throughout this document the correct date is that of the Egyptian calendar.

[3] Hyperberetæus is a Macedonian month, Phamenoth the Egyptian month covering the period Feb. 25–March 26. Throughout the document the two do not correspond.

[4] The epimeletes is a finance official whose competence seems to have stretched over a portion of a nome. *Cf.* Wilcken, *Papyruskunde* I. 1, pp. 149–50.

of them, with the produce of the present year. Year 5, Hyperberetæus 22d, Phamenoth 23d.

Hedulus, son of Hedulus.

Dexandrus, son of Nicon.

II a. 17th.[1] To Horus. Copy of the letter to [Posidonius] Heraclides, the Œconomus.

b. To [Posidonius] Heraclides. Give special orders to turn over the proceeds of the sale of the wine, made through the contract of the agent of Theogenes, into the royal revenues of the fifth year, to the official Mettaleus in amount 42 drachmas . . . and give order that a receipt be made for it.

III a. 18th.[2] Straton to Stratocles and Lamiscus, greeting. I append for you a copy of the letter to Theogenes, that you may act in accordance with its instructions. Year 5, Apellæus 13th, Pachon 13th.

b. To Theogenes. Lamiscus, the official in charge of the syntaxis,[3] wrote to us that ——, adjutant of the Macedonians holding allotments of 30 arouræ of seed-land in the Arsinoite nome, to whom and to whose descendants the land belongs, died upon Tybi 15th of the year 5. . . . sent orders at the same time to Heraclides, the Œconomus, and Horus, the Royal Secretary,[4] to take in charge the allotment for the Basilikon with the produce of this year's seed, until the allotment may be assigned within the period conforming to the decree, if the deceased has sons. Accordingly a letter was sent to you, year 5, Hyperberetæus 11th, Phamenoth 12th, bidding you give orders to take the allotment in charge for the Basilikon with the produce as stated above. Since, then, Stratocles wrote later that . . . and that Lamiscus had assigned. . .

(*Here the papyrus breaks off.*)

[1] Date of the month Apellæus–Pachon, when this letter was sent out from the bureau of Stratocles and Lamiscus.

[2] This letter was received by the bureau of Stratocles and Lamiscus. On the 18th of Apellæus-Pachon it, too, was sent on to Horus.

[3] *τοῦ ἐπὶ συντάξεως*. This official has charge of the changes of the cleruch allotments.

[4] The *βασιλικὸς γραμματεύς*, who had secretarial and administrative duties over an entire nome.

185. Petition in an Action for Damages (218 B.C.)

(Lesquier, *Papyrus de Magdola*, no. 28; Wilcken, *Papyruskunde*, I. 2. no. 338. Translated by W. L. W.)

One of the divisions of the Land under Grant (γῆ ἐν ἀφέσει) was the Land under Gift (γῆ ἐν δωρεᾷ), consisting of great estates donated to favorites of the Ptolemies. The following document shows that these estates were cultivated under a system of sub-leasing and that the cultivators came under the jurisdiction of the king rather than under that of their landlord, even when the case was one which concerned directly the revenues of the landlord, as does this one. The right of the state to change the allotments from one sub-lessee, or cultivator, to another shows that the theory of the state's ownership of the land was strictly maintained. It is also evident from the text of the document that the estates under Gift were large, since they contained different villages in which the cultivators lived.

The document has three parts and probably came from the office of the strategus, Diophanes. First comes the petition sent to the strategus by the cultivator, Idomeneus. The address to the king is purely formal, and the petition certainly never got beyond the strategus. Second comes the note to Hephæstion, the epistates, written, probably, by a secretary at the dictation of the strategus. A copy of these two documents was sent to Hephæstion, and the original petition and note of the strategus remained in the files of the bureau of the strategus. On the back was written a brief summary of the content for easy reference.

To King Ptolemy, greeting, from Idomeneus, one of the cultivators upon the Land Gift of Chrysermus, from the village Camenoë (καμίνων, the village of the Furnaces). I am being wronged by Petobastis, son of Taos, and Horus, son of Keleësis, belonging to the same village. For I lease from the Gift of Chrysermus 2 arouræ [1] and sowed my plot in vetches (ἀράκῳ). But the aforesaid Petobastis and Horus flooded my seed so that my vetch crop was spoiled and I cannot furnish the payments resting upon the plot. I beg of you, therefore, O King, if it seem good to you, to order Diophanes the strategus [2] to write to Hephæstion the epistates [3] to send Petobastis and Horus, who did the flooding, to

[1] An aroura equaled about $\frac{5}{8}$ acre.

[2] The competence of the strategus, like that of the royal secretary, was over an entire nome. Though originally only in charge of the troops of the nome, the office soon came to combine the civil and military headship of the nome.

[3] The duties of the various grades of epistates, of the villages, the cities, and the nomes, are not yet clear. It is clear from this passage that they were connected with the police department.

Crocodilopolis, so that I may accuse them in the court of Diophanes, and, if I prove that they have flooded my seed, compel them to take over my seed land and pay the rental, and give to me in place of what they have flooded an equal share of the land which they cultivate. In that case by having recourse to you, O King, I shall be able to pay my rentals to Chrysermus and shall have met with kindness from you.

I wish you good fortune.

(*2d hand*). To Hephæstion. Above all try to reconcile them. If not, send them to us upon the 10th of Choiax[1] that the case may be decided before the proper tribunal. Year 4, Daisius 27th, Athyr 29th.[2] (Verso) Year 4, Daisius 27th, Athyr 29th, Idomeneus cultivator of the Gift of Chrysermus against Petobastis and Horus regarding the flooding of land.

186. Oath of the Royal Cultivators (107 B.C.)

(Grenfell-Hunt-Smyly, *Tebtunis Papyri*, no. 210; Rostowzew, *Römisches Kolonat*, 214; Wilcken, *Papyruskunde*, I. 2. no. 327. Translated by W. L. W.)

It is evident that the Ptolemaic rulers of Egypt, since they owned all the land in the country and received their rentals in produce, were in the grain, vegetable, and fruit business on a vast scale. The collection of the rentals demanded an army of officials throughout the country. At the head of this great bureau, which was the treasury department of the state, was an official called the Diœcetes, with his office at Alexandria, where also the central granaries were located. The Royal Land, comprising the best of the land in Egypt, was rented out under lease to the Royal Cultivators. These were free men, coming from all the various social strata of the hybrid population of Egypt. It is important, for an understanding of the economic and social conditions of Egypt, to note that the government did not work its domains directly by the use of slaves.

At indefinite intervals, when the needs of the situation seemed to require it, the government announced that it would lease its domains. The old leases then terminated when the new arrangements were completed. The inhabitants of the country who so desired sent in their bids, in the various districts and villages, and the government accepted those most advantageous to itself. The written bid, when signed by the proper government authority, formed a binding contract between the government and the Royal Cultivator. The

[1] Choiax is the Egyptian month from Nov. 27–Dec. 26.

[2] Athyr is the Egyptian month Oct. 28–Nov. 26. Daisius is a Macedonian month.

term of the lease was indefinite, so far as our present knowledge goes, terminating when the government desired to re-lease the Royal Lands.

The Royal Cultivator was further bound by a note which he signed each year when he received his regular loan of seed-corn from the local officials. A badly torn papyrus gives us some knowledge of this paper signed by the Royal Cultivator. It is extremely important in the history of labor conditions in antiquity, because it shows the Cultivator bound by oath to his village during the entire period of the year from the planting of the seed until the harvest was over. It marks an important step in the development of the colonate system of the later Roman period under which the cultivator became a serf bound to the soil. The first lines are too badly mutilated to permit translation. The contract is for a three-year term, and seems, for that reason, to be a case of enforced lease (Rostowzew). The lessee contracts to pay his wheat rental.

In the six-chœnix measure of the village, and on this basis also I shall give the produce with honest measure and, up to the time at which I measure it out, I shall be present for you and the agents of the queen each day, remaining in the places connected with the work of cultivating the soil . . . without taking advantage of temple, altar, sacred precinct or any sanctuary, nor will I devise any scheme of this sort (to escape my obligations as cultivator). If I keep my oath may it be well with me, if I break my oath, the opposite, and . . .

187. The Collection of Rentals

(Mahaffy, *The Flinders Petrie Papyri*, II. no. 20; Wilcken, *Papyruskunde*, I. 2. no. 166; Rostowzew, *Archiv für Papyrusforschung*, III. 211. Translated by W. L. W.)

The collection of the rentals of the state from its Royal Domains and the methods of its transport to the royal granaries were naturally of great importance to the government. When the harvest was gathered by the Royal Cultivators the entire crop was sent by them, under the supervision of state officials called the Custodians of the Crops (γενηματοφύλακες), to the public threshing-floors outside the villages. Nothing was removed until the threshing was completed. Then, in the presence of the Village Secretary, the Village Chief (κωμάρχης), and the Custodians of the Crops on the government's side, and the Elders of the Cultivators and the interested cultivator himself on the other side, the payments to the government were made. Not until all arrears and loans of the government, in addition to the annual payment, were made, could the cultivator remove any grain. The cultivator must still look after the transportation of the grain to the nearest government granary. When once in the Thesaurus (State Granary) the further disposition and transportation lay in the hands of the government officials.

Local officials (σιτολόγοι) looked after the grain transport to the larger granaries along the Nile, where the matter came under the supervision of the higher finance officials, the Royal Steward (Œconomus), epimeletes, and diœcetes. The following papyrus shows that the right of transport to Alexandria by boat was let out to private contractors, using boats which belonged to themselves. The following document is a complaint from Theophilus, an agent of one of these transport contractors whose name is Anticles. Some of the ship-carpenters in the employ of Anticles have been arrested in a neighboring village and detained. Thereby the transport of the grain, for which Anticles is responsible, has been delayed. The document itself is evidently a first draft of the actual petition sent in by the agent Theophilus, as there are numerous erasures and changes in the wording. These are not indicated in the translation.

To Ptolemæus, Epimeletes,[1] from Theophilus, agent of Anticles, in charge of the transport of the state grain in the Arsinoite nome on his own boats. Pinyris and Erianoupis and . . ., ship-carpenters in the Arsinoite nome in charge of the repair of the boats designated for the transport of the state grain . . . (*the sense is not clear to the translator*) . . . for the repair of the boats of Anticles made a visit to Heracleopolis, and Heraclides, Chief of Police,[2] arrested them. But Ptolemæus met Heraclides, the œconomus,[3] and set before him the urgency of the situation, and the latter wrote to Heraclides, Chief of Police, to release them, since I myself refrained from having a personal interview with him (*i.e.* with the officious Chief of Police).

But now I learn that Heraclides (the Chief of Police) has paid no attention to the letter of Heraclides (the œconomus), unless you or the diœcetes [4] write to him. I therefore think it right that you, if it seem best to you after looking into the matter, give orders to write to Heraclides, Chief of Police in the Heracleopolite nome, to release them in order that they may be at hand when needed and

[1] An official of the finance department who seems to have controlled sometimes an entire nome, sometimes only a part thereof. He outranked the œconomus in influence and responsibility. See Wilcken, *Papyruskunde*, I. 1. 149.

[2] ὁ ἀρχιφυλακίτης.

[3] The œconomus is a financial official, subordinate to the epimeletes. His competence covers a nome. Among his duties in the third century B.C. were the sale of the right to collect the taxes and the rigid control of the tax-gatherers. *Cf.* Wilcken, *Papyruskunde*, I. 1. 150–151.

[4] The head of the entire treasury department of the Ptolemaic kingdom.

that the boats may not lie idle. Otherwise the transport of the grain may be brought to a standstill because the boats are not being repaired, and that, too, when quite a considerable quantity of grain has come in, both of the market and of the tax wheat. For I think that you are not ignorant that . . . if it must be transported on beasts of burden, the difference will be five drachmas to the hundred artabæ.

E. HELLENISTIC EDUCATION

188. An Endowment Fund for Public Education (162 B.C.)

(Polybius xxxi. 25. Shuckburgh's translation)

In the Greek city-states in the period after Alexander the private schools of the earlier period (from 500 to 300 B.C.) were at least partially supplanted by a state system of education. Rich private citizens and kings, as in the following extract from Polybius, established endowment funds for the purpose of furthering state education. There is no indication that elementary education was compulsory. The reflections of Polybius upon the too ready acceptance of a gift for school purposes by the Rhodians gives us some notion of an educated and cultured man's ideas upon the value and dignity of education.

The Rhodians, though in other respects maintaining the dignity of their state, made in my opinion a slight lapse at this period. They had received two hundred and eighty thousand medimni of corn [1] from Eumenes,[2] that its value might be invested and the interest devoted to pay the fees of the tutors and schoolmasters of their sons. One might accept this from friends in a case of financial embarrassment, as one might in private life, rather than allow children to remain uneducated for want of means; but where means are abundant a man would rather do anything than allow the schoolmaster's fee to be supplied by a joint contribution from his friends. And in proportion as a state should hold higher notions than an individual, so ought governments to be more jealous of their dignity than private men, and above all a Rhodian government, considering the wealth of the country and its high pretensions.

[1] This is the English use of the word "corn," meaning grain in general.

[2] Eumenes II, king of Pergamum 197–159 B.C.

189. Public Education at Teos (first half of third century B.C.)

(Ditt. *Syll.* no. 523; *Bulletin de corr. hell.* IV (1880). 110 *sqq.* Translated by W. L. W.)

This inscription was discovered near the site of ancient Teos, an Ionic city near Ephesus. It furnishes us detailed and interesting information upon the methods and divisions of the educational system of Teos. An endowment fund had been established by Polythrus, a Teian citizen, the interest of which was to be used for the education of the youth of Teos. The decree of the Teian assembly here recorded arranges for the choice of six teachers, to be selected by popular vote for a year's term, sets a definite salary for each, roughly defines the subjects to be taught, and turns over the execution of details to the regular magistrates in charge of public education, the pædonomus (Superintendent of the Youth) and the gymnasiarch (Director of the Gymnasium). It provides that the regular treasurers be responsible for the endowment fund and empowers them to pay the teachers, and attempts to provide against a diversion of the proceeds of the fund to other purposes.

. . . and that there shall be appointed also, after the choice of the Director of the Gymnasium,[1] a Superintendent of the Youth[2] not less than forty years old. And in order that all the free boys may be educated, as Polythrus, son of Onesimus, had prudently announced to the people, when he gave for this purpose thirty-four thousand drachmas, thereby establishing a most beautiful memorial of his love of honor, it is hereby decreed that there be appointed each year in the elections, after the choice of the Secretaries (of the council and assembly), three Teachers of Letters,[3] who shall teach the boys and girls; and that 600 drachmas a year be paid to the one chosen for the first grade of work,[4] 550 drachmas for the one chosen for the second, 500 drachmas for the one chosen for the third. And a Lyre-player or Harper shall be appointed also, and to the one elected 700 drachmas a year shall be given as pay; and he shall teach to the boys whom it may be fitting to examine for the succeeding grade and to those a year younger, musical theory, and lyre-playing or harp-playing, and to the

[1] γυμνασίαρχος, or Gymnasiarch.

[2] παιδονόμος.

[3] γραμματοδιδάσκαλοι.

[4] ἐπι τὸ πρῶτον ἔργον. There are evidently to be three grades of work through which the pupils are to ascend. It is to be noticed that the lowest of the three grades of work is the best paid.

ephebi[1] musical theory. Let the Superintendent of the Youth decide regarding the age of the boys. Also additional pay shall be given for the month if we insert an intercalary month. Also a Teacher of Heavy-armed Fighting and a Teacher of Archery and Throwing the Javelin shall be hired by the Superintendent of the Youth and the Gymnasiarch, with the understanding that they shall refer their choice to the assembly for ratification. Let these teach the ephebi and the boys who are to learn musical theory as stated above. As pay two hundred and fifty drachmas is to be given to the Teacher of Archery and Javelin-throwing and to the Teacher of Heavy-Armed Fighting three hundred drachmas. The Teacher of Heavy-Armed Fighting shall teach for a period of not less than two months. The Superintendent of the Youth and the Gymnasiarch are to see to it that the ephebi and the boys are carefully trained in the subjects,[2] according as it has been allotted to each of them by the laws. And if the Teachers of Letters come into conflict with each other as to the number of pupils, let the Superintendent of Youth decide the matter, and let them obey as he may give orders. The public exhibitions which must be held the Teachers of Letters shall hold in the gymnasium, the Teacher of Music in the senate-house . . .

. . . if they do not pay the fine, it shall be possible to compel them. In the case of the Teacher of Heavy-armed Fighting and the Teacher of Archery and Javelin-throwing, let the money be contributed, as was written above. If the treasurers in office or those elected from time to time do not pay this money according to the specifications, or any other magistrate or private person speak or act or bring forward[3] or put to vote or propose a law in contravention of this, or in any manner or by any pretext abolish this law, on the plea that it is necessary to divert the money to other uses or not to spend it for that purpose for which the law intends, or in any other manner to assign the money for some special purpose not countenanced in this law, the action taken shall be null and

[1] On the ephebi, see no. 145.

[2] This indicates some form of oversight of the teaching, possibly including a kind of examination.

[3] προθῆι. This probably means "to bring up the matter in the assembly," whereas the words "propose a law" (νόμον προθῆι) refer to the regular action before the boulê and assembly.

void, and the succeeding treasurers are to assign to this account, according to this law, an equal amount of money out of the city revenues and expend the remainder, all of it, according to this law.

190. The Place of Music in the Education of the Arcadians

(Polybius iv. 20. Shuckburgh's translation)

Some appreciation may be gained, from the following quotation from Polybius, of the general Hellenistic attitude toward musical education. It must be remembered that the Arcadians were still one of the backwoods peoples of Greece even in Polybius' day.

For music, and I mean by that *true* music, which it is advantageous for everyone to practice, is obligatory with the Arcadians. For we must not think, as Ephorus in a hasty sentence of his preface, wholly unworthy of him, says, that music was introduced among mankind for the purpose of deception and jugglery; nor must the ancient Cretans and Spartans be supposed to have introduced the pipe and rhythmic movement in war, instead of the trumpet, without some reason; nor the early Arcadians to have given music such a high place in their constitution, that not only boys, but young men up to the age of thirty, are compelled to practice it, though in other respects most simple and primitive in their manner of life. Every one is familiarly acquainted with the fact that the Arcadians are the only people among whom boys are by the laws trained from infancy to sing hymns and pæans, in which they celebrate in the traditional fashion the heroes and gods of their particular towns. They next learn the airs of Philoxenus [1] and Timotheus [2] and dance with great spirit to the pipers at the yearly Dionysia in the theatres, the boys at the boys' festival and the young men at what is called the men's festival. Similarly it is their universal custom, at all festal gatherings and banquets, not to have strangers to make the music, but to produce it them-

[1] Philoxenus of Cythera, a dithyrambic poet who died in 380 B.C. He was a musician as well as a poet and composed the musical accompaniment of his dithyrambs.

[2] A dithyrambic poet of the Athenian school, contemporary with Philoxenus. A portion of a poem of Timotheus, called "The Persians," was found on an Egyptian papyrus in 1902 and edited by Ulrich von Wilamowitz-Moellendorff, *Timotheos. Die Perser.*

selves, calling on each other in turn for a song. They do not look upon it as a disgrace to disclaim the possession of any other accomplishment: but no one can disclaim the knowledge of how to sing, because all are forced to learn; nor can they confess the knowledge, and yet excuse themselves from practising it, because that too is looked upon among them as disgraceful. Their young men again practise a military step to the music of the pipe and in regular order of battle, producing elaborate dances, which they display to their fellow-citizens every year in the theatres, at the public charge and expense.

F. FORMATION OF A GRÆCO-EGYPTIAN HYBRID CIVILIZATION

191. A Family with Mixed Names

(Wilcken, *Papyruskunde*, I. 2. (*Chrestomathie*) no. 51. Translated by W. L. W.)

This is an inscription from Crocodilopolis of the reign of Euergetes I, between 244 and 221 B.C.

Demetrius, a Greek, has married an Egyptian woman named Thasis. Their two daughters have both Greek and Egyptian names. Along with the Egyptian wife, Egyptian religion has evidently come into the life of the family of Demetrius; for Thueris was an Egyptian hippopotamus goddess.

In honor of King Ptolemy and Queen Berenice, his wife and sister, and their children, the shrine and its appurtenances have been dedicated to Thueris by Irene and Theoxena, Cyrenæans, whose Egyptian names are Nepersouchos and Thaues, daughters of Demetrius born from Thasis.

192. A Bilingual Letter

(Witkowski, *Epistulæ privatæ græcæ* (2d ed.), no. 30; Wilcken, *Papyruskunde*, I. 2. (*Chrestomathie*) no. 50. Translated by W. L. W.)

This letter was written in Egypt in the third century B.C. by Ptolemæus to Achilles.

They are either pure Greeks, or hybrids from a mixed marriage. Ptolemæus has had a dream in which Achilles, an Egyptian girl named Taynchis, and some Egyptian deities play a part. The letter of Ptolemæus to Achilles is in Greek, but the dream is related in Egyptian, either because it dealt with Egyptian deities and religious scruples were involved, or because the dream seemed to enact itself in Egyptian. Three fragments only are preserved.

1. After receiving (?). Ptolemæus to Achilles, greeting. After writing regarding the . . .

2. It has seemed best to me now to explain the dream in detail to you, that you may know after what manner the gods care for you. And I have written it below in Egyptian in order that you may understand it exactly. When I was about to go to bed, I wrote two letters, one about Taynchis, daughter of Thermouthis, one about Teteimouthis, daughter of Taues, who is daughter of Ptolemæus and . . .

3. . . . pour out a drink, just as I also have spent a happy day. Farewell. The 2nd year, Phaophi the 25th.

(*The story of the dream in demotic Egyptian*)

I raised my eyes again . . . to those speaking. They bade me stand before the door of the shrine. There sat a priest and a crowd surrounded him. The priest said to the men standing by . . .

The remainder of the demotic text is badly broken. The girl Taynchis appears in the dream: "Taynchis, she said: 'Come, pray, you . . . who is it?' He said: 'It is Nebwotis.'" Achilles also appears in the dream for Ptolemæus says: "Psais, the great god, knew your name."

193. The Will of a Father of a Græco-Egyptian Family

(Grenfell, *An Alexandrian Erotic Fragment and other Greek Papyri*, I. no. 21. Translated by W. L. W.)

This document is dated in the 44th year of Euergetes II — 126 B.C.

Dryton had made three wills. This is a copy of the officially recorded last will, certainly a copy, since it does not have the official attest (that is, the notary's hand and seal) at the end. The first will, which is referred to in this document, was recorded in the 6th year of Philometor, or 164 B.C. Of the second will, we have the recorded copy in a badly shredded condition; P. Grenfell I. 12. It is to be placed presumably about the year 148 B.C. Pathyris is on the west bank of the Nile opposite Thebes.

Year 44, Pauni the 9th, in Pathyris before Asclepiades, the agoranomus. Being in good health and of sound mind, Dryton, son of Pamphilus, Cretan, ranking as a Successor and Hipparch in the Troops of the Reserve.

So long as health remains to me I am to remain in control of my property; but in case of death, I hereby leave and bequeath the real estate and furniture and herds belonging to me and whatsoever else I may possess, as follows:

My war-horse and all my arms to Esthladas, the son born to me and Sarapias, daughter of Esthladas, son of Theon, citizeness, with whom I lived as my wife, in accordance with the laws and a will (deposited) at the record office in Diospolis Parva before Dionysius the agoranomus in the sixth year in the time of Philometor. This will makes the rest clear and has established . . . (?) And of the four household slaves Esthladas is to have the two whose names are Myrsine and . . . The remaining two female slaves, whose names are Irene and Ampelion, are to go to Apollonia and her four sisters, making five in all; likewise, the vineyard belonging to me in the (district of ?) Pathyris, and the well of burnt brick and the other appurtenances, and the wagon with the cow, . . . one dove-cote and a second one unfinished, a yard, next to which on the south are waste fields of the beforementioned Esthladas, on the north a vaulted chamber of Apollonia the Younger, on the east a waste place belonging to Petrasis (?) . . . son of Esthladas, on the west a waste field of Esthladas up to the open doorway upon the west (?). The house to the west and bowls . . . and waste field up to the dove-cote stretching away below the doorway of Esthladas and to the left of the vaulted chamber, I give to Apollonia and Aristo and Aphrodisia and Nicarion and Apollonia the younger, making five daughters born to me and Apollonia, also called Semmonthis, with whom I lived as legal wife. Let them share equally in the two female slaves and the cow and the houses, according as I have made the division. Let Esthladas have the waste field already given him, facing his doorway from east to west, four strips extending to the place of the earthen pot. Of the remaining buildings and empty lots in Diospolis Magna in the Ammonium [1] and among the potters' shops let Esthladas have one half, and Apollonia and her sisters one half, and all my other belongings, contracts for loans in money or wheat, and furniture, let them share by halves. Let Esthladas and Apollonia with her sisters pay the expenditures for building the aforementioned dovecote, until it be completed.

[1] Temple and precinct of the Egyptian God Ammon.

And to Apollonia also called Semmonthis, my wife, let them pay for four years, if she remains at home and without reproach, for the support of herself and the second and third daughters, $2\frac{1}{2}$ artabæ [1] of wheat, $\frac{1}{12}$ artaba of croton, and 200 copper drachmæ each month. And let them give the same amounts out of the common stock to the two youngest daughters for eleven years. And to Tachratis [2] let them give out of the common stock 12 talents in copper as her dowry. Whatsoever additional income Semmonthis appears to have made while living with Dryton, of this she is to have absolute possession,[3] and any one who starts action against her regarding this income . . . (will suffer such and such a penalty). Year 44, Pauni 9th.

194. Petition of the Græco-Egyptian Daughters of Dryton to the Strategus, an Egyptian

(Kenyon, *Greek Papyri in the British Museum,* II. no. 401. Translated by W. L. W.)

The petition is not dated. Other documents bearing the name of the official Phommoutis enable us to place it in the years 116–111 B.C. Dryton has meantime died and his daughters complain that their property in Diospolis Magna is being illegally used.

To Phommoutis, the King's Cousin [4] and Epistrategus and Strategus of the Thebaid.

From Apollonia also called Senmouthis, and Aphrodisia also called Tachratis, both daughters of Dryton dwelling in Pathyris. To us and to our sisters, Aristo also called Senmonthis, and Nicarion also called Thermouthis, and Apollonia the younger also called Senpelais, belongs a half share of our father's estates of which there are four in the Peri-Theban nome and the Pathyrite nome, like-

[1] The Egyptian artaba of the Ptolemaic period was a unit of measure, varying between 24 and 40 chœnices. The chœnix probably equaled about a liter.

[2] The Egyptian name of the second daughter, Aphrodisia.

[3] Apollonia seems to have been a judicious business woman. We have copies of notes made out in her favor in return for loans of money or of grain. One of the loans draws interest at about 60 per cent per annum; Grenfell, *Alex. Erotic Frag.* I. nos. 18–20.

[4] Συγγενής, which is an honorary title given to officials of high rank at this period.

wise the household slaves. Included in these estates, in Cochlax on the Arabian side (eastern bank of the Nile) of the beforementioned Pathyrite nome, is a half share of a vineyard amounting to $2\frac{1}{2}$ arouræ,[1] or as much more as it may be, and the orchard to the east of this, and wells and buildings and . . . and barren land and other land without the . . . , and their appurtenances, all of which our father owned while he lived, and we, his relics, own since his death. . . . Ariston, son of Athenodotus, living in Diospolis Magna has forcibly taken possession of the beforementioned vineyard and its appurtenances in the period when communication ceased (between the two banks of the Nile) and unjustly maintains possession of the half share belonging to us and has planted a certain part in vines, knowing that we are women and that we dwell in another place and cannot easily take action against the possession above stated. Therefore we deem it right to appeal to you, if it seems best, to examine him, and if the matter be as we declare it, to compel him to leave the half share of the vineyard which clearly belongs to us and the vines planted upon it and the places belonging with it, and to pay back the produce which he has taken away from them, and in return for his violent behavior to arrest him as a rogue that we may receive satisfaction. Farewell.

195. A Greek Tutor in an Egyptian Home

(Kenyon, *Greek Papyri in the British Museum*, I. no. 43; Witkowski, *Epist. priv. græc.* no. 59; Wilcken, *Papyruskunde,* I. 2. (*Chrestomathie*) no. 136. Translated by W. L. W.)

This is a letter of a mother to her son, second century B.C. The beginning and the end are lost, as are the names of the writer and addressee. The feminine participle used by the writer proves that she is a woman. The physician, who is certainly an Egyptian, evidently desires his children to be carefully trained in Greek. The cultured and correct Greek style of the writer proves that she is a Greek, not an Egyptian.

When I was informed that you were learning the Egyptian letters I was delighted both for you and for myself, that now when you go to the city you will teach the children in the home of Phalu

[1] An aroura equals about $\frac{5}{8}$ of an acre.

. . . etis, the physician,[1] and will have a means of sustenance in later years.

196. Cosmopolitanism at the Ptolemaic Court

(Plutarch, *Antonius*, 27)

There was a pleasing resonance in her voice (*i.e.* Cleopatra's); and she turned her tongue readily, as though it were some many-stringed instrument, to the use of any dialect she desired, so that she dealt with very few foreigners through an interpreter. To most of them she gave answer herself, for example to the Ethiopians, Troglodytes, Hebrews, Arabs, Syrians, Medians, and Parthians. She is said to have learned the languages of many others besides, although the kings who preceded her did not have the patience to acquire the Egyptian dialect and some of them even abandoned the Macedonian.

G. THE OIL MONOPOLY OF THE PTOLEMIES

197. Various Regulations

(Grenfell, *Revenue Laws of Ptolemy Philadelphus*, no. 39. Adapted from Grenfell's translation)

The Ptolemaic Crown conducted a monopoly in the manufacture and sale of oil, which was practically absolute. The following sources give some idea of the importance of this monopoly and the annihilation of all forms of competition. The most important source is the "Revenue Laws of Ptolemy Philadelphus" of the year 259–58 B.C., edited by Grenfell. The state dictated the amount of the oil-producing plants which had to be set out in each nome, and controlled and sold the seed to the planters. The cultivators could sell the raw product *only* to the state, and that, too, at a price *fixed by the state.*

The contractors (the middlemen who contract with the state to gather the raw product) shall pay to the cultivators 8 drachmæ for an artaba of sesame containing 30 chœnices ready for grinding, 4 drachmæ for an artaba of croton containing 30 chœnices ready for grinding, 1 drachma 2 obols for an artaba of cnecus ready for grinding, 4 obols for an artaba of colocynth, 3 obols for linseed.

[1] Ἰατροκλύστης, the term actually used, means a specialist in the use of clysteries, or injections, *i.e.*, a proctologist, or specialist for the lower bowels. It is another evidence of the tendency toward specialization for which, as Herodotus tells us, Egyptian physicians were famous.

The state not only fixed the price at which it would buy. It also taxed the cultivators for raising what they were compelled to raise.

Ib. 39. The contractors shall receive from the cultivators sesame and croton at the value decreed in the legal tariff for the tax of 2 drachmæ payable on the sesame and 1 drachma on the croton, and shall not exact payment in silver.

Ib. 39–40. The cultivators shall not be allowed to sell either sesame or croton to any persons other than the contractors.

The state was the sole manufacturer of the raw product into the finished oils, in factories absolutely controlled by the state.

Ib. 44. The œconomus and antigrapheus shall appoint . . . to be a factory and shall seal their choice by stamping it. . . . They shall deposit in each factory the requisite amount of sesame, croton, and cnecus.[1] They shall not allow the workmen appointed in each nome to cross over into another nome; any workman who crosses over shall be subject to arrest by the contractor and the œconomus and the antigrapheus. No one shall harbor workmen from another nome; if any one does so knowingly or fails to send back workmen when he has been ordered to restore them, he shall pay a fine of 3,000 drachmæ for each workman and the workman shall be subject to arrest.

The state controlled, in like manner, the sale of the manufactured product by auctioning to the highest bidders in the cities and villages the sole right to sell. Each year the king's decree fixed the retail price at which the contracting small dealer might sell. The profits of the middleman were, therefore, under legal limitation. Naturally the middleman was often tempted to make a larger profit by selling to the consumer at a higher rate than the one legally set. (Mahaffy, *Flinders Petrie Papyri*, II. no. 38 (b); Wilcken, *Papyruskunde*, I. 2 (*Chrestomathie*), no. 300. Date 243–242 B.C. Translated by W. L. W).

Horus to Harmais, greeting. It has come to my ears through several persons who have sailed down [2] from the nome that the oil is being sold at a higher price than that clearly set in the king's

[1] Croton oil is extracted from the seeds of the castor-oil plant. Cnecus oil was made, presumably, from the seed of the artichoke.

[2] Horus was evidently some high official whose residence seems to have been at Alexandria. The verb καταπλεῖν (to sail down) in the papyri usually implies that Alexandria was the goal of the journey.

order; but from you no word has come to us, nor to our son, Imouthes, who is in the district, have you given any information. Explain to me, therefore, even now how the oil is selling in your district, in order that we may bear the information to Theogenes, the Diœcetes.[1] And for the future, if any such thing occurs or the cultivators and the rest are being cheated in the reckoning or any other injustice occurs, see to it that you write to us or give the information to our son, Imouthes, who is in your district, that he may send it to us and we may bear it up to the diœcetes. Keep in good health. Year 5, Pauni the 16th.[2]

BIBLIOGRAPHY

Buckler, W. H., and Robinson, D. M., "Greek Inscriptions from Sardis," in *Am. Journ. Arch.* XVI (1912). 11–82; Droysen, J. G., *Geschichte des Hellenismus* (Gotha, 1877); Dittenberger, W., *Orientis græci inscriptiones selectæ* (Leipzig, 1903); *Sylloge inscriptionum græcarum* (2d ed. Leipzig, 1898); Ferguson, W. S., *Greek Imperialism* (Boston, 1913); Haussoullier, B., "Les Séleucids et le temple d'Apollon didyméen," in *Revue de Philologie*, etc. XXV (1901). 1–42; Köhler, U., "Attische Psephismen aus den Jahren der Theuerung," in *Ath. Mitt.* VIII (1883). 211 *sqq.*; Meyer, P. M., "Zum Ursprung des Colonats," in *Klio*, I. 424–26; Mitteis-Wilcken, *Grundzüge und Chrestomathie der Papyruskunde* (Leipzig, 1912); Niese, B., *Geschichte der griechischen und makedonischen Staaten*, 3 vols. (Gotha, 1893–1903); Jouguet, P., *Papyrus grecs* (Paris, 1907); Kenyon, F. G., *Greek Papyri in the British Museum* (London, 1893–1907); Lesquier, J., *Papyrus de Magdola* (Paris, 1912); Mahaffy, J. P., *The Flinders Petrie Papyri*, 2 vols. (Dublin, 1891, 1893); Grenfell, B. P., *An Alexandrian Erotic Fragment and other Greek Papyri* (Oxford, 1896); *Revenue Laws of Ptolemy Philadelphus* (Oxford, 1896); Grenfell-Hunt-Smyly, *The Tebtunis Papyri* (London, 1902); Rostowzew, M., "Ursprung des Kolonats," in *Klio*, I. 295 *sqq.*; "Studien zur Geschichte des römischen Kolonats," in *Archiv für Papyrusforschung*. Beih. I (Leipzig, 1910); "Kornerhebung und Transport im griechisch-römischen Aegypten," *ib.* III (1906). 211; Schäfer, A., *Demosthenes und seine Zeit*, 3 vols. (2d ed. Leipzig 1885–1887); Tod, N. M., *Greek International Arbitration* (Oxford, 1913); Westermann, W. L., "Interstate Arbitration in Antiquity," in *Class. Journ.* II (1906–1907). 197 *sqq.*; Wilamowitz-Moellendorff, U. von, *Timotheos. Die Perser* (Leipzig, 1903); Wilhelm, A., in *Archaeologisch-Epigraphische Mittheilungen aus Oesterreich*, XX (1897). 57; Witkowski, S., *Epistulæ privatæ græcæ* (2d ed. Leipzig 1911).

[1] Head of the finance bureau of the state with his official seat at Alexandria.

[2] A high import duty upon oils completed what may be called an impregnable monopoly.

CHAPTER XVII

POLITICS OF THE GREEK HOMELAND; THE FEDERAL UNIONS

323–146 B.C.

WHILE those Greeks who had followed eastward in the wake of Alexander's conquests were engaged in imperial enterprises of wide-reaching influence on after time, their kinsmen in the home country were performing a function far humbler yet of no mean value. With remarkable tenacity they were keeping alive the ancient ideals of local freedom and of the dignity and worth of individual man, which ancient imperialism tended to suppress. To illustrate the attachment of the Greeks to these ideals the selections from the *Funeral Oration* of Hypereides are given. Far from losing themselves in dreams of the past, however, the inhabitants of the Greek peninsula were engaged in solving the greatest problem in politics — the problem of combining local freedom with the strength of unity. Their solution was the Federal Union, the most highly developed and most nearly perfect political creation of the ancient world.

198. DEFENDERS OF HELLENIC FREEDOM

(Hypereides, *Funeral Oration*. Selections translated by W. E. C.)

When news of Alexander's death (323) reached the Greeks they undertook to throw off the Macedonian yoke. The prime movers of this attempt were Hypereides and Demosthenes. Under the leadership of Athens a general Hellenic league was formed, and the chief command entrusted to Leosthenes, an Athenian of notable ability and large military experience. At first the allies met with success, and Antipater, the ruler of Macedon, was blockaded in Lamia near Thermopylæ. From the name of this place the conflict is known as the Lamian war. Unfortunately Leosthenes was killed; there was no competent general to take his place, and the war soon ended in the overthrow of the allies (322).

Hypereides was chosen to pronounce the *Funeral Oration* over those Athenians who had fallen in the struggle. His speech, the *Epitaphios*, has been preserved in a slightly mutilated form on an Egyptian papyrus. Stylistically it is the most perfect of his known orations and a beautiful example of that kind of address. Its chief historical value lies in the appeal to the highest patriotic ideal of the city-state.

1. This address, delivered on the occasion of the present funeral, will be concerned with Leosthenes the general and with the other citizens who died with him in the war. That they were good men [is proved by the circumstances of their death. No one ever saw more noble deeds than theirs; hence we must acknowledge][1] that never in all time have there lived men superior to those who lie here or achievements more magnificent than theirs. For this reason I am greatly disturbed lest my words may appear unworthy of the deeds they have wrought, except as I take confidence in the thought that you, my hearers, may make good any short-comings on my part; for the speech will be delivered before no chance audience, but among the very witnesses of their achievements.

2. It is fitting to praise our city because of her policy, in that she chose a course of conduct similar to, and yet grander and more beautiful than, any she has ever followed before; to praise the dead for their manhood in the war, because they have not disgraced the glory of their ancestors; to praise the general Leosthenes for both reasons, because he was the author of the city's policy and because he was chosen general of the army by the citizens.

3. As regards the city, to recount in full one by one her deeds wrought in behalf of all Hellas, neither is the present time sufficient, nor is the occasion suitable for speaking at length, nor is it easy for one man to recall and treat of so many and such great deeds. I shall not hesitate to speak summarily about her; for just as the sun comes upon all the inhabited world, marking out the hours in suitable form and appointing all things beautifully, for the wise and the just of men, caring for the production of sustenance, both fruits and all other necessities of life, so our city continues to chastise the wicked, to aid the just, to guard the equality of all against arrogance, providing for Greeks a public security from individual dangers and extravagances.

4. But I shall cease speaking about the public deeds of the city, as I intimated in the beginning, and shall limit my oration to Leosthenes and his comrades. I am at a loss where to begin speaking or what first to recall; Shall I rehearse the lineage of each

[1] Restoration by Buecheler, cited by Blass.

man? Such a thing I consider absurd. For a man engaged in praising others who have come together from many places to one city to dwell, each bringing with him his own lineage, — for such a man indeed it would be fitting to trace the descent of every one. But in case one is making a speech concerning the men of Athens, to whom a common autochthonous origin gives an unsurpassed nobility of ancestry, I consider it superfluous to praise the descent of individuals . . .

5. First I shall speak about the general, as is just. For Leosthenes, seeing all Hellas abased and cowering, brought to ruin by those who received bribes from Philip and Alexander against their fatherlands,[1] seeing our city in need of a man and all Hellas in need of a city which should be able to stand forth in the hegemony, he devoted himself to the city and the city to the Hellenes for freedom. . . .

6. Who would not justly bestow praise upon those of the citizens who died in this war, who gave their lives for the freedom of the Hellenes, considering this to be the most marked demonstration of their wish to bestow freedom upon Hellas, namely, to die fighting in her behalf? . . .

7. No living men have ever fought in a nobler cause or against heavier odds or with fewer resources. But they judged valor to be strength, and manliness to be magnitude, — not the great number of individuals. Freedom for all in common they established and the glory of their deeds they have placed on the fatherland as a fitting crown. . . .

8. Are they not indeed to be thought fortunate because of this exhibition of valor rather than unfortunate because of their departure from life? For these men of mortal body have gained immortal fame and through their individual bravery have established common freedom for the Greeks. . . . It is fitting that not the threats of a man but the clear tones of the law should be master of the happy, nor should there be merely a fearful accusation among the free, but an opportunity for defence.[2] The safety of

[1] Æschines, for example, was accused of having received such bribes; p. 48.

[2] In these two antitheses the orator contrasts the rule of the Macedonian foreigner with the free republic: on the one hand are the threats of a man and the fear-bringing accusation, on the other the clear voice of the law and the opportunity for defense in case of accusation.

the citizens should not rest upon those who flatter the powerful and deceive the people, but upon confidence in the laws. But the men who lie here, taking upon themselves the burdens of others, have, even by their daily perils, removed for all time the fears of their fellow-citizens and of the Hellenes, and have given their own lives that the rest might live well. . . .

9.[1] O beautiful and memorable the courage exhibited by these men, notable and brave the task they undertook, surpassing the virtue and manliness in perils which they displayed for the common freedom of the Hellenes! It is difficult to comfort those who are in grief for such losses. For sorrow is assuaged neither by speech nor by deed, but each one's nature and fondness for the deceased mark the limit of the grieving. Still we must take courage and lay aside the sorrow as far as is possible, and remember not only the death of those who have gone but also the virtue they have bequeathed. For if their suffering were worthy of tears, so were their deeds worthy of great praise. If they did not meet death as old men, they left a fame that never grows old, and have therefore proved in all respects fortunate. For those who have died childless, their praises among the Greeks will be their deathless children. For those who have left children, the good will of the fatherland will be established as a guardian for their children. As to themselves, if to die is to be as non-existent, they are freed from diseases and grief and the other mischances that befall the life of man. If there is feeling in the realm of Hades and reward from the deity, as we believe, evidently those who aided the perishing honors of the Gods will receive the best of care from the deity.

199. Origin of the Achæan League

(Polybius ii. 37 *sq.*)

In early time there was a league of twelve cities of Achæa (Polyb. ii. 41), which attained to no importance in Hellas. The country is a mountain slope with an extremely narrow plain bordering the Corinthian gulf. As it had no natural resources, the inhabitants remained poor. Under the Macedonian supremacy the league was dissolved; but about the year 280 four cities, Dyme, Patræ, Pharæ, and Tritæa, shook off the foreign yoke, and united in a new league. Other city-states were gradually added till 249, when the accession of

[1] The numbers in this selection have been supplied by the present editor.

Sicyon under the leadership of Aratus made the union a power to be reckoned with in international affairs. From that time Aratus was the inspiring genius of the federation. Under his direction it adopted a vigorous policy of freeing all Peloponnesus from despots and from Macedonian control and of annexing the individual states by negotiation or force. In addition to Polybius an important source is Plutarch, *Aratus* (*cf.* also *Philopœmen*). Pausanias, too, gives a brief sketch, from which a short excerpt is inserted below.

The Achæans, as I have stated before, have in our time made extraordinary progress in material prosperity and internal unity. For though many statesmen had tried in past times to induce the Peloponnesians to join in a league for the common interests of all, and had always failed, because every one was working to secure his own power rather than the freedom of the whole; yet in our day this policy has made such progress, and has been carried out with such completeness, that not only is there in the Peloponnese a community of interests such as exists between allies or friends, but an absolute identity of laws, weights, measures, and currency.[1] All the states have the same magistrates, senate, and judges. Nor is there any difference between the entire Peloponnese and a single city, except in the fact that its inhabitants are not included within the same wall; in other respects, both as a whole and in their individual cities, there is a nearly absolute assimilation of institutions.

It will be useful to ascertain, to begin with, how it came to pass that the name of the Achæans became the universal one for all the inhabitants of the Peloponnese. For the original bearers of this ancestral name have no superiority over others, either in the size of their territory and cities, or in wealth, or in the prowess of their men. For they are a long way from being superior to the Arcadians and Lacedæmonians in number of inhabitants and extent of territory; nor can these latter nations be said to yield the first place in warlike courage to any Greek people whatever. Whence then comes it that these nations, with the rest of the inhabitants of the Peloponnese, have been content to adopt the constitution and name of the Achæans? To speak of chance in

[1] Although each state had a right to legislate for itself, even to the extent of regulating its own weights, measures, and coinage, the advantages of uniformity in such matters brought about an assimilation.

such a matter would not be to offer any adequate solution of the question, and would be a mere idle evasion. A cause must be sought; for without a cause nothing, expected or unexpected, can be accomplished. The cause, then, in my opinion, was this. Nowhere could be found a more unalloyed and deliberately established system of equality and absolute freedom, — in a word, of democracy, — than among the Achæans.[1] This constitution found many of the Peloponnesians ready enough to adopt it of their own accord: many were brought to share it by persuasion and argument: some though acting upon compulsion at first, were quickly brought to acquiesce in its benefits; for none of the original members had any special privilege reserved for them, but equal rights were given to all comers: the object aimed at was therefore quickly attained by the two most unfailing expedients of equality and fraternity. This then must be looked upon as the source and original cause of Peloponnesian unity and consequent prosperity.

(Pausanias vii. 7)

What is called the Achæan league was by common consent the design and the work of the Achæans. This federation was formed at Ægium because, next to Helicê, which had been swept away by a flood, it had been the foremost town in Achæa in former times, and was at this time the most powerful. Of the other Greeks the Sicyonians first joined the Achæan league. Next to the Sicyonians some of the other Peloponnesians joined it, some immediately, others later; and outside the Isthmus the motive that brought people in was the knowledge that the league was becoming more and more powerful. The Lacedæmonians were the only Greeks who were unfriendly to the Achæans and who openly took up arms against them.

[1] Polybius does not mean that the city-states of the league were absolutely democratic; for among them political rights were evidently based on property; the idea is that each enjoyed the rights which in his opinion belonged to him, and was therefore contented with his condition. In like manner each state enjoyed a fair share in the central government.

200. Officers of the League; its Further Progress

(Polybius ii. 43)

At the time (255 B.C.) when a single general was substituted for two, a lieutenant general was instituted as an aid to the commander-in-chief (Polyb. v. 94; xxiii. 16). There were also a hipparch for the cavalry and a nauarch for the navy (Polyb. v. 94 *sq.*). The general was chosen annually and could serve any number of terms though not in successive years.

For the first twenty-five years of the league between the cities I have mentioned, a secretary and two generals for the whole union were elected by each city in turn. But after this period they determined to appoint one general only, and put the entire management of the affairs of the union in his hands. The first to obtain this honor was Margus of Caryneia. In the fourth year after this man's tenure of the office, Aratus of Sicyon caused his city to join the league,[1] which, by his energy and courage, he had, when only twenty years of age, delivered from the yoke of its tyrant. In the eighth year again after this, Aratus, being elected general for the second time, laid a plot to seize the Acrocorinthus, then held by Antigonus; and by success freed the inhabitants of the Peloponnese from a source of serious alarm: and having thus liberated Corinth he caused it to join the league. In his same term of office he got Megara into his hands, and caused it to join also. These events occurred in the year before the decisive defeat of the Carthaginians, in consequence of which they evacuated Sicily and consented for the first time to pay tribute to Rome.[2]

Having made this remarkable progress in his design in so short a time, Aratus continued thenceforth in the position of leader of the Achæan league, and in the consistent direction of his whole policy to one single end; which was to expel the Macedonians from the Peloponnese, to depose the despots, and to establish in each state the common freedom which their ancestors had enjoyed before them.

[1] 249 B.C.; see no. 199.

[2] 242 B.C.

201. A Meeting of the Achæan Assembly

(Polybius xxii. 10–12)

The highest authority in the league was a federal assembly, composed of all the citizens who wished to attend. The voting, however, was not by heads but by states (Livy xxxii. 22 *sq.*; xxxviii. 32). Naturally the citizens of any state first determined among themselves how they would vote, and then the vote of the state was cast according to their resolution. It would have been unfair to make a little state equal in power to a great city like Corinth; and in fact we know that a large state, such as Megalopolis, was divided into cantons for the purpose of federal representation (Weil, in *Zeitschr. f. Num.* IX (1882), 224, *cf.* no. 203 and n. 3). Hence we infer that this principle prevailed throughout the league. In other words the votes were distributed according to population, seemingly on a principle like that which prevailed in the Bœotian league (no. 117). The assembly elected magistrates, declared war, contracted alliances, and in a word transacted all the more important domestic and foreign affairs of the union. There was a council, too, whose number is unknown. Evidently it represented the states according to population. It assembled frequently to attend to the routine duties of administration or to take measures for meeting an emergency such as a hostile invasion (*cf.* Polyb. iv. 7. 5; iv. 9).

Though an admirable institution, the federal union was weak in that the central government possessed too little power to conduct a war efficiently. The troops and supplies were furnished by the individual states; and the federal government could exercise little more than moral suasion in bringing these resources into the field.

10. I have already stated that in the Peloponnese, while Philopœmen [1] was still general, the Achæan league sent an embassy to Rome on the subject of Sparta, and another to King Ptolemy to renew their ancient alliance.

Immediately after Philopœmen had been succeeded by Aristænus as general, the ambassadors of King Ptolemy arrived, while the league meeting [2] was assembled at Megalopolis. King Eumenes [3] also had despatched an embassy offering to give the Achæans one hundred and twenty talents, on condition that it be invested and the interest used to pay the council of the league at the time of the federal assemblies. Ambassadors came also from King Seleucus, to renew his friendship with them and offering a

[1] Philopœmen, about 252–183, was a native of Megalopolis and one of the most distinguished generals and statesmen of the Achæan league; see Plutarch, *Philopœmen*.

[2] 187 B.C.

[3] King of Pergamum.

present of a fleet of ten ships of war. But when the assembly got to business, the first to come forward to speak was Nicodemus of Elis, who recounted to the Achæans what he and his colleagues had said in the Roman senate about Sparta, and read the answer of the senate; which was to the effect that the senate disapproved of the destruction of the walls, and of the execution of the men put to death at Campasium,[1] but that it did not rescind any arrangement made. As no one said a word for or against this announcement, the subject was allowed to pass.

Next came the ambassadors from Eumenes, who renewed the ancestral friendship of the king with the Achæans, and stated to the assembly the offer made by him. They spoke at great length on these subjects, and retired after setting forth the greatness of the king's kindness and affection for the nation.

11. After they had finished their speech, Apollonidas of Sicyon rose and said that, as far as the amount of the money was concerned, it was a present worthy of the Achæans. But if they looked to the intention of the donor, or to the purpose to which the gift was to be applied, none could well be more insulting and more unconstitutional. The laws prohibited any one, whether a private individual or magistrate, from accepting presents from a king on any pretence whatever; but if they took this money, they would every one of them be plainly accepting a present, which was at once the gravest possible breach of the law, and confessedly the deepest personal disgrace. For that the council should take a great wage from Eumenes, and meet to deliberate on the interests of the league after swallowing such a bait, was manifestly disgraceful and injurious. It was Eumenes that offered money now; presently it would be Prusias; and then Seleucus. But as the interests of democracies and of kings are quite opposite to each other, and as our most frequent and most important deliberations concern the points of controversy arising between us and the kings, one of two things must necessarily happen; either the interests of the king will have precedence over our own, or we

[1] As general of the league Philopœmen had conquered Sparta, razed the walls, introduced Achæan laws, and annexed the city to the league. About two years afterward the Spartans massacred some Achæan sympathizers in their city, whereupon the Achæan general retaliated by putting to death some eighty Spartans at Campasium on the border of Laconia. These were the matters referred to the Roman senate.

must incur the reproach of ingratitude for opposing our paymasters. He therefore urged the Achæans not only to decline the offer, but to hold Eumenes in detestation for thinking of making it.[1]

Next rose Cassander of Ægina and reminded the Achæans of the misfortunes which the Æginetans had met with through being members of the Achæan league, when Publius Sulpicius sailed against them with the Roman fleet, and sold all the unhappy Æginetans into slavery. In regard to this subject I have already related how the Ætolians, having got possession of Ægina in virtue of their treaty with Rome, sold it to Attalus for thirty talents. Cassander therefore drew the attention of the Achæans to these facts; and demanded that Eumenes should not seek to gain the affection of the Achæans by offering them money, but that he should establish an incontestable claim to every sign of devotion by giving back Ægina. He urged the Achæans not to accept presents which would place them in the position of being the destroyers of the hopes of Æginetan restoration for all time.

After these speeches had been delivered, the people showed such signs of enthusiastic approval that no one ventured to speak on the side of the king; but the whole assembly rejected the offer by acclamation, though its amount certainly made it exceedingly tempting.

12. The next subject introduced for debate was that of King Ptolemy. The ambassadors who had been on the mission to Ptolemy were called forward, and Lycortas, acting as spokesman, began by stating how they had interchanged oaths of alliance with the king; and next announced that they brought a present from the king to the Achæan league of six thousand stands of arms for peltasts, and two thousand talents in bronze coinage. He added a panegyric on the king, and finished his speech by a brief reference to the good will and active benevolence of the king towards the Achæans. Upon this the general of the Achæans, Aristænus, stood up and asked Lycortas and his colleagues in the embassy to Ptolemy, "which alliance it was that he had thus renewed?"

As no one answered the question, but all the assembly began

[1] From this speech, and from other sources, we learn that Greek statesmen still maintained an independent spirit.

to converse with one another, the hall was filled with confusion. The cause of this absurd state of things was as follows. There had been several treaties of alliance formed between the Achæans and Ptolemy's kingdom, as widely different in their provisions as in the circumstances which gave rise to them; but neither had Ptolemy's envoy made any distinction when arranging for the renewal, merely speaking in general terms on the matter, nor had the ambassadors sent from Achæa; but they had interchanged oaths on the assumption that there was but one treaty. The result was that when the general, quoting all the treaties, pointed out the differences in detail between them which chanced to be important, the assembly demanded to know which it was that it was renewing. And when no one was able to explain, not even Philopœmen himself, who had been in office when the renewal was made, nor Lycortas and his colleagues, who had been on the mission to Alexandria, these men all began to be regarded as careless in conducting the business of the league; while Aristænus acquired great reputation as being the only man who knew what he was talking about; and finally, the assembly refused to allow the ratification, voting on account of this blunder that the business should be postponed.

Then the ambassadors from Seleucus entered with their proposal. The Achæans, however, voted to renew the friendship with Seleucus, but to decline for the present the gift of the ships.[1]

202. Decree of the Achæan League Regarding Orchomenus (about 234 B.C.)

(*Inscr. græc.* V. pt. ii. no. 344, superseding Dittenberger, *Sylloge*, I. no. 229, and Michel, *Recueil*, no. 199. Translated by C. J. O.)

This inscription, one of the very few relating to the Achæan League, was discovered near the site of the ancient Orchomenus in Arcadia. The upper portion was broken away, but the remainder is evidently the conclusion of a decree of the Achæan League regarding the affairs of Orchomenus, which had just become one of its members. The date is most probably 234 B.C. or shortly thereafter, since a number of Arcadian towns are known to have joined the Achæans at that time; but it might possibly be brought down to 199 B.C.

[1] Throughout the proceedings the members of the assembly show a dignity and a soundness of principle that go far toward refuting the charge of degeneracy made against the Hellenes of this age.

(*The first five lines are fragmentary.*)

The same [oath shall be taken] by the Orchomenians and by the Achæans, in [Ægium[1] by the councillors of the Achæans and the] general and the hipparch and the admiral,[2] in [Orchomenus by the archons of the Orchomenians, in these terms:] "I swear by Zeus Amarius, Athena Amaria, Aphrodite, and by all the gods, that I will in all things abide by (the terms of) the stele and the agreement[3] and the decree passed by the commonwealth of the Achæans; and if anyone shall not abide thereby, I will resist to the best of my ability. And may prosperity be mine if I keep my oath, but the reverse if I break it."

None of those who have received a lot or a house in Orchomenus since the people became Achæans shall have power to alienate them within twenty years.[4]

If any charges have been brought against Nearchus[5] or his sons dating from the time before the Orchomenians became Achæans, they shall all be quashed, and no one shall sue Nearchus or his sons, nor shall Nearchus or any of his sons sue anyone, upon charges arising before the Orchomenians became Achæans. Whoever might sue shall be fined 1000 drachmas, and the suit shall be void.

Regarding the golden (statue of) Victory of Zeus Hoplosmius, after pawning which the Methydrians who removed to Orchomenus divided the money, some of them carrying it off to Methydrium, — if they do not repay the money to the Megalopolitans,[6] as the city of Orchomenus has conceded, those who do not give satisfaction shall be liable to prosecution.

[1] A town on the Corinthian Gulf and the capital of the League.

[2] The three chief officials of the League, the last of whom is mentioned in this inscription only.

[3] *I.e.*, the formal act of union by which Orchomenus was admitted into the League.

[4] This provision was intended to assure the permanence of Achæan influence in Orchomenus by forbidding the newly introduced Achæan colonists to sell their properties; *cf.* Dittenberger in *Hermes*, XVI (1881). 181–183.

[5] Probably a tyrant of Orchomenus who had voluntarily abdicated when the city joined the Achæans.

[6] Methydrium was a dependency of Megalopolis, which consequently claimed the proceeds of the pawned statue.

203. Arbitration of the Ætolians between Melitea and Perea (225–200 B.C.)

(*Inscr. græc.* IX. pt. ii. no. 205; Dittenberger, *Sylloge*, II. no. 425; Michel, *Recueil*, no. 22. Translated by C. J. O.)

This inscription, discovered at Avaritza in Southern Thessaly, on the site of the ancient Melitea, records a decision of arbitrators appointed by the Ætolian League in a dispute between the city-state of Melitea and the neighboring settlement of Perea. The two were, at the time, politically united into one community, but the Pereans evidently were dissatisfied and desired the right of seceding if they should choose to do so. This the decision granted to them, and it also provided for the subsequent relations between the two communities, besides defining the boundary line, in the event of a separation. The inscription not only shows the preponderant influence of the Ætolian League in disputes between its member states, but also gives an interesting hint regarding the basis of representation in the federal council (*cf.* n. 3). The date is the last quarter of the third century B.C., when the power of the League extended into Southern Thessaly.

Decision rendered to the Meliteans and the Pereans by the judges chosen by the Ætolians, (namely) Dorimachus, Polemæus, and Argeius, Calydonians, the parties having submitted (their case) by agreement.[1]

The boundary line for the Meliteans and the Pereans shall be . . .[2]

The public domain, namely Carandæ and Phyliadon, shall not be sold by the Meliteans for the purchaser to hold in fee simple, while the Pereans are fellow-citizens of the Meliteans; but they shall lease it for a term, as hitherto.

If the Pereans shall renounce the citizenship of the Meliteans, they shall employ the boundary above described, as regards their territory; and they shall keep a single senator when they secede. They shall pay their share of the loans that the city may owe, according to the ratio borne by their one senator,[3] and they shall

[1] Or, perhaps, "according to the agreements" (by which they had become members of the League).

[2] The description of the boundary consists mainly of a series of obscure geographical names, and has therefore been omitted in the translation.

[3] Hence it appears that the smaller communities, such as Perea, had only one senator, or delegate, to the federal council of the League, whereas the larger, like Melitea, had several, probably according to their population.

contribute the dues accruing to the Ætolians [1] in the proportion of their senator.

The Pereans shall pay to their creditors the accrued tithes,[2] which they owe for three years after obtaining a three years' extension.

The sums that the Pereans were hitherto accustomed to receive from the city yearly, namely three minæ of silver for the archons, ten staters for the herald, ten staters for the oil for the youths, and five staters for the sacrifice of the Soteria, they shall still receive; and in future the city of Melitea shall look after the public funds in Perea as hitherto.

The Pereans shall have the same laws as the Meliteans, and the suits brought before the agoranomi [3] by Pereans against Pereans shall be judged every four months in Perea by the agoranomi from Melitea.

This decision shall be inscribed on stelæ in Melitea and in Delphi and in Calydon and in Thermum.[4]

Witnesses: the entire council in the term of the secretary Lycus; the presidents of the council, Ortholaüs of Spattus and Dysopus of Apollonia; the secretary Lycus of Erythræ; the hipparch [5] Alexon of Hermattus; (also) Pantaleon, son of Petalus, of Pleuron, Nicostratus, son of Nicostratus, of Naupactus, Damoxenus, son of Theodorus, of Heraclea.

204. Decree of the Ætolian League Recognizing the Inviolability of Teos (about 200 B.C.)

(Dittenberger, *Sylloge*, I. no. 280; Michel, *Recueil*, no. 68. Translated by C. J. O.)

Among the ruins of the city of Teos in Asia Minor there have been found a number of inscriptions containing decrees passed by various cities and states

[1] *I.e.*, federal taxes imposed by the League.

[2] Meaning, probably, interest at ten per cent.

[3] *I.e.*, minor commercial cases coming under the jurisdiction of the "controllers of the market-place."

[4] In Melitea, as the city chiefly concerned; in Delphi, as the religious center of the League; in Calydon, as the home of the judges (?); in Thermum, as the political capital of the League. A fragment of the Delphian copy has been found; *cf. Inscr. græc.* IX. pt. ii, *Addenda Ultima*, no. 205 iii B.

[5] The cavalry commander, the highest official of the League after the *strategus* or general.

in answer to the Teians' request that the inviolability of their city and of the surrounding territory might be recognized. According to Greek law, a citizen of one state who had a grievance against a member of another could as a last resort exercise the right of self-help by seizing the person or the property of his adversary, or even of any citizen of the other state, wherever he might find him; but this right came to be greatly abridged through the grant of *asylia*, *i.e.*, inviolability or freedom from seizure, to individuals or to an entire community. (*Cf.* Pauly-Wissowa, *Real-Encyklopädie*, II. 1879–1881, *s. v.* ἀσυλία). In the present case, the Teians also invoked the sanction of religious inviolability by consecrating their entire territory to the god Dionysus. This decree is to be dated shortly before 200 B.C., as appears from a comparison with that of the Delphians in the same matter (Michel, *Recueil*, no. 67). Other decrees of the Ætolians granting inviolability to various states may be found in Dittenberger, *Sylloge*, I. nos. 247, 923; Michel, *Recueil*, nos. 25, 27.

In the generalship of Alexander of Calydon, at the Panætolica.[1]

Whereas the Teians through their ambassadors Pythagoras and Clitus gave renewed assurances of their intimacy and friendship and exhorted the Ætolians to grant that both their city and their land should be sacred to Dionysus and inviolable:

Be it resolved by the Ætolians, that they will maintain the existing friendship and intimacy with the Teians, and that the decrees hitherto passed in their favor regarding all their kindnesses shall remain in force. The consecration and the inviolability of their city and their land shall be recognized by the Ætolians, as the ambassadors requested; and none of the Ætolians or of the dwellers in Ætolia, from wheresoever they may set out, shall seize the Teians or the dwellers in Teos, but these shall enjoy security and inviolability on the part of the Ætolians and the dwellers in Ætolia. If anyone shall seize either their persons or things from their city or land, the general and the councillors in office for the time being shall restore whatever is discoverable, and those who have made the seizure shall be liable for what is not discoverable, the right of claim and other procedure being secured to the Teians in the same manner as the law of the Ætolians ordains for the Dionysiac artists.[2]

[1] A festival held probably in autumn at the same time as the regular annual assembly and election of the League.

[2] *I.e.*, the actors who performed at the festivals of Dionysus, especially in Athens. A decree of the Delphian Amphictiony (*Inscr. græcæ*, II. no. 551) seems to show that they were exempt from seizure except for their personal debts.

In order that the (above-decreed) consecration and inviolability may be embodied in the laws,[1] the revisers of the laws who are appointed shall embody them, when the revision takes place, in the laws.

BIBLIOGRAPHY

I. Political and General. — Thirlwall, C., *History of Greece*, ch. lxvii *sqq.*, not wholly antiquated; Holm, *History of Greece*, IV; Beloch, *Griechische Geschichte*, III; Droysen, J. G., *Geschichte des Hellenismus*, 2 vols. (Hamburg, 1836–1843), still useful; *Geschichte Alexanders des Grossen* (3d ed., Gotha, 1880); Kaerst, *Geschichte des hellenistischen Zeitalters*, I, II (Teubner, 1901), no further publication; *Die antike Idee der Ökumene in ihrer politischen und kulturellen Bedeutung* (Teubner, 1903); Niese, B., *Geschichte der griechischen und makedonischen Staaten seit der Schlacht bei Chaeronea*, 3 vols. (Gotha, 1893–1903), the chief work covering the entire subject; Colin, G., *Rome et la Grèce de 200 à 146 avant Jésus-Christ* (Paris, 1905), valuable; Reuss, F., "Zur Ueberlieferung der Geschichte Alexanders des Grossen," in *Rhein. Mus.* LVII (1902). 559–98; "Hellenistische Beiträge," *ib.* LXII (1907). 591–600; LXIII. 58–78, Alexander's marches, etc.; Kromayer, J., "Alexander der Grosse und die hellenistische Entwickelung in dem Jahrhundert nach seinem Tode," in *Hist. Zeitschr.* C (1908). 11–52; Wheeler, B. I., *Alexander the Great* ("Heroes"); Hogarth, D. G., *Philip and Alexander of Macedon* (Scribner, 1897); Ferguson, W. S., *Hellenistic Athens* (Macmillan, 1911), an original and scholarly work; *Greek Imperialism* (Houghton Mifflin, 1913), Lowell lectures; "Egypt's Loss of Sea Power," in *J. H. S.* XXX (1910). 191–208; Hoffman, O., *Die Makedonen, ihre Sprache und ihr Volkstum* (Göttingen, 1906); Swoboda, H., "Zur Geschichte von Akarnanien," in *Klio*, X (1910). 397–405; Klotsch, C., *Epirotische Geschichte bis zum Jahre 280 v. Chr.* (Berlin), dissert.; Stähelin, *Geschichte der kleinasiatischen Galater*, etc. (Basel, 1897); Bevan, E. R., *House of Seleucus*, 2 vols. (London, 1902); "The Deification of Kings in Greek Cities," in *Eng. Hist. Rev.* XXVI (1901). 625–39; *Jerusalem under the High Priests* (London, 1904); Bouché-Leclerq, *Histoire des Séleucides* (Paris: Leroux, 1913); Tarn, W. W., *Antigonos Gonatas* (Oxford, 1913); Rawlinson, H. G., *Bactria; The History of a Forgotten Empire* (London, 1912); Mahaffy, J. P., *History of Egypt under the Ptolemaic Dynasty* (London, 1899); Tillyard, H. J. W., *Agathocles* (Cambridge, 1908); Sundwall, J., *De institutis reipublicæ Atheniensium post Aristotelis ætatem commutatis* (Helsingforsiæ, 1906); Niccolini, G., "Questioni intorno al re di Sparta Cleomenes III," in *Saggi di storia antica e di archeologia* (Rome, 1910), 1–8; Wiegand, T., and Wilamowitz-Moellendorff, U. von, "Ein Gesetz von Samos über die Beschaffung von Brotkorn aus öffentlichen Mitteln," in *Sitz. Berl. Akad.* 1904. pp. 917–31; Zucker, F., "Beiträge zur

[1] The *nomoi*, or permanent general laws, as distinguished from the *psephismata*, decrees passed for a special purpose.

Kenntniss der Gerichtsorganisation im ptolemäischen Aegypten," in *Philol.* Supplb. XII (1912). 1–130.

II. The Federal Unions. — Holm, *History of Greece*, IV. ch. x *sqq.*; Beloch, *Griechische Geschichte*, III. 1. Abschn. xvii, xx; Thirlwall, C., *History of Greece*, ch. lxi *sqq.*; Schömann, G. F., *Griechische Altertümer*, II. bk. iv; Swoboda, H., *Griechische Staatsaltertümer* (in Hermann's *Lehrb.*), 325 *sqq.*; "Studien zur Geschichte der griech. Bünde," in *Klio*, XI (1911). 450–63; XII. 17–50; Niese, B., *Geschichte der griech. u. mak. Staaten*, vols. II, III (see Contents); Freeman, E. A., *History of Federal Government in Greece and Italy* (2d ed., by Bury, London, 1893); Lipsius, J. H., "Beiträge zur Geschichte griechischer Bundesverfassung," in *Sächs. Gesellsch.* L (1898). 145–76; Dubois, M., *Les ligues étolienne et achéenne* (Paris, 1885); Francotte, A., "Le conseil et l'assemblée générale chez les Achéens," in *Musée Belge*, X (1906). 4–20; Caspari, M. O. B., "The Parliament of the Achæan League," in *Eng. Hist. Rev.* XXIX (1914). 209–20; Seeliger, K., *Messenien und der achäische Bund* (Zittau, 1897), program; Klatt, M., *Studien zur Geschichte des kleomenischen Krieges* (Göttingen, 1877); *Chronologische Beiträge zur Geschichte des achäischen Bundes* (Berlin, 1883); Howard, G. E., *Comparative Federal Institutions: An Analytical Reference Syllabus* (University of Nebraska, 1907), see references to sources and authorities.

CHAPTER XVIII

SCIENCE AND INVENTIONS

About 330–100 B.C.

THE selections of this chapter illustrate various sciences at the highest point of development reached in ancient times. The first excerpt describes the situation and the founding of Alexandria, the chief seat of science and scholarship.

A. ALEXANDRIA

205. THE SITUATION AND THE FOUNDING OF ALEXANDRIA

(Strabo xvii. 1. 6–8)

In sailing toward the west, the sea-coast from Pelusium to the Canobic mouth of the Nile is about thirteen hundred stadia [1] in extent, and constitutes, as we have said, the base of the Delta. Thence to the island of Pharos are a hundred and fifty stadia more.

Pharos [2] is a small oblong island, and lies quite close to the mainland, forming on its side a harbor with a double entrance. The coast abounds in bays and has two promontories projecting into the sea. The island is situated between these projections, and shuts in the bay, lying lengthwise in front of it. Of the extremities of the Pharos the eastern is nearest to the mainland and to the promontory there, called Lochias, which makes the entrance to the port narrow. Besides the narrowness of the passage there are rocks, some under water, others rising above it, which at all times increase the violence of the waves as they roll in upon them from the open sea. The extremity itself of the island is a rock, washed by the sea on all sides, with a tower on it of the same name as the island, admirably constructed of white marble, several stories high. Sostratus of Cnidus, a friend of the kings, erected it for the safety of mariners, as the inscription shows.

[1] A stadium was 600 Greek feet, or about 582 English feet.

[2] For a plan of Alexandria, see Shepherd, *Atlas of Ancient History*, no. 34.

As the coast on both sides is low and without harbors, with reefs and shadows, an elevated and conspicuous mark was required to enable navigators coming in from the open sea to direct their course exactly to the entrance of the harbor.

(The less interesting description of the western entrance is here omitted.)

In addition to its being well enclosed by the mound and by nature, it is of sufficient depth near the shore to allow the largest vessel to anchor near the stairs. Furthermore it is divided into several ports.

The former kings of Egypt, satisfied with what they possessed, and not desirous of foreign commerce, entertained a dislike to all mariners, especially to the Greeks, who on account of their lack of territory, ravaged and coveted the property of other nations. They stationed a guard, who had orders to keep off all persons who approached. To the guard was assigned as a place of residence the spot called Rhacotis, which is now a part of the city of Alexandria, situated above the arsenal. At that time, however, it was a village. The country about the village was given up to herdsmen, who were also able by their numbers to prevent strangers from entering the country.

When Alexander arrived, and perceived the advantages of the situation, he determined to build the city on the harbor. The resulting prosperity of the place was intimated, it is said, by a presage which occurred while the plan of the city was tracing. The architects were engaged in marking out the line of the wall with chalk, and had consumed it all, when the king arrived, whereupon the dispensers of flour supplied the workmen with a part of the flour which was provided for their own use; and this substance was used in tracing the greater part of the divisions of the streets. This, they said, was a good omen for the city.

The advantages of the city are of various kinds. The site is washed by two seas; on the north by what is called the Egyptian Sea, and on the south by the sea of the lake Mareia, which is also called Mareotis. This lake is filled by many canals from the Nile, both by those above and those at the sides, through which a greater quantity of merchandise is imported than through those communicating with the sea. Hence the harbor on the lake is richer than the maritime harbor. The exports by sea from Alexandria exceed the imports. This any person may ascertain, at either Alexandria or Dicæarchia, by watching the arrival and departure of the merchant vessels, and observing how much heavier or lighter their cargoes are when they depart than when they return.

In addition to the wealth derived from merchandise landed at the harbors on each side, on the sea and on the lake, the fine air is worthy of remark: this results from the city's being on two sides surrounded by water, and from the favorable effects of the rise of the Nile. For other cities, situated near lakes, have during the heats of summer a heavy and suffocating atmosphere, and lakes at their margins become swampy by the evaporation occasioned by the sun's heat. When a large quantity of moisture is exhaled from swamps, a noxious vapor rises, and is the cause of pestilential disorders. But at Alexandria, at the beginning of summer, the Nile, being full, fills the lake also, and leaves no marshy matter which is likely to occasion deadly vapors. At the same period the Etesian winds blow from the north over a large expanse of sea, and the Alexandrines in consequence pass their summer very pleasantly.

The shape of the site of the city is that of a chlamys (military cloak). The sides, which determine the length, are surrounded by water, and are about thirty stadia in extent; but the isthmuses, which determine the breadth of the sides, are each of seven or eight stadia, bounded on one side by the sea, and on the other by the lake. The whole city is intersected by streets for the passage of horsemen and chariots. Two of these are very broad, exceeding a plethron [1] in breadth, and cut one another at right angles. It contains also very beautiful public grounds, and royal palaces, which occupy a fourth or even a third part of its whole extent. For as each of the kings was desirous of adding some embellishment to the places dedicated to the public use, each added to the works already existing a building at his own expense; hence the expression of the poet may be here applied, "One after the other springs." All the buildings are connected with one another and with the harbor, and those also which are beyond it.

[1] A plethron is 100 Greek feet.

206. The Museum and other Buildings of Alexandria

(Strabo xvii. i. 8–10)

The Museum is a part of the palaces. It has a public walk and a place furnished with seats and a large hall, in which the men of learning, who belong to the Museum, take their common meal. This community possesses also property in common; and a priest, formerly appointed by the kings but at present by Cæsar, presides over the Museum.

A part belonging to the palaces consists of that called Sema, an enclosure which contained the tombs of the kings and that of Alexander (the Great). . . . Ptolemy carried away the body of Alexander, and deposited it at Alexandria in the place where it now lies; not indeed in the same coffin, for the present one is of alabaster, whereas Ptolemy had deposited it in one of gold. . . . It was plundered by Ptolemy surnamed Cocce's son and Pareisactus, who came from Syria and was quickly deposed, so that his plunder was of no service to him.

In the great harbor on the right hand of the entrance are the island and the Pharos tower; on the left are the reef of rocks and the promontory Lochias, with a palace on it. On the left of the entrance are the inner palaces, which are continuous with those on the Lochias and contain numerous frescoed apartments and groves. Below lies the artificial and closed harbor, appropriated to the use of the kings; and Antirrhodos, a small island facing the artificial harbor, with a palace on it and a small port. It was called Antirrhodos as a rival of Rhodes.

Above it is the theatre, then the Poseidion, a kind of elbow projecting from the Emporium, as it is called, with a temple of Poseidon on it. . . . Next are the Cæsareion, the Emporium, and the Apostaseis (magazines); after them the docks as far as the Heptastadion. This is the description of the great harbor. . . . In short, the city of Alexandria abounds in public and sacred buildings. The most beautiful of the former is the Gymnasium with porticos exceeding a stadium in extent. In the middle of it are a court of justice and groves. Here also is a Paneium, an artificial mound of the shape of a fir-cone, resembling a pile of rock, to the top of which there is an ascent by a spiral path. From the summit may be seen the whole city lying all around and beneath it.

B. ANATOMY AND PHYSIOLOGY

In no department of science was greater progress made than in anatomy, physiology, and surgery. The most eminent representative of this field, in fact the most advanced medical scientist of the ancient world, was Herophilus of Chalcedon, who reached his maturity about the beginning of the third century. His great progress was largely due to the opportunity for the vivisection of criminals granted him by the king of Egypt. To him belongs the discovery of the function of nerves and their classification into sensory and motor and of the fact that the brain is the seat of the mind. He made, too, a great contribution to the knowledge of the eye. Among the most important of his discoveries was that which related to the function of the arteries. Formerly it was supposed that they contained air, whereas he was the first to declare that their function was to convey blood from the heart to various parts of the body (*cf.* Pliny, *Nat. Hist.* xi. 69, quoted below). Substantially, therefore, Herophilus discovered the circulation of the blood. With him, accordingly, begins the observation of the pulse in the diagnosis of illness. Some of his discoveries, particularly those relating to the brain and the function of the arteries, were repudiated by his contemporaries and were thus lost to the world till their rediscovery in modern times; see Beloch, *Griech. Gesch.* III. 1. 485–8; Heiberg, J. L., *Naturwissenschaften und Mathematik im klassischen Altertum* (Leipzig, 1912), 45 *sq.*; Puschmann, T., *History of Medical Instruction* (London, 1891); Sprengel-Rosenbaum, *Geschichte der Medicin*, I. 509 *sqq.*; Gossen, "Herophilus," in Pauly-Wissowa, *Real-Encycl.* VIII. 1104–1110.

207. Vivisection; the Eye, the Nerves and the Brain

(Celsus, *De Artibus*, i. 4 (ed. Daremberg). Translated by E. G. S.)

Aulus Cornelius Celsus was an encyclopædist, somewhat of the same nature as Pliny, who flourished under the princeps Tiberius. His work consisted of six parts: Agriculture, Medicine, Military Science, Rhetoric, Philosophy, and Jurisprudence. We have preserved only the eight books treating of Medicine. In his preface to this part he gives an account of the earlier history of medicine. See Wellmann, M., "A. Cornelius Celsus," in Pauly-Wissowa, *Real-Encycl.* IV. 1273 (no. 82)–76; Schanz, M., *Gesch. d. röm. Lit.* II. 2. (1913) 424–30.

Aside from these matters, since in the inner parts pains and various kinds of diseases have their origin, they think no one can apply remedies to these (parts) who is unacquainted with them. It was therefore necessary to cut into the bodies of the dead and examine their vitals and inner organs. (It was their opinion, too,) that by far the best procedure was that of Herophilus and Erasistratus, who cut into criminals received from the kings out of prison, while living, and who observed, before breathing ceased, those things which nature formerly had kept under seal. (They observed also) their location, color, shape, size, arrangement, hardness, softness, smoothness, touch. . . .

(*Ib.* p. 5. Trans. *id.*)

On the other hand, those who call themselves Empirics, from experience, take account of the apparent causes as being the necessary ones. They insist that the inquiry into hidden causes and actions of nature is superfluous, seeing that Nature is not comprehensible.

(*Ib.* p. 279. Trans. *id.*)

Now under these, at the point where the pupil (of the eye) is, there is an empty space; then below again there is a very thin membrane, which Herophilus describes as like a spider-web (the retina).

(Chalcidius, *Interpretation of Plato's Timæus* (ed. Wrobel, 1876), p. 279. Translated by E. G. S.)

Chalcidius was a Christian of the early fourth century A.D., who wrote in Latin the work with the title given above. It is a Latin translation as well as interpretation; see Kroll, in Pauly-Wissowa, *Real-Encycl.* III. 2042 *sq.*

Likewise of the experts in Nature, renowned men in fact, who with a view to grasping the ingenuity of Nature, investigated the articulation of the human body, by cutting into organic parts, because they thought that thus only they would be definitely sure to a degree above mere suspicion and supposition, if sight were to chime with reason as well as reason with sight. There must therefore be demonstrated the nature of the eye, about which most others and particularly Alcmæon of Croton, a man who was an expert in questions of nature, and who first dared attempt the cutting out (*exsectionem*), and Callisthenes, the pupil of Aristotle, and Herophilus have brought to light many splendid things. (He shows) that there are two narrow paths which from the seat of the brain, in which the highest and dominant power of vitality (*animæ*) is situated, pass to the caverns of the eyes, containing the spirit of nature; which, while issuing from one initial point and from the same root for some distance, are joined together in the innermost parts of the forehead, and being separated in the appearance of two ways, reach the hollow abodes of the eyes at the point where the oblique paths of the eye-brows are extended, and, curved there in the lap of membranes which receive the natural moisture, fill the globes fortified by the shelter of the eyelids, whence they are designated orbs. Furthermore the fact that the light-bearing paths issue forth from one seat, anatomy indeed chiefly teaches. None the less from this consideration we understand that both eyes are moved together, nor can the one be moved without the other.

(Galen, *Works*, vol. III. p. 813, ed. Kühn. Translated by E. G. S.)

Galen, who was born at Pergamum in 129 A.D. and died about 199, was the most famous physician in the period of the Roman empire. His vast writings were published by Kühn in 22 volumes (Leipzig, 1821–1833). The edition, however, so abounds in mistakes that in many places it is scarcely usable. From the time of publication to the present it has been the standard edition, but it is now being displaced by the *Corpus Medicorum*, which is gradually being published. See Mewaldt, "Galenos," in Pauly-Wissowa, *Real-Encycl.* VII. 578–91.

Of the sensory nerves which go down to the eyes from the brain, which Herophilus also calls passages because through them alone the ways of the vital spirit (τοῦ πνεύματος) are perceptible and clear, just as this very (nerve) is beyond belief and above the remaining nerves, so also this is true, that they have their beginning from different localities; but as they advance, they are united with one another, and again they depart and are separated.

208. The Heart, the Arteries, the Veins, and the Circulation of the Blood

(Galen, IV. p. 731. Translated by G. W. B.)

Wherefore when they doubt as to the manner in which the vital spirit (πνεῦμα) may be carried from the heart through the entire body in case the arteries are filled with blood, it is not difficult to clear up the problem, and to assert that the life is not carried but drawn through the arteries, not from the heart alone but from every direction, as is believed by Herophilus, and before him by Praxagoras, Philotimus, Diocles, Pleistonicus, Hippocrates, and ten thousand others. Moreover the force which expands the arteries proceeds from the heart, as it were from a sort of fountain.

(Pliny, *Natural History*, xi. 69, 88, drawing his material in part from Herophilus)

The heart is the principal seat of the heat of the body; it is constantly beating, and moves as though it were one animal enclosed within another. It is enveloped in a membrane equally supple and strong, and is protected by the bulwarks formed by the ribs and the bone of the breast, as the primary source and origin of life. It contains within itself the primary receptacles for the spirit and the blood, in its sinuous cavity, which in the larger animals is threefold and in all at least twofold. Here the mind has its abode. From this source proceed two large veins, which branch into the front part and the back part of the body, and which, spreading out in a series of branches, convey the vital blood by other smaller veins over the whole body. . . .

The pulsation of the arteries is more perceptible on the surface of the limbs, and affords indications of nearly every disease, being either stationary, quickened or retarded, conformably to certain measures and metrical laws, which depend on the age of the patient, and which have been described with remarkable skill by Herophilus, who has been regarded as a prophet in the wondrous art of medicine. These indications, however, have been hitherto neglected in consequence of their remarkable subtlety and minuteness, though at the same time it is by the observation of the pulse, as being fast or slow, that the health of the body, as regulating life, is ascertained.

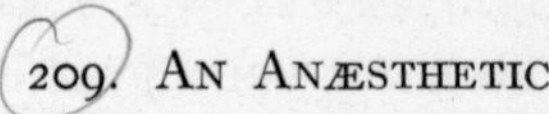

209. An Anæsthetic

(Pliny, *Natural History*, xxv. 13 (94). 147–50)

The subjoined excerpt does not mention Herophilus, but the statement that the "ancients" were accustomed to using mandragora, added to the fact that Herophilus and his contemporaries were great vivisectionists and skilled surgeons, makes it practically certain that they used anæsthetics.

The ancients were in the habit of employing mandragora for diseases of the eye; but more recently the use of it for such purposes has been abandoned. It is a well-ascertained fact, however, that the root, beaten up with rose oil and wine, is curative of defluxions of the eyes and of pains in those organs; in fact the juice of the plant forms an ingredient in many medicaments of the eye. . . .

It is not the mandragora of every country that will yield a juice; but where it does, it is about vintage time that it is collected. In all cases it has a powerful odor, that of the root and fruit the most powerful. The fruit is gathered when ripe and dried in the shade; the juice when extracted is left to thicken in the sun. The same is the case, too, with the juice of the root, which is extracted either by pounding it or by boiling it down to one third in red wine. The leaves are best kept in brine; in fact when fresh their juice is a baneful poison, and these noxious properties are far from being removed even when they are preserved in brine. The very odor of them is highly oppressive to the head, although there are countries in which the fruit is eaten. Persons ignorant of its properties are apt to be rendered unconscious by the odor of the plant when in excess, and too strong a dose of the juice is productive of fatal effects.

Administered in doses proportioned to the strength of the patient, the juice has a narcotic effect, a medium dose being one cyathus. It is given, too, for injuries inflicted by serpents, and before incisions or punctures are made in the body in order to insure insensibility to pain. In fact for this last purpose, with some persons, the odor is quite sufficient to induce sleep.

C. GEOGRAPHY, ASTRONOMY, AND NAVAL ARCHITECTURE

210. Form and Size of the Earth

Ancient science reached the height of its development in the third century B.C. The chief center of culture was Alexandria, which gave its name to the period immediately following its founding. Among the great names of the Alexandrian age is that of Eratosthenes (about 275–195), a man of very versatile genius and for a time Librarian. Although interested in many things, he is chiefly famous for his contribution to mathematical geography. It had long been known that the earth was round, and attempts had been made to compute its circumference; but Eratosthenes made a closer calculation than had previously been reached. He was also the first to suggest the possibility of reaching India by sailing west across the Atlantic. The fragments of his works have been collected by Berger, H., *Die geographischen Fragmente des Eratosthenes* (Teubner, 1880). See also the same author's *Geschichte der wissenschaftlichen Erdkunde der Griechen* (2d ed., Leipzig, 1903); Tozer, H. F., *History of Ancient Geography* (Cambridge: University Press, 1897), ch. ix; Knaack, "Eratosthenes," in Pauly-Wissowa, *Real-Encycl.* VI. 358–89.

The following seems to be the most exact report preserved from antiquity, presenting the mathematical computations of Eratosthenes. It is from Cleomedes, *Concerning the Circular Motion of the Heavenly Bodies*, I. 10 (ed. Ziegler); see Berger, *Eratosthenes*, p. 122. Translated by E. G. S. Verified by T. W. Edmondson.

Under the same meridian, he[1] says, lie Syene and Alexandria. Since then the greatest (lines) in the universe are the meridians,[2] the spherical lines lying under them on the earth must necessarily be the greatest. Consequently whatever extent the theory (of Eratosthenes) will demonstrate for the spherical line running through Syene and Alexandria, so extensive also will be the greatest spherical line of the earth. He then says: And it is so, that Syene lies under the summer solstice.[3] Whenever therefore the sun, having passed into Cancer and, effecting the summer solstice, is precisely at the zenith point of the sky, the gnomon[4] of the sun-dial necessarily becomes shadowless, in accordance with the exact perpendicular of the sun standing overhead;[5] and it is reasonable that this should happen to the extent of three hundred stadia in diameter. At Alexandria at the same hour the gnomons of the sun-dials cast a shadow, since this city lies more to the north than Syene. Inasmuch as these cities lie under the same meridian and the greatest spherical line, if we draw the arc from the apex of the shadow of the sun-dial to the base itself of the sun-dial which is in Alexandria, this arc will prove a segment of the greatest spherical line in the concave sun-dial, since the concave surface of the sun-dial lies under the largest spherical line. If consequently we were

[1] Eratosthenes.

[2] Here Eratosthenes made a slight error in assuming the earth to be an exact sphere, whereas in fact it is slightly flattened at the poles.

[3] Here is another error, due to the imperfection of the ancient method of observation, or we should rather say, to their imperfect instruments. In fact Syene is 37 miles north of the tropic.

[4] "The gnomon which he used as the instrument for his observations was an upright staff set in the midst of a scaphê or bowl, which was so arranged as to correspond to the celestial hemisphere, only inverted, and was marked with lines like a dial"; Tozer, *History of Anc. Geog.* 170.

[5] The demonstration beginning here is clearly explained, and illustrated with a diagram, by Tozer, *op. cit.* 170–2, to which the reader is referred.

to conceive straight lines extended through the earth from each of the sun-dials, they will meet at the centre of the earth. Since then the sun-dial at Syene lies perpendicularly under the sun, if we conceive in addition a straight line drawn from the sun to the apex of the style of the sun-dial, then the line drawn from the sun to the centre of the earth will prove *one* straight line. If then we conceive another straight line from the apex of the shadow of the gnomon drawn up to the sun from the concave dial in Alexandria, this one and the aforesaid straight line will prove to be parallel, passing from different parts of the sun to different parts of the earth. Into these (lines), which are parallel, the line drawn from the centre of the earth to the dial at Alexandria falls as a straight line, so as to render the alternate angles equal. Of these (angles) the one is at the centre of the earth through the meeting of the straight lines which were drawn from the apex of its shadow. The other angle results through the meeting of (the lines drawn) from the apex of the dial at Alexandria and the line drawn upward from the apex of its shadow to the sun through the contact with it. Upon this is constructed the circular line which has been circumscribed from the apex of the shadow of the gnomon to its base; and upon that at the centre of the earth the (line) which passes from Syene to Alexandria. Similar then are the arcs to each other, namely, those based on equal angles. The relation therefore which the line in the concave has to its own circle is the same as the relation of the line drawn from Syene to Alexandria. The line in the concave is to be $\frac{1}{50}$ of its own circle; therefore necessarily also the distance from Syene to Alexandria must be $\frac{1}{50}$ of the largest circle of earth; and this is (a distance) of 5,000 stadia.[1] The whole circle therefore amounts to 250,000 stadia.[2]

Such is the computation of Eratosthenes.

[1] Eratosthenes has overestimated the distance by more than one fifth; Tozer, *op. cit.* 172.

[2] "The general accuracy of the result is very striking; for whereas the real circumference of the earth at the equator is 25,000 English miles, Eratosthenes estimates the great circle of the meridian at 25,000 geographical miles, which is about one seventh part in excess. By the ancients it was regarded as an extraordinary achievement of science, and immense importance was attached to it"; Tozer, *op. cit.* 172. For verifying this statement it is necessary to begin with the English equivalent of the stadium, which contained 600 Greek feet of the Attic standard here used. A foot of that standard is equivalent to 11.65 inches.

211. Evidences of the Rotundity and Size of the Earth

(Strabo i. 1. 20)

Below is a study of the form and dimensions of the earth by Strabo, the geographer, who wrote in the time of the princeps Tiberius, but who drew his information largely from the scientists of the Alexandrian age.

Geometry and astronomy, as we before remarked, seem absolutely indispensable in this science (geography). This in fact is evident, that without some such assistance, it would be impossible to be accurately acquainted with the configuration of the earth; its zones, dimensions, and the like information.

As the size of the earth has been demonstrated by other writers, we shall here take for granted and receive as accurate what they have advanced. We shall also assume that the earth is spheroidal, that its surface is likewise spheroidal, and above all, that bodies have a tendency towards its centre, which latter point is clear to the perception of the most average understanding. However we may show summarily that the earth is spheroidal, from the consideration that all things however distant tend to its centre, and that every body is attracted toward its centre of gravity; this is more distinctly proved from observations of the sea and sky, for here the evidence of the senses, and common observation, is alone requisite. The convexity of the sea is a further proof of this to those who have sailed; for they cannot perceive lights at a distance when placed at the same level as their eyes, but if raised on high, they at once become perceptible to vision, though at the same time further removed. So, when the eye is raised, it sees what before was utterly imperceptible. Homer speaks of this when he says,

> Lifted up on the vast wave he quickly beheld afar.[1]

Sailors, as they approach their destination, behold the shore continually raising itself to their view; and objects which had at first seemed low, begin to elevate themselves. Our gnomons also are, among other things, evidence of the revolution of the heavenly bodies; and common sense at once shows us, that if the depth of the earth were infinite, such a revolution could not take place.[2]

[1] *Odyssey* v. 393.

[2] Strabo holds the opinion that the earth is the center of the universe; but see no. 213.

(Strabo i. 4. 6)

In the subjoined passage Strabo quotes Eratosthenes and comments on his view.

Further, endeavoring to support the opinion that it is in accordance with natural philosophy to reckon the greatest dimension of the habitable earth from east to west, he (Eratosthenes) says that, according to the laws of natural philosophy, the habitable earth ought to occupy a greater length from east to west, than its breadth from north to south. The temperate zone, which we have already designated as the longest zone, is that which the mathematicians denominate a continuous circle returning upon itself. So that if the extent of the Atlantic Ocean were not an obstacle, we might easily pass by sea from Iberia to India, still keeping in the same parallel;[1] the remaining portion of which parallel, measured as above in stadia, occupies more than a third of the whole circle: since the parallel drawn through Athens, on which we have taken the distances from India to Iberia, does not contain altogether 200,000 stadia.[2]

212. Propositions of Aristarchus

(Aristarchus, *On the Sizes and Distances of the Sun and Moon*, translated and edited by Heath, Th., *Aristarchus of Samos, the Ancient Copernicus*. Clarendon Press, 1913)

The greatest astronomer of ancient times was Aristarchus of Samos, who flourished early in the third century. At least a part of his time he spent at Alexandria. Among his achievements were computations of the size and distance of the moon and sun respectively, which were more accurate than the calculations of his predecessors.

In this work Aristarchus still believed the earth to be the center of the universe. Of the propositions given in the treatise cited above, the few here subjoined will perhaps be most interesting to the general reader. For the demonstrations, the reader is referred to Heath.

The moon receives its light from the sun.

The earth is in the relation of a point and center of the sphere in which the moon moves.

[1] This truth, brought to light by Eratosthenes, was afterward lost to the world till its rediscovery in the age of Columbus.

[2] The parallel of longitude passing through Athens is about 36 degrees north. His computation of its circumference corresponds substantially with his estimate of the greatest meridian circle; see p. 637, n. 2 *supra*.

The distance of the sun from the earth is greater than 18 times, but less than 20 times, the distance of the moon (from the earth).

The diameter of the moon is less than $\frac{2}{45}$ but greater than $\frac{1}{30}$ of the distance of the centre of the moon from our eye.

The diameter of the sun has to the diameter of the earth a ratio greater than 19 : 3 but less than 43 : 6.

The sun has to the moon a ratio greater than 5832 : 1 but less than 8000 : 1.

213. The Heliocentric Theory

It was probably after the publication of the work excerpted above that Aristarchus became convinced that the sun is the center, around which the earth and planets move. The theory was rejected by astronomers of the time, and was in this way lost to the world till its rediscovery by Copernicus. On Aristarchus, see the work of Heath mentioned above, and Hultsch, "Aristarchus," in Pauly-Wissowa, *Real-Encycl.* II. 873–6. The treatise in which he expressed his heliocentric view was perhaps termed *Hypotheses*, or *The Construction of Hypotheses*. It is quoted by Archimedes, *Sand-Reckoner*, as follows.

The term world, as it is defined by most astronomers, is here designed to signify a sphere of the heavens, whose center coincides with the center of the earth, and whose semi-diameter is the distance from the center of the earth to the center of the sun. This definition of the term world, as given in the writings of other astronomers, Aristarchus of Samos refutes, and has given it a far more extensive signification; for according to his hypothesis, neither the fixed stars nor the sun are subject to any motion; but the earth annually revolves round the sun in the circumference of a circle, in the centre of which the sun remains fixed. The sphere of the fixed stars, too, whose center he supposes to coincide with the sun's, is of such immense magnitude that the circle, in whose periphery the earth is supposed to revolve round the sun, bears no greater proportion to the distance of the fixed stars than the center of a sphere does to its superficies.

214. The Value of Astronomy for Geography, Architecture, and City-Building

(Hipparchus, quoted by Strabo i. 1. 12 *sq.*)

Hipparchus was a famous geographer and astronomer of the latter half of the second century B.C. He was a prolific writer in both branches of science. See Rehm, "Hipparchos," in Pauly-Wissowa, *Real-Encycl.* VIII. 1666–81.

Many have testified to the amount of knowledge which this subject requires, and Hipparchus, in his Strictures on Eratosthenes, well observes, "that no one can become really proficient in geography, either as a private individual or as a professor, without an acquaintance with astronomy, and a knowledge of eclipses. For instance, no one could tell whether Alexandria in Egypt were north or south of Babylon, nor yet the intervening distance, without observing the latitudes. Again, the only means we possess of becoming acquainted with the longitudes of different places is afforded by the eclipses of the sun and moon." Such are the very words of Hipparchus.

Every one who undertakes to give an accurate description of a place, should be particular to add its astronomical and geometrical relations, explaining carefully its extent, distance, degrees of latitude, and "climate." Even a builder before constructing a house or an architect before laying out a city, would take these things into consideration; much more should he who examines the whole earth: for such things in a peculiar manner belong to him. In small distances a little deviation north or south does not signify, but when it is the whole circle of the earth, the north extends to the furthest confines of Scythia, or Celtica, and the south to the extremities of Ethiopia: there is a wide difference here. The case is the same should we inhabit India or Spain, one in the east, the other far west, and, as we are aware, the antipodes to each other.

215. Hieron's Ship

(Moschion, quoted by Athenæus v. 40–44)

Regarding Moschion little is known. He seems to have belonged to the class of paradoxographists, writers who undertook the task of describing remarkable things of all sorts, literary guides to the wonders of the world. Christ,

Griech. Lit. II. 184, regards paradoxography as a "parasitic growth" on the tree of literature, history, and natural science. The work was pursued with little discrimination between truth and fiction. Moschion, however, was doubtless a contemporary of Hieron, and we have no reason to discredit the essentials of the following account. The selection is given to illustrate the practical mechanics of the age in the construction of perhaps the most wonderful ship known to antiquity.

40. Concerning the ship built by Hieron, tyrant of Syracuse, which also Archimedes the geometrician superintended, I do not think it right to be silent, since a certain man named Moschion has given a description of it, which quite recently I read over with great care.

Moschion writes as follows: Diocleides, a citizen of Abdera, speaks with great admiration of the engine called helepolis, which Demetrius brought against the city of the Rhodians, and applied to their walls. Timæus, too, extols highly the funeral pile made by Dionysius the tyrant of Sicily. Hieronymus also lavishes his admiration on the building and adorning of the chariot in which the body of Alexander was borne to the tomb. Further, Polycleitus speaks in high terms of the candlestick which was made for the king of Persia. But Hieron, king of the Syracusans, who was in every respect a friend of the Romans, was very attentive to the furnishing of temples and gymnasia; and was also very zealous in ship-building, for he made a great number of grain vessels, the construction of one of which I will describe. For the wood he caused such a number of trees to be cut down on Mount Ætna as would have sufficed for sixty triremes; and when this was done, he prepared nails and planks for the sides and for the inside, and wood for every other purpose that could be required, some from Italy and some from Sicily. For ropes he provided cordage from Spain, and hemp and pitch from the river Rhone; and he collected great quantities of useful things from all quarters. Moreover he collected shipwrights and other artisans. Having appointed Archias the Corinthian superintendent of them all, and the principal architect, he bade them labor at the construction with zeal and earnestness, he himself also devoting his days to watching its progress.

In this way he finished half the ship in six months; and every part of the vessel, as soon as it was finished, was immediately covered over with plates of lead. There were three hundred laborers employed in working up the timber, besides the subordinate journeymen whom they had to assist them. The portion that was so far done it was arranged to haul down to the sea that it might receive the finishing touches there. When there arose a great inquiry as to the best method of launching it into the sea, Archimedes the mechanician launched it by himself with the aid of a few persons. Having prepared a helix, he drew this vessel, enormous as it was, down into the sea. Thus Archimedes was the person who first invented the helix. Next the remainder of the ship was also completed in six months more, and was fastened all around with brazen nails, the majority of which weighed ten minas, and the rest were half as big again. They were driven in through holes made beforehand by augers so as to hold the planks firm, and were fastened to the wood with leaden plugs, pieces of cloth being put under, impregnated with pitch. After this was done, after Hieron had completed the external form of the ship, he labored on the interior.

41. The vessel was constructed with twenty banks of oars and three entrances. The lowest entrance led to the hold, to which the descent was by two ladders of many steps each; and the next was contrived for those who wished to go down to the living rooms; and the third was for the armed men. On each side of the middle entrance were apartments for the men, each with four couches in them, thirty in number. The apartment for the sailors was capable of holding fifteen couches, and it had within, three chambers each containing three couches; and the kitchen was toward the stern of the ship. All these rooms had floors of mosaic work, of all kinds of stones tesselated. On this mosaic the whole story of the *Iliad* was presented in a marvellous manner. In all the furniture and in the ceilings and doors everything was executed in the same admirable way. Along the uppermost passage were a gymnasium and walks, with their appointments in all respects corresponding to the size of the vessel. In them were gardens of all sorts of most wonderful beauty, enriched with all varieties of plants and shaded by roofs of lead or tiles. In addition there were tents roofed with boughs of white ivy and of the vine, the roots of which derived their moisture from casks full of earth, and were watered in

the same manner as were the gardens. The tents themselves helped to shade the walks. Near these objects was a temple devoted to Aphrodite, containing three couches with a floor of agate and other most beautiful stones of every kind that the island afforded. Its walls and roof were made of cyprus wood, and its doors of ivory and citron wood. It was furnished exquisitely with pictures and statues and with goblets and vases of every form and shape imaginable.

42. Next to that was a lounging-room with a capacity for five couches, with its doors and walls of box-wood, having a book-case in it, and on the roof a clock imitated from the dial at Achradina. There was also a bath-room with a capacity for three couches, having three brazen vessels for hot water and a bath holding five measures of water beautifully adorned with Tauromenian marble. Many rooms, too, were prepared for the marines and for those who attended to the pumps. Besides all this there were ten stalls for horses on each side of the walls; and near them the fodder for the horses was kept, and the arms and furniture of the horsemen and the grooms. There was a cistern, too, near the head of the ship carefully shut and containing two thousand measures of water, made of beams closely compacted with pitch and canvas. Next to the cistern was a large water-tight tank for fish, made so with beams of wood and lead. It was full of sea-water and in it great numbers of fish were kept.

On each side of the walls were projecting beams, placed at well proportioned intervals; to them were attached stores of wood and ovens and baking places and mills and much other useful apparatus. All round the outside of the ship ran atlases six cubits high, which supported the weight placed above them and the triglyph, all fixed at convenient distances from one another. The whole ship was adorned with suitable pictures.

43. In the vessel were eight towers of a size proportioned to the burden of the ship, two at the stern and as many at the head, and the rest in the middle of the ship. To each were fastened two large beams, or yards, from which port-holes were fixed. Through them stones were discharged upon any enemy who might come against the ship. On each of the towers stood four young men fully armed, and two archers. The whole interior of the towers was full of

stones and darts. A wall with buttresses and decks ran all through the ship supported on trestles; and on these decks were placed a catapult which hurled a stone weighing three talents and an arrow twelve cubits long. This engine was devised and constructed by Archimedes; and it could throw every arrow a furlong. Besides there were mats composed of stout ropes suspended by brazen chains; and as there were three masts, from each of them were suspended two large yards bearing stones, from which hooks and leaden weights were let down upon any enemy which might attack the vessel. There was also a palisade all round the ship made of iron, as a defence against those who might attempt to board it, and iron ravens, as they were called, all round the ship, which, being shot forth by engines, seized on the vessels of the enemy, and brought them round so as to expose them to blows. On each side of the ship stood sixty young men clad in complete armor; and an equal number stood on the masts and on the yards which carried the stones. They were also at the mast-head, which was of bronze. On the first were three men, on the second two, and on the third one. They had stones brought up to them in wicker-baskets by means of pulleys, and arrows were supplied to them by boys within the defended parts of the mast-heads. The vessel had four wooden anchors and eight iron ones. The second and third of the masts were easily found but the first was procured with difficulty among the mountains of Bruttium, and was discovered by a swineherd. Phileas, a mechanic of Tauromenium, brought it down to the seaside.

The hold, although of enormous depth, was pumped out by one man by means of a pulley, with an engine which was the contrivance of Archimedes. The name of the ship was 'the Syracusan,' but when Hieron sent it to sea, he altered its name, calling it 'the Alexandrian.'

It had some small launches attached to it, the first of which was one of the light galleys called cercurus, capable of holding a weight of three thousand talents. It was wholly moved by oars. After that came many galleys and skiffs of about fifteen hundred talents burden. The crews also were proportionally numerous; for besides the men who have already been mentioned, there were six hundred more, whose post was at the head of the ship, always watching for the orders of the captain. There was a tribunal instituted to judge of all offences committed on board the ship, consisting of the captain and pilot, and the officer of the watch. They decided every case according to the laws of the Syracusans.

44. They put on board the ship sixty thousand measures of grain, ten thousand jars of Sicilian salt-fish, twenty thousand talents weight of wool, and of other cargo twenty thousand talents weight. Besides all this, there were the provisions necessary for the crew. When, however, Hieron found that some harbors in Sicily were not large enough to admit this ship and that other harbors were dangerous, he determined to send it as a present to Ptolemy, king of Egypt, at Alexandria.

D. HISTORICAL CRITICISM

It is appropriate to include in this chapter selections from Polybius of Megalopolis, who composed history in a scientific spirit. He was born about 201 and died about 120. His father Lycortas was general, chief executive, of the Achæan league, and at an early age Polybius entered the army and engaged in active service. In time he became a general and diplomatist of distinguished ability. After the defeat of Perseus, king of Macedon, by the Romans (168), Polybius was brought to Rome with a thousand other Achæans as hostages. At this time the Romans must have regarded him as an enemy; but during his stay in the imperial city he became attached to certain great families of Rome, and became an enthusiastic admirer of her people and her institutions. His partiality for Rome may in fact be regarded as a defect of his history.

The composition of his great work required many years, and there is evidence of changes of plan and of views. It contained forty books, of which we have but a small part — books i–v entire, a great part of vi, and fragments of the rest. In the study of this author the first thing to notice is his historical method. No better introduction to the scientific study of history could be found in any modern authority. The moderns have little to change in him and little to add. Apart from the matter of style he is, with the possible exception of Thucydides, the greatest of ancient historians, hence one of the foremost of all time. Whereas Thucydides gives us the finished product only, Polybius takes us into his workshop and shows us the details of his process; hence arises his value for the study of method.

The object of his work is to show how and under what kind of polity Rome gained the supremacy over nearly the whole habitable world (i. 5; *cf.* xxxix. 19). The main period covered extends from 220 to 168, fifty-three years (iii. 1–3, 5). It begins near the opening of the war with Hannibal and the outbreak of the social war in Greece, when the history of the world verges toward a unity which admits of universal treatment (i. 3; ii. 37); it continues the history of Timæus, which breaks off at about this point. To the body of the work he has prefixed a long introduction; and on reaching the year 168 he takes a new start and continues the narrative to the destruction of Carthage in 146.

In his opinion there are three principal elements of historiography. The first is the study of documents, of which he has made extensive use, but which he considers the least important element (xii. 25; *cf.* iii. 21, 33, 56; xvi. 15). The second element is physical and political geography learned in part by personal observation. Polybius himself traveled extensively, facing great dangers and undergoing hardships to obtain the geographical knowledge necessary for his work (iii. 48). In spite of every effort he has made some egregious mistakes. Especially a historian, he asserts, should have a knowledge of the resources of the country of which he treats. While criticising others for their ignorance of such subjects (*cf.* ii. 62), he gives a careful account of the products of the regions with which his narrative is connected: *e.g.*, Lusitania; xxxiv. 8 — silver-mining near New Carthage; xxxiv. 9 — gold-mining near Aquileia; xxxiv. 10. The third element of historiography is political and military science learned by actual experience.

These elements are means to an end, namely the establishment of truth, which is the essential virtue of history (*cf.* ii. 56). In pursuing this object Polybius aims not only to render his own work sound and trustworthy but also to come to the aid of other writers who have made mistakes: "I thought it a point of honor not to look upon the mistakes of others as personal triumphs, after the manner of some writers, but to do the best I could to secure correctness, not only of my own historical writings but of those of other historians also, for the benefit of the world at large" (xvi. 20).

The most important subjects of history are motive and cause, which ordinarily are different sides of the same thing (iii. 7). A general must study the character of his opponent in order to take advantage of his weakness (iii. 80 *sq.*). A statesman must have an eye to the motives for treaties, enmities, and the like, that he may know how to deal with them (iii. 12). Cause must be distinguished from occasion. The latter is the first of a series of actions, whereas the former is the motive which lies back of these actions (iii. 6 *sq.*). In his opinion, however, causation is far broader and deeper than the motives of an individual or of any small group of individuals. The chief cause of the decline of Hellas, for example, is depopulation, and the cause of depopulation is a perverted passion for show and money and for the pleasures of an idle life, which leads to race suicide (xxxvii. 9). The cause of the success of Rome lies in her institutions and in the character of her people (bk. vi). With Polybius, however, causation is not so abstract and so mysterious an idea as with us. Under the influence of the theory of evolution the modern historian has created, so to speak, a reservoir of economic, social, and psychological forces, from which he may draw at pleasure whatever he desires to fit any possible situation. Doubtless this creation is in part imaginary, especially in its excess of abstraction, for which we may find a corrective in the concrete, unclouded vision of Thucydides and Polybius.

Timæus, an historian whom Polybius criticizes with perhaps excessive severity, was a native of Tauromenium, Sicily (about 346–250). His *Histories* (of Sicily and Italy) extended from mythical times to the death of Agathocles, 289 B.C. (Diod. xxi. 17). A later addition continued the narrative through the career of Pyrrhus to 272. As his work contained many references to eastern Hellas, it assumed something of the character of a universal history. The extant fragments may be found in Müller, *Frag. hist. græc.* I. 193–233; IV. 625 *sq.*, 640 *sq.* Further extracts from Polybius will be found in the first volume of this series.

216. Certain Faults of Timæus

(Polybius xii. 4 *a–d*)

(*a*) It is difficult to pardon such errors in Timæus, considering how severe he is in criticising the slips of others. For instance he finds fault with Theopompus for stating that Dionysius sailed from Sicily to Corinth in a merchant vessel, whereas he really arrived in a ship of war. And again he falsely charges Ephorus with contradicting himself, on the ground that he asserts that Dionysius the Elder ascended the throne at the age of twenty-three, reigned forty-two years, and died at sixty-three. Now no one would say, I think, that this was a blunder of the historian, but clearly one of the transcriber. For either Ephorus must be more foolish than Corœbus and Margites,[1] if he were unable to calculate that forty-two added to twenty-three make sixty-five; or, if that is incredible in the case of a man like Ephorus, it must be a mere mistake of the transcriber, and the carping and malevolent criticism of Timæus must be rejected.

(*b*) Again, in his history of Pyrrhus, he says that the Romans still keep up the memory of the fall of Troy by shooting to death with javelins a war-horse on a certain fixed day, because the capture of Troy was accomplished by means of the "Wooden Horse." This is quite childish. On this principle, all non-Hellenic nations must be put down as descendants of the Trojans; for nearly all of them, or at any rate the majority, when about to commence a war or a serious battle with an enemy, first kill and sacrifice a horse. In making this sort of ill-founded deduction, Timæus seems to me

[1] Corœbus and Margites are types of stupidity in Greek literature. The latter is the subject of a mock epic attributed to Homer.

to show not only want of knowledge, but, what is worse, a trick of misapplying knowledge. For, because the Romans sacrifice a horse, he immediately concludes that they do it because Troy was taken by means of a horse.

(*c*) These instances clearly show how worthless his account of Libya, Sardinia, and above all, of Italy[1] is; and that, speaking generally, he has entirely neglected the most important element in historical investigation, namely, the making of personal inquiries. For as historical events take place in many different localities, and as it is impossible for the same man to be in several places at the same time, and also impossible for him to see with his own eyes all places in the world and observe their peculiarities, the only resource left is to ask questions of as many people as possible; and to believe those who are worthy of credit; and to show critical sagacity in judging of their reports.

(*d*) And though Timæus makes great professions on this head, he appears to me to be very far from arriving at the truth. Indeed, so far from making accurate investigations of the truth through other people, he does not tell us anything trustworthy even of events of which he has been an eye-witness, or of places he has personally visited. This will be made evident, if we can convict him of being ignorant, even in his account of Sicily, of the facts which he brings forward. For it will require very little further proof of his inaccuracy, if he can be shown to be ill-informed and misled about the localities in which he was born and bred, and that too the most famous of them.

217. Timæus' Chronological and Archæological Studies

(Polybius xii. 11)

This is the man forsooth who drew out a comparative list of the ephors and the kings of Sparta from the earliest times; as well as one comparing the archons at Athens and priestesses in Argos with the list of Olympic victors, and thereby convicted those cities of being in error about those records because there was a discrep-

[1] In a passage above (ch. 3) Polybius has criticized Timæus' treatment of these countries.

ancy of three months between them! This again is the man who discovered the engraved tablets in the inner shrines, and the records of the guest-friendships on the doorposts of the temples. And we cannot believe that such a man could have been ignorant of anything of this sort that existed, or would have omitted to mention it if he had found it. Nor can he on any ground expect pardon, if he has told an untruth about it: for, as he has shown himself a bitter and uncompromising critic of others, he must naturally look for equally uncompromising attacks from them.

218. Truth the Prime Virtue of History

(Polybius xii. 12)

12. Timæus says that the greatest fault in history is want of truth; and he accordingly advises all, whom he may have convicted of making false statements in their writings, to find some other name for their books, and to call them anything they like except history. . . .

For example in the case of a carpenter's rule, though it may be too short or too narrow for your purpose, yet if it have the essential feature of a rule, that of straightness, you may still call it a rule; but if it has not this quality, and deviates from the straight line, you may call it anything you like except a rule. "On the same principle," says he, "historical writings may fail in style or treatment or other details; yet if they hold fast to truth, such books may claim the title of history, but if they swerve from that, they ought no longer to be called history." Well, I quite agree that in such writings truth should be the first consideration; and, in fact, somewhere in the course of my work, I have said "*that as in a living body, when the eyes are out, the whole is rendered useless, so if you take truth from history what is left is but an idle tale.*" I said again, however, that "there were two sorts of falsehoods, the ignorant and the intentional; and the former deserved indulgence, the latter uncompromising severity." . . . These points being agreed upon — the wide difference between ignorant and intentional lie, and the kindly correction due to the one, and the unbending denunciation to the other — it will be found that it is to the latter charge that Timæus more than anyone lays himself open. And the proof of his character in this respect is clear.

219. The Historian's Need of Practical Experience

(Polybius xii. 25 *e–n*)

(*e*) In the same way the science of genuine history is threefold: first, the dealing with written documents and the arrangement of the material thus obtained; second, topography, the appearance of cities and localities, the description of rivers and harbors, and speaking generally, the peculiar features of seas and countries and their relative distances; thirdly, political affairs. Now, as in the case of medicine, it is the last branch that many attach themselves too, owing to their preconceived opinions on the subject. And the majority of writers bring to the undertaking no spirit of fairness at all: nothing but dishonesty, impudence, and unscrupulousness. Like vendors of drugs, their aim is to catch popular credit and favor, and to seize every opportunity of enriching themselves. About such writers it is not worth while to say more.

(*f*) But some of those who have the reputation of approaching history in a reasonable spirit are like the theoretical physicians. They spend all their time in libraries, and acquire generally all the learning which can be got from books, and then persuade themselves that they are adequately equipped for their task. . . . Yet in my opinion they are only partially qualified for the production of general history. To inspect ancient records indeed, with the view of ascertaining the notions entertained by the ancients of certain places, nations, polities and events, and of understanding the several circumstances and contingencies experienced in former times, is useful; for the history of the past directs our attention in a proper spirit to the future, if a writer can be found to give a statement of facts as they really occurred. But to persuade one's self, as Timæus does, that such ability in research is sufficient to enable a man to describe subsequent transactions with success is quite foolish. It is as though a man were to imagine that an inspection of the works of the old masters would enable him to become a painter and a master of the art himself.

(*g*) This will be rendered still more evident from what I have now to say, particularly from certain passages in the history of Ephorus. This writer in his treatment of war seems to me to have had some idea of naval tactics, but to be quite unacquainted with fighting on shore. Accordingly, if one turns one's attention to the naval battles at Cyprus and Cnidos, in which the generals of the king were engaged against Evagoras of Salamis and then against the Lacedæmonians, one will be struck with admiration of the historian, and will learn many useful lessons as to what to do in similar circumstances. But when he tells the story of the battle of Leuctra between the Thebans and Lacedæmonians, or again that of Mantineia between the same combatants, in which Epaminondas lost his life, if in these accounts one examines attentively and in detail the arrangements and evolutions in the line of battle, the historian will appear quite ridiculous, and betray his entire ignorance and want of personal experience in such matters. The battle of Leuctra indeed was simple, and confined to one division of the forces engaged, and therefore does not make the writer's lack of knowledge so very glaring; but that of Mantineia was complicated and technical, and is accordingly unintelligible, and indeed completely inconceivable to the historian. This will be rendered clear by first laying down a correct plan of the ground, and then measuring the extent of the movements as described by him. The same is the case with Theopompus, and above all with Timæus, the subject of this book. These latter writers also can conceal their ignorance, so long as they deal with generalities; but directly they attempt minute and detailed description, they show they are no better than Ephorus. . . .

(*h*) It is in fact as impossible to write well on the operations of a war, if a man has had no experience of actual service, as it is to write well on politics without having been engaged in political transactions and vicissitudes. And when history is written by the book-learned, without technical knowledge, and without clearness of detail, the work loses all its value. For if you take from history its element of practical instruction, what is left of it has nothing to attract and nothing to teach. Again, in the topography of cities and localities, when such men attempt to go into details, being entirely without personal knowledge, they must in a similar manner necessarily pass over many points of importance; while they waste words on many that are not worth the trouble. And this is what his failure to make personal inspection brings upon Timæus. . . .

(*i*) In his thirty-fourth book Timæus says that "he spent fifty continuous years at Athens as an alien, and never took part in any military service, or went to inspect the localities." Accordingly, when he comes upon any such matters in the course of his history, he shows much ignorance and makes many misstatements; and if he ever does come near the truth, he is like one of those animal painters who draw from models of stuffed skins. Such artists sometimes preserve the correct outline, but the vivid look and life-like portraiture of the real animal, the chief charm of the painter's art, are quite wanting. This is just the case with Timæus, and in fact with all who start with mere book-learning; there is nothing vivid in their presentment of events, for that can only come from the personal experience of the writers. And hence it is, that those who have gone through no such course of actual experience produce no genuine enthusiasm in the minds of their readers. Former historians showed their sense of the necessity of making professions to this effect in their writings. For when their subject was political, they were careful to state that the writer had of course been engaged in politics, and had had experience in matters of the sort; or if the subject was military, that he had served a campaign and been actually engaged; and again, when the matter was one of everyday life, that he had brought up children and had been married; and so on in every department of life, which we may find adequately treated by those writers alone who have had personal experience, and have accordingly made that branch of history their own. It is difficult perhaps for a man to have been actually and literally engaged in everything; but in the most important actions and most frequently occurring he must have been so.

(*j*) And that this is no impossibility, Homer is a convincing instance; for in him you may see this quality of personal knowledge frequently and conspicuously displayed. The upshot of all this is that the study of documents is only one of three elements in the preparation of an historian, and is only third in importance. And no clearer proof of this could be given than that furnished by the deliberative speeches, harangues of commanders, and orations of ambassadors as recorded by Timæus. For the truth is, that the occasions are rare which admit of all possible arguments being set forth; as a rule, the circumstances of the case confine them to narrow limits. And of such speeches one sort is regarded with favor by men of our time, another by those of an earlier age; different styles again are popular with Ætolians, Peloponnesians, and Athenians. But to make digressions, in season and out of season, for the purpose of setting forth every possible speech that could be made, as Timæus does by his trick of inventing words to suit every sort of occasion, is utterly misleading, pedantic, and worthy of a schoolboy essayist. And this practice has brought failure and discredit on many writers. Of course to select from time to time the proper and appropriate language is a necessary part of our art; but as there is no fixed rule to decide the quantity and quality of the words to be used on a particular occasion, great care and training is required if we are to instruct and not mislead our readers. The exact nature of the situation is difficult to communicate always; still it may be brought home to the mind by means of systematic demonstration, founded on personal and habitual experience. The best way of securing that this should be realised is for historians, first, to state clearly the position, the aims, and the circumstances of those deliberating; and then, recording the real speeches made, to explain to us the causes which contributed to the success or failure of the several speakers. Thus we could obtain a free conception of the situation, and by exercising our judgment upon it, and drawing analogies from it, should be able to form a thoroughly sound opinion upon the circumstances of the hour. But I suppose that tracing causes is difficult, while stringing words together in books is easy. Few again have the faculty of speaking briefly to the point, and getting the necessary training for doing so; while to produce a long and futile composition is within most people's capacity and is common enough. . . .

BIBLIOGRAPHY

I. Science. — Marmery, J. V., *Progress of Science* (London: Chapman, 1895), chs. ii, iii; Williams, H. S., *History of Science*, 5 vols. (Harper, 1904) I. chs. ix, xi; Whibley, *Companion to Greek Studies* (Cambridge: University

Press, 1905), 205–7 with references; Beloch; *Griech. Gesch.* III. 1. 473–507; Susemihl, Fr., *Geschichte der griech. Litteratur der Alexandrinerzeit*, 2 vols. (Leipzig, 1891, 1892), see Contents for the various scientists; Günther and Windelband, *Geschichte der antiken Naturwissenschaft* (Müller's *Hdb. der kl. Altwiss.* V, Nördlingen: Beck, 1888); Heiberg, J. L. "Exakte Wissenschaft und Medizin," in Gercke and Norden, *Einleitung in die Altertumswissenschaft*, II (1910). 393–432 with references; *Naturwissenschaften und Mathematik im klassischen Altertum* (Teubner, 1912); Loria, G., *Le scienze esatte nell' antica Grecia* (Modena, 1893–1902).

For mathematics, see Zeuthen, H. G., *Histoire des mathématiques dans l'antiquité et le moyen âge* (Paris, 1902); Cantor, M., *Vorlesungen über Geschichte der Mathematik*, I (3d ed., Leipzig, 1907); Ball, W. W. R., *A Short Account of the History of Mathematics* (Macmillan, 1912); Hultsch, Fr., "Arithmetica," in Pauly-Wissowa, *Real-Encycl.* II. 1066–1116.

For astronomy, geography, and kindred subjects, see *Geographi græci minores*, 2 vols. of text and a third of maps (Paris, 1855–1861); Columba, G. M., *Eratostene e la misurazione del meridano terrestre* (Palermo, 1895); Berger, H., *Die geographischen Fragmente des Eratosthenes neu gesammelt*, etc. (Teubner, 1880); *Geschichte der wissenschaftlichen Erdkunde der Griechen* (2d ed., Leipzig: Weit, 1903); Bunbury, E. H., *History of Ancient Geography*, 2 vols. (2d ed., London, 1883); Tozer, H. F., *History of Ancient Geography* (Cambridge: University Press, 1897); Nissen, H., "Die Erdmessung, des Eratosthenes," in *Rhein. Mus.* LVIII (1903). 231–45; Tannery, P., *Recherches sur l'histoire de l'astronomie ancienne* (Paris, 1893); Heath, Th. L., *Aristarchus of Samos; the Ancient Copernicus* (Oxford: Clarendon Press, 1912); *The Method of Archimedes discovered by Heiberg* (Cambridge: University Press, 1912); Martin, Th. H., "Astronomie," in Daremberg-Saglio, *Dict.* I. 476–504; Hultsch, Fr., "Apollonius," in Pauly-Wissowa, *Real-Encycl.* II. 151 (no. 112)-60; "Archimedes," *ib.* 507 (no. 3)–39; "Aristarchus" (of Samos), *ib.* 873 (no. 25)–6; "Astronomie," *ib.* 1828–62.

On medicine: a *Corpus medicorum græcorum* is being prepared conjointly by the Academies of Copenhagen and Berlin (Teubner); Puschmann, Th., *Geschichte des medizinischen Unterrichts* (Leipzig, 1889); English edition (London, 1891); Neuberger, M., *Geschichte der Medizin*, 2 vols. (Stuttgart, 1906, 1908); Schwalbe, E., *Vorlesungen über die Geschichte der Medizin* (2d ed., Jena. Fischer, 1909); Milne, J. St., *Surgical Instruments in Greek and Roman Times* (Aberdeen University Studies, 1907); Randolph, C. B., "The Mandragora of the Ancients," etc., in *Proceed. Am. Acad. of Arts and Sci.* XL. 485–537; Jones, Ross, and Ellet, *Malaria: a Neglected Factor in the History of Greece and Rome* (Cambridge, 1907); Jones, *Malaria and Greek History* (University of Manchester, 1909); Meyer, E. H. F., *Geschichte der Botanik*, 4 vols. (Königsberg, 1854–1857); Bretzl, *Botanische Forschungen des Alexanderzuges* (Leipzig, 1903). Recent literature on medicine reviewed by Kind, F. E., in *Jahresb.* CLVIII (1912). 132–234.

II. Polybius. — The best edition is that of Büttner-Wobst, Th., 4 vols. (Teubner, 1905); see also the Didot ed. 2 vols with Latin translation (Paris, 1839); *History of the Achæan League as contained in the Remains of Polybius*, ed. with notes by Capes, W. W. (London, 1888). The best English translation is by Shuckburgh, E. S. (Macmillan, 1889), from which the selections for this volume, revised by E. G. S., have been taken. Studies in Polybius are Nissen, H., "Die Oekonomie der Geschichte des Polybius," in *Rhein. Mus.* XXVI (1871). 241 *sqq.*; Bunbury, E. H., *History of Ancient Geography*, II. 16–42; Strachan-Davidson, J. L., "Polybius," in Abbott, E., *Hellenica*, 387–424; Hirzel, R., "Der Einfluss der Philosophie auf die Geschichtschreibung des Polybius," in his *Untersuchungen zu Cicero's philosophischen Schriften*, II. 2. Excurs. vii, 841–907; Thommen, R., "Ueber die Abfassungszeit des Polybius," in *Hermes*, XX (1885). 196–236; Fustel de Coulanges, N. D., "Polybe; ou Grèce conquise par les Romains," in his *Questions historiques* (1893), 119–211; Duff, M. E. G., "Criticism of Polybius' History," in *Royal Historical Society Transactions*, new ser. XI (1897). 1–17; Büttner-Wobst, Th., "Studien zu Polybius," in *Philol.* LIX (1900). 560 *sqq.*; "Polybius als Astronom," *ib.* 151 *sqq.*; Schwartz, E., *Charakterköpfe aus der antiken Litteratur* (3d ed., Leipzig, 1910), 72 *sqq.*; Christ, W., *Griech. Litt.* II. 292 *sqq.*; Bury, J. B., *Ancient Greek Historians* (Macmillan, 1909), ch. vi.

Markhauser, W., *Der Geschichtschreiber Polybius, seine Weltanschauung und Staatslehre* (Munich, 1858); Peter, K. L., *Livius und Polybius: über die Quellen des XXI und XXII Buchs des Livius* (Halle, 1863); Scala, R. von, *Die Studien des Polybios* (Stuttgart, 1890); Bender, F., *Antikes Völkerrecht im Zeitalter des Polybios* (Bonn, 1901); Wunderer, K., *Polybiosforschungen*, 3 vols. (Leipzig, 1901–1909); *Die psychologischen Anschauungen des Geschichtschreibers Polybios* (Erlangen, 1905), program; Cuntz, O., *Polybios und sein Werk* (Leipzig, 1902); Ullrich, H., *Die Reden bei Polybios* (Zittau, 1905), program; Hahn, L., *Roms Sprache und der Hellenismus zur Zeit des Polybios* (Nürnberg, 1906), program; Laqueur, R., *Polybius* (Teubner, 1913).

CHAPTER XIX

SOCIAL CONDITIONS

After 337 B.C.

This chapter connects closely with ch. xvi.

220. In the Streets of Alexandria

(Theocritus, *Idyl*, xv)

For Theocritus, see p. 56.

The poem was composed at Alexandria after the marriage of Ptolemy Philadelphus and Arsinoë, probably therefore about 260 B.C. Arsinoë is giving a festival of Adonis, and two middle-class women from Syracuse, then resident in Alexandria, go out to see the festival. One of them, Gorgo, first calls for the other, Praxinoë, at the house of the latter, and a short conversation takes place before they go out. With them go their two slave maids, Eutychis and Eunoë. Their gossip, the crowded streets, and the wares which they inspect are presented most interestingly by the poet. It is a natural and fascinating picture of life in the great center of the civilized world of that age.

Gorgo. Is Praxinoë at home?

Praxinoë. Dear Gorgo, how long it is since you have been here! She *is* at home. The wonder is that you have got here at last! Eunoë, see that she has a chair. Throw a cushion on it too.

Gor. It does most charmingly as it is.

Prax. Do sit down.

Gor. O, what a thing spirit is! I have scarcely got to you alive, Praxinoë! What a huge crowd, what hosts of four-in-hands! Everywhere cavalry boots, everywhere men in uniform! And the road is endless; yes, you really live too far away!

Prax. It is all the fault of that madman of mine. Here he came to the ends of the earth[1] and took — a hole, not a house, and all that we might not be neighbors. The jealous wretch, always the same, ever for spite!

Gor. Don't talk about your husband, Dinon, like that, my

[1] That is, from Syracuse to Alexandria.

dear girl, before your little boy, — look how he is staring at you! Never mind, Zopirion, sweet child, she is not speaking about papa.

PRAX. Our lady![1] the child takes notice.

GOR. Nice papa!

PRAX. That papa of his the other day — we call every day 'the other day' — went to get soap and dye at the shop, and back he came to me with salt — the great big, stupid fellow!

GOR. Mine has the same trick, too, a perfect spendthrift, Diocleides! Yesterday he got what he meant for five fleeces, and paid seven drachmas apiece for — what do you suppose? — dog-skins, shreds of old leather wallets, mere trash — trouble on trouble. But come take your cloak and shawl. Let us be off to the palace of rich Ptolemy, the king, to see the Adonis; I hear the queen has provided something splendid!

PRAX. Fine folks do everything fitly.

GOR. What a tale you will have to tell about the things you have seen, to any one who has not seen them! It seems nearly time to go.

PRAX. Idlers have always holiday. Eunoë, bring the water and put it down in the middle of the room, lazy creature that you are. Cats like always to sleep soft![2] Come, bustle, bring the water; quicker. I want water first, and how she carries it! give it me all the same; don't pour out so much, you extravagant thing. Stupid girl! Why are you wetting my dress? There, stop, I have washed my hands, as heaven would have it. Where is the key of the big chest? Bring it here.

GOR. Praxinoë, that mantle becomes you wonderfully. Tell me how much did the stuff cost you just off the loom?

PRAX. Don't speak of it, Gorgo! More than a mina, or two, in good silver money — and the work on it! I nearly slaved my soul out over it.

GOR. Well, it is most successful; all you could wish.

PRAX. Thanks for the pretty speech! Bring my shawl and set my hat on my head, the fashionable way. No, child, I don't mean to take you. Boo! Bogies! There's a horse that bites!

[1] Persephone.

[2] In speaking of cats she means lazy servants, like Eunoë. Cats were not common in Greece; the proverb, therefore, must have been Alexandrian.

Cry as much as you please, but I cannot have you lamed. Let us be moving. Phrygia, take the child and keep him amused; call in the dog and shut the street door.

(*They go out.*)

Ye gods, what a crowd! How on earth are we ever to get through this coil? They are like ants that no one can measure or number. Many a good deed have you done, Ptolemy; since your father joined the immortals, there's never a malefactor to spoil the passer-by, creeping on him in Egyptian[1] fashion — O, the tricks those perfect rascals used to play. Birds of a feather, ill jesters, scoundrels all! Dear Gorgo, what will become of us? Here come the king's war-horses! My dear man, don't trample on me. Look, the bay's rearing, see, what temper! Eunoë, you fool-hardy girl, will you never keep out of the way? The beast will kill the man that's leading him. What a good thing it is for me that my brat stays safe at home.

GOR. Courage, Praxinoë. We are safe behind them, now, and they have gone to their positions.

PRAX. There! I begin to be myself again. Ever since I was a child I have feared nothing so much as horses and the chilly snake. Come along, the huge mob is overflowing us.

GOR. (*to an old woman*). Are you from the Court, mother?

OLD WOMAN. I am, my child.

PRAX. Is it easy to get there?

OLD W. The Achæans got into Troy by trying, my prettiest lady. Trying will do everything in the long run.

GOR. The old wife has spoken her oracles, and off she goes.

PRAX. Women know everything, yes, and how Zeus married Hera!

GOR. See Praxinoë, what a crowd there is about the doors.

PRAX. Monstrous, Gorgo! Give me your hand, and you, Eunoë, catch hold of Eutychis; never lose hold of her, for fear lest you get lost! Let us all go in together; Eunoë, clutch tight to me. O how tiresome, Gorgo, my muslin veil is torn in two already! For heaven's sake, sir, if you ever wish to be fortunate, take care of my shawl!

[1] The Greeks looked with contempt on the Egyptians.

STRANGER. I can hardly help myself, but for all that I will be as careful as I can.

PRAX. How close-packed the mob is, they hustle like a herd of swine.

STRAN. Courage, lady, all is well with us now.

PRAX. Both this year and forever may all be well with you, my dear sir, for your care of us. A good kind man! We're letting Eunoë get jammed — come, wretched girl, push your way through. This is the way. We are all on the right side of the door, quoth the bridegroom, when he had shut himself in with his bride.

GOR. Do come here, Praxinoë. Look first at these embroideries. How light and how lovely! You will call them the garments of the gods.

PRAX. Lady Athene, what spinning-women wrought them, what painters designed these drawings, so true they are? How natural they stand and move, like living creatures, not patterns woven. What a clever thing is man! Ah, and himself, Adonis, how beautiful to behold he lies on his silver couch, with the first down on his cheeks, the thrice-beloved Adonis — Adonis beloved even among the dead.

STRANGER II. You weariful women, do cease your endless cooing talk! They bore one to death with their eternal broad vowels!

GOR. Indeed! And where may this person come from? What is it to you if we are chatterboxes! Give orders to your servants, sir. Do you pretend to command ladies of Syracuse? If you must know, we are Corinthians by descent,[1] like Bellerophon himself, and we speak Peloponnesian. Dorian women may lawfully speak Doric, I presume?

PRAX. Lady Persephone, never may we have more than one master. I am not afraid of *your* putting me on short commons.

GOR. Hush, hush, Praxinoë — the Argive woman's daughter, the great singer, is beginning the *Adonis;* she that won the prize last year for dirge-singing. I am sure she will give us something lovely; see, she is preluding with her airs and graces.

(*The song is here omitted.*)

[1] The Corinthians prided themselves on their descent, considering themselves above the Alexandrians, who were a mixed race.

Gor. Praxinoë, the woman is cleverer than we fancied! Happy woman to know so much, thrice happy to have so sweet a voice. Well, all the same, it is time to be making for home. Diocleides has not had his dinner, and the man is all vinegar. Don't venture near him when he is kept waiting for dinner. Farewell, beloved Adonis, may you find us glad at your next coming!

221. The Custom of Shaving the Beard

(Chrysippus, *The Beautiful and the Pleasant;* also a comedy of Alexis, quoted by Athenæus xiii. 18)

Those who are interested in Greek portrait busts and statues notice that before Alexander the Great mature men uniformly wear beards, whereas from his time it is the custom of all excepting the philosophers to shave their faces clean. From the excerpt below we learn that in various states laws were passed to prohibit shaving, but as is usual with such enactments, they were generally disobeyed.

You prefer, however, to have all the objects of your affection with clean-shaven faces. This custom of shaving the beard arose in the age of Alexander, as Chrysippus tells us in the fourth book of his work on *The Beautiful and the Pleasant;* and I think it will not be out of place for me to quote what he says; for he is an author of whom I am very fond, because of his great learning and his gentle good-natured disposition. These are the words of the philosopher: "The custom of shaving the beard was introduced in the time of Alexander, for the people in earlier times did not practise it; and Timotheus the piper used to wear a long beard when playing on the pipe. At Athens, too, they even now remember that the man who first shaved his chin, no long time ago, was given the name Korses. In regard to this circumstance Alexis writes:

> Do you see any man whose beard has been
> Removed by sharp pitch-plasters or by razors?
> In one of these two ways he may be mentioned:
> Either he seems to me to think of war,
> And so to be rehearsing acts of fierce
> Hostility against his beard and chin,
> Or else has some disease that comes from wealth;

For how, I pray you, do your beards annoy you? —
Beards by which you may best be known as men?
Unless in fact you're planning now some deed
Unworthy of the sex and name of men.

Diogenes, too, when he saw a certain smooth-chinned man, remarked: I fear you think you have great reason for accusing nature because it made you a man and not a woman. . . . At Rhodes, though there is a law prohibiting shaving, no one prosecutes another on that charge, for the entire population shaves. At Byzantium also there is a penalty to which every barber is liable who owns a razor, but every one uses a razor none the less for that law." Such is the statement of the admirable Chrysippus.

222. The Make-up of Hetæræ

(Alexis, *Isostasion*, quoted by Athenæus xiii. 23)

For Alexis see introduction to no. 223. *Isostasion* seems to signify Equipoise.

For first of all, to earn themselves great gain,
And better to plunder all the neighboring men,
They use a lot of adventitious aids —
They plot to take in every one. And when
By subtle artifice they've made some money,
They enlist fresh girls and add recruits, who ne'er
Have tried the trade, unto their cunning troop,
And drill them so that they are very soon
Different in manners and in look and semblance
From all they were before. Suppose one's short,
They put cork soles within the heels of her shoes;
If any one's too tall, she wears a slipper
Of thinnest substance, and with head depressed
Between her shoulders, walks the public streets,
And so takes off from her superfluous height.
If any one's too lean about the flank,
They hoop her with a bustle, so that all
Who see her marvel at her fair proportions.
Has any one too prominent a stomach,

They crown it with false bosom, such as perchance
At times you may in comic actors see;
And what is still too prominent, they force
Back, ramming it as if with scaffolding.
Has any one red brows, those they smear
With soot. Has any one a dark complexion,
White lead will that correct. This girl's too fair,
They rub her well with rich vermillion.
Is she a splendid figure, then her charms
Are shown in unclad beauty to the purchaser.
Has she good teeth, then she is forced to laugh,
That all the bystanders may see her mouth,
How beautiful it is; and if she be
But ill inclined to laugh, then she is kept
Close within doors whole days, and all the things
Which cooks keep by them when they sell goats' heads,
Such as a stick of myrrh, she's forced to keep
Between her lips, till they have learned the shape
Of the required smile. And by such arts
They make their charms and persons up for market.

223. Wives are Undesirable

(Alexis, *Soothsayers*, quoted by Athenæus xiii. 7)

Alexis of Thurii, about 390 to about 290, was one of the most famous representatives of the Middle Comedy. He is said to have lived a hundred and six years; and he certainly produced an enormous number of comedies. Although he began to write plays before the middle of the fourth century, and though the date of his *Soothsayers* is unknown, the subjoined selection is grouped with the excerpt from Menander on the same subject because of a similarity in the tone of the three passages.

Oh wretched are we husbands, who have sold
All liberty of life, all luxury,
And live as slaves of women, not as freemen.
We say we have a dowry; do we not
Endure the penalty, full of female bile,
Compared to which the bile of man's pure honey?
For men, though injured, pardon; but the women

First injure us and then reproach us more.
They rule those whom they should not; those they should
They constantly neglect. They falsely swear;
They have no single hardship, no disease;
And yet they are complaining without end.

(Menander, *Woman Carrying the Sacred Vessel of Athena*, quoted by Athenæus xiii. 8)

A. You will not marry, if you're in your senses
And leave this life you're in. For I myself
Did marry; so I recommend you not to.
B. The matter is decided — the die is cast.
A. Go on, then. I do wish you then well over it;
But you are taking arms, with no good reason,
Against a sea of troubles. In the waves
Of the deep Libyan or Ægean sea
Scarce three of thirty ships are lost or wrecked;
But scarcely one poor husband 'scapes at all.

(Menander, *Woman Burned*, quoted by Athenæus xiii. 8)

Oh may the man be totally undone
Who was the first to venture on a wife;
And then the next who followed his example;
And then the third and fourth and after them Metagenes.[1]

224. Hipparchia, the Lady who Became a Philosopher

(Diogenes Laërtius, *Lives and Opinions of Eminent Philosophers*, vi. 96–8)

Little is known of this Diogenes, but it is at least evident that he did not live earlier than the third century A.D. In his fondness for displaying his erudition, and in his lack of critical ability, we may class him with Athenæus, who may have been a contemporary. His work is especially valuable as it contains many quotations from earlier and more important writers. See Christ, *Griech. Lit.* II. 684–8; Schwartz, "Diogenes," in Pauly-Wissowa, *Real-Encycl.* V. 738–63.

Hipparchia was the daughter of well-to-do parents of Maroneia, Thrace, the sister of Metrocles, the Cynic philosopher. Crates, the Cynic philosopher whom she married, lived 340–260 (?). In early Hellas there had been many

[1] Doubtless a character in the play.

intellectual women, but the fifth and fourth centuries were less favorable to them. In the Hellenistic age, however, they reappear. The excerpt below is interesting for its presentation of a woman of this class.

Hipparchia, the sister of Metrocles, was charmed along with others by the doctrines of this school.[1] She and Metrocles were natives of Maroneia. She fell in love with the doctrines and the manners of Crates, and could not be diverted from her regard for him either by the wealth or the high birth or the personal beauty of any of her suitors; but Crates was everything to her. She threatened her parents to make away with herself, if she were not given in marriage to him. When entreated by her parents to dissuade her from this resolution, Crates did all he could; and at last, as he could not persuade her, he arose and placing all his furniture before her, he said: "This is the bridegroom whom you are choosing, and this is the whole of his property. Consider these facts; for it will not be possible for you to become his partner, if you do not apply yourself to the same studies and conform to the same habits as he does." The girl chose him; and assuming the same dress as he wore, went with him as her husband, and appeared with him in public everywhere, and went to all entertainments in his company.

Once when she went to sup at the house of Lysimachus, she attacked Theodorus, who was surnamed the Atheist. To him she proposed the following sophism: "What Theodorus could not be called wrong for doing, that same thing Hipparchia could not be called wrong for doing. But Theodorus does no wrong when he beats himself; therefore Hipparchia does no wrong when she beats Theodorus." He made no reply to what she said, but only pulled her gown. Hipparchia was neither offended nor ashamed, as many a woman would have been; but when he said to her: —

> Who is the woman who has left the shuttle
> So near the warp? [2]

She replied: "I, Theodorus, am the person; but do I seem to you to have come to a wrong decision, if I devote that time to philosophy which otherwise I should have spent at the loom?" These and many other sayings are reported of this female philosopher.

[1] The school of Cynic philosophy.

[2] Euripides, *Bacchæ*, 1228.

225. The Exposed Child and its Belongings

(Menander, *Arbitrants*, 1–178)

In the New Comedy the exposure and later recognition of children are frequent events. In this case Davus, a slave, has found the child and has handed him over to Syriscus, the slave of another master. On hearing that certain trinkets were found with the child, Syriscus demands them of Davus, but is refused, whereupon they ask Smicrines, the first comer, to arbitrate between them. The ring, mentioned in this excerpt among the child's belongings, leads to the identification of the parents. It so happens that Smicrines is father of the child's mother. Its father was her husband Charisius, master of the slave Onesimus introduced at the close of this excerpt. The circumstance that the child was born before the marriage of its parents troubles the situation, which however is happily cleared in the end. The characters of the persons concerned are interesting studies, and there can be no doubt that in general the plays of Menander fairly represent real phases of contemporary life.

Syriscus. You don't choose to do what is just.

Davus. Wretch, you belie me. You have no right to what is not yours.

Syr. We must refer the matter to some one.

Dav. With all my heart.

Syr. Who then —

Dav. Anyone will do for me. But it serves me right, for why did I tell you?

(*An old man enters.*)

Syr. Will you take this gentleman for our umpire?

Dav. By all manner of means.[1]

Syr. (*addressing the old man*). For heaven's sake, noble sir, might it please you to bestow on us a little of your leisure?

Smicrines. On you? What about?[2]

Syr. There is a matter we are disputing over.

Smic. What do I care?

Syr. We are in search of an impartial judge to settle this affair. If then you are not otherwise occupied, decide between us.

[1] ἀγαθῇ τυχῇ, a formula at the head of Attic decrees, "May good fortune attend."

[2] We notice the supercilious air of Smicrines. The part of the play not included in this excerpt shows him not only crabbed but penurious, excessively anxious to dissolve the marriage of his daughter with the prodigal Charisius in order to recover her dowry before it is wasted.

SMIC. A plague take you fellows! What? do you go about in goatskins,[1] and talk of lawsuits?

SYR. Yet for all that — it is no long business, and easy to understand. Do us this favor, father. Do not, for heaven's sake, despise us. On every occasion and everywhere justice should prevail. Whoever happens to be present ought to make it his business to see that it should be so, for this is common to the life of us all.[2]

DAV. (*aside*). I have got myself into a controversy with a very tolerable orator. Why ever did I let myself out to him?

SMIC. Will you abide, tell me, by what I may decide?

SYR. Certainly.

SMIC. I will hear you. For what should hinder me? You, who have held your peace as yet, speak first.

DAV. To make things clear to you, I shall have to go back a little, and not merely tell you what passed between him and me. About the thirtieth, I think, noble sir, I was tending my flock in the waste adjoining the ploughlands yonder, and on that day I was alone by myself. There I found a young child with necklets and other such ornaments.[3]

SYR. That is what it is about.

DAV. He won't let me speak.

SMIC. If you interrupt, I will come down on you with my cane.

DAV. And quite rightly too.

SMIC. Go on.

DAV. I do so. I took up the child. I went home with it. I had in mind to bring it up; that was my purpose at the first. But in the night I took counsel with myself, as we all do, and turned the matter over in my mind. What have I to do with rearing children and such like cares? Where am I to find the means for meeting such a burden? Why store up trouble for myself?

[1] The dress proves them to be slaves, or at best of the poorest and humblest class of free laborers.

[2] Syriscus shows himself throughout a model of uprightness as well as of prudence, a great credit to his class. Davus, on the contrary, is a rascal of small caliber, utterly devoid of consideration for others, intent only on gaining without labor a few drachmas for himself.

[3] Among the ornaments, as explained below, was a ring belonging to the child's father. The mother's object in leaving the ring was undoubtedly to aid in finding the father.

That was how I felt. In the morning I was again tending my flock; this man came up — he is a charcoal-burner — to the spot where I was, to cut logs there. He was an old acquaintance of mine; we chatted together. Seeing I looked thoughtful, he asked, "Why so grave?" "Why indeed," said I, "I have something on my mind," and I told him what had happened, how I had found the child, how I took it up. Thereupon he at once, without giving me time to finish, began to entreat me: "So may good luck attend you, Davus," — that he kept repeating at every word, — "give me the child. So may you be happy, so may you be free. For," says he, "I have a wife; she has lost the child she had just now" — meaning her who has the child now in her arms (*pointing to a woman carrying a child*).

SMIC. Did you entreat him as he says?

SYR. I did.

DAV. The whole day he never let me alone. I gave way to his importunity; I promised; I gave him the child. He went away calling down on me a thousand blessings; he took and kissed my hands.

SMIC. Did you do so?

SYR. I did.

DAV. He took himself off with his wife. Now he meets me, and all at once he claims to have the things that were found with this child — mere trifles they were, not worth speaking of; and he says he is much ill-used because I do not give them up, but claim to keep them myself. On the other hand, I say he ought to be grateful for what he obtained when he entreated me; for even if I do not give him everything, I ought not to be called to account. Even if he had been walking with me and found this in my company, and it were a case of a find in common, he would have taken his share and I mine. But even though I alone found and you were not present, do you suppose that you are to have everything and I nothing at all? In the end I gave you something of my own voluntarily. If then it suits you keep it now. If it does not and you no longer wish for it, give it back to me; thus you will wrong no man or be a loser yourself. But that you should have the whole, partly with my free will and partly by forcing me, that at all events is wrong. I have done; that is all I have to say.

SMIC. He has done. Don't you hear?

SYR. He has done. Very good. I say then in reply: he alone found the child, and all this which he now says is right, and so it was in fact, father. I have nothing to say against it. Praying and entreating I got the child from him; for he speaks the truth. A certain shepherd, one of his mates, to whom he spoke, informed me that he had at the same time found certain ornaments along with the boy. He then, father, comes forward now to claim them. Give me the child, mistress (*taking the boy and holding him up before Davus*).[1] The necklets and the tokens he demands of you, Davus; for he says that these were put upon him as ornaments, not to make up a purse for you; and I who am now his legal guardian, join with him in the claim: you made me that in giving him to me. The case then you have to decide, noble sir, seems to me to be this: are these gold ornaments, or whatever it may be, to be kept safe for the child till he is grown up, according to the intention of his mother, whoever she may be, or is he who stripped him of them to have them because he was the first to find what was another's? What then? I did not, you will say, demand these things of you when I received the child. I was not then entitled to speak in his behalf. Nor am I here to claim anything of you on my own account. "A find in common" indeed! Do not talk of finding anything where another party has a plaint to bring against you. This is not appropriation but expropriation. Consider this, too, father. It may be that this child is of a condition above us, and though reared among rustics will have a soul above these things, and will have the spirit to follow his own nature and to bear himself like a free-born man, to hunt lions, to bear arms, to run in races. You have, I am sure, seen tragedies acted. All this then must be quite familiar to you. Very well. An old goatherd, wearing such a goatskin as I have on now, found those famous men Neleus and Pelias.[2] When however he discovered they were his betters, he declared the matter how he found them,

[1] Here Syriscus is imitating the devices of litigants before the courts. "It must be acknowledged that Syriscus uses this method of arousing pity with exceptional restraint and dignity"; Capps, *Menander*, p. 58.

[2] Neleus and Pelias were sons of Poseidon, who set them adrift in their infancy in a boat. They were reared and recognized in the manner described in this passage. Evidently Syriscus holds strongly to the theory of heredity.

how he took them up. Moreover he gave them a wallet containing the tokens, through which they clearly made out all about themselves, so that they who were then goatherds became kings. If then Davus had got hold of these tokens and sold them, to gain twelve drachmas for himself, these men of such lofty souls, and of so noble a lineage, would have remained all their lives unknown. It is in no way right, father, that I should bring up this child but that Davus should make away with that from which his future welfare was to be looked for. It has been through tokens that one man has been held back from marrying his sister, that another has met with his mother and rescued her, that a third has saved his brother.[1] The lives of all of us are naturally exposed to accident and it behooves us, father, to guard against this by forethought, and foresee these things long in advance, as far as it is in our power. "But give back," he says, "what may not please you." For this he supposes scores against me. There is no justice in that. Because you have to give back some of the child's belongings, do you seek to obtain this besides, so that you may play the knave with more safety in future, if now Fortune has preserved something that was his? I have finished. Decide what you hold to be just.

SMIC. It is no hard matter. All that was with the exposed child is his; so I decide.

DAV. It is very well. But how about the child?

SMIC. I shall not decide, I warrant you, that he is to be yours who would wrong him, but his who has taken his part and stood up against you, who were about to injure him.

SYR. May all good fortune attend you.

DAV. A strange decision truly, by all that is holy! It is I who found everything that am stripped of everything, while he who was no finder carries it off. Must I hand over then?

SMIC. Yes, I say.

DAV. A strange decision truly, may I have no luck if it isn't.

SYR. Come, hand me the wallet.

DAV. My stars, what hard luck is mine!

SYR. At once.

DAV. Take it.

[1] Undoubtedly the audience recognized all these instances as subjects of familiar comedies.

SYR. And show what is inside, for it is there you carry the things.

SMIC. Have you got all?

SYR. I think so, unless indeed he swallowed something while I was pleading and the cause was going against him.

DAV. I never should have thought it.

SYR. Good luck to you, noble sir. (*Smicrines goes away.*) Such a man should be made a judge in every case.

DAV. What an injustice. Bless us all, a strange decision it has proved truly.

SYR. You were a knave.

DAV. O you knave, take care how you yourself keep the things for the child. Bear in mind that I shall always have my eye on you. You may be sure of that.

SYR. Go and be hanged. You, mistress, take these things and bring them into the house to my young master. For we will wait for Chærestratus here, and go out to our work after paying our dues.[1] But first go over these things one by one with me. Have you anything to put them in? Put them then in your bosom.

(*Enter Onesimus, slave of Charisius.*)

ONESIMUS. No one ever saw so slow a cook. At this hour yesterday they had been drinking a good while.

SYR. This seems to be a cock and a very wakeful one. Take it. But what is this set with gems? An axe, I think.

ONES. (*aside*). What is this?

SYR. Here is a ring cased with gold, but itself of steel. The seal is a bull or goat, I can't make out which. One Cleostratus made it, as the letters tell us.

ONES. Let me look at it.

SYR. Here it is. But who are you?

ONES. This is —

[1] As explained above, Syriscus was engaged in charcoal burning some distance from the village in which the action of this play takes place. Periodically he comes to the house of his master, bringing him his profit from the business. None but trustworthy slaves could be given so much freedom; Botsford, *Hellenic History*, xvi. To those who are acquainted with the almost treeless condition of modern Attica the mention of charcoal-burning within her borders necessarily brings great surprise at the vast change that has taken place in the country during the past twenty-five centuries.

SYR. What?

ONES. The ring —

SYR. What ring? for I don't understand.

ONES. Of my master Charisius.

SYR. You are crazy.

ONES. Which he lost.

SYR. Put down the ring, will you?

ONES. Put down what is ours? But where did you get it?

SYR. Bless us and save us! What a misfortune! What a thing it is to keep safe the belongings of an orphan. Every one who comes near you has at once a mind to make off with them.[1] Put down the ring, I tell you.

226. THE BOASTFUL MAN

(Theophrastus, *Characters*, vi)

This passage and those immediately following illustrate certain prominent types of Athenian character. The author, Theophrastus of Eresus, Lesbos, about 372–287 B.C., was the most distinguished of Aristotle's pupils. He collaborated with his master; and after the death of the latter he became for the remainder of his life the head of the Peripatetic School. Theophrastus followed in the footsteps of Aristotle, and extended his researches in various directions. One of his lightest works, but of great interest to us, is his *Characters*. The sketches are fresh and humorous, though necessarily superficial, somewhat after the pattern of comedy. If due allowance is made for the hand of the caricaturist, there will be found a substratum of reality — a human nature akin to that revealed by the private speeches of the fourth-century Attic orators. For an excellent treatment of the characters, see introduction to R. C. Jebb's edition of *The Characters of Theophrastus*, from which the following excerpts have been taken.

Boastfulness would seem to be, in fact, pretension to advantages which one does not possess.

The Boastful Man is one who will stand in the bazaar talking to foreigners of the great sums which he has at sea; he will discourse of the vastness of his money-lending business, and the extent of his personal gains and losses; and, while thus drawing the long-bow, will send his boy to the bank, where he keeps — tenpence.

[1] This statement is partly justified by the actual experience of orphans, for example, Demosthenes, as the Attic orators testify; see no. 156.

He loves, also, to impose upon his companion by the road with a story of how he served with Alexander, and on what terms he was with him, and what a number of gemmed cups he brought home; contending, too, that the Asiatic artists are superior to those of Europe; and all this when he has never been anywhere out of Attica. Then he will say that a letter has come from Antipater[1] — 'this is the third' — requiring his presence in Macedonia; and that, though he was offered the privilege of exporting timber[2] free of duty, he had declined it, that no person whatever may be able to traduce him further for being more friendly than is becoming with Macedonia. He will state, too, that in the famine his outlay came to more than five talents in presents to the distressed citizens; ('he could never say no') and actually, although the persons sitting near him are strangers, he will request one of them to set up the counters; when, reckoning by sums of six hundred drachmas or of a mina, and plausibly signing names to each of these, he will make a total of as many as ten talents. This, he will say, was what he contributed in the way of charities; adding that he does not count any of the trierarchies or public services which he has performed. Also he will go up to the sellers of the best horses, and pretend that he desires to buy; or visiting the upholstery mart, he will ask to see draperies to the value of two talents, and quarrel with his slave for having come out without gold. When he is living in a hired house he will say (to anyone who does not know better) that it is the family mansion; but that he means to sell it, as he finds it too small for his entertainments.

227. The Man of Petty Ambition

(Theophrastus, *Characters*, vii)

Petty Ambition would seem to be a mean craving for distinction.

The Man of Petty Ambition is one who, when asked to dinner, will be anxious to be placed next to the host at table. He will

[1] When Alexander set out on his invasion of Asia, he left Antipater in charge of the government of Macedon, and after the king's death in 323 Antipater became absolute master of Macedon, retaining this position till his death, 319. The reference in the text is probably to this later period; Jebb's note.

[2] Most of the ship timber used by Athens came from Chalcidice, at this time a part of Macedonia.

take his son away to Delphi to have his hair cut.[1] He will be careful, too, that his attendant shall be an Ethiopian;[2] and, when he pays a mina, he will cause the slave to pay the sum in new coin. Also he will have his hair cut very frequently, and will keep his teeth white; he will change his clothes, too, while still good; and will anoint himself with unguent. In the market-place he will frequent the bankers' tables; in the gymnasia he will haunt the places where the young men take exercise; in the theatre, when there is a representation, he will sit near the Generals.[3] For himself he will buy nothing, but will make purchases on commission for foreign friends — pickled olives to go to Byzantium, Laconian hounds for Cyzicus, Hymettian honey for Rhodes; and will talk thereof to people at Athens. Also he is very much the person to keep a monkey; to get a satyr ape, Sicilian doves, deerhorn dice, Thurian vases of the approved rotundity, walking-sticks with the true Laconian curve, and a curtain with Persians embroidered upon it. He will have a little court provided with an arena for wrestling and a ball-alley, and will go about lending it to philosophers, sophists, drill-sergeants, musicians, for their displays; at which he himself will appear upon the scene rather late, in order that the spectators may say to one another, 'This is the owner of the palæstra.' When he has sacrificed an ox, he will nail up the skin of the forehead, wreathed with large garlands, opposite the entrance, in order that those who come in may see that he has sacrificed an ox. When he has been taking part in a procession of the knights, he will give the rest of his accoutrements to his slave to carry home; but, after putting on his cloak, will walk about the market-place in his spurs. He is apt, also, to buy a little ladder for his domestic jackdaw, and to make a little brass shield, wherewith the jackdaw shall hop upon the ladder. Or if his little Melitean dog has died,

[1] The youth wore his hair long till he reached the age of eighteen, when he was enrolled in the register of his deme. On this occasion his hair was cut and a lock dedicated to a god. Those who found it convenient went to Delphi to dedicate the lock to Apollo; Plutarch, *Theseus*, 5.

[2] The opening of the East by Alexander had given the Greeks an opportunity to obtain black slaves; *cf.* Alciphron, *Letters*, ii. 2. 5; Jebb's note. Naturally the wealthier class were inclined to indulge in such curiosities.

[3] The officials had their special seats at the theater, although we learn from this passage, and from others, that they were not very definitely separated from those of private citizens; Jebb's note.

he will put up a little memorial slab, with the inscription, A SCION OF MELITA. If he has dedicated a brass ring in the temple of Asclepius, he will wear it to a wire with daily burnishings and oilings. It is just like him, too, to obtain from the presidents of the Council by private arrangement the privilege of reporting the sacrifice to the people; when, having provided himself with a smart white cloak, and put on a wreath, he will come forward and say: "Athenians! we the presidents of the Council have been sacrificing to the Mother of the Gods meetly and auspiciously; receive ye her good gifts!" Having made this announcement he will go home to his wife and declare that he is supremely fortunate.

228. THE STUPID MAN

(Theophrastus, *Characters*, xiii)

Stupidity may be defined as mental slowness in speech and action.

The Stupid Man is one who, after doing a sum and setting down the total, will ask the person sitting next him "What does it come to?" When he is defendant in an action, and it is about to come on, he will forget it and go into the country; when he is a spectator in the theatre, he will be left behind slumbering in solitude. If he has been given anything, and has put it away himself, he will look for it and be unable to find it. When the death of a friend is announced to him, in order that he may come to the house, his face will grow dark — tears will come into his eyes — and he will say "Heaven be praised!" He is apt, too, when he receives payment of a debt, to call witnesses; and in winter-time to quarrel with his slave for not having bought cucumbers; and to make his children wrestle and run races until he has exhausted them. If he is cooking a leek himself in the country, he will put salt into the pot twice, and make it uneatable. When it is raining he will observe: "Well, the smell from the sky is delicious" (when of course others say, "from the earth"); or if he is asked "How many corpses do you suppose have been carried out at the Sacred Gate?" he will reply, "I only wish that you or I had as many."

229. The Garrulous Man

(Theophrastus, *Characters*, xviii)

Garrulity is the discoursing of much and ill-considered talk.

The Garrulous Man is one who will sit down beside a person whom he does not know, and first pronounce a panegyric on his own wife; then relate his dream of last night; then go through in detail what he has had for dinner. Then, warming to the work, he will remark that the men of the present day are greatly inferior to the ancients; and will tell how cheap wheat has become in the market; and what a number of foreigners are in town; and that the sea is navigable after the Dionysia; and that, if Zeus would send more rain, the crops would be better; and that he will work his land next year; and how hard it is to live; and that Damippus set up a very large torch at the Mysteries; and "How many columns has the Odeum?"[1] and that yesterday he was unwell; and "What is the day of the month?" and that the Mysteries are in Boëdromion, the Apaturia in Pyanepsion, the rural Dionysia in Poseideon.[2] Nor if he is tolerated, will he ever desist.

230. The Penurious Man

(Theophrastus, *Characters*, xxiv)

Penuriousness is too strict attention to profit and loss.

The Penurious Man is one who, while the month is current, will come to one's house and ask for a half-obol.[3] When he is at table with others, he will count how many cups each of them has drunk; and will pour a smaller libation to Artemis than any of the company. Whenever a person has made a good bargain for him and charges him with it, he will say that it is too dear. When a servant has broken a jug or a plate, he will take the value out of

[1] Odeum, music-hall. The Odeum here mentioned is probably that built by Pericles.

[2] The month Boëdromion corresponds roughly with September; Pyanepsion with October; Poseideon with December. The Mysteries were those celebrated annually at Eleusis. The Apaturia was the chief festival of the phratry; see no. 144. The Dionysia were dramatic festivals.

[3] At Athens interest was often due on the last day of the month, but the penurious man was unwilling to wait till that day. By collecting interest before it was due he gained a trifle.

his rations; or if his wife has dropped a three-farthing[1] piece, he is capable of moving the furniture and the sofas and the wardrobes, and of rummaging in the curtains. If he has anything to sell, he will dispose of it at such a price that the buyer shall have no profit. He is not likely to let one eat a fig from his garden, or walk through his land, or pick up one of the olives or dates that lie on the ground; and he will inspect his boundaries day by day to see if they remain the same. He is apt, also, to enforce the right of distraining,[2] and to exact compound interest. When he feasts the men of his deme, the cutlets set before them will be small; when he markets, he will come in having bought nothing. And he will forbid his wife to lend salt, or a lamp-wick, or cummin, or verjuice, or meal for sacrifice, or garlands, or cakes; saying that these trifles come to much in the year. Then, in general, it may be noticed that the money boxes of the penurious are mouldy, and the keys rusty; that they themselves wear their cloaks scarcely reaching to the thigh;[3] that they anoint themselves with very small oil-flasks; that they have their hair cut close; that they take off their shoes in the middle of the day; and that they are urgent with the fuller to let their cloak have plenty of earth, in order that it may not soon be soiled.

231. The Coward

(Theophrastus, *Characters*, xxvii)

Cowardice would seem to be, in fact, a shrinking of the soul through fear.

The Coward is one who on a voyage will protest that the promontories are privateers; and if a high sea gets up, will ask if there is anyone on board who has not been initiated.[4] He will put up

[1] Literally "three chalkoi." A chalkos was an eighth of an obol, the latter being worth about three cents.

[2] This was the forcible appropriation of a sum of money or piece of property adjudged a party at a trial. Although the party was given the legal right to make the seizure, courtesy required that he should make use of it only in the last resort.

[3] The short chiton was the Spartan style. On the other hand, a chiton reaching the ankles seems to have been the mark of luxury or effeminacy; *cf.* Demosth., *On the Mismanaged Embassy*, 314. Evidently the proper length at Athens was a little less than the latter.

[4] Those who were initiated into the Samothracian mysteries were reputed able by prayer to assuage the storm; Diodorus iv. 43. Possibly, as Jebb suggests, the timid

his head and ask the steersman if he is halfway, and what he thinks of the face of the heavens, remarking to the person sitting next to him that a certain dream makes him feel uneasy; and he will take off his chiton and give it to his slave; or he will beg them to put him on shore.

On land also, when he is campaigning, he will call to him those who are going out to the rescue, and bid them come and stand by him and look about them first, saying that it is hard to make out which is the enemy. Hearing shouts and seeing men falling, he will remark to those who stand by him that he has forgotten in his haste to bring his sword, and will run to the tent; where, having sent out his slave to reconnoitre the position of the enemy, he will hide the sword under his pillow, and then spend a long time in pretending to look for it. And seeing from the tent a wounded comrade being carried in, he will run toward him and cry, "Cheer up!" he will take him into his arms and carry him; he will tend and sponge him; he will sit by him and keep the flies off his wound — in short, he will do anything rather than fight with the enemy. Again, when the trumpeter has sounded the signal for battle, he will cry, as he sits in the tent, "Bother! you will not allow the man to get a wink of sleep with your perpetual bugling!" Then, covered with blood from the other's wound, he will meet those who are returning from the fight, and announce to them, "I have run some risk to save one of our fellows;" and he will bring in the men of his deme and of his tribe to see his patient, at the same time explaining to each of them that he carried him with his own hands to the tent.

232. The Oligarch

(Theophrastus, *Characters*, xxix)

The Oligarchical temper would seem to consist in a love of authority, covetousness, not of gain, but of power.

The Oligarchical Man is one who, when the people are deliber-

man was anxious to have such an initiate make a prayer for safety. The form of the sentence seems rather to indicate that he was worrying lest, in case all were lost, there might be on board some uninitiated person who would be debarred from happiness in the next world.

ating whom they shall associate with the archon as joint directors of the procession, will come forward and express his opinion that these directors ought to have plenary powers; and if others propose ten, he will say that "one is sufficient," but that "he must be a man." Of Homer's poetry he has mastered only this one line, —

> No good comes of manifold rule; let the ruler be one;[1]

of the rest he is absolutely ignorant. It is very much in his manner to use phrases of this kind: "We must meet and discuss these matters by ourselves, and get clear of the rabble and the market-place;" "we must leave off courting office, and being slighted or graced by those fellows;" "either they or we must govern the city." He will go out about the middle of the day with his cloak gracefully adjusted, his hair daintily trimmed, his nails delicately pared, and strut through the Odeum Street, making such remarks as these: "There is no living in Athens for the informers;" "we are shamefully treated in the courts by the juries;" "I cannot conceive what people want with meddling in public affairs;" "how ungrateful the people are — always the slaves of a largess or a bribe;" and "how ashamed I am when a meagre, squalid fellow sits down by me in the ecclesia!" "When," he will ask, "will they have done ruining us with these public services and trierarchies? How detestable that set of demagogues is! Theseus," he will say, "was the beginning of the mischief to the State.[2] It was he who reduced it from twelve cities to one, and undid the monarchy. And he was rightly served; for he was the people's first victim himself."

And so on to foreigners and to those citizens who resemble him in their disposition and their politics.

[1] *Iliad*, ii. 204.

[2] Aristotle, *Const. Ath.*, 41. 2, represents Theseus as the founder of constitutional government at Athens, a form of government "which deviated slightly from kingship." With the Theseus of this theory the Oligarch could associate on friendly terms; but there was another view which represented him as the founder of democracy, and it was in this character that he awakened the antipathy of the person under consideration. For the latter view, see Pausanias i. 3.

233. The Profligacy of Demetrius of Phalerum

(Duris, *Histories*, bk. xvi, quoted by Athenæus xii. 60)

Demetrius of Phalerum, a philosopher of the Peripatetic School and a statesman of Athens, was born about 344 B.C. In 318–317 he became governor (superintendent, ἐπιμελητής) of Athens under the Macedonian supremacy, and was overthrown in 307. Among his many legislative acts were sumptuary laws referred to in the selection below. In contrast with their requirements he himself lived in great luxury. See Ferguson, *Hellenistic Athens*, ch. ii; Martini, "Demetrios," in Pauly-Wissowa, *Real-Encycl.* IV. 2817-41.

Demetrius of Phalerum also, as Duris says in the sixteenth book of his *Histories*, possessed as he was of an income of twelve hundred talents a year, and devoting but a small part of it to his soldiers and to the necessary expenses of the state, squandered all the rest in gratifying his innate profligacy, with splendid banquets every day and a great number of guests to feast with him. In the prodigality of expense on these entertainments he outdid even the Macedonians, and at the same time in the elegance of the dinners he surpassed the Cyprians and the Phœnicians. Perfumes were sprinkled over the pavement, and many of the floors in the men's apartments were inlaid with flowers and variously wrought by artists in exquisite patterns. Moreover there were secret appointments with women and youths; and Demetrius, who enacted laws for others and who regulated their lives, directed his own life in the most lawless manner. He paid particular attention, too, to his personal appearance, dyeing the hair of his head with a yellow color, painting his face with rouge, and smearing himself over with perfumed oils; for he was eager to appear agreeable and beautiful in the eyes of all with whom he associated.

234. Alexander as a Drinker

(Various authors, quoted by Athenæus x. 44)

Proteas the Macedonian was also a very great drinker, as Ephippus tells us in his treatise on the *Funeral of Alexander and Hephæstion*. He had an admirable constitution, and he had practiced drinking to a great degree. When accordingly Alexander asked for a cup containing two choes, he drank it and pledged Proteas. Then the latter, taking it and singing the praises of the king at great length, drank it in such a manner as to receive the applause of all present. Soon Proteas asked for the same cup again, and again he drank and pledged the king. Thereupon Alexander, taking the cup, drank it off in a princely manner. He could not endure it, however, but leaned back on the pillow, letting the cup fall from his hands, and afterward fell sick and died. Dionysus, it is said, was angry with him because he had besieged the god's native city Thebes. Moreover Alexander drank so much that once, after a drunken bout, he slept without interruption two days and two nights. This fact is shown in his *Journals*, which were compiled by Eumenes the Cardian and Diodotus the Erythræan. Menander, too, in his *Flatterer*, says: —

A. My good friend, Struthias, I thrice have drunk
 A golden cup in Cappadocia,
 Containing ten full cotylæ of wine.
St. Why, you then drank more than Alexander king.
A. At all events not less, I swear by Pallas.
St. A wondrous feat!

Nicobule, or whoever it was who wrote the books attributed to her, says that Alexander, when supping with Medeus the Thessalian with twenty people present at the gathering, pledged every one of the guests, receiving a similar pledge from all of them; then rising up from the party, he presently went off to sleep.

235. The Luxuries of Alexander the Great and the Splendors of his Court

(Ephippus, Nicobule, Chares, *History of Alexander*, bk. x; Polycleitus, *History*, bk. viii; Phylarchus, and others, quoted by Athenæus xii. 53–5)

Ephippus of Olynthus accompanied Alexander in his march as far as Egypt, where he was left behind on official duty. Little is known of his work *On the Burial of Alexander and Hephæstion* here quoted. Evidently it had much to tell of life at court, and seems to have been unfavorable to Alexander; see Jacoby, in Pauly-Wissowa, *Real-Encycl.* v. 2858 f. Nicobule is still less known; Christ, *Griech. Lit.* II. 158, n. 3. Chares of Mytilene accompanied Alexander the Great and became an officer of ceremony on the introduction of the Persian court customs. We know the work here cited through various quotations; see Schwartz, in Pauly-Wissowa, *op. cit.* III. 2129. 13. Polycleitus of Larissa was probably a contemporary; Christ, *loc. cit.* Phylarchus of Athens, a partisan of the Spartan king Cleomenes, wrote a work entitled *Histories*, in twenty-eight books, extending from Pyrrhus to Cleomenes, 272–220 B.C. It was sensational at the expense of truth (Polyb. ii. 56; Plut. *Them.* 32; *Arat.* 38), and gave unusual attention to the morals of persons and actions; Christ, *op. cit.* 161 *sq.* These sources are therefore practically contemporary.

One of the characteristics of the Hellenistic age, introduced by Alexander, was the extravagant and ostentatious luxury of kings, magistrates, and wealthy individuals, in whose hands the riches of the world were largely concentrated, involving the pauperization of the masses. It is this fact which gives chief interest to the excerpt presented below.

53. Concerning the luxury of Alexander the Great, Ephippus of Olynthus, in his treatise *On the Burial of Alexander and Hephæstion*, relates that he had in his park a golden throne and couches with silver feet, on which he used to sit while transacting business with his companions. Nicobule says, moreover, that while he was at supper all the dancers and athletes sought to amuse the king. At his very last banquet, Alexander, remembering an episode in the *Andromeda* of Euripides, recited it in a declamatory manner, and then drank a cup of unmixed wine with great zest, and compelled all the rest to do the same. Ephippus tells us, too, that Alexander used to wear at his entertainments even the sacred vestments. Sometimes he would put on the purple robe, cloven sandals, and horns of Ammon, as if he had been the god. Sometimes he would imitate Artemis, whose dress he often wore while driving in his chariot; at the same time he had on a Persian robe, which displayed above his shoulders the bow and javelin of the goddess. At times also he would appear in the guise of Hermes; at other times, and in fact nearly every day, he would wear a purple cloak, a chiton shot with white, and a cap with a royal diadem attached. When too he was in private with his friends he wore the sandals of Hermes, with the petasus on his head and the caduceus in hand. Often however he wore a lion's skin and carried a club like Heracles. . . .

Alexander used also to have the floor sprinkled with exquisite perfumes and with fragrant wine; and myrrh and other kinds of incense were burned before him, while all the bystanders kept silence or spoke words only of good omen because of fear. For he was an extremely violent man with no regard for human life, and gave the impression of a man of choleric temperament. At Ecbatana on one occasion, when he was offering a sacrifice to Dionysus, and everything was prepared in a most lavish manner for the banquet . . . (*words lost*) . . . and Satrabates the satrap feasted all the soldiers . . . (*words lost*) . . . But when great numbers were gathered to see the spectacle, says Ephippus, suddenly some arrogant proclamations were issued more insolent even than Persian tyranny used to dictate: while various persons were publishing their different proclamations and proposing to make Alexander large presents, which they called crowns, a keeper of his armory, exceeding all former flattery, having previously arranged the matter with Alexander, ordered the herald to proclaim that "Gorgus, keeper of the armory, presents Alexander son of Ammon with three thousand pieces of gold; and will also present him, when he lays siege to Athens, with ten thousand panoplies and with an equal number of catapults and all weapons required for war."

54. Chares, too, in the tenth book of his *History of Alexander*, says: "When he took Darius prisoner, he celebrated a marriage feast for himself and his companions, having prepared ninety-two chambers in the same place. A house was built with a capacity for a hundred couches; and in it every couch was adorned with wedding furnishings to the value of twenty minas. Each couch was made of silver whereas his own had golden feet. Furthermore he invited to the banquet all his own friends, whom he arranged opposite to himself and to the other bridegrooms. He placed in order also all the land and naval forces and all the ambassadors who were present and all the other strangers who were staying at his court. The reception room was furnished in the most costly and magnificent manner with sumptuous tapestries, and beneath them were carpets of purple and scarlet and gold. To make the structure secure it was supported by columns twenty cubits high, plated over with gold and silver and inlaid with precious stones. All round these columns extended costly tapestries embroidered with figures of animals and of gold, and suspended on gold and silver curtain rods. The circumference of the pavilion was four stadia. The marriage feast took place at the sound of a trumpet, repeated on all other occasions when the king made sacrifice, so that all the army could know it.

This marriage banquet lasted five days. A great number of foreigners and of Greeks brought contributions to it, as well as some Indian tribes. There were present some wonderful conjurors: Scymnus of Tarentum, Philistides of Syracuse, and Heracleitus of Mytilene, after whom Alexis of Tarentum, the rhapsodist, exhibited his skill. Then came harp-players, who played without singing — Cratinus of Methymna, Aristonymus the Athenian and Athenodorus the Teian. Heracleitus of Tarentum, while playing the harp, accompanied himself with his voice, and so did Aristocrates the Theban. Among the pipers who accompanied with song there were present Dionysius of Heracleia and Hyperbolus of Cyzicus. There were besides the following pipers who first of all played the air called the Pythian, and afterward took part in the choruses: Timotheus, Phrynichus, Caphesias, Diophantus, and Evius of Chalcis. Henceforth those who were formerly called Dionysus-flatterers were called Alexander-flatterers on account of the extravagant liberality of their presents, with which Alexander was pleased. There was further the acting of tragedians: Thessalus, Athenodorus and Aristocritus, whilst among the comic actors were Lycon, Phormion and Ariston. Phasimelus the harp-player was also present. The crowns sent by ambassadors and others amounted in value to fifteen thousand talents.

55. Polycleitus of Larissa, in the eighth book of his *History*, states that Alexander used to sleep on a golden couch and that men and women pipers followed him to the camp and that he used to drink till daybreak. Clearchus, too, in his treatise entitled *Lives*, speaking of Darius who was dethroned by Alexander, says: "The king of the Persians offered prizes to those who could invent pleasures for him; by this conduct he allowed his whole empire and sovereignty to be subverted to pleasures. In fact he knew not that he was defeating himself till others had wrested his sceptre from him and had been proclaimed in his place." Phylarchus also, in the twenty-third book of his *Histories*, and Agatharchides of Cnidus, in the tenth book of his *History of Asia*, state that the companions, too, of Alexander gave way to the most extravagant luxury. One of them was a man named Agnon, who used to wear gold studs in his sandals and shoes. Cleitus, surnamed the White, whenever he was about to transact business, was accustomed to walk on a purple

carpet while conversing with those who came to him. Perdiccas and Craterus, who enjoyed athletic exercises, had men accompany them with hides fastened together so as to cover a space an entire stadium in extent. They selected within the encampment a space, which they covered with these skins as an awning; and under it they practised their gymnastics. They were followed, too, by many beasts of burden, which carried sand for the use of the palæstra.

Leonnatus and Menelaüs, who were fond of hunting, brought curtains with them sufficient for enclosing a space a hundred stadia in circumference. With this material they fenced in a large space, within which they practised hunting. As for the golden plane-trees and golden vine, bearing bunches of grapes made of emeralds and Indian carbuncles and all sorts of other stones of the most costly and magnificent description, under which the kings of Persia were accustomed often to sit while engaged in business — the expense of all this, says Phylarchus, was far less than the sums squandered every day by Alexander; for he had a tent with a capacity for a hundred couches and fifty golden pillars supported it. Over it were spread golden canopies wrought with the most superb and costly embroidery, for the purpose of shading all the upper part of it. First of all, five hundred Persian melophori stood round the interior of it, clad in robes of purple and apple-green. Besides them there were archers to the number of a thousand, some clad in garments of fiery red, others in purple, and many others in blue cloaks. In front of them stood five hundred Macedonian Argyraspides. In the middle of the pavilion was placed a golden throne, on which Alexander used to sit and transact business, surrounded by his personal guards. Round the tent on the exterior was a squad of elephants fully equipped, and a thousand Macedonians in their native dress; then ten thousand Persians, five hundred of whom wore purple, the gift of Alexander. With all this retenue of friends and servants, no one dared approach Alexander of his own accord, so great was his dignity and the veneration in which he was held. At that time Alexander wrote letters to the cities of Ionia, first of all to the Chians, to send him a great amount of purple, for he wished all his companions to wear robes of that color. When his letter was read to the Chians, Theocritus the philosopher, who was present, said: 'He fell by purple death and mighty fate.'[1]

236. State aid for the Poor in Rhodes

(Strabo xiv. 5)

The custom continuing in the time of Strabo is declared by him to be in accordance with an ancient usage, which must have been as old at least as the Hellenistic age. It is an interesting fact that the distribution of cheap grain at the expense of the state, initiated at Rome by Gaius Gracchus and further developed by his successors, was already in vogue in the Hellenic states. The custom must not be too hastily condemned as socialistic or as a pernicious device of demagogues; for the pauperization of the masses had resulted from economic conditions over which they could have exercised but little influence. If the people were not to starve, they had to be helped, and the best minds of the ancient world could devise no better plan than the distribution of cheap or free grain. Undoubtedly it encouraged idleness and helplessness, but that is true of all charity and paternalism, modern as well as ancient.

Although their form of government is not democratic, the Rhodians are attentive to the welfare of the people, and exert themselves to support the masses of the poor. The people receive allowances of grain and the rich support the needy in accordance with an ancient usage. The state has public offices, whose object is to procure and distribute provisions, that the poor may obtain subsistence, and the city may not suffer for want of persons to serve her especially in manning her fleets.

237. Bœotian aid to the Poor and Suspension of Suits for the Collection of Debts

(Polybius xx. 6)

The condition here described belongs to the latter part of the third century B.C.

Bœotia as a nation had fallen to so low a state that for nearly twenty-five years the administration of justice had been suspended in private and public suits alike. Their magistrates were engaged in despatching bodies of men to guard the country or in proclaiming national expeditions, and thus continually postponed their

[1] Homer, *Iliad*, v. 83.

attendance at the law-courts. Some of the generals also dispensed allowances to the needy from the public treasury, whereby the common people learned to support and to invest with office those who would help them escape the penalties of their offences and of their undischarged liabilities, and to be enriched from time to time with some portion of the public property obtained by official favor. No one contributed to this lamentable state of things more than Opheltas, who was always inventing some plan calculated to benefit the masses for the moment, while perfectly certain to ruin them in the future.

238. THE EXTENSIVE INDEBTEDNESS OF THE ÆTOLIANS AND THE VAIN ATTEMPT AT REPUDIATION

(Polybius xiii. 1)

This passage refers to the close of the third century B.C.

From the unbroken continuity of their wars and the extravagance of their daily lives, the Ætolians became involved in debt, not only without others noticing it but without being aware of it themselves. Disposed naturally therefore to a change in their constitution, they elected Dorimachus and Scopas to draw up a code of laws, because they saw that these men were not only by disposition innovators but were themselves deeply involved in debt. These men accordingly were appointed to the office and drew up the laws . . . (*lacuna*) . . .

When they reported their code, they were opposed by Alexander of Ætolia, who tried to show by many instances that innovation was a dangerous growth which could not be checked, and which invariably ended with inflicting grave evils upon those who fostered it. He urged them therefore not to look solely to the exigencies of the hour and their relief from the existing contracts, but to the future as well. For it was a strange inconsistency to be ready to forfeit their very lives in war to preserve their children, and yet in their deliberations to be entirely careless of the future.

239. Suspension of the Payment of Debts in the Achæan League

(Polybius xxxviii. 9)

Critolaüs, general of the Achæan league, was determined to bring on a war with Rome (winter of 147–46 B.C.). The magistrates mentioned in the following excerpt are those of the states of the league. It is clear that the debtors affected by the suspension of payments were not the proletarians, but the holders of property, ordinarily farms, for there could be no loans without security and the principal form of property was still land; *cf.* Beloch, *Griech. Gesch.* III. 328 *sq.* The passage is evidence, therefore, of an extensive mortgaging of farms throughout Peloponnese, due at least in part to an extravagant standard of life.

Critolaüs . . . sent round orders to the magistrates not to exact money from debtors, nor to receive prisoners arrested for debt, and to cause loans on pledge to be held over until the war should be decided. By this kind of appeal to the interests of the vulgar everything he said was received with confidence; and the common people were ready to obey any order he gave, incapable as they were of taking thought for the future, but caught by the bait of immediate indulgence and relief.

240. Luxury of the Lacedæmonians

(Phylarchus, *Histories*, xv, xx, quoted by Athenæus iv. 20)

Subsequently the Lacedæmonians relaxed the rigor of this way of living. At all events Phylarchus, in the fifteenth and again in the twentieth book of his *Histories*, writes thus concerning them: "The Lacedæmonians had given up assembling for the phiditia [1] according to the custom of the country; and whenever they met, after having had a few things brought round for the sake of a seeming compliance with the law, they had other things prepared: couches furnished in a very expensive way and of exceeding size, and all differing from one another in their adornment; so that some of the strangers who were invited used to be afraid to put their elbows on the pillows; and those who formerly used to rest on a bare bench

[1] Another term for the syssitia, public messes, described by Plutarch, *Lycurgus*, 10–12; *cf.* Botsford, *Hellenic History*, ch. vi.

during the whole banquet, perhaps once leaning on their elbows for a few minutes, had now come to such a pitch of luxury as I have spoken of, and to a serving of many cups of wine and of all sorts of food procured from all countries and dressed in every kind of luxurious style; and in addition they had come to use foreign perfumes and also foreign wines and sweetmeats. The people who lived a short time before the age of Cleomenes began this fashion, namely Areus [1] and Acrotatus, rivalling the indulgences of the court of Persia. They in their turn were so far exceeded in extravagance by some private individuals who lived in Sparta at that time that Areus and Acrotatus appeared to be people of such rigid economy as to have surpassed the most simple of their predecessors in self-denial."

241. The Attempted Social Reform of Agis, King of the Lacedæmonians

(Plutarch, *Life of Agis*)

Agis ascended the throne in 245 or 244 and was executed in 241; Beloch, *Griech. Gesch.* III. 2. 118 *sq.* The condition which he attempted to reform is fully described in the following excerpts from Plutarch. The number of Spartans had shrunk to seven hundred, of whom only one hundred were "peers," — who enjoyed a sufficient income to enable them to take part in the syssitia — public messes — and in political affairs. Among the hundred peers, who owned most of the land of Lacedæmon, some were heavily indebted. The chief representative of this class was Agesilaüs, a member of one of the royal families, and uncle of Agis. According to Plutarch the idea of a thoroughgoing reform of the social and political condition originated with Agis, who was not yet twenty years of age. It was only to rid himself of his vast debts, however, that Agesilaüs supported the measure. After this object had been accomplished, Agesilaüs and other large debtors had every reason for wishing to put a stop to the reform, and their desires were seconded by the circumstance that during the absence of Agis the proletariat ceased to take an interest in the reform; so that on his return he found no support. Undoubtedly Agis had a high moral aim. His enthusiasm, too, was sufficient, but he lacked the experience and the political wisdom essential to overcoming the formidable opposition. These defects were to be made good by Cleomenes, his successor.

It is quite natural that Plutarch should find the lives of Agis and Cleomenes paralleled by those of the two Gracchi, and that some modern scholars should

[1] Areus, king of the Lacedæmonians, died in 265–264; Beloch, *Griech. Gesch.* III. 2. 113. For Cleomenes, see no. 243.

assume that the two young Roman statesmen derived their ideas and their inspiration from the two Spartan reformers who lived about a century before their time. The attempted reform of Agis, however, was far more sweeping than that of the Gracchi. The property which the Spartan king planned to distribute was private; the land distributed by the Gracchi was public. On Agis, see Beloch, *Griech. Gesch.* III. 1. 646–51; Niese, B., "Agis," in Pauly-Wissowa, *Real-Encycl.* I. 819 (4)–21; *Griech. u. mak. Staat.* II. 296 *sqq.*

3. After the desire of silver and gold had penetrated into Sparta, the acquisition of wealth produced greed and meanness, while the use and enjoyment of riches was followed by luxury, effeminacy, and extravagance. Thus it resulted that Sparta lost her high and honored position in Greece, and remained in obscurity and disgrace until the reign of Agis and Leonidas. Agis was of the Eurypontid [1] line, the son of Eudamidas and sixth in descent from king Agesilaüs,[2] who invaded Asia and became the most powerful man in Hellas. . . .

Leonidas, son of Cleonymus, was of the other royal family, that of the Agiadæ, and was the eighth in descent from the Pausanias who conquered Mardonius at the battle of Platæa.[3] . . . Leonidas, who had spent much of his life at the courts of Asiatic potentates, and had been especially attached to that of Seleucus, seemed inclined to outrage the political feeling of the Greeks by introducing the arrogant tone of an Oriental despot into the constitutional royalty of Sparta.

4. On the other hand, the goodness of heart and intellectual power of Agis proved so greatly superior, not only to that of Leonidas, but to every king since Agesilaüs the Great, that before he arrived at his twentieth year, in spite of his having been brought up in the greatest luxury by his mother Agesistrata and his grandmother Archidamia, the two richest women in Sparta,[4] he abjured all frivolous indulgence, laid aside all personal ornament, avoided extravagance of every kind, prided himself on practising the old

[1] On the two royal families of Lacedæmon, see Gilbert, *Const. Antiq.* 4–7; Busolt, *Griech. Gesch.* I. 544–7. The Agiadæ and Eurypontidæ claimed descent from Agis and Eurypon respectively. Historians generally consider these two persons mythical, and offer various explanations of the double kingship, no one of which is absolutely convincing.

[2] Early in the fourth century; Botsford, *Hellenic History*, ch. xxi.

[3] *Op. cit.* ch. xi.

[4] On the wealth and power of Spartan women, *op. cit.* ch. xxv.

Laconian habits of dress, food, and bathing, and was wont to say that he would not care to be king unless he could use his position to restore the ancient customs and discipline of his country.

5. The corruption of the Lacedæmonians began at the time when, after having overthrown the Athenian empire, they were able to satiate themselves with the possession of gold and silver.[1] Nevertheless, as the number of houses instituted by Lycurgus was still maintained, and each father still transmitted his estate to his son, the original equal division of property continued to exist, and preserved the state from disorder. But a certain powerful and self-willed man, named Epitadeus,[2] who was one of the ephors, having quarrelled with his son, proposed a rhetra[3] permitting a man to give his house and land to whomsoever he pleased, either during his life or by his will after his death. This man proposed the law in order to gratify his own private grudge; but the other Spartans through coveteousness eagerly confirmed it, and ruined the admirable constitution of Lycurgus. They now began to acquire land without limit, as the powerful men kept their relatives out of their rightful inheritance. As the wealth of the country soon got into the hands of the few, the city became impoverished, and the rich began to be viewed with dislike and hatred. There were left at that time no more than seven hundred Spartans, and of that number about one hundred possessed an inheritance in land, while the rest, without money and excluded from all the privileges of citizenship, fought in a languid and spiritless fashion in the wars, and were ever on the watch for some opportunity to subvert the existing condition of affairs at home.

[1] *Loc. cit.*

[2] The law here ascribed to Epitadeus is mentioned by Aristotle, *Polit.* ii. 9. 14, 1270 a, and must therefore have been enacted before his time. From the fact, however, that no extant writer of the fourth century or earlier hints at an equality of land in early Lacedæmon, Grote, *History of Greece*, II. 393 *sqq.*, argues that the idea of an equal distribution of land by Lycurgus was a fiction of the third century, connected with the attempted reform of Agis. The argument is very strong, and has not been satisfactorily met by those who think differently. See, for example, Busolt, *Griech. Gesch.* I. 521 *sqq.*, who assumes an original equality of land, which was soon disturbed by the Messenian wars, and by differences in the size of families. Epitadeus, however, seems to have been a real person, who was an ephor, and who may have passed a law relating to the gift or inheritance of landed property; *cf.* Niese, "Epitadeus," in Pauly-Wissowa, *Real-Encycl.* VI. 217.

[3] The Lacedæmonian term for statute.

6. Agis, therefore, thinking that it would be an honorable enterprise, as indeed it was, to restore these citizens to the state and to reëstablish equality for all, began to sound the people themselves as to their opinion about such a measure. The younger men quickly rallied round him, and with an enthusiasm which he had hardly counted upon began to make ready for the contest. Most of the elder men, however, who had become more thoroughly tainted by the prevailing corruption, feared to be brought back to the discipline of Lycurgus as much as a runaway slave fears to be brought back to his master. They bitterly reviled Agis when he lamented over the condition of affairs and sighed for the ancient glories of Sparta. His enthusiastic aspirations, however, were sympathised with by Lysander, son of Libys, Mandrocleides, son of Ecphanes, and Agesilaüs. Lysander was the most influential of all the Spartans, while Mandrocleides was thought to be the ablest politician in Greece, as he could plot with subtlety and execute with boldness. Agesilaüs was the uncle of King Agis and a fluent speaker, but of a weak and covetous disposition. It was commonly supposed that he was stirred to action by the influence of his son Hippomedon, who had gained great glory in the wars and was exceedingly popular among the younger citizens; but what really determined him to join the reformers was the amount of his debts, which he hoped would be wiped out by the revolution. As soon as Agis had won over this important adherent, he began to try to bring over his mother to his views, who was the sister of Agesilaüs, and who from the number of her friends, debtors and dependents, was very powerful in the state and took a large share in the management of public affairs.

7. When she first heard of the designs of Agis, she was greatly startled, and attempted to dissuade the youth from an enterprise which she thought was neither practicable nor desirable. When however Agesilaüs pointed out to her what a notable design it was, and how greatly to the advantage of all, while the young king himself besought his mother to part with her wealth in order to gain him glory, arguing that he could not vie with other kings in riches, as the servants of the Persian satraps and the very slaves of the intendants of Ptolemy and Seleucus possessed more money than all the kings that ever reigned in Sparta; but that if he could

prove himself superior to those vanities by his temperance, simplicity of life, and true greatness of mind, and could succeed in restoring equality among his countrymen, he would be honored and renowned as a truly great king. By this argument the young man entirely changed his mother's mind, and so fired her with his own ambition, as if by an inspiration from heaven, that she began to encourage Agis and to urge him on, and invited her friends to join them, while she also communicated their design to the other women, because she knew that the Lacedæmonians were in all things ruled by their women, and that they had more power in the state than the men possessed in their private households. Most of the wealth of Lacedæmon had fallen into female hands at this time, and this fact proved a great hindrance to the accomplishment of Agis' schemes of reform; for the women offered a vehement opposition to him, not merely through a vulgar love of their idolized luxury, but also because they saw they would lose all the influence and power which they derived from their wealth. They betook themselves to Leonidas and besought him, as the elder man, to restrain Agis and check the development of his designs. Leonidas was willing enough to assist the richer class, but he feared the people, who were eager for reform, and would not openly oppose Agis, although he endeavored secretly to ruin his plan and to prejudice the ephors against him by imputing to him the design of hiring the poor with the plunder of the rich to make him despot, and insinuating that by his redistribution of lands and remission of debts he meant to obtain more adherents for himself than citizens for Sparta.

8. In spite of all this opposition Agis contrived to get Lysander appointed ephor, and immediately induced him to propose a rhetra before the gerousia,[1] the main points of which were that all debts should be cancelled; that the land should be divided, — that between the valley of Pellene and Mount Taÿgetus, Malea and Sellasia, — into 4,500 lots and the outlying districts into 15,000; that the latter district should be distributed among those of the periœci who were able to bear arms; and the interior district among the Spartans themselves; that these be reinforced from the periœci and from all those foreigners who had a liberal education and a

[1] The council of twenty-eight elders, senators.

good physique and were in the prime of life; and that these citizens should be divided into fifteen companies, some of four hundred and some of two hundred, for the public meals, and should conform in every respect to the discipline of their forefathers.

9. When this rhetra was proposed, as the gerousia could not agree whether it should become a law, Lysander convoked an assembly of the people and himself addressed them. Mandrocleides and Agesilaüs also besought them not to allow a few selfish voluptuaries to destroy the glorious name of Sparta, but to remember the ancient oracles, warning them against the sin of covetousness, which would prove the ruin of Sparta, and also of the responses which they had recently received from the Oracle of Pasiphaë. . . . The oracular responses which had come from this shrine bade the Spartans all become equal, as Lycurgus had originally ordained. After these speeches had been delivered, king Agis himself came forward, and after a few introductory words, said that he was giving the strongest pledges of his loyalty to the new constitution; for he declared his intention of surrendering to the state before any one else, his own property, consisting of a vast extent of land, both arable and pasture, besides six hundred talents in money; and he assured the people that his mother and her friends, the richest people of Sparta, would do the same.

10. The people were astounded at the magnanimity of the youth, and were filled with joy, thinking that at last after an interval of three hundred years, there had appeared a king worthy of Sparta. Leonidas, on the other hand, opposed him as vigorously as he could, reflecting that he would be forced to follow his example, and divest himself of all his property, and that Agis, not he, would get the credit for the act. . . .

11. The people espoused the cause of Agis, while the rich begged Leonidas not to desert them, and by their entreaties prevailed upon the members of the gerousia, who had the power of originating all laws, to throw out the rhetra by a majority of one vote. . . .

The parts thus far omitted refer to the less important details of the conflict. Lysander now succeeded in having Leonidas dethroned, and Cleombrotus, son-in-law of the latter, made king in his stead.

12. At this crisis Lysander was forced to lay down his office, as the year for which he had been elected had expired. The ephors

at once took Leonidas under their protection, restored him to the throne, and impeached Lysander and Mandrocleides as the authors of illegal measures for cancelling debts and redistributing land. As these men were now in danger of their lives, they prevailed upon the two kings to act together and overrule the decision of the ephors; for this, they declared, was the ancient rule of the constitution, that if the kings were at variance, the ephors were entitled to support the one whom they judged to be in the right against the other; but their function was merely to act as arbitrators and judges between the kings when they disagreed, and not to interfere with them when they were of one mind. Both the kings agreed to act upon this advice, and came with their friends into the assembly, turned the ephors out of their chairs of office, and elected others in their room, one of whom was Agesilaüs. They now armed many of the younger citizens, released the prisoners, and terrified their opponents by threatening a general massacre. No one, however, was killed by them; for although Agesilaüs desired to kill Leonidas, and when he withdrew from Sparta to Tegea, sent men to waylay and murder him on the road, Agis, hearing of his intention, sent others on whom he could rely, who escorted Leonidas safely as far as Tegea.

13. Thus far all had gone well, and no one remained to hinder the accomplishment of the reforms; but now Agesilaüs alone upset and ruined the whole of this noble and genuinely Spartan scheme by his detestable vice and covetousness. He possessed large tracts of the best land in the country, and also owed a great sum of money; and as he desired neither to pay his debts nor to part with his land, he persuaded Agis that it would be too revolutionary a proceeding to carry both measures at once, and that if the moneyed class were first propitiated by the cancelling of debts, they would afterward be inclined to submit quietly to the redistribution of lands. Lysander and the rest were deceived by Agesilaüs into consenting to this plan, and they brought all the written securities for money which had been given by debtors, which are called by them klaria,[1] into the market-place, collected them into one heap and burned them. As the flames rose up, the rich and those who had lent money went away in great distress, but Agesilaüs, as if exulting at their misfortune, declared that he had never seen a brighter

[1] Κλάρια derived from κλᾶροι, "lots."

blaze or a purer fire. As the people at once demanded the division of the land, and called upon the kings to distribute it among them, Agesilaüs put them off with various excuses, and managed to spin out the time till Agis was sent out of the country on military service. . . .

During the absence of Agis Leonidas regained the throne, and the reform was effectually blocked. On his return Agis had to take sanctuary for his safety. As he went out one day to bathe, he was seized, imprisoned, and after a mock trial, hanged. The execution of his mother and grandmother immediately followed. Agis was the first king who was put to death by the ephors.

242. The Democratic Table of Cleomenes, King of the Lacedæmonians

(Phylarchus, *Histories,* quoted by Athenæus iv. 21)

For Phylarchus, see no. 56.

Cleomenes, the son of King Leonidas referred to in the preceding selection, came to the throne in 235 and died in exile, 219. He was a military commander of brilliant ability and a statesman who not only saw the miserable condition of Lacedæmon but possessed sufficient political skill for overcoming opposition and carrying through the reforms of Agis. The simple hospitality of Cleomenes contrasts with the extravagant luxury prevailing among the Spartan rich during this period; *cf.* no. 240.

Although he was but a young man, Cleomenes possessed eminent wisdom in his discernment of affairs, and was exceedingly simple in his manner of life. King as he was, and with so important affairs intrusted to his management, he displayed such behavior to all who were invited to a sacrifice, as to make them see that what they had daily prepared at home for themselves was in no respect inferior to what he allowed himself. Though many embassies were sent to him, he never made a banquet for the ambassadors at an earlier hour than the regular time; and there was never anything more laid than a common pentaclinum;[1] and when there was no embassy, there was laid simply a triclinium. There were no orders issued by the regulator of the feasts, as to who should come in or sit down first; but the eldest led the way to the couch, unless he invited some one else to do so. Cleomenes was generally seen supping

[1] As the name indicates, pentaclinum was a table with five couches for guests; triclinium, just below, was a table for three.

with his brother, or with some of his friends of his own age. There was placed on a tripod a brazen wine-cooler and a cask and a small silver cup holding two cotylæ[1] and a cyathus; and the spoon was of bronze. Wine was not brought round to drink unless some one asked for it; but one cyathus was given to each guest before supper, generally to himself first. Then when he had given the signal, the rest asked for some wine. What was served up was placed on a very common-looking table; and the dishes were such that there was neither anything left nor anything deficient, but just a sufficient quantity for every one; so that those who were present could not feel the want of anything. He did not think it right to receive guests as sparingly in respect of soup and meat as men are treated at the phiditia,[2] nor again to have so much superfluity as to waste money for no purpose, exceeding all moderation and reason in the feast; for the one extreme he counted illiberal and the other arrogant. When he had company the wine was of a somewhat better quality. While they were eating all kept silence; but a slave stood by, holding in his hand a vessel of mixed wine, and poured for every one who asked for it. In the same manner after supper there were given to each guest not more than two cyathi of wine, and this too was brought to each person as he made a sign for it. There was no music of any kind accompanying the meal, but Cleomenes himself conversed all the time with each of the guests, having invited them as it were for the purpose of listening and talking; so that all departed charmed with his hospitality and affability.

243. The Political and Social Reform of Cleomenes, King of the Lacedæmonians

(Plutarch, *Life of Cleomenes*)

Cleomenes had the advantage of Agis in experience, as he was about thirty when he came to the throne. It was a great advantage to him also that the attempt and the failure of Agis lay before his eyes as an example and especially as a warning to him to prepare a solid basis of power before attempting a revolution. It was his good fortune to possess military talent, and the interstate relations of Hellas at that time gave him a favorable opportunity for building up a reputation for military leadership.

[1] Cotyle, .578 pint liquid measure. A cyathus is a sixth of a cotyle.
[2] Phiditia, see no. 240, n. 1.

For some time the Ætolian league had been the chief power in the Greek peninsula. But more recently the Achæan league (see no. 199) under Aratus was coming to the front. In fact it bade fair to absorb all Peloponnese. This development naturally provoked the hostility of Sparta. Taking the field, Cleomenes gained several brilliant successes over the forces of the league, and thus built up for himself a military support. At the same time he was busy with political intrigues. As the other throne of Lacedæmon became vacant, Cleomenes succeeded in having it filled by the brother of Agis, Archidamus, who had been in exile. Some time afterward, however, Archidamus was assassinated by the party which had put Agis to death, as Phylarchus states, though some suspected Cleomenes (Plut. *Cleom.* 5). It is important to notice, too, that the wife of Cleomenes was Agiatis, widow of Agis, a woman of estimable character, who used her powerful influence in favor of reform. For further details regarding the political situation, see Beloch, *Griech. Gesch.* II. 1. 718–26; Niese, *Griech. u. mak. Staat.* II, 314 *sqq.* The chief source of Plutarch seems to have been Phylarchus, who was a warm admirer of Cleomenes, though he also drew from writers who were less favorable. The importance of the selection given below lies in the fact that it is an account of one of the most interesting social reforms in antiquity — a reform in thorough accord with the general trend of political thought. The theory that it had an influence on the Gracchi, though unproved, is possible.

7. After this victory Cleomenes became inspired with fresh confidence, and was convinced that if he only were allowed undisputed management, he would easily conquer the Achæans. He explained to his stepfather Megistonous that the time had at length come for the abolition of the ephorate, the redistribution of property, and the establishment of equality among the citizens. After these reforms Sparta might again aspire to recover her ancient ascendancy in Hellas. Megistonous agreed, and communicated his intention to two or three of his friends. It chanced that at this time one of the ephors who was sleeping in the temple of Pasiphaë dreamed an extraordinary dream, that in the place where the ephors sat for the despatch of business he saw four chairs removed and one alone remaining, while as he wondered he heard a voice from the shrine say, "This is best for Sparta." When the ephor related this dream to Cleomenes, he was at first much alarmed, and feared that the man had conceived some suspicion of his designs, but finding that he was really in earnest, recovered his confidence. Taking with him all those citizens whom he suspected of being opposed to his enterprise, he captured Heræa and Alsæa, cities belonging to the Achæan league, revictualed Orchomenus, and threatened Mantineia. By

long marches and countermarches he so wearied the Lacedæmonians that at last, at their own request, he left the greater number of them in Arcadia, while he with the mercenaries returned to Sparta. During his homeward march he revealed his intention to those whom he considered to be most devoted to his person, and regulated his march so as to be able to fall upon the ephors while they were at their evening meal.

8. When he drew near the city, he sent Eurycleides into the dining-room of the ephors on the pretence of carrying a message from the army. After Eurycleides followed Phœbis and Therycion, two of the foster-brothers of Cleomenes, called Mothaces [1] by the Lacedæmonians. They were accompanied by a few soldiers. While Eurycleides was talking with the ephors, these men rushed in with drawn swords and cut them down. Their president, Agylæus, fell at the first blow and appeared to be dead, but contrived to crawl out of the building unobserved into a small temple sacred to Fear, the door of which was usually closed, but which then chanced to be open. In it he took refuge and shut the door. The other four were slain together with a few persons, not more than ten, who came to their assistance. No one who remained quiet was put to death, nor was any one prevented from leaving the city. Even Agylæus, when he came out of his sanctuary on the following day, was not molested. . . .

10. On the following morning Cleomenes published the names of eighty citizens whom he required to leave the country, and removed the chairs of the ephors, except one, which he intended to occupy himself. He now convoked an assembly and made a speech in justification of his recent acts. In the time of Lycurgus, he said, the kings and the gerousia shared between them the supreme authority in the state; and for a long time the government was carried on in this manner without any alteration being required, until during the long wars with Messene, as the kings had no leisure to attend to public affairs, they chose some of their friends to sit as judges in their stead. These persons at first acted merely as the servants of the kings, but gradually got all power into their own hands, and thus insensibly established a new power in the state.

[1] The Mothaces or Mothones were a class of freedmen, many of them the sons of Spartan fathers and helot mothers; Gilbert, *Const. Antiq.* 34.

A proof of the truth of this fact is to be found in the custom which still prevails, that when the ephors send for the king, he refuses to attend at the first and second summons, but rises and goes to them at the third. Asteropus,[1] who first consolidated the power of the ephors, and raised it to the highest point, flourished in comparatively recent times, many generations after the original establishment of the office. If, he went on to say, the ephors had behaved with moderation, it would have been better to allow them to remain in existence; but when they began to use their ill-got power to destroy the constitution of Sparta, when they banished one king, put another to death without trial, and kept down by terror all who wished for the introduction of the noblest and most admirable reforms, they could no longer be borne. Had he been able without shedding a drop of blood to drive out of Lacedæmon all those foreign pests of luxury, extravagance, debts, money-lending, and those two more ancient evils, poverty and riches, he should have accounted himself the most fortunate of kings, because like a skilful physician he had painlessly performed [2] so important an operation upon his country. As it is, the use of force is sanctioned by the example of Lycurgus, who though only a private man appeared in arms in the market-place, and so terrified King Charilaüs that he fled for refuge to the altar of Athena. Being an honest and patriotic man, however, he soon joined Lycurgus, and acquiesced in his reforms. The acts of Lycurgus prove that it is hard to effect a revolution without armed force, of which he declared he had made a most sparing use, and had put out of the way those only who were opposed to the best interests of Lacedæmon. He announced to the rest of the citizens that the land should be divided among them,

[1] We do not know when this ephor lived, or precisely what change he made in the constitution of the office which he filled. It has been conjectured, however, that previously the ephors had been appointed by the king, but that he proposed and carried a law for making the office elective; *cf.* Gilbert, *Const. Antiq.* 20. The theory of the early ephorate, as contained in this alleged speech of Cleomenes, is substantially correct; and it is interesting in this connection to observe the practical effect of research in early Lacedæmonian history. The ephors had existed from an early period in subordination to the kings, but in the course of the sixth century they became the chief magistrates; Botsford, *Hellenic History*, ch. vi. The discovery of these facts made the overthrow of the office by Cleomenes appear to be a return to the original constitution.

[2] In a period in which anæsthetics were used in surgical operations this simile was especially appropriate; *cf.* no. 209.

that they should be relieved from all their debts, and that all resident aliens should be submitted to an examination in order that the best of them might be selected to become full citizens of Sparta, and help defend the city from falling a prey to the Ætolians and Illyrians from want of men to defend her.

11. Then he first threw his inheritance into the common stock, and his example was followed by his step-father Megistonous, his friends, and the rest of the citizens. The land was now divided; and one lot was assigned to each of those whom he had banished, all of whom he said it was his intention to bring back as soon as order should be restored. He recruited the number of the citizens by the admission of the most eligible of the periœci to the franchise, and organized them into a body of 4000 heavy infantry, whom he taught to use the sarissa, or Macedonian pike, which was grasped with both hands, instead of the spear, and to sling their shields by a strap [1] instead of using a handle. Next he turned his attention to the education and discipline of the youth, a task in which he was assisted by Sphærus. The gymnasia and the common meals were soon reëstablished; and the citizens, most of them willingly, resumed their simple Laconian habits of living. Fearing to be called a despot, Cleomenes appointed his own brother Eucleides as his colleague. Then for the first time were two kings of the same family seen at once in Sparta.

12. . . . At this period his was the only army, Greek or foreign, which was not attended by actors, jugglers, dancing girls, and singers; but he kept it free from all licentiousness and buffoonery, as the younger men were nearly always being practised in martial exercises, while the elders acted as their instructors. When they were at leisure, they amused themselves with witty retorts and sententious Laconian pleasantries. The high value of this kind of discipline is described at greater length in the life of Lycurgus.

13. In everything Cleomenes acted as their teacher and example, offering his own simple frugal life, so entirely free from vulgar superfluities, as a model of sobriety for them all to copy; and this

[1] In the seventh century the Spartans had used man-covering shields suspended in this way (Botsford, *Hellenic History*, ch. vi), but had afterward abandoned them for the lighter round shields. The change here mentioned seems to have been a return to earlier conditions.

added greatly to his influence in Hellas. In fact when men attended the courts of other kings of that period, they were not so much impressed by their wealth and lavish expenditure as they were disgusted by their arrogant, overbearing manners; but when they met Cleomenes, who was every inch a king, and saw that he wore no purple robes, did not lounge on couches and litters, and was not surrounded by a crowd of messengers, door-keepers, and scribes, so as to be difficult of access, but that he himself dressed in plain clothes, came and shook them by the hand, and conversed with them in a kindly, encouraging tone, they were completely fascinated and charmed by him, and declared that he alone was a true descendant of Heracles.

As long as Cleomenes had only the Achæan league to cope with, he more than held his own. Afterward, however, when Antigonus, king of Macedon, joined the Achæans against him, he gradually lost ground. His last step in social reform was taken under these circumstances in order to increase his power of resisting the enormous odds opposed to him.

22. Antigonus now advanced, took Tegea, and allowed his troops to plunder Orchomenus and Mantineia. Cleomenes, who was confined to the territory of Lacedæmon, proceeded to emancipate all helots who could pay a sum of five Attic minas for their freedom. By these means he raised a sum of five hundred talents. He also organized a special corps of 2000 men, armed after the Macedonian fashion, with which he hoped to be able to meet the Leucaspids, or white-shielded troops of Antigonus, and proceeded to attempt a wonderful and astonishing feat of arms.

244. Miscellaneous Social Conditions and Sentiments

The selections under nos. 244–246 have been taken from the Anthology of Epigrams. The first anthology of epigrams, as far as we know, was made by Meleagros of Syrian Gadara, in the first century B.C. This collection seems to have been erotic. Copious additions, perhaps involving a radical recasting, were made by Philippus of Thessalonica in the first century A.D., and again by the Byzantine Agathias in the sixth century. The present arrangement, if it can be so called, we owe to a certain Constantinos Kephalas, who probably lived in the tenth century. It is his manuscript which is known as the Palatine, and which is the chief source of our knowledge. There is an attempt at a division of this collection into books, as Erotica, Dedicatoria, Epitaphia, etc.; but it was subject to every conceivable irregularity and contained in addition a mass of irrelevant Byzantine material. Finally in the fourteenth century a grammarian Planudes undertook to rearrange, expurgate, and probably also to enrich the work of Kephalas. The smaller collection of Planudes long held the field alone, and was published in 1484 at Florence, and often thereafter. It was not till 1606 that the work of Kephalas was discovered, at Heidelberg in the library of the Count Palatine. The Planudean manuscript is our only source for 397 epigrams, and these are now usually printed as a supplement, book xvi, of the Palatine collection. Of the latter, bks. i–iii and viii are wholly Byzantine non-classical interpolations, and should not be reprinted or edited as a part of the classical "Anthology." The Didot edition has a literal Latin translation and useful notes. The Teubner text is critical but incomplete.

The date and the authorship of the poems are so uncertain that the present editor has thought it best to make the selections for this volume without regard to chronological limitations.

(The following selections have been translated by W. C. L.)

Anthology v. 134 — Little Brown Jug

Anonymous

Rotund, fairly-turned, one-eared, long-necked, high-throated, eloquent with narrow mouth, thou jolly handmaid of Bacchus, of the Muses, and of Cythereia, sweet-laughing merry mistress of the feast, why, pray when I am sober art thou full of wine; but again, if I be drunk, then hast thou not a drop? Thou sinnest against the drinking bout's good comradeship!

Ib. 275 — The First of Many Gifts

This wimple I bring thee, my bride, shining, inwrought with golden threads. Lay it upon thy locks, and drawing it over thy shoulders, press this clasp to thy faultless white breast. Ay, to thy breast: so it may serve for bodice, as it winds its embrace about thee. This thou mayst wear while yet a virgin. But may wedlock be thine and fruitful harvest of children, so that then I may provide for thee a silvern coronet and jewel-studded headband.

Ib. 296 — Woman's Secluded Life

Leontios, sixth century A.D.

This complaint of women is a favorite commonplace, best handled perhaps by the Euripidean Medeia, emancipated though she seems. The modern touch in the "moving pictures" is of course accidental, and probably refers to real life.

The task of youths is not so great as falls to us delicate women. They have their comrades, to whom with fearless utterance they tell the pains of their anxiety. They are busy with diverting games, and roaming about the streets, enjoy bright colored pictures. 'Tis not permitted us to see the daylight, but in dim rooms we are hidden, wasted with worries.

245. Miscellaneous Social Conditions and Sentiments (*Continued*)

(The following selections have been translated by W. C. L.)

Anthology vi. 174 — The Three Spinning Girls' Dedications

Antipatros of Sidon, second century B.C.

To Pallas these three girls of like age, knowing, as does the spider, how to shape the delicate thread, have offered: Demo the fairwoven basket, Arsinoë the distaff, worker of the fairspun thread, and Bacchylio the fair-wrought comb, a nightingale among the weavers, wherewith she used to part the well woven warp-threads. For free from shame, each, stranger, chose to live, winning from her handiwork her sustenance.

Ib. 203 — A Case of Divine Healing

Doubtful authorship

The old woman, the handworker, with crippled feet, came on a wise quest for the healing water, creeping with aid of the oaken staff that supported her in her helplessness. Pity seized the Nymphs, who upon the foothills of loud-thundering Ætna abode in the watery home of eddying Symæthus, their father. And the hot Ætnæan liquid strengthened, without harming, her doubly-crippled legs. Her staff she left to the Nymphs, who had assured her they would send her away needing no support: and pleased were they with the gift.

Ib. 226 — A Tiny Estate

Leonidas of Tarentum(?), third century B.C.

"Low is my porch as is my fate:
Both void of state."

This is Cleiton's humble cot.
Tiny is the well-tilled field,
Small the neighboring vineyard plot,
Scant is the little woodlot's yield.
Yet in this his home content
Eighty years has Cleiton spent.

Ib. 280 — A Bride's Farewell to Childhood

Anonymous

Timarete, before her marriage, dedicated to Artemis her tambourine and beautiful ball, the coronal that upheld her hair, and, O Lady of Limnæ, a maid to a maid, as is fitting, she gave to thee these little maids, her dolls and the dolls' dresses. O daughter of Leto, extend thy hand over Timareteia, and sacredly keep safe the sacred child.

Ib. 306 — A Cook's Gift to Hermes

Ariston, second century B.C.

A kettle and this flesh-hook, the bent key of the pigsty, this ladle to stir soup, a well-feathered fan, a good brass pot, with an axe, the throat-cutting knife,[1] a dipper to reach the broth between the spits, the wiping sponge lying by the strong carving-knife, this double-headed salt-pestle,[2] with a good stone mortar, and the meat-holding trencher — these the cook Spinther, having cast off the burden of slavery, has dedicated to Hermes as signs of his art.

246. Miscellaneous Social Conditions and Sentiments (*Concluded*)

(The selections below have been translated by W. C. L.)

Anthology ix. 9 — Homeward Bound

Julius Polyænus, first century A.D.(?)

The sailor, or the poet, is seemingly unconscious of the universal application of his prayer.

Many a time have I prayed to thee, and always thou hast granted, O father Zeus, the goal of stormless prosperous voyaging.

[1] The cook had to kill the pigs, as a modern one might chickens.

[2] The pestle was dumb-bell shaped.

Grant me this voyage also, and keep me safe, and from troubles bring me to anchorage in harbor. Home and fatherland are the grace of life. Excessive cares for men are not life but hardship.

Ib. 89 — The Old Gleaner

Philippus of Thessalonica, first century A.D.

To keep off grievous hunger the aged Nico was gleaning wheat-ears with the young girls — and died from the heat. Her companions, in lack of wood, heaped up from the grain for her a funeral pyre of straw. Be not angry, O Demeter, if the maidens clad [1] her who was a mortal child of earth in the product of earth.

Ib. 151 — A Dirge for Corinth

Antipatros

Corinth was destroyed by the Romans in 146 B.C.

Where is now thy farseen beauty, O Dorian Corinth? where thy crown of towers, where thy ancient possessions? Where are the temples of the Blessed and where the homes? Where are the dames descended from Sisyphus, and where the tens of thousands, thy people of old? Nay but not even a trace of thee has remained, O thou of many evil dooms, but all hath been seized on and devoured by war. Undestroyed alone are we the Nereids, daughters of Ocean, who remain the halcyons of thy woes.

Ib. 174 — The Pedagogue's Pecuniary Pains

Palladas of Alexandria, 400 A.D.

Here instruction is given by those who are under the anger of Serapis: those that begin with the 'Fatal Wrath.' Here the boy's nurse each month brings his fee, under compulsion, tying to his book and paper the pittance. As if it were incense she brings to the master's chair, as to a tomb, that bit of paper, throwing it down beside him. Even from that little she steals her own gains; she changes the copper and puts in lead; she takes her regular (toll). If someone is to bring a piece of gold for a year, in the eleventh month, before he has paid, he changes to another

[1] "Clothed" is often applied to the earth, dust, or ashes, in which the bones of the dead found rest; *cf.* bk. vii *passim.*

teacher, openly ungrateful, reviling the former master while he deprives him of his pay for the whole year.

Ib. 251 — To the Bookworm

Evenus, date uncertain

Thou whom the Muses most detest,
  Devourer of their pages,
Thou thievish devastating pest,
  Browsing upon the stolen sweets of sages,
  Why with thy dusky skin
  Lurkest thou here within
The holy records, bookworm, thou who art
Of envy the true sign and counterpart.

Ib. 359 — The Pessimist

Probably Poseidippus, third century B.C.

What path of life may a man tread? In the marketplace are quarrels and troubles, at home worries. In the country abundant weariness, on the sea terror. In an alien land, fear if thou hast anything; if thou art destitute, discomfort. Thou art married? Thou'rt not free from worry. Thou art not married? Yet more lonely dost thou live. Youth is senseless, forceless again are gray hairs. The choice is one or other of these two: either never to be born or to die straightway at birth.

Ib. 360 — The Optimist

Metrodorus, third century B.C.

Any path of life thou mayst tread. In the marketplace is glory and wise action, at home rest. In the fields the charm of nature, on the sea gain. In the alien land if thou hast anything, good name; if thou art in lack, thou alone knowest it. Thou art married? So shall thy household be best. Thou art unwedded? Thou livest yet more easily. Children are the desire of the heart, a childless life is carefree. Youth is vigorous, revered again are gray hairs. The choice is not one of the two; never to have been born or to die; for all is good in life.

Ib. 418 — The Waterpower Mill

Antipatros

Withhold the hand that turns the mill, O grinding women. Sleep late, even though at dawn the cocks' note gives the signal. For Deo [1] has laid upon the Nymphs your wearisome handicraft. Leaping upon the summit of the wheel, they twirl the axle about; and he with his revolving spoke turns the hollow mass of the Nisyrian [2] millstones. We again have a taste of the old (carefree) life, since without toil we learn to feast on Deo's creation.

[1] Short form for Demeter.

[2] From the island Nisyrus, which Poseidon tore from the neighboring island of Cos, to hurl it upon the giant, Polybotes. The whirling millstones make the poet think of Nisyrus.

INDEX

The numbers refer to the pages.

RECORDS OF CIVILIZATION

SOURCES AND STUDIES

Edited by JAMES T. SHOTWELL

IN PREPARATION

Announcement of the appearance of these volumes will be made from time to time in the Monthly Book List of the Columbia University Press, which will be mailed regularly upon request.

THE DOCUMENTS OF THE EARLY PAPACY. By JAMES T. SHOTWELL, Ph.D., Professor of History in Columbia University, and LOUISE R. LOOMIS, Ph.D. 8vo, cloth.

THE EARLY RECORDS OF CHRISTIANITY. By HAROLD H. TRYON, M.A., B.D., Associate Professor in Union Theological Seminary. 8vo, cloth.

OTTO OF FREISING. Translated with commentaries and notes by CHARLES C. MIEROW, Ph.D., Professor of Classical Languages and Literatures in Colorado College. 8vo, cloth.

THE SOURCES OF IRISH HISTORY IN THE MIDDLE AGES. By JAMES F. KENNEY. 8vo, cloth.

THE SOURCES FOR THE SOCIAL HISTORY OF ENGLAND, 1750–1850. By JUDITH B. WILLIAMS, Ph.D. 8vo, cloth.

THE BEGINNINGS OF MODERN PHYSICAL SCIENCE. By FREDERICK BARRY, Ph.D. 8vo, cloth.

COLUMBIA UNIVERSITY PRESS

Columbia University, New York City